8th Edition

HIGHER EDUCATION LAW
IN AMERICA

EASY-TO-USE FORMAT COVERING TOPICS SUCH AS:

- Cheating and Plagiarism
- Sexual Assault
- Disciplinary Actions
- Copyrights and Patents
- Tuition Issues

- Employee Rights
- Freedom of Speech and Religion
- Sex Discrimination
- Student Privacy
- Athletics

Center for
Education & Employment Law

Center for Education & Employment Law
P.O. Box 3008
Malvern, PA 19355

> "This publication is designed to provide accurate and authoritative information in regard to the subject matter covered. It is sold with the understanding that the publisher is not engaged in rendering legal, accounting or other professional services. If legal advice or other expert assistance is required, the service of a competent professional person should be sought." *-from a Declaration of Principles jointly adopted by a Committee of the American Bar Association and a Committee of Publishers and associations.*

Library of Congress Cataloging-in Publication Data

Higher Education Law in America.
    p. cm.
    Includes index.
    ISBN 978-1-933043-27-2 (pbk.)
    1. Universities and colleges--Law and legislation--United States. I. Center for Education & Employment Law.
    KF4225 .H54 2000
    378.73--dc21

                      00-055074

ISBN 978-1-933043-27-2

Cover Design by Jen Erb

Other Titles Published
By Center for Education & Employment Law:

Deskbook Encyclopedia of American School Law
Deskbook Encyclopedia of Employment Law
Deskbook Encyclopedia of Public Employment Law
Federal Laws Prohibiting Employment Discrimination
Private School Law in America
Statutes, Regulations and Case Law Protecting Individuals with Disabilities
Students with Disabilities and Special Education
U.S. Supreme Court Education Cases
U.S. Supreme Court Employment Cases

TABLE OF CONTENTS

CHAPTER ONE
Student Rights

CHAPTER TWO
Discrimination Against Students

TABLE OF CONTENTS

CHAPTER FIVE
Employment

CHAPTER SIX
Employment Practices and Labor Relations

CHAPTER SEVEN
Employment Discrimination

CHAPTER EIGHT
Intellectual Property

CHAPTER NINE
School Liability

TABLE OF CONTENTS

INTRODUCTION

Higher Education Law in America provides an encyclopedic compilation of federal and state court decisions in the area of college and university law. We have reviewed hundreds of federal and state court decisions involving higher education law and have included the most important ones in this deskbook. The chapters have been arranged topically, and the cases have been presented in an easy-to-use manner.

Each chapter contains explanatory passages at the beginning of each section to help you develop an overall understanding of the legal issues in that particular area. The case summaries have been written in everyday language, and at the start of each case is a brief note highlighting the holding or the significant issues discussed within. Further, the case summaries themselves contain boldface type to emphasize important facts, issues and holdings.

We feel that *Higher Education Law in America* will help you understand your rights and responsibilities under state and federal law. It has been designed with professional educators in mind, but also has tremendous value for lawyers. We hope you will use this book to protect yourself and to gain greater wisdom and understanding. Hopefully, we have succeeded in making the law accessible to you regardless of your level of understanding of the legal system.

Jim Roth, Esq.
Senior Legal Editor
Center for Education & Employment Law

ABOUT THE EDITORS

James A. Roth is Senior Editor of *Special Education Law Update* and *Legal Notes for Education*. He is also a co-author of the deskbook *Students with Disabilities and Special Education*. He is a graduate of the University of Minnesota and William Mitchell College of Law. Mr. Roth is admitted to the Minnesota Bar and is an adjunct program associate professor at St. Mary's University of Minnesota – Twin Cities Campus.

Steve McEllistrem is Senior Legal Editor of Center for Education & Employment Law. He co-authored the deskbook *Statutes, Regulations and Case Law Protecting Individuals with Disabilities* and is editor of *Special Education Law Update*. He graduated *cum laude* from William Mitchell College of Law and received his undergraduate degree from the University of Minnesota. Mr. McEllistrem is admitted to the Minnesota Bar.

Thomas D'Agostino is a Managing Editor at the *Center for Education & Employment Law*. He graduated from the Duquesne University School of Law and received his undergraduate degree from Ramapo College of New Jersey. He is a past member of the American Bar Association's Section of Individual Rights and Responsibilities as well as the Pennsylvania Bar Association's Legal Services to Persons with Disabilities Committee. Mr. D'Agostino is admitted to the Pennsylvania bar.

Curt J. Brown is the Group Publisher of the Center for Education & Employment Law. Prior to assuming his present position, he gained extensive experience in business-to-business publishing, including management of well-known publications such as *What's Working in Human Resources, What's New in Benefits & Compensation, Keep Up to Date with Payroll, Supervisors Legal Update,* and *Facility Manager's Alert*. Mr. Brown graduated from Villanova University School of Law and graduated magna cum laude from Bloomsburg University with a B.S. in Business Administration. He is admitted to the Pennsylvania Bar.

How to Use Your Deskbook

We have designed *Higher Education Law in America* in an accessible format for both professional educators and attorneys to use as a research and reference tool toward prevention of legal problems.

Research Tool

As a research tool, our deskbook allows you to conduct your research on two different levels – by topics or cases.

Topic Research

◆ If you have a general interest in a particular **topic** area, our **table of contents** provides descriptive chapter headings containing detailed subheadings from each chapter.

➢ For your convenience, we also include the chapter table of contents at the beginning of each chapter.

Example:
For more information on liability, the table of contents indicates that a discussion of instructor misconduct takes place in Chapter Nine, under Intentional Conduct, on page 401:

CHAPTER NINE
School Liability

How to Use Your Deskbook

◆ If you have a specific interest in a particular **issue**, our comprehensive **index** collects all of the relevant page references to particular issues.

Example:
For more information on student activities, the index provides references to all of the cases dealing with student activities instead of only those cases dealing with fraternities and sororities:

Statewide testing, 51, 356-358
Student activities
    Fraternities and sororities, 127-130
        Hazing, 132-136
        Injuries, 130-132
        Operation and school supervision, 125-127
        Organizational liability, 128-130
Student activity fees, 171-174

Case Research

◆ If you know the **name** of a particular case, our **table of cases** will allow you to quickly reference the location of the case.

Example:
If someone mentioned a case named *Gonzaga Univ. v. Doe,* looking in the table of cases, which has been arranged alphabetically, the case would be listed under section "G" and would be found on p. 46 of the text.

G

Ginn v. Stephen F. Austin State Univ., 201
Glenn v. Univ. of Southern California, 410
Godinez v. Siena College, 408
Goldberg v. Northeastern Univ., 380
Gomes v. Univ. of Maine, 18
 Gonzaga Univ. v. Doe, 46
Goodman v. Bowdoin College, 93
Gordon v. Purdue Univ., 2

✓ Each of the cases summarized in the deskbook also contains the case citation, which will allow you to access the full text of the case if you would like to learn more about it. See *How to Read a Case Citation,* p. 503.

◆ If your interest lies in cases from a **particular state**, our **table of cases by state** will identify the cases from your state and direct you to their page numbers.

Example:
> If cases from California are of interest, the table of cases by state, arranged alphabetically, lists all of the case summaries contained in the deskbook from that state.

CALIFORNIA

Barnhart v. Cabrillo Community College, 396
→ Bessard v. California Community Colleges, 154
Brown v. Li, 167
California School of Culinary Arts v. Lujan, 262

✓ Remember, the judicial system has two court systems — state and federal court — which generally function independently from each other. See *The Judicial System,* p. 499. We have included the federal court cases in the table of cases by state according to the state in which the court resides. However, federal court decisions often impact other federal courts within that particular circuit. Therefore, it may be helpful to review cases from all of the states contained in a particular circuit.

Reference Tool

As a reference tool, we have highlighted important resources which provide the framework for many legal issues.

◆ If you would like to see specific wording of the **U.S. Constitution**, refer to **Appendix A**, which includes relevant provisions of the U.S. Constitution such as the First Amendment (freedom of speech and religion) and the Fourteenth Amendment (which contains the Equal Protection Clause and the Due Process Clause).

How to Use Your Deskbook

◆ If you would like to review **U.S. Supreme Court decisions** in a particular subject matter area, our topical list of U.S. Supreme Court case citations located in **Appendix B** will be helpful.

The book also contains a glossary, which provides definitions of legal terms and certain statutes. The glossary can be found on p. 505.

We hope you benefit from the use of *Higher Education Law in America.* If you have any questions about how to use the deskbook, please contact James Roth at jroth@pbp.com.

TABLE OF CASES

TABLE OF CASES

TABLE OF CASES

TABLE OF CASES

TABLE OF CASES

TABLE OF CASES

TABLE OF CASES BY STATE

COLORADO

CONNECTICUT

DELAWARE

TABLE OF CASES BY STATE

MICHIGAN

MINNESOTA

OKLAHOMA

OREGON

PENNSYLVANIA

TABLE OF CASES BY STATE

TABLE OF CASES BY STATE

CHAPTER ONE

Student Rights

I. THE CONTRACTUAL RELATIONSHIP

The relationship between students and colleges or universities is a contractual one, and may be defined by the terms of a tuition agreement, college catalogue or brochure and student handbooks. Generally, when a contract has been breached, extra-contractual damages (like punitive damages) are not available. Only when there has been some egregious behavior, like fraud, will such damages be recoverable.

A. Breach of Contract

◆ *The Indiana Court of Appeals held a student had to show a university acted with a dishonest purpose in order to prove bad faith.*

An Indiana student who was pursuing a doctorate in economics received an "Unsatisfactory" grade in a thesis research course. An economics policy committee met and told the student he would be dismissed from the doctoral program if he did not find a new faculty advisor and submit a plan and timetable for completing his thesis. Despite receiving an extension, the student did not complete these tasks. The economics policy committee dismissed him from the doctoral program. After exhausting internal appeals with the university, the student sued the university and the professor who had assigned an unsatisfactory grade for breach of contract, negligence and defamation. A state trial court held the university's actions constituted academic judgment that it would not disturb, absent bad faith. The court later held the contractual relationship between the parties and the question of bad faith required further consideration. The student received permission to file an amended complaint. He responded by filing an amended complaint alleging a claim of bad faith.

The court dismissed the amended complaint. On appeal, the state court of appeals upheld the dismissal of the amended complaint. **Courts do not rigidly apply contract law principles to education disputes, even though the relationship between students and educational institutions is contractual in nature.** Courts recognize that implied contracts exist between students and universities, and the nature of contractual terms varies. **To prove bad faith, the student had to show more than bad judgment or negligence. Instead, he needed to show the university acted with a dishonest purpose.** The amended complaint did not support a claim of bad faith. It simply alleged that the university failed to comply with obligations set forth in the policies and procedures manual and the university bulletin. As the complaint did not support a claim for bad-faith breach of contract, the court upheld the lower court's decision. *Gordon v. Purdue Univ.*, 862 N.E.2d 1244 (Ind. Ct. App. 2007).

◆   *Breach may be found if the institution failed to fulfill a specific contractual promise distinct from any overall obligation to offer a reasonable program.*

Yale University School of Medicine's student handbook required all students to take and pass Step 1 of the U.S. Medical Licensing Examination (USMLE). The handbook allowed students three chances to pass. Students were expected to pass all phases of the USMLE within six years. An African-American student was dismissed after two unsuccessful attempts at passing Step 1 of the USMLE. He appealed the decision, alleging the dean of student affairs never told him he faced dismissal if he failed on his second try. The student enrolled in two review courses to prepare for taking the exam a third time. He later asked for a 30-day extension. When the school found out the student had not taken the exam, it dismissed him again. Several months later, the student took and passed Step 1 of the USMLE on his third try. When the school refused to readmit him, he filed a federal district court action for race discrimination and breach of contract, among other state claims.

The court agreed with Yale's contention that Connecticut courts have resisted claims of "educational malpractice" and generally defer to educational institutions in their academic decisions. However, the Supreme Court of Connecticut recognized at least two situations where courts will entertain a claim for breach of a contract for educational services in *Gupta v. New Britain General Hospital*, 239 Conn. 574 (Conn. 1996). Breach of contract may be found if the educational program failed in some fundamental respect, like not offering any of the courses necessary to become certified in a particular field. The court found the student's contract claim fell within the second exception.

The handbook granted a student three opportunities to pass the exam before dismissal. That was a distinct contractual promise independent of the medical school's obligation to offer a reasonable educational program. The court denied the school's motion for dismissal and scheduled the case for a trial. *Morris v. Yale Univ. School of Medicine*, No. 05CV848 (JBA), 2006 WL 908155 (D. Conn. 4/4/06).

◆ *The relationship between private schools and their students is contractual.*

A student enrolled in a joint program offered by the University of Scranton and the Wyoming Valley Health Care System. The program had a clinical component, and he received positive evaluations for over 200 clinical cases. The student later received two less favorable evaluations, and the program director accused him of "refusing to communicate" and being unprepared. After meeting with the director, the student was placed on probation and then terminated from the program for failing to progress in his probationary period. The student sued the university and health care system in a federal district court for breach of contract. He also claimed breach of the covenant of good faith and fair dealing, denial of due process and tortious interference with contract.

The court refused to dismiss the student's breach of contract claim. **Under state law, the relationship between private schools and students was contractual by nature. Students can file claims for breach of contract when a school violates the contract.** In this case, the student presented evidence of policies and procedures which the defendants should have followed when taking disciplinary action against him. However, he failed to allege viable claims for breach of the covenant of good faith and fair dealing. The court also dismissed the due process claim, which was premised on failure to follow handbook procedures. Finally, the court dismissed the student's claims for tortious interference with contract and punitive damages. *Kimberg v. Univ. of Scranton*, No. 3:06cv1209, 2007 WL 405971 (M.D. Pa. 2/2/07).

◆ *The District Court of Appeal of Florida held a university did not exercise its discretion arbitrarily by dismissing a student.*

The student attended a master's program in social work. After he received a failing grade in a field practicum course, the university dismissed him. The student was granted two administrative appeals. Both times, his failing grade and dismissal were affirmed. The student sued the university, alleging it denied him due process because the university acted in bad faith when it dismissed him. He claimed the dean of the school of social work and a member of the student review and termination committee were biased against him.

The state court of appeal found no evidence to support the student's claims. **The court held university authorities have wide discretion in determining whether a student has met academic requirements. Courts will not interfere unless school authorities acted in bad faith or exercised their discretion arbitrarily.** The court of appeal found the student's field instructor indicated the student needed improvement in 10 out of 38 areas evaluated. The field director also noted his difficulties with staff and clients at the agency where he performed his field practicum. The student's clients were unhappy with his performance and demeanor and did not want to participate in any more sessions with him. For all these reasons, the court of appeal held the university did not act in bad faith or exercise its discretion arbitrarily when it dismissed the student. It affirmed the judgment. *Karlan v. Florida Int'l Univ. Board of Trustees*, 927 So.2d 91 (Fla. Dist. Ct. App. 2006).

♦ *A federal district court held a Maryland university did not breach a contract by interfering with a student's ability to complete a thesis.*

The student attended a private university's school of health to pursue a doctorate degree. He fulfilled the requirements for his degree except for completing his thesis. Under university policy, students were allowed a maximum of seven years from the date they enrolled to obtain the degree. The university extended the deadline for the student several times. He conducted research for his thesis in an empty on-campus office. After the last extension, the university denied the student further access to the office space.

The student sued the university in a federal district court, alleging it breached a contract by sabotaging his ability to complete the thesis, among other things. He contended his enrollment in the university established an implied contract. According to the student, the university undermined his thesis research by insisting he include a mental health survey, refusing to allow him to compensate those who participated in the study with federal grant money, and denying him the office space. **The court agreed that the relationship between a student and a private university is largely contractual in nature. Such a contract requires a university to act in good faith, and to act fairly.** There was evidence that the university reasonably accommodated the student above and beyond any reasonably-imagined contractual requirement. **Courts intervene into academic decisions only if a student completes all academic requirements and the school's refusal to grant a degree is "arbitrary and capricious."** Many of the events the student complained about were academic judgments. As nothing suggested the university acted in an arbitrary or capricious manner, there was no breach of contract. The court also dismissed the student's race and national origin discrimination claims. *Onawola v. Johns Hopkins Univ.*, 412 F.Supp.2d 529 (D. Md. 2006).

♦ *An Ohio university did not breach a contract by using exams from one semester for the following semester.*

A student attended a private university in Ohio and earned a bachelor's degree in 2000. In 2001, the student enrolled in the university's graduate program. He earned a master's degree in 2003. The student sued the university in the state court system, alleging it breached a contract with him by permitting several instructors to reuse exams from one semester to the next. The university moved for summary judgment. Relying on *Elliott v. Univ. of Cincinnati*, 134 Ohio App.3d 203, 730 N.E.2d 996 (Ohio 1999), the court said **the relationship between a university and a student who enrolls, pays tuition, and attends class is contractual. A court looks to university guidelines for the terms of the contractual relationship**. The court said the terms of the contract between the student and the university in this case were contained in the university's undergraduate and graduate bulletins. It found nothing in those bulletins mentioned prohibiting the reuse of exams.

No specific passage in the bulletin disallowed reusing exams. Instead, the student relied on language in bulletins that read, "Faculty must not tolerate academic dishonesty nor discrimination or harassment from students to other students." The student asserted the provision implied a prohibition against reusing exams. The court disagreed. **It stated that if a contract is clear and unambiguous, the court cannot create a new one.** As the handbook did not prohibit instructors from using old exams, the court found no breach of contract existed. Ohio courts do not recognize a cause of action for educational malpractice, and the court awarded summary judgment to the university. *Leiby v. Univ. of Akron*, No. 2004-10094, 2005 WL 3163943 (Ohio Ct. Cl. 11/9/05).

◆ *The Supreme Judicial Court of Maine held a handbook reservation clause, which allowed a college to unilaterally change the terms of its handbook without notice to students, defeated a student's breach of contract claim.*

A college hearing board conducted disciplinary proceedings against a male student for sexual assault of a female student. The board held for the male student. The student handbook said nothing about appeals from the hearing board. A handbook reservation clause gave the college the right to unilaterally change the terms of the handbook without notifying students. The dean advised the female student she had a right to appeal. The appeals board found the male student guilty of sexual assault. The board prohibited the male student from living in campus housing, eating in college dining halls, and being on campus after 11:00 p.m. It placed him on permanent disciplinary probation. The college president refused the male student's request to overturn the board's decision.

The student sued the college in a state court for breach of contract. The court found the college did not breach any contractual obligation to the student and held for the school. The student appealed, arguing the college breached its contract because the decision by the college to allow the female student to appeal did not meet his reasonable expectations. He said the disciplinary process described in the student handbook did not authorize the female student's appeal to the dean's hearing board. The Supreme Judicial Court of Maine court found the handbook was not a contract *per se*. **The handbook had a reservation clause, which allowed the college to unilaterally change handbook terms without notice to the students.** The court affirmed the judgment for the college. *Millien v. Colby College*, 874 A.2d 397 (Me. 2005).

◆ *A federal district court held a Virginia university did not breach a contract by dismissing a student from a master's program.*

The university graduate school policy made two failing grades grounds for dismissal. The student failed a required course, but was allowed to retake it. He failed the class a second time and was dismissed from the program. Two months later, the student met with his professor to discuss a grade change. The professor told him he could obtain a withdrawal from the course retroactively, which would remove the failing grade and allow him to stay in the program. The student requested the withdrawal, but it was denied because he filed it outside the allotted time under the university catalogue. He sued the university in a federal district court for breach of contract, among other claims. The university moved for dismissal. **The court dismissed the case, finding the**

catalogue was not a contract. It characterized the catalogue as an
"unenforceable illusory contract," because it promised specified
performance that was entirely optional. The court also held the student had
no property interest in continued enrollment at the university, defeating his due
process violation claim. *Davis v. George Mason Univ.*, 395 F.Supp.2d 331
(E.D. Va. 2005).

◆   *A Virginia federal district court held that a law school student's challenge
to the terms of a student handbook will proceed to trial.*

The law school policies and procedures manual and its student handbook
stated that at the end of each semester, students may evaluate a course
anonymously. The student completed three course evaluations for courses
taught by different instructors. On the evaluation forms, she wrote similar
accounts of sexual harassment and race discrimination. The student was
suspended until she agreed to undergo a psychiatric evaluation. University
officials later suggested she withdraw until she received psychiatric treatment.
The student agreed to withdraw under threat of expulsion. Almost two years
later, she sued the university in a federal district court for breach of contract,
contending the university's manual and handbook were a contract. Because the
manual stated that student evaluations could be completed anonymously, the
student argued the university breached the contract when it investigated and
identified her as the author of the student evaluations.

The court explained that to interpret the intent of a contract, a court must
look to its language. Where the intent is clear, and the language can only be
interpreted one way, courts should evaluate the language in accordance with its
plain and ordinary meaning. The university argued the student mistook
"anonymity" for "confidentiality." It argued that anonymity is defined as "not
named or identified," whereas confidential is defined as "meant to be kept
secret." **The court said the university's interpretation did not meet the
plain and ordinary meaning of the word "anonymous." Anonymity could
imply the author of the evaluation would not be identified.** If the university
wanted to be able to police the contents of the evaluations, it should have
spelled that out in the contract. It denied the university's dismissal motion and
ordered the case to proceed to trial. *Truell v. Regent Univ. School of Law*, No.
Civ.A. 2:04 CV 716, 2005 WL 1926645 (E.D. Va. 8/5/05).

◆   *A Connecticut court held a university course catalogue was not an
enforceable contract for educational services.*

A post-graduate student became dissatisfied with his clinical rotation and
the credentials of his instructors. He withdrew from a course when he had
problems with it. The student could not graduate in four years because of his
light course load. He took a leave of absence and sued the university in a state
superior court for breach of contract, claiming the university program did not
live up to what was represented in its course catalogue. The court stated a
contractual relationship exists between private universities and their students.

**A university may not be held liable for breach of contract unless its
program fundamentally fails to satisfy a specific contractual promise.** See
Gupta v. New Britain General Hospital, 239 Conn. 574, 687 A.2d 111 (1996).

The student did not show the university program failed in any fundamental way in its educational offerings. "Fundamental" items included the number of days or hours of instruction and other objective criteria. As the student did not offer any concrete evidence of a fundamental failure that made it impossible for him to obtain a medical degree, there was no support for his breach of contract claim. The student did not show the university broke a particular contract promise. The catalogue was not a contract and the court awarded summary judgment to the university. *Cullen v. Univ. of Bridgeport*, No. CV-020396010, 2003 WL 23112678 (Conn. Super. Ct. 2003).

◆   *The U.S. Supreme Court held that the doctrine of substantial performance applied to contracts in an academic setting.*

An overweight Rhode Island student joined a college's nursing program in her sophomore year. During her junior year, the college began pressuring her to lose weight. She received a failing grade in a clinical nursing course, for reasons related to her weight rather than her performance. By school rules, the failing grade should have resulted in expulsion from the program. However, the school offered her a contract that allowed her to stay in the program if she lost at least two pounds per week. She failed to lose the weight, was asked to withdraw from the program, and transferred to another nursing program. She sued the college in a federal district court, alleging that it had violated the Rehabilitation Act and that it had breached an implied contract to educate her. She was awarded damages for breach of contract. The jury determined that the student had substantially performed her obligations under the contract so as to enable her to prevail on her claim against the school. The school appealed.

The U.S. Court of Appeals, First Circuit, affirmed the decision, deferring to the district court's determination of how the state courts would have ruled on the issue. The school further appealed to the U.S. Supreme Court. The Supreme Court held that the court of appeals should have reviewed the case *de novo* (as if hearing it for the first time). The appellate court should not have deferred to the district court's determination of what state law would be. Instead, **it should have examined the doctrine of substantial performance to ascertain whether it ought to be applied to a contract in an academic setting**. The Court reversed and remanded the case. *Salve Regina College v. Russell*, 499 U.S. 225, 111 S.Ct. 1217, 113 L.Ed.2d 190 (1991).

B. Fraudulent Misrepresentation

◆   *A student did not show breach of contract or fraudulent misrepresentation by a college that accused him of selling copies of an upcoming examination.*

After an investigation and hearing, the college concluded the student had engaged in academic misconduct and dismissed him from the program. He sued the college in a state court for breach of contract, fraudulent misrepresentation, and fraudulent nondisclosure. The student filed a separate breach of contract claim against the teacher of the class he was accused of cheating in. A jury ruled in his favor on the fraudulent misrepresentation claim against the college and awarded him $20,000 in damages. It also ruled for the student on his breach of contract claim against the teacher and awarded him

$10,000 on that claim. The court set aside the verdict against the college on the fraudulent misrepresentation claim. On the breach of contract and fraudulent nondisclosure claims against the college, the jury found against the student.

The Supreme Court of Missouri reversed the judgment on the breach of contract claim against the teacher. The claim was based on the employment contract between the teacher and the college, and the student was not entitled to third-party beneficiary status under it. The court upheld the trial court's decision to set aside the fraudulent misrepresentation verdict. Any alleged misrepresentation regarding the disciplinary hearings did not harm the student because he did almost nothing to prepare for them. **Because the student did not present evidence showing he relied on representations that the college would follow certain due process procedures at his appeal hearing, he could not prove fraudulent misrepresentation.** *Verni v. Cleveland Chiropractic College*, 212 S.W.2d 150 (Mo. 2007).

◆ *A federal district court in New York refused to dismiss students' claims that a university engaged in deceptive business practices and breached a contract when it made changes to its drama program, including a change in its name.*

Current and former students sued the university, claiming the changes were deceptive business practices and in breach of contract. To address the contract claim, the court referred to a catalogue the university published every other year to promote the drama program. The catalogue included a policy relating to changes, which said course offerings, academic requirements, degree programs, tuition, fees and faculty were subject to change at any time.

The court held "the relationship between a university and its students is contractual." It would be inappropriate to grant judgment to the students on the claim that the change in the name of the program was a breach of contract. Although the catalogue clearly stated that degree programs were subject to change, it also emphasized the prestige and uniqueness of the program and promised students they would receive diplomas bearing the previous name. Under these circumstances, a factual issue existed as to whether the university breached its contract with the students when it changed the name of the program. The court also refused to award pretrial judgment to the university on the deceptive business practices claims. There was a factual question as to whether the catalogue was likely to mislead a reasonable consumer and as to whether it fully disclosed the university's right to change the program name. *Deen v. New School Univ.*, No. 05 Civ. 7174 KMW, 2007 WL 1032295 (S.D.N.Y. 3/27/07).

◆ *Two university employees could be sued for fraud where they allegedly misled a student about a music media program.*

A student enrolled at an Alabama university because its catalogue indicated it had a music media major and "state of the art" equipment. However, the student encountered problems when he tried to take classes in music media. His academic advisor first required him to take the university's core-requirement courses, then told him the university was seeking an instructor to teach music media classes. When the student was finally placed in a "basic recording" course, the instructor missed the first four classes. Another instructor later showed him the university's outdated recording studio, in which some of the equipment did not work. He informed the student that he was not qualified to teach basic recording. The student withdrew from school and sued the university, its board, a number of officials and his advisor for breach of contract and fraud. A state court dismissed his claims, but the Supreme Court of Alabama reinstated fraud claims against the advisor and a vice president of academic affairs. **There was evidence that they made misrepresentations to the student with the intent to deceive him, and that he relied on those misrepresentations.** *Byrd v. Lamar*, 846 So.2d 334 (Ala. 2002).

◆ *A college was potentially liable for fraud and breach of contract where questions existed about representations it had made to incoming students.*

A college established a satellite campus in Alabama after acquiring the facilities of a psychotherapy institute. Four students enrolled in the college, but it experienced financial difficulties and had to close before they could complete their degrees. One of the reasons for its failure was its inability to get licensure for former students of the institute. This resulted in fewer students enrolling and less tuition revenue. The students sued the college for breach of contract and fraud, among other claims. An Alabama trial court granted pretrial judgment to the college, and the students appealed.

The Court of Civil Appeals of Alabama found factual issues existed as to whether the college had breached the contract or committed fraud. The contract with the students was ambiguous, being made up of different documents and oral representations. There were questions as to whether the college had promised to do more than simply provide an education for each semester in exchange for tuition. The students stated a potential fraud claim. **In Alabama, a party can be liable for fraud even where a misrepresentation is "made by mistake and innocently," if another party acted on the misrepresentation and suffered harm.** Because the college was potentially liable, the court reversed and remanded the case for a trial. *Craig v. Forest Institute of Professional Psychology*, 713 So.2d 967 (Ala. Civ. App. 1997).

C. Tuition Issues

Courts may enforce tuition contracts based on enrollment agreements, school handbooks or bulletins. Where a private school has breached its contractual obligations, courts may award tuition refunds. In addition to general contract considerations, the Higher Education Act (HEA) and its amendments require institutions to develop "fair and equitable" policies for refunding unearned tuition in the event the student fails to complete the enrollment period. Some of the regulations specify the order for reimbursement, while other regulations govern the calculation of the appropriate amount of the student's refund.

◆ *A federal court did not have jurisdiction over a dispute that did not raise a federal question and did not involve more than $75,000.*

St. Francis College refused to award a diploma to a student that owed it approximately $5,000. He sued St. Francis in a federal district court for $5,000.

He contended he was under tremendous stress, which led to a nervous breakdown because of the actions by St. Francis. The court noted that the claim pertained to a private dispute. For that reason, a federal court did not have jurisdiction over the matter. **The student had not raised a federal question of law, and the amount in controversy did not exceed $75,000.** Accordingly, the court dismissed the lawsuit. *Korshikova v. St. Francis College*, No. 06-CV-2722 (NGG), 2006 WL 2265099 (E.D.N.Y. 8/6/06).

◆   *An Ohio college lost a claim against a student for unpaid tuition, because he withdrew prior to a withdrawal deadline and it failed to establish a contract.*

A student attended a college in Ohio for two or three weeks in 2002. He had a problem with his financial aid package and did not have enough money to pay his tuition. The college told the student he could no longer attend until he paid what he owed. The student withdrew before the withdrawal deadline. The college sued the student in an Ohio trial court for $6,000 plus interest and other expenses. According to the student, he did not participate in any college activities or use the technologies he was billed for. The court agreed, and the college appealed to the Court of Appeals of Ohio. **To prevail on its claim for unpaid tuition, the college had to prove it had a binding agreement with the student.** A binding contract could be established if the college could prove the student agreed to pay under an agreement that included a date when payment was due. The contract also had to indicate a date it could be cancelled, if applicable, without a penalty. The court relied on *Lake Ridge Academy v. Carney*, 66 Ohio St.3d 376, 613 N.E.2d 183 (Ohio 1993), which involved a parent's reservation of a seat for a student in a private elementary school.

In *Lake Ridge Academy*, the Supreme Court of Ohio held "[u]nder a **school reservation agreement, when a parent is given the option to cancel the agreement before a certain date without incurring a penalty for the full tuition and does not do so, the parent may become liable for the full tuition if the contract so provides.** The parent's notification of cancellation, if given after the option date, is ineffective to discharge this liability. Subsequent failure to make scheduled tuition payments is a breach of contract." The court of appeals found the same reasoning could be applied to this case. However, without a contract, the court could not determine if the student owed the college tuition. The judgment in his favor was therefore affirmed. *Hiram College v. Courtad*, 162 Ohio App.3d 642, 834 N.E.2d 432 (Ohio Ct. App. 2005).

◆   *A college that expelled a student did not have to pay him damages for future wages beyond the time necessary to complete his degree.*

A Georgia private college student was accepted into a Columbia University-sponsored program called "Biosphere 2." According to the student, the college agreed to send him a financial aid check while in the program. He would take the check to the comptroller of the program and his expenses would be deducted from the check. The college sent the student a check made payable to the program for $8,905. The comptroller's office returned $7,000 to him, which he used to repay student loans. The student completed the program and returned to the college. Later, the college expelled him for defrauding

Columbia. He sued the college in a Georgia trial court for breach of contract and failing to follow proper procedures regarding expulsion. The college reduced the expulsion to a one-semester suspension. However, the student did not return to school. He argued the college should pay him damages for income he lost based on an estimate of what he would earn if he had a degree.

The court awarded the student $698,500 in damages, and the college appealed to the Court of Appeals of Georgia. According to the college, the trial court should not have permitted evidence about future lost wages because they are not recoverable in a breach of contract action for expulsion from school. **The court applied Georgia employment cases holding that employees may recover future lost wages if discharged, but must take other employment to mitigate their damages. In this case, there was no evidence that the student could not return to school and obtain a degree.** No discipline appeared on his transcript. As the student did not show an inability to return to school and earn a degree, he was entitled to lost income only for additional time needed to complete his degree. The trial court had erred by considering future lost wages beyond the time necessary to complete his degree. The case was returned to the trial court to redetermine the student's damages. *Morehouse College v. McGaha*, 277 Ga. App. 529, 627 S.E.2d 39 (Ga. Ct. App. 2005).

◆   *The Court of Appeals of Maryland held state universities were not liable to students who claimed unreasonable mid-year tuition increases.*

When the state board of university regents learned it was about to lose funding, it approved tuition increases of up to 5% during a semester. Several students sued the board in a state circuit court for breach of contract and related claims. The court granted the board's motion for summary judgment and dismissed the case. The students appealed the contract issue to the Court of Appeals of Maryland. It held **the board was protected by sovereign immunity against the contract claim because the students did not establish they had a written contract**. The legal relationship between the students and universities was characterized as a "quasi-contract." Under a quasi-contract theory, the board could make unilateral changes within the parties' reasonable expectations. The court held the board qualified for sovereign immunity as an arm of the state government. Since the state code provided for a sovereign immunity waiver only in tuition cases that involve a refund, waiver did not apply. The court affirmed the judgment for the board. *Stern v. Board of Regents, Univ. System of Maryland*, 836 A.2d 996 (Md. 2004).

◆   *A Massachusetts student was no longer entitled to reduced tuition after her mother resigned from her job with the university.*

A Boston University student received tuition remission because her mother worked for the university. At the start of her junior year, the university sent her a "projected tuition remission" for the year. However, during the fall semester, the student's mother resigned. The university notified the student that she was no longer entitled to tuition remission benefits as of the spring semester, and the student sued. A trial court ruled for the university, and the Appeals Court of Massachusetts affirmed. **The projected tuition remission was not an**

unconditional offer of financial aid for one year but rather was conditioned on the student's mother continuing her employment with the university. When the mother resigned, the university's obligation to offer remission benefits ended. *Lindley v. Boston Univ.*, 778 N.E.2d 31 (Mass. App. Ct. 2002).

◆ *Where the Texas community college system improperly raised student services fees, it had to reimburse students who paid too much.*

A Texas community college district, composed of seven junior colleges, decided to adopt a sliding scale fee schedule for student services, which included a technology fee. Five students brought a class action lawsuit against the district, arguing that the fee increase violated the Texas Education Code and that the technology fee was unlawful. A court and a jury ruled in favor of the class, and the Court of Appeals of Texas affirmed in part. Here, the district failed to comply with the statutory guidelines when it imposed the technology fee because it did not set forth a proposal in a resolution that was approved by the state attorney general. Also, **the increase in the student services fee was unlawful because the district imposed the increase without a majority vote of the students or the student governments** at the seven junior colleges. Moreover, the fees were paid under implied duress because if the students refused to pay, the district could prevent them from registering for classes and/or deny them academic credit. The court affirmed the award to the class of over $15 million in damages for the improperly collected fees. *Dallas County Community College Dist. v. Bolton*, 89 S.W.3d 707 (Tex. Ct. App. 2002).

D. Educational Malpractice

Claims for educational malpractice usually stem from accusations that a school has failed to evaluate and properly place a student, or failed to provide the educational services necessary to educate the student. However, courts have been extremely reluctant to recognize lawsuits based upon educational malpractice. For example, in Leiby v. Univ. of Akron, *summarized in subsection A, above, an Ohio court rejected a student's educational malpractice claim based on his contention that his diplomas were "worthless." It held Ohio does not recognize claims based on educational malpractice.*

Claims for educational malpractice lack readily acceptable standards of care, cause or injury. Educational malpractice claims are further disfavored due to public policy considerations, such increased litigation and appropriate deference by the courts to the academic decisions of educators.

◆ *A student could not avoid the bar against educational malpractice claims by suing a school for constructive discharge.*

A dental student claimed to have witnessed rampant cheating that school officials refused to address. She asserted that this devalued her education and breached the university's promise to abide by its code of conduct. She also asserted that she had been constructively discharged from the dental program due to mistreatment by a faculty member. The faculty member in question had flunked her in a class, and she had subsequently failed the exam twice more. In her lawsuit against the university, a federal district court ruled in favor of the school. **It noted that her breach of contract claim was in essence a claim for educational malpractice, and that such a claim could not survive. The student failed to present specific promises that the school had breached.** Rather, she was asserting that the school had failed to provide an effective education. Further, the court refused to create a new cause of action for constructive discharge from a university. Doing so would undermine the public policy of leaving to professional educators decisions related to education, and would allow students to avoid the bar against educational malpractice claims. *Gally v. Columbia Univ.*, 22 F.Supp.2d 199 (S.D.N.Y. 1998).

◆ *Although educational malpractice claims cannot succeed in most states, including Minnesota, claims alleging consumer fraud or deceptive trade practices can be used where a school fails to perform specific promises.*

A group of students filed a lawsuit against a for-profit, proprietary trade school, claiming fraud, misrepresentation, breach of contract and violation of the Minnesota consumer fraud and deceptive trade practices statutes in connection with a computer program offered by the school. A trial court characterized the students' claims as educational malpractice claims and granted the school's motion for pretrial judgment. The trial court further determined that neither the consumer fraud nor the deceptive trade practices statutes applied, and that neither of these statutes allowed damages.

The state court of appeals noted that **while educational malpractice claims were barred by public policy, claims for breach of contract, fraud or other intentional torts alleging the failure to provide promised educational services were actionable**. Under this analysis, the trial court correctly granted pretrial judgment to the school on the claims challenging the instructors and quality of education provided. The claims arising from the alleged failure to fulfill certain representations and promises were actionable; therefore, the trial court erred in granting pretrial judgment to the school on those claims. They were remanded to the trial court along with the claims based on the state consumer fraud statute (which allowed the recovery of money damages) and the state deceptive trade practices statute (which did not allow the recovery of money damages, but did allow for injunctive relief). *Alsides v. Brown Institute, Ltd.*, 592 N.W.2d 468 (Minn. Ct. App. 1999).

◆ *New York courts have declined to consider actions of educational malpractice because they require courts to make decisions as to the validity of broad educational policies such as the appropriateness of a textbook.*

Two New York residents registered for a Pascal computer programming course at a private university. Prior to registration, they read the university's catalogue, which encouraged students without a computer programming background to attend. They also read the class schedule, which indicated no prerequisites for the Pascal course. Their advisor assured them that the course did not require an advanced math background and that their rudimentary high school math skills would suffice. They paid $855 to the university under its installment plan. The professor assigned readings from a course textbook designed for computer science majors, scientists and engineers. He also assigned problems requiring an extensive math background. The students' advisor instructed them to keep working on the admittedly difficult problems. The students then withdrew from the class in frustration. They were unable to contact their advisor for nearly three weeks, at which time they were no longer eligible for any type of tuition refund. The students sued the school in a state court, seeking relief for breach of contract, rescission, breach of fiduciary duty, educational malpractice, and unfair and deceptive business practices.

The court held that the professor's use of an unsuitable textbook coupled with his inappropriate classroom examples intentionally drawn from math and science constituted a breach of the college's educational contract with the students. Rescission of the contract was justified because it was unconscionable and because the students were induced to enter into the contract in reliance upon the college's gross misrepresentations. Further, the college assumed the obligations of a fiduciary when it assigned the students an advisor who made misrepresentations on which the students relied to their detriment. The court also held that the college was liable for educational malpractice, ruling that use of the improper textbook was a per se example of negligence, incompetence and malpractice. The school's actions also violated a New York law prohibiting deceptive business practices. The court ordered the school to reimburse the students and imposed punitive damages against it. *Andre v. Pace Univ.*, 618 N.Y.S.2d 975 (N.Y. City Ct. 1994).

The university appealed to the New York Supreme Court, Appellate Term, which noted that, as a matter of public policy, New York courts have declined to consider actions of educational malpractice because they require courts to make decisions as to the validity of broad educational policies. It noted that the claims asserted in this case entailed **an evaluation of the adequacy and quality of the textbook and the effectiveness of the teaching methods. These are determinations best left to the educational community**, and the trial court erred by making them. The court also found that the trial court erroneously dismissed the university's counterclaim for the remainder of the tuition owed. The students were aware of the university's policy and did not present any evidence showing that their delay in requesting a refund was caused by the university. Thus, they were liable for the full tuition. The court reversed the trial court's decision and entered judgment for the university. *Andre v. Pace Univ.*, 655 N.Y.S.2d 777 (N.Y. Sup. Ct. 1996).

◆   *In rejecting an educational malpractice claim, the Seventh Circuit noted that the claim lacked a satisfactory standard of care, involved uncertainties about damages, created the potential for a flood of litigation, and embroiled courts in the day-to-day operations of schools.*

A Kansas high school basketball star was recruited by a private university in Nebraska to play on its team. The student was unprepared for a university education, but was assured that he would receive sufficient tutoring so that he would receive a meaningful education. During the student's four years at the university, his language and reading skills never rose to even a high school level. The university then made arrangements with an Illinois preparatory school to provide him a year of remedial education. Afterward, the student attended another university in Chicago, but had to withdraw for lack of funds.

Following a depressive and destructive episode, the student sued the Nebraska university for negligence and breach of contract. The negligence claims were based on educational malpractice and negligent admission. A federal district court granted the university's motion to dismiss the case. *Ross v. Creighton Univ.*, 740 F.Supp. 1319 (N.D. Ill. 1990).

The student appealed to the U.S. Court of Appeals, Seventh Circuit, which noted that courts in at least 11 states have considered and rejected educational malpractice claims. The main reasons for doing so included: 1) the **lack of a satisfactory standard of care** by which to evaluate an educator, 2) the inherent **uncertainties about the cause and nature of damages**, 3) the **potential for a flood of litigation** against schools, and 4) the threat of **embroiling courts in the day-to-day operations of schools**. With respect to the negligent admission complaint, the court applied many of the same reasons. On the breach of contract claim, the court found a student would have to show more than that the education provided by the university was not good enough. This would be nothing more than a repackaging of an educational malpractice claim. Instead, a student "must point to an identifiable contractual promise that the [university] failed to honor." Here, the student had alleged a breach of promise with respect to certain services, which effectively cut him off from *any* participation in and benefit from the university's academic program. The court affirmed in part the dismissal of the student's complaint, but allowed the breach of contract claim to proceed. *Ross v. Creighton Univ.*, 957 F.2d 410 (7th Cir. 1992).

II. DISCIPLINARY ACTIONS

A. Due Process

1. Hearings and Procedural Safeguards

The Due Process Clause of the Fourteenth Amendment requires state entities to provide notice and an opportunity to be heard when individual liberty or property interests are at stake. Due process includes the notion of fundamental fairness and notice and an opportunity to be heard at some point during disciplinary procedures. A federal district court explained that informal procedures may minimize the risk of lawsuits in higher education disciplinary cases. These include: 1) use of an impartial decisionmaker; 2) providing notice of the charges and the evidence against the student; 3) an opportunity for the student to appear before the decisionmaker; 4) an opportunity for the student to suggest witnesses; 5) avoiding the imposition of sanctions against witnesses; and 6) permitting the student to either voluntarily accept discipline or the ruling of the decisionmaker. A. v. C. College, 863 F.Supp. 156 (S.D.N.Y. 1994).

◆ *A Connecticut college did not violate a student's due process rights as he received notice and a chance to be heard regarding the charges against him.*

The student contacted a female classmate in a chat room. He made several attempts to date her, but she rejected his advances. The student continued to pursue the classmate, appearing uninvited at her dormitory room and giving her gifts. The student e-mailed a professor about his "excessive interest" in the classmate. The professor was disturbed by the e-mail, in which the student asked him to protect the classmate from other males. After an investigation, the student was told to have no further contact with the classmate. About a month later, he offered to pay a person to spy on her. The university held a disciplinary hearing, after which a hearing officer found the student had stalked the classmate. The student was suspended for 15 months, barred from student activities and prevented from earning credits. After an unsuccessful internal appeal, the student filed an action in state court, seeking an order that would require the university to reinstate him as a full-time student in good standing.

The court found the student was entitled to the requested order only if he could show the suspension proceeding did not meet due process requirements. He failed to make this showing as **he could not prove a violation of any due process rights. There is no fundamental right to attend college. The student received notice of the charges against him, and neither the form nor content of the notice prejudiced his ability to defend the charges.** Because the student was not denied due process with respect to the university's procedures, the court denied his request for a preliminary injunction. *Danso v. Univ. of Connecticut*, 50 Conn.Supp. 256, 919 A.2d 1100 (Conn. Super. Ct. 2007).

◆   *The U.S. Court of Appeals, Sixth Circuit, held an Ohio medical college did not violate a student's due process rights during his disciplinary hearing.*

The student was arrested for a felony drug crime. The college notified him by letter that it was suspending him until investigations and hearings on his drug charge were completed, and advised him of his right to an investigation. The student decided not to schedule an investigation until the pending criminal charges were resolved. The student was not permitted on campus until the completion of a disciplinary hearing. A few months later, the student pled guilty to a felony drug charge, then asked for a hearing. The college sent him a written notice to appear before its student conduct and ethics committee to answer questions about his arrest. The student was not entitled to be represented by an attorney at the hearing because the criminal proceedings had ended. However, the college allowed his attorney to be present. At the hearing, the officer who had arrested the student testified. The committee questioned the officer, but denied the student's attorney an opportunity to do so.

The college expelled the student for violating its zero-tolerance drug policy. The student sued the college in a federal district court for due process violations. The court dismissed the case. On appeal, the Sixth Circuit stated **the Due Process Clause of the Fourteenth Amendment protects individual liberty and property interests. The student's interest in pursuing an education was a protected property interest. Due process is flexible, and its basic requirements are notice and an opportunity to be heard. Additional procedures vary based on the circumstances of each case.** The student argued the college fell short of the process his circumstances demanded, because he had a significant interest in continuing his medical education. The court held the college provided him sufficient notice of the disciplinary charges against him and the procedures that would follow. While the college did not permit the student's attorney to cross-examine the officer, the procedures it used were fundamentally fair. The judgment for the college was affirmed. *Flaim v. Medical College of Ohio*, 418 F.3d 629 (6th Cir. 2005).

◆ *A New York college violated a student's right to due process by not complying with its own procedures.*

The student applied for admission to a master's degree program while he was an undergraduate at the college. The program sent him a conditional acceptance letter stating he would be accepted if he earned at least a B in his first four program courses and completed all admission requirements. Later, the director of the graduate program sent the student a letter stating she had reviewed his grades and discussed them with his professors. She did not believe he should continue in the program because his personal beliefs about teaching and learning were too different from the goals of the program. The college did not allow the student to register for additional courses and withdrew his registration for the upcoming spring semester. The student sued the college in a state court, alleging due process violations for failure to provide the procedures for dismissal expressed in the college's own rules and regulations.

The court dismissed the case, and the student appealed to a state appellate division court. The court rejected the college's argument that he was not fully matriculated because he had only been "conditionally accepted" by the graduate program. The student satisfied admission requirements and the conditions of the acceptance letter. The college said nothing in the letter about a later review and did not mention in its handbook or catalogue that it would review a student's personal goals before making a decision. **The court found the college could not dismiss the student without following the due process procedures stated in its rules and regulations.** The judgment was modified with directions to reinstate the student. *Matter of McConnell v. Le Moyne College*, 25 A.D.3d 1066, 808 N.Y.S.2d 860 (N.Y. App. Div. 2006).

◆ *A Pennsylvania university did not deprive a student of due process when it suspended him for sexually assaulting another student. The university judicial board adhered to statutory procedures for student disciplinary hearings.*

A Pennsylvania university dean received an e-mail from a female student alleging a male student had pulled her shirt up and fondled her breasts at a campus party. The university scheduled a discipline hearing before the judicial board to determine if the student violated the student code of conduct. The university informed him in writing of the date and time of the hearing and of the charges against him. During the hearing, the female student testified to the authenticity of the e-mail she wrote and answered the student's questions.

The dean informed the student in writing of the board's decision to suspend him for two years. The student appealed to the Commonwealth Court of Pennsylvania. He claimed the evidence was insufficient to support the board's finding and that the hearing violated his due process rights by failing to provide sufficient time to prepare a response and secure witnesses. The court stated **the student was entitled to due process, which includes basic principles of fundamental fairness. At a minimum, the university had to provide him notice of the charges and an opportunity for a hearing. However, the**

university did not have to provide a "full-dress judicial hearing," subject to the rules of evidence or representation by an attorney. Pennsylvania state universities must comply with 22 Pa. Code § 505.3. The court held the university did so by providing the student with the date, time and place of the hearing, an opportunity to submit written, physical or testimonial evidence, allowing him to question witnesses, and affording him sufficient time to prepare a defense. **The university adhered to its procedures and applied the correct standard of review, affording the student adequate due process.** *Ruane v. Shippensburg Univ.*, 871 A.2d 859 (Pa. Commw. Ct. 2005).

◆ *The University of Maine did not have to provide all due process protections of a criminal trial in a lawsuit involving the discipline of two football players.*

The football players were accused of sexually assaulting a female student at her off-campus apartment. Police investigated but did not file criminal charges against them. The university charged them with violating the student conduct code. After a hearing, a panel found the players guilty of sexual assault, and they were suspended from school and thrown off the football team. They also lost their scholarships. The players sued the university and school officials in a federal district court for due process and contract violations. They claimed the university did not provide them copies of witness and evidence lists, the victim's statement to the police, and a third party's statement regarding her credibility. The players asserted their attorney could not effectively cross-examine the victim because she remained behind a partition at the hearing.

The court noted that education is not a fundamental right or liberty interest. The substantive due process claim was dismissed. Regarding the procedural due process claim, the court explained that **colleges and universities must inform a student facing discipline of the charges and the nature of the evidence, and provide the student an opportunity to respond. A student may only be punished based on substantial evidence.** The court found that the student conduct code required the university to conduct disciplinary hearings with fundamental fairness. The code was considered a contract between the players and university. The players' procedural due process allegations raised sufficient questions as to whether the university complied with its contractual promise of fundamental fairness. While they could proceed with their procedural due process and contract claims, their remaining claims were dismissed. *Gomes v. Univ. of Maine*, 304 F.Supp.2d 117 (D. Me. 2004).

After further consideration, the court found the university complied with the requirements for a fair hearing because it gave the students an opportunity to answer, explain and defend themselves. **The university was not required to follow all of the procedural safeguards of a criminal trial.** The court granted the university's motion for summary judgment and dismissed the case. *Gomes v. Univ. of Maine*, 365 F.Supp.2d 6 (D. Me. 2005).

◆ *A Kentucky university did not violate a student's constitutional right to due process when it dismissed him from the school's doctoral program.*

A doctoral student alleged the university violated his due process rights when it arbitrarily terminated his enrollment in the school of education's doctoral program. The university said his work was unsatisfactory. It claimed it warned him his work was below the required standards and offered him help to improve his performance. The student sued the university in a federal district court. The university sought summary judgment. The court held the student failed to establish a due process violation. **The court noted "the essence of due process is the requirement that a person in jeopardy of serious loss be given notice of the case against him and an opportunity to meet it."** The student appealed. The Sixth Court of Appeals found the student presented no evidence to support his claim that the university acted arbitrarily. **The court found the university satisfied the student's due process rights because it told him his performance was unsatisfactory, explained how his poor performance impacted on his ability to remain in the program, and carefully and deliberately dismissed him.** *Amaechi v. Univ. of Kentucky,* 118 Fed. Appx. 32 (6th Cir. 2004).

◆ *A South Carolina student who was recently dismissed from his academic program was still a "student" when he received an on-campus parking ticket.*

The University of South Carolina dismissed the student for academic reasons. While his dismissal was on appeal, he agreed to be placed on conduct probation for 15 months in settlement of an earlier nonacademic incident. The student signed a form acknowledging the board had explained his rights to him. He later argued with a university police officer over a parking citation. The officer issued him a notice of policy violation for harassment. The university then denied the student's academic dismissal appeal. He failed to attend a campus judicial board hearing on the parking citation and the board expelled him. The student appealed his expulsion, arguing he was not a student at the time of the citation incident and did not have to adhere to university policies.

The university denied the student's appeal and he sued it in a state court. The court granted the university's motion for summary judgment, and the student appealed to the Court of Appeals of South Carolina. The court noted the student had settled his disciplinary appeal by agreeing to conduct probation for 15 months. He clearly considered he would be a student in the future. The court found no change in his student status between the date he signed the agreement and the parking violation. **The court rejected the student's contention that the university handbook definition of "continuing student relationship" was vague. The academic appellate process was still taking place at the time of the parking violation and the dismissal became final long after the incident.** The student held himself out to be a student and continued his student relationship with the school. The court affirmed the decision for the university. *Carter v. Univ. of South Carolina,* 360 S.C.App. 428, 602 S.E.2d 59 (S.C. Ct. App. 2004).

◆ *A university could consider evidence of a student's off-campus misconduct during a hearing regarding his on-campus misconduct.*

The University of Minnesota charged the student with violating its student conduct code for on-campus misconduct. He challenged the charge at a hearing before the campus committee on student behavior, which permitted evidence of his off-campus sexual encounters and past assaults at the hearing. They were deemed relevant to his on-campus behavior. The committee recommended a two-year suspension, but a review panel advised the president of the university not to accept the recommendation. The president personally reviewed the record, then accepted the recommended suspension. The student appealed to the Minnesota Court of Appeals, which upheld the president's decision.

Although **the university would have to be careful to avoid unduly prejudicial testimony at future disciplinary hearings**, the student was issued written notices of the charges against him, received an opportunity to confront his accusers, and was represented by an advocate. Thus, the off-campus evidence did not taint the proceeding so as to render it unfair. The student would have to serve the suspension. *R.T. v. Univ. of Minnesota*, No. C9-01-1596, 2002 WL 1275663 (Minn. Ct. App. 2002).

◆ *Academic dismissals require less procedural protection than disciplinary dismissals; however, even an academic dismissal requires adequate notice.*

A graduate student at the University of Alaska Anchorage applied for and was accepted to an advanced practicum in special education. He worked with a host teacher at the school district to which he was assigned and was supervised by a university professor. After the host teacher notified the professor of problems with the student, the professor met with the student and attempted to rectify the problem. However, the school's principal later told the professor that things were worse than they had appeared at the previous meeting.

The professor met with the principal and the host teacher before determining that the student should be removed from the practicum. The student was notified of his removal from the practicum and was subsequently notified that he was being removed from the special education program. He appealed under the university's procedures, and the case ultimately reached the Supreme Court of Alaska, which held **the university had complied with its internal guidelines for dismissing a student from the practicum. However, an issue remained as to whether the student had been given proper notice that he was at risk of being removed from the special education program.** The court remanded the case. *Nickerson v. Univ. of Alaska Anchorage*, 975 P.2d 46 (Alaska 1999).

2. Private Schools

Private schools have broad discretion to establish disciplinary rules and procedures through their contractual relationships with students. Generally, private school students are only entitled to receive the procedural safeguards specifically provided for by the institution.

◆ *A federal district court held in favor of a Pennsylvania university that expelled a male student for bizarre behavior and threats against others.*

The student was accused of bizarre behavior by several female students who feared he might harm them. They complained to the university that he graphically described how he would kill people. After two hearings, the university found the student guilty of threatening the safety of others and suspended him for the rest of the school year. When he reapplied for admission, the university denied his application and permanently expelled him. The student appealed the denial of his application in a letter that was splattered with blood. He then sued the university in a federal district court.

The court found no basis for the lawsuit. The university committed no constitutional violation by disciplining him. The student argued that the university treated his case differently from the way it handled a claim against a student stalker. **According to the court, at the very most, the university may have treated the student more harshly than the student stalker. However, that was not enough to prove the university violated his constitutional rights.** The court granted the university's motion for dismissal. *Hubler v. Widener Univ.*, No. Civ.A. 05-01785-JF, Civ.A. 05-01920-JF, 2006 WL 437542 (E.D. Pa. 2/22/06).

◆ *A New York university violated its own disciplinary rules by failing to give a student adequate time to prepare for a hearing to consider his expulsion.*

A New York student was involved in a dorm room fight. An associate director of security interviewed others involved and concluded the student had struck one of them without warning or provocation. A university hearing officer told the student he was charged with an unprovoked attack on another student. He gave the student an opportunity to be heard and handed him a copy of the undergraduate disciplinary rules, which permitted the university's dean of students to suspend students pending completion of hearing procedures. The rules also required notice to students of the exact charges and a reasonable notice of the time and place for the interview. Students could prepare oral and written defenses and present them to university hearing officers. They could appeal hearing officer decisions to the vice president of academic affairs.

The school expelled the student after officials interviewed him. It allowed him to choose between voluntary withdrawal, with no mark on his academic records, or expulsion with the right to appeal, which would remain on his permanent record. The student voluntarily withdrew and petitioned a state court for an order annulling the discipline, reinstating him as a student, removing all references to his expulsion from his record, and allowing him to complete his courses. The student claimed he was forced to withdraw and asked the court to review the school's actions. **The court held the university violated its rules by failing to give the student adequate time to prepare for the interview and adequate time to prepare a written defense. It returned the case to the university for a hearing under its own rules.** The court denied the student's request to be reinstated as a student in good standing, since university rules allowed suspension pending the completion of disciplinary procedures. His request for an order striking references to his expulsion was also denied. *In re Ebert v. Yeshiva Univ.*, 780 N.Y.S.2d 283 (N.Y. Sup. Ct. 2004).

◆ *The U.S. Court of Appeals, Fifth Circuit, held private religious university campus police had probable cause to arrest a student who tried to register for classes after he was suspended from school.*

The school suspended the student for violating the student code of conduct by stalking two female students. When the student appeared at school to register for a summer session, campus police arrested him for criminal trespass and turned him over to county police. Although the student was charged with criminal trespass, the district attorney's office later dropped the charges. The student sued the university, campus police and a university dean in a federal district court for false arrest, false imprisonment and malicious prosecution, among other claims. The school, campus police, and dean requested summary judgment and dismissal of the charges, as the student did not offer facts to show they acted with malice. The district court agreed and dismissed the action. The student appealed to the Fifth Circuit, which found the university and its officials had probable cause to arrest and prosecute the student. It affirmed the district court judgment. *Barnes v. Johnson*, 99 Fed. Appx. 534 (5th Cir. 2004).

◆ *A federal district court refused to dismiss an action by a Florida law school student who was expelled without the use of school academic procedures.*

The student allegedly threatened to blow up an office at the school and frightened three students with intimidating behavior. A school counselor called him "the most volatile and frightening student she had encountered." The school dean issued the student an expulsion letter based on "serious threats" and "physically intimidating conduct." The student claimed he did not receive any notice of the charges and was not provided with a hearing. He sued the school and several of its officials in a federal district court for negligence, defamation and breach of contract. The school and officials moved to dismiss the case for failure to state a claim upon which relief could be granted.

The court agreed to dismiss the negligence claim. Under Florida law, a student may be suspended or expelled for breaching a university's code of conduct. Even if school officials were mistaken in issuing the notice, they were not liable unless they acted with malice. As there was no finding of malice in this case, the negligence claim was dismissed. There could also be no liability for defamation. The dean's statements were privileged because they were based on the school's interest or duty to investigate and resolve the case. The court held a contract existed between the student and school, which was governed by the terms of the student handbook. **The law school's code of academic integrity specified that students would receive procedural protections before any expulsion decision.** The court denied the school's motion to dismiss this claim, as it had apparently breached these contract terms. The court dismissed the remaining claims. *Jarzynka v. St. Thomas Univ. School of Law*, 310 F.Supp.2d 1256 (S.D. Fla. 2004).

◆ *The Supreme Court of Kentucky held a state licensing statute did not create a duty for a private college to provide due process procedures.*

College officials searched the student's dormitory room after others reported he threatened to harm a classmate. The search yielded three pocket knives and a large Army survival knife with a blade over five inches long. The college's student handbook prohibited dangerous weapons and included dismissal as a sanction for weapons possession. College officials met with the student and told him of the accusation of threats and the discovery of the knives. The student did not deny the threats and admitted he owned the knives. An official handed him a dismissal letter, but told him he could be readmitted if he agreed to psychiatric treatment and evaluation. The student instead sued the college and its officials in a state court for due process violations. The court granted the college's motion for summary judgment, finding the handbook clearly warned students that weapons possession could result in dismissal. The state court of appeals reversed the judgment, finding that state licensing regulations imposed due process requirements upon private colleges.

The Supreme Court of Kentucky explained that the main purpose of the licensing statute was to "protect the Commonwealth's citizens from fraudulent or substandard educational institutions." **The appeals court erroneously held that state law authorized recovery for a violation of the licensing statute. The statute did not impose due process obligations on private colleges. According to the court, a private college "does not necessarily subject itself to the entire panoply of due process requirements that would be applicable at a state-sponsored education institution." The college had great flexibility with regard to its due process obligations.** While a contract had been formed between the parties, the court found the handbook did not guarantee due process rights. The handbook stated that under "unusual circumstances," due process procedures would not be followed. **Since the student breached college rules by possessing weapons on campus, the college was not obligated to perform under the contract. His admission of misconduct justified immediate dismissal and nullified any reason for a hearing.** The supreme court reinstated the judgment for the college. *Centre College v. Trzop*, 127 S.W.3d 562 (Ky. 2003).

◆ *Brandeis University did not violate its obligations in conducting an investigation and disciplinary proceeding against a student accused of rape.*

In March 1996, a female student filed a complaint with the Brandeis student judicial system, alleging that a male student had engaged in intercourse with her without her consent. Following a hearing, the university board on student conduct determined that the male student engaged in unwanted sexual activity and created a hostile environment. As a penalty, he was suspended for the four-month summer term and was placed on disciplinary probation until he graduated. The male student filed a complaint against Brandeis listing various tort, civil rights and contractual claims. He argued that he was unfairly disciplined and sought injunctive relief and compensatory damages. The trial court dismissed the complaint, but the court of appeals reversed on the breach of contract claim. The student appealed. The Massachusetts Supreme Judicial Court found that although a contractual relationship existed, the student failed to establish that the school did not meet his reasonable expectations.

The student contended Brandeis: (1) did not interview him at the investigatory stage; (2) did not apply the "clear and convincing evidence" standard of proof to its decision; (3) excluded his expert's testimony; and (4) failed to make a complete record of the proceedings. In rejecting the student's allegations, **the court strictly construed the language of the handbook in favor of Brandeis.** As to the first assertion, the court determined the section at issue did not apply to investigations of student misconduct, but to invasion of privacy claims in connection with room inspections. **The court also found nothing in the handbook that required the university to interview the**

student or to seek evidence from him at the investigatory stage. Next, the court found "ample evidence" to conclude that the board reached its decision based on clear and convincing evidence. Third, the handbook did not mention the admission of witness testimony. As to the student's fourth allegation, the court acknowledged that the 12-line report of the disciplinary proceeding was brief, but concluded that the handbook did not require the report to be of a specific length. Accordingly, the student failed to state a claim upon which relief could be granted, and the judgment of the trial court was affirmed. *Schaer v. Brandeis Univ.*, 432 Mass. 474, 735 N.E.2d 373 (Mass. 2000).

◆ *An Illinois private university had a rational basis for expelling a student who failed to earn credits for two consecutive semesters.*

The student failed two required field work assignments for her master's in social work program. The student accused the university of failing to offer her a remediation plan as described in the university handbook. The university claimed she did not qualify for remediation and expelled her from the program under a handbook policy requiring dismissal of any student failing to earn credit in consecutive semesters. She sued the university in a state court for breach of contract and other claims. The court held the university handbook created a contract and found the university breached the contract by not creating a remediation plan. It ordered the university to refund her tuition.

The university appealed to the Appellate Court of Illinois, which found the university adequately documented the student's problems. It held the relationship between a student and private university is not purely contractual. Courts are generally unwilling to interfere with private university student regulations. **A student may prevail on a contract claim against a private university only if an adverse academic decision is arbitrary, capricious or in bad faith.** A student must show a dismissal was without any discernable rational basis. As there was no such showing in this case, the court reversed the judgment. *Raethz v. Aurora Univ.*, 805 N.E.2d 696 (Ill. App. Ct. 2004).

3. Search and Seizure

◆ *The pre-eminent search and seizure case in the public school context is New Jersey v. T.L.O. The courts have applied the principles of this case to colleges and universities based on the strong state interest in protecting student safety. In T.L.O., the Supreme Court held a school search need only be reasonable at its inception, and not overly intrusive under the circumstances.*

A New Jersey high school teacher found two girls smoking in the lavatory in violation of school rules. She brought them to the assistant vice principal's office where one of the girls admitted smoking in the lavatory. The other denied even being a smoker. The assistant vice principal then asked the latter girl to come to his private office, where he opened her purse and found a pack of cigarettes. As he reached for them he noticed rolling papers and decided to thoroughly search the entire purse. He found marijuana, a pipe, empty plastic bags, a substantial number of one dollar bills and a list of "people who owe me money." He then turned her over to the police. A juvenile court hearing was held, and the girl was found delinquent. She appealed the juvenile court's determination, contending that her constitutional rights had been violated by the search of her purse. She argued that the evidence against her obtained in the search should have been excluded from the juvenile court proceeding.

The U.S. Supreme Court held that the search did not violate the Fourth Amendment prohibition against unreasonable search and seizure. **When police conduct a search, they have to meet the probable cause standard. However, school officials are held to a lower standard: reasonable suspicion.** Two considerations are relevant in determining the reasonableness of a search. First, the search must be justified initially by reasonable suspicion. Second, the scope and conduct of the search must be reasonably related to the circumstances that gave rise to the search, and school officials must take into account the student's age, sex and the nature of the offense. **The Court upheld the search of the student in this case because the initial search for cigarettes was supported by reasonable suspicion.** The discovery of the rolling papers then justified the further searching of the purse since such papers are commonly used to roll marijuana cigarettes. The "reasonableness" standard was met by school officials in these circumstances and thus the evidence against the girl was properly obtained. *New Jersey v. T.L.O.*, 469 U.S. 325, 105 S.Ct. 733, 83 L.Ed.2d 720 (1985).

◆   *The use of deadly force by police was justified based on probable cause to believe an intruder threatened serious bodily harm.*

A security guard at a Minnesota college noticed a car driving on a sidewalk near campus. He followed the car and local police were called. When the car finally stopped some 20 minutes later, the guard and local police officers approached it. The driver did not respond when instructed to put his hands where they could be seen. He then attempted to get away, putting the car in reverse and ramming the guard's security vehicle before accelerating toward two police officers, who were on foot. The driver was shot 14 times and later pronounced dead at the scene. The college security guard did not fire any shots. All of the officers who fired weapons later said they did so because they feared for their lives or the lives of their fellow officers. The driver's widow alleged that her husband had bipolar disorder. She sued the police department, officers, security guard and college in a federal district court for violating his constitutional right to be free from unreasonable searches and seizures. The widow also claimed the police violated the Americans with Disabilities Act (ADA) by failing to train officers how to approach people with mental illness.

The case reached the U.S. Court of Appeals, Eighth Circuit, which rejected the constitutional claim against the police. **The use of deadly force was justified, as the officers had probable cause to believe the driver posed a threat of serious bodily harm.** The court held constitutional claims against private actors, such as the college and security guard in this case, were viable "only if they are willing participants in a joint action with public servants acting under color of state law." In this case, the security guard did nothing more than follow the suspect into the alley. **His level of involvement was insufficient to subject him or the college to liability for any constitutional violation.** The court rejected the widow's ADA claim that the shooting could have been avoided if the officers had been trained how to approach people with mental illness. The suspect's threatening behavior, not a lack of training, caused the shooting. *Sanders v. City of Minneapolis*, 474 F.3d 523 (8th Cir. 2007).

◆ *A "seizure" does not occur every time police stop and question a person. Officers may rely on trustworthy reports from staff to make investigatory stops.*

An African-American library patron was using a computer in a library at the New Jersey Institute of Technology. An assistant librarian called the security department to report him for taking a stapler. The patron agreed to answer questions by the police, then let them search his bag. After they did not find the stapler, the patron left the building. He sued the officers, institute and library staff in a federal district court for constitutional rights violations. He claimed the officers and staff falsely accused him of stealing computer software rather than a stapler and subjected him to an unreasonable search and seizure. The court awarded summary judgment to the institute and staff.

The patron appealed to the U.S. Court of Appeals, Third Circuit, asserting the police violated his Fourth Amendment right to be free from unreasonable searches and seizures. While he admitted consenting to the questioning and the search of his bag, he claimed the consent was invalid because one officer failed to inform him that he had a right to refuse the search. The court found there was no such requirement. The patron's consent was valid, as the investigation lasted only seven minutes, took place in public, and was not threatening or intimidating. The district court had properly held that no jury could have found a Fourth Amendment violation. **The U.S. Supreme Court has held a seizure does not occur every time police officers approach someone to ask a few questions. The court found the patron obviously did not feel coerced or threatened into remaining in the library or responding to questions.** After the brief search of his bag, he walked out of the library without responding to the officer's request for his name. In any event, the court held the brief stop of the patron was based on reasonable suspicion, because it was based on information from the assistant librarian. **Officers may rely on a trustworthy secondhand report and need not base an investigatory stop on personal observation.** The court rejected the patron's additional arguments and affirmed the judgment. *Only v. Cyr*, 205 Fed.Appx. 947 (3d Cir. 2006).

◆ *A Delaware university did not need to allow an appeal from an expulsion decision, as the procedures it used satisfied due process requirements.*

The case involved a student who was arrested off campus for possessing marijuana and a handgun. Police and a university security officer searched his dormitory room and found a round of 9mm ammunition and a small bag of marijuana. The university charged the student with possession of illegal drugs, a weapon, ammunition and drug paraphernalia. The student was advised of his right to a hearing before the Zero Tolerance Subcommittee, where he could be represented by a student, faculty member or staff member. He was further informed that he could have witnesses testify on his behalf and could ask that his accuser be present at the hearing. The committee upheld the charges for possessing ammunition and marijuana, and the university expelled the student.

The student's appeal was denied. He then sued the university in a federal district court for due process and civil rights violations. He claimed he was wrongfully denied a jury trial and subjected to cruel and unusual punishment. **The court held the Eighth Amendment applies to criminal offenses, not to disciplinary measures taken against students.** The student had no right to a jury trial under the Seventh Amendment, which applies only to federal court proceedings. The court found no evidence that the expulsion was racially motivated. Instead, the evidence showed the student was expelled because he admitted to possessing the ammunition and was responsible for the marijuana found in his dormitory room. There was no merit to his due process claim. **The university was not required to allow him to appeal its expulsion decision, and the procedures it used satisfied due process requirements.** Nor did the expulsion decision violate any of the student's protected liberty interests. **The decision to expel the student was rationally related to the legitimate purpose of fostering a safe and drug-free campus.** *Marsh v. Delaware State Univ.*, No. CIVA 05-00087 JJF, 2007 WL 521812 (D. Del. 2/15/07).

◆ *Private security guards employed by a New York university did not have to follow the same rules as municipal police.*

University of Rochester security guards searched a man for weapons. A metal scanner registered positive and a guard removed three baggies filled with white powder from the man's pocket. When asked what the substance was, he replied "crack." A police officer field-tested the substance, determining that it was cocaine. The man was arrested for possession of a controlled substance. He sought to suppress the evidence, claiming the security officers had no reasonable basis to take him into custody or search him. He also claimed that any incriminating statements or identification of him had to be excluded.

A New York court held **university-employed private security guards did not have to follow the same rules as city police. They did not work for the state and thus were not bound by the Fourth Amendment.** As for the incriminating statements and the identification issues, the man was entitled to have that evidence precluded as to the police because he did not receive the notice he should have received under New York law. However, the statements he made to the private security guard were not precluded. The man was entitled to a hearing to determine whether these statements were made voluntarily. *People v. Capers*, No. 06-16941, 2007 WL 171901 (N.Y. City Ct. 1/23/07).

◆ *University police officers did not make an unconstitutional seizure of a student who failed to respond to the officers.*

While driving through campus, an Indiana student lapsed into diabetic shock. His vehicle ended up on a sidewalk. When university police arrived on the scene, the student was unresponsive. The police officers forcibly removed him from his car and handcuffed him until an ambulance arrived, even though they had noticed his medical alert bracelet. The student sued the university and officers under 42 U.S.C. § 1983 for violating his Fourth Amendment rights. A federal court ruled in favor of the university and the officers. **The forcible**

removal and the detainment were justified by the student's unresponsiveness. The Seventh Circuit Court of Appeals affirmed the decision. The student's failure to respond added an element of unpredictability to the situation, and the police reasonably believed he was an intoxicated driver. Also, the police did not use excessive force in removing the student from his car. *Smith v. Ball State Univ.*, 295 F.3d 763 (7th Cir. 2002).

◆ *College security officers did not need probable cause before searching a New Hampshire student's dorm room.*

College safety and security officers entered a student's dorm room and found marijuana. State authorities then charged the student with marijuana possession. The student filed a motion to suppress the evidence, asserting that the search of his room was unconstitutional under the Fourth and Fourteenth Amendments and the New Hampshire Constitution. A state court suppressed the evidence, but the Supreme Court of New Hampshire reversed. Here, the student did not have the same constitutional rights he would have had if the police had searched his room. **The campus security officers were not acting as agents of the police; therefore, there was no governmental action so as to justify increased constitutional protection.** The marijuana confiscated during the search could be used against the student in the criminal proceeding. *State v. Nemser*, 807 A.2d 1289 (N.H. 2002).

B. Academic Dismissals

Courts have traditionally left grading policies to the special expertise of educators, but may review a grading policy that is arbitrary and capricious, irrational, made in bad faith or contrary to federal or state law. See, for example, Susan M. v. New York Law School, *556 N.E.2d 1104 (N.Y. 1990). Courts do not substitute their judgment for that of university faculty on matters such as degree requirements and academic dismissals.*

1. Poor Performance

◆ *Schools and universities are generally given a great deal of latitude by courts in making academic decisions. Their choices, however, must have some rational basis and not be arbitrary. The Supreme Court upheld a university's decision to dismiss a student from an advanced academic program based on poor performance.*

A student was enrolled in the University of Michigan's "Inteflex" program, which is a special six-year course of study leading to both an undergraduate and medical degree. The student struggled with the curriculum for six years, completing only four years' worth of study and barely achieving minimal competence. Because he was given a grade of "incomplete" in several important classes and was forced to delay taking his examinations, he was placed on an irregular program. Finally, he completed the four years of basic study necessary to take the NBME Part I, a test administered by the National Board of Medical Examiners which is a prerequisite to the final two years of study under the Inteflex program. Unfortunately, the student failed the exam, receiving the lowest score ever in the brief history of the Inteflex program.

The university's medical school executive board reviewed the student's academic career, decided to drop him from registration in the program, and denied his request to retake NBME Part I. The executive board was not swayed by arguments that his failure on the exam was due to his mother's heart attack 18 months previously, the excessive amount of time he had spent on an essay contest that he had entered, and his breakup with his girlfriend. The student brought suit in federal court claiming breach of contract under state law and also alleging a violation of his due process rights under the U.S. Constitution.

At trial, the evidence showed that **the university had established a practice of allowing students who had failed the NBME Part I to retake the test one, two, three, or even four times. The student here was the only person ever refused permission to retake the test.** The district court ruled against him on the contract claim and further held that his dismissal was not violative of the Due Process Clause. The U.S. Court of Appeals, Sixth Circuit, reversed and held that the student had possessed a property interest in his continued participation in the Inteflex program, and that the university had arbitrarily deprived him of that property interest by singling him out as the only student ever denied permission to retake the NBME Part I.

The U.S. Supreme Court unanimously reversed the court of appeals' decision and reinstated the district court's ruling against the student. **The Due Process Clause was not offended because the university's liberal retesting custom gave rise to no state law entitlement to retake NBME Part I.** Furthermore, the university had based its decision to dismiss the student upon careful, clear and conscientious deliberation, which took his entire academic career into account. The university had acted in good faith. The Supreme Court further observed that the discretion to determine, on academic grounds, who may be admitted to study is one of the "four essential freedoms" of a university. The Court thus held that the Due Process Clause was not violated by the student's dismissal. *Regents of Univ. of Michigan v. Ewing*, 474 U.S. 214, 106 S.Ct. 507, 88 L.Ed.2d 523 (1985).

◆ *Unlike dismissals for disciplinary reasons, dismissals for academic reasons do not require the procedural requirements of* Goss v. Lopez, *419 U.S. 565 (1975), a public high school case involving suspensions of students for misconduct. In disciplinary cases, school officials must give a student notice of the charges and an opportunity to respond to them. School officials have broader discretion in dealing with academic expulsions and suspensions than in disciplinary actions involving misconduct.*

The academic performance of students at the University of Missouri-Kansas City Medical School was assessed periodically by the Council of Evaluation, a faculty-student body with the power to recommend probation or dismissal subject to approval by a faculty committee and the dean. Several faculty members expressed dissatisfaction with the performance of a medical student. As a result, the Council of Evaluation recommended that she be advanced to her final year on a probationary status. Faculty complaints continued, and the council warned the student that absent "radical improvement," she would be dismissed. She was allowed to take a set of oral and practical examinations as an "appeal" from the council's decision.

The student spent a substantial portion of time with seven practicing physicians who supervised the examinations. Two recommended that she be allowed to graduate. Two recommended that she be dropped immediately from the school. The remaining three recommended that she not be allowed to graduate in June and be continued on probation pending further reports of her progress. Subsequent reports regarding the student were negative, and she was dropped from the program following the council's recommendation. The student sued, alleging that she had not been accorded due process prior to her dismissal. The district court determined that the student had been afforded due process. The U.S. Court of Appeals, Eighth Circuit, reversed.

On appeal, the U.S. Supreme Court held that **the student had been given due process as guaranteed by the Fourteenth Amendment**. The procedures leading to the student's dismissal, under which the student was fully informed of faculty dissatisfaction with her progress, and the consequent threat to the student's graduation and continued enrollment did not violate the Fourteenth Amendment. **Dismissals for academic reasons do not necessitate a hearing before the school's decision-making body.** *Board of Curators v. Horowitz*, 435 U.S. 78, 98 S.Ct. 948, 55 L.Ed.2d 124 (1978).

◆ *A California student could not bring a federal lawsuit based on claims that had already been considered in a state court action.*

The student failed a course during his first semester in an executive MBA program. The entire grade for the course was based on a group project. The student claimed the group in which he had participated turned in a version of the project that excluded his name and work product. The professor allowed the student to submit his own project. The student did so and received an F grade. The university dismissed him because the grade caused his average to drop below the minimum program requirement. The student's administrative appeals were denied, and he sued the university in the state court system for an order that would require the university to allow him to make up his grade.

The San Francisco Superior Court denied the student's request for a restraining order and other relief. Instead of appealing within the state court system, the student filed a new action against the university in a federal district court. He asserted a new set of claims based on the F grade, dismissal from the program and exclusion from campus. In the federal lawsuit, the student alleged discrimination under state and federal law. He also claimed violations of due process, breach of contract and infliction of emotional distress. The court noted that a valid final judgment on the merits of a claim prevents a party from later asserting claims that were raised – or could have been raised – in the first action. Claims arising out of the same facts that were previously litigated will be barred. **The claims in the federal action were clearly the same as the ones that formed the basis for the state court action. As the student should have included his discrimination claims in the state court action, the court dismissed the case.** *Green v. Univ. of San Francisco*, No. C 06-3321 JF (PVT), 2006 WL 3545024 (N.D. Cal. 12/8/06).

◆   *The Court of Appeals of Tennessee held in favor of a college that refused to reinstate a student who was dismissed after he failed a course twice.*

The student attended a school of dentistry at a college in Tennessee. He repeated his freshman year because he had previously failed courses in gross anatomy and microscopic anatomy. The college had an academic policy of dismissing students who failed the same course twice. During the fall semester, the student failed the same two courses. The college notified the student it was dismissing him. The student evaluation and promotion committee dismissed the student for poor academic performance. The dean of the school of dentistry rejected the student's appeal and dismissed him from the college.

The student's appeal was denied, and he sued the college in a state court for breach of contract. He based his claim on breach of the terms of the college academic policies and procedures and the student affairs handbook. The court dismissed the case, and the student appealed to the Court of Appeals of Tennessee. The student argued the college violated its policies by not providing him an opportunity to have his grades recalculated or giving him supportive assistance to appeal. **The court stated it was not equipped to review a university's academic policies. Courts do not substitute their judgment for that of university faculty on matters such as degree requirements and academic dismissals. The court rejected the student's breach of contract claim because college policies did not form a contract.** It affirmed the judgment for the college. *Lord v. Meharry Medical College School of Dentistry*, No. M2004-00264-COA-R3-CV, 2005 WL 1950119 (Tenn. Ct. App. 8/12/05).

◆   *A federal district court denied a District of Columbia student's request for an order to require a university to allow him to graduate.*

The student intended to graduate from the university with a degree in Computer Science in May 2005. He missed two required classes in computer science because of a medical condition, and received incomplete grades, making him unable to graduate in May. The student and his professors agreed he could complete the courses if he complied with certain conditions. The student failed to meet the conditions, and the university refused to let him graduate. He sued the university in a federal district court for breach of contract and race discrimination. The court considered his motion for a temporary restraining order. Even though the student admitted breaching the terms of the agreement with his professors, he asked the court to direct the university to let him graduate as if he received incomplete grades in the courses. **The court held the student failed to establish a strong likelihood of prevailing on his pending claims for breach of contract, race discrimination and equal protection against the school. It denied the request for a temporary restraining order.** The court believed the university and the other students who did meet their requirements could be harmed by allowing the student to receive his degree without meeting university requirements. *Habte v. George Washington Univ.*, No. Civ. 050962JGP, 2005 WL 1204882 (D.D.C. 5/19/05).

◆   *The Supreme Court of Alaska held a university did not violate a student's due process rights by dismissing him and denying him readmission.*

The student did not get along with a field instructor who supervised his field course work toward a social work degree. Although the field instructor did not recommend a failing grade, a faculty liaison professor assigned him an incomplete grade that was later changed to failure. An academic review panel upheld the grade, and the university later denied his reapplication. The student sued the university in the state court system, alleging due process violations for allegedly not following its own rules and failing to provide him with proper notice and an opportunity to be heard. The student added discrimination claims based on his gender and a disability. The court held the professor gave the student adequate notice of his academic deficiencies. She warned him several times about ongoing lateness and inferior work. The state supreme court affirmed the decision, agreeing that the university had provided the student with due process. **A person has no due process interest in admission to a professional school in the absence of dishonesty or publication of the reason for denying admission.** *Hermosillo v. Univ. of Alaska, Anchorage*, No. S-10563, 2004 WL 362384 (Alaska 2004).

◆   *A Tennessee state university did not have to provide a medical student a formal hearing to suspend him for academic reasons.*

The student was informed of his academic deficiencies and unprofessional conduct by a dean toward the end of his second year. Although he eventually passed all his second-year courses, he failed the USMLE Step 1 the following summer. Early in his third year, after a negative report to the student promotion committee, a recommendation was made that the student be suspended, and the suspension was upheld. The student appealed internally without success, then sued the state under 42 U.S.C. § 1983 for violating his Fourteenth Amendment due process rights. A federal district court ruled in his favor, but the Sixth Circuit reversed, noting that academic decisions, unlike disciplinary decisions, do not require a formal hearing to satisfy the Fourteenth Amendment's procedural due process requirements. **The medical school reached a careful and deliberate decision** based on an evaluation of the student's medical knowledge, ethical conduct and interpersonal skills. This adhered to its internal procedures and provided the student with sufficient procedural due process. *Ku v. State of Tennessee*, 322 F.3d 431 (6th Cir. 2003).

◆   *An Alaska university student could be removed from a program where he failed a competency exam.*

The student applied for admission to the elementary education program and was accepted on the condition that he pass the Praxis exam, which measures teacher competency. He failed the reading and writing portions of the exam, and school officials notified him that if he failed again, he would be removed from the program. When he failed a second time, he was removed. He appealed his removal internally, but the academic appeals committee upheld the decision. The case reached the Alaska Supreme Court, which also ruled against the student. Even though the university did not require all elementary education students to pass the Praxis exam, **its decision was not arbitrary because the student showed a real weakness in his reading and writing skills.** The university could have rejected him on that basis alone. Further, since passing the Praxis exam was a requirement for obtaining a teaching license, the decision to require the student to pass the test was reasonable. *Hunt v. University of Alaska, Fairbanks*, 52 P.3d 739 (Alaska 2002).

◆ *Where a failing student received notice and an opportunity to respond, she was appropriately dismissed from school.*

A graduate student in a nurse anesthesiology program began receiving poor grades. Counselors advised her on how to improve her performance, but she continued to miss program goals and was placed on probation. After her third failing term, a clinical education committee unanimously recommended her dismissal. She received notice of the committee's decision and requested a due process hearing, but her dismissal was upheld. She sued the university trustees for breach of contract and intentional infliction of emotional distress. A state court ruled in favor of the trustees, and the Michigan Court of Appeals affirmed. Even though there was an implied contract between the student and the university, it required only that dismissal not be arbitrary. Here, **the university followed all appropriate procedures when dismissing the student**, and she received proper due process. The trial court was correct in deferring to the university's judgment that her academic performance warranted dismissal. *Carlton v. Trustees of Univ. of Detroit Mercy*, No. 225926, 2002 WL 533885 (Mich. Ct. App. 2002).

◆ *A California law school did not have to readmit a student during his lawsuit challenging his academic dismissal.*

The student did poorly in his first semester and was notified that he was not in good academic standing. His performance improved in his second semester, but by the end of his fourth semester, his GPA in required courses plummeted to 1.96 (the mandatory minimum GPA in required courses was 2.05). The law school dismissed him, and the academic standards committee upheld the dismissal. The student then sued for breach of contract, among other claims, and sought an injunction ordering the school to reinstate him while the lawsuit was pending. A court refused to issue the injunction, and the California Court of Appeal affirmed that decision. To be entitled to injunctive relief, the student would have to show he was likely to succeed on his claims at trial, and he would suffer more harm than the law school if he was not reinstated. Because he failed to show a reasonable likelihood of success on the merits, the law school did not have to re-enroll him. *Rosenberg v. Golden Gate Univ.*, No. A097304, 2002 WL 31439753 (Cal. Ct. App. 10/31/02).

◆ *The Gonzaga University School of Law was not negligent in the process it followed to increase its minimum cumulative grade point average requirement and was justified in dismissing a student for having a substandard GPA.*

Gonzaga Law School required students to maintain both a semester and a cumulative GPA of 2.2. If they did not, they would be placed on academic probation for one semester. If their grades did not improve, Gonzaga dismissed them. In Fall 1994, the school revised its academic standing rule to eliminate probation and base dismissal solely on failure to achieve a 2.2 cumulative GPA after the first year. It also required students with a low-semester or cumulative GPA to negotiate and establish an individual academic plan with their faculty advisor. The new rule was distributed to all students, but was not implemented until the following year, after a task force of students and faculty reviewed the changes. In the beginning of the Fall 1995 semester, Gonzaga distributed the new handbook and implemented the revised rule, notifying all students through a memorandum placed in their mailboxes. A student began his second year of law school in the Fall of 1995 in good standing. During that semester, however, he earned a GPA of 1.7 and his cumulative GPA fell to 2.047. As a result, he was dismissed. The student sued, claiming he was notified of the change in academic rules seven weeks into the Fall 1995 semester. He also claimed that by enrolling in the law school, he had formed a contract with Gonzaga, one term of which was the academic standing rule, and that the university had breached the contract by changing the rule without adequate notice to him.

A Washington trial court ruled for Gonzaga, and the student appealed. The state court of appeals held that while the relationship between a student and a university is "primarily contractual in nature," contract law cannot be rigidly applied when addressing student-university relationships. The court concluded that **Gonzaga did not act arbitrarily and capriciously by changing the academic standard rule**. The trial court's ruling in Gonzaga's favor was correct. **Gonzaga's administration, faculty and students worked for more than a year on the rule before it was implemented.** As to timely notification, the student admitted he received the memo and the Law Student Handbook, which contained a copy of the disputed academic policy. *Ishibashi v. Gonzaga Univ. School of Law,* 101 Wash. App. 1078 (Wash. Ct. App. 2000).

◆ *Courts may review a grading policy that is arbitrary and capricious, irrational, made in bad faith or contrary to federal or state law.*

A New York Law School student performed below a 2.0, or "C," cumulative average. The law school rules required students to maintain a 2.0 or better, or be subject to academic dismissal by the Academic Status Committee. The student appeared before the committee to state her case, but the committee was not persuaded by the student's excuses and voted unanimously to dismiss her. The student asked the committee to reconsider its decision. When the committee declined, the student filed suit in a New York trial court challenging the committee's decision and the grades she received in three of her classes. The trial court dismissed all of the claims, but the appellate division reversed and remanded the case with respect to the student's grade in one of her classes to determine if the grade was a rational exercise of discretion.

Both parties appealed to the Court of Appeals of New York. The student claimed that when she met with the professor he indicated she had received a zero on an essay question, worth 30% of her grade, because she had analyzed the problem under Delaware and New York law when only Delaware law was asked for. The student explained she analyzed the problem under New York law to get extra credit. **Courts have traditionally left grading policies to the special expertise of educators**, but may review a grading policy that is arbitrary and capricious, irrational, made in bad faith or contrary to federal or state law. The court determined **the student failed to meet this standard of** review because the allegations went to the heart of the professor's evaluation of her academic performance. The court dismissed the claim in its entirety. *Susan M. v. New York Law School*, 556 N.E.2d 1104 (N.Y. 1990).

2. Cheating and Plagiarism

◆ *Due process requires that an individual with a constitutionally protected interest receive notice and a meaningful opportunity to be heard.*

A student enrolled in the University of Michigan school of dentistry. Like all students, she signed an acknowledgement to abide by the school honor code. The student was accused of violating the code in a class. When the university notified her of the violation, she waived her right to an honor council hearing. Instead, the student chose to have a three-member *ad hoc* faculty committee hear her case. After a hearing, the faculty committee members unanimously agreed that she committed a violation and recommended the school expel her. The student appealed to an executive committee which held another hearing where she admitted the violation. The committee suspended her until the next semester and placed her on probation. After the student returned to school, she was again accused of code violations. The committee formally expelled her, and she sought a state court order to prevent the action.

The court denied the request, and the student appealed. The Court of Appeals of Michigan **held due process requires that an individual receive notice and a meaningful opportunity to be heard. To prove a constitutional risk of bias, an individual must show the risk or probability of unfairness was too high to be tolerated.** The court held the student did not prove an unacceptable risk of bias. Members of the honor council and *ad hoc* committee only submitted recommendations to the executive committee. The court rejected the student's contention that two honor council members who were classmates could not be impartial. As familiarity with a case does not disqualify a decision maker, the judgment was affirmed. *Imitiaz v. Board of Regents of Univ. of Michigan*, No. 253107, 2006 WL 510057 (Mich. Ct. App. 3/2/06).

◆ *A Florida university followed its code and did not violate any due process rights pertaining to the waiver of a student hearing.*

The student enrolled in "Senior Project," a required course for a degree in construction management. He dropped the class after two weeks, but reenrolled in it the next year. As part of the course, students were required to develop a hypothetical construction company. When the student submitted documentation for his company, the course instructor believed parts of it were identical to those submitted by others in the previous semester. The instructor and department chairman confronted the student and told him a formal academic misconduct charge would be filed. The university's vice provost for academic affairs wrote the student a letter informing him of the charge and sent him a copy of the student handbook. The letter explained that the matter could not be resolved informally because the student had previously received an F grade in a course for cheating. The student requested an administrative hearing.

The vice provost conducted the hearing, at which the instructor presented evidence and testified about the student's cheating, plagiarism and academic dishonesty. The student admitted hiring an architect to design part of his project and using part of the classmates' work from the previous semester. He claimed he had continued working with the group after he dropped the course. The vice provost upheld charges of plagiarism, cheating and collusion, and expelled the student. After unsuccessful appeals within the university, the student sought review by a Florida district court of appeal. **The court found the university had followed the procedures specified in its code and did not violate any due process rights pertaining to the waiver of a review board hearing.** The vice provost's letter directed the student to read handbook provisions on academic misconduct, grievance procedures and student rights. The court found the letter gave the student the same opportunity to waive a review board hearing as a specific waiver form. The court held the university's failure to strictly comply with state administrative code requirements was harmless error and did not violate the student's due process rights. The hearing transcript revealed that he never tried to cross-examine the instructor, who identified 27 items in his work that were identical to work submitted by other students. As sufficient grounds for expulsion existed, the court affirmed the decision. *Matar v. Florida Int'l Univ.*, 944 So.2d 1153 (Fla. Dist. Ct. App. 2006).

◆ *A federal district court held a New York college did not discriminate against a disabled student when it dismissed him for plagiarism.*

The student was allowed certain accommodations he requested from his graduate psychology program, but denied some others. One of his professors gave him a B+ for a course despite the submission of a late paper. The student wrote to the college vice president, alleging the professor discriminated against him because of his disability. The college dean investigated the complaint, and the department chair reviewed the student's paper. While reading the paper, the chair suspected plagiarism. She submitted the student's paper to an online service for plagiarism and confirmed her suspicion. The student received a zero for the assignment. The student filed a grievance which resulted in a finding that a failing grade was appropriate. The college dismissed him.

The student sued the college in a federal district court, alleging it violated the Americans with Disabilities Act and Section 504 of the Rehabilitation Act. He asserted the college discriminated against him when it refused to let him resubmit his research paper. **The court found nothing suggested the student could not resubmit his paper based on his disability. The college presented evidence of another incident where a non-disabled student was also denied a chance to resubmit her paper.** The vice president had confirmed her suspicions through the online service. The court held the college was not motivated by discrimination and dismissed the case. *O'Connor v. College of Saint Rose*, No. 3:04-CV-0318, 2005 WL 2739106 (N.D.N.Y. 10/24/05).

◆ *The Appeals Court of Massachusetts held a university fully complied with its disciplinary procedures in finding a student guilty of plagiarism.*

A Brandeis University professor noticed a second-term senior student did not properly attribute four secondary sources in a paper. She filed a student judicial system referral report, accusing him of verbatim plagiarism. The university's board of student conduct unanimously found the student guilty of plagiarism, and he unsuccessfully challenged the finding through the university appeal process. The student sued Brandeis in a Massachusetts trial court for breach of contract and breach of fiduciary duty. The court granted Brandeis's motion for summary judgment, and the student appealed. **The state court of appeals explained the university was expected to conduct hearings with basic fairness.** In reviewing the record, the court found Brandeis satisfied that expectation by providing the student all of the process he was due under the terms of the handbook, from notification of the charge through the hearing process. **The handbook clearly warned him that violation of academic honesty policies could lead to serious penalties.** Moreover, the sanction was consistent with those imposed on other upperclassmen for similar infractions. The trial court did not err in granting summary judgment to the university. *Morris v. Brandeis Univ.*, 804 N.E.2d 961 (Mass. App. Ct. 2004).

◆ *A Connecticut university complied with its disciplinary regulations and did not act arbitrarily by disciplining a student for cheating on an exam.*

A teaching assistant believed the student was suspiciously looking about during the exam, and her answers were very similar to those of a classmate. The student denied the charge, but the university's executive committee suspended her. The student sued the university in a state court for breach of contract and moved for summary judgment. The student argued the university breached its contract by improperly carrying out its disciplinary procedures. She claimed the committee disregarded pertinent evidence, which included that her exam answers were similar to the answers of other students who took the test in another building where the exam was also given. The court rejected the student's arguments, stating the similarity of answers was not the issue. She did not refute a professor's detailed evidence of her cheating.

The court found the university complied with its disciplinary regulations and the university did not act arbitrarily by ordering a suspension. The court refused to interfere with a decision to expel or discipline a student as long as the university did not act arbitrarily. The university relied on information gathered during its investigation before deciding to charge the student with cheating. The student never refuted the professor's assertions or offered her own comparative analysis of the two exams. She failed to present any evidence that the school acted maliciously. **As the school relied on credible evidence of cheating, the court dismissed the case**. *Okafor v. Yale Univ.*, No. CV980410320, 2004 WL 1615941 (Conn. Super. Ct. 2004).

◆ *A federal district court held a Texas university did not violate federal disability protection laws by disciplining a student for academic dishonesty. There was an objectively reasonable basis for suspecting him of cheating.*

The student left an examination room during an examination. A university employee observed him with a copy of the exam in a men's room stall. He observed a camera flash in the stall. Videotapes from campus security cameras confirmed that a student in a different section of the same class was sitting in the next stall of the men's room at the time the student was observed there. **A federal district court found the student did not show the university discriminated against him due to his disability. The university had an**

objectively reasonable basis for suspecting the student of cheating and had accommodated his disabilities. *Sadik v. Univ. of Houston*, No. Civ. A. H-03-4296, 2005 WL 1828588 (S.D. Tex. 8/1/05).

♦ *The Court of Appeal of California held a law school provided a student with due process before suspending him for one semester for plagiarism.*

A second-year law student at the UCLA Law School submitted a 49-page paper to a professor who discovered "substantial portions" of it had been copied from a book without acknowledgment. The school's assistant dean and law school librarian agreed that the student had committed plagiarism. During an informal meeting, the student admitted his work was "fast and loose," but he denied any intent to commit plagiarism. The school allowed the student's request to postpone a disciplinary meeting so he could take a final examination. He then attended the disciplinary meeting, where he was represented by counsel. After reviewing the evidence, the school dean found he had committed plagiarism in violation of the Student Conduct Code. The school retroactively suspended the student and required him to complete 300 hours of community service. After unsuccessfully appealing his suspension, he complied with the disciplinary terms. Following his graduation, the student filed a state court action to set aside his suspension on the basis that he did not receive procedural due process. The court granted UCLA's summary judgment motion.

The student appealed to the Court of Appeal of California. The court noted that before any disciplinary action was initiated, the student's paper was reviewed by several school officials and even fellow students. All of these individuals concluded he had plagiarized the book. **The student received notice of the accusation against him and was informed of the definition of plagiarism in the Student Conduct Code.** The school provided him with an explanation of disciplinary procedures, and it was his obligation to learn UCLA's disciplinary procedures. Moreover, the student admitted the plagiarism. For this reason, he was not entitled to a hearing before the student conduct committee. **UCLA had provided the student with several opportunities to explain his actions.** Even had he received a hearing, it was unlikely he could have presented any new evidence to change the conclusion that he committed plagiarism, especially since he had admitted this conduct. The judgment for UCLA was affirmed. *Viriyapanthu v. Regents of the Univ. of California*, No. B157836, 2003 WL 22120968 (Cal. Ct. App. 2003).

♦ *A state court upheld the academic suspensions of two Texas university students who were disciplined for making "strikingly similar" answers on an organic chemistry examination.*

The students were a husband-wife couple who created suspicion because they gave incorrect answers to questions despite "millions of possible incorrect solutions." They were tested together in a hotel room while attending an off-campus conference. Their incorrect answers led to charges of violation of the school honor code. The university honor council held a hearing and found the students violated the code. The students were assigned F grades for the course and were suspended for two months. The students failed to appear at a second hearing they requested. They then sought a state court order to remove their academic suspensions and the F grades from their transcripts.

The court rejected the students' argument that the university blue book created a contract. They appealed to the Court of Appeals of Texas, which noted the record of their suspensions would appear only on internal school records. Since the students would not suffer any irreparable harm in the absence of a court order, the court affirmed the decision. *Law v. Rice Univ.*, 123 S.W.3d 786 (Tex. Ct. App. 2003).

◆ *A North Carolina state university was immune from a lawsuit brought by an expelled law student.*

A state university law school student attempted to obtain the answers a study group had prepared for previous exams used in a particular course. She was unable to do so. On the day of the exam, she went to the emergency room complaining of stomach problems and missed the test. After the test, she called a fellow student and asked for the answers, claiming she already had taken the test and wanted the answers to prepare for the bar exam. When a dean learned of her dishonesty, she refused to let the student take a makeup exam. Disciplinary proceedings were initiated, and the student was eventually expelled. She sued the university in a federal court under 42 U.S.C. § 1983 and also asserted a negligence claim. The court dismissed her lawsuit on Eleventh Amendment immunity grounds because she could not show that an exception applied to permit her suit to continue. **North Carolina never waived its immunity, and Section 1983 did not eliminate states' immunity in such situations.** *Pfouts v. North Carolina Cent. Univ.*, No. 1:02CV00016, 2003 WL 1562412 (M.D.N.C. 2003).

◆ *Union University's Albany College of Pharmacy could not expel or fail three students for cheating where the college relied on statistical evidence showing that they had given the same incorrect answers on various exams.*

All three students were in their fourth year at the college when several professors accused them of cheating on tests in various courses over a two-year period. The Student Honor Code Committee found the students guilty based on evidence that they gave the same incorrect answers on various exams, similarly calculated answers to questions (although the students had arrived at the answers through different methods), and two anonymous notes questioning whether the students were cheating. Two of the students were found guilty of cheating in six courses and were expelled. The other student was charged with cheating in one course and received a failing grade for the class. The students appealed the committee's decision to a state trial court, which upheld the committee's decision as rational.

On appeal, the New York Supreme Court, Appellate Division, reviewed whether the committee's decision was arbitrary or capricious. It noted that the committee relied on a compilation of statistics showing the similarities in the students' answers, but **the statistical evidence only gave rise to a suspicion of cheating**. The court pointed to an affidavit from an expert statistician who said the statistics were not valid because they lacked "randomness," specifically that the students had no knowledge of the subject matter on the tests, and that there was "independence," in that the students had not studied together. The court also found the notes used as evidence by the committee to be inadmissible hearsay. Overall, **the court found the committee's decision irrational because it found the students guilty of cheating based merely on a statistical compilation of information, even though the students had taken the exams in separate rooms, and the exam proctors discerned no evidence of cheating**. The court annulled the committee's determination. *Basile v. Albany College of Pharmacy of Union Univ.*, 719 N.Y.S.2d 199 (N.Y. App. Div. 2001).

◆ *A Texas university student accused of plagiarism lost his appeal claiming the school's decision to expel him was an act of racial discrimination.*

The matter arose after the student turned in his final project to his theater professor. The project was a script titled "Return to Live," which the student submitted as his own original writing. Upon receiving a B for the project, he complained to an administrator in the College of Arts and Sciences that he deserved a higher grade. Suspicious of the script's originality, the professor researched similar plays in the public library and discovered that the student's script replicated another work called "Resurrection" almost word for word. As a result, the student failed the theater course and was expelled. The student sued for discrimination, among other claims, but his lawsuit was dismissed.

The student appealed, claiming he had told his professor he would be using an existing work and therefore did not plagiarize. He cited testimony by the administrator that finding the allegedly plagiarized play in the library would be like finding a "needle in a haystack." The student noted that the professor would therefore not be aware of the previously published play unless he himself had told her. The court determined the administrator's "needle in a haystack" reference referred to trying to find a play before limiting the search to a particular category. The professor explained that she limited her search to Afro-American dramas, a much smaller collection to search than all of the plays in the library. **The court rejected the student's argument that his expulsion constituted racial discrimination. A white student who was caught plagiarizing but denied the charge also was expelled.** The district court decision was affirmed in full. *Ntreh v. Univ. of Texas at Dallas*, No. 05-99-01165-CV, 2000 WL 1093233 (Tex. Ct. App. 2000).

◆ *Where Texas professors did not take allegations of cheating into account when grading a student, a federal court held he had no cause of action against them for being dismissed from the university.*

A graduate student in psychology received two grades of C that subjected him to possible expulsion. A number of his professors also knew of allegations against him for cheating. However, they asserted they did not take the allegations into account when grading him. After the student's second C, he was placed in a remediation program. He then received two more Cs and failed two oral comprehensive examinations. A second, more demanding remediation plan was then drafted, calling for the student to enroll in a specific class. When he failed to do so, he was dismissed from the program because of his failure to comply with program academic requirements. He sued, claiming that the decision to dismiss him was tainted by the allegations of cheating and that he was not given a chance to address those allegations.

A federal district court ruled in favor of the university, and the Fifth Circuit Court of Appeals affirmed. **The dismissal had been for academic reasons, not disciplinary reasons. The protections available to the student were not as great. Even if the dismissal had been for disciplinary reasons, the student had essentially been given a hearing** when he went over the remediation plans with school personnel. It was only after he failed to meet the requirements of the second remediation plan that he was dismissed from the program. *Wheeler v. Miller*, 168 F.3d 241 (5th Cir. 1999).

◆ *A loss of credit for two classes in which a student was found to have violated a university honor code was fair punishment.*

The University of Tennessee Board of Trustees' honor code created a violation for failure to report the giving or receiving of unauthorized aid on an examination. Four students reported observing a group of other students who apparently gave or received aid during several examinations. One of the accused students was charged with cheating on five examinations under the honor code. An administrative law judge found the student not guilty on three charges and guilty on two others. He imposed as a punishment one year of probation and the loss of credit for the two classes in which she was held in violation of the honor code. The student appealed the decision to a Tennessee trial court, stating that a 19-day delay by the administrative law judge in issuing his opinion caused her to delay retaking the two courses. The student nonetheless graduated. The court held for the university, and the student appealed to the Court of Appeals of Tennessee. **The court of appeals found ample evidence in the record that the student had violated the honor code. There was evidence that the student had been looking at another person's examination papers.** The administrative law judge's delay did not violate state law, and the court affirmed the trial court's judgment for the university. *Daley v. Univ. of Tennessee at Memphis*, 880 S.W.2d 693 (Tenn. Ct. App. 1994).

C. Nonacademic Dismissals

Depending on the circumstances, dismissal for cheating may be an academic dismissal or a "nonacademic dismissal." Educational institutions should follow reasonable procedures and provide students facing discipline with appropriate notice and an opportunity to be heard.

◆ *The suspension of a New York business school student was not disproportionate to the offense of harassing other students.*

A New York Appellate Division Court dismissed a student's petition to annul his suspension by Columbia University's business school for one year. The court refused to annul the decision to ban him for life from using the university's Career Services and Alumni Affairs and from certain recruiting-related student activities. The student had sent harassing communications to and about several other students at the business school. The student received an opportunity to present his side of the story and to appeal internally. **The court found the school fulfilled all the required process rights due to the student for a disciplinary proceeding on a nonacademic matter. It said the university's actions were not disproportionate to the student's conduct,** and it dismissed the student's petition. *Fernandez v. Columbia Univ.*, 790 N.Y.S.2d 603 (N.Y. App. Div. 2005).

◆   *A federal appeals court found no merit to a student's claim that a Texas university maintained a "zero tolerance" drug policy.*

A Southwest Texas State University student claimed the university's drug policy, as written in the student handbook, mandated automatic dismissal if a student was found guilty of the possession, use or distribution of illegal drugs. In protest of what he deemed a "zero tolerance drug policy," he lit a marijuana cigarette at an on-campus rally. The university suspended him for two semesters. He sued the university and various officials in a federal district court, alleging the policy violated his Equal Protection rights. The court granted summary judgment to the university, and the student appealed.

The U.S. Court of Appeals, Fifth Circuit, found that although the handbook had some conflicting language, there was no evidence it contained a "zero tolerance" drug policy. **The court found the policy provided disciplinary options to impose suspensions or dismissals, undermining the "zero tolerance" policy argument. Student code penalty provisions were not automatic.** Moreover, students were entitled to a hearing before a disciplinary committee with the discretion to consider mitigating factors and reduce suspensions to probation. The court held the student's Equal Protection claim lacked merit, and it affirmed the judgment. *Anderson v. Southwest Texas State Univ.*, 73 Fed.Appx. 775 (5th Cir. 2003).

◆   *A Georgia dental college properly expelled a student for drug use and falsifying documents.*

The student performed well academically, but was suspected of trafficking in narcotics. After university police searched his apartment and found controlled substances, he admitted using drugs. He was granted a medical leave to enter a rehabilitation program. Subsequently, the university learned that he had let his insurance coverage lapse in violation of school policy. After a hearing, he was dismissed from school. When he applied for readmission six months later, the university denied his application based on additional charges of possessing a loaded weapon and falsifying his financial aid application. He sued, and a federal court ruled in favor of the university. First, the court determined that he was not disabled under Section 504 because he was considered a current drug user. Only two months passed between his admittance to the treatment program and his dismissal. Second, **there was no due process violation.** Not only is attendance at a dental school not a fundamental right, but **the student had been given notice and an opportunity to be heard during the proceedings** against him. *Federov v. Board of Regents for the Univ. of Georgia*, 194 F.Supp.2d 1378 (S.D. Ga. 2002).

◆ *A university could expel a student for murdering a classmate even though he had completed all his degree requirements.*

A student enrolled at Johns Hopkins University and completed his degree requirements in three and a half years. However, because the university held its graduation ceremonies only once a year at the end of the spring semester, he had to wait to receive his diploma. During the spring semester, the dean of students contacted him about complaints of harassment filed by another student, and told him that he would have to notify her and campus security when he intended to be on campus. He informed the dean that he would be on campus on a particular date to attend a student organization meeting. As promised, he attended the meeting, where he got into a confrontation with the student who had accused him of harassment. He shot and killed the student, then pled guilty to murder. When the dean informed him that the university had expelled him and that he was not going to receive his diploma, he sued.

A state trial court dismissed his action, and the Court of Special Appeals of Maryland affirmed. It did not matter that the student would have already received his diploma had the university conducted a fall graduation ceremony. What mattered was that the student had not yet been awarded his degree, and that he remained subject to the student handbook rules. **Since the student handbook required him to not only complete his course work, but also to comply with the university's conduct code, and since murder was a violation of that code, the university was justified in expelling the student despite his completion of all degree requirements.** The student was not entitled to a diploma. *Harwood v. Johns Hopkins Univ.*, 747 A.2d 205 (Md. Ct. Spec. App. 2000).

◆ *An Arkansas community college nursing student who tried to get drugs with a fraudulent prescription could be expelled.*

The student was arrested for attempting to obtain a controlled substance with a fraudulent prescription. She was suspended pending the police charges against her and pleaded no contest to a misdemeanor offense. The college then expelled her from school. It later conducted a new hearing to give the student another opportunity to review all the evidence and participate in the hearing with the help of counsel. The college again upheld the decision to expel the student. She sued the college in a federal court under 42 U.S.C. § 1983, asserting that the college had violated her constitutionally protected due process rights. The court dismissed her lawsuit.

The Eighth Circuit affirmed the ruling for the college. First, **the college's Standards of Conduct were not void for vagueness.** They required students to obey all rules and regulations formulated by the college as well as all federal, state and local laws. This was sufficient to notify the student that criminal conduct was not acceptable. Second, the student had been provided with adequate notice of the charges against her and an opportunity to present her side of the story. As a result, her claim against the college could not succeed. *Woodis v. Westark Community College*, 160 F.3d 435 (8th Cir. 1998).

◆ *A Pennsylvania court held it should not interfere with internal disciplinary matters unless they were biased, prejudicial or lacking in due process.*

A student attending a private school operated by a Pennsylvania charitable foundation was suspended for one year after he repeatedly photographed and accosted visitors and scholars of the foundation. He was suspended for an additional two-year period after impersonating a foundation employee on three occasions in order to gain access to an area containing unique and priceless art.

The student filed a lawsuit in a Pennsylvania trial court seeking a decree rescinding his suspension from the school. The trial court dismissed the lawsuit for lack of jurisdiction, and the student appealed to the Superior Court of Pennsylvania. The superior court held that because the student's lawsuit sounded in equity, the trial court had improperly declined to assert jurisdiction. However, pursuant to *Schulman v. Franklin & Marshall College*, 371 Pa. Super. 345, 538 A.2d 49 (1988), **courts should not interfere with internal disciplinary matters unless the process has been found to be biased, prejudicial or lacking.** Here, the school reasonably suspended the student for his harassing behavior and unauthorized entries into areas containing priceless art. *In re Barnes Foundation*, 661 A.2d 889 (Pa. Super. 1995).

◆ *Schools generally receive greater deference with respect to dismissals involving academic deficiency than for those involving nonacademic reasons.*

A student at a private college of osteopathic medicine failed several courses during his first year. He also failed his spring clinical rotations and a neurobiology class during his third year. However, he later passed the classes after retaking them. During his fourth year, the student refused the college's request to return from an internship in Minneapolis after problems arose there. He finally returned, was placed on probation, and then assigned to do his clinical rotations in Des Moines. After serious attendance problems, two alleged incidents of unauthorized practice of medicine, and one alleged incident of forgery, the student was dismissed following a series of notices and hearings. The student challenged his dismissal in an Iowa trial court.

The court held that the dismissal was arbitrary and capricious, but it denied reinstatement and awarded him the equivalent of four years' tuition. Both parties appealed their adverse rulings to the Supreme Court of Iowa. The court stated that **schools generally are accorded greater deference with respect to dismissals involving academic deficiency** than for those involving nonacademic reasons. Here, the school's admission at trial established that the student's dismissal was nonacademic. **Although professional training violations were academic matters, they also were considered nonacademic disciplinary violations.** However, even under the stricter burden applied to nonacademic disciplinary actions, the court held that the two incidents of unauthorized practice of medicine coupled with the events that led to his probation justified his dismissal. The holding of the district court was reversed. *Pflepsen v. Univ. of Osteopathic Medicine*, 519 N.W.2d 390 (Iowa 1994).

III. STUDENT PRIVACY RIGHTS

State and federal laws provide for the protection of students' privacy interests, particularly in their academic records. The laws provide guidelines and procedures for the maintenance and disclosure of records.

A. The Family Educational Rights and Privacy Act

The Family Educational Rights and Privacy Act of 1974 (FERPA), 20 U.S.C. § 1232(g), also called the Buckley Amendment, applies to any educational institution receiving federal funds. The act, along with U.S. Department of Education regulations at 34 C.F.R. Part 99, contains extremely detailed requirements regarding the maintenance and disclosure of student records. These requirements become applicable only upon a student's attendance at the school.

FERPA, at 20 U.S.C. § 1232g(d), requires schools to allow college students the right to inspect and review their education records. When students request access to their education records, schools must grant that access within a reasonable time, not to exceed 45 days. Students also must be given the opportunity for a hearing to challenge the content of their education records, or to ensure that the records are not inaccurate, misleading, or otherwise in violation of their privacy or other rights.

Education records include those records, files, documents and other materials that contain information directly related to a student and that are maintained by the school or by an agent of the school. Records maintained by a law enforcement agency of a school (for the purpose of law enforcement) do not constitute education records for purposes of FERPA. Schools cannot release, or provide access to, any personally identifiable information in education other than directory information without the parents' written consent. Violating FERPA results in a loss of federal funds.

At times, FERPA seems to come into conflict with other laws, like the 1990 Student Right-to-Know and Campus Security Act, 20 U.S.C. § 1092(f), which requires all institutions of higher education that participate in federal funding programs to prepare, publish and distribute to all current students and employees an annual campus security report. Because colleges and universities sometimes deal with student crime through disciplinary boards, rather than through campus police, there can be pressure to seal student disciplinary records (under FERPA) that would otherwise be public under the Campus Security Act.

Further, FERPA provides that a college or university can include in the education record of any student "appropriate information ... concerning disciplinary action taken against such student for conduct that posed a significant risk to the safety or well-being of that student, other students, or other members of the school community." 20 U.S.C. § 1232g(h). Since schools often benefit more from designating a particular act a violation of the student code (and being able to keep the information private) rather than designating it a crime (and having to release the information to the public), reports on campus security are not always accurate.

◆ *A student who claimed that a university violated FERPA could not sue under 42 U.S.C. § 1983 to enforce individual "rights" under the act.*

A student attended a private university in Washington, intending to teach in the state's public school system after his graduation. At the time, the state required new teachers to obtain an affidavit of good moral character from the dean of their college or university. When the university's teacher certification specialist overheard a conversation implicating the student in sexual misconduct with a classmate, she commenced an investigation of the student and reported the allegations against him to the state teacher certification agency. She later informed the student that the university would not provide him with the affidavit of good moral character required for certification as a Washington teacher. The student sued the university and the specialist under state law and under 42 U.S.C. § 1983, alleging a violation of FERPA.

A jury awarded the student over $1 million in damages. The case reached the U.S. Supreme Court, which ruled that **FERPA creates no personal rights that can be enforced under Section 1983**. Congress enacted FERPA to force schools to respect students' privacy with respect to educational records. It did not confer upon students enforceable rights. As a result, the Court reversed and remanded the case for further proceedings. *Gonzaga Univ. v. Doe*, 536 U.S. 273, 122 S.Ct. 2268, 153 L.Ed.2d 309 (2002).

◆ *Using students to correct other students' work and call out the grades in class did not violate FERPA.*

An Oklahoma parent sued a school district and various administrators under FERPA after learning that students sometimes graded other students' assignments and called out the results in class. A federal court held this practice did not violate FERPA because calling out grades did not involve "education records" within the meaning of the statute. The Tenth Circuit reversed, but the U.S. Supreme Court noted that **student papers are not "maintained" within the meaning of FERPA when students correct them and call out grades**. Moreover, correcting a student's work can be as much a part of the assignment as taking the test itself. The momentary handling of assignments by students was not equivalent to the storing of information in a records room or a school's permanent secure database. *Owasso Independent School Dist. No. I-011 v. Falvo*, 534 U.S. 426, 122 S.Ct. 934, 151 L.Ed.2d 896 (2002).

◆ *As FERPA creates no individually enforceable rights, a disabled student could not pursue an action for wrongful disclosure of his condition.*

A Massachusetts university baseball coach told the team that the student had bipolar disorder. The student sued the university in a federal district court for violations of FERPA. The court determined it was unclear as to whether the coach's statement violated the nondisclosure rules of FERPA. **Even if it did, the student had no right of action in court to redress such a violation,**

because FERPA does not create any individually enforceable rights.
Violations of FERPA are redressed by the Secretary of Education, who may
direct in certain circumstances that funds be withheld from the educational
institution. Accordingly, the court dismissed the FERPA claim. *Zona v. Clark
Univ.*, 436 F.Supp.2d 287 (D. Mass. 2006).

◆ *A North Carolina University obtained a court order to seal depositions and
a student's academic transcript in a sexual harassment lawsuit.*

The university, coach and employee sought summary judgment in the
lawsuit, and filed the depositions of two students and their parents. The
university, coach and employee also filed the affidavit of the university's
registrar with the student's final official transcript attached. The university
moved to seal the depositions and affidavit. Because the First Amendment gives
the public a right to see and hear all evidence in a civil trial, courts may seal
documents filed with a motion for summary judgment only if the government
has a compelling interest to do so. Because the depositions contained private
information on other students, the university argued they should be sealed to
protect their privacy interests. The court disagreed.

The court found no violation of the other students' privacy rights because
they had no reasonable expectation of privacy in information exchanged with
team members. **The depositions were not protected by FERPA, as they were
not "education records."** FERPA was only one of the considerations in
deciding if the student's interest was a compelling governmental interest. It
placed great weight on the student's decision to file the lawsuit. She previously
took no position on her privacy interests, leaving the court to assume she had
no significant interest in having her academic records sealed. A FERPA
exception allows the disclosure of relevant educational records on a student
who initiates legal action against a university. Because the student had ample
opportunity to respond to the motion to seal the record, the court concluded she
effectively consented to the release of her academic records. *Jennings v. Univ.
of North Carolina*, 340 F. Supp.2d 679 (D.N.C. 2004).

◆ *An Illinois student's defamation and invasion of privacy claims were
barred because they arose from remarks made by a professor that were deemed
to be within the scope of his employment.*

An Illinois political science professor suspected a colleague of having a
sexual relationship with a graduate student. He informed the department chair
about their behavior and discussed the matter with four other professors. He
also informed the student's boyfriend of his suspicions. During this time, other
students complained that the colleague was generally unavailable and did not
keep his office hours. The student filed a grievance against the professor,
charging him with sexual harassment and violating her privacy, and made a
charge against him with the Illinois Department of Human Rights. The
professor sued the student in a federal district court, alleging deprivation of his
First Amendment speech rights and retaliation. The student counterclaimed for
defamation, intentional infliction of emotional distress and invasion of her
privacy rights. The court awarded summary judgment to the professor.

The Seventh Circuit held the professor showed his comments were made
within the scope of his employment. Evidence indicated the university was

concerned about inappropriate professor-student relationships and encouraged professors to report suspicious relationships. The professor communicated his concerns during the academic year within normal office hours. The court rejected the student's characterization of his remarks as gossip. The professor spoke to other professors about the colleague's lack of professionalism and his observations were motivated, at least in part, by an intent to serve the university. **The court rejected the FERPA claim based on *Gonzaga Univ. v. Doe*, above, in which the Supreme Court held there is no private cause of action for FERPA violations under 42 U.S.C. § 1983.** *Shockley v. Svoboda*, 342 F.3d 736 (7th Cir. 2003).

◆ *University disciplinary records were held to be "education records" under FERPA and thus could not be disclosed to the press.*

A student newspaper at an Ohio university sought student disciplinary records from the University Disciplinary Board for an article about crime trends on campus. After a lawsuit, the Ohio Supreme Court held that student disciplinary records were not "education records" under FERPA. As a result, the university had to hand over the records, without name, Social Security number and student identification number. Another newspaper then requested disciplinary records from two Ohio universities. The U.S. Department of Education (DOE) asked a federal district court for an order to prevent the universities from disclosing the disciplinary records. The court agreed with the DOE that disciplinary records are "education records" under FERPA, and issued an injunction to prevent the release of the information.

The Sixth Circuit Court of Appeals affirmed, noting that **because the disciplinary records related to students and were kept by the universities, they were education records under FERPA.** Since university disciplinary proceedings are not like criminal trials, which have been traditionally open to the press and the public, an order preventing release of the information was appropriate. *U.S. v. Miami Univ.*, 294 F.3d 797 (6th Cir. 2002).

◆ *Student applicant information was not protected by FERPA where it was not personally identifiable.*

The University of Wisconsin System received a request for records of applicants applying for admission to the system's 11 undergraduate campuses, its law school and its medical school over a six-year period. The system partially complied with the request, but withheld information on standardized test scores, race and gender because it believed the information was protected by FERPA and because it believed the release of such information would require it to create new records. The case reached the Supreme Court of Wisconsin, which held that **FERPA did not prevent disclosure of the requested data because it was not personally identifiable information.**

Even though it might be possible for the data to create a list of identifying characteristics, the court concluded that the information was not personally identifiable. Also, the court noted that the system would not have to create new records to comply with the request. It merely would have to redact personally identifiable information from records it already maintained. Doing so would be burdensome; however, the system could charge a fee for photocopying records to alleviate its costs. The system had to provide the requested information. *Osborn v. Board of Regents of Univ. of Wisconsin System*, 647 N.W.2d 158 (Wis. 2002).

◆ *A state university was immune to suit where it negligently disseminated confidential student records.*

A freshman basketball player at a Texas university was suspended from the team when he failed to maintain good academic standing. Various newspapers reported the story. The day after the suspension, a fax containing a portion of his educational records was sent from the men's basketball office to two local radio stations. The stations broadcasted that information. The student sued the university and several officials for negligence under the state tort claims act and for violating FERPA. A state court dismissed the lawsuit on the grounds that the university had immunity, and the Texas Court of Appeals affirmed. Here, **there was no tangible personal property that led to his injury so as to bring his claim within the exception to immunity under the tort claims act**. The fax machine used to disseminate his confidential information did not cause his injury. Also, he conceded on appeal that the FERPA claim could not survive. *Axtell v. Univ. of Texas at Austin*, 69 S.W.3d 261 (Tex. Ct. App. 2002).

◆ *Neither FERPA nor school policy provide a means by which a student may obtain information on how a particular grade was assigned.*

A Texas university student received a grade of C in a physics class. He was disappointed with the grade and sought to challenge the assignment of the grade in a federal district court, or in the alternative to strike it from the record. The university and the teacher moved to dismiss the case. FERPA provides that no federal funds shall be made available to any educational agency or institution unless the parents of a student who has been in attendance at such institution are provided an opportunity for a hearing for the purpose of ensuring that the content of the student's education records are not inaccurate, misleading, or otherwise in violation of the privacy rights of the student. **Neither FERPA nor school policy provide a means by which a student may obtain information on how a particular grade was assigned**. The court ruled that **at most, the student was only entitled to know whether the assigned grade was recorded accurately** in the records. Therefore, the court granted the defendants' motion to dismiss the case. *Tarka v. Cunningham*, 741 F.Supp. 1281 (W.D. Tex. 1990).

◆ *A student newspaper had to be allowed to attend student Organization Court meetings and had to be granted access to the court's records.*

After the student newspaper at the University of Georgia was denied access to Organization Court records and proceedings involving hazing at fraternities, the newspaper sued, seeking access to records and disciplinary proceedings of the student Organization Court. The university claimed that FERPA required it to keep confidential those records and proceedings. However, the Supreme Court of Georgia disagreed. It noted that even if FERPA could be construed as prohibiting the release of education records, **the access being sought here was not access to "education records." What the newspaper was seeking was**

documentation of hazing charges against fraternities. The court determined that the newspaper was entitled to the records of proceedings as well as to Organization Court proceedings under the state's Open Meetings Act. *Red & Black Publishing Co. v. Board of Regents*, 427 S.E.2d 257 (Ga. 1993).

B. State Law Privacy Rights

States laws modeled on FERPA may create enforceable privacy rights for students. Students may also bring common law claims based on enrollment contracts or other agreements with their institutions.

◆ *A New York court held two student rape victims could not compel the school newspaper to exclude their names from a news report.*

The students sued New York University (NYU) for allowing them to be raped through negligent security. They learned the NYU student newspaper had obtained documents with their names and planned to publish them. The students sought the court's permission to replace their names with pseudonyms and to seal court records containing their true names. The newspaper sought to intervene in the lawsuit, asserting its interests diverged from that of NYU. The court found NYU had different interests than the newspaper and could not adequately represent it. State regulations made all court documents "court records" that were open to the public unless there was "good cause" to seal them. The students argued their identities should be concealed because they would be embarrassed and humiliated if the newspaper published their names.

The court rejected the students' argument. It explained that their right to privacy was limited. The statute they relied on only applied to public employees. **The newspaper had lawfully obtained the students' names through court records. The court rejected their "good cause" argument, as embarrassment, damage to reputation and the general desire for privacy did not constitute good cause to seal court records.** While the court denied the students' request to exclude their names, the use of pseudonyms was a viable option to avoid any sensational publicity. The newspaper was entitled to intervene, and court records were to remain open. Student names were not to be excluded, but they could proceed anonymously by using pseudonyms. *Jane Doe 1 and Jane Doe 2 v. New York Univ.*, 786 N.Y.S.2d 892 (N.Y. Sup. 2004).

◆ *A private Georgia university did not violate the state's Open Records Act by refusing to grant a student's request to see the records of other students.*

The student stated she had been sexually assaulted on campus. She asked the university for records of other students who were victims of rapes and sexual assaults on campus. The university refused the request, and the student sued the university in a Georgia trial court, alleging it violated the state's Open Records Act. The court found the school's police force performed public functions in the enforcement of state laws. It held the records sought by the student were subject to the act and allowed her to view them. The university appealed to the Court of Appeals of Georgia.

The court explained the state Open Records Act generally required that all "public records" be open to inspection by the general public. It held the act was intended to encourage public access to information and promote public confidence in government through access to public records. The university was a nonprofit corporation, not a government agency. Campus officers were not public officials based on the state's decision to authorize them to perform certain duties. The court found the records were not "public records" because they were not prepared, maintained or received in the course of the operation of a public office or agency. The court reversed the judgment, as the documents maintained by the school police were not covered by the Act. *Mercer Univ. v. Barrett and Farahany, LLP*, 610 S.E.2d 138 (Ga. Ct. App. 2005).

◆ *Parts of a statewide test that were owned by the state were public records and had to be disclosed to a student.*

The Ohio Department of Education (ODE) administers the Ohio Proficiency Test to high school seniors to ensure that they have requisite knowledge in selected academic areas. Ohio State University also administered a statewide test to high school students that was developed to accelerate the modernization of vocational education in the state. Part of that test was developed and owned by a private entity. Both tests used a new format each time a test was administered and the tests were owned in part by the state agencies that administered them. An Ohio student who had taken both examinations requested access to the tests after they had been administered. The ODE refused to release test information for review unless the student signed a nondisclosure agreement. The family refused to sign the agreement and instead sued to compel state education officials to release relevant portions of both tests pursuant to the state Public Records Act.

The Supreme Court of Ohio ruled **the state-owned parts of both tests were public records within the meaning of state law**. Further, none of the exceptions to the state law presumption in favor of public disclosure applied. The student sought release of the information for educational purposes and did not seek to use it for a commercial purpose. A state law that prohibits assisting a student in cheating on proficiency tests was not applicable to this case. The student was entitled to an order for disclosure of the requested information. However, the portion of the test devised by the private entity was not a public record and was not subject to release. *State ex rel. Rea v. Ohio Dep't of Educ.*, 81 Ohio St.3d 527, 692 N.E.2d 596 (Ohio 1998).

◆ *A Colorado student could sue a college for ordering an HIV test without his permission.*

A student in a medical assistant training program told his instructor that he had tested positive for HIV and asked him to keep that information confidential. The instructor informed the class that all students were required to be tested for rubella. The student consented to the test with the understanding that his sample would be tested for rubella only. However, the instructor contacted the lab and asked that the student's sample be tested for HIV. She did not request such testing for any other student. After the sample tested positive, the lab reported the student's name, address and HIV status to the state of health (as required by law) and informed the college of the results. The student sued the college for invasion of privacy, asserting it unreasonably disclosed private facts and intruded upon his seclusion. The court dismissed the intrusion upon seclusion claim, but a jury found the student was entitled to damages for the college's unreasonable disclosure of private facts.

On appeal, the Colorado Court of Appeals held in his favor. **The claim for intrusion upon seclusion involved the college's authorization of a test that the student had not authorized, which was the improper appropriation of confidential information. The claim for unreasonable disclosure of private facts involved the dissemination of that information.** That the student suffered harm because of the disclosure of information did not mean he could not have suffered harm because of the improper appropriation of the information. The court reversed and remanded the case. *Doe v. High-Tech Institute, Inc.*, 972 P.2d 1060 (Colo. Ct. App. 1998).

◆   *An Ohio court found that a university's maintenance of a student's summer law program grades with his undergraduate grades was reasonable.*

A student enrolled in Ohio Northern University's summer law school qualification program. The program was designed for students who were not qualified for admission under regular criteria. Those who achieved a "B-" average would be admitted to the law school. The student failed to maintain the required grade point average and thus was not enrolled in the law school. Prior to enrollment in the summer program, the student had received an undergraduate engineering degree from the university. He sued the university in state court claiming that on at least two occasions it released his undergraduate transcript containing a record of his performance in the law school summer program. He sought a court order prohibiting the university from maintaining a record of his performance in the summer program and asking for money damages. An Ohio court ruled against him, and he appealed.

The Court of Appeals of Ohio held **the student failed to show that the maintaining of his summer law program grades together with his undergraduate record was unreasonable, arbitrary, or in violation of any federal or state law.** Further, the court held that whether the student had been "admitted" to the law school or had merely been "participating" in the summer program was irrelevant. The important fact was that the student had attended courses at the law school. Accordingly, the university was entitled to maintain records of his law school attendance. The lawsuit was dismissed. *Smith v. Ohio Northern Univ.*, 514 N.E.2d 142 (Ohio Ct. App. 1986).

C. Computer Privacy

◆   *The remote search of a dormitory computer did not violate a Wisconsin student hacker's reasonable expectation of privacy in the computer.*

A California-based Qualcomm computer system administrator informed the University of Wisconsin – Madison that someone had hacked Qualcomm's network through a computer connected to the university's network. A university investigator confirmed the report and discovered the hacker had also gained access to the university network. Concerned that the university's 60,000-account e-mail system was in immediate jeopardy, the investigator accessed the computer from a remote location. After viewing the computer's temporary directory, the investigator confirmed the unauthorized activity and took the computer off line to protect the university's e-mail system. He contacted university police and a federal agent who was working on the case. The investigator and university went to the hacker's dorm room and unplugged the computer from the network. The hacker arrived and gave the investigator permission to run a few commands. The test confirmed that the computer had been used to hack the networks. Federal agents obtained a warrant and seized the computer. The hacker was indicted on multiple offenses. A federal district court denied his motions to suppress evidence gathered via the remote search.

On appeal, **the U.S. Court of Appeals, Ninth Circuit, held the student hacker had a reasonable privacy expectation in his personal computer, which was not eliminated by attaching it to the university's network. The investigator's actions were not taken for law enforcement purposes, and a search warrant was not needed because he was acting in his role as a system administrator.** University policy authorized the investigator to rectify emergency situations that threatened the integrity of campus computers or communication systems. His actions were justified because he needed to act at once to protect the system. Under the circumstances, the court found the remote search of the computer was "remarkably limited." The investigator was logged in to the computer for just 15 minutes, and did not view, delete or modify any files. As the investigator's actions were taken to secure the university's e-mail server, the court held the evidence obtained during the searches was admissible. *U.S. v. Heckencamp*, 482 F.3d 1142 (9th Cir. 2007).

◆ *A student who allegedly saved child pornography on university computer lab computers was not entitled to privacy under the Fourth Amendment.*

A Maine student left an image on a university computer screen that a university employee considered pedophilic. University authorities investigated the incident and discovered similar images on the hard drives of other computer-lab computers. The university contacted the police, and the student was indicted for receiving child pornography in violation of 18 U.S.C. § 2252A(a)(2). The prosecution obtained two hard drives from the university that allegedly contained illegal images, as well as the university's computer usage logs, which indicated when the student used the computers. The student filed a motion to have the hard drives and logs suppressed as the product of searches that violated his Fourth Amendment right against unreasonable searches and seizures. A federal court judge ruled the student had no right to privacy in this matter and denied the motion to suppress. **To assert a right under the Fourth Amendment, a defendant must show that he believes he had a right to privacy and that society would find his expectation objectively reasonable.**

Because the usage logs were maintained for the benefit of the university, they could not be suppressed. The judge cited *Smith v. Maryland*, 442 U.S. 735 (1970), in which the U.S. Supreme Court held that a telephone customer had no legitimate expectation of privacy in telephone numbers he had dialed because, in dialing, he voluntarily conveyed the information to the telephone company and assumed the risk that the information could be disclosed. As for the hard drives, the judge found the student pointed to no computer privacy policies at the university, no statements made to him about the use of the computer lab, no practices concerning access to and retention of the contents of the hard drives or even password requirements. **The student was simply using university computers under circumstances where images on the monitor were visible to others.** *U.S. v. Butler*, 151 F.Supp.2d 82 (D. Me. 2001).

IV. GRADING AND CURRICULUM

◆   *The U.S. Court of Appeals, Sixth Circuit, held a Vanderbilt University student deserved a chance to convince a jury that his professor was negligent in his method of returning graded papers.*

The student was enrolled in an organic chemistry class. The professor placed graded answer sheets for the class in a stack on a table outside the classroom. Students had to go through the stack to find their answer sheets. The professor allowed students to resubmit their answer sheets for a "re-grade" if they believed he incorrectly marked them. The student found one of his correct answers was marked incorrect and returned the paper for re-grading. The professor believed the student had changed the answer and reported the student to Vanderbilt's honor council. The honor council conducted a hearing, and found the student guilty of cheating. He received a failing grade for the organic chemistry class and was suspended for the summer session. After an unsuccessful appeal, the student sued Vanderbilt in a federal district court for negligence, among other claims. The court held criteria to determine a standard of care for a teacher returning graded exams has never been established. Consequently, the student could not prove negligence.

On appeal, the Sixth Circuit found **Vanderbilt owed its students a duty not to engage in conduct that posed an unreasonable and foreseeable risk of harm.** Vanderbilt argued it could not have foreseen that a student would sabotage another student's test to improve his own position in the curve. The Sixth Circuit disagreed, in view of the competitive environment in academic institutions. The court found it unclear whether the manner in which the professor distributed graded answer sheets posed an unreasonable risk of harm. **A jury could conclude the burden on the professor to use another method for returning tests was minimal and find the harm to students was foreseeable.** The gravity of harm created by the professor's method was severe. A wrongful conviction by a disciplinary committee could ruin a student's chances of getting into graduate school. The professor breached the university's duty of care by acting in a way that posed an unreasonable and foreseeable risk of harm. A jury would have to decide whether Vanderbilt injured the student. The court reversed and remanded the judgment. *Atria v. Vanderbilt Univ.*, 142 Fed.Appx. 246 (6th Cir 2005).

◆   *The U.S. Court of Appeals, Ninth Circuit, rejected an appeal by a former student who claimed the University of California violated the First Amendment and state law by offering a curriculum that included religious studies classes.*

The court held the former student alleged no facts supporting a conclusion that the course offerings advanced a non-secular purpose, had a primary effect of advancing or inhibiting religion and fostered an

excessive entanglement with religion. The former student had filed multiple lawsuits against the university in federal courts, many of them alleging race discrimination. The university expelled him in 1999 for misconduct after he unsuccessfully challenged a C grade in a rhetoric class. *LaFreniere v. Regents of Univ. of California*, 207 Fed.Appx. 783 (9th Cir. 2006).

◆ *A New York student, who was homeschooled through high school, lost his equal protection claim in a federal district court against a state college.*

After the college admitted the student, it notified him by letter that college records showed he had not provided any papers to prove he had graduated from a high school or received a GED. The letter also informed the student that the state education department required students to have a high school diploma or equivalent before they could graduate from a New York state college. The college told the student to obtain a GED. The student deliberately did not try to get a GED, asserting it carried the stigma of being a substitute for a high school diploma used primarily for high school dropouts. He then sued the college in a federal district court, alleging it violated his equal protection rights by treating him differently from similarly situated public school graduates. He argued that because his homeschool education was substantially equivalent to a public school education, the college had no rational basis to treat him differently.

The court stated **the college did not have to take the word of the student that he received the equivalent of a public high school education.** In *Univ. of Pennsylvania v. EEOC*, 493 U.S. 182 (1990), the U.S. Supreme Court stated that **courts should avoid second-guessing legitimate academic judgments and respect a faculty's professional judgment.** The court held the actions of the college were rationally related to its legitimate interests in maintaining academic standards and the integrity of its degree-granting programs. It granted the request of the college to dismiss the equal protection claim. A year after the student filed the lawsuit, New York amended its regulations governing homeschooling. The new regulations stated that as long as students who were homeschooled met certain instructional requirements, they could graduate from a New York college. The college later issued the student an associate degree. *Owens v. Parrinello*, 365 F. Supp.2d 353 (W.D.N.Y. 2005).

◆ *A temporary grade reduction did not sufficiently injure a student such that he was entitled to damages.*

A Texas community college teacher responded to a tardiness problem in an 8:00 a.m. English class by stating that attendance would be taken and that those not present at the beginning of class would be counted absent. The department's attendance policy stated that students who were absent six days from a class were subject to a failing grade. However, when a student reached his sixth absence for the class, the teacher lowered his grade from an A to a B rather than issuing a failing grade. The student waited for one year to challenge the grade and filed a complaint with the dean of the department. The teacher agreed to change the grade to an A, but the student filed a lawsuit against the college and some of its employees in the U.S. District Court for the Northern District of Texas. The court dismissed the complaint, and the student appealed to the U.S. Court of Appeals, Fifth Circuit.

The court found that the only injury claimed by the student was the reduction of the grade for approximately 12 months, which allegedly denied him an opportunity to compete for academic scholarships. **The student had failed to state that he actually applied for scholarships and thus failed to show that he was injured because of the grade reduction.** Any injury he suffered was purely speculative. Accordingly, the claim was frivolous and insufficient to invoke the jurisdiction of a federal court. The court affirmed the order to dismiss the lawsuit. *Dilworth v. Dallas County Community College Dist.*, 81 F.3d 616 (5th Cir. 1996).

◆ *A grading complaint at a community college was deemed to be of an academic nature. Thus, the dean had final decisionmaking power in the area.*

Nursing students attending a Missouri community college complained that testing procedures in a required course caused them to fail the class. The claims included typographical errors, testing on materials not covered in classes and inability to review quizzes after grading. One of the students who failed the class met with the college dean to discuss retaking the final test, but her request was denied. The students complained to the state board of nursing, which conducted an investigation. The college responded by submitting a compliance proposal and offered the course again to the students. One of the failing students who subsequently retook and passed the class sued the college and some of its officials in a Missouri federal court under 42 U.S.C. § 1983, alleging civil rights violations. The court granted pretrial judgment to the college and administrators, and the student appealed to the Eighth Circuit.

The student claimed she had suffered procedural due process violations when the college failed to follow its handbook grievance procedure for resolving grading disputes and that administrators used arbitrary and capricious administrative methods. She also complained of substantive due process violations in the college curriculum requirements and claimed that college administrators were motivated by bad faith. The court held the complaint was related to an academic matter for which the dean held final decisionmaking power. It rejected the student's assertion that her complaint was a procedural and not an academic matter. **The alleged procedural irregularities did not rise to the level of a constitutional violation** or bring the question of grading outside the realm of academics. The administrators had appropriately rescheduled the course. The court affirmed the district court decision. *Disesa v. St. Louis Community College*, 79 F.3d 92 (8th Cir. 1996).

◆ *Academic freedom could be used as a defense to a claim brought under the Establishment Clause.*

A New York resident audited a community college course entitled "Family Life and Human Sexuality" and claimed that it promoted eastern religions and disparaged traditional Jewish and Christian teachings on marriage, procreation and adultery. He re-enrolled in the course the following semester and joined a number of New York taxpayers in filing a lawsuit against the community college, its administrators and board in the U.S. District Court for the Eastern District of New York, seeking declaratory and injunctive relief that the course offering violated the state and federal constitutions and New York law. The court considered several preliminary motions by the parties.

The court rejected the college and officials' dismissal motion based upon their claim that their right to academic freedom barred the plaintiffs from challenging college policies, activities and course materials. **Although the principles of academic freedom could provide a defense to the claims, they did not bar the claims altogether.** The individual taking the course did not have a viable claim because the class would have ended before the litigation did. Taxpayer status alone was insufficient to confer standing to allow a free exercise claim, and these claims were dismissed. The court was unable to construe a New York law requiring course offerings in college catalogues to be plainly disclosed, and this claim was dismissed. It also was unwilling to grant the requested order prohibiting the college from offering the course the following semester. However, **the court denied pretrial dismissal of the remaining taxpayers' claim that the course offering violated the Establishment Clause of the Constitution or the New York Constitution**. It dismissed the other claims. *Mincone v. Nassau County Community College*, 923 F.Supp. 398 (E.D.N.Y. 1996).

◆ *A grade of F was properly assigned where a South Dakota student turned in his assignments late.*

After being dismissed for academic reasons, a student was readmitted to a medical school in South Dakota. He then received a grade of F in internal medicine and was again dismissed from the school. He sued in federal court, asserting that the grade he received should have been I (incomplete), because although he failed to do all the requisite work before the end of the semester, he did complete the work shortly after the next semester began. He maintained that the professor had stated that incompletes would be given where a student failed to get all the work done on time, and he allegedly relied on that statement. He asserted that the grade of F in place of I was arbitrary and capricious conduct in violation of his substantive due process rights. A federal court granted pretrial judgment to the school, and the student appealed.

The U.S. Court of Appeals, Eighth Circuit, held that there was no genuine issue of material fact as to whether the grade of F was arbitrary. **The student had failed the final written examination, failed to properly present patients during rounds, and failed to turn in required work on time. Thus, the grade was justified.** There had been no substantive due process violation, and the student had been properly dismissed from the school. The court affirmed the lower court's decision for the medical school. *Hines v. Rinker*, 667 F.2d 699 (8th Cir. 1981).

V. HOUSING

◆ *A medical school may have violated the New York City Human Rights Law by denying two lesbian couples the right to seek campus housing in the same manner as a married couple.*

Yeshiva University's Albert Einstein College of Medicine, a private institution, owns a number of apartments near its campus and offers them at discounted rates to its students on a first come, first served basis. Priority is given to married couples. Two lesbian students requested housing for themselves and their life partners, but the university did not give them priority because they could not produce proof of marriage. The American Civil Liberties Union (ACLU) filed suit on behalf of the students, claiming the university violated the state's human rights law, the Roommate Law (Real Property Law Section 235-f) and the New York City Human Rights Law by discriminating against them based on marital status. The complaint further alleged the housing policy had a disparate impact on lesbians and gay men and therefore discriminated on the basis of sexual orientation.

A trial court dismissed the complaint, finding no cause of action for marital-status discrimination. The court also ruled that the Roommate Law did not apply to temporary college housing. Finally, it ruled that the disparate impact theory held no weight because the students were able to obtain student housing without their partners. The Supreme Court, Appellate Division, affirmed, noting Yeshiva's policy impacted all unmarried students, whether homosexual or heterosexual, and therefore was not discriminatory.

The ACLU appealed to the New York Court of Appeals, arguing the policy had an adverse impact on gay and lesbian students and discriminated based on sexual orientation. New York Human Rights Law Section 8-107(17) creates a cause of action for plaintiffs who can demonstrate that a seemingly neutral policy has a disparate impact on a protected group. It specifically prohibits discrimination based on sexual orientation. **The court held that the lower courts erred by comparing gay and lesbian students only to other unmarried students without including married students in its comparison of how the policy affects potential housing residents**. To determine whether the housing policy had a disparate impact on the basis of sexual orientation, "there must be a comparison that includes consideration of the full composition of the class actually benefited under the changed policy." The disparate impact claim was wrongly dismissed, and the case was remanded for further proceedings. *Levin v. Yeshiva Univ.*, 96 N.Y.2d 484 (N.Y. 2001).

◆ *The Second Circuit dismissed a challenge to Yale University's rule requiring unmarried freshmen and sophomores to live in co-ed dormitories.*

A group of Orthodox Jewish students claimed Yale's housing rule violated their religious beliefs. They asserted constitutional violations against the university under 42 U.S.C. § 1983. A federal district court granted Yale's motion to dismiss, finding the university was not a state actor or instrumentality subject to Section 1983. The court rejected the students' claims that the university's mandatory on-campus housing requirement is an attempt to monopolize the local housing market and violates the Fair Housing Act by denying students of certain religions the right to live in a single-sex dormitory. The students appealed to the Second Circuit.

The Second Circuit noted that only two of Yale's 19 board members were appointed by the state. Therefore, **Yale was not considered a state actor, and the Section 1983 claims were invalid.** The court rejected the claim that Yale's underclass dormitory policy was an attempt to monopolize the local student housing market in violation of the Sherman Antitrust Act, 15 U.S.C. §§ 1-2, because Yale forced students to live in its housing facilities. The Second Circuit rejected this argument because students could receive an equally beneficial education at other universities around the nation. Also, Yale's refusal to exempt certain religious observers from co-educational housing did not violate the Fair Housing Act. The decision of the district court was affirmed. *Hack v. President and Fellows of Yale College*, 237 F.3d 81 (2d Cir. 2000).

◆   *A college's insurer could not sue a student to recover for fire damage to a dorm room.*

When a college student negligently caused a fire that damaged his dorm room, the college's insurer paid for the damage. It then sought to recover the amounts paid from the student. The Massachusetts Superior Court ruled that it could not do so. Here, the dorm agreement was not explicit enough to put the student on notice that he would be liable for fire damage. Also, the college did not require students to obtain fire insurance on their dorm rooms. As a result, the student was an implied co-insured under the policy, and the insurer could not recover from him under subrogation (standing in the shoes of the college). *Endicott College v. Mahoney*, No. 00-589C, 2001 WL 1173303 (Mass. Super. 2001).

CHAPTER TWO

Discrimination Against Students

I. DISABILITY DISCRIMINATION

A. Eligibility for Disability Law Protection

The Americans with Disabilities Act of 1990 (ADA), 42 U.S.C. § 12101, et seq., *states that **no qualified individual with a disability shall, by reason of such disability, be excluded from participation in or be denied the benefit of services, programs, or activities of a public entity, place of public accommodation or other covered entity. The ADA is based on the anti-discrimination principles of Rehabilitation Act Section 504,** 29 U.S.C. § 794.*

Courts reviewing student disability claims must first determine if the student is "disabled." The ADA defines "disability" as a physical or mental impairment that substantially limits one or more major life activities; a record of such impairment; or being regarded as having such an impairment.

*The U.S. Court of Appeals, Seventh Circuit, has held Section 504's protection extends not just to handicapped individuals who are direct participants in federally funded programs or activities, but also to those who are intended ultimate beneficiaries of such programs or activities. The court noted that **discrimination on the basis of a handicap is actionable upon a simple showing that discrimination has resulted in diminution of the benefits a disabled individual would otherwise receive from a federally funded program.** Simpson v. Reynolds Metals Co., 629 F.2d 1226 (7th Cir. 1980).*

◆   *The non-disabled parent of a disabled student could sue a university under*
Section 504 to vindicate her rights.

A job applicant unsuccessfully applied for a position with the University of
Missouri. She sued the university in a federal district court, alleging it did not
hire her because of her son's disability. The university argued Section 504 did
not allow the applicant to claim discrimination on the basis of another person's
disability. The court disagreed, finding Section 504 extends to "any persons
aggrieved by" violations. **Courts have held that individuals and entities who
are injured by discrimination on the basis of a disability may sue under
Section 504 even though they are not themselves disabled.** Congress
intended to prohibit discrimination against any disabled individual who would
benefit from a federally funded program or activity. *Feurer v. Curators of Univ.
of Missouri*, No. 4:06CV750 HEA, 2006 WL 2385260 (E.D. Mo. 9/17/06).

◆   *The U.S. Court of Appeals, Fourth Circuit, allowed a student who suffered
migraine headaches to proceed with an ADA suit against a Virginia law school.*

The student had "intractable migraine syndrome" for which she took
prescription medicine. While taking a final exam, she got a migraine headache
and asked exam administrators for more time. The administrators refused. The
student failed the exam, and her appeals to take it again were denied. She
complained to the dean about the construction of the exam and the university's
grade appeal process. The dean allowed the student to retake the exam, but a
dispute arose over the date for doing so. The student asked a federal district
court for a temporary restraining order, which was denied. The student took the
exam and failed it again. She could not graduate on time and could not begin a
judicial clerkship she had accepted. The student sued the university in a federal
district court for violating the ADA. The court granted the university's motion
to dismiss the case for failure to state a claim.

The student appealed to the Fourth Circuit, which rejected the university's
claim to Eleventh Amendment immunity. The ADA expressed the clear intent
of Congress to abolish a state institution's Eleventh Amendment immunity. The
Fourteenth Amendment authorizes Congress to enact appropriate legislation to
enforce its constitutional guarantees. One of those guarantees is the right to be
free from irrational disability discrimination. **Title II of the ADA was
appropriate legislation as it was created to enforce the prohibition on
irrational disability discrimination. Title II of the ADA forbids state
universities from excluding disabled persons from its programs, services
or benefits because of a disability. It requires state universities to make
reasonable accommodations for disabled students.** The ADA claim should
not have been dismissed, and the question of whether the student had a
qualified disability was returned to the trial court. *Constantine v. Rectors and
Visitors of George Mason Univ.*, 411 F.3d 474 (4th Cir. 2005).

◆   *A Virginia university did not discriminate against a student by dismissing
him from a program and revoking an offer to medical school.*

A student applied to a university's school of medicine. As an alternative to
placing the applicant on a waiting list, the university offered him a spot in its
Medical Academic Advancement Post-baccalaureate (Postbacc) program. The

medical school would accept the student after a year if he completed the Postbacc program's requirements, which included maintaining a 2.75 grade-point average, with no grade lower than C. The student did not meet the program requirements, but he was allowed to remain on a probationary basis. A program committee insisted the student arrange for tutoring and contact the university's learning needs and evaluation center to be tested for a learning disability. After conducting a series of tests, the center concluded the student had difficulties with short-term memory and reading speed.

The center recommended that professors allow the student twice the allotted time to complete timed exams. His cumulative GPA for the entire year was well under the overall 2.75 standard for the academic year, and he was dropped from the Postbacc program. After an unsuccessful appeal to the dean of the school of medicine, the student sued the university in a federal district court for violating the ADA. **The court held the student was not disabled, and that his perceived disability did not lead to his dismissal. It said the university dismissed the student solely because his grades fell below the GPA requirements.** The Fourth Circuit agreed. It held the university did not violate the ADA because it dismissed the student for reasons unrelated to a perceived disability and provided him reasonable accommodations for any perceived disability. *Betts v. The Rector and Visitors of the Univ. of Virginia*, 145 Fed.Appx. 7 (4th Cir. 2005).

◆ *In determining when a statute of limitations starts to run, the Sixth Circuit considers when the complaining party had reason to know of an injury.*

A Tennessee medical college student was diagnosed with ADD during his first semester. An increased academic workload and his duties as a student body president exacerbated his symptoms. The student experienced mania and amphetamine psychosis and received a failing grade on a take-home exam for a second-year course. The college believed he cheated on the exam and directed him to appear before its student promotions committee to discuss the failing grade. In January 2001, the committee found the student guilty of an honor code violation without conducting an investigation, and the college placed him on a leave of absence. He entered a rehabilitation program and started seeing a psychiatrist. At the same time, he sought readmission to the college medical program, which was denied on May 22, 2002. One year later, the student sued the school in a federal district court, alleging it violated his due process rights under 42 U.S.C. § 1983 when it did not investigate or allow him to defend himself. The court dismissed the complaint as untimely.

The student appealed to the U.S. Court of Appeals, Sixth Circuit. It stated the statute of limitations in Tennessee for civil rights actions under Section 1983 was one year. The student filed his claim on time if the period began to run on or after May 22, 2002. **In determining when the statute of limitations starts to run, the Sixth Circuit looks to when an individual knew or had reason to know of the injury that is the basis of the complaint.** In this case, the court found the typical lay person would have been alerted as to the need to protect his rights more than a year before May 22, 2002. It affirmed the judgment. *Roberson v. State of Tennessee*, 399 F.3d 792 (6th Cir. 2005).

◆ *The University of Connecticut did not violate federal disability law by dismissing a student after multiple failures on part of a medical licensing exam.*

The student failed her first-year course requirements, then completed one of the courses with the help of a tutor. She was promoted to second year, but again failed her course requirements. The student failed Step I of the medical licensing exam twice. Step I was a prerequisite to the third year of medical school. The university provided the student with two years of free tutoring to help her satisfy her third-year requirements, and conditionally promoted her to the third year if she passed Step I. The student failed Step I twice more, despite additional tutoring assistance from the university. The university initiated dismissal proceedings. A university neuropsychologist reported the student's academic problems were caused by dyslexia, attention deficit disorder anxiety and depression. The National Board of Medical Examiners declined the student's request for accommodations on Step I, stating she was not disabled.

The student sued the board and university in a federal district court for refusing to meet her requests for accommodation. The court held for the board and university, and the student appealed. The Second Circuit explained that qualified disabled individuals are entitled to reasonable accommodations under the ADA and Section 504 for access to and participation in public services and accommodations. **To establish a violation, the student had to show she was a "qualified individual" with a disability. The court held she never proved she was a qualified individual with a disability or was otherwise eligible to continue her medical studies.** School records showed she was an average student throughout her academic career. The court found the school in no way discriminated against the student and actually went the extra mile to support her. The board did not discriminate against her by refusing to accommodate her, as she did not show she was disabled. The judgment was affirmed. *Powell v. National Board of Medical Examiners*, 364 F.3d 79 (2d Cir. 2004).

◆ *A California medical school student with a learning disability was not disabled under the ADA or the Rehabilitation Act.*

The student earned an undergraduate degree in biochemistry with a 3.54 grade average, then earned a master's degree in cellular/molecular biology. The university admitted the student into medical school after he took the medical college admission test four times, with no accommodations. He completed the first two years of the program on a normal schedule, earning a B average with no accommodations. The student also passed the national board exam without accommodations. He failed a required third-year clinical clerkship and took time off school to prepare for others, eventually passing three of them. The university's disability resource center evaluated the student and found he had a learning impairment. It recommended extra reading and preparation time for his clerkships. The student took several weeks off to prepare for a clerkship rotation. He passed those clerkships, but the university denied his request for eight weeks off to read for his next one. The university dismissed the student after he failed another clerkship, stating he did not meet its academic standards.

The student sued the university in a federal district court for violating the ADA. The court awarded summary judgment to the university, and the student appealed. The Ninth Circuit Court of Appeals centered its review on whether the student was disabled. The university itself had evaluated the student and recognized his limitations involved major life activities such as learning, reading and working. However, **he failed to prove he was substantially limited in any of those activities. The student's ability to achieve academic success without accommodations contradicted his argument that his impairment significantly limited his learning and reading.** The court held he was not disabled, and affirmed the judgment. *Wong v. Regents of the Univ. of California*, 379 F.3d 1097 (9th Cir. 2004). In 2005, the Ninth Circuit amended its decision slightly and denied the student's petition for a rehearing.

◆ *A Massachusetts law school student did not show her school violated the ADA by failing to reasonably accommodate her carpal tunnel syndrome.*

The student complained of pain due to carpal tunnel syndrome. The law school allowed her to cut her class load. The student then underwent treatment for anxiety and depression and performed poorly on her final examinations. The school dismissed her for failing to meet its academic standards. She sued the school in a federal district court for ADA violations. The court awarded summary judgment to the school, ruling the student did not show that carpal tunnel syndrome substantially limited her ability to learn or work.

The student appealed. The First Circuit Court of Appeals found the student never proved she was disabled or that the school regarded her as impaired. The only evidence she presented to show the school considered her disabled was that it provided her with certain accommodations. **She offered nothing to prove her physical limitations would disqualify her from a broad range of jobs or otherwise substantially limit her ability to work, when compared to the average person in the general population.** As the student presented no evidence that carpal tunnel syndrome substantially limited her ability to learn or work, the court could not determine she had a disability. The judgment was affirmed. *Marlon v. Western New England College*, 124 Fed.Appx. 15 (1st Cir. 2005).

◆ *A Kentucky university did not discriminate against a law school student on the basis of disability by refusing to readmit him to the program.*

During his first semester of law school, the student became depressed. A few of his professors suggested he take a leave and return the next fall. The student withdrew before taking his final exams. The university denied his application for readmission, which was submitted one day late. After the university refused to reconsider the reapplication, the student sued the university in a state court for disability discrimination in violation of the Kentucky Civil Rights Act, which mirrors the language of the ADA and the Rehabilitation Act. The court awarded summary judgment to the university, and the student appealed to the Court of Appeals of Kentucky.

The student argued he was qualified for readmission because his test scores and undergraduate grade point average remained the same as in his original application. The court rejected this argument, stating that only his second application was under review. **To prevail under the act, the student had to show he was otherwise qualified apart from his disability. The court explained that an "otherwise qualified" person under Section 504 is one who**

is able to meet all program requirements in spite of a disability. Educational institutions are not required to disregard the disabilities of an applicant, provided the disability is relevant to reasonable qualifications for admittance. Institutions need not make substantial modifications in reasonable standards or programs to accommodate individuals with disabilities. The court held the university had considered the student's disability and other valid factors in reaching its decision and found he was not a qualified applicant. The court affirmed the judgment for the university. *Hash v. Univ. of Kentucky*, 138 S.W.2d 123 (Ky. Ct. App. 2004).

◆ *A federal district court held a New York university dismissed a Ph.D. student for poor performance, not on the basis of disability.*
The student was a Ph.D. candidate in the university's sociology department. During her second year, she was diagnosed with a pelvic tumor and underwent surgery to remove her uterus. The university granted her request for a medical leave for a full academic year. When she returned, she did not inform the university she was claiming a disability. The university denied the student's request to take a reduced class load and eventually dismissed her from the program for poor performance and failure to take a required exam. The university also stated concern for her inability to speak and write English well and to complete a mandatory American Language Exam.
The student sued the university for disability discrimination under the ADA and Rehabilitation Act. **The Rehabilitation Act defines an "individual with a disability" as one who has a physical or mental impairment which substantially limits one or more of the person's major life activities, has a record of such impairment, or is regarded as having such an impairment. Major life activities are functions such as caring for oneself, walking, seeing, hearing, speaking, breathing, learning and working.** The court found that since reproduction is a major life activity, the student had a disability. However, she did not refute evidence that she had not completed language proficiency requirements. As the student did not convince the court that she was dismissed because of her disability, the court awarded summary judgment to the university. *Chen v. Trustees of Columbia Univ.*, No. 00 Civ. 7532 (RCC), 2004 WL 1057637 (S.D.N.Y. 2004).

◆ *A Minnesota student with a sleep disorder did not tell his college he needed accommodations and rejected some that were offered.*
The student had narcolepsy and had to repeat certain course work to gain readmittance to the college nursing school. He did not contact the college Office for Students with Disabilities (OSD) to request accommodations. A teacher accused the student of falling asleep in class. The day before a final examination, an instructor advised him to meet with the OSD. The student brought a doctor's letter that did not mention the need for any accommodations. He declared he did not want to be treated differently than other students and rejected an offer for a private testing room and more time. The student failed his examination and sued the college in a state court for violating the ADA and state law. He claimed violation of his equal protection rights because the college allowed another student who failed the exam to take the next course.

The court found the two students were not similarly situated. The ADA claim was barred by sovereign immunity and the college was entitled to judgment on the state law claim. The student appealed to the state court of appeals, which found **the student did not show he was "disabled" because he did not show narcolepsy limited a major life activity. He also failed to tell the college about his disability and rejected accommodations because he did not want different treatment.** The court affirmed the judgment for the college. *Redden v. Minneapolis Community and Technical College*, No. A03-1202, 2004 WL 835768 (Minn. Ct. App. 2004).

◆ *A student with multiple personality disorder was not protected by the ADA or the Rehabilitation Act.*

The student had 17 distinct personalities and enrolled in a North Carolina university's teacher certification program. However, she was suspected of plagiarism on one assignment and began exhibiting aggressive behavior. She also became hysterical after picking up a final exam when she could not find "Michael," one of her personalities. After she was removed from the program, she sued under the ADA and Section 504, asserting that she had been dismissed because of her disability. A federal court ruled against her, and the Fourth Circuit affirmed. It found that **she was not substantially limited in a major life activity as a result of her multiple personalities.** She was simply unable to obtain a teaching certificate. Thus, she was not entitled to the protections of either act. *Davis v. Univ. of North Carolina*, 263 F.3d 95 (4th Cir. 2001).

◆ *A disabled graduate student who could not meet a school's academic requirements even with a reasonable accommodation was not entitled to be reinstated to the program after his dismissal.*

A student in an M.D./Ph.D. program at a Massachusetts school suffered from bipolar disorder. After failing three courses in the M.D. program, he continued in the Ph.D. program with the accommodation of extra time to complete his written examinations. He was later dismissed from that program because of the generally poor quality of his research and because he failed to make sufficient progress in lab experiments that were basic program requirements for his thesis. He sued the school under Title III of the ADA and Section 504 of the Rehabilitation Act, seeking reinstatement to the programs. A federal court ruled against him, noting that he was not an "otherwise qualified" person with a disability due to academic failure, disruptive behavior and insufficient progress in required lab experiments. **It was his lack of scientific aptitude and not a lack of time that caused his academic failure.** *El Kouni v. Trustees of Boston Univ.*, 169 F.Supp.2d 1 (D. Mass. 2001).

◆ *A New Mexico medical school student with test anxieties in two subjects was not considered disabled under the ADA.*

The student suffered from "chemistry and mathematics anxiety." However, he overcame this in undergraduate and graduate programs. The student informed his basic biochemistry professor of his anxiety, but stated that he needed no test-taking accommodations. After receiving marginal grades in two first-year courses, he was notified that he would have to repeat the first year. Instead, he sued the medical school for disability discrimination under the ADA. The court granted pretrial judgment to the school, and the student appealed. The U.S. Court of Appeals, Tenth Circuit, affirmed the lower court's decision. Here, **the student failed to show that his math and chemistry anxiety substantially limited him in the major life activity of learning. As a result, he was not a disabled person within the meaning of the ADA.** Further, even if he was, he could not demand an unreasonable accommodation from the school. Requiring the school to advance the student to the next level would require an unreasonable accommodation. *McGuinness v. Univ. of New Mexico School of Medicine*, 170 F.3d 974 (10th Cir. 1998).

B. Reasonable Accommodation

◆ *The U.S. Supreme Court held that schools do not have to make accommodations that fundamentally alter the nature of the programs offered.*
    A nursing school applicant with severe hearing impairments claimed the school's denial of her admission violated Section 504, which states that an "otherwise qualified individual with a disability" may not be excluded from a federally funded program "solely by reason of her or his disability." The school explained the hearing disability made it unsafe for the applicant to practice as a registered nurse. The school pointed out that even with a hearing aid, she had to rely on her lip-reading skills, and that patient safety demanded the ability to understand speech without reliance on lip-reading.
    Agreeing with the school, **the Supreme Court held the term "otherwise qualified individual with a disability" meant an individual who is qualified in spite of his or her disability**. The applicant's contention that her disability should be disregarded for purposes of determining whether she was otherwise qualified was rejected, as was her contention that Section 504 imposed an obligation on the school to undertake affirmative action to modify its curriculum to accommodate her disability. **While a school may be required in certain cases to make minor curricular modifications to accommodate a disability, the applicant here was physically able to take only academic courses. No accommodations were required since clinical study would be foreclosed due to patient safety concerns.** The Court held that Section 504 did not require a major curricular modification such as allowing the applicant to bypass clinical study. The school's denial of admission was upheld. *Southeastern Community College v. Davis*, 442 U.S. 397, 99 S.Ct. 2361, 60 L.Ed.2d 980 (1979).

◆ *A New York graduate institute did not make reasonable attempts to accommodate a student with lupus in a P.h.D. distance learning program.*
    The program in clinical psychology had a 300-hour residency requirement. The institute denied the student's request to transfer to a different residency group because it was oversubscribed. It also denied her permission to fulfill her residency requirement by video-conferencing. The student sued the institute under the ADA and Rehabilitation Act. A federal district court held for the institute, and the student appealed. The U.S. Court of Appeals, Second Circuit,

held the institute did not violate the ADA or Rehabilitation Act by denying the request for a different group. However, a jury might find that the institute failed to properly evaluate the student's request for a delay in the start of her program and to fulfill her residency requirement through video-conferencing. **The court found evidence that the institute had failed to engage in an interactive process of finding an accommodation for her.** The case was remanded to the district court for further proceedings. *Hartnett v. Fielding Graduate Institute*, 198 Fed.Appx. 89 (2d Cir. 2006).

◆ *A deaf California student was entitled to input in choosing an interpreter, despite evidence that this accommodation would be costly.*

The student sued her college under the ADA and Rehabilitation Act for failing to provide her with adequate sign-language interpreter services. She also claimed the college forced her to "sign away her rights" by completing an application for the services. **A federal district court explained that federal disability laws required the college to provide "meaningful access" to its programs through reasonable modifications. Modifications that could be classified as "fundamental" or "substantial" are not required.**

Under Title II of the ADA, the college had the discretion to offer other aids aside from interpreter services. The college had the burden of showing another alternative was equally effective. The court was unable to determine from the record whether any alternatives were equally effective. This question could not be decided on a pretrial motion. The college presented evidence showing that providing the student a personal interpreter would constitute almost 7% of its annual budget. However, the college did not conclusively show that allowing her to choose an interpreter would create an undue administrative burden. Instead, it suggested the student's input in selecting an interpreter was required. The pretrial motions were denied. *Hayden v. Redwoods Community College Dist.*, No. C-05-01785 NJV, 2007 WL 61886 (N.D. Cal. 1/8/07).

◆ *The University of Minnesota Medical School was not required to allow a disabled student the accommodation of missing some lectures.*

The student was given a written warning for failing to meet attendance requirements. The university disability services office rejected his request to be excused from lectures but suggested other accommodations. The school then learned that a complaint was pending against the student with the state medical ethics board for having a sexual relationship with a patient. After an investigation, the student was dismissed from the program. He sued the university, claiming it failed to accommodate his disabilities. A state court held for the university, and the student appealed.

The Court of Appeals of Minnesota held **the university was not required to provide the accommodation of the student's choosing. Instead, it was only required to provide a reasonable accommodation.** The university did so by offering to allow the student to tape-record lectures and to move around during lectures. His request to be excused from meeting the lecture attendance requirement was unreasonable, because the university deemed attendance an essential element of its program. There was no evidence to raise any inference of discrimination, as the university offered several legitimate reasons for its decision, including the student's unethical sexual relationship with a patient, failure to attend lectures, and his inappropriate interactions with female peers. *Tori v. Univ. of Minnesota*, No. A06-205, 2006 WL 3772316 (Minn. Ct. App. 12/26/06).

◆ *A Pennsylvania student with multiple disabilities was unable to meet a university's academic requirements, despite accommodations.*

The student did not request any accommodations from her university until she had been in attendance for two years. By that time, she had been placed on academic probation due to poor academic performance. The university then provided the accommodations she requested, including extended time to complete assignments, freedom to move about during class, and certain furniture. Despite the accommodations, the student's academic performance did not improve significantly and she was dismissed. She sued the university in a federal district court, claiming it violated the ADA. The court granted the university's pretrial motion for judgment, finding no evidence of discrimination based on disability. Instead, the evidence showed the university made several efforts to accommodate the student. Despite the provision of accommodations, she was unable to meet the university's academic requirements. **Noting that professors are to be given great deference when it comes to evaluating the academic performance of students, the court held for the university.** *Millington v. Temple Univ. School of Dentistry*, No. Civ.A. 04-3965, 2006 WL 2974141 (E.D. Pa. 10/13/06).

◆ *A graduate student will be permitted to pursue his ADA lawsuit against a university in a District of Columbia federal court.*

The student claimed the university refused to allow his return to a Ph.D. program after a five-year leave. During this time, his candidacy lapsed and his core course credits expired. The court stated that **reasonable accommodations are those necessary to give a disabled person the same opportunity to obtain the offered benefit that he would have had, if not for limitations caused by a disability.** The university contended that the student failed to show that the requested modifications were reasonable because he did not establish that his disability required a need to modify its academic policies. The court held it could not reach this conclusion without further consideration. A jury would have to consider whether **the accommodations were reasonable or if modifications would fundamentally alter the nature of the doctoral program.** The court denied pretrial judgment. *Long v. Howard Univ.*, 439 F.Supp.2d 68 (D.D.C. 2006).

◆ *Federal disability law did not require a New York college to provide every single accommodation that a blind student requested.*

The college coordinator attempted to meet with the student to discuss his needs. Because the student failed to keep any appointments, the coordinator was unable to make arrangements. The college later provided most of his requested accommodations. The student failed to pick up books on tape and missed many appointments related to accommodations. He became belligerent in his dealings with college staff members. The college informed the student his treatment of college staff members violated its code of conduct, and he was dismissed. The student sued the college in a federal district court for violating the ADA and Section 504. The court noted the college had hired readers to record textbooks and contacted professors to make sure the tapes were accurate. The college provided an assistant at its learning center and offered access to its disability coordinator. **Federal law did not require the college to provide every single accommodation that the student requested.** Even if he had been able to prove a failure to accommodate, he would not be able to recover monetary damages. **The student's claim was filed under Title III of the ADA, which does not allow recovery of monetary damages.** *Melendez v. Monroe College*, No. 04-CV-2266, 2006 WL 2882568 (E.D.N.Y. 10/6/06).

◆ *The U.S. Court of Appeals, Eighth Circuit, held a Missouri student failed to prove a university violated the ADA by refusing requested accommodations.*

The student was wheelchair-bound and sight impaired due to cerebral palsy. The chair of the Department of American Studies refused to allow the student to enroll in a graduate-level American studies course until he completed his graduate school application, eliminated some incomplete undergraduate grades, and was admitted to the graduate school. The student petitioned the graduate school to attend as an unclassified graduate student in the American Studies Department. The university granted the petition. However, the student attempted 12 credit hours the next semester and earned none. The student was disqualified from federal financial aid and complained of disability discrimination. The university barred him from entering its campus after learning he had threatened a professor.

The student sued the university in a federal district court for violating the ADA. The court granted the university's motion for dismissal, and the student appealed to the Eighth Circuit. The court found the university offered him many accommodations, such as changes in his academic status and classes. On the list of accommodations he stated he did not receive, he failed to specify which ones had been rejected. Also, he did not explain why he needed each requested accommodation. **An accommodation is reasonable only if it is related to a disability.** As the student failed to substantiate with sufficient evidence that the university did not provide certain requested accommodations, and that reasonable accommodations would have qualified him for admission into the graduate school, the court affirmed the judgment. *Mershon v. St. Louis Univ.*, 442 F.3d 1069 (8th Cir. 2006).

◆ *An Indiana university did not violate the ADA when it terminated a student from an assistantship and refused to allow him more space in class.*

A state university accepted the student into a graduate program and offered him a graduate research assistantship that was contingent on his academic performance. He requested and received roomier seating from the program coordinator because he was larger than average. However, he was denied a request for more room to stand and move around to control his narcoleptic condition. The student's grade average fell below 3.0, and a supervisor concluded his work was unacceptable. The university terminated his assistantship, and he filed a discrimination claim with the Equal Employment Opportunity Commission (EEOC), alleging the university violated the ADA.

The EEOC dismissed the complaint, and the student sued the university in a federal district court, alleging ADA violations for failing to grant him further accommodations. **The court held Title II of the ADA requires universities to make reasonable accommodations for disabled students so they can participate in educational programs.** However, **the student in this case never established he had a disability. The court found he did not clearly state what his impairment was and did not offer evidence to support a finding that he had an impairment.** The student's statement about his narcoleptic condition was not supported with medical records to show his condition significantly affected a major life activity. The court dismissed the case. *Brettler v. Purdue Univ.*, 408 F.Supp.2d 640 (N.D. Ind. 2006).

◆ *A Connecticut court ruled in favor of Yale Divinity School on a student's claims that it breached a contract to educate her and violated Section 504.*

The student claimed Yale Divinity School breached its contract to provide her educational services when it denied her request for more time to complete her assignments and finish her dissertation after she injured her right hand. The student also said Yale refused to extend the time she could remain a school resident. She said she did not have time to complete her course requirements when they were due and was unable to graduate on time. The student sued the school in a Connecticut court for breach of contract and Section 504 violations.

The court rejected the student's arguments that the school violated specific contractual promises separate from its overall educational program. **The school presented evidence that it never promised the student she could remain a student for an indefinite period of time so she could complete her studies.** It also proved she had reasonable time to complete her courses. The student alleged she became "handicapped" under Section 504 when she hurt her hand. Yale presented evidence that it gave her time extensions to complete her program. It allowed her 645 hours of typing assistance and provided her a laptop computer. The school also submitted medical reports that refuted the student's claim to disability status. **On appeal, the state appellate court held the student failed to show the university denied her reasonable accommodations or a right to continue her education because of a disability.** It affirmed the judgment. *Little v. Yale Univ.*, 884 A.2d 887 (Conn. Ct. App. 2005). The Supreme Court of Connecticut denied the student's petition for review. *Little v. Yale Univ.*, 891 A.2d 1 (Conn. 2006).

◆ *A federal district court held a Colorado university did not violate Section 504 because it did not deny a student reasonable accommodations.*

The student, a native of Zaire, attended the university's pre-med program. She sued the university in a federal district court, alleging it discriminated against her because of a disability in violation of Rehabilitation Act Section 504. The student claimed she suffered from an unspecified disability due to injuries she sustained while working for the university. She claimed four professors failed to honor letters of accommodation issued by the university's office of disabilities services, and did not provide other accommodations. The university argued the student never gave one of her professors a letter of accommodation. Instead, she gave the professor a letter from the program coordinator seeking extra time on exams because English was her second language. The letter did not mention the student needed an accommodation due to a disability. **The court found the professor provided her extra time to sit for an exam. The student failed to present any evidence that the university denied her request for accommodation,** and the court granted the university's motion for summary judgment. *Buhendwa v. Univ. of Colorado at Boulder,* No. Civ. A03CV00485 REBOES, 2005 WL 2141581 (D. Colo. 8/22/05).

On appeal, the U.S. Court of Appeals, Tenth Circuit, held the student's disability bias claim failed. **The student later admitted that the professor refused to grant her extra time on the final examination because she fell asleep and not because she had test-taking anxiety.** Her race bias claim, filed under Title VI of the Civil Rights Act of 1964, also failed. Although the student claimed she was treated differently than similarly situated "blond students," the other students were not similarly situated because they did not fall asleep during the final examination. In addition, there was no evidence that any of the blond students had missed any quizzes. The court affirmed the district court's judgment for the university. *Buhendwa v. Univ. of Colorado at Boulder,* 214 Fed.Appx. 823 (10th Cir. 2007).

◆   *A California university violated the ADA when it refused to provide a student the seating accommodations she requested.*

The student had impairments affecting her spine and right foot. She asked for special seating directly in front of her professors, permission to stand up or move as needed, extra time to complete exams, and other accommodations. The university rejected each accommodation except the seating. The student withdrew from the university and sued it in the state court system for disability discrimination. The university removed the action to a federal district court. **Under the ADA, a "disability" is defined as a physical or mental impairment that substantially limits one or more of the major life activities of an individual. To be substantially affected, a person must have an impairment that prevents or severely restricts him or her from carrying out activities that are of central importance to most people's daily lives.** The university argued the student failed to establish that her impairments substantially limited the major life activities of sitting, standing, walking and lifting. The student submitted reports from her doctors stating she was limited to standing only five to 10 minutes, walking 10 to 15 minutes at a slow to moderate pace, and sitting 20 to 25 minutes.

The court found the student showed that her impairments substantially limited one or more major life activities. It held the university mischaracterized the evidence about the student's sitting limitations. Most of the medical evidence supported the student's allegations. **Courts have generally found that being unable to sit for an hour or less may constitute a substantial limitation.** The university also failed to show the student was not substantially limited in her abilities to stand and walk. As she presented enough evidence to avoid pretrial dismissal, the court scheduled the case for a trial. *Selandia v. The Regents of the Univ. of Calif.,* No. CIVS031551LKKPANPS, 2006 WL 463127 (E.D. Cal. 2/24/06).

◆ *A federal district court denied a California university's motion to dismiss a disability discrimination lawsuit.*

Before the student enrolled in the university's nursing program, he stated he had a learning disability in reading, writing, and comprehension. He asked the university for special assistance, including an interpreter, but the university denied the request. According to the student, he got a D in a pharmacology class because he did not receive the accommodations. The student transferred to another school and sued the university in a federal district court for violating Title III of the Americans with Disabilities Act of 1990. The court found he established his ADA claim. The university did not challenge the sufficiency of the student's allegations. Rather, it argued the law did not require the university to provide an interpreter based on his alleged dyslexia.

The court said the university could be right in asserting the law did not require it to provide an interpreter. **An ADA regulation, 28 C.F.R. Part 36.303(b)(1), states that "auxiliary aids and services" includes qualified interpreters as aids for the hearing impaired.** The university also contended the student's complaint presented very few factual allegations concerning "special assistance" and "reasonable accommodations." However, the court held the student's complaint provided allegations sufficient to proceed on his ADA claim. It denied the university's motion to dismiss the case for failure to state a claim. *Turner v. Univ. of San Francisco School of Nursing*, No. C 05-02048 JSW, 2005 WL 3097874 (N.D. Cal. 11/18/05).

◆ *A Minnesota university provided reasonable accommodations to a medical school student before dismissing him from the program.*

The university allowed the student extra testing time, flexible deadlines and tutoring. He dropped to a part-time schedule due to poor performance. The student completed only five of 14 required first-year courses, and failed human genetics. The committee on student scholastic standing required him to complete his nine remaining first-year classes or face dismissal. The university agreed to provide further accommodations such as double time for testing in a private testing room, a microscope and slides to use at home, notes, and regular meetings with his faculty mentor. Even with these accommodations, the student failed two courses. The committee allowed him to take make-up exams in those courses. The student completed his two years of classroom courses and began clinical rotations. He failed a rotation and appeared again before the committee. The student explained he failed his clinical rotation because he was scared to death of babies, intimidated by the faculty, and unprepared for the rotation.

After the student failed several other rotations, the university dismissed him. He sued the university in a federal district court, alleging it violated Section 504 by failing to provide him with reasonable accommodations and by dismissing him solely because of his disability. The court held for the university, and the student appealed. The Eighth Circuit found the university dismissed the student because he could not synthesize data to perform clinical reasoning, with or without accommodations. **Section 504 did not require the university to lower its standards for a professional degree by eliminating or substantially modifying its clinical training requirements.** As the university offered the student many accommodations, and he did not prove the others would have cured his deficiencies, the court affirmed the judgment. *Falcone v. Univ. of Minnesota*, 388 F.3d 656 (8th Cir. 2004).

C. Liability Issues

◆ *The Supreme Court determined that a lower court had failed to consider a public university's argument that it should not have to pay for a handicapped student's special educational requirements in a case filed under Section 504.*

A deaf graduate student at a Texas university requested a sign language interpreter. The university refused to pay for an interpreter because he did not meet university financial assistance guidelines. The student sued the university in a federal district court under Section 504. He sought an order requiring the appointment of an interpreter at the university's expense for as long as he remained there. The court granted his request for a preliminary order requiring the university to pay for the interpreter. However, the court stayed further consideration of the case pending a final administrative ruling.

The university appealed to the U.S. Court of Appeals, Fifth Circuit, which affirmed the preliminary order but vacated the stay pending administrative action. The university complied with the order by paying for the interpreter. The student completed his graduate program. The U.S. Supreme Court granted review to address the university's argument that the lower courts should make a final ruling on who was to pay for the interpreter. The student argued that the case was now moot in view of his graduation. The Court vacated the appeals court's decision and remanded the case for a trial on the merits to allow the university a full opportunity to argue for recoupment of its payments for the interpreter. *Univ. of Texas v. Camenisch*, 451 U.S. 390, 101 S.Ct. 1830, 68 L.Ed.2d 175 (1981).

◆ *A federal court in Nebraska recently restated the rule that employees and administrators are not individually liable for violations of federal laws protecting disabled individuals, since they do not "operate" an institution.*

A Nebraska student was diagnosed with attention deficit hyperactivity disorder during his first semester of medical school. He was treated with Ritalin and passed his first-semester courses. The next semester, the student failed two classes. The medical school allowed him to repeat his first year, but also required him to obtain a psychiatric evaluation and follow any treatment plans. The student was reevaluated, and his medication was increased, causing side effects such as headaches and lack of concentration. The next year, he failed another class and was not allowed to retake a final examination. The school's Advancement Committee voted to dismiss the student. A review committee upheld the action, and he sued the university, medical school, administrators and employees in a federal district court for disability discrimination, breach of contract, infliction of emotional distress and related claims. The court noted that other federal courts have held **university employees and administrators do not "operate" a university in a way that exposes them to liability under the Americans with Disabilities Act and the Rehabilitation Act**.

The court explained that to prevail on a breach of contract claim, the student first had to state there was a promise between himself and the university. As he was unable to show any promise, his breach of contract claim failed. The student did not allege facts to support his claim for intentional infliction of emotional distress. He did not show intentional or reckless conduct that was so outrageous and extreme as to go beyond all possible bounds of decency, and the court also dismissed this claim. *White v. Creighton Univ.*, No. 8:06 CV 536, 2006 WL 3419782 (D. Neb. 11/27/06).

◆ *An Illinois university was not liable for violating a learning disabled student's rights under the Americans with Disabilities Act.*

In spite of his learning disabilities, the student earned a bachelor's degree in philosophy, completed pre-med courses, and attained high scores on the MCAT exam. In 1999, an Illinois university admitted him to a medical scholars program that allows students to pursue M.D. and Ph.D. degrees simultaneously. The student took only philosophy courses during his first year and did well. However, the following year, he failed three medical courses and was required to retake the entire first-year medical school curriculum. A psychiatrist confirmed the student had visual perception problems and dysgraphia.

The medical college extended the student's exam time but did not implement other accommodations recommended by his psychiatrist. The next year, he failed a clinical lab sciences exam and the college decided to dismiss him from the program. The student alleged he did not receive the same accommodations as other students, and sued the university in a federal district court for ADA violations. The university argued it was entitled to sovereign immunity under the Eleventh Amendment. The court referred to *Tennessee v. Lane*, 541 U.S. 509 (2004), in which the U.S. Supreme Court held Title II of the ADA validly abrogated Eleventh Amendment immunity. The Illinois court dismissed the case, noting that **education is not considered a fundamental constitutional right. Title II as applied to the state university program in this case exceeded Congress's power.** *Doe v. Board of Trustees of Univ. of Illinois*, 429 F.Supp.2d 930 (N.D. Ill. 2006).

◆ *The U.S. Court of Appeals, Fifth Circuit, held a state university was not immune from liability in a disability discrimination lawsuit.*

Two hearing-impaired students attended a Louisiana state university. They sought language interpreters and note takers for their classes, and certain study aids. The university provided some assistance, but not on a regular basis. The students sued the university in a federal district court, alleging it violated the ADA and Section 504 by denying their requests. The court agreed with the university that the accommodations it provided were adequate and that it was immune from suit under the Eleventh Amendment. The students appealed.

The U.S. Court of Appeals, Fifth Circuit, relied on *Grove City College v. Bell*, 465 U.S. 555 (1984), a sex discrimination case filed under Title IX. In this case, the Fifth Circuit found that just as in *Grove City*, Congress has expressly stated that one purpose of the relevant student aid provisions was "to assist in making available the benefits of postsecondary education to eligible students … by … providing assistance to institutions of higher education." Federal assistance supplemented university financial aid, enhancing its ability to enroll needy students. **The Fifth Circuit held the university did not waive** immunity under Section 504 or the ADA. Because the students claimed they were excluded from classes without the accommodations required for their disabilities, the court reversed the judgment. *Bennett-Nelson v. Louisiana Board of Regents*, 431 F.3d 448 (5th Cir. 2005).

◆ *A federal district court refused to dismiss a Connecticut student's ADA claim because he presented strong evidence of disability discrimination.*

The student was blind and an accomplished musician. He received a Bachelor of Music and Jazz degree, and a Connecticut university accepted him into its Grade K-12 Music Education Certification Program. During the student's first semester in the program, he asked for accommodations for his disability. The student claimed the university denied his requests and that he did not succeed because he was not reasonably accommodated.

The student sued the university in a federal district court for ADA violations. The university sought dismissal. The court found the student alleged conduct that, if proven true, would establish discrimination or ill will due to his disability. **In further court activity, he would receive the opportunity to show university officials denied reasonable accommodations because of their mistaken and irrational belief that he would never be able to become a competent music teacher.** *Corey v. Western Connecticut State Univ.*, No. 3:03CV0763 (DJS), 2004 WL 514837 (D. Conn. 2004).

Several courts have held that university employees and administrators may not be held individually liable for violating the Americans with Disabilities Act or Section 504 of the Rehabilitation Act.

◆ *The U.S. Court of Appeals, Third Circuit, held Congress did not intend to impose personal liability on each person involved in a student's education.*

Instead, the institution has the power to make accommodations and thus "operates" the place of public accommodation. *Emerson v. Thiel College*, 296 F.3d 184 (3d Cir. 2002).

II. SEX DISCRIMINATION AND HARASSMENT

College and university students have federally protected rights to be free from sex discrimination and sexual harassment. Title IX of the Education Amendments of 1972 prohibits recipients of federal funding from denying any person educational participation or benefits on the basis of gender.

A. Discrimination

◆ *The U.S. Supreme Court held the categorical exclusion of women from the Virginia Military Institute (VMI) denied equal protection to women.*

The U.S. Attorney General's office filed a complaint against the state of Virginia and VMI on behalf of a female high school student seeking admission to the state-affiliated, male-only college. A federal court found that because single gender education conferred substantial benefits on students and preserved the unique military training offered at VMI, the exclusion of women did not violate the Equal Protection Clause. The U.S. Court of Appeals, Fourth Circuit, vacated the judgment, ruling that Virginia had failed to state an adequate policy justifying the male-only program. On remand, the district court found that the institution of coeducational methods at VMI would materially affect its program. It approved the state's plan for instituting a parallel program for women even though the program differed substantially from VMI's in its academic offerings, educational methods and financial resources. The court of appeals affirmed, and the U.S. Supreme Court agreed to review the case.

The Court stated that parties seeking to defend gender-based government action must demonstrate an exceedingly persuasive justification that is genuine and not invented as a response to litigation. Virginia had failed to show an exceedingly persuasive justification for excluding women from VMI. There was evidence that some women would be able to participate at VMI, and the lower courts had improperly found that most women would not gain from the adversative method employed by the college. **The remedy proposed by Virginia left its exclusionary policy intact and afforded women no opportunity to experience the rigorous military training offered at VMI.** The parallel women's program was substantially limited in its course offerings, and participants would not gain the benefits of association with VMI's faculty, stature, funding, prestige and alumni support. The proposal did not remedy the constitutional violation, and the Court reversed and remanded the case. *U.S. v. Virginia*, 518 U.S. 515, 116 S.Ct. 2264, 135 L.Ed.2d 735 (1996).

◆ *Gender-based distinctions in academic fields generally will not withstand constitutional scrutiny. The Supreme Court held that a university for women could not justify a policy that denied men the opportunity to enroll for credit.*

The policy of the Mississippi University for Women, a state-supported university, was to limit its enrollment to women. The university denied otherwise qualified males the right to enroll for credit in its School of Nursing. One male, who was denied admission, sued in federal court claiming that the university's policy violated the Fourteenth Amendment's Equal Protection Clause. The lower federal courts agreed, and the school appealed to the U.S. Supreme Court. The Court held **the university's discriminatory admission policy against men was not substantially and directly related to an important governmental objective**. The school argued that women enrolled in its School of Nursing would be adversely affected by the presence of men. However, the record showed that the nursing school allowed men to attend classes in the school as auditors, thus fatally undermining the school's claim that admission of men would adversely affect women students. The Court held that the policy of the university, which limited enrollment to women, violated the Equal Protection Clause. *Mississippi Univ. for Women v. Hogan*, 458 U.S. 718, 102 S.Ct. 3331, 73 L.Ed.2d 1090 (1982).

◆ *The Court of Appeals of Kentucky held a university did not discriminate against a student by terminating him from its medical program.*

The student completed his first and second years of medical school with honors. A female classmate complained to the university that he threatened to hurt her. The university suspended the student from his clinical activities while it investigated the complaint. The student was charged with violating the university's student professional behavior code. A hearing committee concluded he physically threatened the classmate in violation of the student code and inappropriately behaved on several other occasions. A psychiatric report on the student stated his hostile and inappropriate behavior was not easily treated. The student refused to seek treatment and the school terminated his enrollment without the possibility of readmission. He sued the university in a state court, which held for the university. The student then appealed.

The Court of Appeals of Kentucky held that to prevail in his sex discrimination case, **the student had to show the university treated him less favorably that female students whose situation was nearly identical. Federal authorities can be relied on in interpreting a state discrimination case.** The court looked to the Civil Rights Act of 1964, which states that "for two or more employees to be considered similarly situated for purposes of creating an inference of disparate treatment in a reverse gender discrimination case, **the plaintiff must prove that all of the relevant aspects of his employment situation are nearly identical to those of the female employee who he alleges was treated more favorably.**" The student based his claim on the records of four minority students. Of the four, only the female who complained about him was female. The court found the classmate's conduct was different from the student's. She had not made physical threats and had apologized for any inappropriate behavior. The court affirmed the judgment for the university. *Stathis v. Univ. of Kentucky*, No. 2004-CA-000556-MR, 2005 WL 1125240 (Ky. Ct. App. 5/13/05).

◆   *The Sixth Circuit affirmed a district court's ruling that a university did not violate Title IX by expelling a male student for committing a sexual assault.*

Two Ohio University students celebrated a birthday by drinking at an off-campus bar. They eventually left the bar together and had sexual contact in a dormitory room. The university investigated the incident and later charged the male student with sexual assault under its student code. Following a hearing, a university disciplinary board recommended his expulsion, which was upheld by the university president. The student sued the university and officials in a federal district court for sex discrimination under Title IX. The court granted summary judgment to the university, and he appealed to the Sixth Circuit.

The court relied on the Second Circuit's decision in *Yusuf v. Vassar College*, 35 F.3d 709 (2d Cir. 1994) to analyze the Title IX claim. The Second Circuit decision distinguished between "erroneous outcome" claims and "selective enforcement" claims. Under the erroneous outcome analysis, the student produced no evidence that the expulsion was discriminatory or motivated by a "chauvinistic view of the sexes." Under the selective enforcement theory, he did not establish the university treated similarly situated females more favorably. The court acknowledged that both students were intoxicated. However, the female could not remember what happened that night. This evidence did not show the university took action against the student based on his sex. Accordingly, the judgment for the university was affirmed. *Mallory v. Ohio Univ.*, No. 01-4111, 2003 WL 22146132 (6th Cir. 2003).

B. Harassment

1. Sexual Harassment by Employees

In Franklin v. Gwinnett County Public Schools, *503 U.S. 60, 112 S.Ct. 1028, 117 L.Ed.2d 208 (1992), a high school student who was harassed and sexually abused by a teacher sued her school under Title IX. The case reached the U.S. Supreme Court, which held she could recover monetary damages under Title IX for the teacher's harassment.*

The liability standards from Franklin, Gebser v. Lago Vista Independent School Dist., *524 U.S. 274 (1998), and* Davis v. Monroe County Board of Educ., *526 U.S. 629 (1999) apply in the higher education setting. When a sexual harassment claim is based on the conduct of an employee, the student must prove a school official with authority to take corrective action actually knew of the conduct, but remained deliberately indifferent to it to prevail under Title IX. The student must also show the harassment was so severe, pervasive and objectively offensive that it caused a deprivation of educational benefits.*

◆ *The U.S. Supreme Court found that an award of damages would be inappropriate in a Title IX case unless an official with the authority to address the discrimination failed to act despite actual knowledge of it, in a manner amounting to deliberate indifference to discrimination.*

The Supreme Court examined the potential liability of a Texas school district in a case involving a student who had a sexual relationship with a teacher. The Court rejected the liability standard advocated by the student and by the U.S. government, which resembled *respondeat superior* liability under Title VII. Title IX contains an administrative enforcement mechanism that assumes actual notice has been provided to officials prior to the imposition of enforcement remedies. An award of damages would be inappropriate in a Title IX case unless an official with the authority to address the discrimination failed to act despite actual knowledge of it, in a manner amounting to deliberate indifference to discrimination. Here, **there was insufficient evidence that a school official should have known about the relationship so as to impose liability on the school district.** *Gebser v. Lago Vista Independent School Dist.,* 524 U.S. 274, 118 S.Ct. 1989, 141 L.Ed.2d 277 (1998).

◆ *An Arkansas student failed to show university officials were legally responsible for sexual harassment by a professor.*

The student visited the professor's home to prepare a grant proposal. She said they had dinner and that the professor kissed her, held her down on his bed, and told her he wanted to have sex with her. The student said he later tried to contact her, resulting in "emotionally distressing meetings." She complained to university officials, who forced the professor to resign within a week. The student sued the university and officials in a federal district court for Title IX and constitutional violations. The court refused to dismiss monetary damage claims against the officials, and they appealed to the U.S. Court of Appeals, Eighth Circuit. **The court noted the officials had no direct contact with the**

professor during the relevant time period. The student did not present sufficient evidence that they did not respond to her complaints or act to prevent sexual harassment. The university had a strong, published policy against sexual harassment. **The student did not prove the officials were deliberately indifferent to sexual harassment. As a result, they could not be held liable for damages.** The court returned the case to the district court with directions to separate the claims against the professor and dismiss the remaining federal claims against the officials. *Cox v. Sugg*, 484 F.3d 1062 (8th Cir. 2007).

◆ *An Oklahoma college did not violate Title IX as it was not deliberately indifferent to a complaint about a professor's sexual behavior.*

A student was enrolled in two classes taught by a tenured professor. She claimed that the professor touched her inappropriately several times. The professor also made many sexual comments, she said, in front of her peers, and others while they were alone. The student sued the university in a federal district court, alleging it violated Title IX because it was deliberately indifferent to the sexual harassment. She claimed the college knew the professor sexually harassed others before she enrolled at the college. The court found the college did not have actual knowledge of prior incidents. In addition, those incidents were too dissimilar, too infrequent, and too distant in time. On appeal, the U.S. Court of Appeals, Tenth Circuit, applied the Supreme Court's reasoning in *Gebser v. Lago Vista Independent School Dist.*, above.

There was evidence that the college dean had actual knowledge of discrimination in the college's programs from the prior incidents. The court found this sufficient to satisfy Title IX's "actual knowledge" requirement. The court stated that the courts have differed on whether notice sufficient to trigger liability may consist of prior complaints or must consist of notice regarding current harassment in the recipient's programs. There was evidence in this case that the professor had dated two students close to his age. The court held this did not provide the college with the knowledge that the professor posed a substantial risk of sexual harassment to college students. The other student complaints of inappropriate sexual behavior against the professor occurred almost 10 years earlier. Those complaints involved significantly different behavior, including inappropriate touching and name-calling. **The court rejected the student's contention that the college was deliberately indifferent to her allegations, and affirmed the judgment for the college.** *Escue v. Northern Oklahoma College*, 450 F.3d 1146 (10th Cir. 2006).

◆ *The U.S. Court of Appeals, Seventh Circuit, held a professor did not sexually harass a student by leaving flowers and notes on her doorstep.*

An Indiana university professor left flowers and notes on a student's doorstep. She showed them to several administrators, then filed a complaint with the university's equal opportunity office. Although the university made a formal finding of no sexual harassment, it warned the professor to leave the student alone and not to retaliate against her. Even though the U.S. Department of Education's Office for Civil Rights declined the student's request to investigate the case, she sued the professor and the university in federal district court, alleging they violated Title IX and her equal protection rights via 42 U.S.C. § 1983. The court awarded summary judgment to the university.

The student appealed to the Seventh Circuit, which held that to prevail in a Title IX action, there must be sexual harassment so severe or pervasive that it changes the conditions of education. It must also be shown that the institution knew of harassment, yet remained deliberately indifferent to it. The court relied on Title VII employment discrimination cases considering the frequency and severity of allegedly discriminatory conduct. **The student never explained how the professor's conduct deprived her of educational opportunities.** Even had she shown his actions could be deemed severe or pervasive harassment, the university was not deliberately indifferent. Instead, the university promptly investigated the student's complaints and warned the professor not to contact or retaliate against her. The court affirmed the judgment for the university. *Hendrichsen v. Ball State Univ.*, 107 Fed.Appx. 680 (7th Cir. 2004).

◆   *The Court of Appeals of Michigan ruled a university was not liable for the alleged sexual harassment of a student by her music professor.*

The student attended the university's school of music. She soon complained that her music professor harassed her regularly by making sexual comments, commenting about what she wore, and asking her if she would massage him. The university advised the student to submit a formal complaint, and she did so. The associate dean met with the professor and told him the school would reprimand him or he could resign. The professor refused to resign, but the associate dean never placed a letter of reprimand in his file. However, the dean gave the professor a harsh warning and threatened to discharge him. The university excused the student from the class and gave her an A for the semester, but she did not enroll the next semester. The university did not give the professor teaching assignments or office space the next year.

The student sued the university in a state court for hostile environment sexual harassment under the Elliott Larsen Civil Rights Act (CRA), an anti-discrimination statute that parallels federal law and creates a legal cause of action for hostile environment sexual harassment. The court denied the university's request for summary judgment. A jury found the university liable for sexual harassment, and the university appealed to the Court of Appeals of Michigan. **The court held the university acted appropriately, as its conduct reasonably served to prevent further harassment by the professor.** The university did not have to fire the professor to show it acted appropriately. The court reversed the judgment and held for the university. *Johnson v. Univ. of Michigan Regents*, No. 247975, 2004 WL 2873831 (Mich. Ct. App. 2004).

◆   *The U.S. Court of Appeals, Third Circuit, held a Pennsylvania university was not liable in a student's Title IX sexual harassment action.*

The student claimed a professor sexually harassed her. She sued the university in a federal district court, arguing the university was deliberately indifferent to the harassment. The court conducted a jury trial, at which another professor testified she had reported her concerns about the professor's conduct to a university equity director. The professor stated nothing was done and the director never followed up with her about her reports. However, the director denied knowing about the professor's misconduct. She said had she been told about the sexual harassment, she would have called the student to her office for further action. The jury found the student failed to prove that a university employee with authority to take action against the professor knew of his harassment of students or that the university failed to adequately respond.

The student appealed to the Third Circuit. It noted that **in a Title IX sexual harassment claim, the university could be found liable if an official was authorized to institute corrective measures, knew about the professor's misconduct, but remained deliberately indifferent to it**. The court held the jury was entitled to find that the student did not establish the university knew about sexual harassment or failed to adequately respond to it. The judgment for the university was upheld. *Pociute v. West Chester Univ.*, 117 Fed.Appx. 832 (3d Cir. 2004).

◆ *To prevail in a Title IX action alleging harassment by an employee, the student must prove a school official with authority to take corrective action actually knew of the conduct, yet remained deliberately indifferent to it.*

An Illinois university music student was hired as an office assistant to her voice teacher. The student claimed the teacher asked her if she loved him and asked to rub her shoulders, tickle her and have her hug him. She told a female teacher and a counselor what happened, but neither of them reported the teacher's behavior. Two years earlier, a school dean had investigated sexual harassment charges against the voice teacher by faculty members. The investigation revealed the voice teacher made advances to three other female students who never filed complaints and to a fourth student who did file a complaint. The student transferred from the university and then filed a complaint about the voice teacher's conduct. The university ordered the teacher to take training and placed a reprimand letter in his personnel file.

The student sued the university under Title IX for sexual harassment and added a sexual harassment claim against the teacher under Title IX and 42 U.S.C. § 1983. A federal district court granted summary judgment to the university and teacher, and the student appealed to the Seventh Circuit. **The court held a student seeking to hold a university liable for Title IX violations must prove a school official with authority to take corrective measures against the harasser actually knew of the behavior, but was deliberately indifferent to it.** The court found the university had no actual notice of the teacher's misconduct and affirmed the judgment in its favor. **The student's Section 1983 claim against the teacher was not foreclosed by Title IX.** The court reinstated her action against him and remanded it to the district court. *Delgado v. Stegall*, 367 F.3d 668 (7th Cir. 2004).

◆ *The Second Circuit reversed a decision against a student on her sexual harassment claim against a former professor, but affirmed the judgment on her Title IX claim for the state university that had employed him.*

A New York student accused a tenured professor of referring to her as "Monica," based upon her physical resemblance to Monica Lewinsky. She did not report his conduct until meeting with the department chair midway through the academic year. At least five officials met to discuss his conduct, and the student delivered a handwritten complaint to the chair. The professor admitted making the comments, but insisted they were jokes or punishment for classroom disruptions. Within three months, he resigned. The student stopped attending her classes and received all failing grades. She sued the professor in a federal district court for violating her equal protection rights under 42 U.S.C. § 1983. She also claimed university officials violated Title IX. The court awarded judgment to the professor and university, and the student appealed.

The U.S. Court of Appeals, Second Circuit, held **a professor employed by a state university is a state actor under Section 1983**, based on the authority position held by professors over student educational and advancement opportunities. **There was evidence that the professor's remarks may have been pervasive enough to create a hostile environment.** The district court had improperly used a rigid, mathematical methodology to calculate the number of instances of misconduct to determine "pervasiveness." The court vacated the judgment for the professor and remanded the claim against him for additional proceedings. **University officials could not be held liable for his conduct, as the record indicated they adequately responded to the student's complaint.** The court affirmed the judgment for the university. *Hayut v. State Univ. of New York*, 352 F.3d 733 (2d Cir. 2003).

2. Sexual Harassment by Peers

◆   *The U.S. Supreme Court held schools may be held liable for incidents of peer sexual harassment under Title IX.*

The case involved a fifth-grade Georgia student who claimed that a classmate subjected her to unwanted sexual comments, physical abuse and ongoing harassment for about five months. She complained to her teacher and the school's principal, but claimed that they did nothing in response. When the case reached the Supreme Court, it held that **a recipient of federal funds may be held liable for student-on-student sexual harassment under Title IX where the funding recipient is deliberately indifferent to known student sexual harassment and the harasser is under the recipient's disciplinary authority.** The Court additionally held that in order to make a finding of deliberate indifference, the recipient's response to harassment must be clearly unreasonable in light of the known circumstances. **In order to create Title IX liability, the harassment must be so severe, pervasive and objectively offensive that it deprives the victim of access to the funding recipient's educational opportunities or benefits.** *Davis v. Monroe County Board of Educ.*, 526 U.S. 629, 119 S.Ct. 1661, 143 L.Ed.2d 839 (1999).

◆   *A Massachusetts maritime academy supervisor was immune to claims that he did not do enough to stop male cadets from sexually harassing females.*

Two female cadets asked whether there had been prior instances of sexual misconduct by male cadets before they enrolled. They said officials at the academy told them there had never been such an incident. At an orientation program, the supervisor said the academy had a zero-tolerance policy with respect to sexual harassment. The female cadets claimed male cadets verbally abused them, then sexually assaulted them in their dormitory room. After they reported the assaults to the supervisor, they said the harassment worsened.

The female cadets claimed the supervisor told them the "problem would go away" if they stopped talking about it. They withdrew from the academy and filed a state court action for violation of their equal protection rights. The state court of appeals held the supervisor was entitled to qualified immunity. **Although supervisors can be held liable for student-on-student harassment if they are "deliberately indifferent" to it, this legal rule was not clearly established until the U.S. Supreme Court's decision in** *Davis v. Monroe County Board of Educ.*, above. This decision came after the cadets had left the academy and the alleged harassment against them had already ended. Because the legal rule was not clearly established until after the events giving rise to the lawsuit took place, the supervisor was entitled to qualified immunity. *White v. Gurnon*, 67 Mass. App. Ct. 622, 855 N.E.2d 1124 (Mass. App. Ct. 2006).

◆ *A federal district court held a South Carolina student may pursue a claim that a college was deliberately indifferent to her sexual assault complaint.*

The student claimed a male student sexually assaulted her in a dorm room. She said a college dean told her she could press criminal charges or pursue the matter through the college. According to the student, the dean was very compassionate during her first meetings with her. However, she said the dean started to act rudely towards her when she learned the identity of the rapist. The student took a medical withdrawal from school. After her return, the college discipline and appeals committee conducted a hearing, then found her guilty of sexual misconduct. The committee found the male student was not guilty of sexual assault. The student sued the college in a federal district court, alleging it violated Title IX by failing to take prompt and effective action to resolve her complaint. The college argued its response was not deliberately indifferent, and that any sexual harassment did not deny the student access to the school's educational opportunities. The court denied the college's motion for pretrial judgment. **A jury would have to decide if the college was deliberately indifferent to the student's complaint.** *Doe v. Erskine College*, No. Civ.A. 8:04-23001RBH, 2006 WL 1473853 (D.S.C. 5/25/06).

◆ *A Georgia student who sued a university for sexual assault by student-athletes in a dorm room presented enough evidence to advance to a trial.*

The student went to a student-athlete's dorm room, where she consented to sexual relations. She did not know one of his teammates was hiding in a closet. The teammate sexually assaulted the student and invited another teammate to sexually assault and rape her. The student filed criminal charges against the student-athlete and teammates. She withdrew from the university. The student-athletes were charged with disorderly conduct under the university's code of conduct and suspended from athletics. A university judiciary panel held hearings almost a year after the incident and decided not to punish them. The student sued the university in a federal district court for violating Title IX. The court held for the university, and the student appealed.

The U.S. Court of Appeals, Eleventh Circuit, held **student-on-student harassment violates Title IX. A university may be held liable if it acts with**

deliberate indifference to known acts of harassment that is so severe, pervasive and objectively offensive that it bars a victim's access to an educational opportunity or benefit. The student claimed the university had accepted the student-athlete even though it knew of his history of similar misconduct at other schools. The court found the university did not sufficiently respond to the student's allegations. Within 48 hours of the incident, the university had a preliminary report of the incident. However, it exercised almost no control over the student-athlete and failed to enforce its harassment policies. As the student presented evidence of discrimination that effectively barred her access to an educational opportunity or benefit, the court reversed the judgment. *Williams v. Univ. of Georgia*, 441 F.3d 1287 (11th Cir. 2006).

◆ *A federal district court found a Colorado university could not be liable in a Title IX case where it did not know of the conduct giving rise to the action.*

Two female students claimed that a football player and a female tutor for the athletic department planned a football recruiting event to provide recruits an opportunity to have sex with intoxicated female students. They further claimed recruits and players sexually assaulted them and sued the university for violating Title IX. The court relied on *Davis v. Monroe County Board. of Educ.*, above. The students argued the university should have been aware that female students faced a risk of severe and pervasive sexual harassment and assault from participants in the football program because of previous similar incidents.

The students contended the university had control over recruits and players, but failed to control or eliminate the risk. They also claimed the university was deliberately indifferent to the acts of the recruits and players when it did not implement rules for the recruiting program or exercise supervision over the program. The court rejected the students' argument. It said the other incidents did not involve the same risk. **The court found the university could not be deliberately indifferent to acts it knew nothing about. The students could not prove the harassment was caused by the university without showing it had actual knowledge and was deliberately indifferent to the misconduct.** The court awarded judgment to the university. *Simpson v. Univ. of Colorado*, 372 F. Supp.2d 1229 (D. Colo. 2005).

III. RACE AND NATIONAL ORIGIN DISCRIMINATION

The Equal Protection Clause of the Fourteenth Amendment, Title VI of the Civil Rights Act of 1964, 42 U.S.C. § 1981 and state anti-discrimination laws all prohibit discrimination against individuals in educational settings.

A. Affirmative Action

◆ *While achieving a diverse student body may be a worthy goal, the means to achieve that goal must comply with the Equal Protection Clause. The U.S. Supreme Court allowed race to be used as a "plus" factor in admissions.*

The University of Michigan had an admissions policy for its law school that used race as a "plus" factor for underrepresented minorities. The policy was flexible, utilized an individualized assessment system, and did not create quotas. The policy was challenged as unconstitutional by white students who were not accepted for enrollment. The case reached the U.S. Supreme Court, which upheld the policy. **The Court first noted that the goal of achieving diversity in the student body was a compelling governmental interest.** As a result, the policy would not violate the Equal Protection Clause if it was narrowly tailored to achieving that goal. Since the law school's policy did not set impermissible quotas, and since **it utilized an individualized assessment system by using race/ethnicity as a "plus" factor when evaluating individual applicants for admission,** it was constitutional. The Court also noted that race-conscious admissions policies should be limited in time so that racial preferences can be ended as soon as practicable. *Grutter v. Bollinger*, 539 U.S. 306, 123 S.Ct. 2325, 156 L.E.2d 304 (2003).

◆ *The Supreme Court found unconstitutional the University of Michigan's undergraduate admissions policy, which awarded applicants in underrepresented minority groups 20 points out of 100 needed for admission.*

Applying the same strict scrutiny analysis it used in *Grutter*, above, the Court held the undergraduate policy was not narrowly tailored to achieve the compelling governmental interest in a diverse student body. **The undergraduate admissions policy did not assess points on an individualized basis,** but rather awarded them to all minority applicants. The failure to review each applicant individually doomed the policy under the Equal Protection Clause. *Gratz v. Bollinger*, 539 U.S. 244, 123 S.Ct. 2411, 156 L.Ed.2d 257 (2003).

◆ *In 1978, the Supreme Court held a special admissions program at a California medical school that reserved close to one-sixth of the school's openings each year for minority students violated the Equal Protection Clause.*

The Medical School of the University of California at Davis had two admission programs for its entering class of 100 students. Under the regular procedure, candidates whose overall undergraduate grade point averages fell below 2.5 on a scale of 4.0 were summarily rejected. The special admissions policy, designed to assist minority or other disadvantaged applicants, reserved 16 of the 100 openings each year for medical school admission based upon criteria other than that used in the general admissions program. Special admission applicants did not need to meet the 2.5 or better grade point average of the general admission group, and their Medical College Admission Test scores, measured against general admission candidates.

A white male brought suit to compel his admission to medical school after he was twice rejected for admission even though candidates with lower grade point averages and lower test score results were being admitted under the special admissions program. The plaintiff alleged that **the special admissions excluded him from medical school on the basis of his race** in violation of the Equal Protection Clause of the Fourteenth Amendment, the California Constitution, and Title VI of the 1964 Civil Rights Act. Title VI of the Civil Rights Act provides that no person shall on the ground of race or color be excluded from participating in any program receiving federal financial assistance. The Equal Protection Clause states that no state shall deny to any person within its jurisdiction the equal protection of the law. The California Supreme Court concluded that the special admissions program was not the least intrusive means of achieving the state's goals of integrating the medical profession under a strict scrutiny standard.

On appeal, the U.S. Supreme Court held that **while the goal of achieving a diverse student body is sufficiently compelling to justify considerations of race in admissions decisions under some circumstances, the special admissions program, which foreclosed consideration to persons such as the plaintiff, was unnecessary to achieve this compelling goal and was therefore invalid under the Equal Protection Clause**. Since the school could not prove that the plaintiff would not have been admitted even if there had been no special admissions program, the Court ordered that he be admitted to the medical school. *Regents of the Univ. of California v. Bakke*, 438 U.S. 265, 98 S.Ct. 2733, 57 L.Ed.2d 750 (1978).

◆   *The Supreme Court held that a university could avoid liability for a race-based admission policy if it could show that the applicant would have been denied admission absent the policy.*

An African immigrant of Caucasian descent applied for admission to the Ph.D. program in counseling psychology at a Texas public university. The university considered the race of its applicants at some stage of the review process and denied admission to the applicant. He sued for money damages and injunctive relief, asserting that the race-conscious admission policy violated the Equal Protection Clause. The university moved for summary judgment, arguing that even if it had not used race-based criteria, it would not have admitted the applicant because of his GPA and his GRE score. A federal court granted summary judgment to the university, but the Fifth Circuit Court of Appeals reversed. The case reached the U.S. Supreme Court, which noted that its decision in *Mt. Healthy City Board of Educ. v. Doyle*, 429 U.S. 274, 97 S.Ct. 568, 50 L.Ed.2d 471 (1977), made clear that **if the government has considered an impermissible criterion in making an adverse decision to the plaintiff, it can nevertheless avoid liability by demonstrating that it would have made the same decision absent the forbidden consideration**. Therefore, if the state could show that it would have made the decision to deny admission to the applicant absent the race-based policy, it would be entitled to summary judgment on the claim for damages. With respect to the claim for injunctive relief, it appeared that the university had stopped using a race-based admissions policy. However, that issue had to be decided on remand. *Texas v. Lesage*, 528 U.S. 18, 120 S.Ct. 467, 145 L.Ed.2d 347 (1999).

◆   *A Michigan constitutional amendment barring racial preferences by state universities did not violate the First Amendment or Equal Protection Clause.*

In November 2006, Michigan voters approved Proposal 2, a ballot initiative to bar preferential treatment based on race or gender in public education. The proposal would amend the state's constitution and was set to take effect in December 2006. A day after the measure passed, individuals and groups who opposed it sued the governor and two state universities. They sought a declaratory judgment that the amendment was invalid, and a permanent injunction barring its enforcement. The universities filed a cross-claim for permission to continue using their existing admissions and financial aid policies. A white male who had applied for admission to the University of Michigan Law School sought to intervene in the case, as did a public interest group. They wanted the amendment to take effect on schedule. The court issued a temporary order barring the application of Proposal 2 to the universities' admissions and financial aid policies until July 1, 2007. It then allowed the student to intervene. On appeal, the Sixth Circuit held the preliminary order did not state a sufficient ground for blocking Proposal 2 under federal law.

The court rejected the argument that the amendment violated the Equal Protection Clause of the Fourteenth Amendment. It found a state constitutional amendment that eliminates racial distinctions "would seem to be an equal protection virtue, not an equal protection vice." The court also rejected the argument that Proposal 2 was preempted by Title VI of the Civil Rights Act of 1964. Nor did Title IX preempt the amendment. As the student showed a strong likelihood of reversing the district court's order, the Sixth Circuit granted his motion for a stay pending his appeal. *Coalition to Defend Affirmative Action v. Granholm*, 473 F.3d 237 (6th Cir. 2006).

◆ *The University of Washington Law School's admission policy did not discriminate against applicants on the basis of race.*

The law school had no racial quotas, targets or goals for admission or enrollment, but considered race, ethnicity and other diversity factors as a "plus" in admission decisions. The school also relied on nonracial diversity factors. Several white applicants who were denied admission to the law school sued the university in a federal district court for race discrimination. The court denied summary judgment to the applicants, and they appealed to the Ninth Circuit. The court relied on *Grutter v. Bollinger*.

In *Grutter*, the University of Michigan Law School sought to enroll a "critical mass" of underrepresented minority students to ensure that minority students could make unique contributions to the school. The Michigan law school targeted African-Americans, Hispanics and Native Americans in this effort. In *Grutter*, the U.S. Supreme Court held the school established a compelling interest in attaining a diverse student body and upheld its admissions policy. The Ninth Circuit found the University of Washington Law School acted in good faith to implement its admissions process and satisfied the factors described in *Grutter*. **The school did not establish quotas, targets or goals for admission or enrollment of minorities, nor did it direct the admission of a certain number of minority applicants.** As the law school followed the guidelines in *Grutter* by conducting a "highly-individualized, holistic review of each applicant's file," the court affirmed the judgment. *Smith v. Univ. of Washington Law School*, 392 F.3d 367 (9th Cir. 2004).

◆ *The Florida Supreme Court held the NAACP had associational standing to challenge an executive order abolishing the use of race and gender preferences for admission to Florida state institutions of higher learning.*

The state board of regents amended three sections of the state administrative code in response to Executive Order 99-281, which asked the board to immediately prohibit racial or gender set-asides, preferences, or quotas in admissions to all Florida institutions of higher education. The NAACP and its members brought a rule challenge under state law. An administrative law judge denied a motion for dismissal by the board of regents and the state board of education, finding the NAACP had "associational standing" because its members included students in middle school, high school and college. The Florida District Court of Appeal reversed and remanded the case. It held the NAACP could not establish associational standing because it failed to show how its members would suffer a real and immediate injury.

The Supreme Court of Florida held an association that challenges a state rule must demonstrate a substantial number of its members are substantially affected by the rule. The rule's subject matter must be within the association's general scope of interest and activity, and the relief requested must be of the type appropriate for a trade association representing its members. The record indicated some NAACP members were prospective state university candidates and were minorities who would be affected by these changes. The appellate decision required the NAACP to prove actual harm to gain associational standing. State law did not impose this requirement. **As the NAACP showed the amendments would have a sufficient impact on its membership, it satisfied the requirement of "substantial impact" for "associational standing."** The court quashed the appellate decision and remanded the case. *NAACP v. Florida Board of Regents*, 863 So.2d 294 (Fla. 2003).

◆ *The University of Georgia's admissions policy, which offered additional points to minority applicants, was unconstitutional because it restricted the use of other factors in violation of the Equal Protection Clause.*

In 1995, the University of Georgia (UGA) developed a three-stage admissions process. The initial stage evaluated the applicant based on objective academic criteria without regard to race or gender. At stage two, UGA assessed the applicant's total student index (TSI). Candidates were awarded points based on a variety of factors including race, extracurricular activities, state residency and academic achievement. At this stage of the admissions process, candidates with a TSI score of 4.93 were automatically accepted; applicants with a TSI score below 4.66 were automatically rejected. The candidates whose scores fell between 4.66 and 4.92 moved to the third stage. At the "edge read" (ER) stage, all applicants start with a score of zero and race is not a factor. Three white female applicants were denied admission to the UGA 1999 freshman class. One of the applicants would have automatically been admitted if she received gender and minority credit; the other two women would have qualified for consideration at the ER stage. The women sued for race discrimination in violation of the Equal Protection Clause and Title VI, and gender discrimination in violation of the Equal Protection Clause and Title IX. The court concluded that UGA's admissions policy violated Title VI, and by extension the Equal Protection Clause, because striving for a diverse student body was not a compelling interest able to withstand strict scrutiny.

The court held for the women. UGA appealed to the Eleventh Circuit. The court of appeals ruled that regardless of whether diversity is a compelling interest, UGA's admissions policy, which restricted the use of other factors relevant to diversity, could not satisfy strict scrutiny and therefore violated the Equal Protection Clause. First, **UGA's policy lacked flexibility; it "mechanically" assigned bonus points for race without conducting individual evaluations of each candidate** and limited the factors at the TSI stage to only 12. Second, the policy failed to fully consider race-neutral factors, such as income level and language skills. Third, the value assigned to race was "arbitrary." In addition, only an SAT score between 1200 and 1600 was accorded more value than a race factor and, **among the nonacademic factors, no factor was worth more than the race**. Finally, UGA did not show that before adopting its race-conscious admissions policy, it had considered race-neutral factors and rejected them as inadequate. For these reasons, UGA's admissions policy violated the Equal Protection Clause. *Johnson v. Board of Regents of Univ. of Georgia*, 263 F.3d 1234 (11th Cir. 2001).

◆ *Although a university's use of racial preferences for admissions to law school was unconstitutional, four students failed to show that they would have been admitted to the school absent the discrimination.*

Four white students applied for admission to the University of Texas School of Law. After they were denied admission, they sued under Title VI of the Civil Rights Act of 1964 and 42 U.S.C. §§ 1981 and 1983, asserting that the law school's use of racial preferences for the purpose of achieving a diverse student body violated those laws. A federal district court held that although the government had a compelling interest in achieving a diverse student body, and a compelling interest in overcoming the present effects of past race discrimination, the school's use of separate admissions procedures for minority and nonminority students was not narrowly tailored to achieve those compelling interests. The students had the ultimate burden to prove that they would have been admitted to the law school absent the unconstitutional procedures used by the university. The court held they did not meet that burden.

On appeal, the Fifth Circuit held **the law school's use of racial preferences served no compelling state interests** and that the burden should have been on the law school to show that under a constitutional admissions procedure, the students would not have been admitted. On remand, the district court held **the university showed the students would not have been admitted even if its procedures had been constitutional**. *Hopwood v. Texas*, 999 F.Supp. 872 (W.D. Tex. 1998). On second appeal to the Fifth Circuit, the court upheld the district court's determination that the students would not have been admitted to the law school even if the admissions policy was constitutional. *Hopwood v. Texas*, 236 F.3d 256 (5th Cir. 2000).

B. Discrimination and Equal Protection

◆ *The U.S. Supreme Court held individuals cannot sue colleges, schools and states for policies that unintentionally discriminate against minorities under Title VI. They may still sue entities for acts of intentional discrimination.*

Alabama amended its constitution in 1990 to declare English its official language. It began administering driver's license exams only in English, and a federal court agreed with a class of individuals that the state violated a Title VI regulation published by the U.S. Department of Justice. Title VI is one of the principal federal laws preventing discrimination on the basis of race, color or national origin. It prohibits recipients of federal funding, including states and educational institutions, from practicing discrimination in any covered program or activity and is commonly cited in education cases alleging discrimination on those grounds. The case reached the U.S. Supreme Court, which noted **Title VI prohibits only intentional discrimination** and cannot be used to enforce a disparate-impact action. **Because disparate-impact regulations of the kind at issue in this case did not apply to Title VI, the private right of action under Section 601 did not include a private right to enforce disparate-impact regulations.** The lower court judgments were reversed. *Alexander v. Sandoval*, 532 U.S. 275, 121 S.Ct. 1511, 149 L.Ed.2d 517 (2001).

◆ *A Texas student did not prove a university law school rejected him based on race because he could not refute he had a poor academic record.*

The student claimed the law school deactivated his file because it was incomplete and that the fall class was closed. He sued the university in a federal district court for intentional discrimination based on race. The court found the student's law school application reflected his Law School Admissions Test (LSAT) was in the bottom 2% of those who took it. His undergraduate grade point average was 2.43. The law school stated it had not admitted any applicant of any race with a similar LSAT score and grade point average. **The court held the student failed to establish race discrimination. He did not show he was qualified for admission and could not refute the university's legitimate nondiscriminatory reason for not admitting him.** The court held the applicant did not establish a Title VI intentional discrimination claim and awarded judgment to the law school. *Gant v. Southern Methodist Univ. School of Law*, No. CIVA305CV1455K, 2006 WL 2691301 (N.D. Tex. 9/19/06).

◆ *A Pennsylvania university did not discriminate against a student based on her race when it dismissed her for academic failure.*

The student had to repeat her first year of college, then failed four courses in her repeat year. She met with a professor to talk about her study habits. The professor suggested that the student study from her notes instead of index cards and suggested that she visit the university's Recruitment, Admission and Retention Office (RAR) for extra help. RAR is a federally funded program that actively recruits minority students and offers them support services. All African-American students received an RAR invitation, regardless of their academic qualifications or background. A different professor later advised the student to study from old exams and expressed surprise that the other professor had not made the same suggestion. A Caucasian student told the student that the professor who had advised her to go to RAR had told the Caucasian student to study from past tests. At the end of her repeat year, a university committee dismissed the student because she received several failing grades while on probation. She sued the university in a federal district court for race discrimination in violation of 42 U.S.C. § 1983.

The court held for the university, and the student appealed to the U.S. Court of Appeals, Third Circuit. The student argued the professor's suggestion that she go to the RAR program for help stereotyped her. She said the RAR program implied that African-American students were less qualified or capable of meeting the demands of the university. **The court found no evidence to show a connection between racial stereotyping and the academic dismissal. The student failed to prove the university dismissed her because of race.** The only evidence she offered to prove discrimination was that the professor gave her different advice than she gave to a Caucasian student. The court held that offering different students different advice did not mean the professor did so because of race. The judgment for the university was affirmed. *Manning v. Temple Univ.*, No. 05-1215, 157 Fed. Appx. 509 (3rd Cir. 2005).

◆   *A Maine college did not discriminate against a student who was dismissed after he got in a fight with a minority student.*

The student threw a snowball at a student shuttle. The student claimed that the driver – a Korean college student – threatened to run him down and backed the van onto the sidewalk towards him. According to the student, he began to walk away, but the driver got out of the van. The student struck the driver in the face, breaking his nose and causing extensive bleeding. The college judicial board held the student violated the college code of conduct and barred him for two years. The board determined the driver did not throw a punch and cleared him of any charges. The student sued the college in a federal district court for race discrimination. The court awarded summary judgment to the college, and the student appealed to the U.S. Court of Appeals, First Circuit.

The student argued the college dismissed him for discriminatory reasons, and that the evidence corroborated his version of the events. **The court found the reason the college dismissed him was that he severely injured another student, which was a legitimate nondiscriminatory reason.** After reviewing the hearing record, the court agreed with the board's finding that the driver did not throw a punch. The evidence did not support the student's argument that race was the only possible reason for the different outcomes between him and the driver. The court affirmed the judgment for the college. *Goodman v. Bowdoin College*, 380 F.3d 33 (1st Cir. 2004).

◆   *A Nebraska college did not discriminate against a student by rejecting her applications for a post-graduate program.*

The student applied to the college's post-graduate physician's assistant program. After being rejected for the third time, she sued the college in a federal district court for race discrimination. The court dismissed the case, based on evidence that the student failed many classes, had a poor attendance record and did not hand in her assignments. She failed to rebut the college's legitimate, nondiscriminatory reasons for denying her application. The student appealed to the Eighth Circuit, where she asserted a college academic advisor coerced her into taking three challenging science courses at one time rather than sequentially, as a college policy required. She failed two of those courses and got a D in the other. The student also said interviewers asked her inappropriate questions and gave her a low interview score because of race discrimination. The court held that even if it disregarded the three courses she took because of alleged coercion, the nine courses she needed to retake were ample evidence of her academic ineptitude. She offered no evidence that the interview process was unfair or the calculation of her initial grade average was ill-motivated. As the student could not disprove the college's legitimate, nondiscriminatory reasons for denying her admission, the court affirmed the judgment. *Baker v. Union College*, 95 Fed. Appx. 844 (8th Cir. 2004).

◆ *A university may have discriminated against a black student by expelling him but not three white students.*

A black student lived with a white student in a mobile home on the campus of a Missouri university. One night, they had a party with two white female students and several non-students. Everyone but the black student drank alcohol. When campus police entered the home, the black student cooperated with them. However, since the university did not allow students who lived on campus to possess alcohol or have visitors of the opposite sex, the black student and the other three students were expelled. Shortly thereafter, the three white students were readmitted, but the black student was not. He sued the university under 42 U.S.C. § 1981 for race discrimination. A federal court granted pretrial judgment to the university, but the Eighth Circuit reversed. The court held that **the black student had presented sufficient evidence of intentional discrimination to warrant a trial.** He was the only student at the party not drinking, and he cooperated the most with campus police. Further, he presented evidence that students expelled for violating the alcohol and/or visitation rules were always readmitted. Finally, he alleged that university officials made repeated references to his race during the investigation. *Williams v. Lindenwood Univ.*, 288 F.3d 349 (8th Cir. 2002).

C. National Origin

◆ *A Wisconsin court found an Iranian student presented ample evidence to show a university's reason for dismissing him was a cover-up for racial bias.*

The student had lived in the U.S. since he was 10 years old and was a U.S. citizen. He received a scholarship to attend a Wisconsin dental school. After he was to begin his studies at the dental school, the student was required to travel to the U.S. Embassy in Naples, Italy so he could complete a process that would allow his wife to immigrate to the U.S. He was away for about 10 days. At the end of the fall 2000 semester, the student received two Fs and one D. The university sent him a letter advising him he was subject to dismissal. The student met with an academic review committee to discuss his grades, and the committee voted to allow the student to repeat his first year under academic probation. It was agreed that any failing grade received during the repeat year could lead to dismissal. The student received two failing grades because he did not take medication that had been prescribed for depression and anxiety.

Two years after he was dismissed from the program, the student sued the university in a state court, claiming racial discrimination. The court dismissed the case, and the student appealed to the Court of Appeals of Wisconsin. **To establish a case of discrimination, the court held the student had to show the university gave preferential treatment to another student who was "similarly situated."** The student contended the university gave another student many more chances than it gave him. The court stated there is no magic formula for determining whether two parties are similarly situated. A court must determine whether parties are similarly situated based on the facts of each case. **In this case, there was enough evidence to infer the university's real reason for treating the student unfavorably was discrimination.** As there was doubt concerning the reason given by the university for dismissal, a trial court would need to hear further facts. The court reversed the judgment and returned the case to the trial court for this purpose. *Amir v. Marquette Univ.*, 297 Wis.2d 326, 727 N.W.2d 63 (Wis. Ct. App. 2006).

◆ *A citizen of the Dominican Republic was permitted to proceed with a Title VI complaint against a New York university.*

The student claimed he was harassed by peers and had to complete a group project by himself because no one would work with him. He claimed this caused feelings of inferiority and adversely affected his education. The student claimed he was "teased, insulted, mocked, degraded and ridiculed" in another class as a member of a minority group by a professor and other students. A female student brought harassment allegations against him. A student services panel held he would be permitted to complete his degree, but would be considered a "persona non grata" in university facilities. The student sued the university in a federal district court for race discrimination. He included a claim under Title VI. **A federal magistrate judge found the student failed to show race had anything to do with the sexual harassment and disciplinary proceedings against him.** However, the judge permitted him to amend his Title VI claim against the university by alleging intentional discrimination. He recommended that this claim proceed. *Rodriguez v. New York Univ.*, No. 05 Civ. 7374 JSR, 2007 WL 117775 (S.D.N.Y. 1/16/07).

◆ *A Texas federal district court dismissed a Cameroon native's race and national origin discrimination claim against an associate professor.*

The University of Houston admitted the student to a doctoral degree program in the Department of English. She claimed an associate professor questioned her about her country of origin and academic profile. The professor allegedly threatened to ruin the student's transcript and delay her graduation. She brought grading and discrimination complaints against the professor under a university policy. The English department dismissed the accusations as unfounded. At about the same time, another professor in the English department accused the student of plagiarism.

The university honesty panel, which included the associate professor, concluded the student had plagiarized and she received an F for that class. The student was later expelled after another charge of plagiarism by the same professor. The student sued the university, professor, and others in a federal district court for discrimination and retaliation under Title VI. The university argued that **Title VI claims may only be brought against entities that receive federal funding, not individual employees. The court agreed, and granted a motion to dismiss the Title VI claim against the associate professor.** *Bisong v. Univ. of Houston*, Civil Action No. H-06-1815, 2006 WL 2414410 (S.D. Tex. 8/18/06).

◆   *A federal district court dismissed a Greek student's charge that a Virginia law school discriminated against him based on his national origin.*

The student attended a law school in Virginia. He claimed the assistant dean verbally assault him with bigoted comments for more than a year. The assistant dean allegedly said "Greeks own restaurants and diners and are not cut out to be lawyers." The student decided to appeal a grade he received in one class, but claimed he was discouraged from doing so by school staff. He claimed a professor made bigoted remarks to him and encouraged a student to harass him about his Greek origins. The student sued the university in a federal district court, alleging it violated Title VI of the Civil Rights Act of 1964.

The court found the student did not sufficiently state that the acts by the assistant dean and professor were based on national origin or that the university could be found vicariously liable for those acts. While there were comments referring to his Greek heritage, others were unrelated to it. For example, the assistant dean said she discouraged the student from appealing his grade because she did not want him to set a precedent that grades could be overturned. Just because the student was the only fully ethnic, bilingual Greek American full-time law student, this did not mean every action he complained about had to do with being Greek. **The court found the student would have been subjected to the same conduct even if he were not Greek.** The conduct he alleged was not severe or pervasive enough to support his hostile environment claim. At most, the student described an ongoing saga of rudeness, insensitivity, and personality clashes. **As educational institutions can be held liable under Title VI only for intentional conduct, the court dismissed the case.** *Langadinos v. Appalachian School of Law*, No. 1:05 CV 00039, 2005 WL 2333460 (W.D. Va. 9/25/05).

◆   *A Korean doctoral student did not show a District of Columbia university discriminated against him on the basis of national origin.*

The student's Ph.D. program required him to complete course work and pass a comprehensive written and oral exam. Grades for the exam were pass, bare pass, minimum pass, or fail. Candidates had two chances to pass the comprehensive exam, but were terminated from the program if they failed twice. The student fulfilled the course work requirements but failed the exam twice, and was terminated from the program. He sued the university for violating the District of Columbia Human Rights Act. The case reached the District of Columbia Court of Appeals, where the student argued that comments made about Korean students by a professor were direct evidence of discrimination. **The court found the comments reflected a generalized assessment of the analytical abilities of Korean students and were not enough to prove discrimination.** As the student showed no link between the comments and his dismissal, the university was entitled to judgment. *Jung v. George Washington Univ.*, 875 A.2d 95 (D.C. App. Ct. 2005).

◆   *A federal district court dismissed two Missouri teachers from a student's race and national origin discrimination lawsuit.*

The student alleged two teachers gave him poor grades because of his race and nationality. After he received the poor grades, the college dismissed him.

The student sued the teachers in a federal district court, alleging they discriminated against him because of his race and nationality by giving him poor grades and participating in the decision to dismiss him. The teachers argued the charges against them individually should be dismissed because the student did not allege any facts that could reasonably infer they were personally involved in any discrimination. They claimed the student did not show they were personally involved in giving him his grades or that they participated in the decision to dismiss him. **The court agreed, holding the student could not sue teachers in their individual capacities under Title VI.** *Ajiwoju v. Cottrell*, No. 04-0715-CV-W-FJG, 2005 WL 1026702 (W.D. Mo. 5/2/05).

◆   *A federal district court held a New York university did not discriminate against a Moroccan-born student based on her national origin.*

The student alleged her French professor severely mistreated her and prevented her from getting course credit. The professor failed her for the course. The student claimed the department chair would not allow her to return to the classroom and told her if she did, security would escort her out. The student alleged the chair said, "You're from Morocco, you're Arab," and told her an Arab student who frightens a French professor could go to jail. She said she spoke with a staff member who asked her how she knew French. When she told him she was from Morocco, the staff member said, "Oh My God, Arab. Bin Laden is here." The student claimed she was not allowed to take the French final exam, and the university gave her a failing grade for the class. The grade was later converted to a "W" (withdrawn). The student sued the university in a federal district court for violating Title VI. She alleged that after September 11, 2001, most people questioned the motives of Arabs in America.

The court found the student failed to prove the university's actions were motivated by discrimination. It said **unspecified comments cannot provide a rational basis to infer the university acted out of discrimination**. The student did not allow officials a chance to respond to charges of discrimination because she never told them about any discrimination. The court dismissed the case. *Aoutif v. City Univ. of New York*, No. 05-CV-496 (ILG), 2005 WL 3334277 (E.D.N.Y. 12/8/05).

◆   *An Ohio university did not discriminate against a medical student because of her national origin by demanding she improve her English.*

The student was born in Poland. She moved to the United States when the University of Cincinnati College of Medicine accepted her into a residency program in its anesthesia department. The student received high scores and positive comments in her first two quarters. However, professors noted her poor command of English was a language barrier that interfered with patient care. Her evaluations declined and she continued to have communication problems. The college placed the student on academic probation and assigned a professor to help her. The professor urged the department chair to accommodate the student's request for guidance and counseling for her language deficiency. The university assigned her to a pediatric surgery unit during her fourth quarter, but did not provide her with any language instruction. The scoring on her evaluation was lower than before, but the college kept her on probation and required her to enroll in an English course. The student transferred to a medical school in New York, where she completed her first year of residency.

The student sued the University of Cincinnati in an Ohio state court for national origin discrimination. **The court held the university could lawfully take its action on her foreign accent, based on evidence that it interfered with her ability to perform. The student was unqualified for the position because the medical profession demands the ability to communicate effectively.** The court found the school did not treat the student less favorably than others outside the protected class. Four other residents who were trained in foreign countries successfully completed the program. Apart from the student, the only other resident to fail was an American. The court stated that if the university treated her differently at all, it was because of her communication difficulties, not her Polish heritage. Since the university was not motivated by discrimination, the court dismissed the case. *Sarach-Kozlowska v. Univ. of Cincinnati College of Medicine*, No. 2001-07505, 2004 WL 823433 (Ohio Ct. Cl. 2004).

◆ *A federal district court held a Florida university did not discriminate against an Iranian-American by suspending him for a firearms arrest.*

The university placed the student on "interim suspension" after his arrest for firearms possession. He filed a grievance against the university, claiming the dean did not investigate the arrest. The student claimed the university could not suspend him for violating the university's code of conduct as a consequence of the arrest, because the police did not charge him with any crime. The state later charged the student with a misdemeanor for exhibiting a weapon. When the university learned the student had been charged with a misdemeanor but not a felony, it entered into negotiations with him for his return to school. The university later found the student had violated the code of conduct.

The student sued the university in a federal district court for national origin discrimination. **To prove national origin discrimination under 42 U.S.C. § 1981, the student had to show the university treated him less favorably than other similarly situated persons who were outside his protected class. No other student had been arrested and held on bond for a criminal offense.** The court held the interim suspension was not proof of discrimination. Because the offense was so serious, the university justifiably suspended him before an investigation or hearing. The court granted the university's motion for summary judgment. *Ali v. Stetson Univ.*, 340 F.Supp.2d 1320 (M.D. Fla. 2004).

IV. AGE DISCRIMINATION

In addition to state laws, the Age Discrimination Act of 1975 (42 U.S.C. § 6101, et seq.) provides the basis for claims of age discrimination by students. Similar to Title IX claims, however, the Age Discrimination Act applies only to programs or activities receiving federal funding. Since the Age Discrimination in Employment Act (ADEA) is a broader statute (albeit only in employment), the Age Discrimination Act is not used very often, but its protections should be noted.

◆ *The U.S. Court of Appeals, Second Circuit, held Cornell University had a valid reason to expel a student that was not based on her age or gender.*

The female student attended Cornell's veterinary program. She twice failed required exams, and the university expelled her. The student sued the university in a federal district court, alleging discrimination based on her gender and because of her age in violation of the Age Discrimination Act. The court held the student did not prove the motivation to expel her was based on gender or age discrimination and dismissed the claims. The student appealed to the Second Circuit. The court found she had failed to exhaust her administrative remedies before she filed suit. **The court agreed with the district court's finding that the student failed to prove the university had expelled male students who twice failed required exams. It affirmed the judgment.** *Curto v. Edmundson*, 392 F.3d 502 (2d Cir. 2004).

◆ *An older student's claim of age discrimination failed where he could not show that he was qualified for entrance into a medical school's class.*

A 53-year-old psychologist applied to be a member of a first-year medical class at the Albert Einstein College of Medicine. The psychologist was called for an interview and was recommended for acceptance by the interviewer. However, the psychologist was not accepted. He alleged age discrimination in violation of New York Education Law and filed suit in a state court. The complaint alleged that faculty members indicated that the problem was not with the psychologist's qualifications, but with his age. The school contended that the psychologist's qualifications clearly precluded him, and that it had followed its established and published admittance regulations. The school was granted a dismissal, and the psychologist appealed to the state appellate division.

The issue in this case was whether the psychologist was otherwise qualified for admittance, ignoring his age. A court's review of a school's policies is limited to determining whether it acted in good faith or irrationally and arbitrarily. The school showed that the psychologist's grades, as reflected by his science classes and overall grade point average, were clearly unacceptable. It also alleged that his Medical College Aptitude Test score was lower than any student accepted. The psychologist pointed out that he was called for an interview and not summarily dismissed. He also noted his accomplishments in his current field, which included having hosted a weekly television show on mental health. The court ruled that **the psychologist was trying to create his own entrance standards, which the court had no power to allow**. The dismissal of claims was affirmed. *Brown v. Albert Einstein College of Medicine*, 568 N.Y.S.2d 61 (N.Y. App. Div. 1991).

◆ *The Age Discrimination Act applies only to recipients of federal funding.*

In February 1983, a man sued Yale University alleging that Yale had discriminated against him on the basis of both handicap and age. Yale had dismissed him as a student in the graduate English department in 1967 and denied him readmission in 1975 and 1981. The issue before a U.S. district court was whether Yale discriminated against the man in violation of the

Rehabilitation Act of 1973 and the Age Discrimination Act of 1975 when it denied him readmission.

The court observed that a July 1986 evidentiary hearing revealed that the Yale English department received no federal funding, which would trigger the application of the acts. **The fact that a few of the English department's professors participated in Yale's summer program, which was federally funded, did not trigger the application of the acts** since the seminars did not involve Yale graduate students. The summer program office administered the federal grants relating to the English department professors. The man could not meet his threshold burden that the specific program that allegedly discriminated against him, in this case the English department, received federal financial assistance. The man was not protected by the acts, and therefore his case was dismissed. *Stephanidis v. Yale Univ.*, 652 F.Supp. 110 (D. Conn. 1986).

◆ *A student's Age Discrimination Act claim failed where he was unable to show that his age had anything to do with the denial of his readmission to medical school.*

A student at Thomas Jefferson University Medical School who also was a practicing attorney sued the school for age discrimination after he was denied readmission to the school. Asserting a claim under the Age Discrimination Act (among other claims), **the student averred that he was treated differently because he was older than his classmates**. He maintained that he was improperly failed in Family Medicine, that he was given lower than average evaluations in Pediatrics, that his request for transfer of his Internal Medicine clerkship was denied, and that his application for readmission to the school was denied after his withdrawal. He further claimed that he had been fraudulently induced to sign an agreement withdrawing from the school and that he had signed the agreement under duress. He also contended that the school's attorney induced him to sign the agreement by stating that he had received a failing grade in his Family Medicine written examination when in fact the exam had not yet been graded. However, the student had drafted the agreement himself. It specified that if he were allowed to resign from the school in good standing, he would agree to withdraw an age discrimination complaint he had filed with the U.S. Department of Health and Human Services.

A Pennsylvania federal court noted that the student was an experienced attorney. **It rejected his age discrimination claim, noting that younger students also had failed courses under similar circumstances and had received evaluations based on the same criteria as were used to evaluate him.** Since he was the one who had drafted the agreement, and since the agreement had been drafted before the conversation with the school's attorney took place, the student could not show that the school's attorney fraudulently induced him to sign the agreement. The court further held that the school did not have to make extraordinary efforts to enable the student to practice law and study medicine at the same time. The court ruled for the school. *Petock v. Thomas Jefferson Univ.*, 630 F.Supp. 187 (E.D. Pa. 1986).

CHAPTER THREE

Athletics and Student Activities

I.   ATHLETIC PROGRAMS

The National Collegiate Athletic Association (NCAA) is a voluntary, nonprofit association which regulates college athletics, defines eligibility for players and imposes sanctions for violating its rules. NCAA rules limit a student's period of eligibility for interscholastic competition to five years. NCAA regulations prevent athletic participation for one year after transfer from one institution to another. The NCAA's core course requirement excludes from consideration for initial eligibility all courses taught below regular high school instructional levels, including remedial and special education.

A. Eligibility of Participants

◆ *A federal district court denied a Kansas student-athlete's request for an order to prevent the enforcement of an NCAA athletic eligibility rule.*
      The student transferred to the University of Kansas (KU) in 2004 after beginning college at another school three years earlier. He earned a spot on the KU football team as a walk-on and eventually became an alternate starter on the defensive line. The NCAA denied KU's request for a waiver of the NCAA's five-year eligibility rule. After an unsuccessful appeal, the student sued KU and the NCAA in a federal district court for civil rights violations. He petitioned a federal district court for an order preventing the university from enforcing the NCAA's eligibility ruling. After a hearing, **the court found the five-year eligibility period begins to run when a student-athlete initially registers and attends the first day of classes in a regular term of an academic year**

for a minimum full-time program of studies. The NCAA may grant a waiver of the eligibility rule for reasons beyond the control of the student or institution which deprive the student-athlete of the opportunity to participate for more than one season in his/her spot within the five-year period.

An NCAA member school may grant a one-year extension of the five-year period for a female student-athlete for reasons of pregnancy. The student contended that he missed the chance to participate in football when his girlfriend became pregnant some time before he enrolled at KU. He said he decided not to attend college so he could work and care for his daughter. The student argued a female could have taken advantage of the pregnancy exception under NCAA bylaws. The court rejected the student's gender discrimination claim. It also found no merit to his claim that he would be unable to complete his education and lose any chance to be recruited by a professional football team. The student's financial aid package was not an athletic grant and the threat of losing a professional career was speculative. **The court denied the student's request for relief, finding it was in the public interest to allow the NCAA to enforce its own rules without court intervention.** *Butler v. NCAA*, Civ. Act. No. 06-2319 KHV, 2006 WL 2398683 (D. Kan. 8/15/06).

◆ *A soccer player who was subject to sanctions after transferring from one school to another failed to demonstrate that an athletic conference transfer rule violated federal antitrust laws.*

The player decided to attend the University of Southern California (USC). USC athletic officials purportedly told her that she would be free to transfer to another school without penalty as long as she finished her freshman year at USC and met all academic requirements. After allegedly learning that USC athletes received fraudulent academic credit, the player transferred to the University of California, Los Angeles (UCLA). Both USC and UCLA are members of the Pacific 10 collegiate athletic association. USC opposed the transfer and sought sanctions against the player pursuant to the Pac-10's transfer rule, which would not allow her to play soccer for UCLA during her first year there. As a result, the player sued USC, the USC officials who recruited her and the Pac-10. She alleged that USC had enforced Pac-10 sanctions only against her and never against other transferring athletes because she participated in an investigation into possible academic fraud at USC. She asserted that the transfer rule conflicted with the federal Sherman Act, 15 U.S.C. § 1, which prohibits contracts or conspiracies that restrain trade or commerce. A federal district court dismissed the complaint, and the player appealed to the U.S. Court of Appeals, Ninth Circuit.

The student claimed Sherman Act violations under the "rule of reason analysis." A restraint such as the transfer rule violates the rule of reason if its harm to interstate competition outweighs its competitive benefits. The player had to prove that the transfer rule produced significant anti-competitive effects in relevant geographic and product markets. A geographic market is an area where consumers can obtain a product from more than one source. A product market is the group of competing goods. The player claimed the relevant geographic market in this case was the Los Angeles area, and the relevant product market was the UCLA women's soccer program. The Ninth Circuit rejected this interpretation. First, it noted that schools outside the Los Angeles area attempted to recruit the player for similar soccer programs, so the relevant geographic market should extend to the national market of women's collegiate soccer programs. Similarly, her contention that the UCLA program was the relevant product market was rejected because it was interchangeable with many programs across the country. Even if the player had correctly asserted that the relevant market was national in scope, her suit would have failed because she objected to a Pac-10 transfer rule, which only applies to member schools and not the entire national market of college soccer programs. Finally, **because the player admitted she was the only USC athlete to suffer sanctions under the transfer rule, she conceded that the transfer rule did not affect all relevant consumers, thereby foiling her antitrust claim.** *Tanaka v. Univ. of Southern California*, 252 F.3d 1059 (9th Cir. 2001).

◆ *In a secondary school case, the U.S. Supreme Court noted that students have a lesser expectation of privacy than the general populace, and that student-athletes have an even lower expectation of privacy in the locker room.*
     The Court upheld a random drug testing program imposed by an Oregon school district because the insignificant invasion of student privacy was outweighed by the school's interest in addressing drug use by students who risked physical harm while playing sports. Similarly, drug testing programs applicable to private schools have been upheld under the notion that student athletes have a lower expectation of privacy. *Vernonia School Dist. 47J v. Acton*, 515 U.S. 646, 115 S.Ct. 2386, 132 L.Ed.2d 564 (1995).

◆ *Student-athletes have a lower expectation of privacy than the general student population, and the NCAA has an interest in protecting the health and safety of student-athletes involved in NCAA-regulated competition.*
     In 1986, the NCAA instituted a drug testing program for six categories of banned drugs including steroids and street drugs. Under the program, the drug tests took place at championship competitions. In order to participate, all students had to sign a consent form at the start of each school year allowing the drug tests. Two Stanford athletes instituted an action in a California trial court, alleging that the drug testing program violated their right to privacy. The court granted a preliminary injunction prohibiting the NCAA from enforcing its drug testing program against Stanford or its students, except in football and men's basketball. After a trial, the court permanently enjoined the NCAA from enforcing its drug-testing program against Stanford or its student-athletes.
     The case reached the Supreme Court of California, which reversed the decisions of the lower courts, noting that student-athletes had a lower expectation of privacy than the general student population. Observation of urination obviously implicated privacy interests. However, by its nature, participation in highly competitive post-season championship events involved close regulation and scrutiny of the physical fitness and bodily condition of student-athletes. **Required physical examinations (including urinalysis) and the special regulation of sleep habits, diet, fitness and other activities that intrude significantly on privacy interests are routine aspects of a college athlete's life not shared by other students or the population at large.**

Further, the court noted that drug testing programs involving student-athletes have routinely survived Fourth Amendment privacy challenges. The court concluded that the NCAA had an interest in protecting the health and safety of student-athletes involved in NCAA-regulated competition. *Hill v. NCAA*, 26 Cal.Rptr.2d 834 (Cal. 1994).

◆ *A drug testing program was struck down where it was not voluntary, and where the college athletes did not have a diminished expectation of privacy.*

The University of Colorado conducted a drug testing program for intercollegiate athletes that entailed a urine test at each annual physical with random tests thereafter. A program amendment substituted random rapid eye examinations for urinalysis, and the university prohibited any athlete refusing to consent to the testing from participating in intercollegiate athletics. The program called for progressive sanctions ranging from required participation in rehabilitation programs to permanent suspension from athletics. A group of athletes filed a class action suit against the university in a Colorado trial court seeking declaratory and injunctive relief. The court ruled for the athletes.

The Colorado Court of Appeals affirmed this decision, and the university appealed to the Supreme Court of Colorado. The court observed that the program did not ensure confidentiality and was mandatory, inasmuch as refusal to participate disqualified students from participating in university athletic programs. **The university was unable to articulate an important governmental interest for the program. Unlike cases involving high school athletes, college students did not have a diminished expectation of privacy under the Fourth Amendment that justified government searches in the absence of an important governmental interest.** Random, suspicionless urinalysis was unconstitutional. University student athletes did not consent to participation in the program because there could be no voluntary consent where the failure to consent resulted in denial of a governmental benefit. The court affirmed the decision for the athletes. *Univ. of Colorado v. Derdeyn*, 863 P.2d 929 (Colo. 1993).

◆ *A wrestler who transferred from a Rhode Island university had to sit out for one year because he was not in good academic standing.*

The student, a talented wrestler, failed a course during his first semester at Nebraska and did not repeat the course before transferring to Brown. The NCAA notified him he would be prohibited from wrestling the next academic year because he had not successfully repeated the course. The student sued the NCAA in a federal district court, seeking an injunction to restrain the NCAA from preventing him from wrestling. The court denied the injunction. **NCAA regulations prevent athletic participation for one year after transfer. There is an exception to this rule for students in good academic standing who would have been eligible to participate had they remained at their previous institution.** Since he had failed the course, he would have been ineligible at Nebraska, so he was also ineligible at Brown. In addition, the student could not bring constitutional claims since the NCAA is a private actor, not a state agent. *Collier v. NCAA*, 783 F.Supp. 1576 (D.R.I. 1992).

B. Students with Disabilities

◆ *The University of North Carolina at Greensboro did not violate federal disability laws when it dismissed a disabled student from its golf team.*

The student earned a partial golf scholarship and was the fourth best player on the team in his freshman year. The next year, the student's father informed the golf coach of his diagnosis with Obsessive-Compulsive Disorder (OCD). The father explained that his son's condition caused him to repeat certain ritualistic behaviors and have negative thoughts. The coach responded by suggesting that the student red-shirt for the season and agreed to allow him to attend therapy sessions that sometimes conflicted with team practices. The coach began to emphasize procedures to be followed when a player was late or absent from practice. Throughout the season, the student was late to many practices and workouts, or absent. He did not play in any more tournaments. The coach did not excuse the absences as a disability-related accommodation because the student did not register with the university office of disability services. At the end of the season, the coach removed him from the team for misconduct and rules violations. As a result, the student lost his scholarship. He transferred to another college where he played on the golf team.

The student sued the university in federal court for violating the Americans with Disabilities Act (ADA) and Section 504 of the Rehabilitation Act by dismissing him from the team and failing to renew his scholarship. The court granted the university's motion for pre-trial judgment, because the student failed to show he had a "disability" within the meaning of the Rehabilitation Act. **Although he had a mental impairment, he did not show it substantially limited his ability to perform any major life activity.** He was typically on time for appointments, completed course work and was able to follow school rules. The student's condition had improved significantly as a result of therapy and medication. The coach's red-shirt offer did not prove he regarded the student as disabled. University officials met to discuss his condition and consulted with its counseling and testing center. This conduct did not prove a perception of disability. *Costello v. Univ. of North Carolina Greensboro*, No. 1:03CV01050, 2006 WL 3694579 (M.D.N.C. 12/14/06).

◆ *A student-athlete's challenge to the NCAA's core course requirement was allowed to proceed in the following case.*

A student with a learning disability who was deemed ineligible to play Division I football during his freshman year sued the NCAA, two universities that stopped recruiting him once he was declared ineligible, and the ACT/Clearinghouse, claiming the NCAA "core course" requirement violated Rehabilitation Act Section 504 and the Americans with Disabilities Act (ADA). The **court denied the NCAA's motion for summary judgment, finding evidence that its blanket exclusion of all courses taught "below the high school's regular instructional level (e.g., remedial, special education or compensatory)" from consideration as core courses was not facially neutral and was premised on a specified level of academic achievement that persons with disabilities were less capable of meeting.** The court determined that the student should receive a trial to determine whether the

NCAA was liable for monetary damages and should be granted full athletic eligibility. The court held that his claim based on the alleged deprivation of a chance to play professional football was too speculative to survive pretrial dismissal. Further, it held he was without legal standing to challenge NCAA initial eligibility rules because he would never again be subject to them.

The NCAA moved the court for reargument, noting that the court had presumed that the student could never regain his full allotment of four years of athletic eligibility. The NCAA argued that its rules had been changed as the consequence of a 1998 consent decree between it and the U.S. Department of Justice. Under current NCAA regulations, partial and non-qualifying student athletes eventually could gain a fourth year of athletic eligibility. Since the student had not lost any athletic eligibility, the NCAA argued that his claim for injunctive relief was now moot. It further alleged that the student lacked standing to seek injunctive relief because he could not prove that he lost any years of eligibility due to its discriminatory conduct. The court agreed with the NCAA that the prior order had presumed that the student had forever lost a year of eligibility under pre-1998 NCAA rules. Under the current rules, he could regain a fourth year of athletic eligibility. The court held the student no longer had standing to seek injunctive relief against the NCAA. It amended its order to dismiss the claims seeking injunctive relief under the ADA and Section 504. **The student was otherwise entitled to proceed with his ADA claims against the universities, and his Section 504 claims against the universities and NCAA.** *Bowers v. NCAA,* 130 F.Supp.2d 610 (D.N.J. 2001).

When Temple University sought an order requiring the University of Memphis (which also had recruited the student) to contribute to any potential damage award, the University of Memphis claimed sovereign immunity, but the court ruled that **Congress had validly eliminated immunity under Title II of the ADA,** and that the acceptance of Rehabilitation Act funds amounted to a waiver under that act. *Bowers v. NCAA,* 171 F.Supp.2d 389 (D.N.J. 2001).

◆ *A college football player with a disability could be prohibited from continuing to play without violating Section 504 of the Rehabilitation Act.*

A University of Kansas student who was on a football scholarship experienced an episode of transient quadriplegia during a scrimmage. The team physician discovered that the student had a congenital condition that put him at an extremely high risk for suffering severe and potentially permanent neurological injuries, including quadriplegia. **The university disqualified the student from participating in intercollegiate football.** Although he obtained opinions from three other doctors stating that his risk of injury was no greater than any other player's, the university denied his request to rejoin the football team. He filed a lawsuit against the university in a federal district court, claiming it had violated Section 504, which prohibits discrimination by recipients of federal funding against individuals on the basis of disability, if the individual is otherwise qualified to participate in the recipient's programs or activities. The court denied the university's motion to dismiss the lawsuit, and the student sought order to require his reinstatement to the football team.

Because Section 504's definition of a person with a disability involves a consideration of whether the individual is impaired in some major life activity, the court considered whether intercollegiate athletic participation was a major life activity. The university argued that it was not, because the general population cannot participate in college athletics. The student argued that his grades improved, and he gained many other opportunities for personal development by playing on the team. **The court agreed that playing football was related to the major life activity of learning, but held that his disqualification was not a substantial limitation on his continuing ability to learn.** The university had not revoked the student's athletic scholarship, and he retained the opportunity to participate in the football program in a role other than player. The court accepted the conclusion of the university's physicians that there was a reasonable basis for his exclusion from the team that did not violate Section 504. The court denied the student's motion. *Pahulu v. Univ. of Kansas*, 897 F.Supp. 1387 (D. Kan. 1995).

C. Academic Restrictions

The National Collegiate Athletic Association (NCAA) imposes academic requirements on collegiate student-athletes. The academic requirements may include specific course requirements or designated grade point averages.

◆ *A college baseball player who alleged he was given improper academic advice by a counselor could proceed with a lawsuit for damages.*

The player attended St. Leo College on a partial scholarship. After three years, he transferred to Clemson University. He contacted one of Clemson's academic advisors about enrolling in classes. His main objective was to remain eligible to play baseball. Clemson did not offer the player's major, so the advisor suggested that he declare a different major. Under the NCAA's 50-percent rule, student-athletes must complete at least half of the course requirements of their degree programs to be eligible to compete during the fourth year of school. The advisor gave the player erroneous advice about what classes to take. Realizing the mistake, Clemson sought a waiver of the 50-percent rule. The NCAA denied the waiver, and the student did not play. The next year, the player returned to St. Leo College, completed his degree and played baseball for a final season. He then sued Clemson in a South Carolina court for negligence, breach of fiduciary duty and breach of contract.

The court granted Clemson's motion for pretrial judgment, holding that the player did not advance any tort theory under the South Carolina Tort Claims Act because the university's course of action did not constitute gross negligence. The state court of appeals agreed with the player that the trial court should not have decided the issue of gross negligence. There were issues of fact as to whether the advisor committed gross negligence. Although the advisor realized her mistake not even two weeks into the semester, she did not contact the athletic department supervisor or the NCAA compliance director, which was standard procedure. **The appeals court also agreed that there may have been a breach of fiduciary duty and a breach of contract on the part of the university.** The court remanded the case for reconsideration. *Hendricks v. Clemson Univ.*, 339 S.C. 552, 529 S.E.2d 293 (S.C. Ct. App. 2000).

♦ *A non-qualifying student whose scholarship was withdrawn could not sue Kansas State University (KSU) because of the Eleventh Amendment.*

A student was offered an NCAA-approved track scholarship at KSU that covered her tuition, fees, room, board and books. However, after she enrolled, KSU withdrew the scholarship when it learned **the NCAA Initial-Eligibility Clearinghouse had failed to certify the student because she was a "nonqualifier," having failed two high school classes.** The clearinghouse report was not produced until after the student had enrolled.

When KSU sought to recover tuition and other expenses for the fall semester, the student and her father sued KSU for breach of contract and fraud, also suing several KSU officials, including the track coach. A federal district court held KSU was immune to suit under the Eleventh Amendment, which prohibits a suit by an individual against a state in federal court. Since KSU had not consented to be sued, the student and her father could not maintain their action against it. Further, the officials had been acting in their official capacities; thus, they also were entitled to Eleventh Amendment immunity. *Adams v. Kansas State Univ.*, 27 F.Supp.2d 469 (S.D.N.Y. 1998).

♦ *An Illinois court held a student's religious courses and computer classes were not "core courses" under the NCAA academic eligibility requirements.*

The NCAA sets eligibility requirements for Division I competition, which mandate that students take at least 13 high school "core courses" and that students achieve a specified minimum grade point average in those courses as well as a specified minimum score on either the SAT or ACT. The higher a student's test score, the lower the required GPA needed. An 18-year-old black student who excelled at basketball graduated from a private, Catholic high school. He was heavily recruited by colleges and universities, and selected a private Illinois university. The NCAA ruled the student was not qualified to compete in Division I play during his freshman season, and he sued the NCAA in a federal district court for an order allowing him to play in his freshman year.

The student asserted that the NCAA had improperly found him to be ineligible by excluding from the "core course" requirements two religion and two computer classes. The court determined the religion courses **were taught from a particular religious point of view – based on a Christian ideology**. The court also determined that, based on the syllabi **for the computer classes, at least 50% of the course instruction included keyboarding or word processing**, which took the classes outside core status. As a result, the student did not have even a negligible chance of success on the merits of his claim, and he was not entitled to injunctive relief. Further, the student's claims of breach of contract and misrepresentation likewise had a very slim chance of success. The court refused to overrule the NCAA's eligibility determination, and the student was not allowed to play basketball during his freshman season. *Hall v. NCAA*, 985 F.Supp. 782 (N.D. Ill. 1997).

♦ *Although the NCAA arbitrarily denied a student's request for an academic eligibility waiver, there was no finding of any dishonest purpose.*

A high school senior intended to attend a private university on a basketball scholarship. However, the NCAA held he failed to complete the minimum of

13 "core courses" required under its eligibility standards. It notified the student that he was ineligible under NCAA guidelines to play college basketball for or receive financial aid from the university. The university sought a waiver of the eligibility requirements, which the NCAA denied on the ground that there were neither exceptional circumstances present nor independent evidence of the student's academic qualifications that warranted granting relief. The student sought a preliminary injunction from the U.S. District Court for the District of Connecticut to prevent the NCAA from further interfering with his opportunity to attend the university and play basketball for its team. The district court granted the motion for an injunction, reasoning that the student would suffer irreparable harm if the injunction were denied, and that he was likely to prevail on his argument that the NCAA breached its duty to the student by arbitrarily refusing to grant him a waiver of its eligibility requirements. The NCAA appealed to the U.S. Court of Appeals, Second Circuit.

The court held that the district court had erred in finding that the NCAA had exhibited bad faith simply by acting arbitrarily. Under Connecticut law, bad faith means more than mere negligence; it involves a dishonest purpose. Here, **despite determining that the NCAA had arbitrarily refused to grant the student a waiver because it had granted waivers in similar cases in the past, the court failed to make a factual finding of bad intent**. The court remanded the case and left the injunction intact. However, it conditioned the maintenance of the injunction upon commencement of a trial on the merits within four months. *Phillip v. Fairfield Univ.*, 118 F.3d 131 (2d Cir. 1997).

D. Eligibility of Schools

◆ *The Fifth Circuit found that the NCAA's suspension of all athletic programs at a private university did not violate any property interests.*

An alumnus of Southern Methodist University (SMU) sued the NCAA in a federal district court on behalf of SMU, other SMU graduates, current SMU students, football team members and cheerleaders. The action challenged the NCAA's suspension of all 1987 SMU athletic programs and alleged that the NCAA had violated federal antitrust laws by restricting compensation to college football players. This allegedly violated price-fixing restraints under the Sherman Anti-Trust Act. The SMU suspension allegedly constituted a "group boycott" by NCAA members. The complaint also contained civil rights claims, which alleged that the suspension destroyed the careers of SMU football players and caused the cheerleaders emotional distress. The NCAA allegedly imposed these penalties on SMU repeatedly in a manner that violated due process of law. The lawsuit requested an order preventing the suspension as well as the payment of monetary damages in excess of $200 million.

The court dismissed the lawsuit. The alumnus appealed to the U.S. Court of Appeals, Fifth Circuit, which noted that SMU had failed to represent itself in the lawsuit. The alumnus could not properly bring a suit on SMU's behalf, and the complaint failed to state any legal grounds. **No property interests were violated by the NCAA suspension and the damages were insufficient to support an antitrust lawsuit.** According to the court, **NCAA eligibility rules were reasonable and did not constitute price fixing**. They were an appropriate means to integrate athletics with academics. Enforcement of the rules did not constitute an illegal group boycott. The district court had properly dismissed the civil rights claims. State participation in a private entity such as the NCAA does not make the entity a state actor unless the entity enforces state laws. Because no state action existed in the enforcement of NCAA rules, there was no basis for the federal civil rights complaint. *McCormack v. NCAA*, 845 F.2d 1338 (5th Cir. 1988).

◆ *A federal district court refused to order the NCAA to declare a private university eligible for post-season play.*

Howard University's football team compiled a regular season record of nine wins and one loss in 1987. This was one of the best records for all NCAA Division I-AA schools. Howard won the championship of its conference, the Mid-Eastern Athletic Conference (MEAC). All MEAC schools, including Howard, are known as traditionally black institutions. Despite its fine season, Howard was excluded from the Division 1-AA championship. Howard brought an antitrust action in a federal district court, seeking to prevent the NCAA from holding its championship playoffs until a decision by the court was issued.

The court noted that in order to obtain an injunction, Howard would have to show that it was likely to prevail in its case, that it would be irreparably harmed without the injunction, that other parties would not suffer substantial harm, and that the public interest would be served. While noting that Howard's low ranking by the committee ran contrary to logic, the possibility that Howard would suffer irreparable harm was balanced by the potential that any of the other 16 teams already in the playoffs would suffer equal harm if displaced by Howard. Because **the playoff games were already set and scheduled with television arrangements**, the district court was unwilling to delay the playoff schedule. **Any delay of the playoff games would be disruptive and cause severe hardships to the teams already selected.** Howard's interest was outweighed by that of the general public, and the games would commence as scheduled. *Howard Univ. v. NCAA*, 675 F.Supp. 652 (D.D.C. 1987).

E. Discrimination and Harassment

1. Gender Equity in Athletics

Title IX of the Education Amendments of 1972 (20 U.S.C. § 1681, et seq.) addresses sex discrimination in school athletics. It applies only to athletic programs that receive federal financial assistance. One of the most important Title IX implementing regulations provides as follows:

A recipient that operates or sponsors interscholastic, intercollegiate, club or intramural athletics shall provide equal athletic opportunity for members of both sexes. In determining whether equal opportunities are available the Director will consider, among other factors:
(1) Whether the selection of sports and levels of competition effectively accommodate the interests and abilities of members of both sexes;
(2) The provision of equipment and supplies;

(3) Scheduling of games and practice time;

(4) Travel and per diem allowance;

(5) Opportunity to receive coaching and academic tutoring;

(6) Assignment and compensation of coaches and tutors;

(7) Provision of locker rooms, practice and competitive facilities;

(8) Provision of medical and training facilities and services;

(9) Provision of housing and dining facilities and services;

(10) Publicity.

Unequal aggregate expenditures for members of each sex or unequal expenditures for male and female teams if a recipient operates or sponsors separate teams will not constitute noncompliance with this section, but the Assistant Secretary may consider the failure to provide necessary funds for teams for one sex in assessing equality of opportunity for members of each sex. 34 CFR § 106.41(c).

◆   *A federal district court let members of an Ohio university women's rowing team pursue a class action discrimination suit alleging unequal access to athletic facilities, benefits and opportunities.*

The women claimed the rowing team never had enough boats to train properly and did not have a meeting room large enough to accommodate the entire team. Team members claimed they were assigned the least desirable times for weight training, had too few coaches and little access to trainers. They claimed they lacked adequate event and practice apparel and had to sleep four to a room and two to a bed when traveling. Scholarships were not substantially proportionate to men's and women's rates of athletic participation.

The team members sought to have the case certified as a class action on behalf of all present, prospective and future participants in the women's athletic program at the University of Cincinnati. The court held the members of the rowing team inadequately represented the interests of unnamed class members who might seek to participate in other sports at the university. In fact, there was an inherent conflict between the rowing team members and participants in other athletic programs at the university. This conflict existed because **Title IX compliance could conceivably be achieved by taking resources away from the rowing program and allotting them to other women's varsity sports. The team members did not show there were legal or factual questions common to the entire class, or that their claims were typical of the claims of the proposed class.** The court allowed the team members to amend their complaint by limiting the class to current and future members of the rowing team. *Miller v. Univ. of Cincinnati*, 241 F.R.D. 285 (S.D. Ohio 2006).

◆   *A women's tennis coach was allowed to further pursue her federal sex discrimination lawsuit against Purdue University.*

During a 13-year career, the coach was recognized for her commitment to academics and community service. She led the women's tennis team to its best season ever in 2003. Nonetheless, Purdue notified the coach it was not renewing her appointment because the university's athletic director wanted to take the team in a different direction. The coach sued Purdue in a federal district court, alleging it violated Title VII of the Civil Rights Act of 1964.

According to the coach, male coaches were treated more favorably than their female counterparts. The women's tennis team only had two athletic scholarships, while the men's team had four. Male coaches had larger offices than did females. Purdue moved for summary judgment, asserting it had legitimate reasons for not renewing the coach. She left some players behind after a road match in Tennessee, acted rudely and unprofessionally during the NCAA tournament, failed to meet legitimate performance expectations and used foul language. **The court found the coach met all of the expectations for her position. Foul language was common in college athletics.** The only objective piece of evidence to support non-renewal was an annual review following the 1999 season. The court denied Purdue's motion for summary judgment, as it sought further information on whether the coach met legitimate job expectations and whether Purdue treated male head coaches better than women coaches. *Peirick v. Indiana Univ.-Purdue Univ. Indianapolis Athletics Dep't*, No. 1:03 CV 1965 LJM WTL, 2005 WL 1518663 (S.D. Ind. 6/27/05).

◆   *The University of North Dakota was allowed to cut its men's wrestling program to help it comply with Title IX.*

The University of North Dakota issued a report on gender equity in athletics in 1995, recommending that women's golf, tennis and soccer be added in the next few years to increase female athletic participation and decrease the difference between male and female athletic participation at the university. The report did not recommend any changes in men's athletics. Three years later, the university faced a budget crunch and eliminated the men's wrestling program in an effort to cut $95,000 from the athletic department's budget. The move also was made to comply with the dictates of Title IX. When wrestlers and recruits sued the university, claiming that the program elimination actually violated Title IX by discriminating against them on the basis of gender, a federal court ruled in favor of the university. The Eighth Circuit Court of Appeals affirmed. It noted that **the elimination of men's teams is a permissible means of complying with Title IX.** By eliminating wrestling, the university was following the "substantially proportionate" standard set forth in the regulations interpreting Title IX. The U.S. Department of Education has allowed universities to cut men's programs as a way to provide substantially proportionate participation opportunities for both male and female students. *Chalenor v. Univ. of North Dakota*, 291 F.3d 1042 (8th Cir. 2002).

◆   *Four student-athletes were allowed to bring a class action Title IX lawsuit against a New Mexico university.*

Four female student-athletes at a New Mexico university filed a proposed class action lawsuit against the university under Title IX and the state constitution, seeking compensatory and equitable relief. While the judge deliberated on whether to grant class certification, a trial ensued and **a jury ruled in favor of the student-athletes, awarding them compensatory damages.** When the judge denied class certification, the athletes' request for declaratory and injunctive relief was denied. The athletes appealed to the Tenth Circuit Court of Appeals, which reversed the denial of class status. Here, the evidence indicated that one of the students was on the soccer team at the time the suit was filed. As a result, the lower court should not have ruled that the plaintiffs were not entitled to class status. The court also reversed the order denying injunctive and declaratory relief. *Paton v. New Mexico Highlands Univ.*, 275 F.3d 1274 (10th Cir. 2002).

◆ *A female place kicker who was dropped from the Duke University football team because of her sex was not entitled to punitive damages under Title IX.*

A female student who made the Duke University football team but was later dropped from it sued the university in a federal district court. She alleged discrimination in violation of Title IX when the football coach refused to allow her to participate in summer camps, games, and practices, and made offensive comments to her regarding her attempts to participate in the football program. After the case was initially dismissed, the Fourth Circuit concluded that once the student was allowed to try out for football, the university could not discriminate against her based on her sex. Although Title IX regulations made a distinction between contact and non-contact sports operated for members of one sex, the court concluded that this distinction vanished once a member of the opposite sex was allowed to try out for a single-sex contact sport team. Since the student was a member of the university's male football team at one point, her allegations of discrimination under Title IX stated a cause of action.

At trial, a jury awarded the student $2 million in punitive damages. Duke sought to set aside the punitive damages award, arguing that even if the evidence supported the judgment, there is no clear-cut legal authority stating that punitive damages are allowable under Title IX. The Fourth Circuit again heard the case and agreed that the student was not entitled to punitive damages under Title IX. **Since Title IX is modeled after Title VI, and since the Supreme Court has held that punitive damages are not available in private actions brought under Title VI** (see *Barnes v. Gorman*, 536 U.S. 181 (2002)), **the court concluded that they are not available under Title IX either.** The court remanded the case for a determination of whether the student was entitled to her attorneys' fees. *Mercer v. Duke Univ.*, 50 Fed. Appx. 643 (4th Cir. 2002).

◆ *An Ohio university could eliminate three men's teams to come into compliance with Title IX.*

An Ohio university with a history of disproportionately few women athletes determined that the best way to achieve gender equity under Title IX was to eliminate three men's teams. It eliminated men's soccer, tennis and wrestling. In the lawsuit that followed, the men's teams asserted that the decision to cut their teams violated Title IX and the Equal Protection Clause. A federal court ruled in favor of the university, and the Sixth Circuit affirmed. The policy interpretation of Title IX allowed the elimination of men's sports to comply with the law, and the men's teams were not challenging the constitutionality of either Title IX or its regulations. Moreover, **participation in collegiate athletics is not a constitutional right. Nor does Title IX grant rights to male athletes.** The court determined that there was no equal protection violation in the elimination of the teams. *Miami Univ. Wrestling Club v. Miami Univ.*, 302 F.3d 608 (6th Cir. 2002).

2. Sexual Harassment

◆ *The informal atmosphere of collegiate athletics includes profanity, slang, and sarcasm that does not always create a hostile educational environment.*

A student who played on a North Carolina university women's intercollegiate soccer team claimed a coach asked players about their sexual activities. She alleged the coach commented on players' legs and breasts and called one player a "slut." The coach met with the student in his hotel room while the rest of the team was at an out-of-town tournament. He asked her about her social life and who she was sleeping with. The student told him it was not his business, and he soon dismissed her from the team. After the university investigated the student's complaint against the coach, he apologized to her and promised to refrain from further discussing sexual matters with players. However, the student sued the university in a federal district court, alleging he had created a hostile sexual environment. The court granted the university's motion for summary judgment and the student appealed.

The U.S. Court of Appeals, Fourth Circuit, held **a Title IX hostile environment claim requires proof of harassment that is so severe or pervasive that it creates an abusive educational environment.** Laws prohibiting sexual harassment are designed to protect people from extreme conduct that can make work or school hellish because of a person's sex, not to purge or punish all vulgarity. **To hold the university liable for harassment by the coach, the student had to show the university was aware of his conduct but failed to address it.** The evidence showed the coach used vulgar language and participated in sexual banter at practice. His comments were not directed at the student, and he never touched, threatened, ogled, or propositioned her. **The court emphasized the difference between the atmosphere in a classroom and a sports environment.** Coaches have more informal and casual contact with student-athletes than instructors have with students. They use profanity, slang, sarcasm, and yelling to motivate their teams. This does not equal a sexually hostile educational environment, even for a man coaching women. Courts analyze the facts of each case in assessing whether a coach crossed the line separating "vulgarity and mildly offensive" conduct from "deeply offensive and sexually harassing" conduct. The court found no reasonable jury could find the coach's remarks created a hostile environment. It affirmed the judgment. *Jennings v. Univ. of North Carolina*, 444 F.3d 255 (4th Cir. 2006).

Title IX has been construed by the courts as precluding sexual harassment and retaliation against those who complain about sex discrimination.

◆ *The Supreme Court recognized a retaliation claim under Title IX, finding coaches are often in the best position to vindicate the rights of student-athletes.*

An Alabama high school teacher discovered the girls' basketball team did not receive the same funding or access to equipment and facilities as boys' teams. The teacher claimed his job was made difficult by lack of adequate funding, equipment and facilities, and he began complaining to supervisors. He stated the district did not respond to his complaints and gave him negative evaluations before removing him as girls' coach. The teacher sued the school board in a federal district court, claiming the loss of his supplemental coaching contracts constituted unlawful retaliation in violation of Title IX. The court dismissed the case, and its decision was affirmed by the Eleventh Circuit.

The Supreme Court **held Title IX covers retaliation against a person for complaining about sex discrimination**. "Retaliation is, by definition an intentional act," and is a form of discrimination, since the person who complains is treated differently than others. **A program that retaliates against a person based on a sex discrimination complaint intentionally discriminates in violation of Title IX.** Without finding that actual discrimination had occurred, the Court held the teacher was entitled to bring his case before the district court and attempt to show the board was liable. A private right of action for retaliation was within the statute's prohibition of intentional sex discrimination. Title IX did not require the victim of retaliation to also be the victim of discrimination. The Court stated "if retaliation were not prohibited, Title IX's enforcement scheme would unravel." Teachers and coaches were often in the best position to vindicate the rights of students by identifying discrimination and notifying administrators. **The text of Title IX itself gave the board sufficient notice that it could not retaliate against the teacher after he complained of discrimination. Title IX regulations have been on the books for nearly 30 years.** The Court found a reasonable school board would realize it could not cover up violations of Title IX by retaliating against teachers. It reversed and remanded the case to allow the teacher to try to prove retaliation by the board. *Jackson v. Birmingham Board of Educ.*, 544 U.S. 167 (U.S. 2005).

◆ *A federal district court dismissed sexual harassment claims against an Illinois college by a student-athlete who quit the women's basketball team.*

The student spoke out against homosexuality during a team luncheon. She claimed the college then subjected her to repeated harassment. The student said an assistant coach tried to indoctrinate her about lesbian activity. She said coaches reduced her playing time because she disagreed with their views and rejected their instructions not to wear ribbons in her hair because they were "too feminine." She alleged she was forced to leave the team as a result of their indoctrination efforts, dress code requirements, and biased personal criticism.

The student alleged she suffered same-sex discrimination and harassment as a result of being heterosexual. She sued the college in a federal district court under Title VII and Title IX. **The court noted that while Title VII covers same-sex harassment claims, the student did not claim she was a target of any sexual proposals. Also, there was no indication the coaches were motivated by hostility toward females in an athletic setting.** While harassment that relies on stereotypical notions of how men and women should appear and behave can be attributed to sex, this is not harassment based on sexual orientation or preference. The court characterized this as "gender stereotyping." The student's allegations suggested it was her views about homosexuality that motivated her harassers. Since she did not state a claim for sexual harassment, the court dismissed the case. *Howell v. North Cent. College*, 320 F.Supp.2d 717 (N.D. Ill. 2004).

◆   *The Ohio State University could not be held liable under Title IX where a jury found no sexual harassment was committed by an assistant coach.*

A student at Ohio State University participated on the track and cross-country teams. After her eligibility expired, an assistant coach allegedly offered to let her continue to train with the team and become a volunteer assistant coach. He then asked her out on two occasions. She refused to date him and allegedly was unable to continue training with the teams as a result of her refusal. She sued the university, the assistant coach and the athletic director under Title IX and 42 U.S.C. § 1983. The defendants moved to dismiss the lawsuit. The U.S. District Court for the Southern District of Ohio dismissed the case against the university, finding that **once the student informed school officials of the assistant coach's actions, they took prompt action to ensure that the "harassing" behavior, which had already ceased, would not recur**.

However, the court found that a genuine issue of fact remained as to whether the assistant coach's actions in asking the student out amounted to a request for sexual favors. Accordingly, the case against the assistant coach could not be dismissed. A jury then ruled that the assistant coach had not sexually harassed the student by demanding sexual favors in return for coaching her. Nor had he created a sexually hostile environment. When the student appealed the ruling in favor of the university to the Sixth Circuit, the court held there could not be institutional liability under Title IX where there had been no underlying discrimination on the part of the assistant coach. *Klemencic v. Ohio State Univ.*, 263 F.3d 504 (6th Cir. 2001).

3. Race Discrimination

◆   *Former University of Arkansas basketball coach Nolan Richardson was unable to prove his discharge was based on race.*

Richardson became Arkansas' first African-American head coach in 1985 and his team won the NCAA men's basketball championship in 1994. In 2000, a sportswriter wrote an article in which he said Richardson had called Arkansas fans "redneck SOBs." Fans complained about the comment. A former board member contacted the athletic director (AD) and told him Richardson should be fired for the statement. Shortly after that, the AD allegedly asked the columnist if he would write a column equating Richardson's comment with a white person calling the coach a "nigger." The columnist said he wanted to avoid controversy and later told Richardson about the conversation. After losing a game against Kentucky in 2002, Richardson said "if they go ahead and pay me my money, they can take the job tomorrow." The university chancellor felt the statement was damaging to basketball recruiting and recommended firing Richardson. When he refused to retire, the university discharged him. Richardson sued the university in a federal district court for violating Title VII of the Civil Rights Act of 1964. The court found Richardson failed to prove the university fired him because of his race and held in favor of the university.

Richardson appealed to the U.S. Court of Appeals, Eighth Circuit. The court held he would have to show a specific link between the alleged discrimination and the decision to discharge him. **The court agreed with the district court's conclusion that when the university discharged Richardson**

– two years after his remark to the columnist – Richardson and the AD had already made amends, and Richardson had signed a new contract. The court found this evidence severed any possible link between the remark and the discharge. *Richardson v. Sugg*, 448 F.3d 1046 (8th Cir. 2006).

◆ *Two African-American student-athletes could pursue their race discrimination lawsuit against the NCAA under Proposition 16.*

The NCAA uses Proposition 16 to determine which first-year college students can play Division I and II sports. The rule uses a combination of high school grades in NCAA-approved "core courses" and scores on such standardized tests as the SAT and the ACT to determine eligibility. Two African-American students who signed national letters of intent to play sports at Division I schools failed to meet the NCAA's test score requirements. They were not allowed to play intercollegiate athletics their freshman year.

The students sued the NCAA in a federal district court, alleging the NCAA intentionally discriminated against them on the basis of race in violation of Title VI of the Civil Rights Act of 1964 and 42 U.S.C. § 1981, and violated the Americans with Disabilities Act (ADA) and Section 504 regarding one of the athletes. In evaluating the ADA and Section 504 claims, the court noted one athlete had suffered an injury by being denied athletic eligibility. She proved causation by claiming the design of Proposition 16 discriminated against her because of a disability. However, these claims failed because an NCAA rule change allows student-athletes who do not qualify for their initial year of eligibility to recoup that lost year with good grades. As a result, **the athlete was not denied a year of eligibility by failing to meet the initial qualifying requirements, and lacked standing to bring her ADA and Section 504 claims**. The court then dismissed the race discrimination claims brought under Title VI and Section 1981. On appeal, the Third Circuit reversed in part, noting **the students sufficiently alleged race discrimination** under Section 1981 to survive pretrial dismissal. Their claim that the NCAA considered race when it adopted Proposition 16 could proceed further. However, the Title VI, ADA, and Section 504 claims were properly dismissed. *Pryor v. NCAA*, 288 F.3d 548 (3d Cir. 2002).

◆ *The NCAA was not liable for Title VI claims alleging Proposition 16 had a disparate impact on African-American students.*

A number of African-American high school student-athletes graduated from high school with GPAs exceeding NCAA requirements. However, they all scored lower than the minimum SAT score required for participation in Division I collegiate athletics as freshmen. They sued the NCAA, asserting that the minimum SAT score requirement of Proposition 16 had a disparate impact on African-American athletes in violation of Title VI. A Pennsylvania federal district court held the NCAA could be sued under Title VI, and that Proposition 16 had a disparate impact on African-Americans. The NCAA appealed to the Third Circuit, which assumed the NCAA received indirect federal financial assistance through its member institutions. It stated **Title VI was intended to be program specific. In other words, it only prohibited discrimination in programs or activities that received federal funds.** Even though Congress had enacted the Civil Rights Restoration Act to broaden the protections of Title VI and Title IX, the Department of Education had not yet enacted regulations to implement that statute. It was unclear if those regulations could prohibit neutral actions that had a discriminatory effect. As a result, **the NCAA did not come under the umbrella of Title VI. It was not a direct recipient of federal funds and did not exert sufficient authority over its member institutions to make it liable under Title VI.** *Cureton v. NCAA*, 198 F.3d 107 (3d Cir. 1999).

In response to the Third Circuit's decision, the students moved the district court to amend their original complaint with a claim alleging intentional discrimination. The judge denied the motion, finding the plaintiffs had waited too long to amend the complaint, and that allowing the amendment would result in impermissible prejudice to the NCAA. The Third Circuit upheld the district court's decision. *Cureton v. NCAA*, 252 F.3d 267 (3d Cir. 2001).

F.   Injuries

Collegiate athletic participants assume the risks inherent in sports competition. The Supreme Judicial Court of Massachusetts explained that to hold a university liable for injuries to a student-athlete during a competitive athletic event, there must be a showing of willful, wanton or reckless conduct by participants. In Gauvin v. Clark, *404 Mass. 450, 537 N.E.2d 94 (Mass. 1989), the court said players engaging in sports agree to undergo some physical contacts which could amount to assault and battery without their consent. For that reason, college hockey participants only had a duty to refrain from reckless misconduct. This standard applies to non-contact sports, but may not apply to cheerleading injuries, as seen in* Torres v. Univ. of Massachusetts, *below.*

◆ *A Connecticut student-athlete's signed waiver of liability did not protect a university from liability for negligence.*

The student was a pitcher on the university baseball team. During a batting practice he was behind an L-screen, which is a safety device placed in front of pitchers. The screen has an opening so the pitcher can throw the ball to the batter. A batter hit a ball that struck the student on the head. He sued the university in a state court for negligence. The student claimed the screen was defective, damaged, worn and improperly repaired. The university contended the student had voluntarily and knowingly signed a waiver releasing it from liability caused by or arising out of his athletic participation.

The court found the university's release form did not expressly refer to negligence. In *Wagenblast v. Odessa School Dist.*, 110 Wash.2d 845, 758 P.2d 968 (Wash. 1988) – a case involving minors – the court found **"exculpatory releases from any future university district negligence are invalid because they violate university policy."** The superior court found that waiver agreements that do not explicitly refer to negligent conduct should not bar negligence claims by students – adults or minors – who engage in sports activities that present a risk of injury. The court denied the university's motion for dismissal on the student's negligence claim against the university. *Zides v. Quinnipiac Univ.*, No. CV020470131S, 2006 WL 463182 (Conn. Super. 2/7/06).

♦ *The Supreme Court of California held a community college was not liable for injuries to a student who was hit by a pitch during a baseball game.*

During a preseason road game against another community college, the host team's pitcher hit the student in the head with a pitch, cracking his batting helmet. The student said he was intentionally hit in retaliation for an earlier pitch thrown by a pitcher for his team that hit an opposing batter. The student staggered, felt dizzy, and was in pain, but his manager and first base coach told him to stay in the game. He was later told to sit on the bench, but his injuries were not immediately treated. The student sued the host community college in a state superior court. The case was dismissed, but the Court of Appeal of California reversed the judgment, finding the college owed the student a duty of supervision. The Supreme Court of California agreed to review the case.

The court held the college players were co-participants, and its coaches and managers had supervisory authority over the game. **Co-participants had a duty not to act recklessly, outside the bounds of the sport. Coaches and instructors had a duty not to increase the risks inherent in sports participation.** Colleges derive economic and marketing benefits from a major sports program. These benefits justified finding that **a host school owed a duty to home and visiting players to not increase the risk inherent in the sport**. The court found the host college did not fail in its duty to supervise and control the pitcher. **Being hit by a pitch was an inherent risk of baseball. The failure to provide umpires did not increase the inherent risk.** The host college had no duty to provide medical care, as the student did not submit evidence of injury. **Colleges are not vicariously liable for the actions of their student-athletes during competition.** The court reversed the judgment. *Avila v. Citrus Community College Dist.*, 38 Cal.4th 148, 131 P.3d 383 (Cal. 2006).

♦ *A Massachusetts cheerleader was allowed to proceed with a negligence action against her university after being severely injured at practice.*

The cheerleader was injured when she fell during a pyramid stunt called "the flying squirrel." The maneuver required two cheerleaders to stand on the shoulders of two others, who launched her about 10 feet up to the shoulders of cheerleaders on the upper tier. Although she was experienced, the cheerleader had never tried this maneuver before. The coach talked her through the exercise and placed spotters at the front and sides of the pyramid, but none in the rear. He spent about five minutes instructing the spotters. The squad attempted the stunt when the coach was not there. The cheerleader fell from the top of the pyramid and landed in the rear, suffering serious neck fractures that caused her to become disabled and unable to cheerlead or run again. She sued the university in a Massachusetts superior court, alleging negligence by the coach.

The university argued it could not be held liable for negligence under *Gauvin v. Clark*, 404 Mass. 450, 537 N.E.2d 94 (Mass. 1989) unless there was evidence of willful or reckless conduct in the context of a sporting event. **The court disagreed and denied a summary judgment motion by the university. It held the university owed the student a duty to exercise reasonable care. The failure to do so in this case caused her injuries.** *Torres v. Univ. of Massachusetts*, 20 Mass.L.Rptr. 310 (Mass. Super. 2005).

◆   *A federal district court held a Vermont student waived any claims against his school for injuries suffered during an intercollegiate hockey game.*

The student signed a "Student Athlete Agreement to Participate in Intercollegiate Sports" before his first season on the team. The agreement stated in part: "I understand the dangers and risks of trying out for and playing and practicing in the above sports." It also indicated "I hereby voluntarily assume all risks associated with participation and agree to hold harmless [the university and coaches] . . . except in the event of their gross negligence."

An opposing player checked the student during a game, causing him to fall backward and strike his head on the ice. He continued to play on the team, but two years later, he suffered a concussion. The student was diagnosed with mild but permanent neuropsychological deficits from the checking incident two years earlier. The university required the student to sign an additional release, but he failed to do so. He left the university the next year to play professional hockey. The student sued the university in a federal district court for negligence. The university contended the participation agreement barred the action and that the student assumed the risk of injury. The student argued the "hold harmless" language of the agreement was ambiguous and unenforceable. **The court held the words "hold harmless" did not make the agreement ambiguous. The agreement clearly demonstrated the intent to relieve the university from liability except in cases of gross negligence.** The court granted the university's motion for summary judgment and dismissed the negligence claim. *Sanders v. Univ. of Vermont*, No. 2:00-CV-424 (D. Vt. 2004).

◆   *An Indiana university was not liable to a varsity baseball player for injuries he suffered while practicing with the team. Student-athletes assume the risk of foreseeable and inherent dangers in collegiate athletics.*

The injury occurred during a baseball team practice inside a university gym. During a practice drill, the student was struck in the eye by a ball thrown by a teammate, causing severe and permanent injury. The student sued the university, coaching staff and teammate in a state court for negligence. The court dismissed the case, and the student appealed.

The Court of Appeals of Indiana stated that while the state supreme court has held secondary schools owe their students a duty to exercise ordinary and reasonable care, it has never imposed this duty on colleges or universities. The student argued the trend is for courts to find a "special" relationship between colleges or universities and their student-athletes. The court disagreed, stating the reasonable care standard was created to guide people in their everyday lives, not for athletes who choose to participate in sports. The court found being hit by a ball during team practice is an inherent and foreseeable danger of athletic participation. **Athletes assume the risk of a certain amount of foreseeable and inherent danger.** The court held that avoiding reckless or malicious behavior or intentional injury was the standard of care for sporting events and practices. **Athletes should not recover in negligence cases unless they prove malicious, reckless or intentional conduct.** As the university, coaches and teammate owed no duty of care to the student, the judgment was affirmed. *Geiersbach v. Frieje*, 807 N.E. 2d 114 (Ind. Ct. App. 2004).

◆ *The Court of Appeals of Massachusetts dismissed a Boston College season ticket holder's challenge to the loss of his season tickets, finding Boston College had the right to revoke his ticket privileges due to his disorderly conduct.*

A group of spectators who were tailgating during a Boston College football game got into a fight with college police. The college revoked one spectator's season tickets for disorderly conduct and barred him from entering the campus. The spectator sued the college in a state court for "unlawful trespass warning," revocation of his season tickets, and intentional infliction of emotional distress. The court granted Boston College's motion for summary judgment and the spectator appealed to the Court of Appeals of Massachusetts.

The court noted each season ticket issued by Boston College clearly indicated it was a "revocable license." Consequently, **the college had the right to revoke the ticket privileges at any time and for any nondiscriminatory reason. With regard to his trespass claim, the court stated that as a private college, Boston College could bar the spectator from its campus, regardless of his guilt or innocence.** The evidence did not support the intentional infliction of emotional distress claim. The actions of the college police were not "so extreme and outrageous as to be beyond all bounds of decency." The court upheld the trial court's decision to dismiss the case. *Dischino v. Boston College*, 799 N.E.2d 605 (Mass. App. Ct. 2003).

◆ *A freak weightlifting injury entitled a wrestler to an award of $50,000.*

A wrestler at the University of North Carolina (UNC) was lifting weights in the student recreation center when a cable came loose on a weight machine. This resulted in a head injury to the wrestler. Although he was able to continue wrestling for the rest of the year, he had to give it up after suffering a second concussive injury. He entered medical school, suffered continuing problems, and sued UNC under the North Carolina Tort Claims Act, alleging that the machine that caused his injury had been negligently maintained by the university. An Industrial Commission deputy commissioner ordered UNC to pay the wrestler $500,000, but the full commission **reduced the award to $50,000.** The North Carolina Court of Appeals upheld the award of $50,000. Although the student continued to be affected by his injuries, he did not present sufficient evidence that he was permanently injured or that his future earning capacity had been negatively impacted so as to justify the larger award. However, he was entitled to the $50,000 because he lost one wrestling season, endured many headaches, and had his normal activities restricted for at least six months. *Hummel v. Univ. of North Carolina*, 576 S.E.2d 124 (N.C. Ct. App. 2003).

◆ *Universities have an affirmative duty of care toward student-athletes who participate on school-sponsored, intercollegiate teams.*

A University of North Carolina cheerleader was injured in 1985 while the JV cheerleading squad was warming up before a women's basketball game. The squad did not use mats during the warm-up. While practicing a pyramid, the cheerleader fell off the top, and spotters were unable to prevent her head and shoulders from hitting the hardwood floor. The cheerleader suffered permanent brain damage. UNC did not provide a coach for the JV cheerleading squad during the 1984–1985 school year, but the varsity squad had a faculty supervisor who oversaw their stunts. A part-time UNC employee was the "administrative supervisor" for the JV team. The supervisor arranged travel plans and performed other managerial duties, but did not supervise the team's stunts, training or safety during games and practice. The JV cheerleaders essentially coached themselves, deciding how and when to perform stunts.

The case reached the North Carolina Court of Appeals, which found UNC owed the cheerleader a duty of care because she had a "special relationship" with the university. UNC depended on the JV cheerleading team to act as school representatives at athletic events. The university provided the squad with uniforms and transportation, as well as the use of school facilities for practice. Cheerleading satisfied one credit hour of UNC's physical education requirement. Additional evidence of a special relationship included the fact that UNC exerts a considerable degree of control over its cheerleaders. They must maintain a certain GPA and refrain from drinking alcohol in public. The court further ruled that **UNC not only had an affirmative duty of care, but also voluntarily undertook a separate duty of care by assuming certain responsibilities with regard to teaching the varsity cheerleaders about safety**, which legally obligated it to educate the JV squad about safety. The court reversed and remanded the Industrial Commission's decision, leaving the commission to determine whether UNC breached its duty to the cheerleader. *Davidson v. Univ. of North Carolina at Chapel Hill*, 543 S.E.2d 920 (N.C. Ct. App. 2001).

◆ *A university could not be held liable for injuries a student suffered when he was punched in the face during an intramural soccer game.*

A student at a California university was punched in the face by a member of the opposing team while playing in an intramural soccer game. He sued the university for negligent supervision. The university asserted that it had no duty to the student and that, even if had, it fulfilled that duty by providing referees for the game. It also asserted that a statute immunized it from liability because the student had engaged in a hazardous recreational activity. A trial court found that the university had no duty to the student and dismissed the case.

The California Court of Appeal affirmed, noting that **the university had no general duty of care toward the student** by virtue of *in loco parentis* (a doctrine that places an entity in the place of the parents) because the student was not a child. Further, there was no special relationship between the student and the university such that the university had to protect the student from the criminal act of a third party. Finally, **because soccer is an intensely physical game, fraught with risk of serious injury, the student's participation in the game amounted to a "hazardous recreational activity" for purposes of the immunizing statute**. *Ochoa v. California State Univ., Sacramento*, 85 Cal.Rptr.2d 768 (Cal. Ct. App. 1999).

◆ *A Georgia court held a student presented sufficient facts demonstrating that the college's gross negligence caused his injuries and that his waiver did not encompass assumption of the risk.*

A member of a private college men's varsity team was injured when he was struck in the back by another boat operated by members of the women's varsity team. The usual traffic pattern for boats on the river was the right-hand rule. However, on the day of the injury, the traffic pattern was changed to a left-hand rule to enable boats to practice on the actual course. The coach of the men's team, who also was the supervisor of the entire rowing program, notified the team that the left-hand rule was in effect. However, it was uncertain whether the coach of the women's team informed his team of the changed traffic pattern, or whether he was aware of the change on that day. After the accident, the injured rower sued the college and the coaches, among others, asserting that their gross negligence caused his injuries. The college and coaches maintained that at worst they were negligent and that, because the rower had signed a release document releasing all participants from any claims except those arising out of gross negligence, the case should not even go to the jury. The court denied their motion for a directed verdict, and the jury returned a verdict for the rower.

The college and coaches appealed to the Court of Appeals of Georgia. The court found **sufficient facts presented to the jury to show gross negligence**. The jury could have concluded that the coach of the women's team was grossly negligent in failing to advise the team of the change in the traffic pattern, in failing to be aware of the change himself, and in failing to be on the water supervising his team at the time of the accident. The jury also could have concluded that the men's coach was grossly negligent in failing to stop the men's boat when he became aware of the women's boat on the course, and in failing to ensure that the women's team was advised of the traffic pattern change. The question had therefore been properly given to the jury, and it had concluded, within reason, that the defendants were grossly negligent. **With respect to the release form, even though the rower was aware of and assumed the general risks inherent in rowing, it could not be said that he had assumed the particular risk to which he was subjected** as a result of the defendants' gross negligence. The court upheld the verdict. *Trustees of Trinity College v. Ferris*, 491 S.E.2d 909 (Ga. Ct. App. 1997).

◆   *The following Massachusetts case illustrates the principle that if the risk that results in the harm is reasonably foreseeable, liability follows.*

A senior at the Massachusetts Institute of Technology (MIT) majored in aeronautical engineering and also was a member of the men's track and field team. He had been pole vaulting since his freshman year. While practicing under his coach's direct supervision, the student was injured after vaulting when he fell backward and struck his head on the hard track surface. Although the NCAA recommended a length of 16 feet for the pole-vaulting pit, the pit at MIT was only 13 feet in length. The coach had witnessed, or was at least aware of, a vaulter bouncing off the pit mattress, resulting in second-impact injuries. On the day of the accident, there were no pads at the back or sides of the pit.

After noticing that the student was running too fast, the coach failed to instruct him to slow down or abort his vault. The student was later diagnosed as having a skull fracture with associated contusions to the brain. He sued the university and two of its track and field coaches for injuries. The court entered judgment upon the jury verdict for the student. The defendants appealed to the Appeals Court of Massachusetts. On appeal, they argued there was no evidence to support a finding that they should have reasonably foreseen the student would land beyond the back of the pit and hit his head on the track surface. However, the court held **it is only the risk that results in the harm that must be reasonably foreseeable, not the precise manner of the accident or the extent of the harm**. The court held that from the evidence, the student's accident was reasonably foreseeable. The length of the landing pit and its location near a hard surface did not provide a safe environment for pole-vaulters. The lower court decision was affirmed. *Moose v. Massachusetts Institute of Technology*, 683 N.E.2d 706 (Mass. App. Ct. 1997).

◆ *Although some risks are inherent to activities like weightlifting, the risk of a spotter intentionally failing to provide necessary assistance is not.*

A scholarship player on an Ohio university basketball team was required by the university to lift weights to improve as a player. While lifting weights at the university's gym, the student attempted to bench-press a 365-pound weight. The weight fell on the student, injuring him. He claimed that a university employee agreed to act as a spotter for him, though the employee claimed that he had not done so. The student sued the employee and the university for his injuries, claiming that the employee's reckless and wanton misconduct had caused his injuries. The trial court held that the employee was at most negligent and granted pretrial dismissal to the defendants.

The Court of Appeals of Ohio noted that **where individuals are engaged in recreational or sports activities, they assume the ordinary risks of the activities and cannot recover for any injury unless they can show that their injury resulted from reckless or intentional conduct**. Here, it was undisputed that the student was engaged in a recreational activity at the time he was injured. However, there was a dispute over whether the employee had agreed to perform as a spotter for the student. As a result, the action should have gone to trial. The court reversed and remanded the case. *Sicard v. Univ. of Dayton*, 660 N.E.2d 1241 (Ohio Ct. App. 1995).

II. STUDENT ACTIVITIES

Colleges and universities may limit official recognition of particular organizations and impose restrictions on them. One state court has held imposing liability on colleges for conduct relating to fraternity and sorority activities would require them to "baby-sit" each student.

A. Operation and School Supervision

◆ *Texas A&M University officials could not be held liable for the collapse of a bonfire stack that killed 12 students and injured 27 others.*

After the tragic collapse of a bonfire stack that killed or injured several students, the students' representatives sued the university and its officials for violating student constitutional rights to bodily integrity. The representatives claimed the university encouraged unqualified students to build the bonfire and failed to provide adequate supervision. A federal district court dismissed the claims against university officials, finding them barred by sovereign immunity.

The U.S. Court of Appeals, Fifth Circuit, found the representatives stated a claim under the "state-created danger" theory, and the case was returned to the district court for more proceedings. The district court again held for the officials, this time on the basis of qualified immunity. The representatives filed another appeal to the Fifth Circuit, which found the officials were entitled to immunity as long as their conduct was objectively reasonable in light of clearly established law. **Although the state-created danger theory was a valid theory, it was not clearly established as a basis for recovery at the time of the accident. Because the theory was not clearly established when the bonfire stack collapsed, the university officials did not have fair notice that their conduct may have violated the students' constitutional rights.** As a result, the officials were entitled to qualified immunity. *Breen v. Texas A&M Univ.*, 485 F.3d 325 (5th Cir. 2007).

◆ *A college could use money from a fund-raising campaign to eliminate single-sex fraternities and sororities.*

A New Hampshire college initiated a five-year fund-raising campaign that raised about $568 million from alumni. Several years later, the board of trustees announced that it was going to use some of the money raised to eliminate single-sex fraternities and sororities. A group of alumni who had contributed to the campaign sued the college to prevent it from using the funds for that purpose. They asserted that the college had engaged in misrepresentation in violation of the state Consumer Protection Act, and that the board of trustees had withheld information about its intent to eliminate traditional fraternities and sororities. They also alleged that the board was in a fiduciary relationship to the alumni because there were alums on the board.

A state court dismissed their lawsuit, and the Supreme Court of New Hampshire affirmed the judgment. First, the board of trustees did not owe a fiduciary duty to the alumni despite the existence of alums on the board. Second, **the alumni failed to show that the board engaged in intentional, fraudulent nondisclosure**. And third, since the fund-raising campaign was not commerce (the transactions were in the nature of a gift), there was no violation of the Consumer Protection Act. *Brzica v. Trustees of Dartmouth College*, 791 A.2d 990 (N.H. 2002).

◆ *The University of Pittsburgh was entitled to strip a fraternity house of its status as a recognized student organization after the arrest of several members.*

Pi Lambda Phi had a local chapter at the University of Pittsburgh. On April 30, 1996, city police raided the fraternity house, finding drugs and drug paraphernalia. Four members were arrested and charged with possession of controlled substances. One of these members was the fraternity's "risk manager" and another was the president of the university's Interfraternity Council. A fourth was later convicted of possession and distribution of controlled substances and expelled. As a result, the university suspended the fraternity's campus chapter, pending an investigation. The university's vice chancellor later decided to revoke the fraternity's chapter for one year. In addition, he prohibited Pi Lambda Phi from participating in school-sponsored

Greek activities and from recruiting new members. When the Interfraternity Council subsequently voted not to recertify Pi Lambda Phi, the fraternity sued the university in federal court, alleging First Amendment violations. The court determined that the fraternity was not protected by the First Amendment.

The Third Circuit affirmed. First, it described the two types of constitutionally protected associations. Intimate associations generally are seen as family relationships or other private relationships involving a relatively small group of people. Pi Lambda Phi did not satisfy this definition. Expressive associations are more broadly defined, and while political expression is not necessary to meet the definition of expressive organizations, there must be some public activity that involves an issue of political, social or cultural importance in order for the association to gain constitutional protection. Here, the fraternity raised $350 for charity and helped run a haunted house for the Pittsburgh School for the Blind. These "few minor charitable acts" were insufficient to meet the definition of expressive associations. Moreover, the university's actions did not significantly affect the group's ability to advocate its views. **The school's action in decertifying the fraternity had more to do with its involvement with drugs, which has no protected expressive element and which was unrelated to any expressive activity.** *Pi Lambda Phi Fraternity v. Univ. of Pittsburgh*, 229 F.3d 435 (3d Cir. 2000).

◆ *A university's residential policy, which required all students to live in college-owned facilities, may constitute a violation of the Sherman Act.*

A New York private college announced a policy requiring all students to live in college-owned facilities and to purchase college-sponsored meal plans. Four college fraternities sued the college and its president, alleging that the residential policy violated the Sherman Act by unlawfully monopolizing the market for residential services in the city where the college was located. The court held the policy was not "trade or commerce" as it lacked a substantial connection to interstate commerce. The court dismissed the complaint, and the fraternities appealed to the U.S. Court of Appeals, Second Circuit, arguing that the residential plan had the commercial purpose of eliminating competition in the provision of residential services in order to raise revenues.

The college maintained that its purpose was to create an academic environment that was more appealing to female applicants who were unable to enjoy the privileges of fraternity life. The court noted the Sherman Act would apply only if the residential policy constituted trade or commerce. It then stated that in determining whether particular conduct was commerce, the principal focus had to be on the nature of the activity, rather than the form or objectives of the organization. Here, **the fraternities had provided facts to support a connection between the residential policy and interstate commerce.** The college collected approximately $4 million in room and board fees from students who came from outside New York State. **The fraternities and other private landlords in the city would lose approximately $1 million per year as a result of the new policy**, a substantial portion of which would have been collected from out-of-state residents. Because the allegations were sufficient to survive dismissal, the court reversed and remanded the case. *Hamilton Chapter of Alpha Delta Phi v. Hamilton College*, 128 F.3d 59 (2d Cir. 1997).

◆ *A court's role was limited to determining whether a private university had substantially complied with its own disciplinary guidelines.*

A fraternity at a private university was burglarized, and records of the fraternity's activities were stolen. Portions of these records later appeared in the university's newspapers and were mailed to the university's officials. The published records alleged violations of the school's anti-hazing policy as well as other infractions. The dean of the university then conducted an investigation of the fraternity, which resulted in several penalties. The fraternity brought suit against the school in a state court and alleged that its members' Fourteenth Amendment due process rights had been violated. A New York trial court dismissed the claim, and the fraternity appealed to the Supreme Court, Appellate Division. **Private school students cannot allege violations of constitutionally protected due process rights absent a showing of state involvement in the university activity.** Here, no such state involvement was shown. A court's role in due process actions concerning a private institution, absent state involvement, is limited to determining whether the school had substantially complied with its own disciplinary guidelines. The court reviewed the record concerning the university's regulations and actions and affirmed the dismissal of the claim. *Mu Chapter Delta Kappa Epsilon v. Colgate*, 578 N.Y.S.2d 713 (N.Y. App. Div. 1992).

B. Organizational Liability

◆ *The Phi Kappa Tau fraternity chapter at the University of Mississippi was not liable in negligence for a woman's injuries.*

A fraternity brother provided beer to an underaged fraternity member at the fraternity house during the summer of 2001, when school was not in session. The woman was riding on the back of a four-wheeler on the grounds of the house. The fraternity member confronted the driver and threw a bottle that struck the woman in the face, injuring her. She sued the local and national chapters of the fraternity for negligence in a federal district court. The court held for the fraternity chapters, finding they did not owe the woman any legal duty under state law. She appealed to the U.S. Court of Appeals, Fifth Circuit.

The court affirmed the district court judgment. **As unincorporated associations, the chapters were not liable for the wrongful acts of their members unless they "encouraged, promoted, or subsequently ratified them." There was no evidence that the chapters encouraged or ratified the member's behavior.** There was no duty on the part of the national chapter to supervise the local chapter more closely, as no special relationship existed in this case. *Lewis v. Univ. of Southern Mississippi*, No. 06-60375, 2007 WL 1112660 (5th Cir. 4/12/07).

◆ *The family of a Louisiana student who killed herself after an alleged rape was allowed to proceed with claims that local police and a fraternity caused her death by threatening and harassing her after the attack.*

The student was raped by a member of a fraternity at an off-campus residence. Her family claimed the fraternity and a local police officer continually harassed her in an attempt to dissuade her from reporting the rape.

The officer, who was a fraternity alumnus, allegedly told the student the authorities would do nothing if she reported the incident. The family said the officer also told her she would be sued for defamation or slander if she insisted on pressing charges. The student then hanged herself. A trial court threw out the family's negligence claims against the officer and police department, but the Court of Appeal of Louisiana reversed the judgment. **Although state law generally immunizes the government from liability for discretionary actions, an exception applies to acts that constitute malicious, intentional or willful misconduct.** If the family's allegations about the police officer's actions were true, this exception might apply. *Garza v. Delta Tau Delta Fraternity National,* No. 2006 CA 0698, 2007 WL 914875 (La. Ct. App. 3/28/07).

◆   *A Texas fraternity and its members were not liable to a student for allegedly defamatory statements that resulted in the withdrawal of his pledge invitation.*

A student who had pledged to join the Phi Gamma Delta Fraternity was accused of sexual misconduct. He denied the allegations, claiming they were part of an extortion scheme to gain money. Phi Gamma withdrew its pledge invitation. A year later, the student pledged to join a chapter of the same fraternity at a different Texas university campus. He was denied admittance based on information communicated between fraternity members at the different chapters. The student sued the fraternity and various fraternity members in the state court system for damaging his reputation and subjecting him to increased hazing based on the allegations of sexual misconduct. The court awarded summary judgment to the fraternities and their members.

The student appealed, arguing that Phi Gamma owed him a duty of care because its members made statements in the course and scope of their fraternity membership. The Court of Appeals of Texas rejected his arguments. There was no evidence indicating the fraternity was incorporated in the state. **As an unincorporated entity, the fraternity did not owe the student any duty of care.** Moreover, he was unable to show a member's remarks were made in the course of his official duties as a fraternity historian. **There was no evidence these comments were communicated to other fraternities at the University of Texas.** The court agreed with the trial court that the hazing claim was untimely filed under a two-year state statute of limitation. The entry of summary judgment was affirmed. *Waddill v. Phi Gamma Delta Fraternity Lambda Tau Chapter, Texas Tech Univ.,* 114 S.W.3d 136 (Tex. Ct. App. 2003).

◆   *A Kansas fraternity pledge could not sue the fraternity or its members when he passed out after drinking too much.*

A student attended a Pledge Dad night at a fraternity at the University of Kansas. While there, he consumed a large amount of alcoholic beverages. At 2:00 a.m., his pledge dad found him passed out in the living room of the fraternity house and took him to a local hospital emergency room, where his blood alcohol level was measured at .294. The student later sued the national fraternity, the local chapter and five individual members for negligence, and the company that owned the property for premises liability. The court ruled in favor of all the defendants, and the Kansas Supreme Court affirmed. **The local chapter was not a legal entity and therefore could not be sued.** Further, the individual members could not be liable because **they did not breach any duty they owed him; he voluntarily drank alcohol** that night. As far as the national fraternity was concerned, there was no special relationship between the student and the fraternity so as to give rise to liability. Finally, the company that owned the property could not be held liable for conditions on the premises at a fraternity party. *Prime v. Beta Gamma Chapter of Pi Kappa Alpha*, 47 P.3d 402 (Kan. 2002).

◆ *The U.S. Supreme Court has held that the NCAA is not a recipient of federal funds and is therefore not subject to suit under Title IX.*

The case was filed by a college graduate who had played two years of intercollegiate volleyball at a private college before enrolling in postgraduate programs at two other colleges. Because she had exhausted only two years of her athletic eligibility, she sought a waiver from the NCAA's Postbaccalaureate Bylaw, which allows postgraduate student-athletes to compete in intercollegiate sports only at the institution where they received an undergraduate degree. The student sued the NCAA in a Pennsylvania federal court after it denied her requests for a waiver. She claimed that the NCAA discriminated against her on the basis of gender in violation of Title IX. The complaint asserted that the NCAA granted more waivers to male postgraduate students than it did to females. The case reached the U.S. Supreme Court, which noted that Title IX covers entities that receive federal financial assistance – whether direct or indirect – whereas those entities that only benefit economically from federal financial assistance are not covered. **Because the NCAA only benefited economically from institutions that received federal financial assistance, it could not be sued under Title IX.** *NCAA v. Smith*, 525 U.S. 459, 119 S.Ct. 924, 142 L.Ed.2d 929 (1999).

◆ *A national fraternity could not be held liable for a student's injuries because it was not in a position to control the actions of its chapters on a day-to-day basis and had no knowledge of any hazing activity.*

A student at a private university in Louisiana was accepted into a fraternity. During the intake process, he was physically beaten and abused by several members of the fraternity while they were conducting hazing activities. The student and his parents filed suit against the national fraternity, among others, to recover damages for the injuries sustained as a result of the hazing.

A state court granted summary judgment to the national fraternity, and the student and his parents appealed to the Court of Appeal of Louisiana. They argued the national fraternity should be liable for the actions of its chapter members because it had a duty to prevent injury to new members. They also asserted that the national fraternity's action in forbidding hazing activities showed a clear knowledge and former approval of those activities. The court, however, noted that the national executive director of the fraternity had stated by affidavit that he had no knowledge of any hazing activity at the local chapter and that the **national fraternity took numerous steps to inform local chapters and members that hazing activities were clearly prohibited.**

Further, deposition testimony by several local chapter members indicated that **any hazing activity that occurred was purposely hidden from the national fraternity**. Because the national fraternity was not in a position to control the actions of its chapters on a day-to-day basis, and because it had no knowledge of any hazing activity, it could not be held liable for the student's injuries. The trial court decision was affirmed. *Walker v. Phi Beta Sigma Fraternity (RHO Chapter)*, 706 So.2d 525 (La. Ct. App. 1997).

C. Injuries

◆ *An Ohio football fan assumed the risk of injury when he left the seating area and joined an unruly crowd on the playing field.*

After a football game at the University of Toledo ended, a throng of fans stormed the field and began tearing down the goal posts. The fan injured his back when one of the goal posts broke, sending fans and pieces of the post on top of him. The fan sued the university for negligently failing to either install collapsible goal posts or provide better crowd control. The university responded by arguing that he assumed the risk of harm when he joined the crowd on the field. **The court explained that an individual who consents to subject himself to an appreciated or known risk is totally barred from recovering for any injuries.** The court held the fan ignored barriers and risked injury to himself when he climbed over a railing and slid down a concrete wall to get onto the field. The university's duty was simply to refrain from "wanton or reckless conduct" that was likely to injure him. As the fan assumed the risk of getting hurt, the university was not liable for his injuries. *Moening v. Univ. of Toledo*, No. 2005-09774, 2006 WL 3530587 (Ohio Ct. Cl. 11/17/06).

◆ *A fraternity could not be held responsible for the deaths of six Texas students who were struck by a pickup truck on their way to a fraternity party.*

After a football game, a fraternity threw a party. Nine students drove to the party and parked on the road, after which they walked to the fraternity. Three of the students walked on the grass; the other six walked on the paved shoulder with their backs to oncoming traffic. Another student was driving a pickup truck along the road at that time and fell asleep at the wheel. The truck collided with some of the vehicles parked on the road and fatally injured the six students walking on the shoulder. **Their estates sued the fraternity for negligence, alleging that it engaged in "dangerous conduct" and that it created a foreseeable risk of harm.** A trial court ruled for the fraternity, and the Texas Court of Appeals affirmed. The appeals court noted there were two causes of the accident: the student driver falling asleep, and the six students walking on the shoulder with their backs to oncoming traffic. As a result, the fraternity could not be held liable for negligence. *Calp v. Tau Kappa Epsilon Fraternity*, 75 S.W.3d 641 (Tex. Ct. App. 2002).

◆ *A Missouri student could pursue his claims against a college and a fraternity after he was shot.*

A student enrolled in a college and moved into a fraternity house. During a party, he got into a heated telephone conversation with a man who was not a student at the college. He then tried to lock the front door of the fraternity but was unable to do so because the lock was broken. When the man appeared later and shot him, he sued the college and the fraternity for negligently failing to maintain the premises. A state court granted pretrial judgment to the defendants, but the Supreme Court of Missouri reversed and remanded the case. Here, there were material issues of fact concerning who was a landlord and who was a tenant such that a trial had to be conducted. **Without knowing the status of the parties, the court could not determine the respective duties of the college, the fraternity and the student.** *Letsinger v. Drury College*, 68 S.W.3d 408 (Mo. 2002).

◆   *Fraternity sponsors of a paint ball game could be liable for a player's injuries if their actions were negligent. They were not entitled to assert that the game was inherently dangerous.*

A prospective pledge at a fraternity participated in a "war game," wherein players shot paint balls at each other. During the game, the student's goggles were snagged by a tree limb and lifted away from his eyes. When he stood and fired another round without replacing them, a paint ball hit him, permanently blinding him in one eye. He sued the fraternity, the chapter that had sponsored the war game, and the chapter president, alleging that they had sponsored an unreasonably dangerous activity, that they had provided inadequate supervision and equipment, and failed to train him properly. A state trial court granted summary judgment to the defendants, finding that the student had engaged in a competitive contact sport, thereby assuming the risk of injury.

The student appealed to the Texas Court of Appeals, contending that **sponsors of an event cannot assert the "competitive contact sports" doctrine because they are not participants.** The court agreed. Participants in a competitive contact sport are judged under the intentional or reckless conduct standard because they are caught up in the spirit of the contest. Sponsors, however, have the benefit of time to reflect before they act. Thus, they are to be judged by concepts of ordinary negligence. The court reversed and remanded the case for further proceedings. *Moore v. Phi Delta Theta Co.*, 976 S.W.2d 738 (Tex. Ct. App. 1998).

◆   *A college and national fraternity did not owe students a special duty of care to prevent underage drinking, which violated the college's alcohol policy.*

A minor freshman student was socializing at a fraternity house at a Pennsylvania university. Kegs of beer arrived shortly after noon, and the students decided to tap them earlier than allowed by school policy. While the minor student socialized at the fraternity house, he sat in a hot tub provided for the party and drank beer. The student left the house hours later on his motorcycle, which had a dim or burnt out headlight. While driving down a local highway, he attempted to pass a car in front of him. A fatal head-on collision resulted and a subsequent analysis revealed that the minor was legally intoxicated at the time he was killed. The administratrix of the minor's estate filed suit against the college and the national fraternity. She alleged that the college's alcohol policy and lack of adult supervision impliedly sanctioned underage drinking on campus, that the college was negligent for these reasons, and that the college's policies and inaction were a direct cause of the minor's fatal collision. The administratrix also alleged that the national fraternity was responsible for control of the actions of its members.

A Pennsylvania trial court granted summary judgment in favor of both the college and the fraternity, and the administratrix appealed to the Superior Court of Pennsylvania. On appeal, the court noted that **both the college and the national fraternity counseled against the use of alcohol, and neither defendant owed the student a special duty of care, which had been breached**. The holding in favor of both defendants was affirmed. *Cooperstein v. Liberty Mutual*, 611 A.2d 721 (Pa. Super. Ct. 1992).

◆ *An Illinois university had no duty to protect a student from fraternity members who had been drinking. The state appellate court held imposing liability on the university would have the effect of requiring it to "baby-sit" each student.*

A student at a private university was in her dormitory room when a fraternity member called her to the lobby. When she arrived, the fraternity member grabbed her, then threw her over his shoulder and ran out of the building. The student asserted the fraternity member fell, crushing her underneath him. She claimed that as a result of the fall, she completely lost her sense of smell and also suffered hearing loss. The student sued the fraternity member, the fraternity and the university in a state court, seeking monetary damages for doctors' bills, surgical treatments, medicine and nursing care.

The student claimed that the fraternity member had gone to the dormitory after a fraternity party at which members of the fraternity drank alcohol. She alleged the university had failed to control the on-campus activities of the fraternity and its members. The student also asserted that by installing safety devices in the dormitory, the university assumed the duty of protecting dormitory residents and that this duty was breached. The university sought a dismissal of the case before trial. An Illinois appellate court noted that although college students were once considered minors subject to control by colleges and universities, they are now generally considered adults. **Universities are educational rather than custodial institutions, and requiring the university to baby-sit each student would be inappropriate.** The university had no duty to protect the student from fraternity members who had been drinking. *Rabel v. Illinois Wesleyan Univ.*, 514 N.E.2d 552 (Ill. App. Ct. 1987).

D. Hazing

◆ *Although a fraternity had a duty to a Pennsylvania student, it did not breach that duty when local chapter members hazed him.*

A University of Pittsburgh student applied to the Beta Epsilon chapter of the Kappa Alpha Psi fraternity after Kappa lifted a restriction on inducting new members that had been imposed when a Kappa pledge died in Missouri. The student attended a fraternity gathering and was paddled more than 200 times by four fraternity brothers. He went to the hospital the next day and remained there for three weeks with renal failure, seizures and hypertension.

He later sued Kappa, the local chapter, the chapter advisor and a number of others for negligence. A Pennsylvania trial court ruled in favor of the defendants, and an appellate court largely affirmed. Here, even though Kappa owed a duty of care to the student, the student failed to show that it breached that duty. For example, he failed to show that the two-year moratorium on new members was merely a symbolic gesture and not a sincere attempt to curb hazing. However, **he was allowed to proceed with his lawsuit against the chapter advisor**. The evidence indicated that the chapter advisor failed to discuss hazing with local chapter members and did not advise them to read the executive orders that imposed sanctions for hazing. *Kenner v. Kappa Alpha Psi Fraternity*, 808 A.2d 178 (Pa. Super. Ct. 2002).

◆ *Corps of Cadets officials at Texas A&M were entitled to immunity in the following hazing case.*

The Texas A&M Corps of Cadets is a voluntary student military training organization consisting of approximately 2,000 students (about 5% of the student population). Members of the Corps live together, drill together, stand for inspections and physically train on a daily basis. A freshman student enrolled as a member of the Corps and joined a precision rifle drill team. **During "hell week," he was allegedly subjected to numerous hazing incidents by the drill team advisors, including having his head taped like a mummy, and endured several beatings.** He also was allegedly beaten after the drill team lost a competition to another school's team. He never reported the incidents to school authorities; however, he did tell his parents, who then informed school authorities that hazing was occurring. When asked about hazing by the faculty advisor, the student downplayed the seriousness of it. Near the end of his first year, he went to a "hound interview" (seeking to become an advisor to the drill team) where he was beaten and forced to cut himself with a knife. He and his parents then met with the Commandant of the Corps, who took them to the university police to file criminal charges. All the drill team advisors were then expelled or suspended for hazing.

He sued a number of Corps officials under 42 U.S.C. § 1983 and Texas' hazing statute, alleging that the officials' failure to supervise the Corps' activities demonstrated a deliberate indifference to his constitutional rights. The U.S. District Court for the Southern District of Texas held that **the actions of the Corps officials in educating students about the illegality of hazing were reasonable**. They disseminated brochures and other materials to students what hazing was and how to prevent it. They met with students and their parents to discuss hazing and to encourage parents to report it if they saw evidence of it, and they reasonably believed that their efforts were sufficient to prevent constitutional violations. **As a result, the court found that the officials were entitled to qualified immunity from suit.** On appeal, the Fifth Circuit Court of Appeals affirmed the grant of immunity to the officials. The student failed to show that the officials were deliberately indifferent to his constitutional rights. *Alton v. Hopgood*, 168 F.3d 196 (5th Cir. 1999).

◆ *A university could not be held liable for a student's hazing where it had no reason to know that hazing was going on.*

A student transferred to Cornell University after spending his first two years at other institutions. He was accepted to pledge a fraternity, the national organization of which prohibited hazing, as did Cornell. After allegedly enduring beatings and torture, psychological coercion, and embarrassment, the student sued Cornell for negligent supervision, premises liability and breach of an implied contract to protect him. The U.S. District Court for the Northern District of New York dismissed the action, finding that there was no special relationship between the university and the student, and that the university published information about the dangers of hazing and its prohibition on campus. **Further, the university did not have sufficient reason to believe that hazing activities were going on; and once it became aware of the hazing, it took disciplinary action against the perpetrators.** Finally, the court could find no evidence of any specific promises by the university that could be deemed part of an implied contract. The university was not liable for the hazing of the student. *Lloyd v. Alpha Phi Alpha Fraternity*, 1999 U.S. Dist. LEXIS 906 (N.D.N.Y. 1/26/99).

◆ *Fraternity members could be sued for negligence and for violating an anti-hazing statute in the following case.*

A 17-year-old college freshman was invited to pledge a fraternity and died after consuming excessive amounts of alcohol during a hazing ritual. His parents sued several members of the fraternity for negligence and also asserted claims under two New York statutes. The fraternity members sought to have two of the causes of action against them dismissed, and the case reached the Supreme Court, Appellate Division. The court held the fraternity members were not entitled to dismissal. **The parents alleged their son's intoxication was not entirely voluntary and that careless acts by the fraternity members went beyond the mere furnishing of intoxicants.** The action against the fraternity members could proceed. *Oja v. Grand Chapter of Theta Chi Fraternity*, 684 N.Y.S.2d 344 (N.Y. App. Div. 1999).

◆ *A university that knew about prior instances of hazing had a duty to protect a student from such behavior.*

Four or five members of a fraternity at a Nebraska university kidnapped a pledge, handcuffed him to a radiator and gave him a large quantity of alcohol. After the pledge became ill from his intoxication, he was taken to a third-floor restroom where he was handcuffed to a toilet pipe. The pledge escaped from the handcuffs and attempted to escape by exiting a restroom window and sliding down a drainpipe. However, he fell and suffered severe injuries. He sued the university, claiming that it had acted negligently in failing to enforce prohibitions against acts of hazing, the consumption of alcohol, and acts of physical abuse, when it knew or should have known that the fraternity was in violation of those prohibitions. The university moved for a pretrial judgment, asserting that it owed the pledge no duty to supervise the fraternity and protect the pledge from harm. The court granted the university's motion, and appeal was taken to the Supreme Court of Nebraska.

The supreme court held **the university could be liable to the pledge as an invitee on its property.** Because the university knew of two prior instances of hazing at fraternities on campus, and because it was aware of several incidents involving members of that fraternity, the acts taken against the pledge were reasonably foreseeable. The university had a duty to protect the pledge. Whether it breached that duty was a question of fact that had to be decided at trial. The court reversed the pretrial judgment in favor of the university. *Knoll v. Board of Regents of the Univ. of Nebraska*, 601 N.W.2d 757 (Neb. 1999).

◆ *Where the consumption of alcohol is coerced by social pressure or otherwise, it may not be voluntary, and liability may result.*

A Missouri university student was invited to become a member of a campus organization that was responsible for organizing the annual St. Pat's festivities. To gain membership to the organization, the student had to undergo an initiation that allegedly consisted of the coerced chugging and excessive consumption of alcohol, as well as other physical and verbal abuse. Members of the organization allegedly forced the student to consume a heated preparation of grain alcohol and green peas until he became unconscious, then left him unattended despite knowing that a participant in the initiation had died three years earlier. The student died two days later, and his parents filed a wrongful death lawsuit against the organization and the individual members who had conducted the initiation, as well as the fraternities on whose property the initiation took place. The trial court dismissed the action, and the parents appealed to the Court of Appeals of Missouri.

The court of appeals reversed and remanded the case. **Here, despite the apparently voluntary consumption of alcohol by the student, there may have been great social pressure to drink**. That coercion may have overcome any decision the student might have made about whether he should consume alcohol and, if so, how much he should consume. The case should not have been dismissed. *Nisbet v. Bucher*, 949 S.W.2d 111 (Mo. Ct. App. 1997).

◆ *A university was liable to a student for hazing injuries where it knew or should have known that hazing was going on.*

After receiving a full football scholarship, a student at the University of Delaware decided to join a fraternity and began his pledge period. The university prohibited hazing, as did the national organization. However, hazing continued. At the end of the pledge period – on "hell night" – the student was subjected to physical and emotional abuse as part of the hazing process. The night culminated when a lye-based liquid oven cleaner was poured over his back and neck. He suffered first and second-degree chemical burns, withdrew from the university and relinquished his scholarship. The national organization revoked the local fraternity's charter, but the university, due to a lack of cooperation, was unable to discipline students after the incident. The student sued the university, the fraternity and the perpetrator who poured the lye on him, and a jury awarded him $30,000, apportioning 93% of the liability against the university and 7% against the perpetrating student. The court then overturned the jury verdict against the university.

On appeal to the Supreme Court of Delaware, the court held that the student could be deemed an invitee of the university. Accordingly, once the university knew or had reason to know that a third party's actions could cause harm to the student, it had a duty to protect him. **The court found that there**

was sufficient evidence before the university that hazing activities still were taking place, and that the university thus had a duty to protect the student. Further, the university's anti-hazing and security regulations indicated that the university had control over the premises sufficient to justify the award of damages against it. The court reversed the lower court's decision to overturn the jury verdict. *Furek v. Univ. of Delaware*, 594 A.2d 506 (Del. 1991).

◆   *A fraternity member was convicted under a hazing statute after the death of a pledge. His challenge to the constitutionality of the statute failed.*

A fraternity member at a university in Missouri subjected pledges to repeated physical abuse, including kicks, punches, caning of the soles of the feet, and other forms of beating. As a result of the abuse, one of the pledges blacked out. He never regained consciousness and died the following afternoon. An autopsy revealed that he had broken ribs, a lacerated kidney, a lacerated liver, upper body bruises and a subdural hematoma of the brain, which proved fatal. The fraternity member was charged with five counts of hazing and, after his conviction, was sentenced to six months imprisonment for each count. He appealed to the Supreme Court of Missouri, asserting that the hazing statute violated the First Amendment's right to associate, as well as the Fifth and Fourteenth Amendments' rights to due process and equal protection.

The supreme court found that **the hazing statute did not prevent fraternity members from meeting at any time and place they might choose.** Further, the statute did not infringe upon constitutional rights once the fraternity members met. It merely prohibited recklessly endangering the mental or physical health or safety of a prospective member as a condition of admission into or preservation of membership in the fraternity. Accordingly, the statute was constitutional, and the fraternity member's conviction was affirmed. *State v. Allen*, 905 S.W.2d 874 (Mo. 1995).

CHAPTER FOUR

Freedom of Speech and Religion

I. EMPLOYEES

The First Amendment prohibits the government from abridging the freedom of speech and press. The Supreme Court's decision in Garcetti v. Ceballos, *126 S.Ct. 1951 (U.S. 2006), below, restated the general rule that public employees have a limited First Amendment right to speak as private citizens on matters of public concern. However, the Court explained that while the First Amendment invests public employees with certain rights, it does not empower them to "constitutionalize" their employee grievances. The* Garcetti *decision clarified that a public employee's speech made pursuant to official duties is not protected by the First Amendment. The Court held that "when public employees make statements pursuant to their official duties, the employees are not speaking as citizens for First Amendment purposes."*
Prior First Amendment cases held that public employee speech about purely private matters is unprotected by the Constitution. For example, in Pickering v. Board of Education, *below, the Supreme Court held a public*

employee may not be disciplined for speaking on matters of public concern unless there is proof that the communication was made in reckless disregard for the truth. In Connick v. Myers, *461 U.S. 138 (1983), the Court held **a public employee's speech upon matters of purely personal interest has no constitutional protection.** In* Rankin v. McPherson, *483 U.S. 378 (1987), the Court held that whether an employee's speech addresses the public concern is determined by the content, form, and context of the speech.*

Under Pickering *and* Connick, *school employees were entitled to First Amendment speech protection if they spoke on matters of public concern and their interest in public comment outweighed the government interest in efficient public service. When a public employee's speech addresses a matter of public concern, rather than a purely private matter, courts balance the interests of the employee against the interests of the government employer. While speech concerning the public interest is due protection, it cannot jeopardize the employer's interest in workplace efficiency.*

◆   *Garcetti v. Ceballos* involved a California deputy district attorney who questioned a search warrant affidavit presented by a defense attorney. He determined that it contained serious misrepresentations and recommended dismissing the case. At a subsequent meeting, a heated discussion ensued. The DA's office decided to proceed with the prosecution, and the deputy district attorney was reassigned, then transferred to another courthouse and denied a promotion. He claimed the transfer was retaliatory, and sued county officials under 42 U.S.C. § 1983 for First Amendment violations. The case reached the U.S. Supreme Court, which held that **public employees who make statements pursuant to their official duties are not speaking as citizens for First Amendment purposes, and are not insulated from employer discipline when they do so.** It was part of the deputy district attorney's job to advise his supervisors about the affidavit, and if his supervisors thought his speech was inflammatory or misguided, they had the authority to take corrective action against him. *Garcetti v. Ceballos,* 126 S.Ct. 1951, 164 L.Ed.2d 689 (U.S. 2006).

A. Protected Speech

◆   *When an employee speaks on a matter of public concern, and is then disciplined, courts use a balancing test to determine whether the employee's right to speak outweighs the employer's right to promote workplace efficiency.*

An Illinois school district fired a high school teacher for sending a letter to the editor of a local newspaper criticizing the board and district superintendent for their handling of school funding methods. The letter particularly criticized the board's handling of a bond issue and allocation of funding between school educational and athletic programs. The teacher also charged the superintendent with attempting to stifle opposing views on the subject. The board held a hearing at which it charged the teacher with publishing a defamatory letter. It then fired the teacher for making false statements. An Illinois court affirmed the board's action, as did the Illinois Supreme Court, which held the teacher's speech was unprotected by the First Amendment because his teaching position required him to refrain from statements about school operations.

The U.S. Supreme Court disagreed that public employment subjected the teacher to deprivation of his constitutional rights. **The state interest in regulating employee speech must be balanced with individual rights. The Court outlined a general analysis for evaluating public employee speech, ruling that employees are entitled to constitutional protection to comment on matters of public concern.** The public interest in free speech and debate on matters of public concern was so great that it barred public officials from recovering damages for defamatory statements unless they were made with reckless disregard for their truth. Because there was no evidence presented that the letter damaged any board member's professional reputation, **the teacher's comments were not detrimental to the school system, but only constituted a difference of opinion.** Since there was no proof of reckless disregard for the truth by the teacher and the matter concerned the public interest, the board could not constitutionally terminate his employment. The Court reversed and remanded the case. *Pickering v. Board of Educ.*, 391 U.S. 563, 88 S.Ct. 1731, 20 L.Ed.2d 811 (1968).

◆ *Where employees can be disciplined or discharged for legitimate reasons, the First Amendment will not protect them from the adverse action.*

An untenured Ohio teacher was not rehired after a number of incidents that led the school board to conclude he lacked tactfulness in handling professional matters. After the board decided not to reemploy the teacher, he asked for and received a list of the board's reasons. The board gave general reasons and noted that he had made an obscene gesture and had given an on-air opinion about school dress codes at a local radio station. The teacher sued for reinstatement on the grounds that his discussion with the radio station was protected by the First Amendment and that to refuse reemployment was a violation of his speech rights. A federal district court agreed, and ordered reinstatement with back pay. The Sixth Circuit affirmed the decision and the board appealed.

The U.S. Supreme Court first rejected the school board's argument that the Eleventh Amendment barred private lawsuits against local political subdivisions such as a school district. City and county governments were not "states" within the meaning of the Eleventh Amendment. However, the Court overturned the lower court decisions, holding that apart from the actions for which the teacher might claim First Amendment protection, the board could have chosen not to rehire him on the basis of several other incidents. The radio station incident, while clearly implicating a protected right, was not the substantial reason for non-renewal. The board could have reached the same decision had the teacher not engaged in constitutionally protected conduct. **A marginal employee should not be able to prevent dismissal by engaging in constitutionally protected activity and then hiding under a constitutional shield as protection from all other actions that were not constitutionally protected.** The lower courts were instructed to determine whether the board's decision could have been reached absent the constitutionally protected activity of phoning the radio station, and, if such a decision could have been reached, whether remedial action to correct the violation would be necessary. *Mt. Healthy City School Dist. v. Doyle*, 429 U.S. 274 (1977).

◆ *Under* Garcetti v. Ceballos, *this chapter, public employees who speak in the context of their job duties are not insulated from employment discipline by virtue of the First Amendment.*

A Georgia university student aid counselor reported fraudulent student aid practices in the Federal Work Study program. She said her supervisor "was dismissive and made no corrections" when confronted with evidence of fraud. The counselor met with the university president and a vice president, but she stated they took no action and claimed that her evaluations were lowered following her complaints. The university then informed her that it would not renew her contract. The counselor met with state education officials and turned over a 32-page analysis of student files and documents indicating possible fraud at the university. An independent state audit of the university revealed serious noncompliance with federal regulations. The supervisor resigned, and the university and state reached a $2.1 million settlement regarding the audit.

The counselor sued university officials, including the supervisor and president, in a federal district court. The court held the officials were entitled to qualified immunity on her First Amendment claims, and she appealed. The U.S. Court of Appeals, Eleventh Circuit, **explained that to prevail on a First Amendment claim, public employee speech must address a matter of public concern. Even if the speech initially qualifies for protection by touching on the public concern, courts will not hold for an employee unless his or her First Amendment interest in engaging in the speech outweighs the employer's interest in promoting the efficiency of public services.** The court cited *Garcetti v. Ceballos*, this chapter, which held that **when employees speak in the context of their job duties, the Constitution does not insulate them from discipline.** In this case, the counselor's employment duty was to ensure the accuracy and completeness of student files and to report mismanagement or fraud in student financial aid files. Since the speech that she claimed had led to her non-renewal was made pursuant to her job duties, it did not warrant First Amendment protection. The court affirmed the judgment for the university officials. *Battle v. Board of Regents for State of Georgia*, 468 F.3d 755 (11th Cir. 2006).

◆ *The First Amendment does not protect speech that a public employee makes as part of his or her official job duties.*

A Florida community college vice president for external affairs was responsible for supervising grants, legal affairs, government affairs and cultural affairs. She also provided strategic planning and reported directly to the college president. During her tenure, the vice president objected to the president's behavior. She complained to the college provost that the school had apparently entered into an advertising contract without allowing for competitive bidding, as required by state law. Following her expression of this and other objections, the college notified her it was not renewing her contract.

The vice president sued the president and college in a federal district court, asserting retaliation for exercising her First Amendment rights. The court held for the president and college, and she appealed. The Eleventh Circuit found the First Amendment claim failed because the vice president's complaints were made pursuant to her job duties. **Although a state employee cannot be discharged in retaliation for engaging in protected speech, the First Amendment does not protect speech a public employee engages in as part of his official job duties.** The vice president was directly responsible for the legal affairs of the college, and it was her job to make sure the college followed applicable laws. She raised her concerns internally and did not present them to any government agency or media outlet until after she was informed her contract was not being renewed. Her statements "fell squarely within her job duties" and therefore were not protected by the First Amendment. The court affirmed the judgment. *Vila v. Padrón*, 484 F.3d 1334 (11th Cir. 2007).

◆ *A public employee's speech made pursuant to official job duties is not entitled to First Amendment protection.*

In 1986, Sharron Bessent started a nonprofit agency for improving adult literacy in Dyer County, Tennessee. The program was funded entirely by private donations until 1991, when Tennessee began funding adult education programs in all counties. In 1997, Bessent and Dyersburg State Community College began a relationship by which the college acted as the fiscal agent for state grants allocated to the program while Bessent continued to administer it. After this arrangement was formed, there were allegations that Bessent falsified information relating to overtime, time sheets and clients served.

The college notified Bessent that the state intended to conduct an audit and that it planned to take complete control of the program. It then hired her in a supervisory position. Bessent expressed opposition to the move and was placed on probation, then discharged. She sued the college in a federal district court, claiming it retaliated against her for exercising her First Amendment rights. The court ruled against her, and she appealed to the U.S. Court of Appeals, Sixth Circuit. Bessent's First Amendment claim failed because her statements were made pursuant to her official duties. **As a public employee, statements made pursuant to official job duties were not entitled to First Amendment protection.** The court also rejected Bessent's due process claims, as she did not show any deprivation of a constitutional liberty interest. *Bessent v. Dyersburg State Community College*, No. 06-5305, 2007 WL 959420 (6th Cir. 4/2/07).

◆ *Institutions are entitled to direct their instructors to keep personal discussions about sexual orientation or religion out of their classes.*

An Illinois college instructor gave a gay student religious pamphlets on the sinfulness of homosexuality. One was entitled "Sin City" and told the story of a man who was beaten when he tried to stop a gay pride parade and was arrested by police. It also said a demon urged on a minister who preached that "God loves even gay people." The student complained to college officials and urged them to fire the instructor. In a follow-up letter, the student reported that the instructor had accused him of trying to get her fired. The college investigated and the Affirmative Action Office (AAO) and Equal Employment Opportunity Commission (EEOC) concluded that the instructor had sexually harassed the student based on sexual orientation. The college did not offer the instructor a position the following semester, and she sued the college in a federal district court for speech rights violations. The court held for the college and the instructor appealed to the U.S. Court of Appeals, Seventh Circuit.

The court relied on *Garcetti v. Ceballos*, this chapter, noting the case signalled the Court's concern that the courts give appropriate weight to a public employer's interests in First Amendment cases. In this case, **the college had an interest in ensuring that instructors stayed on the subject matter of their clinics and classrooms. The court affirmed the judgment for the college, as it could lawfully direct instructors to keep personal discussions about sexual orientation or religion out of a class or clinic.** *Piggee v. Carl Sandburg College*, 464 F.3d 667 (7th Cir. 2006).

◆ *A South Dakota university did not violate an untenured physics professor's speech rights by not renewing his contract.*

The professor claimed the department director declined to address his concerns. He then accused the director of lying and badmouthing him. The university informed him by letter his contract might not be renewed, and it scheduled a meeting with the department chair and others. In the meeting, the professor admitted calling his department director "a lying, backstabbing sneak." The university did not renew his contract based on his lack of civility. The professor sued the university in a federal district court, alleging First Amendment violations and seeking an order to prevent the university from not rehiring him. The university asserted the professor's remarks were complaints that were not of public concern and therefore not protected by the First Amendment. The court agreed, because **the professor's speech was personal, and not a matter of public concern**. It also rejected his claim that he required a preliminary injunction because having to pursue a career outside the university would cause him irreparable harm. The court balanced the damage to the professor against the harm the university would suffer if it was forced to reemploy him. Because forced reemployment would be disruptive to the university, the court dismissed the case. *Keating v. Univ. of South Dakota*, 386 F.Supp.2d 1096 (D.S.D. 2005).

◆ *A department manager was entitled to go before a jury with his claim that a New Mexico university retaliated against him for speaking out about financial dealings between the university and a state agency.*

The employee was the program manager of a university subdivision. An employee from the state health department told him the department would extend a grant to the school, but insisted the bulk of the funds flow through a nonprofit organization headed by a recent department retiree and the girlfriend of the program manager's supervisor. The manager suspected the employee was trying to avoid a state procurement law requiring the department to use a competitive bidding process. He declined the grant offer. The supervisor told the manager to resign or be fired. The manager resigned and sued the university in a state court. The case was removed to a federal district court, which granted the university's summary judgment motion.

The manager appealed to the U.S. Court of Appeals, Tenth Circuit. It held the statements about the grant were a matter of public concern because it alleged official wrongdoing. **The form and content of the manager's speech indicated he intended to vindicate the public interest, not to benefit himself. The manager's interest in speaking outweighed the university's interest in regulating him.** Since he was entitled to go before a jury to determine whether the university would have reached the same decision regardless of his speech, the court remanded the case. *Baca v. Sklar and the Board of Regents of the Univ. of New Mexico*, 398 F.3d 1210 (10th Cir. 2005).

◆ *An Ohio university employee who was fired eight months after engaging in protected speech could not prove her discharge was wrongful.*

The employee accused her immediate supervisor of improperly allocating university funds to cover the funeral expenses of a deceased university president. The supervisor sent her a termination notice eight months later based on four incidents involving gross insubordination and an unhealthy environment. The employee sued the university in a federal district court for violations of the First Amendment. The court granted summary judgment to the university, and she appealed to the U.S. Court of Appeals, Sixth Circuit.

The employee claimed the university fired her because she spoke out about the president's funeral expenses. The university countered with evidence of insubordination. **The Sixth Circuit held the eight-month delay between the time the employee spoke out and the time she was fired was a long time for an employer to wait to retaliate against an employee.** The court believed the university offered credible non-retaliatory reasons for the action. As the employee did not show the university treated her differently from other similarly situated non-protected employees, the court affirmed the judgment. *Timm v. Wright State Univ.*, 375 F.3d 418 (6th Cir. 2004).

◆ *An Arkansas associate professor did not prove she was not rehired because she criticized the university's academic program.*

The professor was a tenure-track associate professor in the history department and also taught and researched in the university's Middle East studies program. After her first year, she believed Arab administrators in the Middle East program were discriminating against her because she was not Arab. She also complained that the administrators were discriminating against all non-Arab women students. Students complained to the dean that the associate professor had aired her views to them in class. They said she told them the administrators were prejudiced against women, and the university improperly used funds to send non-program faculty on trips to the Middle East and to make private purchases there.

The history department recommended reappointing the professor, but the college personnel committee did not, finding she fell short of the standards for progress toward tenure. After considering both recommendations, the university dean did not reappoint the professor. She sued the university in a federal district court for speech rights violations. The court held for the professor and the university appealed to the U.S. Court of Appeals, Eighth Circuit. **The court found the professor spoke in part about a matter of public concern. However, even if her speech was protected, the university**

decided against reappointing her because she did not sufficiently progress toward tenure. For that reason, the court affirmed the judgment. *Schilcher v. Univ. of Arkansas*, 387 F.3d 959 (8th Cir. 2004).

◆ *The Tenth Circuit upheld a jury verdict which found an Oklahoma administrator had participated in the wrongful termination of a professor.*

An Oklahoma university assistant professor was appointed to a tenure-track position. He complained to an administrator about overcrowding in his classroom and other safety concerns, and e-mailed university officials and the state fire marshal about these issues. Department faculty and an interim department chair approved the professor's tenure application, but the university vice president of academic affairs recommended against renewing his one-year contract. The professor sued university officials in a federal district court after his contract was not renewed, alleging retaliation for exercising his speech and association rights. A jury returned a verdict in his favor, finding the board of regents liable for $34,959 and the vice president liable for $53,063.

The court denied the vice president's motion to vacate the judgment and he appealed. The Tenth Circuit held a court will grant a motion for judgment to set aside a verdict only if the evidence leads to one conclusion that is not susceptible to reasonable inferences supporting the verdict. **The vice president failed to present sufficient evidence from the trial transcript that he was not personally involved in undermining the professor's tenure application. He could be held liable for wrongful termination if he set in motion a series of events that he knew or should have known would cause others to deprive the professor of his constitutional rights.** The court affirmed the judgment for the professor. *Garrett v. Hibler*, 80 Fed.Appx. 82 (10th Cir. 2003).

◆ *The Court of Appeals of California held a professor did not show a university deprived him of his First Amendment and due process rights.*

The professor agreed to teach a course abroad and arranged for substitutes to teach his classes without informing his department. The university claimed this was unprofessional conduct and demoted him. An arbitrator reversed the decision, and the professor sued the university for civil rights violations and breach of contract. A court awarded the university summary judgment. Two years later, the professor sued the university again, alleging it retaliated against him for filing a grievance and filing the previous lawsuit. A court again held for the university. The professor filed a third action against the university for First Amendment violations and defamation. The court awarded summary judgment to the university, and he appealed to the Court of Appeal of California.

The court stated that to succeed on a First Amendment retaliation claim, the professor had to establish his prior lawsuits involved the public concern. Evaluation of the constitutional protection due an employee's speech requires examining its content, form, and context. The court characterized the grievance and lawsuits as "speech involving individual personnel disputes," which would not be relevant to the public's evaluation of the university. The professor did not inform the public about his demotion, nor did he use it as an example of how the university was interfering with its obligations to students or taxpayers. There was no evidence that the professor personally heard any of the statements forming the basis for his defamation claim. The court affirmed the judgment in all respects. *Aviel v. California State Univ., Hayward*, No. A102092, 2003 WL 22810321 (Cal. Ct. App. 2003).

◆ *A Virginia law prohibiting state employees from accessing sexually explicit material on state-owned computers did not violate the First Amendment.*

A Virginia law required state employees to obtain written approval from an agency head before using an agency-owned or leased computer to access, download, print or store information with sexually explicit content. Six professors from various public universities in Virginia sued state officials in federal court, asserting that the law violated their First Amendment rights of free speech and academic freedom. The court granted pretrial judgment to the professors, finding that the law infringed on their constitutional rights.

The state officials appealed to the U.S. Court of Appeals for the Fourth Circuit, which reversed. The court noted that the law did not prohibit all access to explicit material by state employees, since they still could view such material on computers not owned or leased by the state. Access to materials through the use of state-owned or leased computers involved a professor's role as an employee, not as a private citizen. **Since the law did not regulate state employee speech that was of public concern, it did not violate the professors' First Amendment speech rights.** The court also rejected the professors' argument that the law violated their particular right to academic freedom. Any right of academic freedom belonged to the university and was not an individual right. *Urofsky v. Gilmore*, 216 F.3d 401 (4th Cir. 2000).

◆ *In* Waters v. Churchill, *511 U.S. 661 (1994), the U.S. Supreme Court held a reasonable belief of workplace disruption can be enough to outweigh a speaker's rights under the First Amendment.*

In *Waters,* the Supreme Court held public employee termination is permitted where only a likelihood of disruption existed. It was unnecessary to demonstrate an actual disruption if termination was based on the employer's reasonable belief that a disruption could occur. *Waters v. Churchill*, 511 U.S. 661, 114 S.Ct. 1878, 128 L.Ed.2d 686 (1994).

B. Religion and Free Speech

The First Amendment's Establishment Clause prohibits Congress from making any law respecting the establishment of religion. The Free Exercise Clause of the First Amendment bars Congress from making any law that prohibits the free exercise of religion.

Like the speech provisions of the First Amendment, the religion clauses apply only to governmental action and do not bind private institutions and their employees.

◆ *A Kansas university's display of a controversial statue did not violate the Establishment Clause, because the display had a secular purpose and its primary effect was not hostility toward the Roman Catholic Church.*

Washburn University selected five statues to be placed on its campus as part of an annual sculpture exhibit. One of the statues was titled "Holier than

Thou." It depicted a Roman Catholic bishop wearing a miter and a stole, with a "grotesque" negative expression. A tenured professor of biology and a student president of a Catholic campus center sued the university and its officials in a federal district court, asserting the statue had an anti-Catholic message that violated the Establishment Clause. The university moved for dismissal of the lawsuit.

The court utilized the test from *Lemon v. Kurtzman*, 403 U.S. 602 (1971) to determine if the university violated the Establishment Clause. **It rejected arguments by the student and professor that the statue promoted bigotry and hatred toward Catholics and their faith. There was no evidence the statue was selected because of its religious message, or that the university had a policy of antagonism towards Catholicism.** A reasonable person would not find the statue conveyed an anti-Catholic message. The court held the display of the statue had a secular purpose that did not foster hostility toward the Catholic Church. The university did not violate the Establishment Clause, and the court entered judgment in its favor. *O'Connor v. Washburn Univ.*, 305 F.Supp.2d 1217 (D. Kan. 2004).

◆ *The Supreme Court held the act of certifying a union by the National Labor Relations Board (NLRB) infringed on a Catholic school's rights.*

The right of employees of a Catholic school system to join together and be recognized as a bargaining unit was successfully challenged in a case decided by the U.S. Supreme Court. In this case, the unions were certified by the NLRB as bargaining units, but the diocese refused to bargain. The court said that the religion clauses of the U.S. Constitution, which require religious organizations to finance their educational systems without governmental aid, also free the religious organizations of the obviously inhibiting effect and impact of unionization of their teachers. The court agreed with the employer's contention that **the very threshold act of certification of the union by the NLRB would necessarily alter and infringe upon the religious character of parochial schools**, since this would mean that the bishop would no longer be the sole repository of authority as required by church law. Instead, he would have to share some decision making with the union. This, said the Court, violated the religion clauses of the U.S. Constitution. *NLRB v. Catholic Bishop of Chicago*, 440 U.S. 490, 99 S.Ct. 1313, 59 L.Ed.2d 533 (1979).

◆ *Two nuns hired to perform secular services for a New Jersey university could bring a breach of contract action after being discharged.*

A Catholic university hired the nuns for computer science department positions. Their probationary contracts had no religious conditions and were used for both lay and clerical faculty. The university later decided the nuns were a "disruptive influence" and should be dismissed. Instead of following university procedures, university officials consulted a Marist brother who was an administrator for the university. He conferred with the nuns' Ursuline superiors who refused the nuns permission to renew their contracts. The university dismissed the nuns under Roman Catholic canon law, which prohibited "accepting duties outside the institute without permission of the legitimate superior." The nuns sued the university in a state court, which upheld their breach of contract claim. A state appeals court reversed the decision.

The nuns appealed to the New Jersey Supreme Court, which considered **whether matters of religion precluded a civil court action under the Free Exercise Clause**. It distinguished between religious school employees who "spread the faith" and those with "secular obligations." The court held the "ministerial function test" prohibited court intervention only when the employment activity involved direct participation in religious activities. The nuns had not counseled students as to spiritual affairs or moral matters and had performed primarily secular tasks. The court found **the nuns had not performed any "ministerial functions." They had been hired for their computer skills, not for their clerical value.** There was no indication that the contracts were to be governed by canon law. The court held that state courts had jurisdiction over their claims and reversed the holding of the court of appeals. *Welter v. Seton Hall Univ.*, 608 A.2d 206 (N.J. 1992).

◆   *If a public college or university creates a public forum for speech, it cannot prohibit religious speech. However, where no public forum is created, reasonable restrictions can be imposed.*

A physiology professor at the University of Alabama occasionally mentioned his religious beliefs during classes. He also scheduled an after-class discussion group entitled "Evidence of God in Human Physiology," which several of his students attended. Although he stated that his remarks were his own personal bias, a group of his students complained to the head of the physiology department. **The department head, after meeting with the dean and the school's attorney, drafted a memo directing the professor to stop interjecting his personal religious beliefs in class and not to hold the optional classes.** The professor petitioned the president of the university for a rescission of the order, but the president affirmed the restrictions. The professor filed suit in federal court under 42 U.S.C. § 1983 seeking an injunction lifting the restrictions placed on his speech. The professor moved for summary judgment. **The trial court determined that the university had created a public forum for the exchange of ideas, and that the university's interests were not sufficient to justify restricting the professor's freedom of speech.** The court granted summary judgment in favor of the professor. The university appealed to the U.S. Court of Appeals, Eleventh Circuit.

The appeals court rejected the district court's determination that a classroom constituted a public forum. It relied on the U.S. Supreme Court's decision in *Hazelwood School Dist. v. Kuhlmeier*, 484 U.S. 261, 108 S.Ct. 562, 98 L.Ed.2d 592 (1988), in which the Court stated that "school facilities may be deemed to be public forums only if school authorities have ... opened those facilities for indiscriminate use by the general public." If the facilities, as in this case, have been reserved for other intended purposes, no public forum has been created. **Where no public forum exists, school officials may impose reasonable restrictions on the speech rights of students and teachers. Accordingly, the appeals court held that the professor's classroom was not a public forum and the university could reasonably regulate his speech.** In addition, the university could prohibit the professor from promoting and scheduling optional classes. The court reversed the district court's award of summary judgment in favor of the professor. *Bishop v. Aronov*, 926 F.2d 1066 (11th Cir. 1991).

C. Electronic Communications

◆ *University of Houston Downtown (UHD) officials did not violate an adjunct professor's constitutional rights by limiting e-mail access for all adjuncts to times when they had actual course loads.*

The adjunct professor complained about a number of UHD policies, including compensation and treatment of adjunct professors. He claimed UHD denied access to his e-mail account after he attempted to use the system to distribute his complaints. The adjunct sued UHD and several administrators in a federal district court, asserting constitutional rights violations. He claimed UHD cut his course load from three courses to two in order to deprive him of benefits, terminate his retirement system status and cut his pay. The adjunct claimed Texas law violated the Constitution by prohibiting the unionization of state employees and the ability of non-citizens to become labor officials.

The court held for UHD, and the adjunct appealed to the Fifth Circuit. It **noted the U.S. Supreme Court has held a public school system's internal mail system is not a "state-created forum" for unlimited expression.** States may reserve forums for their intended purposes, as long as regulations are reasonable and not intended to suppress expression. **The court found no First Amendment violation. Restrictions created by a spam filter and the adjunct e-mail access policy were uniformly applied and were not based on content.** The policies were reasonable in view of UHD's goal of controlling the amount of data on its computer system. Any reduction in the adjunct's course load was not retaliatory. He was not treated differently than other UHD adjuncts, most of whom also taught only two courses. Adjunct faculty members are not similarly situated to full-time faculty members. They typically teach fewer classes than tenured or tenure-track professors and are not held to the same publishing expectations. As the adjunct could not compare himself to full-time faculty members, his Equal Protection Clause claim failed. Texas law prevented state political subdivisions, including UHD, from entering into collective bargaining agreements or recognizing labor organizations as bargaining agents for public employees. The law did not prevent employees from filing individual grievances. The adjunct lacked standing to challenge Texas Labor Code Section 101.109. He could still file his own individual grievances, and he did not even claim he had tried to become a union officer or organizer. The court affirmed the judgment for UHD. *Faculty Rights Coalition v. Shahrokhi*, 204 Fed.Appx. 416 (5th Cir. 2006).

◆ *A University of Virginia employee's e-mail to a member of a local NAACP chapter regarding the university pay scale may be protected speech.*

The employee and a co-worker were both NAACP members. The employee e-mailed the local NAACP chapter regarding a university pay scale restructuring. The chapter met to discuss this. The co-worker asked the employee to send her copies of documents distributed at the meeting. She used her university e-mail account to send the documents, and these were later forwarded to hundreds of others. University officials investigated the action. The employee refused to answer questions involving her NAACP membership. Supervisors notified her "she was facing termination." They told the employee she should "present her defense" the day before her hearing. According to the employee, she was not informed of the nature of the claims or told what she had done wrong. The employee stated that the "hearing" amounted to being handed two pink slips. Supervisors allegedly denied her request to speak.

The employee sued the university in a federal district court for violations of the First Amendment, Due Process Clause and state law. The court noted she was a 17-year university employee with a protected property interest in continued employment. **The university failed to provide an essential requirement of due process by not informing her of the nature of the charges.** The due process claim was valid, as the employee stated the charges were only vaguely outlined. **The court held public employment cannot be conditioned on grounds that infringe upon an employee's First Amendment rights.** The fact that the e-mail was sent to the NAACP was evidence that it involved the public concern. **As the employee stated sufficient facts that she was speaking as a citizen on a matter of public concern, her First Amendment claims should not be dismissed.** The court awarded pretrial judgment to the university on the state law claims, but denied it on her federal claims. *Bowers v. Rector and Visitors of Univ. of Virginia*, No. 3:06CV00041, 2006 WL 3041269 (W.D. Va. 10/24/06).

◆ *A Wisconsin university could prevent a student-employee from using a vulgar phrase as part of her e-mail signature.*

A part-time university student worked at one of the university's graduate schools. She altered her e-mail messages so that the phrase, "The truth shall set you free, but first it will piss you off! Gloria Steinem," would automatically appear as part of her e-mail signature. When her supervisor instructed her to remove the quote from work-related e-mails because the word "piss" was vulgar and inappropriate, she did so and then challenged the directive internally. After she lost her internal challenge, she sued the university and her supervisor for violating her speech rights under the First Amendment. A federal district court ruled in favor of the defendants, and the Seventh Circuit Court of Appeals affirmed. It rejected the employee's argument that the university had created a limited public forum with its e-mail system such that it could not engage in viewpoint discrimination against her. The court also found that her speech was not on a matter of public concern. Further, **even if her speech had been of a public nature, the university's interest in regulating inappropriate language outweighed her interest in speaking**. The university had appropriately directed her to cease using the e-mail signature. *Pichelmann v. Madsen*, 31 Fed.Appx. 322 (7th Cir. 2002).

D. Academic Freedom

1. Classroom Speech

The notion that academic freedom belongs to professors is generally inaccurate. The U.S. Court of Appeals, Sixth Circuit, recently restated the general rule that academic freedom applies to the institution, not the professor.

◆ *An Ohio university did not violate a lecturer's First Amendment rights by telling her to communicate grading requirements more clearly to her students.*

The lecturer gave incomplete grades to 13 of 17 students in a writing class for improper formatting, improper citations, and/or textual changes to their work. She left it up to each student to determine which reason applied in his or her own case. The lecturer's listserv postings did not specify particular reasons for which students received incomplete grades, and at least one student complained. A supervisor told the lecturer her listserv postings were not sufficiently clear to inform students how to complete the course. She asked her to send each student in the class a letter with individualized instructions for earning a final grade. Five weeks later, several students complained that the lecturer did not provide this information. The supervisor again asked the lecturer to draft letters to each student and emphasized that incomplete grades were a serious problem affecting student academic and financial aid status. The lecturer never responded and did not prepare the letters. She later sued the director of the English department and the supervisor for violating her rights to speech and academic freedom. A federal district court dismissed the case, and the lecturer appealed to the U.S. Court of Appeals, Sixth Circuit.

The court rejected the lecturer's claim that an instruction by a supervisor to communicate with students violated the First Amendment. Any right to academic freedom recognized by the First Amendment applied to the university, not the lecturer. A university is entitled to determine who may teach, what may be taught, how it is taught, and who may be admitted. These freedoms give a university the right to decide how classes are taught and how grades are assigned. **Professors have certain protections under the First Amendment, like making decisions about instruction and grading that differ from those of the university. They do not have to agree with the views of the university when it comes to a grade or a way to teach.** In this case, the university did not make the lecturer adopt the ideas of others as if they were her own. It simply asked her to explain to students exactly what was required to obtain a final grade. As the university did not violate the lecturer's rights, the court affirmed the judgment in its favor. *Johnson-Kurek v. Abu-Absi*, 423 F.3d 590 (6th Cir. 2005).

◆ *An Indiana university did not violate a professor's academic freedom by terminating his employment for poor job performance.*

Indiana State University hired an African history professor under a contract specifying a seven-year probationary period. A personnel committee recommended against reappointing him after two years, based on its finding that his performance was mediocre. The professor claimed a department chairperson advised him not to associate with other African professors and to become more involved with African-American activities. After exhausting his university appeals, the professor sued the university in a state court for due process and First Amendment violations. The university removed the case to a federal district court, which held his constitutional claims were meritless.

The professor appealed to the U.S. Court of Appeals, Seventh Circuit. It held that to succeed on a due process claim, the professor had to show the existence of a mutually explicit understanding of continued employment. A review of the contract showed the university had broad discretion to decide whether to reappoint him. As the professor did not establish a property interest in continued employment, his due process claim failed. His liberty interest claim failed because he could not show the university publicly communicated its denial of his reappointment and that the communication damaged his good name. **The professor's academic freedom claim was meritless. The statements by the department chairperson resembled employment advice. They were not connected with the performance of employment duties**, and did not suppress the professor's First Amendment rights. Moreover, he was never sanctioned for having spoken about any issue. Accordingly, the court affirmed the judgment. *Omosegbon v. Wells*, 335 F.3d 668 (7th Cir. 2003).

◆ *If a professor's "philosophical counseling activities" were on a matter of public concern, a university might have violated his First Amendment rights by ordering him to cease those activities.*

A professor at the City College of New York, who was involved in "philosophical counseling activities" on campus, was instructed by college officials to cease those activities. He sued under 42 U.S.C. § 1983, alleging First Amendment and due process violations. A federal court granted the college's motion to dismiss the lawsuit, but the Second Circuit vacated that decision. Here, **the lower court should have determined what was involved in the professor's "philosophical counseling activities"** to ascertain whether the speech was on a matter of public concern so as to be protected under the First Amendment. The court remanded the case. *Marinoff v. City College of New York*, 63 Fed. Appx. 530 (2d Cir. 2003).

◆ *A college inappropriately fired a professor for conduct and comments he made during class.*

A former professor at a Colorado junior college sued the college for terminating his employment on the basis of allegedly inappropriate classroom conduct and speech. The case arose when **a number of students complained he used an inappropriate teaching style and made offensive comments in class.** He allegedly discussed the presence of tampons in a sewer plant while lecturing about animal parasites, referred to human oral and anal sex and male orgasms during a lecture about the transmission of parasites, used euphemisms to describe feces, and implied that students were "dumb." He inappropriately referred to student evaluations and discussed matters unrelated to course content during class. A jury awarded the professor over $550,000.

The Tenth Circuit Court of Appeals affirmed the ruling for the professor. It noted that teachers enjoy some First Amendment protection in their classroom speech and cited to *Keyishian v. Board of Regents*, and *Tinker v. Des Moines Independent Community School Dist.*, 393 U.S. 503 (1969). Although not every word uttered in class is protected by academic freedom, the jury found the termination was not reasonably related to legitimate pedagogical interests. As the college had failed to object to having the jury decide that question, the verdict could not be set aside. *Vanderhurst v. Colorado Mountain College Dist.*, 208 F.3d 908 (10th Cir. 2000).

◆ *A public university professor did not have a right to determine what would be taught in his classroom.*

A professor at a Pennsylvania university taught a course entitled "Introduction to Educational Media." One of his students complained that he used the class to advance religious ideas. For example, his syllabus for at least one class included an emphasis on bias, censorship, religion and humanism, and listed numerous publications discussing those issues as required or recommended reading. The vice president for academic affairs wrote the professor, directing him to cease and desist from using "doctrinaire materials" of a religious nature. When **the new chair of the education department became concerned that the professor was still advancing religious issues**, he and the department faculty voted to reinstate an earlier syllabus, and he cancelled certain book orders. Eventually, the professor was suspended with pay, although he returned the next semester to teach several courses.

The professor sued the university for violating his speech rights, and the case reached the U.S. Court of Appeals, Third Circuit. The court held that **a public university professor does not have a First Amendment right to determine what will be taught in the classroom**. Outside the classroom, the professor had a right to advocate for the use of certain curriculum materials. However, inside the classroom, he did not have a right to use those materials without permission. The university was allowed to make content-based decisions when shaping its curriculum. *Edwards v. California Univ. of Pennsylvania*, 156 F.3d 488 (3d Cir. 1998).

2. Loyalty Oaths

Several employee claims based on political speech and association were upheld by the courts in the 1950s. For example, in Sweezy v. New Hampshire, *354 U.S. 234 (1957), the Supreme Court declared unconstitutional a university policy aimed at prohibiting the employment of communist party members.*

◆ *A Washington statute aimed at prohibiting subversives from becoming teachers was too vague to be constitutional.*

Faculty members at the University of Washington brought a class action suit to declare two state statutes unconstitutional. One statute required all state employees to take loyalty oaths, and the other required all teachers to take an oath as a condition of employment. Both oaths dealt with employee loyalty to the U.S. Constitution and to the government. The public employee statute applied to all public employees and defined a "subversive person" as one who conspired to overthrow the government. The Communist Party also was named as a subversive organization. Persons designated as subversives or Communist Party members were ineligible for public employment.

The U.S. Supreme Court held that the statutes were vague and overbroad, and violated the Fourteenth Amendment's Due Process Clause. The statutes were too unspecific to provide sufficient notice of what conduct was prohibited. This constituted a denial of the teachers' due process rights. **The university could not require its teachers to take an oath that applied to some vague behavior in the future,** especially since there were First Amendment freedom of speech and association claims at stake. *Baggett v. Bullitt,* 377 U.S. 360, 84 S.Ct. 1316, 12 L.Ed.2d 377 (1963).

◆ *An Arizona statute that prohibited even associating with the Communist Party was struck down. The statute should have targeted only those employees with a "specific intent" to do something illegal.*

An Arizona teacher who was a Quaker refused to take an oath required of all public employees under Arizona law. The oath swore that the employees would support both the Arizona and the U.S. Constitutions as well as state laws. The legislation also stated that anyone who took the oath and supported the Communist party or the violent overthrow of government would be discharged from employment and charged with perjury. The teacher sued for declaratory relief in the Arizona courts, having decided she could not take the oath in good conscience because she did not know what it meant.

The case eventually reached the U.S. Supreme Court, which held that political groups may have both legal and illegal aims and that there should not be a blanket prohibition on all groups that might have both legal and illegal goals. Such a prohibition would threaten legitimate political expression and association. The Court held that mere association with a group cannot be prohibited without a showing of "specific intent" to carry out the group's illegal purpose. It went on to say that **the Arizona statute was constitutionally deficient because it was not confined to those employees with a "specific intent" to do something illegal**. The statute infringed upon employee rights to free association by not punishing specific behavior that yielded a clear and present danger to government. The statute was struck down as unconstitutional. *Elfbrandt v. Russell,* 384 U.S. 11, 86 S.Ct. 1238, 16 L.Ed.2d 321 (1965).

◆ *A state could not require teachers to file annual affidavits listing every organization they belonged to in the past five years.*

The Arkansas legislature established **a statute that required every teacher employed by a state-supported school or college to file an annual affidavit listing every organization to which he or she had belonged in the past five years**. A teacher who had worked for an Arkansas school system for 25 years and who was a member of the NAACP was told he would have to file such an affidavit before the start of the next school year. After he failed to do so, his contract for the next year was not renewed. He filed a class action lawsuit against the school district in a federal district court.

The court found that the teacher was not a member of the Communist Party, or any organization advocating the violent overthrow of the government. It upheld the statute, finding that the information requested by the school district was relevant. The Supreme Court of Arkansas had previously upheld the statute's constitutionality in a case brought by other teachers. The U.S. Supreme Court agreed to hear both cases and consolidated them for a hearing. The Court noted that the state certainly had a right to investigate teachers, since education of youth was a vital public interest. It stated that the requirement of the affidavit was reasonably related to the state's interest. However, the Court held that **requiring teachers to name all their associations interfered with teacher free speech and association rights**. The Court ruled that because fundamental rights were involved, governmental screening of teachers was required to be narrowly tailored to the state's ends. Because the statute went beyond what was necessary to meet the state's inquiry into the fitness of its teachers, the Court ruled it unconstitutional. *Shelton v. Tucker,* 364 U.S. 479, 81 S.Ct. 247, 5 L.Ed.2d 231 (1960).

◆ *A loyalty oath could not be administered to two applicants who objected to it on religious grounds.*

Two Jehovah's Witnesses applied for positions with the California Community College District. As part of state-mandated preemployment procedures, the district required the applicants to sign an oath swearing "true faith and allegiance" and to "support and defend" the United States and California Constitutions. The applicants refused to take the oath due to their religious beliefs, and the district rejected their applications.

The applicants sued the district under the Religious Freedom Restoration Act of 1993 (RFRA), challenging the validity of the loyalty oath as a condition precedent for employment. A California federal court held that **requiring the applicants to take an oath that violated their religious tenets placed an undue burden on their right to free exercise of religion**. The district failed to assert that the loyalty oath furthered a compelling government interest or was the least restrictive means of achieving that interest. Although employee loyalty was a compelling interest, the evidence failed to establish that a loyalty oath effectively achieved this goal. An alternative oath directed to an applicant's actions rather than his or her beliefs would be equally effective and less restrictive. Because the loyalty oath could not be justified under the compelling interest test articulated in the RFRA, the court enjoined the district from administering the loyalty oath to the applicants. *Bessard v. California Community Colleges,* 867 F.Supp. 1454 (E.D. Cal. 1994).

[*Editor's Note:* The U.S. Supreme Court held that the RFRA was unconstitutional as applied to state actions in *City of Boerne, Texas v. Flores,* 521 U.S. 507, 117 S.Ct. 2157, 138 L.Ed.2d 624 (1997).]

II. DEFAMATION

Defamation consists of a communication that injures a person's reputation. The defamatory material must have been "published" to third parties who understand that the material refers to the plaintiff. Also, the plaintiff's reputation must have suffered in the minds of the third parties, and there must be a tangible (usually economic) injury. There are several defenses to defamation lawsuits including truth, consent and opinion. The defense of **privilege** is common in employment cases.

◆ *The Court of Appeal of California rejected a student's defamation claim against a state university.*

Professors said the student stalked them and later refused to abide by an order to stay away from them. The university expelled the student and she filed a state court action for defamation, claiming the reports about her were false. The Court of Appeals of California held that **statements reporting suspected criminal activity to law enforcement were privileged and could not form the basis of a defamation claim.** *Fink v. California State Univ. Northridge*, No. B183977, 2006 WL 465947 (Cal. Ct. App. 2/28/06).

◆ *An e-mail by a Kentucky professor did not exceed the scope of his qualified privilege, and there was no showing he sent it with malice.*

An annual piano competition among students at the University of Kentucky School of Music generated some controversy. Students e-mailed all School of Music faculty members and several university administrators, questioning the impartiality of the judging. The pianist judge chose one of his former students as the winner. When the professor received the e-mail, he sent an e-mail that later became the basis of a defamation lawsuit against him. The professor suggested that a female professor had encouraged the students to send the e-mail. It also noted that the professor's husband "has been known to create situations like this before." The professor expressed anger at the students for suggesting that he had rigged the competition. He indirectly asked for an investigation by stating "I leave it to impartial colleagues to sort this out." The female professor and her husband sued the professor in a state court for defamation. The entire case was based on the content of his e-mail. The court held the e-mail was privileged. There was no defamation, as the e-mail was sent in good faith and without actual malice. The court held for the professor, as he did not use defamatory language or cause injury to the couple's reputation.

The professor and her husband appealed to the Court of Appeals of Kentucky. The court noted that the professor's e-mail was a response to an e-mail that referred to him specifically by name. He sent the e-mail to appropriate supervisory personnel and people who had a direct interest in the matter. **This indicated he did not exceed the scope of his qualified privilege. Moreover, there was no showing of malice.** The e-mail did not meet the test for defamatory communications, as nothing it said could reasonably be construed as a statement of fact concerning the female professor or her husband. It merely requested an investigation. The professor's e-mail showed restraint in light of the allegation that he had rigged the music competition. The court affirmed the decision in his favor. *Vorobiev v. Hersh*, No. 2005-CA-002522-MR, 2007 WL 706816 (Ky. Ct. App. 3/9/07).

◆ *The U.S. Court of Appeals, First Circuit, held a university did not violate employee First Amendment rights by maintaining secret files.*

Full-time university employees for a Puerto Rico university alleged that for ten years, the university gathered information about them without their consent and "in a suspicious manner." The information was allegedly collected to identify or classify employees based on their membership in some unidentified professional association and their speech about the university. The employees sued the university in a federal district court for violation of their speech rights.

The district court dismissed the case and the employees appealed. The First Circuit found the complaint failed to identify the associations or expressions about which the university had allegedly gathered information. **Without more specifics, the court had no means to determine whether the university targeted free association.** The court dismissed the case because it found the complaint was insufficient to support a First Amendment claim. *Aponte-Torres v. Univ. of Puerto Rico*, 445 F.3d 50 (1st Cir. 2006).

◆ *Comments made by a Pennsylvania university professor about a lecturer during a private internal grievance proceeding were not privileged.*

The lecturer had a one-year appointment in a veterinary school, after working for the university for the previous 12 years. She told the department chair she wanted a tenured faculty position. A faculty search committee unanimously rejected her application for tenure based on her history of poor interpersonal relations. The faculty member continued to work at the university and filed a grievance, alleging gender discrimination, among other things. The chair testified at the grievance hearing that the faculty member had lied on two separate occasions and had misused grant funds earmarked for clinical work. The faculty member alleged the remarks by the chair during the hearing were defamatory. She sued the university in a federal district court for defamation, employment discrimination and fraudulent misrepresentation. The court granted the university's motion for summary judgment.

The faculty member appealed to the U.S. Court of Appeals, Third Circuit. The court stated **"all communications pertinent to any stage of a judicial proceeding are accorded an absolute privilege which cannot be destroyed by abuse."** However, **internal grievance proceedings were not entitled to the same absolute immunity as regular judicial proceedings**. The district court incorrectly held the chair's statements were absolutely privileged. The court noted that **Pennsylvania cases have found that a judicial privilege applies only to proceedings before government bodies or those pursuant to a statute or administrative regulation**. The reason for distinguishing private proceedings from public ones is that government hearings typically involve basic procedural safeguards that may be lacking in private proceedings. No transcript was kept during the grievance hearing, so there was no record of what the chair said when he allegedly defamed the faculty member. The court reversed and remanded the order for summary judgment on the defamation claim. *Overall v. Univ. of Pennsylvania*, 412 F.3d 492 (3d Cir. 2005).

◆ *A federal district court held two faculty members did not defame a New York instructor during a closed faculty meeting.*

A tenure-track instructor learned she would not be reappointed, and she contended that faculty members who voted against her reappointment did so because she was pregnant. The president of the institute overturned the vote and reappointed her for a semester, making her eligible for tenure the following spring. The department again met to discuss the instructor's reappointment. She claimed two faculty members made inaccurate statements about her that resulted in the loss of her reappointment and her claim to tenure. The instructor sued the faculty members in a federal district court for defamation. **The court held a statement is defamatory if "it tends to expose the plaintiff to public contempt, ridicule, aversion, or disgrace, or induce an evil opinion of him in the minds of right-thinking persons." Under New York law, individuals are given absolute immunity for statements of opinion.** The faculty members asked the court for summary judgment, based on the absolute privilege given to statements of opinion. **The court dismissed the case, finding the instructor did not prove the remarks were false. She also failed to show the remarks were not opinion.** *Donofrio-Ferrezza v. Nier*, No. 04 Civ. 1162 (PKC), 2005 WL 2312477 (S.D.N.Y. 9/21/05).

◆ *A District of Columbia law school admissions council did not defame a student by issuing him a low score on a law school admissions test.*

After the student received his results for the Law School Admissions Test (LSAT), he complained to the university that it had been incorrectly scored. University representatives told him the council would not review his test score. The score would remain on file for five years in accordance with council policy. The student sued the council for defamation in a federal district court, arguing it publicized an incorrect score. **The court held a test score cannot be considered defamatory. The student failed to show the score was made public. Liability for defamation exists if a statement "tends to injure a person in his trade or lower him in the estimation of the community or subject him to ridicule, shame, contempt or embarrassment." A low LSAT score did not injure the student in his trade, as he did not claim to be employed in a trade in which a low LSAT score would harm him.** He did not prove the score subjected him to scorn, ridicule, shame, contempt or embarrassment or that the council communicated the score to anyone else. For these reasons, the court dismissed the case. *Coates v. Law School Admission Council*, No. Civ.A. 105CV0641JDB, 2005 WL 3213960 (D.D.C. 10/25/05).

◆ *A student's claim for defamation against a Connecticut university resident advisor could proceed to trial.*

A university judicial board charged the student with violating community standards. A resident advisor testified at a board hearing that he saw the student enter a women's restroom and tear down posters in a hallway. The board found the student violated community standards and suspended him. He sued the university and resident advisor in a state trial court, alleging statements made in the board hearing were defamatory. **The court held that communications uttered or published in the course of judicial proceedings are absolutely privileged as long as they are in some way pertinent to the subject of the controversy.** In *Chada v. Charlotte Hungerfold Hospital*, 272 Conn. 776, 854 A.2d 1163 (Conn. 2005), the Supreme Court of Connecticut held an **absolute privilege is a defense to potentially defamatory communications**. The court found the student was entitled to more procedural safeguards than he received. The resident advisor was entitled to a qualified privilege for statements made during board proceedings. The case should go forward to decide if the resident advisor's statements were defamatory. *Rom v. Fairfield Univ.*, No. CVO203915128, 2006 WL 390448 (Conn. Super. Ct. 1/30/06).

◆ *The Supreme Court of Iowa held a security guard failed to show a university wrongfully discharged him or defamed him.*

The white security guard saw an African-American football player holding a white student in a headlock. The security guard told the player to let go of the student, but the player lunged toward him. The guard pepper-sprayed the player and hit him on the thigh with his baton. The student later said they were just horseplaying. After the media covered the incident, the NAACP and Black Student Coalition demanded an investigation. A university panel concluded the guard had overreacted and used unnecessary force. It found his actions were not racially motivated, but noted minority students had complained about him in the past. The university fired the guard, and he sued the university and its president in a state court for wrongful discharge and defamation.

The court held for the university, and the guard appealed to the Supreme Court of Iowa. He alleged he could not find jobs in security and related law enforcement fields, and claimed the panel report was defamatory. The guard pointed to parts of the report that called him immoral and a racist. It also suggested he had a confrontational mindset, overreacted and used force too quickly. The court noted the trial court had not ruled on the panel's remarks about any alleged racism, and the guard did not ask the trial court to do so. **As for the other statements in the report, the supreme court believed they could not reasonably be interpreted as defamatory.** The court affirmed the judgment. *Lloyd v. Drake Univ.*, 686 N.W.2d 225 (Iowa 2004).

◆ *A Minnesota state university was not liable to a demoted faculty member for defamation resulting from remarks printed in a school newspaper.*

The faculty member was Dean of the College of Social Sciences at St. Cloud State University (SCSU). He filed an age discrimination claim against the university for demoting him. Shortly after the demotion, the university's bi-weekly student-run newspaper published an article about the dean that he considered defamatory. The dean sued SCSU in a state court for defamation, but the court found SCSU had no editorial control over the newspaper, and could not be held liable for defamation. The dean appealed. **The Court of Appeals of Minnesota explained that a state university cannot control or be responsible for possible libel printed in a student-run paper. It said a university is almost completely barred from censoring a student paper. To allow this would impede the free flow of ideas and expression of ideas.** The trial court had correctly found the relationship between SCSU and the student newspaper significantly differed from a private publisher's relationship to its newspapers. Because SCSU had no editorial control over the newspaper's content, the court affirmed the judgment. *Lewis v. St. Cloud State Univ.*, 693 N.W.2d 466 (Minn. Ct. App. 2005).

◆ *A Florida court held a state university had no immunity against a former student's claim for negligently defaming him in an alumni newsletter.*

The former student had attended the university's Department of Oceanography, where a current member of the faculty had been his classmate. While the two were there, a priceless fossil specimen had disappeared from the lab. The faculty member wrote an article for the university's alumni newsletter, in which he identified an unconfirmed rumor in the department that the missing specimen was seen for sale by the former student's company. The former student sued the faculty member and university in the state court system. He alleged the faculty member defamed him, and the university negligently published defamatory materials by failing to verify the facts. The university argued it was protected from liability by sovereign immunity. The court agreed and dismissed the university from the lawsuit.

The former student appealed to the District Court of Appeal of Florida, which noted a claim for negligent defamation is distinct from a typical defamation claim. As the former student had alleged the university was negligent, the court had to determine whether the university owed him a duty of care. If there was no duty of care, sovereign immunity did not bar a claim for negligent defamation. **The court stated that publishers owe nonpublic figures a duty of care regarding the content of their publications. The university did not enjoy blanket immunity for anything editors of its alumni publications published.** The court found the former student was alleging "operational" conduct that did not involve basic governmental policymaking. The university was not entitled to sovereign immunity. The court reversed and remanded the judgment. *Rudloe v. Karl*, 899 So.2d 1161 (Fla. Dist. Ct. App. 2005).

◆ *An Ohio college did not defame a medical student after he pled guilty to charges of drug possession.*

The student attended the college's medical school. In his third year, he was arrested and charged with several felony drug offenses. The college suspended him immediately and eight months later, he pled guilty to the criminal charges. After a hearing, the college dismissed the student. He attended a friend's graduation party where he learned several medical school students believed he was a drug dealer. A classmate stated there had been a debate at the medical school about when to get rid of the student. Up until that point, the student had not discussed the details of his drug conviction to other students.

The student sued the college in an Ohio court for defamation. The student argued the rumors about his dismissal constituted defamation. **The court held that to prevail, he had to show a defamatory statement was published by word or in writing to another person for which the college was responsible. The court refused to infer the college was the source of the rumors.** Even if the statements concerning the debate about the student's status at the college could be attributed to college employees, the student presented no evidence from which a jury could find they were false or defamatory. The court awarded summary judgment against the student. *Flaim v. Medical College of Ohio at Toledo,* No. 2004-04132, 2004 WL 2521293 (Ohio Ct. Cl. 10/6/04).

◆ *The Court of Appeal of California held newly discovered evidence found in an e-mail could undermine a university's defense in a defamation case.*

A state university vice president received an external review report which stated that an assistant health education professor was not meeting standards for a tenured university professor, "resulting in a weak program." The report was distributed to seven other administrators. The professor sued the university and several others for defamation and invasion of privacy in a state trial court. The court granted their motion for summary judgment, and the professor appealed to the court of appeal. While his appeal was pending, new evidence was found on a computer hard drive, and he requested a special writ.

The court granted the writ and reversed entry of summary judgment. **To establish his defamation claim, the professor had to show there was an intentional publication of a factual statement that was false, unprivileged, and had a natural tendency to injure him or cause special damages.** The trial court had found the allegedly defamatory statements were protected by a common interest privilege. It held there was no triable issue concerning malice by the university officials, which would defeat the privilege. Newly found evidence on a computer hard drive revealed an e-mail including the report and an allegedly defamatory statement. As the e-mail raised a triable issue of fact on the issue of malice, the court granted the writ and reversed the entry of summary judgment. *Fischbach v. Trustees of California State Univ.*, Nos. B159589, B165926, 2004 WL 179471 (Cal. Ct. App. 2004).

◆ *A professor deemed to be a public figure could not succeed on his defamation lawsuit against a student reporter.*

When a student reporter wrote that a professor obtained tenure only after successfully suing the college for race discrimination, and added that the lawsuit was a possible explanation for the professor's outspoken racial views and the administration's reluctance to openly censure the professor, the professor sued the reporter for defamation. A state court ruled that **the professor was a public figure based on his participation in public lectures and writings that attracted national media attention**. The court then made several evidentiary rulings and held that no defamation occurred. The Massachusetts Court of Appeals affirmed. The trial court properly allowed into evidence an editorial calling for the professor's removal (due to his use of a book published by the Nation of Islam) because it showed that the professor's reputation could have been damaged by articles other than the one written by the student. *Martin v. Roy*, 767 N.E.2d 603 (Mass. App. Ct. 2002).

III. STUDENTS

A. Protected Speech

1. Religious Speech

◆ *A Texas state university policy that was used to prohibit students from distributing pro-life leaflets was held unconstitutional.*

The university policy required each organization handing out leaflets to include the organization's name on the leaflets. A student anti-abortion group distributed leaflets on campus without stating its name. The university attempted to prohibit members from passing out the leaflets. They sued the university in a federal district court, alleging the policy unconstitutionally restricted anonymous speech in a designated public forum. The court held the policy was unconstitutional, and the university appealed.

The U.S. Court of Appeals, Fifth Circuit, noted the Supreme Court has held anonymous pamphleteering is a form of advocacy that exemplifies the purpose behind the First Amendment. However, the right to anonymous speech on a public street differs from that of a student on the campus of a public university. Public universities can and typically do restrict access to campus facilities. Students often must identify themselves to university officials before they can use campus facilities. The Fifth Circuit held that on-campus speech is almost never totally anonymous. The university contended the policy served a significant state interest by preserving the campus for speech by students, faculty and staff. The students argued the university permitted non-affiliated people to speak anonymously on campus and hold anonymous signs. **The court agreed, and held the policy was too far-reaching, as it required the speaker to identify him or herself to every person receiving literature.** As the policy required speakers to sacrifice more anonymity than needed, the court affirmed the judgment. *Justice for All v. Faulkner*, 410 F.3d 760 (5th Cir. 2005).

◆ *A Tennessee university did not violate a student's speech rights by removing his anti-war messages from university buildings. A federal district court noted the First Amendment does not protect acts of vandalism.*

The student and some friends went to a university art and architecture building at 1:30 a.m. after drinking for two hours. They used university art supplies to make anti-war banners. The student then wrote "no war" in yellow paint on the art building, elevator doors, and the front doors of the college athletic center. He taped banners from the interior railings of the art building and a bulletin board outside it. The student was arrested and charged with vandalism. He sued the university in a federal district court, alleging First Amendment violations. **The court stated "the guarantees of the First Amendment have never meant that people who want to propagandize protests or views have a constitutional right to do so wherever or however they please." Taking paint and writing on university buildings was simple vandalism, which is not protected by the First Amendment.** The university did not take the banners down because of their messages. They were removed as evidence related to the vandalism charges. For these reasons, the court dismissed the lawsuit. *Wilson v. Johnson*, No. 3:04-CV-59, 2005 WL 2417057 (E.D. Tenn. 9/30/05).

◆ *A Pennsylvania student who opposed a university play depicting Jesus Christ as a homosexual was entitled to a trial on his First Amendment rights.*

Temple University put on a play depicting Jesus Christ and his disciples as homosexuals who engaged in sexual acts with one another. The student asked the university to prohibit the production on campus and planned an alternative event to portray Jesus according to the student's beliefs. A university vice president assured the student a stage would be provided for an alternative event. However, university trustees met and decided not to provide a stage or any assistance for the student's planned event. The student became upset at the meeting and had to be restrained. The vice president ordered campus police to handcuff the student and take him to a hospital for a psychiatric evaluation.

A university official applied for a warrant to involuntarily commit the student for an emergency psychiatric evaluation, but doctors released him. The student sued the university and its officials in a federal district court for First Amendment violations and other claims. **He alleged the university violated his First Amendment rights by involuntarily committing him and refusing to assist him in retaliation for exercising his religious beliefs and speech rights.** The university conceded the student was engaged in protected activity. **The court held that a hearing was necessary to determine whether the university acted in retaliation for the student's protected activity.** It denied summary judgment and ordered a trial on the First Amendment claims. *Marcavage v. Board of Trustees of Temple Univ.*, No. Civ.A. 00-5362 (PBT), 2004 WL 1151835 (E.D. Pa. 2004).

◆ *A federal district court dismissed claims that an assignment to read a religious-related book violated student free exercise rights.*

An orientation program held by the University of North Carolina, Chapel Hill (UNC) required incoming freshmen to read a book that explored Islam. UNC stated it was highly relevant in light of the then-recent terrorist attacks. Although the program had an exception for students with religious objections, several incoming students sued UNC in a federal district court for Free Exercise Clause violations. **The court considered UNC's motion for dismissal, and noted the book was not a religious reading.** It found the orientation program was an academic exercise.

The court stated UNC had attempted to engage students in a scholarly debate about a religious subject, and encourage them to express their opinions. Students who objected to reading the book could refrain from doing so. **UNC did not compel the affirmation of any particular religious belief, favor any religious dogma, or punish the expression of any particular religion.** As UNC did not ask students to compromise or give up their religious beliefs, the court granted its motion to dismiss the action. While the court dismissed the claims against the university, it permitted the students to file a second amended complaint to add new factual allegations. *Yacovelli v. Moeser*, 324 F.Supp.2d 760 (M.D.N.C. 2004).

◆ *Virginia Military Institute's daily "supper prayer" violated the Establishment Clause by coercing cadets to participate in a religious ritual.*

Virginia Military Institute (VMI) is a state-operated college that closely regulated the personal behavior of cadets. Each night, cadets marched in formation and were called to attention in the mess hall for a prayer read by a chaplain. Cadets had to remain standing and silent while the prayer was read, but were not obligated to recite the prayer, close their eyes, or bow their heads. VMI denied a request by some cadets to ignore the supper prayer, and they commenced a federal lawsuit, asserting it violated the Establishment Clause. The court granted summary judgment to the cadets, and issued an order prohibiting VMI from continuing the prayers. It held VMI's superintendent was entitled to qualified immunity in the action. The parties appealed.

The Fourth Circuit Court of Appeals applied the "coercion test" of *Lee v. Weisman*, 505 U.S. 577 (1992) and *Santa Fe Independent School Dist. v. Doe*, 530 U.S. 290 (2000). Under *Lee* and *Santa Fe*, **"school officials may not, consistent with the Establishment Clause, compel students to participate in a religious activity." The record showed VMI's educational philosophy was based on coercion.** Because of VMI's coercive atmosphere, the Establishment Clause precluded school officials from sponsoring an official prayer, even for mature adults. However, VMI's superintendent was entitled to qualified immunity, as the cadets' rights to be free from prayer at a public military college were not clearly established at the time. *Mellen v. Bunting*, 341 F.3d 312 (4th Cir. 2003).

◆ *Where a Washington college allowed secular demonstrations, it could not place restrictions on a demonstration based on religion.*

The dean of a community college allowed an anti-abortion demonstration on campus. His office received a number of complaints, leading him to ask campus security to remove the demonstrators. When they refused to leave, police were called, and a demonstrator was arrested. He later sued the dean and the head of campus security under 42 U.S.C. § 1983 for violating his First Amendment rights. A federal court granted pretrial judgment to the defendants, but the Ninth Circuit Court of Appeals reversed the judgment. The court held a **"no religious instruction or worship" condition imposed by the college dean violated the First Amendment as a content-based restriction on speech.** Only if that restriction was necessary to achieve a compelling state interest, and was narrowly designed to accomplish that interest, would it be constitutional. The court also held that the dean was not entitled to immunity under Section 1983 because he should have known that placing the "no religion" restriction on the demonstration violated the First Amendment. There also was a question of fact, requiring a trial, as to whether the security head was entitled to immunity. *Orin v. Barclay*, 272 F.3d 1207 (9th Cir. 2001).

◆ *A theater student was allowed to continue with his production of a play alleged to be anti-Christian after a Seventh Circuit panel ruled that the play's production at a public university did not violate the Establishment Clause.*

The dispute arose after a theater student at an Indiana university chose to produce the play "Corpus Christi" for his senior performance project. The play depicts a homosexual Christ-like character who engages in sex with his apostles. A group of individuals, including taxpayers, members of the state General Assembly, and members of the Board of Trustees of Purdue University objected to the production of the play. In a lawsuit, they alleged that the publicly funded university would be violating the Establishment Clause by allowing the performance. The plaintiffs further asserted that if production of "Corpus Christi" were permitted, it would give the impression that the university endorsed the play's allegedly anti-Christian ideals.

The plaintiffs sought a preliminary injunction from a federal district court to stop production. The court refused to grant the injunction, finding the theater was a limited public forum because it allowed students and community members to stage performances. **Because the theater was a limited public forum, the university could not discriminate against the viewpoint of those who stage performances.** The university was conducting itself in a viewpoint-neutral manner by allowing opponents of the play to hand out literature at the performance, holding an assembly to air both sides of the dispute and including a disclaimer in the playbill stating the university did not endorse the viewpoints presented within the play. On appeal, the U.S. Court of Appeals for the Seventh Circuit upheld the district court decision. The court found the plaintiffs' assertion that the First Amendment prevents state universities from providing venues for un-Christian ideas "absurd." There was no evidence the university was hostile to Christianity because it did not tell the student to produce the play. Nor was there any indication that the play would have been prohibited if it were antagonistic toward other religions. *Linnemeir v. Board of Trustees of Purdue Univ.*, 260 F.3d 757 (7th Cir. 2001).

◆ *Requiring a Mormon student to perform scripts containing language she found religiously offensive did not violate her First Amendment rights.*

When a student who belonged to the Church of Jesus Christ of Latter-day Saints auditioned for the university's Actor Training Program, the instructors asked her if there was anything she would be uncomfortable doing as an actor. She replied that she would not take her clothes off, take the name of God or Christ in vain, or use the word "fuck." The student was accepted into the program, and her professors encouraged her to overcome her objection to certain language. Nevertheless, she omitted words and phrases she found objectionable from one of her performances without approval. At the end of her first semester, she was informed by her instructors that she would no longer be allowed to censor language she found objectionable. The student then left the program and sued in federal court, claiming the requirement to use religiously objectionable language violated her constitutional rights to free exercise of religion and free speech. She sought damages under 42 U.S.C. § 1983.

The court found that the student's constitutional rights were not violated. The instructors' stance on using offensive language derived from an aesthetic principle encouraging all actors to challenge themselves and not to specifically deprive the student of her free exercise rights. As such, the court rejected the student's free exercise claim. The court also rejected the student's free speech claim. Citing *West Virginia State Board of Educ. v. Barnette*, 319 U.S. 624 (1943), the court recognized that a state entity cannot force a student to advocate a particular ideological point of view. Here, **the instructors were not forcing the student to adopt or promote an ideological view**: they merely asked her to read some lines that she found offensive. The court dismissed the case. *Axson-Flynn v. Johnson*, 151 F.Supp.2d 1326 (D. Utah 2001).

◆ *Graduation prayers were allowed at Indiana University.*

In a case involving graduation prayers at Indiana University, the Seventh Circuit distinguished the ceremonies from public school ceremonies involving younger students. **There was no element of coercion requiring students to participate in the large, impersonal university commencement exercises**, and many students and family members remained in their seats during the prayer. Adult students were unlikely to succumb to peer pressure and could choose not to attend the ceremony without suffering any severe consequences. The court agreed with the university that the prayers solemnized the ceremony, did not endorse any particular religion and allowed the university to continue a 155-year-old tradition. *Tanford v. Brand*, 104 F.3d 982 (7th Cir. 1997).

2. Academic Practices

◆ *An Illinois university did not violate a graduate student's speech rights by dismissing her for a fraudulent scientific presentation.*

The student submitted research to a scientific journal and presented it at a conference. The university suspected her of academic misconduct. After a hearing, a university investigatory panel concluded the student fabricated scientific data she knew were invalid when she presented them at the conference. The university dismissed the student, and she sued the university in a federal district court for speech rights violations. The court held the university's interest in academic integrity outweighed her speech interests.

On appeal, the U.S. Court of Appeals, Seventh Circuit, found the university had a strong interest in its reputation in the academic and scientific community. **Public presentation of false data by a graduate-level student affiliated with the university significantly compromised that reputation. The First Amendment protects the marketplace of ideas but does not protect students from the consequences of their own fraudulence.** *Pugel v. Board of Trustees of Univ. of Illinois*, 378 F.3d 659 (7th Cir. 2004).

◆ *A Pennsylvania private college's display of a Confederate flag did not violate a student's speech rights even though he found it offensive.*

The student attended Gettysburg College, which is located near the Civil War battleground. Two days before the college held an art exhibition featuring the Confederate flag, the student asked the court to forbid the college from doing so, asserting he and the community would be irreparably harmed by the display of such a racially charged symbol. The court noted the college was a private institution, and no government actor was involved in the display. Without state action, the student could not allege a constitutional violation.

The court held that simply being offended was insufficient to support a First Amendment speech rights violation claim. The First Amendment protected speech rights by preventing the government from intruding on

individual expression. The court held it could intervene only if speech would potentially cause immediate and cognizable harm. There was no such showing here. The student was free to protest the exhibit or to publish leaflets and editorials in opposition to the display. The court dismissed the case. *Coleman v. Gettysburg College*, 335 F.Supp.2d 586 (M.D. Pa. 2004).

◆   *A former student unsuccessfully sued a New York university for violating his equal protection rights after it forbade him from entering campus.*

After the former student graduated, he threatened to attack the dean with a baseball bat unless he changed a grade. An associate vice president notified the former student he was barred from campus and university activities for a year. The former student filed three lawsuits against the university in different courts. The courts eventually dismissed all the actions. The former student applied for a graduate program at the university and continued to enter the campus. Campus police ticketed him for criminal trespass. The university allowed the former student to attend a friend's on-campus law school graduation but excluded him from a swearing-in ceremony. He phoned a university vice president and left a voice mail calling him an "asshole," threatening to punch him in the face, and saying he would attend the swearing-in ceremony.

The university then revoked the former student's visitor privileges for one year. He sued university officials in a U.S. District Court, alleging exclusion from campus violated his equal protection and due process rights. **A federal magistrate judge found that as a visitor, the former student had no due process interest in being on campus. Members of the general public have no liberty or property interest in remaining on a university campus.** A public university is an educational institution subject to state rules and regulations. Those rules are designed to ensure order is maintained on college campuses. **New York state education regulations allowed universities to eject students from campus for violating rules of conduct.** While the former student stated no clear basis for an equal protection claim, the magistrate interpreted it to concern the difference between rights of campus access for visitors and students or employees. The magistrate recommended that the court grant summary judgment against the former student. *Moore v. Black*, No. 03-CV-0330A (SR), 2004 WL 1950338 (W.D.N.Y. 2004).

◆   *A federal district court held a Pennsylvania university's code of conduct was overbroad and thus violated the First Amendment.*

Shippensburg University's catalogue contained a code of conduct establishing student rights and responsibilities and regulating student behavior. The code prohibited "acts of intolerance directed toward other community members." The term "acts of intolerance" was not defined. The university's racism and cultural diversity statement prohibited racial and ethnic intimidation and harassment. Two students sued the university in a federal district court, asserting the code and diversity statement violated their First Amendment rights to speech, association and free exercise of religion. The university sought dismissal, asserting the provisions were not subject to First Amendment scrutiny because they were "merely aspirational and precatory."

The court held five of the provisions disputed by the students restricted speech and conduct that was protected by the First Amendment. Among the provisions held unconstitutional were the statements that "acts of intolerance directed toward other community members will not be tolerated" and "the expression of one's beliefs should be communicated in a manner that does not provoke, harass, intimidate, or harm another." **The court held unconstitutional the code provisions stating a student's actions should mirror the university's racial and diversity ideals and the university's definition of racism.** The university did not show it had a history of campus disruption that would allow these provisions. The court granted the students' motion for a preliminary injunction concerning the five unconstitutional provisions and denied the university's motion to dismiss the case. *Bair v. Shippensburg Univ.*, 280 F.Supp.2d 357 (M.D. Pa. 2003).

◆ *A student had no First Amendment right to have his master's thesis kept by the university library where he failed to comply with professional guidelines.*

A graduate student at a California university wrote his master's thesis and obtained approval of the version he submitted for review. He later attempted to file his thesis in the university library with two new pages in which he criticized administrators with profanity. The thesis committee and a dean refused to allow the thesis to be filed because the extra pages did not meet professional standards for publication. Even though the university never filed a copy of the thesis, the student received a master's degree. He then sued the university, asserting he should have been allowed to file the revised thesis, and asserting due process violations because he did not receive a formal hearing.

A federal court ruled against the student, and the Ninth Circuit affirmed. Here, **the thesis was a curriculum assignment with pedagogical objectives that required him to comply with professional guidelines. Because he failed to do so, he could not claim a First Amendment right** to have his thesis filed. He also failed on his due process claim because the defendants' decision to defer granting his degree was an academic one that was careful and deliberate. *Brown v. Li*, 308 F.3d 939 (9th Cir. 2002).

3. Retaliation

◆ *The Third Circuit upheld the dismissal of a case filed by a Pennsylvania student who claimed he was arrested in retaliation for accusing an instructor of discrimination.*

A white Jewish student argued with an African-American computer lab instructor over his use of computer lab facilities. A college policy permitted computer use by students enrolled in active, ongoing classes, but prohibited access for personal use. At the time, the student was not enrolled in an active, ongoing class and was using computers for his own use. He wrote a letter to the college president complaining about the denial of lab use. The dispute continued for eight months and resulted in the student's forcible removal from the computer lab by Pittsburgh police officers. He was arrested for trespass, but charges were later withdrawn.

The student sued the college and officials including the instructor in a federal district court for speech rights violations and breach of contract. He claimed violation of his First Amendment rights based on the letter he wrote to the college president. A federal district court held for the college and officials, and the student appealed. The U.S. Court of Appeals, Third Circuit, said that **to prevail on a speech rights retaliation claim, the student had to show he engaged in protected speech and the college retaliated against him for making the speech. The court found his letter was not a matter of public concern and was thus not protected activity.** The student's contract claim failed because no contract ever existed between the college and student. The college was not required to provide him with written notice of every regulation governing the use of its facilities to enforce its regulations. The court affirmed the judgment for the college and officials. *Feldman v. Community College of Allegheny*, 85 Fed. Appx. 821 (3d Cir. 2004).

◆   *An expelled student could proceed with his First Amendment retaliation claim against Connecticut university officials.*

A Connecticut university student criticized the university administration and filed an ethics complaint against the university president. After the interim vice president and dean of student affairs accused him and two other students of making unauthorized changes to over 30 grades in violation of the university handbook, a hearing was conducted and the student was expelled. The university upheld the student's expulsion, but dropped proceedings against the two others. The student sued the university in a federal district court, alleging violations of his speech and due process rights.

The university sought to dismiss the lawsuit on Eleventh Amendment immunity grounds, and a federal court granted the motion in part. As an arm of the state, the university could not be liable for negligence. Also, the student received appropriate due process in the hearing and expulsion procedures used by the university. However, **there was a fact issue as to whether he had been expelled in retaliation for his speech against the administration**. The court refused to dismiss that claim and ordered a trial. *Brown v. Western Connecticut State Univ.*, 204 F.Supp.2d 355 (D. Conn. 2002).

B. Newspapers and Yearbooks

◆   *The U.S. Supreme Court has held that, at the collegiate level, the conduct of students and the dissemination of ideas – no matter how offensive could not be curtailed based solely on the "conventions of decency."*

A graduate student at the University of Missouri was expelled for distributing on campus a newspaper that violated university bylaws since it contained forms of "indecent speech." The newspaper was found objectionable for two reasons. First, on the front cover was a political cartoon of policemen raping the Statue of Liberty and the Goddess of Justice with a caption that read "... with Liberty and Justice for All." Secondly, the issue contained an article entitled "Mother Fucker Acquitted," which discussed the trial and acquittal on an assault charge of a New York youth. The student sued the university in a federal district court, for First Amendment violations.

The court denied relief, and the Eighth Circuit affirmed. On further appeal, the U.S. Supreme Court held the student should be reinstated. It stated that

while a university has an undoubted prerogative to enforce reasonable rules governing student conduct, it is not immune from the sweep of the First Amendment. The Court noted that *Healy v. James*, 408 U.S. 169 (1972), made it clear that the mere dissemination of ideas – no matter how offensive to good taste – may not be shut off in the name of "conventions of decency" alone. *Papish v. Univ. of Missouri*, 410 U.S. 667 (1973).

◆   *The U.S. Court of Appeals, Seventh Circuit, held a university dean was entitled to immunity for prior restraint of the content of a student newspaper.*

Students at an Illinois state university held positions on the student newspaper and student communications media board. According to board policy, only students determined newspaper content. No censorship or prior approval by university officials was allowed. The university became interested in the school paper, the *Innovator*, after it printed articles attacking the integrity of the dean of the college of arts and sciences. The dean and university president issued statements accusing the *Innovator* of irresponsible and defamatory journalism. The newspaper refused to retract comments that officials insisted were false, or even to print their responses. When the dean of student affairs notified the newspaper's printing company that a university official had to review and approve the newspaper's content before each issue was printed, the students sued the university for speech rights violations.

A federal district court refused to dismiss the claims against the dean. The Seventh Circuit held in 2003 that she was not entitled to qualified immunity because the prohibition against censorship within the university setting was clearly established at the time she acted. **The Supreme Court held that high school officials have broad powers to censor school-sponsored newspapers if their actions are supported by valid educational purposes in** *Hazelwood School Dist. v. Kuhlmeier*, **484 U.S. 260 (1988).** The Court allowed prior restraint in *Hazelwood* because the student newspaper was prepared as part of a high school journalism curriculum. In this case, the Seventh Circuit found the greater maturity of college students made censorship of college newspapers untenable. *Hosty v. Carter*, 325 F.3d 945 (7th Cir. 2003).

The dean petitioned the Seventh Circuit for reconsideration. The petition was granted, and the court reversed its 2003 decision. **The court held the** *Hazelwood* **standard could apply to a public university. However, its application in this case was unclear. Since public officials need not predict the resolution of constitutional uncertainties, the court held the dean was entitled to qualified immunity.** *Hosty v. Carter*, 412 F.3d 731 (7th Cir. 2005).

◆   *A university violated the First and Fourteenth Amendment rights of the yearbook editor when it confiscated yearbooks for being "inappropriate."*

The editor of Kentucky State University's (KSU's) yearbook during the 1993–1994 school year decided to be innovative and, for the first time, gave the yearbook a theme: "Destination Unknown." The theme reflected the students' uncertainty about life after college and the pending question of whether the university was to become a community college. The yearbook included pictures from KSU events as well as current national and world events. KSU's vice president for student affairs objected to the final product. She opposed the yearbook's cover, theme, the lack of captions under many photos and the inclusion of current events unrelated to KSU. **The vice president and other university officials prohibited the yearbooks from being distributed and confiscated them.** The editor and another student sued the school on behalf of all KSU students in federal court, claiming their First and Fourteenth Amendment rights were violated. The court dismissed the suit, finding that the yearbook was a nonpublic forum because it was not intended to be a journal of expression, but rather a record of the events at KSU for its students. The students appealed to the U.S. Court of Appeals, Sixth Circuit.

The court noted it is well established that a high school yearbook is not a public forum and is subject to strict control by school officials. It held **a college yearbook was a limited public forum**. KSU's written policy toward the yearbook gave the student editors control over the publication because it did not allow a faculty/staff advisor to change the yearbook in order to alter the content. In addition, **the language of the university's student publication policy indicated that such publications were intended to be limited public forums.** The policy begins by saying, "The Board of Regents respects the integrity of student publications and the press, and the rights to exist in an atmosphere of free and responsible discussion and of intellectual exploration." The Sixth Circuit remanded the matter to the district court for further proceedings. *Kincaid v. Gibson*, 236 F.3d 342 (6th Cir. 2000).

◆   *Insulting statements that cannot be reasonably interpreted as stating facts cannot form the basis of a defamation action.*

A Virginia university student newspaper published an article describing a university official as a student program's "Director of Butt Licking." The official sued the newspaper for defamation and use of insulting words in violation of state law. A state trial court held that the newspaper reference was void of any literal meaning and not reasonably susceptible to interpretation as containing factual information. On appeal, the Supreme Court of Virginia held that **statements that cannot reasonably be interpreted as stating facts about a person cannot form the basis of a defamation action**. The court rejected the official's claim that she was entitled to present her case to a jury on grounds that literal interpretation of the offensive phrase imputed to her a criminal violation of the state sodomy statute and was defamatory. It also rejected her assertion that the statement injured her reputation and held her up to ridicule by implying that she lacked integrity. The court affirmed the judgment for the newspaper. *Yeagle v. Collegiate Times*, 497 S.E.2d 136 (Va. 1998).

◆   *Where student editors refused to publish an advertisement they believed was defamatory, they could not be held liable under the First Amendment.*

An attorney wrote two articles that were highly critical of his law school, which were published in the law school's newspaper. He sought to have a classified advertisement placed in the paper, soliciting material that would discredit certain faculty and administrators at the school for the purpose of assisting him in a federal civil rights action against the school. He also sought in the ad to urge students who had been discriminated against by the school's criminal defense clinic to join his Office for Civil Rights complaint against the clinic. When the paper's three student editors refused to publish the ad, fearing that it was defamatory and would expose them and the paper to litigation, the attorney sued the students and the school under the First Amendment. The U.S. District Court for the Eastern District of New York noted that **the student editors were not state actors (a requirement for a claim brought under the First Amendment) and** that **the school did not exercise control over the newspaper**. As a result, the attorney's claim could not succeed. The court dismissed the lawsuit. *Leeds v. Meltz*, 898 F.Supp. 146 (E.D.N.Y. 1995).

◆   *A Texas university could not forbid some newspapers while allowing others to be distributed.*

Southwest Texas State University had a policy forbidding the distribution of newspapers that contained advertisements. The university did not regulate the distribution of newspapers or literature without advertisements. The regulation also did not apply to the student-run university newspaper, which contained many advertisements. Aside from these restrictions, the university fostered an environment of free expression. A group of students and a small, politically oriented, local newspaper that had attempted free distribution on campus sued the university, claiming that its "no solicitation" policy violated the First Amendment.

A federal district court held for the university, and the students appealed to the U.S. Court of Appeals, Fifth Circuit, which stated that **the university was a limited public forum. As such, its ability to regulate expressive conduct was limited.** There was no evidence that handing out free newspapers would affect the university's academic mission or crime rate. The regulation was not narrowly tailored to meet the privacy, litter, or congestion interests of the university. Moreover, the fact that the university did not regulate publications without advertisements illustrated the tenuous nature of those arguments. The regulation was declared unconstitutional. *Hays County Guardian v. Supple*, 969 F.2d 111 (5th Cir. 1992).

C. Student Activity Fees

◆   *The University of California did not violate the First Amendment by barring the use of student fees to campaign against a state ballot initiative.*

The Associated Students of the University of California at Santa Barbara (ASUCSB) opposed a state ballot initiative called Proposition 76. The proposition would have given the governor the power to limit or cut certain appropriations. ASUCSB passed a resolution allocating $1,000 in student funds to print flyers opposing the proposition. The university refused to disburse the funds from the student fee accounts. ASUCSB sued university officials in a federal district court for First Amendment violations.

The court held the organization had no constitutional right to spend student fees on ballot initiative campaigning. **Student fees were public money which belonged to university regents,** and therefore the government. **The decision to withhold the funds did not violate the First Amendment.** A written agreement between student organizations and the university specifically indicated the university's chancellor was empowered to impose and collect student activity fees. In addition, students paying the fees made their checks out to the regents and not to the organizations. University regents, not student organizations, had the power to raise, collect and control the fees. *Associated Students of the Univ. of California at Santa Barbara v. Regents of the Univ. of California*, No. C 05-04352 SI, 2007 WL 196747 (N.D. Cal. 1/23/07).

◆   *The U.S. Supreme Court held a university could not withhold authorization for payments to a printer on behalf of a Christian student organization.*

The University of Virginia collected a mandatory $14 student activity fee from full-time students each semester. The fees supported extracurricular activities that were related to the educational purposes of the university. University-recognized student groups could apply for funding by the activities fund, although not all groups requested funds. University guidelines excluded religious groups from student funding as well as activities that could jeopardize the university's tax-exempt status. A university-recognized student group published a Christian newspaper for which it sought $5,862 from the activities fund for printing costs. The student council denied funding because the group's activities were deemed religious under university guidelines. After exhausting appeals within the university, group members filed a lawsuit in the U.S. District Court for the Western District of Virginia, claiming constitutional rights violations. The court granted summary judgment to the university, and its decision was affirmed by the U.S. Court of Appeals, Fourth Circuit.

The students appealed to the U.S. Supreme Court. The Court observed that **government entities must abstain from regulating speech on the basis of the speaker's opinion**. Upon establishing a limited public forum, state entities must respect the forum by refraining from the exclusion of speech based upon content. **Because the university had opened a limited public forum by paying other third-party contractors on behalf of student groups, it could not deny the religious group's claim for funds on the basis of its viewpoint.** Allowing the payment of the group's printing costs amounted to a policy of government neutrality for different viewpoints. The Court distinguished the student fee from a general tax and placed emphasis on the indirect nature of the benefit. The Court reversed the lower court decisions, ruling that access to public school facilities on a neutral basis does not violate the Establishment Clause of the First Amendment. *Rosenberger v. Rector and Visitors of Univ. of Virginia*, 515 U.S. 819, 115 S.Ct. 2510, 132 L.Ed.2d 700 (1995).

◆   *The U.S. Supreme Court held that the University of Wisconsin could assess a mandatory activity fee to fund student extracurricular programs.*

The University of Wisconsin required all students to pay the university a non-refundable activity fee to support registered student groups. Students who objected to the collection and use of their student fees to support objectionable political and ideological expression sued university regents in a federal district court, asserting that the program violated their speech rights. The court held that the fee program compelled students to support political and ideological activity with which they disagreed in violation of the First Amendment. It prohibited the university from using student fees to fund registered student organizations engaged in such activity. The U.S. Court of Appeals, Seventh

Circuit, affirmed in part, finding that the student activity fee program was not germane to the university's mission and burdened student speech.

The U.S. Supreme Court found that the university assessed the fee to facilitate the free and open exchange of ideas among students. Objecting students could insist upon certain safeguards regarding the compelled support of expressive activities. To insist upon germaneness to the university's mission would contravene the purpose of the program, which was to encourage a wide range of speech. The Court found it inevitable that the fees would subsidize some speech that students would find objectionable, and it declined to impose a constitutional requirement upon the university compelling it to refund fees to students. Viewpoint neutrality was the proper standard for the protection of the First Amendment rights of the objecting students. **The university could require students to support extracurricular speech of other students in a viewpoint neutral manner**, and the parties had stipulated in this case that the program was viewpoint neutral. The university had wide latitude to adjust its extracurricular speech programs to accommodate students. The Court reversed and remanded the case for further proceedings. *Board of Regents of Univ. of Wisconsin System v. Southworth*, 529 U.S. 217, 120 S.Ct. 1346, 146 L.Ed.2d 193 (2000).

On remand, the district court determined the university's updated fee system, which set forth the criteria groups had to meet before obtaining funding and required the student government to determine which groups received funding, was unconstitutional because it was not viewpoint neutral. Under the new system, the university's student government made funding decisions with little or no oversight. The court further held the criteria used to determine whether a group received funding was too subjective. The university was ordered to establish a viewpoint neutral funding system. *Fry v. Board of Regents of Univ. of Wisconsin System*, 132 F.Supp.2d 744 (W.D. Wis. 2000).

◆ *Oregon students could be required to pay fees that supported a non-political public interest research group.*

The University of Oregon required students, as a condition of matriculation, to pay incidental fees that contributed to the support of the Oregon Student Public Interest Research Group (OSPIRG) Education Fund. A number of students sued to have the fees declared unconstitutional. The Ninth Circuit Court of Appeals first held that the university and the state board of higher education were immune from liability under the Eleventh Amendment. However, the officials responsible for the administration of the fees could be sued. The court then held that the fees were not unconstitutional.

This was not a case of compelled membership in an objectionable organization. Students were not required to join the OSPIRG Education Fund. Nor did the fees go to an organization that did political lobbying because the OSPIRG Education Fund was separate from the OSPIRG (the political arm of the group). Here, the fees were allocated among scores of campus organizations representing many diverse viewpoints. Further, the OSPIRG Education Fund provided college students with hands-on experience in recognizing, researching and solving the problems of society. This furthered the university's educational mission. *Rounds v. Oregon State Board of Higher Educ.*, 166 F.3d 1032 (9th Cir. 1999).

◆ *A California university could require students to pay student fees that funded political activities.*

The Associated Students of the University of California (ASUC) administers student government and extracurricular activities at the University of California, Berkeley. The ASUC senate conducts student government through 30 elected student representatives. During the school year, the senate meets weekly and sometimes debates controversial public issues including gay and lesbian rights, gun control, and marijuana legalization. A group of students and student organizations challenged the mandatory collection of student fees of which a part funded ASUC senate political activities. They filed a lawsuit against university regents in a California superior court. The court held for the regents, and the Court of Appeal of California affirmed the judgment. The Supreme Court of California remanded the case to determine whether senate activities violated the speech and association rights of dissenting students by using their fees to support certain ideological and political views.

The superior court again held for the regents, and the dissenting students appealed to the court of appeal. The court reviewed superior court findings that the financial burden on the dissenting students was minimal and that senate activities accounted for only four percent of total ASUC expenditures. The senate's primary function was to administer and govern ASUC activities, and the senate was not dedicated to achieving a particular political or ideological outlook. **The expenditure of mandatory fees did not violate the test described by the supreme court since the educational benefits provided by the ASUC senate outweighed the advancement of political and ideological interests** and was not merely incidental to those interests. The court affirmed the judgment for the regents. *Smith v. Regents of the Univ. of California*, 65 Cal.Rptr.2d 813 (Cal. Ct. App. 1997).

D. Student Elections

◆ *A college president's cancellation of a student election may have violated the First Amendment.*

The student newspaper at the College of Staten Island endorsed student union candidates, some of whom were also part of the newspaper's staff, for elected student government positions. After a complaint was filed, the Student Election Review Committee postponed the election. The college president then reviewed the disputed issue of the newspaper and agreed that it improperly endorsed the student union candidates, compromising the electoral process. She declared the results of the election void and ordered a new election. The student union candidates swept both elections. When a lawsuit was filed against the president and the university, asserting that the president violated the First Amendment by canceling the election, a court held that there were **issues of fact as to whether the president's decision was a constitutionally permissible content-based determination** or impermissible viewpoint discrimination. As a result, it refused to award pretrial judgment to the student plaintiffs. *Husain v. Springer*, 193 F.Supp.2d 664 (E.D.N.Y. 2002).

The president later moved for summary judgment. **The court found she sought reprisal when the newspaper promoted a particular viewpoint. Therefore, the president discriminated according to viewpoint in violation of the students' First Amendment rights.** *Husain v. Springer*, 336 F. Supp.2d 207 (E.D.N.Y. 2004).

◆ *A university could not put spending limitations on student council candidates without violating the First Amendment.*

A California university student ran unopposed for a seat on the student-run legislative council. After he was elected, the elections commission discovered that he spent $233.40 on his campaign despite student association regulations limiting campaign spending to $100. He was disqualified from holding the position and sued under the First Amendment. He sought a preliminary injunction reinstating him to the position during the litigation, and a federal court ruled in his favor. It stated that the Eleventh Amendment did not preclude awarding injunctive relief. Further, the student met the requirements for obtaining such relief. He was likely to succeed on the merits of his claim because campaign spending restrictions directly affect freedom of speech; he would suffer irreparable injury if the injunction was not granted; and **allowing him to represent the students who elected him was in the public interest**. The student was reinstated to his seat on the legislative council. *Welker v. Cicerone*, 174 F.Supp.2d 1055 (C.D. Cal. 2001).

IV. USE OF CAMPUS FACILITIES

A. Students and Student Groups

The location of a person's speech on campus determines the limits the government may apply. The U.S. Supreme Court has devised a "forum analysis" to analyze campus speech cases. While the government cannot restrict speech in traditional public forums, such as sidewalks, parks and public streets, public institutions may designate areas for expression and limit their use to certain groups or topics, so long as there is no viewpoint discrimination.

◆ *The Establishment Clause does not prevent private citizens from using public facilities for religious purposes. In fact, if a facility is made available to the public, religious groups cannot be excluded from using it.*

The University of Missouri at Kansas City, a state university, made its facilities available for the general use of registered student groups. **A registered student religious group that had previously received permission to conduct its meetings in university facilities was informed that it could no longer do so because of a university regulation that prohibited use of its facilities for the purposes of religious worship or teaching.** Members of the group sued in federal court, alleging that the regulation violated their First Amendment rights to free exercise of religion and freedom of speech. The court upheld the school's regulation, but the U.S. Court of Appeals, Eighth Circuit, reversed, stating that the regulation was discriminatory against religious speech and that the Establishment Clause does not bar a policy of equal access in which facilities are open to groups and speakers of all kinds.

The Supreme Court agreed with the court of appeals' assessment, stating **that the university policy violated the fundamental principle that state regulation of speech must be content-neutral**. It is obligatory upon the state to show that the regulation is necessary to serve a compelling state interest and that it is narrowly drawn to achieve that end. The state was unable to do that here. The state's interest in achieving greater separation of church and state than is already ensured under the Establishment Clause was not sufficiently "compelling" to justify content-based discrimination against religious speech of the student group in question. *Widmar v. Vincent*, 454 U.S. 263, 102 S.Ct. 269, 70 L.Ed.2d 400 (1981).

◆ *A student Christian organization obtained a preliminary order preventing a law school from revoking its official status.*

The dean of an Illinois law school revoked the official student organization status of the Christian Legal Society (CLS) because the organization excluded those who engaged in or affirmed homosexual conduct. The dean found the tenets of the national CLS violated the university's affirmative action/equal opportunity (EEO) policy. That policy said that the university would provide equal employment and education opportunities for all qualified people without regard to sexual orientation. All recognized student organizations had to comply with federal or state nondiscrimination laws. The CLS sued the university in a federal district court for First Amendment violations. The court denied its request for an order requiring the university to restore its official status. The CLS appealed to the U.S. Court of Appeals, Seventh Circuit.

The court found it unclear whether the CLS had violated any university policy. **It was likely that the university impermissibly infringed on the CLS's right of expressive association, and its speech rights.** The university failed to identify which federal or state law it believed the CLS had violated. CLS membership requirements did not exclude members on the basis of sexual orientation. Rather, the organization required members to adhere to certain standards of sexual conduct. **The university's affirmative action/EEO policy did not apply to CLS because the organization did not employ anyone.** The court reversed the judgment and granted the CLS its requested order. *Christian Legal Society v. Walker*, 453 F.3d 853 (7th Cir. 2006).

◆ *A New Jersey university with a religious affiliation was exempt from a state law prohibition against discrimination based on sexual orientation.*

An openly gay student asked the university to formally recognize a gay and lesbian student organization. A university student activities committee recommended approval of the organization. The vice president of student affairs denied the request, but offered to work with students to foster a positive, safe and caring community. The student sued the university in a state court under the state Law Against Discrimination (LAD), which prohibits sexual orientation discrimination. The court denied the university's motion to dismiss the case, and it appealed to the New Jersey Superior Court, Appellate Division.

The court considered the university's claim to an exemption from the LAD. **The LAD states that its prohibitions do not apply to any educational facility operated by a bona fide religious or sectarian institution.** The court noted that federal employment law has been used for guidance in developing standards to decide LAD claims. **Courts have held exemptions under Title VII of the Civil Rights Act of 1964 reflect a decision by Congress that religious organizations have a constitutional right to be free from governmental intervention.** The court held the university was entitled to the LAD exemption. It reversed the judgment and dismissed the case. *Romeo v. Seton Hall Univ.*, 875 A.2d 1043 (N.J. Super. Ct. App. Div. 2005).

◆ *A federal district court held a Texas university did not violate a student's speech rights by limiting where he could speak on campus.*

The student wanted to express his religious and political views that "homosexuality is a sinful, immoral, and unhealthy lifestyle" through delivering a speech and passing out literature on campus. The student submitted a request to the university to speak at a location across the street from the student union building. The university denied the request, but allowed him to speak at a different location. The student sued the university in a federal district court for First Amendment violations. To determine what restrictions a university may impose on student speech rights on campus, the U.S. Supreme Court has focused on the "forum," or place of the speech.

While the Supreme Court has found colleges are afforded a certain degree of latitude to control conduct on campus based on the need for order, this must be balanced with the need to protect First Amendment freedoms. **The Supreme Court has held a public university campus resembles a public forum, but this did not mean that students or teachers had absolute rights to use all parts of a campus for unlimited expressive purposes. The university allowed the student to speak about what he wanted at the time he requested, and did not violate his speech rights.** Its decision to limit where he could speak was reasonable, as the student himself admitted. The court held the university did not violate the student's First Amendment right to free speech when it directed him to deliver his speech elsewhere on campus. *Roberts v. Haragan*, 346 F.Supp.2d 853 (N.D. Tex. 2004).

◆ *In the following case, the Supreme Court held that rights to association may not be disregarded or limited.*

A group of students desired to form a local chapter of Students for a Democratic Society (SDS) at a state-supported college. **They were, however, denied recognition as a campus organization.** The students sued for declaratory and injunctive relief. A federal district court held the college's refusal to recognize the group, in light of the disruptive and violent nature of the national organization, was justifiable. The U.S. Court of Appeals for the Second Circuit affirmed, stating that the students had failed to avail themselves of the due process of law accorded to them and had failed to meet their burden of complying with the prevailing standards for recognition.

The U.S. Supreme Court held that **the lower courts erred in disregarding the First Amendment interest in freedom of association that the students**

had in furthering their personal beliefs. It also held that putting the burden on the students (to show entitlement to recognition) rather than on the president (to justify nonrecognition) was also in error. The Court stated that insofar as the denial of recognition was based on the group's affiliation with the national SDS, or as a result of disagreement with the group's philosophy, the president's decision violated the students' First Amendment rights. A proper basis for nonrecognition might have been that the group refused to comply with a rule requiring them to abide by reasonable campus regulations. Since it was not clear that the college had such a rule, and whether the students intended to observe it, the case was remanded to the district court for resolution. *Healy v. James*, 408 U.S. 169, 92 S.Ct. 2338, 33 L.Ed.2d 266 (1972).

B. Commercial Speech

◆   *A student newspaper lost its First Amendment challenge to a Pennsylvania statute sanctioning businesses that advertise alcohol in any school publication.*

The Pitt News filed suit seeking to prevent the enforcement of "Act 199," a 1996 amendment to the state's liquor code that sanctioned advertisers of alcohol products in school newspapers. The U.S. Court of Appeals, Third Circuit, ruled that the newspaper could not sue because it could not demonstrate that its constitutional rights were being violated, and it could not sue on behalf of third parties. **The paper's loss of advertising revenue and subsequent decrease in the length of the publication did not demonstrate that its First Amendment rights were violated.** *The Pitt News v. Fisher*, 215 F.3d 354 (3d Cir. 2000), *cert. denied*, 121 S.Ct. 857 (U.S. 2001).

◆   *A university's radio station did not have to allow the KKK to underwrite a program.*

A not-for-profit public broadcast radio station operated by the University of Missouri (and a member of National Public Radio) received a request from the state coordinator for the Ku Klux Klan to underwrite a number of 15-second spots on the station's "All Things Considered" program. This would require the station to acknowledge the gift by reading a message from the Klan stating that it was a white Christian organization standing up for the rights and values of white Christians and leaving contact information. The university's chancellor decided that allowing the underwriting would result in a loss of revenue to the station of at least $5 million, and rejected the offer. The state coordinator and the Klan sued the station manager, asserting that the station could not reject the offer because it was a public forum, and could not discriminate by viewpoint.

The U.S. District Court for the Eastern District of Missouri held that **the station did not have to accept the Klan's offer to underwrite "All Things Considered." The station's employees had the discretion to choose which underwriting offers to accept, and the underwriting program could not be deemed a public forum.** Further, the decision to reject the offer was not based on viewpoint but on business considerations. The court granted pretrial judgment to the station manager. The Eighth Circuit Court of Appeals affirmed. It noted that the underwriting spots constituted governmental speech and that the government could exercise discretion over what it chose to say. Since the station had the right to reject the proposed spots, the Klan's lawsuit could not succeed. *KKK v. Bennett*, 203 F.3d 1085 (8th Cir. 2000).

◆ *The Supreme Court has held that restrictions on commercial free speech need not be subjected to as rigorous an analysis to determine the restrictions' reasonableness. As long as the restriction is reasonable, it will be upheld.*

The State University of New York (SUNY) prohibited private commercial enterprises from operating in SUNY facilities. Campus police prevented a housewares manufacturer from demonstrating and selling its products at a party hosted in a student dormitory. The manufacturer and a group of students sued SUNY in a federal district court, stating that the policy violated the First Amendment. The court held for SUNY, stating that the student dormitories did not constitute a public forum for purposes of commercial activity, and the restrictions were reasonable in light of the dormitories' purpose. The Second Circuit Court of Appeals reversed, stating that it was unclear whether the policy directly advanced SUNY's interest and whether it was the least restrictive means of achieving that interest. The U.S. Supreme Court granted review and stated that the court of appeals erred in requiring the district court to apply a least restrictive means test. The Court stated that **regulations on commercial speech require only a reasonable "fit" between the government's ends and the means chosen to accomplish those ends.** The Court reversed and remanded the case. *Board of Trustees of the State Univ. of New York v. Fox*, 492 U.S. 469, 109 S.Ct. 3028, 106 L.Ed.2d 388 (1989).

C. Non-Student Groups

◆ *An Indiana university did not violate the First Amendment when it prohibited a traveling evangelist from preaching on its campus.*

Traveling preacher James Gilles appeared in public places and preaching for many years. His confrontational style led to disturbances and he was arrested many times. In 2001, Gilles began preaching at Vincennes University without an invitation to be on the campus. His preaching led to a disturbance, and campus police asked him to leave. Following that incident, the university adopted a new policy requiring prior approval by the dean of students for all sales and solicitations on campus. Approved solicitors could solicit only on a walkway in front of the student union. Gilles sued university officials in a federal district court, claiming the policy violated his right to free speech. The court granted summary judgment against him, and he appealed.

The U.S. Court of Appeals, Seventh Circuit, held **public universities are not required to make all their facilities equally available to students and nonstudents. As owners of public property, public universities have the right to ensure the property is used only for lawfully dedicated purposes.** The university had the right to bar access to any outsider, as long as the exclusion was not based on the content of the speaker's message. In this case, the university had placed the area where Gilles sought to speak completely off limits to those who were not invited by a faculty member or student group. Confining solicitors to the walkway in front of the student union was reasonable. Because the university could lawfully bar uninvited guests from using a particular area to speak, the district court's ruling was affirmed. *Gilles v. Blanchard*, 477 F.3d 466 (7th Cir. 2007).

◆ *An Ohio university did not violate the First Amendment rights of a preacher it excluded from its campus because he was not invited to speak there.*

James Gilles, the traveling preacher who lost *Gilles v. Blanchard*, above, visited Miami University in Ohio and spoke at an outdoor area of the campus. After Gilles and a colleague had spoken for about 45 minutes, a university security officer told them they needed to leave because they did not have permission to speak on campus. Gilles sued university officials in a federal district court for violation of his First and Fourteenth Amendment rights.

The court found the university's speech policy did not impermissibly restrain free expression. **The policy was content-neutral, because it did not discriminate against speakers based on the nature of their speech.** As an institution of higher learning, the university had a significant interest in "protecting the educational experience of its students." **By requiring outside speakers to gain permission to speak from the university or a student group, the university permissibly limited speech to subjects that drew interest from at least one student group.** In light of the educational purpose served by the campus forum, it was permissible for the university to limit access to its campus in this way. Therefore, the policy did not violate Gilles' First Amendment rights. *Gilles v. Hodge*, No. 104-CV-00702, 2007 WL 1202706 (S.D. Ohio 4/20/07).

◆ *A federal district court dismissed a lawsuit filed against a Pennsylvania university by a traveling preacher.*

The preacher came to the university to preach and hand out literature regarding his beliefs on religion and abortion. He was not invited or sponsored, and he failed to comply with a written university policy that required him to register with the university at least two hours in advance. A university official and police chief warned the preacher he could not continue with his activities, but he refused to leave campus. As a result, he was issued a citation for criminal trespass. The preacher sued the university and university officials in a federal district court for violation of his First Amendment rights and his rights to due process and equal protection.

The university then instituted a new, more permissive policy regarding expressive activities on campus. The new policy removed the two-hour registration requirement and allowed non-sponsored presentations and demonstrations as long as they did not "disrupt the normal operation of the university or infringe on the rights of other members of the university community." The court noted the preacher's claims for injunctive and declaratory relief were based on a policy that had been replaced. **Because the new policy provided the preacher all the relief he sought, the court dismissed the case.** *Marcavage v. West Chester Univ.*, No. 06-CV-910, 2007 WL 789430 (E.D. Pa. 3/15/07).

◆   *A North Carolina university's anti-discrimination policy may have violated a Christian fraternity's constitutional rights.*

The university's anti-discrimination policy required all officially recognized student organizations to open their memberships without regard to age, race, color, national origin, religion, disability, veteran status, or sexual orientation. The fraternity notified the university that the policy conflicted with its Christian statement of faith and tenets of belief. The university withdrew the fraternity's official recognition. The fraternity sued the university in a federal district court for violating its constitutional rights to freedom of association and free exercise of religion. The court held the policy might have prohibited the fraternity from excluding members. The university was ordered not to apply the policy. **The court order ensured the university would treat the fraternity like non-religious student organizations which are permitted to limit membership to those who share their beliefs and goals.**

The university published a statement which offered official recognition to student organizations that select their members on the basis of commitment to a set of beliefs. The fraternity received official recognition for the next academic year. The university then filed a motion to dismiss the complaint as moot. The court found the university had made the new policy as public and permanent as possible. As the university should be trusted to abide by the new policy, the case was dismissed. *Alpha Iota Omega Christian Fraternity v. James Moeser*, No. 1:04CV00765, 2006 WL 1286186 (M.D.N.C. 5/4/06).

◆   *The U.S. Supreme Court held a federal law requiring higher education institutions to provide equal access to military recruiters or forfeit certain federal funding did not violate school speech or association rights.*

Congress enacted the Solomon Amendment to address restrictions put on military recruiting by law schools that disagreed with the U.S. government's policy on homosexuals in the military. The amendment disqualified institutions of higher learning from receiving certain federal funds, if any part of an institution denied access to military recruiters that was equal to that provided other recruiters. An association of law schools and faculties sued the U.S. government in a federal district court, asserting the Solomon Amendment violated the schools' First Amendment speech and association rights. The association claimed the amendment unconstitutionally required law schools to choose between federal funding and their speech and association rights. The court denied the association's request for a preliminary order against enforcement of the Amendment. Congress took note of the court's finding that the law could be interpreted as allowing schools to promote non-discrimination policies by limiting military recruiting to undergraduate campuses. It amended the law to require "equal access" for military recruiters. Meanwhile, the association appealed to the U.S. Court of Appeals, Third Circuit. The court held the Solomon Amendment regulated speech, and it reversed the decision. The U.S. Supreme Court agreed to review the case.

The Supreme Court explained that the First Amendment protects rights of association, as well as free speech. The law schools "associated" with military recruiters only in the sense of their interactions with them. The Solomon Amendment forbade higher education institutions from

applying their general non-discrimination policies to military recruiters. Law schools had to provide the military the same access they provided to all other employment recruiters. The broad power of Congress to provide for defense included the authority to require campus access for military recruiters. Congress was free to attach reasonable conditions to federal funding. The Solomon Amendment regulated conduct, not speech. Law schools remained free to express their views on government policy while remaining eligible for federal funds. As there was no restriction on speech, the Amendment did not place unconstitutional conditions on receiving federal funds. The Court held the Solomon Amendment did not force the schools to associate with the military by granting it equal access. A military recruiter's presence on campus did not violate law school association rights. Students and faculty remained free to associate and voice their disapproval of the military's message. The association had exaggerated the reach of prior First Amendment cases. The Court reversed the judgment. *Rumsfeld v. Forum for Academic and Institutional Rights*, 547 U.S. 47 (2006).

◆   *A federal district court held a Colorado university's director violated a pro-life organization's speech rights by preventing the group from handing out leaflets in an area of the campus that was deemed a designated public forum.*

The organization sought to distribute flyers on a major pedestrian route of the campus. The director denied the request, asserting an unwritten university policy allowed him to choose a location for the group's activities. The organization sued the director in a federal district court for speech rights violations. **The court found no legal justification to bar the organization from an area of campus under an unwritten policy.** It stated there may be significant governmental reasons to differentiate between the speech rights of student and non-student groups on campus. However, the director failed to offer valid reasons in this case. The court rejected his request for qualified immunity, finding his actions violated the organization's clearly established First Amendment rights. *Mason v. Wolf*, 356 F.Supp.2d 1147 (D. Colo. 2005).

◆   *A California state university did not violate an anti-abortion group's rights to speech, assembly or religious free exercise by asking group members to leave the campus.*

The group arrived on campus to deliver a pro-life message. None of the group members were students or had any association with the university, and the group did not make any arrangements for their visit. The university office responsible for approving all demonstrations, literature distribution and similar activities on campus allowed the group to hand out literature, but prevented it from displaying posters. The university expressed concern that posters might interfere with and distract from the peacefulness of another event on campus that day. The group displayed signs and police directed members to leave the campus. It later sued the university in a U.S. district court for First Amendment violations. **The court held the group's constitutional rights were not clearly established in this case. University officials reasonably believed the group violated a state penal code provision governing non-students entering a campus to interfere with the peaceful conduct of**

campus activities. The court held the university was protected by qualified immunity and dismissed the case. *Milton v. Serrata*, No. C 03-4541 CRB, 2004 WL 2434941 (N.D. Cal. 2004).

CHAPTER FIVE

Employment

I. BREACH OF CONTRACT

Breach of contract claims arise from written contracts, academic custom and usage, faculty handbooks and reliance on written and oral statements implying or modifying an employment contract.

A. Written Contracts

◆ *A librarian failed to show a Texas university breached its employment contract with her or constructively discharged her from employment.*

The university hired the librarian in 1972 and granted her tenure on the faculty of the library in 1981. Things went smoothly until the university hired a new library director in 1987. The director was not satisfied with the librarian's work performance, and he reassigned some of her duties. In 1993, the director and another official documented the librarian's alleged history of "low quality and quantity of work," rude behavior toward staff and the public, and excessive absenteeism. The director changed the librarian's title, and she complained that he had demoted her. The librarian requested retirement, then sued the university, director and another official in the state court system for breaching her employment contract and constructive discharge. The court held a trial. It refused to instruct the jury to consider the question of breach. Instead, it had the jury focus on constructive discharge. The jury found for the university.

The state court of appeals found that the jury was given improper instructions and reversed the judgment. The university appealed to the Supreme Court of Texas, which reinstated the verdict. Although the librarian claimed she was demoted in breach of her contract, there was no evidence that she ever held any job other than as a tenured librarian. Her contract with the university did not specify any particular job functions. Nor did the librarian show she was constructively discharged from employment. **Constructive discharge does not take place merely because job assignments have changed. Instead, an employee must show she was subjected to unendurable working conditions.** As the librarian did not show this, the court reversed the judgment. *Baylor Univ. v. Coley*, 221 S.W.3d 599 (Tex. 2007).

◆ *The U.S. Court of Appeals, Third Circuit, held a Pennsylvania college did not breach a professor's employment contract by discharging her.*

The college hired the professor to be its Director of Athletics and Professor and Head of Physical Education and Athletics. She continued to work after her initial 2.5 year term and received salary letters advising her of annual increases. The college faculty handbook provided further guidance as to the terms and conditions of employment for faculty members. The college later discharged the professor, stating it believed the athletic department needed new leadership. It notified her a year and a half before the termination was to be effective. Assuming she was tenured, the professor tried to appeal the decision. The college president refused to accept the professor's claim she was tenured. He explained that she had never been tenured, but instead the professor served at the pleasure of the president as stated in her appointment letter. The professor wrote to the president again and requested a hearing before a faculty tenure review appeals committee.

The president denied the request, and the professor sued the college in a federal district court for breach of contract. **The court noted the professor's appointment letter clearly provided that the term of her position is "at the pleasure of the President of the College." This language expressly negated any possibility of tenured status as a faculty member.** The professor argued the words "at the pleasure of the president" referred only to her role as athletics director and department head. The court disagreed. It said the professor's attempt to interpret her letter as stating she was entitled to tenure was an attempt to create ambiguity where there was none. The court found the language was unambiguous and dismissed the case. *Atkinson v. LaFayette College*, 460 F.3d 447 (3rd Cir. 2006).

◆ *A Kentucky state university was immune from liability in a lawsuit filed by an assistant football coach for breach of contract.*

The coach alleged the university hired him for a two-year term, while the university claimed the contract was for one year. After coaching for one year, the coach received a termination notice. He sued the university in a federal district court, alleging it breached his contract, among other things. The university moved for dismissal based on immunity from liability under the Eleventh Amendment. The Eleventh Amendment protects state-funded universities from lawsuits filed in federal courts by individuals. The coach contended governmental immunity does not apply to civil actions that arise out of the operation of a college football program. He said football at this level is a commercial activity and a big business. The court rejected this argument, holding that **lawsuits arising out of athletic programs should not be treated differently from other lawsuits against state universities. The Sixth Circuit has held the Eleventh Amendment bars suits against state university athletic programs.** The court dismissed the case. *English v. Univ. of Hawaii*, No. Civ.A. 3:04-7-JMH, 2005 WL 2456247 (E.D. Ky. 10/5/05).

◆ *A South Carolina faculty member could not sue a university for missing office items after he signed a release agreeing not to file further claims.*

The university suspended the faculty member after a student filed a sexual harassment complaint against him. The faculty member was instructed to leave the campus immediately and was not allowed to return pending a criminal investigation. He left behind several volumes of his private library in his locked office, along with teaching materials, maps, and personal mementos. After the faculty member was acquitted of the criminal charge he sued the university, alleging it wrongfully suspended him. The parties settled the case through mediation. Under the terms of the agreement, the faculty member released the university of any claims arising out of his employment and retained tenure.

The faculty member returned to the university and discovered his property was gone. The university never located the missing items, and he sued it in a state trial court for negligence. The court determined the release was comprehensive and dismissed the action. The faculty member appealed to the state court of appeals. It held **a valid release barred subsequent claims arising from the same circumstances, even if the parties may not have intended to release a specific claim.** The court held the release in this case clearly precluded future claims arising out the faculty member's employment with the university. *Abu-Shawareb v. South Carolina State Univ.*, 613 S.E.2d 757 (S.C. Ct. App. 2004).

◆ *A Colorado state college followed appropriate procedures in terminating an employee's position when it became unable to fund it.*

A certified employee held a classified position under the state personnel system. His position did not receive regular state funding, and when special funding and interim funds were exhausted, the college eliminated it and dismissed him. An administrative law judge held the decision was not arbitrary or an abuse of discretion, and the state personnel board agreed. The employee appealed to the Court of Appeals of Colorado, which stated reorganizations and layoffs involve practical and financial concerns.

There are no credibility determinations to be made in terminating an employee based on a lack of funds. In contrast, disciplinary terminations do require credibility determinations and require the employer to act on the basis of "merit and fairness." The court held the employee lacked a property interest in his abolished position. **Although a public employee has a continued interest in employment, there can be no reasonable expectation that a position will never be abolished**. The human resources manager who processed the layoff complied with a statutory layoff matrix based on classification structure, employment history, performance evaluations, and veteran status. As there was no error in the board's order, the court affirmed it. *Velasquez v. Dep't of Higher Educ.*, 93 P.3d 540 (Colo. Ct. App. 2003).

◆ *A professor who served as a dean under a four-year appointment was properly terminated when the appointment expired.*

A Tennessee state university entered into a contract with a professor for a four-year appointment as Dean of the College of Education. At the end of four years, the professor was terminated and demoted to the rank of tenured professor with a corresponding reduction in pay. He brought an action before the Tennessee Claims Commission, asserting breach of contract and wrongful discharge. The commission ruled that the university had to pay the professor the difference between his salary as a dean and his salary as a professor. However, the Court of Appeals of Tennessee reversed. It found **no evidence that the professor was entitled to continue receiving a dean's salary after his appointment expired**. The contract only provided that he would be entitled to a tenured position. *Emans v. Board of Regents of State of Tennessee*, No. M2000-02187-COA-R3-CV, 2002 WL 31443206 (Tenn. Ct. App. 2002).

◆ *A doctor who signed a non-compete agreement could violate it where he was not harming the university's legitimate business interests.*

A Florida university hospital employed a doctor who signed a non-compete agreement stating that he would not engage in a "community-based clinical practice within a radius of 50 miles" of the university hospital for a two-year period following his employment. After leaving the university, the doctor began working in a community-based clinical practice within 50 miles of the university hospital. The university sued, seeking to enforce the non-compete agreement. The doctor argued that he was not causing irreparable injury to the university hospital's "legitimate business interests" because no former patients of the university hospital followed him to his current practice. A trial court found that the doctor violated the terms of the non-compete agreement but that his new practice did not interfere with the university hospital's legitimate business interests. The Florida District Court of Appeal affirmed. Since **none of the doctor's former patients were receiving treatment from him**, and since his current practice was not attempting to recruit prospective university patients, the court refused to enforce the agreement. *Univ. of Florida, Board of Trustees v. Sanal*, 837 So.2d 512 (Fla. Dist. Ct. App. 2003).

◆ *Despite some procedural irregularities, a board of trustees could vote not to renew a college president's contract.*

A Texas college hired a president under a three-year contract, which contained an option for a three-year extension. Toward the end of the initial term, the board of trustees met by teleconference and voted not to renew the president's contract. He was given notice of the non-renewal in compliance with the terms of his contract. He then sued the college for breach of contract, asserting that the termination notice was invalid because the vote against renewing his contract occurred at a meeting that was not called in compliance with the college's bylaws. A state court granted pretrial judgment to the college, and the Texas Court of Appeals affirmed. Even though the teleconference was called in an irregular manner, that was insufficient to void the board's decision not to renew the president's contract. **Although the board's actions at that meeting were voidable, they could be ratified (and were) at a later meeting.** Further, the president lacked standing to challenge the procedural violations. The president was not able to regain his job. *Swain v. Wiley College*, 74 S.W.3d 143 (Tex. Ct. App. 2002).

◆ *In the absence of approval by University of Louisiana trustees, a coach who sought a promotion to athletic director had no claim against the system.*

The men's basketball coach for Northwestern State University (NSU) also sought the athletic director (AD) position when the AD announced his retirement. The coach was informed of a plan to name him athletic director/head basketball coach. The university president sent a letter to the coach outlining the plan, but noting that it would not be official until approved by the Board of Trustees for the University of Louisiana System. The board never approved the appointment of the coach to the AD position. When the president retired and an acting president was appointed, the acting president initiated a nationwide search for a new AD and invited the coach to apply. The coach instead sued the board for breach of contract and detrimental reliance. A Louisiana trial court ruled in favor of the board, finding no contract existed.

The court determined that since the board of trustees never approved the change in positions, no contract was ever formed. It also rejected the coach's contention that he turned down a job offer to be athletic director at the University of South Alabama because he had been promised the same position at NSU. The only evidence offered in support of this position was a letter from Southern Alabama's AD stating what the contract terms would be if the coach were offered a position. This letter was not a job offer. **Because the coach could not establish a contract or that he relied on a promise made by NSU to his detriment, he failed to establish a case** under state law, and the university was entitled to a judgment in its favor. The trial court decision was affirmed. *Barnett v. Board of Trustees*, 809 So.2d 184 (La. Ct. App. 2001).

◆ *A New Mexico public university was not immune to suit in an action brought under a written contract.*

A tenured professor in pediatric medicine at the University of New Mexico began serving as the director of the division of developmental disabilities under a written contract that provided $5,000 for his administrative duties. After the professor helped the university obtain a grant to establish a center for training and research in developmental disabilities, he became the director of the center and his administrative salary increased to $10,000. A few years later, after a review of the center, the dean of the medical school informed the professor that his directorship would be on probation for the rest of the year. The following year, he was removed as director of the center, and the year after that, his administrative salary returned to $5,000. The professor sued the university for breach of contract, and a state trial court denied the university's claim of governmental immunity. The Supreme Court of New Mexico affirmed that decision, noting that the professor's action against the university was based on a written contract. Since a state statute provided that governmental entities were immune from actions based on unwritten contracts, **the implication was that the government could be sued under valid written contracts.** *Handmaker v. Henney*, 992 P.2d 879 (N.M. 1999).

◆   *A liquidated damages clause was valid as the harm caused by a coach's early departure was difficult to ascertain, and the amount was reasonable.*

After a Vanderbilt University football coach joined another school, a Tennessee federal court awarded Vanderbilt $281,886.43 under the employment contract. The sum included a liquidated damages amount for the two-year time period covered by a contract extension the coach had signed. The coach appealed, alleging that the liquidated damages provision was unenforceable as a penalty and that the contract extension was not binding upon him. The U.S. Court of Appeals, Sixth Circuit, reversed and remanded the case.

The liquidated damages clause was not a penalty and was enforceable. By leaving early, the coach would harm Vanderbilt more than by just the cost of replacing him. However, a question of fact existed as to whether the two-year contract extension was enforceable. Although the coach had signed the contract, he had told the athletic director that the extension would not be "final" until his attorney-brother looked at it. The court remanded the case for a determination as to whether the brother had to approve the contract extension before the coach could be bound by its terms for damages and, if so, whether the brother's failure to object to the contract's language constituted *de facto* approval. *Vanderbilt Univ. v. DiNardo*, 174 F.3d 751 (6th Cir. 1999).

◆   *Transferring a professor to a non-teaching staff position was not a breach of contract where there was no reduction in pay and where the contract called for the professor to teach and/or serve the college.*

A professor employed by a Georgia private art college developed personality conflicts with several colleagues in the video department. His colleagues complained and requested that the college transfer the professor out of the department. The college complied with the request, reassigning the professor to a non-teaching "staff" position in an ancillary video production unit with no reduction in salary. The new position was consistent with his training and experience. The professor wanted to teach but refused to accept the college's offer to place him as a visiting teacher in a county public school system. He filed a lawsuit in a Georgia trial court, alleging breach of contract and seeking damages. The trial court granted pretrial judgment to the professor. The college appealed to the Court of Appeals of Georgia.

The court of appeals held that the professor's contract, which required him to devote his time "to teaching and/or service to the college," recognized the flexibility necessary in the effective administration of a college. The trial court's reliance on the professor's transfer from "faculty" to "staff" as the basis for its ruling was misplaced. **Considering the nature of the new position, as opposed to its classification, the court held that the transfer was not a breach of contract.** *Johnson v. Savannah College of Art*, 460 S.E.2d 308 (Ga. Ct. App. 1995).

◆ *Professors who were contractually entitled to the rank of professor for life were not entitled to lifetime employment where they signed annual contracts.*

Two faculty members at a Pennsylvania private university were promoted to professor in 1965. The contracts provided that "the distinctive rank of professor is an appointment for life." However, the contract also provided that they would receive a salary for the following academic year only. Between 1965 and 1990 both professors entered into similar annual contracts with the university, except that the appointment for life clause was deleted. In 1982, the university modified its retirement policy to make retirement mandatory for tenured faculty members who reached the age of 70. Pursuant to this policy, both professors were retired from active faculty status. The professors challenged the mandatory retirements in court, and the case eventually reached the Superior Court of Pennsylvania.

The university contended that **while the rank of professor was a lifetime rank, employment as a member of the faculty was year by year.** The superior court agreed, noting that employment relationships are generally terminable at will. In holding for the university, the superior court noted its reluctance to interpret employment contracts as guaranteeing employment for life. Rather, it gave effect to the intent of the parties as reasonably manifested by the language of their written agreement. Here, the language of the contract clearly entitled the professors to retain their rank for the remainder of their life. However, the faculty members were not guaranteed employment for life. The duration of each employment contract was for a period of one academic year only. *Halpin v. LaSalle Univ.*, 639 A.2d 37 (Pa. Super. Ct. 1994).

B. Handbooks

◆ *Two California professors were entitled to a trial to consider if a Christian college discharged them based on marital status.*

The professors taught in the marriage and family counseling department of the college, which was affiliated with the Church of Christ. The church looked to the Bible as its ultimate constitution and required professors to accept the Bible as the word of God. The professors' teaching contracts indicated they were to comply with the faculty handbook. The handbook also stated that faculty members should conduct their on- and off-campus activities and relationships in a Christ-like manner. One of the professors filed for divorce, and a rumor circulated that he was having an affair with the other professor. The dean asked the divorcing professor to step down from his chair position but allowed him to keep teaching. When the professors announced their wedding, the college refused to renew their teaching contracts.

Both professors sued the college in a state court, alleging discrimination on the basis of marital status and breach of their continuing contracts. The court denied the college's request for summary judgment. **The college appealed to** the California Court of Appeal, arguing it was entitled to the "ministerial exception," which allows religious institutions to enjoy immunity from examination into religious doctrine. The college argued it fired the professors for violating a rule prohibiting married co-workers from making up one department, not because of their marital status. The court found no evidence that the college cared about the professors' marital status. It showed concern only for whether the professors were perceived to be committing adultery. The court said the claim was based on a contract, not marital status discrimination. It held the trial court had to further consider whether the professors fell within the ministerial exception. *Hope Univ. v. Superior Court*, 119 Cal.App.4th 719, 14 Cal.Rptr.3d 643 (Cal. Ct. App. 2004).

◆ *A college that failed to provide a professor with written evaluations as required by the faculty handbook did not have to renew his contract.*

A private college in New York employed an untenured probationary assistant professor in its accounting department under a series of one-year contracts. The faculty handbook called for written evaluations to be provided each teacher, but the college failed to provide them. After the professor organized and participated in a student protest aimed at the accounting department's curriculum, the college sent him a letter along with his proposed contract notifying him that upon expiration of the contract, it would not be renewed. The letter indicated that **the basis for non-renewal was the impaired collegiality and confidence between the professor and the accounting department**. He signed the one-year, non-renewable contract that accompanied the letter and became unemployed at the end of the year.

The professor sued the college for breach of contract in a state trial court where pretrial judgment was granted to the college. The New York Supreme Court, Appellate Division, affirmed the lower court decision in favor of the college. It noted that the non-renewal of the professor's contract was solely related to his failure to get along with his colleagues and was not related to his teaching skills, which the college conceded were excellent. Also, even though the college failed to provide written evaluations as called for in the faculty handbook, **there was no duty to automatically renew the professor's contract if he was found to be an excellent teacher**. The college's decision not to renew the professor's contract did not amount to breach of contract. *DeSimone v. Siena College*, 663 N.Y.S.2d 701 (N.Y. App. Div. 1997).

◆ *Where a professor maintained that a handbook created a contract, and that the university breached that contract, her claim failed because the university followed the procedures outlined in it.*

A private Iowa university hired a part-time lecturer into a faculty position under a one-year contract and told that she would be evaluated annually. She received excellent reviews and eventually became a tenure track professor. Before becoming eligible for tenure, the professor began to have difficulties with the art department's new chairperson concerning the submission of her work for review as part of her annual evaluation. The professor objected to the lack of stated criteria and noted that her graphic design work, often created in a commercial setting, did not easily fit into the category "scholarly and artistic development." The chairperson found her work insufficient in this area. After three more annual appointments she was fired. She challenged this decision before an academic committee, stating she was denied her procedural rights, but the committee disagreed. The professor sued the university for breach of contract, and the case reached the Supreme Court of Iowa.

The court found that although the professor was employed under a series of one-year contracts, she was more than an at-will employee. **In order for the professor to prove that her faculty handbook was an enforceable employment contract, she had to show that it was sufficiently definite in its terms to create an offer, that it was communicated and accepted by her so as to create acceptance and that she continued working, so as to provide consideration.** The court found that here, **the handbook created an enforceable contract but also found that the university did not breach that contract.** The handbook did not state that any particular criteria should be used to evaluate the professor's work and it did not allow her to demand that the university use more or different criteria than what was currently used. Furthermore, **all the grievance procedures described in the handbook were given to the professor.** She was given adequate warning, told she could remedy the situation by providing sufficient documentation of her commercial work and given full access to the appeals process. *Taggart v. Drake Univ.*, 549 N.W.2d 796 (Iowa 1996).

◆   *Where a college failed to follow procedures in a handbook on achieving tenure, it was required to conduct another tenure review.*

A New York private college hired an art history professor for a newly created tenure track position. According to the faculty manual, once a professor was hired, consideration for tenure was governed by procedures set forth in the manual. The evaluation subcommittee and the advisory committee recommended that tenure be granted. However, the dean gave a negative recommendation based on declining enrollment in art history courses. During the tenure review, the president's participation was limited to his consultation with the dean in contravention of express provisions in the faculty manual. The board of trustees voted to deny tenure to the professor. A New York trial court vacated the denial and directed the college to conduct another tenure review.

The college appealed. The New York Supreme Court, Appellate Division, held the college had failed to follow its own procedures in conducting the professor's tenure review. **The college did not adhere to the process set forth in the faculty manual** insofar as that process contemplated an active role for the president of the college. The court also held that the college had failed to apply its own substantive criteria in evaluating the professor for tenure. Student involvement, the crucial factor in the dean's negative recommendation, was not among the enumerated criteria in the faculty manual. While enrollment could be an appropriate consideration in the decision whether to create or continue a tenure-track position, it was not an appropriate consideration in the tenure review of a particular faculty member. The appellate division court affirmed the order requiring the college to conduct another tenure review. *Bennett v. Wells College*, 641 N.Y.S.2d 929 (N.Y. App. Div. 1996).

C. AAUP Guidelines

◆ *A university followed the proper procedures when it fired a professor for sexual harassment.*

A tenured anthropology professor at Baylor University took several students on a university-sponsored academic field trip to Guatemala. While there, he engaged in inappropriate sexual contact with female students and made crude sexual remarks to them. A student reported his conduct to university officials upon returning, and an investigation found the student's accusations to be true. When the professor refused to accept a demotion and mandated counseling, a hearing was conducted, after which the tenure committee recommended the professor's termination.

The president fired the professor, who sued for breach of contract and defamation. A jury found the university breached its contract with the professor, but the Texas Court of Appeals reversed. The inclusion of an American Association of University Professors (AAUP) statement in the employment manual did not mean that the manual incorporated the AAUP's termination procedures. **The university had clearly set forth its termination procedures and followed them in this case.** The professor received written notice of the charges against him and had an opportunity to challenge the evidence and confront witnesses at the hearing. The termination was upheld. *Fox v. Parker*, 98 S.W.3d 713 (Tex. Ct. App. 2003).

◆ *A professor could not use the American Association of University Professors (AAUP) guidelines, which had been incorporated into his contract, to modify the intent of the contract.*

A professor and a New Jersey private university entered into five separate employment contracts, each of which incorporated the terms of the university's collective bargaining agreement with the AAUP guidelines. However, the professor's applications for tenure were denied due to his lack of a doctorate degree and his failure to publish. His contract for a sixth academic year stated that his associate professor position was a "non-tenured position." In the following year, he was appointed as an associate dean but continued to teach three credits per semester without additional compensation. He was fired several years later because his overall performance was found to be "significantly below expectations." The professor filed a lawsuit in a New Jersey superior court, alleging that he had acquired *de facto* tenure under the provisions of the AAUP contract. The AAUP contract required that faculty members who had taught for 14 continuous academic semesters be granted tenure. The superior court held for the university, and the professor appealed.

A state appellate division court noted that **the provision requiring tenure for faculty members teaching 14 continuous semesters was a subsidiary provision that should not be interpreted so as to conflict with the principal purpose of the contract**. The court rejected the professor's disproportionate emphasis on the provision to support his tenure claim. The interpretation of the probationary appointments provision urged by the professor unlawfully conflicted with the principal purpose of the university's formal tenure policy, which placed substantive and procedural prerequisites on the acquisition of tenure. The superior court ruling was affirmed. *Healy v. Fairleigh Dickinson Univ.*, 671 A.2d 182 (N.J. Super. Ct. App. Div. 1996).

◆ *Where a part of the AAUP guidelines was excluded from an employment contract, the university did not have to follow the procedures listed in that part.*

A private Louisiana university dismissed a tenured professor for alleged professional incompetence. She sued the university for reinstatement of tenure and employment. She argued that the university, after agreeing to modify her existing employment contract, failed to apply Paragraph Seven of the AAUP guidelines, which provide procedures for the termination of a tenured professor. The trial court held that the college had no obligation to comply with Paragraph Seven, and the professor appealed to the state court of appeal.

On appeal, the professor argued Paragraph Seven of the AAUP guidelines was an implied provision in her employment contract. Her contract incorporated the provisions listed in the university's faculty handbook, which provided procedures for the termination of faculty appointments. The appellate court held that **the faculty handbook and the contract clearly excluded Paragraph Seven of the AAUP guidelines. As a result, the paragraph did not apply to any procedures established by the university for the termination of tenured professors.** The court further stated that there was no merit to the professor's argument that the college agreed to modify her original employment contract. The court affirmed the trial court's decision. *Olivier v. Xavier Univ.*, 553 So.2d 1004 (La. Ct. App. 1989).

◆ *A seminary breached a professor's employment contract by refusing to follow its own regulations.*

The executive committee of a seminary's board of trustees ordered the president of the seminary to reduce the budget by at least $50,000. As a result, a 62-year-old tenured faculty member, who had taught there for 31 years, was fired. The faculty member sued for breach of contract. The seminary agreed that the contract was subject to the AAUP Recommended Institutional Regulations on Academic Freedom and Tenure. This document, along with the faculty promotion and tenure policy of the seminary, contained provisions governing the firing of a tenured faculty member.

The seminary claimed that the document did not require it to allow the fired teacher to participate in "any way at any stage" of the proceedings. The court observed, however, that **the regulations required any faculty member facing termination to be allowed to participate in the dismissal proceedings before a faculty group and the governing board**. It noted that without an opportunity to be heard, the faculty member had no opportunity to have pertinent issues reviewed and discussed in a meaningful way. The court therefore ruled that the seminary failed to follow its own regulations since the language of the document clearly expressed that an aggrieved faculty member had a "contractual right to request a review of his termination." In this case, the discharged faculty member was denied that opportunity, which meant that the seminary had breached his contract. *Linn v. Andover-Newton Theological School*, 638 F.Supp. 1114 (D. Mass. 1986).

◆ *The AAUP guidelines were held not to apply in a case where teachers' contracts were not terminated but rather not renewed.*

Three teachers were employed at Talladega College under employment contracts with a term of one year from August 1984 to August 1985. In May 1985, each received a letter from the college president notifying them that their employment with the college would end in August 1985. The teachers sued the college in an Alabama circuit court for breach of contract. The court ruled for the college, and the teachers appealed to the Alabama Supreme Court. They claimed that the *Procedural Standards in Faculty Dismissal Proceedings* published by the AAUP were incorporated within their employment contracts. The teachers filed a breach of contract and wrongful termination lawsuit, alleging that the AAUP standards favored them because the standards applied to any untenured teacher "whose term appointment has not expired."

The state supreme court stated that although the AAUP standards were neither expressly nor impliedly a part of the teachers' contracts, it would apply the standards for purposes of the appeal. The court concluded that the title of the publication and the publication's provisions indicated that the standards applied only to dismissals of college faculty members. **The standards did not apply here since the teachers' contracts were not cancelled prior to their completion.** The teachers completed their performance through August 1985 and were paid for the entire term. They had no valid claims since they were not dismissed but rather were simply not reemployed for the next year. One of the teachers claimed that he had achieved *de facto* tenure status since he had been employed for more than seven years. The court disagreed, noting that the faculty handbook required that permanent tenure be extended only to persons specifically elected by the board of trustees and that the "acquisition of tenure ... is not automatic after seven years of teaching..." The decision in favor of the college was affirmed. *Hill v. Talladega College*, 502 So.2d 735 (Ala. 1987).

D. Implied Contracts

◆ *The U.S. Court of Appeals, Ninth Circuit, held against an instructor who sued an Oregon community college for misrepresentation.*

The instructor was offered a contract and was assured his position was "as official as it gets." Based on these assurances, he resigned from a prior tenured teaching position. Because of budget shortfalls, the college president refused to recommend the approval of his contract and the board declined to do so. The college then claimed the contract was not binding without board approval and denied the instructor the secure position he originally had been offered.

The instructor sued the college in a federal district court. **The case reached the Ninth Circuit, which held he could not show the type of justifiable reliance required to establish a claim for misrepresentation.** It then granted a petition for a rehearing. After the rehearing, the Ninth Circuit found the instructor again did not show he justifiably relied on representations. Without the board's approval, no offer was within the community college's powers. *Oja v. Blue Mountain Community College*, 184 Fed.Appx. 597 (9th Cir. 2006).

♦   *A Texas university did not breach an oral contract by firing a volleyball coach who claimed he was told he could work there until he retired.*

The university athletic director told the coach he could work there until he retired if he ran a clean program and treated his players appropriately. The university then joined the Big 12 Athletic Conference, and the athletic director told the coaches they had to strengthen and develop their programs to be competitive in the new conference. The volleyball coach scheduled tougher opponents, and the team's win-loss record took a dive. The university fired the coach and he sued it in a state court for breach of contract. The university argued the case should be dismissed because there was never a written contract. The court agreed and awarded summary judgment to the university. The Court of Appeals of Texas affirmed the judgment. **The contract claim was barred by the statute of frauds, a common law rule that requires indefinite term employment contracts to be in writing.** *Sonnichsen v. Baylor Univ.*, No. 10-02-00125-CV, 2004 WL 1903418 (Tex. Ct. App. 2004).

♦   *The Court of Appeals of Wisconsin held Ripon College did not misrepresent information to an applicant for an assistant professor position.*

A college vice-president interviewed the applicant, who asked him about the college's financial condition. The vice-president described the college's endowment, and discussed past and present student enrollment numbers. He told the applicant that the college intended to raise faculty salaries so it could better compete with comparable institutions. The applicant turned down a higher-paying offer from another institution and accepted the job at the college.

The college eliminated the applicant's position at the end of an academic year, and she sued the college in a Wisconsin trial court for misrepresentation. The court awarded judgment to the college and the applicant appealed. The state court of appeals found the information disclosed to the applicant during her interview, including its intention to increase salaries, was true. **The court found she was asking the court to impose a duty on the college to provide her with predictions, not facts. Failure to offer predictions is not a misrepresentation.** As the college had no duty to predict future economic events, the court affirmed the judgment. *Bellon v. Ripon College*, 278 Wis.2d 790, 693 N.W.2d 330 (Wis. Ct. App. 2005).

♦   *A private New Jersey college did not breach its employment contract with an employee by firing her without a hearing for not revealing a criminal matter.*

The college hired the employee as its director of graduate programs. She did not reveal that she and her husband were defending federal criminal charges of embezzling over $1 million in employee pension and profit-sharing funds from a previous venture. The college learned of the employee's indictment and guilty plea and suggested she resign. The employee agreed to resign but then changed her mind. The college stated it could discharge her without a hearing or other due process protections because she was an at-will employee. The employee sued the university in a U.S. district court for breach of contract.

The court dismissed the case, finding the employee was not a full-time faculty member and that there was no employment contract. The professor appealed to the U.S. Court of Appeals, Third Circuit. **Under New Jersey law,**

the professor was an employee at-will unless she presented evidence to show the parties intended to renew a fixed term contract. As she did not submit such evidence, the court held she was an employee at-will. The college was not obligated to offer the professor due process when it terminated her employment. Since there was no employment contract at the time of the alleged breach, the court affirmed the judgment. *Fanelli v. Centenary College*, 112 Fed.Appx. 210 (3d Cir. 2004).

◆   *The Supreme Court of New Hampshire upheld a jury verdict which found that reappointment letters created an employment contract.*

A New Hampshire college audio-visual director worked for 11 years under annual reappointment letters describing terms such as his salary, employment period and duties. The college discharged the director prior to the end of the term of a reappointment letter. He sued the college for breach of contract in the state court system, alleging termination without good cause. The case went to trial, which resulted in a verdict for the director. The court denied the college's motion for a directed verdict. The college appealed to the state supreme court. It reviewed the terms of the reappointment letters and held a reasonable jury could find they constituted an employment contract. The fact that they stated 12-month terms was persuasive evidence that the director was not an "at-will" employee. The reappointment rights section of the College Handbook stated employees could be disciplined for just cause. The court held a reasonable jury could find the college was obligated to follow this provision. Since there was sufficient evidence for a jury to find an employment contract existed, the denial of a directed verdict was not an abuse of discretion. The jury verdict was upheld. *Dillman v. New Hampshire College*, 838 A.2d 1274 (N.H. 2003).

◆   *An Alabama coach who relied on an athletic director's (AD's) invalid commitment to a two-year position was entitled to compensatory damages.*

When the Savannah State University head basketball coach expressed reservations about taking a one-year position with Alabama State University (ASU), the ASU AD advised him by letter that if he was not appointed head coach for a second season, he could be assured a position as first assistant coach. The coach then quit his job and moved his family to Alabama. The AD had made the commitment without securing approval from ASU's president, who had sole authority to bind the university in employment matters. The president rejected the assurance and told the AD to inform the coach that he only had a one-year contract. The AD waited until after the 1995–96 season to reveal to the coach his true status. The coach was not hired permanently. He sued ASU and various officials in a state trial court. Citing statutory immunity, the court dismissed all the claims, except those brought against the AD.

After a jury sided with the coach and awarded him compensatory and punitive damages, the AD appealed to the Alabama Supreme Court. The AD argued that the coach had failed to prove the elements of promissory fraud. He also questioned whether the coach had proven that the AD had intentionally deceived him. The court noted that **the jury had evidence from which it could find that the AD, knowing his lack of authority and knowing the coach's insistence upon a term of more than one year, made an offer that exceeded**

his authority. Further, the AD was not entitled to state-agent immunity because his misrepresentations were willful, malicious, fraudulent or in bad faith. The court upheld the compensatory damage award, noting the coach's lost income, mental anguish and mounting debts, all arising from the fact that he left his Georgia position to take the ASU job, and once terminated, was unable to find suitable work in Alabama. The court, however, reversed the award of punitive damages. The coach was ordered to give back the punitive damage portion of the award; if he refused, the court would reverse the entire award and order a new trial. *Williams v. Williams*, 786 So.2d 477 (Ala. 2000).

II. EMPLOYEE MISCONDUCT

Employee misconduct includes a variety of actions such as inappropriate, unethical, or criminal behavior. In addressing such actions, educational institutions may be bound by faculty handbooks or requirements for hearings.

◆ *A Kansas court held a campus police officer's conduct was improper, but did not constitute gross misconduct or conduct unbecoming an officer.*

A Kansas university police officer stopped a student for speeding. Most of the stop was recorded by an in-car video camera. The student became greatly upset when the officer ran a license check and said her license was suspended. The officer then turned off the camera. His written report stated he informed the student her license was suspended, issued her a citation, noted her car was legally parked, and suggested that a friend drive her car away. The police department investigated to determine what happened after he turned off the camera. The student claimed the officer said she could park her car in front of her apartment herself. After the investigation, the university dismissed the officer for falsifying his incident report and violating the in-car video policy. An administrative tribunal upheld the action, finding his actions were "gross misconduct or conduct unbecoming a state officer or employee."

A Kansas state court upheld the discharge, and the officer appealed. The Court of Appeals of Kansas stated that to prove "intentional" conduct, there had to be evidence he willfully concealed wrongdoing. Under the state employment securities law, **"gross misconduct" was "conduct evincing extreme willful or wanton misconduct." In order for misconduct to be "gross," "it must be aggravated, extreme, or wanton in nature, evincing a knowing and reckless disregard for the rules, policies, or other standards of appropriate behavior."** The court held that while the officer's report was inaccurate, the evidence was insufficient to support a finding of intentional falsification of a police report. His deactivation of the camera was a technical violation that did not constitute gross misconduct. The court reversed the judgment and ordered the officer to be reinstated with back pay and benefits. *Jones v. Kansas State Univ.*, 81 P.3d 1243 (Kan. Ct. App. 2004).

◆ *An Ohio university had good reason to discharge an employee who disclosed private information about a student to a newspaper reporter.*

The employee was a program assistant in a research and graduate studies program. When she started work there, she received a letter from the university explaining she must ensure the confidentiality of sensitive and protected record information. The assistant also received a copy of the university's policy for retaining and disseminating student information. She signed an agreement acknowledging she was familiar with the university's policies on student education records. The agreement stated employees who violated its terms might be reprimanded, suspended, dismissed or subjected to other disciplinary action. A student who was a candidate for student government participated in the program. The campus newspaper published a story listing grade averages of student candidates. It reported the student's GPA as 2.92. The assistant contacted the newspaper to tell them this was incorrect, and revealed that the student's correct GPA was 2.68. The newspaper printed a story with the headline "KSU staff member claims candidate lied about GPA." The student sued the university for disclosing her GPA. After providing a full hearing procedure, the university discharged the assistant for violating the agreement.

The assistant sued the university in the state court system. The case reached the Court of Appeals of Ohio. **The court held the assistant's good reputation did not outweigh the harm she caused by knowingly disclosing confidential student information.** A good reputation could not mitigate intentional acts and their consequences. The assistant argued that as a secretarial staff member, she could not be expected to comply with a federal law – which is "at best confusing for lawyers." The court of appeals disagreed. **The order of removal stated she was removed for violating her agreement, not for violating federal law.** As the assistant knew she was violating her agreement, the court affirmed the judgment. *Swigart v. Kent State Univ.*, No. 2004-P-0037, 2005 WL 1077176 (Ohio Ct. App. 5/6/05).

◆ *A North Dakota instructor failed to counter a college's evidence that there was adequate cause to fire her for neglect of duties and incompetence.*

Bismarck State College (BSC) notified a tenured commercial art instructor it intended to dismiss her for disclosing a student's confidential information to a classroom of students. BSC alleged the disclosure violated state higher education board policy and federal law and demanded she apologize to the student. BSC later found the instructor's apology inappropriate and told her it considered her behavior to be a neglect of duty. She challenged the sufficiency of this notice. BSC amended the notice to include charges of neglecting teaching responsibilities by ending a class a month early and failing to clean up her classrooms. It also alleged incompetent teaching, an inappropriate pattern of behavior and incompetence. BSC then fired the instructor for cause. An administrative law judge upheld the dismissal and a state district court affirmed the decision, granting BSC's motion for summary judgment.

The Supreme Court of North Dakota found the trial court had properly ordered summary judgment on the instructor's breach of employment contract claim. She failed to present any facts to show why a jury would not have found adequate cause to fire her. The instructor presented no facts to support her wrongful termination and conspiracy charges, and the order for summary judgment was affirmed. *Peterson v. North Dakota Univ. System*, 678 N.W.2d (N.D. 2004).

◆ *An Idaho State University accountant was properly fired for misconduct that amounted to insubordination.*

The accountant received satisfactory performance reviews until she got a new boss, who became more critical. After an argument with her supervisor, she was given a written reprimand for refusing to accept a reasonable assignment (insubordination and conduct unbecoming a state employee). While on a medical leave, she made a threatening phone call to a university medical clinic and was issued a second written reprimand. She later raised a commotion in the financial services office and exhibited contumacious behavior at a grievance meeting, which led her supervisor to recommend termination. She challenged the dismissal, and the case made its way to the Idaho Supreme Court, which upheld it. Here, **the record established four incidents of misconduct that supported the decision to let her go.** *Horne v. Idaho State Univ.,* 69 P.3d 120 (Idaho 2003).

◆ *A professor was fired for assaulting his department chair and not for complaining about the university's smoking policy.*

A Texas state university hired an associate professor who soon complained about the university's lack of a no-smoking policy. Over the next two years, he continued to complain about the policy even though the university agreed to designate certain areas as smoke-free zones. The university continued to renew his contract but refused to do so in the third year after he pushed his department chairman and engaged in other misconduct. He sued the university for violating the Texas Whistleblower Protection Act, but a state court ruled against him. The Texas Court of Appeals affirmed, noting that **there was insufficient evidence that the professor was fired for his complaints about the smoking policy.** It was not until after he assaulted the department chair that he was fired. *Ginn v. Stephen F. Austin State Univ.,* No. 03-02-00443-CV, 2003 WL 1882264 (Tex. Ct. App. 2003).

◆ *A professor's good-faith refusal to turn over student grades to her supervisor was not insubordination.*

A tenured associate professor refused to comply with her supervisor's request to turn over student grades to evaluate the professor's program. She asserted the student handbook's privacy policy permitted only the registrar to release grades and that no other department could release them without written student consent. The supervisor then issued the professor a written reprimand. An administrative law judge (ALJ) upheld the reprimand, finding her refusal to comply with the request amounted to insubordination because compliance would not threaten her health or safety.

A state court affirmed the ALJ's decision. The West Virginia Supreme Court of Appeals held **the professor was not insubordinate because the privacy policy was ambiguous, and she reasonably believed the request was invalid.** As a result, she had a good-faith belief that she should not comply. The court ordered the reprimand to be expunged from her personnel file. *Butts v. Higher Educ. Interim Governing Board/Shepard College,* 569 S.E.2d 456 (W.Va. 2002).

◆ *Where an employee refused to discuss matters relating to a grievance she had filed, she could not be discharged for insubordination.*

An administrative employee and her supervisor at the University of Alaska did not get along. The supervisor delivered a memorandum to the employee requiring her to meet regarding problems in the office. The employee attended the meeting. The supervisor then delivered a second memorandum which gave the employee three months to improve her performance and which required a written response. The employee notified her supervisor that the information contained in the second memorandum was inaccurate and that she was going to file a grievance. She then refused to discuss any matters relating to the grievance. The next day, the supervisor delivered a third memorandum, which placed the employee on unpaid leave and scheduled a pre-termination hearing. After the hearing, the employee was discharged. She sought a review of the decision, and the case reached the Supreme Court of Alaska.

The supreme court found insufficient evidence that the employee had been insubordinate so as to justify her discharge. She had provided a written response to the second memorandum in the form of a grievance letter, and **her refusal to talk with her supervisor about matters relating to the grievance was not insubordination.** Further, even if, as the university contended, the employee refused to communicate at all with her supervisor, that refusal resulted from an ambiguous and unclear order. **As the employee reasonably believed the supervisor was asking her to discuss grievance-related matters, she was entitled to refuse to do so.** The court found the termination unjustified. *Nyberg v. Univ. of Alaska*, 954 P.2d 1376 (Alaska 1998).

III. TENURE AND PROMOTION DENIALS

State tenure laws create property rights in public employment that vest school employees with certain procedural rights. Tenured employees are typically entitled to notice and an opportunity to respond to the charges, a hearing with the right to confront and cross-examine witnesses, and the right to be represented by counsel. These and related procedural protections are referred to as due process rights.

A. Supreme Court Decisions

◆ Board of Regents v. Roth, *408 U.S. 564 (1972) and* Perry v. Sindermann, *408 U.S. 593 (1972), help define employee due process rights.*

Roth and *Sindermann* emphasize, first, that there must be an independent source for a liberty or property interest to exist. Such interests are not created by the Constitution, but arise by employment contract or by operation of state tenure laws. Second, if a liberty or property interest is not established, no requirement of due process exists under the Fourteenth Amendment. Third, **if a teacher possesses a liberty or property interest in employment, then due process is required and the teacher may not be dismissed without a hearing.** A tenured teacher, or an untenured teacher during the term of his or her contract, possesses a property interest in continued employment. An untenured teacher who is not rehired after expiration of his or her contract is entitled to a due process hearing if the decision not to rehire is accompanied by a finding of incompetence or immorality, because the teacher's liberty of employment would be impaired by such a finding. However, probationary employees or at-will employees generally do not enjoy due process protections.

The *Roth* case explained that **in order for a teacher to be entitled to due process, the teacher must have a "liberty" or "property" interest at stake.** The teacher in *Roth* was hired at a Wisconsin university for a fixed contract term of one year. At the end of the year, he was informed that he would not be rehired. No hearing was provided and no reason was given for the decision. In dismissing the teacher's due process claims, the Supreme Court stated that no liberty interest was implicated. In declining to rehire the teacher, the university made no charge against him such as incompetence or immorality. Such a charge would have made it difficult for the teacher to gain employment elsewhere and thus would have deprived him of liberty. As no reason was given for the nonrenewal of his contract, the teacher's liberty interest in future employment was not impaired and he was not entitled to a hearing on these grounds.

The Court declared that because the teacher had not acquired tenure he possessed no property interest in continued employment at the university. To be sure, the teacher had a property interest in employment during the term of his one-year contract, but upon its expiration the teacher's property interest ceased to exist. The Court stated: **"To have a property interest in a benefit, a person clearly must have more than an abstract need or desire for it. He must have more than a unilateral expectation of it. He must, instead, have a legitimate claim of entitlement to it."** *Board of Regents v. Roth*, 408 U.S. 564, 92 S.Ct. 2701, 33 L.Ed.2d 548 (1972).

◆   The *Sindermann* case involved a teacher employed at a Texas university for four years under a series of one-year contracts. When he was not rehired for a fifth year, he brought suit contending that due process required a dismissal hearing. The Supreme Court held that "a person's interest in a benefit is a 'property' interest for due process purposes if there are such rules and mutually explicit understandings that support his claim of entitlement to the benefit that he may invoke at a hearing." Because the teacher had been employed at the university for four years, the Court felt that he may have acquired a protectable property interest in continued employment. The case was remanded to the trial court to determine whether there was an unwritten "common law" of tenure at the university. If so, the teacher would be entitled to a dismissal hearing. *Perry v. Sindermann*, 408 U.S. 593, 92 S.Ct. 2694, 33 L.Ed.2d 570 (1972).

B. Claims of Discrimination

◆   *The Supreme Court of Rhode Island refused to overturn a $455,000 jury verdict for a professor who was denied tenure for unlawful reasons.*

After serving in the engineering division for three years, the professor had a falling out with the division's director of undergraduate programs over a grading controversy. The professor eventually changed the grades under protest, but his relationship with the director remained sour. The director asked the professor to interview a minority candidate for a vacant position. The professor claimed the director's secretary told him the interview was being conducted for "some affirmative action considerations." The professor refused to conduct the interview, saying he was concerned it might be illegal to interview a candidate for a job that had already been set aside for someone else.

The professor was subsequently denied tenure, and after his internal grievance was denied, he sued the university in a state court. He claimed the university tolerated and condoned an ethnically hostile work environment and that the director retaliated against him for opposing discriminatory practices. The director further said he was denied tenure based on his national origin. A jury sided with the professor with respect to his retaliation claim and awarded him $400,000 in back pay, $175,000 in compensatory damages and $100,000 in punitive damages. The university appealed. **The state supreme court upheld the verdict with respect to the retaliation claim. Although a rational jury could have reached a contrary verdict, there was enough evidence to support the conclusion that tenure was denied because the professor opposed the university's hiring practices.** The jury was entitled to credit the professor's testimony over that of the university's witnesses. Moreover, the proximity between his refusal to participate in the interview and the denial of tenure supported his retaliation claim. *Shoucair v. Brown Univ.*, 917 A.2d 418 (R.I. 2007).

◆   *An Ohio university did not breach its employment contract when it fired a medical department professor who was a native of India.*

The professor worked in the department of psychiatry under a one-year, non-tenured contract. The university renewed his contract for a second year, when it also hired a new department chair. The professor alleged the chair disliked him because he was Indian. At the end of the year, the chair notified him his contract would not be renewed. A university grievance committee found the non-renewal decision was not motivated by discrimination or personal animosity. The professor sued the university in a state court for breach of contract and intentional infliction of emotional distress. He added claims against the department chair for intentional infliction of emotional distress.

The court granted summary judgment to the university and chair, and the professor appealed. **The Court of Appeals of Ohio held that all employment in the state is "at-will" so that either party may sever the employment relationship at any time and for any reason. The renewal of an untenured professor is discretionary.** Since the professor had not published or applied for funding for the past two years, he failed to fulfill his contract performance requirements. The university had a legitimate reason not to renew his contract. The court affirmed the judgment, rejecting the professor's claims for intentional infliction of emotional distress against the university and chair as they did not engage in outrageous conduct. *Adityanjee v. Case Western Reserve Univ.*, 806 N.E.2d 583 (Ohio Ct. App. 2004).

◆   *A female professor who failed to meet publishing requirements for tenure candidates could not succeed on her sex discrimination claim.*

An Indiana university hired an assistant professor for the anatomy department at its medical school. Her tenure track required her to demonstrate proficiency in three areas: research, teaching and service. In order to meet the research standards, she had to publish one-to-two peer-reviewed research papers per year and be listed as either the first or a senior author. After three years, the promotion and tenure committee admonished her for her low publishing rate. When she submitted her candidacy for tenure, she had published only five peer-reviewed papers – only once as a senior author and never as the first author. The anatomy department denied tenure, and she sued for gender discrimination. A federal court ruled for the university, and the Seventh Circuit affirmed. Here, **the professor was unable to show that less qualified male candidates had been awarded tenure** because the males with similar publishing rates had received tenure under less stringent standards. Their departments did not have the same publishing standards. *Lim v. Trustees of Indiana Univ.*, 297 F.3d 575 (7th Cir. 2002).

◆ *A professor from the University of Redlands lost her discrimination case because she failed to prove she was denied tenure because she is Jewish.*

A professor in the university's art department applied for tenure in 1995. The Faculty Review Committee subsequently denied her tenure. An appeals committee recommended tenure, but the university president ultimately decided not to grant tenure, advising her to apply the next year. Once again, she was denied tenure. The appeals committee concluded her review was not fair because the dean may have been prejudiced against her. It recommended she be allowed to reapply in three years. The president upheld the denial and rejected the committee's recommendation to allow the professor to reapply, finding no prejudice by the dean. As a result, the professor sued the university for breach of implied contract, breach of implied covenant of good faith and fair dealing, fraud, and religious discrimination. A state superior court ruled for the university.

The professor appealed, contending that the university's proffered reasons for the denial were merely pretextual. The California Court of Appeal concluded that the denial of tenure was not related to the fact that the professor was Jewish, it was due to academic politics at the university. **The court conceded she may have been treated unfairly, but it did not find any of the university's decisions about denying her tenure were related to her religion.** A reasonable juror would conclude that any perceived prejudice was based on the incident with her colleague and not the fact that she was Jewish. Even if various faculty members made comments about her not teaching classes on certain Jewish holidays, this did not demonstrate discrimination since she suffered no adverse consequences for not teaching on those days. The court affirmed the trial court's decision. *Slatkin v. Univ. of Redlands*, 88 Cal.App.4th 1147, 106 Cal.Rptr.2d 480 (Cal. Ct. App. 2001).

◆ *A tenured professor was unable to show a New York university discriminated against him because he suffered no adverse employment action.*

An East Indian was hired by the University of Rochester in 1963 as a professor of statistics and assigned to the program in statistics, which was part of the math department. In 1967, the professor received tenure. That same year, the university established a department of statistics. Five years later, he was promoted to the rank of full professor of statistics and biostatistics. In 1997, the university conducted a reorganization, which included the professor's department. As a result, the professor retained his full-tenure status, with a primary appointment in the program of statistics and a secondary appointment in the biostatistics department. The professor sued the university for discrimination on the basis of race, national origin, religion and age. The district court held for the school, and the professor appealed.

The Second Circuit affirmed, finding the professor failed to establish a *prima facie* case of discrimination. While he was a member of a protected class and qualified for his position, **he failed to show that he suffered an adverse employment action**. Inconvenience or alteration in job responsibilities was not enough to constitute an adverse employment action. **The professor retained full-tenure status, remained on faculty committees and received the same pay and benefits.** Except for a subjective perception that his current position was less prestigious, the professor made no showing of materiality and offered no evidence that the reorganization had a discriminatory purpose. *Mudholkar v. Univ. of Rochester*, 229 F.3d 1136 (2d Cir. 2000).

◆ *Where a professor obtained tenure through an internal grievance process, she was not subjected to discrimination in violation of Title VII.*

Despite a departmental recommendation to grant tenure to a professor of philosophy employed by Vanderbilt University, the acting dean of the relevant college informed the professor that her employment with the university would end the following year. The professor filed a grievance with the professional ethics committee, which concluded that irregularities had occurred and forwarded the matter to the promotion and tenure committee. Meanwhile, the professor sued the college in a Tennessee federal court for national origin and gender discrimination in violation of Title VII. However, before the court considered the case, the tenure committee awarded the professor tenure and granted her an award of back pay. The professor claimed the back pay award was insufficient to compensate her for the emotional distress and damage to her reputation, but the district court granted pretrial judgment to the university. The U.S. Court of Appeals, Sixth Circuit, affirmed, holding that **because the professor successfully obtained tenure through the university's internal grievance process, no adverse employment action ever occurred**. Accordingly, no violation of Title VII was committed. *Dobbs-Weinstein v. Vanderbilt Univ.*, 185 F.3d 542 (6th Cir. 1999).

C. Collegiality and Animosity

◆ *A federal district court dismissed an Illinois professor's constitutional rights violation claims.*

The professor was disciplined after having confrontations with other faculty members. After a no-confidence vote by the faculty, he lost his position as a member and chair of a college personnel committee. He was also removed from the University Council Personnel Committee position. The professor sued university officials in a federal district court for denial of due process and equal protection rights. The court dismissed the claims against the board and officials on Eleventh Amendment grounds, finding they were not subject to constitutional claims for damages. The claims of deprivation of property and liberty without due process lacked merit. Although the professor had a property interest in his employment as a tenured faculty member, he did not have any interest in membership on committees. As he did not show damage to his good name, reputation, honor or integrity, the court dismissed his claim based on deprivation of a liberty interest. Since the university did not take adverse employment action against the professor, such as termination, demotion, or a loss of pay and benefits, he failed to allege any significant legally cognizable injury, and the case was dismissed. *Ganesan v. NIU Board of Trustees*, No. 02 C 50498, 2003 WL 22872139 (N.D. Ill. 2003).

◆   *Even though collegiality was not listed as a specific factor for tenure or promotion review, a university could consider it when evaluating a teacher.*

A teacher at a Maryland university sought an early review for tenure and a promotion. When both were denied, she sued the university for breach of contract, asserting that it had improperly considered **"collegiality" (defined by the court as "the capacity to relate well and constructively to the comparatively small bank of scholars on whom the ultimate fate of the university rests" and as "the relationship of colleagues")** in its decision-making process. She claimed that the university could only evaluate teaching, research and service. The university claimed that although nothing in the contract mentioned collegiality, it was inherently a part of the contract and therefore a proper consideration in both tenure and promotion decisions.

The Court of Special Appeals of Maryland ruled in favor of the university, finding that **collegiality was a proper factor for review**. It noted that the American Association of University Professors had even contemplated as much in its Statement on Professional Ethics. **Collegiality plays an important role in both teaching and service.** Finding insufficient evidence that the university breached either the contract or its implied covenant of good faith and fair dealing, the court ruled that the teacher's claim could not succeed. *Univ. of Baltimore v. Iz*, 716 A.2d 1107 (Md. Ct. Spec. App. 1998).

◆   *While a university professor may have been denied tenure because of personal animosity, the law could offer him no remedy.*

An English and drama professor sued Wesley College for wrongfully denying him tenure. The professor claimed that the president of the college held such personal animosity towards him that he intentionally undermined his tenure application by providing misleading materials to the board of trustees. The trustees, after assessing negative financial figures for the college and a lack of students interested in the degree program for drama, denied the professor tenure. Without tenure, the college would only renew the professor's employment contract for one additional year. The Court of Chancery of Delaware ruled in favor of the trustees. Because the college faced a $300,000 operating deficit and was in danger of facing financial insolvency, the trustees could properly adopt plans to eliminate the budget deficit, including personnel cutbacks. Even though the professor presented evidence of personal animosity toward him, he did not present evidence that the president lied to the trustees.

Finally, the court held that **personal animosity, in and of itself, could not constitute the foundation of a lawsuit.** *Hudson v. Wesley College,* No. 1211, 1998 WL 939712 (Del. Ch. 1998).

◆ *A university could deny tenure to a professor based on lack of collegiality.*

A professor employed part-time by a Louisiana private university was promoted to full-time probationary faculty status in 1987. He was again promoted to associate professor in 1991 and entered into a series of one-year contracts with the university. Each contract constituted a new appointment with the university for that respective year. The faculty handbook provided that "each non-tenured member of the ordinary faculty is considered to be on probation" but that "tenured faculty contracts may not be terminated except for cause." Although the faculty exercised the primary right of determination in matters of faculty status, the university conciliation committee could request reconsideration of tenure decisions. The faculty ultimately denied the professor's application for tenure based on his alleged lack of "collegiality" and refused the conciliation committee's request for reconsideration. The professor filed suit in a Louisiana trial court, alleging breach of contract. The trial court held for the university, and the professor appealed. The Court of Appeal of Louisiana held that **any ambiguity with regard to the employment relationship should be construed in favor of employment-at-will.** The professor was a non-tenured employee who could be terminated at the expiration of his annual contract without cause. Consequently, he was permissibly denied tenure based on lack of collegiality. A contrary ruling would improperly destroy the distinction between probationary and tenured faculty. The holding of the trial court was affirmed. *Schalow v. Loyola Univ. of New Orleans,* 646 So.2d 502 (La. Ct. App. 1994).

D. Handbooks and Procedures

◆ *A trial court was ordered to re-examine claims that changes to an employment handbook wrongfully deprived professors of vested tenure rights.*

Until 2002, the Metropolitan State College of Denver was a part of the Colorado State Colleges System. At that time, the state removed the college from the system and created a board of trustees to govern it. In 2003, the board issued a new handbook describing the rights of professional personnel at the college. The new handbook superseded one that had been in place since 1994, and it included some changes that did not sit well with tenured professors. For example, it did not afford tenured faculty priority over nontenured faculty in the event of a layoff. In addition, it removed the requirement that the college try to relocate dismissed faculty and eliminated a hearing committee procedure that was used when tenured faculty members sought to challenge their dismissal.

Five tenured professors filed a state court action against the board of trustees for injunctive and declaratory relief, claiming the new handbook breached their employment contracts and violated their procedural due process rights. The court held the new handbook did not breach their employment contract. It also rejected the due process claim, because none of the professors had been subjected to dismissal or layoff under the terms of the new handbook.

On appeal, the Court of Appeals of Colorado held the board lacked the authority to unilaterally modify handbook provisions that afforded the professors substantive and vested rights. **Provisions in the new handbook relating to priority and relocation in the event of layoffs affected the professors' substantive rights.** It was up to the trial court to determine whether those rights were vested. The new handbook violated the professors' due process rights because it allowed the college president to institute and resolve dismissal proceedings. Based on these and other errors, the case was returned to the lower court. *Saxe v. Board of Trustees of Metropolitan State College of Denver*, No. 05CA1251, 2007 WL 686067 (Colo. Ct. App. 3/8/07).

◆ *When Harvard University followed its handbook in denying tenure, a professor's breach of contract action against it was dismissed.*

After an associate professor of government at Harvard was denied tenure, he grieved the matter, claiming that Harvard's provost was biased against him and influenced the ad hoc committee that had recommended against tenure. The reviewing committee ruled that the grievance was without merit, and the professor sued for breach of contract. A state court refused to dismiss the lawsuit, but the Appeals Court of Massachusetts reversed, holding that the lawsuit should have been dismissed. Nothing in the university's handbook prevented the provost from submitting an opinion regarding the professor's abilities. Also, there was no requirement that the ad hoc committee be composed of specialists in the professor's field. Since **Harvard did not violate the tenure evaluation procedures outlined in its handbook**, the breach of contract lawsuit should have been dismissed. *Berkowitz v. President & Fellows of Harvard College*, 789 N.E.2d 575 (Mass. App. Ct. 2003).

◆ *A Mississippi court dismissed a professor's lawsuit because she failed to exhaust the university's grievance process.*

Mississippi Valley State University discharged an assistant professor who also served as director of the Department of Field Experience. The professor did not appeal the decision through the university's three-step appeal process. Nearly two years after being discharged, she sued the university and university officials in a state court for tortious discharge and interference with her employment contract. The court dismissed the case as untimely under a one-year statute of limitations. The Court of Appeals of Mississippi agreed with the university that the triggering event for the statute of limitations was the date of the termination letter, not the professor's last day of work. Therefore, an action brought two years after the date of the letter was untimely. Regardless of the timeliness of the claims, the professor failed to exhaust her administrative remedies by not first proceeding through the university's appeal process. Therefore, the court did not have jurisdiction. *Black v. Ansah*, No. 2001-CA-01909-COA, 2003 WL 21267089 (Miss. App. 2003).

◆ *A professor lost her challenge to tenure denial by failing to follow procedural court rules.*

An assistant professor of health, physical education, recreation and coaching was evaluated for tenure after five years. She was rated above average in teaching and service, but below average in scholarly activity, and was denied tenure. She sued the university under Title VII and the Fourteenth Amendment, asserting equal protection violations. After pretrial judgment was granted to the university, the professor appealed to the Seventh Circuit, which affirmed. Here, the professor committed procedural errors by failing to comply with local court rules. Also, she was unable to show an equal protection violation. She was not treated differently than other similarly situated tenure candidates, and **she had no liberty interest claim because the university did not make any stigmatizing remarks in connection with the denial of tenure.** *Hedrich v. Board of Regents of Univ. of Wisconsin System,* 274 F.3d 1174 (7th Cir. 2001).

◆ *Where procedural errors by a tenure committee did not prejudice a professor, his breach of contract claim failed.*

An Ohio university professor sought tenure consideration and was notified by a superior that the Retention, Promotion and Tenure Committee wanted to discuss his monitoring of two former graduate students, whose master's theses he rejected. Although tenure track procedures called for a two-week notice, he was only given one day's notice prior to the committee meeting. After the meeting, the committee denied him tenure based on his conduct toward the two graduate students. He received the minutes from the tenure meeting later than he should have. When he sued for breach of contract, the Ohio Court of Appeals ruled against him, finding that the two procedural errors did not substantially prejudice his rights. **There was no indication that the professor had been unable to prepare an adequate response as a result of the improper notice or the delay in receiving the minutes.** *Galiatsatos v. Univ. of Akron,* No. 00AP-1307, 2001 WL 1045513 (Ohio Ct. App. 2001).

◆ *A university did not have to grant tenure to an assistant professor merely because a handbook described tenure procedures.*

A Louisiana private university assistant professor was classified as a probationary regular appointment, with the prospect of tenure. The faculty handbook explained that appointments during the probationary period were made for one year, with written notification of reappointment made annually. Tenure-track professors were eligible for tenure if they met the university's expectations for tenured faculty. During the professor's third-year review, he was informed that he had a low number of publications. During his sixth-year review, the provost rejected all recommendations that he be given tenure. A committee determined that the provost had not acted improperly. Thereafter, the professor sued the university for breach of contract in a state court, which granted the university's motion for pretrial judgment. The professor appealed to the Court of Appeal of Louisiana, Fourth Circuit.

On appeal, the professor argued the university had breached his contract by denying him promotion and tenure. The university argued that there was no factual support for his claim that a contract existed that promised him tenure. The professor asserted that a contract was formed by the parties mutually agreeing to be bound by certain terms and conditions described in the faculty handbook. However, a handbook is a unilateral expression of company policy, and the publishing of that policy does not evidence a meeting of the minds.

Here, the professor did not claim that he was promised tenure; he claimed that he understood that the faculty handbook constituted such a promise because each party mutually agreed to be bound by the terms and conditions set forth therein. Because there was no proof of a contract promising tenure, the trial court correctly ruled for the university. *Schwarz v. Administrators of the Tulane Educ. Fund*, 699 So.2d 895 (La. Ct. App. 1997).

◆ *A handbook designed as a guide for the faculty did not create a property right to tenure.*

An assistant German professor at a Texas university was notified his contract would not be renewed for financial reasons. The professor asked to undergo the tenure approval process so he could tell potential employers he was being considered for tenure. According to the faculty handbook, he was eligible for tenure consideration. He was not, however, granted tenure. He sued the university in a federal district court, claiming he was denied due process of law in being refused tenure and in being fired. A jury agreed, but the judge overturned the jury's decision. The professor appealed to the U.S. Court of Appeals, Fifth Circuit. The court stated **the handbook was a guide for the faculty and not a self-contained policy document. It did not create a constitutionally protected property right in continued employment or an assurance of tenure. The handbook was not a contract.** The only process due to the professor was the exercise of professional judgment in a non-arbitrary fashion. Since there was evidence to support the termination, it was not arbitrary. *Spuler v. Pickar*, 958 F.2d 103 (5th Cir. 1992).

E. Other Tenure and Promotion Cases

◆ *The Court of Appeals of North Carolina held a university employee was not entitled to priority consideration for a vacant position just because she worked for the university for more than 10 years.*

The employee worked in the university's Animal Science Department. She left for three years and returned as an administrative billing assistant in the Communication Technologies Department. The university promoted the employee to the position of Telecom Project Manager/Telecom Analyst II. A few months later, she was laid off, but a Telecom Analyst I position soon became vacant. The employee applied for the job, but the university hired a less experienced former employee who had also been let go. The employee filed a complaint with the state office of administrative hearings, alleging she was entitled to priority consideration for the job under North Carolina General Statutes Section 126-7.1. This law provides state employees with more than 10 years of service priority consideration over state employees with less than 10 years of service in the same or a related job classification. A state trial court held the employee was entitled to priority consideration for the job.

The university appealed. The Court of Appeals of North Carolina held the trial court misinterpreted the law. Under the trial court's reading, a state employee with over 10 years of service, regardless of the position, should receive priority consideration over another person with less than 10 years of service in the same or a related position classification. **As the employee did** not have more than 10 years in the same or a related classification as the position for which she applied, she was not entitled to priority consideration for the job. The court reversed the judgment. *Wilkins v. North Carolina State Univ.*, 178 N.C.App. 377, 631 S.E.2d 221 (N.C. Ct. App. 2006).

◆ *A District of Columbia professor did not prove a university interfered with her bid for tenure in a way that breached its duty of good faith and fair dealing.*

The professor worked in a tenure track position for five years, then applied for a tenured associate professor position. The tenure committee voted against tenure because it considered her research weak. A scholarly journal notified the professor that it had rejected a paper she authored due to serious criticism by reviewers. The university again denied the professor's request for tenure based on lack of progress in publishing. The professor sued the university in a District of Columbia court for breach of contract and breach of the covenant of good faith and fair dealing. The court held for the university, and she appealed.

On appeal to the District of Columbia Court of Appeals, the professor argued the university failed to provide her with sufficient lab space and arbitrarily cancelled her research grant. This made her unable to perform her contractual publishing obligations, breaching both her contract and the covenant of good faith and fair dealing. **The court noted all contracts contain an implied duty of good faith and fair dealing. This means neither party may do anything which has the effect of destroying or injuring the rights of the other party under the contract.** The university took steps to make lab space available to the professor, but she failed to progress in her scholarly productivity. The court agreed with the university that **courts are reluctant to interfere with tenure decisions**. The professor failed to satisfy the requirements for tenure as set forth in the faculty handbook. The court affirmed the judgment. *Allworth v. Howard Univ.*, 890 A.2d 194 (D.C. 2006).

◆ *A Kentucky tax professor will receive a trial in an action against a university for negligence and fraudulent representation.*

The university hired the professor for an academic year and agreed to pay him a $25,000 supplement funded by an endowment fund. The professor believed his appointment to the endowed professorship was permanent. After he accepted the position, the professor learned his appointment to the endowed professorship was temporary and his future supplemental salary was determined at the discretion of the dean. He left the university and sued it in a Kentucky trial court for negligently or fraudulently misrepresenting the terms of his contract verbally and through e-mails.

The court found no bad faith and dismissed the case. The professor appealed to the Court of Appeals of Kentucky. **The court noted the professor introduced oral communications, e-mails, and other correspondence that created doubt about the university's good faith.** The dean would be entitled to official immunity for negligently performing discretionary acts as long as he acted in good faith. However, the hiring process included the non-discretionary aspect of representing or communicating the compensation package. **If the dean negligently represented the compensation package to the professor, a court could find the university liable.** The court held the trial court's finding that no facts supported a finding of bad faith was premature. It reversed and remanded the judgment to the trial court for further action. *Westin v. Shipley*, No. 2003-CA-001548-MR, 2004 WL 2260299 (Ky. Ct. App. 2004).

◆ *Kentucky university trustees were entitled to official immunity for their discretionary acts in denying a professor's application for tenure.*

A University of Louisville assistant professor applied for tenure after 11 years with the university. The university board of trustees denied the application and discharged him. The professor sued the university and trustees in a state court, which dismissed his claims for tortious interference with contractual relationships and breach of contract. The professor appealed to the Court of Appeals of Kentucky, where the trustees claimed official immunity. **The court held qualified official immunity applies to the negligent performance by an officer or employee of discretionary acts or functions performed in good faith within the scope of the employee's authority. The court found the trustees' evaluations were based on personal deliberations and were discretionary.** Because the professor offered no evidence of bad faith on the part of the board members, the court correctly dismissed the tortious interference claim. His contract expired at the end of its present term, and the court affirmed the judgment. *Haeberle v. Univ. of Louisville*, No. 2003-CA-000433-MR, 2004 WL 595257 (Ky. Ct. App. 2004).

◆ *The Ohio State University did not breach a contract with an instructor by refusing to increase her responsibilities or reappoint her.*

The instructor rejected a job offer outside the university, then changed her mind. After she decided to stay with the university, she talked with a vice provost about a new job title, salary and increased responsibilities. The university's office of academic affairs approved a new restructuring plan. The instructor alleged that she and the vice provost signed a position description confirming her duties and responsibilities in the restructuring process. The vice provost resigned and an interim provost changed the restructuring plan.

Dissatisfied with the changes, the instructor sued the university in a state court for breach of contract. The instructor claimed her agreement with the vice provost created both an oral and written contract. She said the vice provost promised her a new job title, increased management and supervisory responsibilities, and a salary adjustment. **The court held nothing in the position description or the vice provost's words or conduct constituted a binding obligation. The evidence showed instead that the position description was subject to change and depended on the vice provost.** The court found no contract guaranteeing the instructor the position of business manager or a particular salary range. The court held for the university. *White v. Ohio State Univ.*, 815 N.E.2d 1160 (Ohio Ct. Cl. 2004).

◆ *A California court held a temporary community college instructor was not a regular employee under the college system's academic classification system.*

The instructor taught less than 60% of the hours required for a full-time assignment and was deemed a temporary employee. He submitted three grant requests and worked on them during the intercession so as to not exceed the 60%

rule. The college later rescinded one of the grant awards because it believed his work during the intercession might count toward the 60% rule. The college denied a request by the instructor's union for reclassification as a permanent employee and he petitioned a state court for relief. The court held his projects constituted "teaching" and that he exceeded the 60% rule. It ordered the college to reclassify the instructor as a permanent employee, and the university appealed to the Court of Appeal of California.

The court noted the California Code established three classifications for community college instructors including probationary contract employees, tenured regular employees, and temporary employees, who could be terminated at the discretion of the governing board. **Pursuant to the code, a temporary employee who teaches full time for a complete school year and is rehired for the next school year will automatically be reclassified as a contract employee.** The court held an instructor teaching adult or community college classes less than 60% of a full-time assignment must be classified as a temporary employee. It distinguished statutory teaching requirements from the research and grant projects, which it characterized as "faculty work." Since these projects could not be considered "teaching" under the statute, the instructor did not exceed the 60% rule and should not be reclassified. The trial court's judgment was reversed. *Kamler v. Marin Community College Dist.*, No A098114, 2003 WL 21493662 (Cal. Ct. App. 2003).

◆ *Where a university conducted a fair review of a professor's record before denying tenure, the professor could not succeed in his lawsuit against it.*

Washington State University hired a professor with eight years' teaching experience and promised to review him for tenure after three years instead of six. However, at the review, his research record revealed that he had been a co-author on all his publications, and they were not in top-tier journals. He had also received poor teaching scores. After he was denied tenure, he sued the university for breach of contract, discrimination and misrepresentation. The case reached the Supreme Court of Washington, which ruled in favor of the university. **The court found that the university had considered the professor's full teaching and publication record, and that the procedure used had been fair.** None of the professor's claims could survive. *Trimble v. Washington State Univ.*, 993 P.2d 259 (Wash. 2000).

◆ *Athens State College did not violate the Alabama Fair Dismissal Act when the director of a volunteer program lost her job.*

During the 1970s, the college began sponsoring the Retired Senior Volunteer Program (RSVP). In 1989, the Alabama Department of Examiners of Public Accounts (DEPA) determined that state law prohibited the college's sponsorship of RSVP. Six years later, the DEPA found that providing operating space and equipment constituted monetary support in violation of the attorney general's conditions. The college discontinued the RSVP program and discharged its director. Although the director kept her job when the United Way began sponsoring the program, she appealed the college's decision to discontinue the program. An employee panel decided that the college should have reinstated the director to a non-teaching position.

A state court upheld the panel's decision, and the case reached the Alabama Supreme Court. The court drew a distinction between teachers, who are certified to teach in a specific field, and non-teachers, who may not be "presumptively qualified" to perform in another non-teaching position. The intent of the Fair Dismissal Act is to provide non-teacher employees with procedural protections in connection with their terminations. In applying the act to the director's claim, **the high court found no evidence to suggest that she was qualified to perform other non-teaching positions at the college**. When the college withdrew its sponsorship of the program, the director's position was eliminated. Consequently, she lost her job due to a "justifiable decrease in jobs in the system." **The college complied with the procedures set forth in the Fair Dismissal Act.** *Ex parte Athens State College*, 795 So.2d 709 (Ala. 2000).

◆ *A professor's position as associate dean was not a protected property interest preserved by her tenured faculty position.*

The University of North Dakota hired a professor in the School of Communication. She was also given administrative duties as the director of the School of Communication and as the associate dean of the College of Fine Arts and Communication. In 1995, she was told by her senior administrators to improve her administrative performance. Eventually, she was dismissed from her administrative duties, but remained a faculty member. She sued in federal court, alleging that her discharge from the administrative positions violated her protected property interests under tenure. The court dismissed her claim that she had a protected property interest in her administrative positions. Citing the North Dakota State Board of Higher Education Policy Manual, which was included in her employment contract, the district court noted that tenure does not extend to administrative positions.

The Eighth Circuit Court of Appeals agreed, noting that the professor's administrative position was at will, and thus did not evoke a protected property interest. In fact, the letter of understanding supplementing her employment contract stated, "Associate Deans have no specific term, but rather serve at the pleasure of the Dean." The circuit court found that the professor's position as director of the School of Communication included a three-year contract, but **her protected property interest had been satisfied because the university had fully compensated her for the salary associated with the position even though she did not serve out the full term**. *Rakow v. State of North Dakota*, 208 F.3d 218 (8th Cir. 2000).

◆ *The spouse of a member of a board of trustees was not eligible for promotion due to the potential conflict of interest that would occur.*

An accountant employed by the Long Beach Community College District for over 25 years applied for a new accounting position. At the time she applied, her husband had been a member of the college's board of trustees for over two years. The accountant was deemed ineligible for the position by the college's director of human resources because of her husband's position, the California conflict of interest statute, and several state Attorney General opinions interpreting the conflict of interest statute. The college hired the top-ranked external candidate. The accountant then filed a petition with a state trial court seeking the job. The trial court denied her request, finding that Section 1091.5 of the California Conflict of Interest statute allowed her to keep her present position once her husband was elected to the board of trustees, but that the same section barred her promotion to a different position.

The state court of appeal held that the conflict of interest statute barred the accountant from being promoted to the disputed supervisory position. The accountant's assertion that she was entitled to the position based on one of the exceptions contained in the statute was rejected by the court, as the disputed exception only allowed the spouse of a board of trustees member to retain any position held for at least one year as of the time the spouse was elected to the board. Since the accountant had held her position for approximately five years before her husband's election, she was statutorily allowed to keep that position, but was barred from being promoted to the new position. The judgment was affirmed. *Thorpe v. Long Beach Community College Dist.*, 83 Cal.App.4th 655, 99 Cal.Rptr.2d 897 (Cal. Ct. App. 2000).

◆ *A tenured professor's challenge to an amended appraisal policy, which permitted consideration of previous evaluations, passed constitutional muster because it was not applied retrospectively.*

In 1997, the Colorado State Board of Agriculture, which oversees Colorado State University, amended its performance appraisal policy and adopted a new policy for review of tenured faculty. A professor who was granted tenure in 1981 received unsatisfactory performance reviews for 1997 and 1998, based in part on previously issued evaluations. He sued, alleging the amended policy was improper because it was applied retrospectively. The court held for the university, and the professor appealed.

The Colorado Court of Appeals evaluated the policy, first to determine if the drafters intended a retroactive effect and second to determine if the policy, as applied, was retrospective. The court found that the new policy did not alter disciplinary provisions, but provided for a new two-step review of tenured faculty. The court also noted that the policy was "retroactive," though not necessarily unconstitutional. Therefore, the critical issue became whether the policy affected any of the professor's vested rights. In making this determination, the court determined that the amended policy "[did] not take away or impair vested rights, [did not] create a new obligation, [did not] impose a new duty, or attach a new disability." Instead, **the professor had previously been subjected to disciplinary provisions and was still subjected to those provisions, regardless of the amended policy. The new policy merely created a new procedural framework.** As the university's new policy was not retrospective, the court affirmed the judgment. *Johnson v. Colorado State Board of Agriculture*, 15 P.3d 309 (Colo. Ct. App. 2000).

◆ *A university could deny tenure to a professor with electronic publications on the ground that her work was not published in refereed journals.*

An associate professor at a New York university went before a tenure review committee and received a 3 to 2 vote in her favor. Nevertheless, the dean of the school of education recommended to the university president that she be denied tenure because of her lack of publications in peer-reviewed, scholarly (refereed) journals. The professor specialized in computer applications in occupational therapy and had developed a number of computer applications. **Her work had been published electronically or in non-print media.** After tenure was denied, she claimed that the review process had been flawed and that she had not been allowed to demonstrate her computer materials to the committee. The case reached the New York Supreme Court, Appellate Division, which held that there was no record of the review being arbitrary, capricious or tainted by bad faith. Here, the dean had recommended against tenure because she believed that the professor needed to theoretically justify and validate through research the computer applications she had developed. However, **the university had conducted the review process in substantial compliance with its procedures.** As a result, the court refused to overturn the university's decision to deny tenure. *Loebl v. New York Univ.,* 680 N.Y.S.2d 495 (N.Y. App. Div. 1998).

◆ *An associate professor could not sue a university for denying him a promotion where he was found to have withdrawn his request for it.*

An assistant professor of anesthesiology at the University of West Virginia's School of Medicine attained tenure and a promotion to associate under guidelines that called for him to demonstrate "excellence" in teaching and service, and a level of "satisfactory" in the area of research. The university modified the guidelines to require "excellence" in research. When the associate professor applied for the position of professor, he was informed that he would be evaluated under the new guidelines and that he did not qualify for promotion under them. **He then wrote two letters, informing the university that he declined to be evaluated under the new guidelines,** and filed an administrative grievance, requesting that the old guidelines be used in evaluating him for promotion. He also asserted that the university was retaliating against him for two earlier grievances he had filed in which he had obtained substantial dollar amounts. An administrative law judge (ALJ) determined that the associate professor had withdrawn his request for promotion, and the case reached the state Supreme Court of Appeals.

The court agreed with the ALJ that the associate professor had withdrawn his request for promotion. Even though his letters stated that he declined to be evaluated under the new guidelines, and there was some question as to whether this meant that he was withdrawing his promotion request, the ALJ had concluded that the letters were a withdrawal. Since this determination was not clearly wrong, it could not be reversed. The associate professor's claim had to be dismissed. *Graf v. Univ. of West Virginia Board of Trustees,* 504 S.E.2d 654 (W.Va. 1998).

◆ *An Oregon university did not have a duty to avoid making negligent misrepresentations to a teacher.*

A professor at an Oregon community college took a leave of absence to work as a visiting professor at a nearby university and, at the end of the year, applied for a permanent tenure-track position there. He was offered the position but before accepting, he received his student evaluations. They were well below those of the average teacher at the university and the professor asked a dean whether the poor evaluations would affect his chances of obtaining tenure. The dean told him that the evaluations would not be a problem. The professor resigned his position at the community college and accepted the job at the university. Over the next year, **his student evaluations did not improve, and the following year he was offered a nonrenewable one-year contract**.

The professor sued the university, alleging the dean negligently misrepresented the affect of his poor evaluations on tenure. A jury found for the professor, and the university appealed. The Supreme Court of Oregon found that the university did not owe the professor a duty to avoid making negligent misrepresentations. The parties were in a contractual relationship and both were acting on their own behalf. **The university employee handbook did not require the university to provide employees information regarding their job security** and created no duty to avoid negligent misrepresentations. Finally, the court held that the employer-employee relationship does not create a special duty of care. The court affirmed the decision for the university. *Conway v. Pacific Univ.*, 924 P.2d 818 (Or. 1996).

◆ *Even though two physicians had an understanding that tenure would be a formality, a university was not required to grant it.*

A private, Maryland university recruited two physicians to join its pediatric cardiology department. Both were tenured professors at different universities and dealt primarily with the department director in their negotiations. After interviews with other university officials, the physicians were offered professor positions. The physicians began to have difficulties in the department. Other doctors and staff complained that they were difficult to get along with, had poor management skills and failed to adequately monitor research projects. Because the physicians had not yet been approved for tenure, the university terminated their employment. They sued the university for breach of contract, alleging that the director had orally assured them that the approval process was a formality and that they would receive tenure. The jury found that the physicians had accepted contracts for tenured professorships and that the university did not have just cause to fire them. The university appealed.

The Court of Special Appeals of Maryland held that the jury could have found that the approval process was a formality and that the physicians' tenured positions were assured. However, **the director did not have the authority to bind the university to a guarantee of tenure since the university never told him that the physicians could bypass the approval process.** Although the director may have believed the physicians would have little difficulty obtaining tenure, there was no indication that the tenure committees shared this belief. The court reversed the trial court's decision. *Johns Hopkins Univ. v. Ritter*, 689 A.2d 91 (Md. Ct. Spec. App. 1996).

IV. LETTERS OF INTENT

A letter or statement of intent regarding future employment is generally not enforceable against an employer unless the letter evinces a bilateral understanding that employment will be forthcoming. A unilateral, subjective expectation on the part of an employee (or future employee) is insufficient to subject an employer to liability.

◆ *A department chair was immune from personal liability in a lawsuit arising out of a rescinded job offer.*

An assistant professor at a New York university decided to pursue other positions and interviewed with the department chair at a Wisconsin public university. She received an offer from a school in Buffalo but contacted the department chair to find out if he had made a decision before deciding whether to accept the Buffalo job. When he offered her a job, she turned down the Buffalo job and resigned from her current position. However, after a committee refused to extend the tenure track for her from three to five years, she was notified that the Wisconsin university did not intend to offer her a position. She sued the chair and the board of regents. After granting her partial relief against the board, a trial court held that the chair was entitled to immunity. The Wisconsin Court of Appeals affirmed. **The department chair's actions were neither ministerial nor "malicious, willful and intentional."** His discretionary acts were within the scope of his employment and he was entitled to immunity. *Bicknese v. Sutula*, 635 N.W.2d 905 (Wis. Ct. App. 2001).

◆ *Where an employee received a letter that only confirmed his compensation, and not the duration of the employment, he could be discharged during the school year.*

A manager employed by a Missouri university received letters each year confirming his reappointment and compensation for the following school year. Ten years after his initial hiring, he received a letter that confirmed only his proposed compensation. The school discharged him in November of that same year. The manager filed a wrongful discharge lawsuit against the university in a Missouri trial court. The trial court dismissed the claim, and the manager appealed to the Missouri Court of Appeals. The court of appeals held that the compensation letter sent to the manager was insufficient to establish a contract. The court noted that **a statement of duration was an essential element of an employment contract**. An indefinite hiring at a set amount per year was a hiring at will and could be terminated by either party at any time. Moreover, even if the letters received from the university in prior years formed a series of one-year contracts, the university purposely excluded the language "reappointing" the manager for another year. Any previous contract the manager had with the university had expired by the time he was discharged, and the university was not under any obligation to rehire him. *Clark v. Washington Univ.*, 906 S.W.2d 789 (Mo. Ct. App. 1995).

◆ *A letter addressing the use of laboratory facilities at a university did not amount to a contract requiring the university to provide such facilities.*

A Northwestern University medical school professor sued the university claiming that it had harassed him into resigning from his tenured position. He alleged that the university had failed to assign him new patients for research and removed him from the patient rotation hospital calendars. He filed a lawsuit against the university in an Illinois court, which held in his favor. The court issued a temporary restraining order preventing the university from changing the professor's research practices. A state appellate court reversed the decision and remanded the case for additional proceedings.

On remand, the circuit court enjoined the university from evicting the professor from his laboratory facilities. It based its decision on a partially written agreement allegedly requiring the university to provide the professor with adequate facilities to continue and expand his research. The university sought a reversal of the injunction. The university's request was denied and it again appealed to an Illinois appellate court. The court held that **although the agreement mentioned the laboratory facilities, it did not clearly reflect an agreement between the university and professor for his continued use of the facilities.** The professor was not entitled to the injunction allowing him continued use of the laboratory facilities. *Williams v. Northwestern Univ.*, 523 N.E.2d 1045 (Ill. App. Ct. 1988).

V. INVESTIGATIONS, HEARINGS AND PROCEDURES

A. Investigations

When public institutions and administrative agencies investigate discrimination charges, they are bound to respect the due process rights of public employees during such investigations.

◆ *A Minnesota community college did not violate a part-time English instructor's right to due process by declining to renew his contract after an investigation established he had sexually harassed a student.*

The instructor's contracts ran from semester to semester. Near the end of his sixth consecutive semester, the college legal affairs director advised him that a student had filed a sexual harassment complaint against him. According to the student, the instructor had spent weeks coming to the bookstore to stare at her while she worked, trying to talk to her and asking her out despite her repeated refusals. The legal affairs director told the instructor to stay away from the bookstore. She did not, however, give him written notice or a copy of applicable college policies and procedures or tell him he could submit a written response to the allegations. At a later interview, the director failed to give the instructor notices required by state law. After interviewing the instructor, the student and three witnesses, she wrote up a report concluding he had violated the college's sexual harassment policy. After she completed her report, she threw away her notes. The college notified the instructor it would not renew his contract, and he sued the college and various officials in a state court for violating his due process rights and illegally disposing of evidence.

The court held for the college, and the instructor appealed. The Court of Appeals of Minnesota found the instructor had to establish he was deprived of a constitutionally protected property or liberty interest in continued employment. **He could not show any property interest in continued employment because the terms of his contract called only for part-time,**

temporary employment that ended each semester. The court was not persuaded by his argument that ordering textbooks for the classes he expected to teach showed he had a property interest in continued employment. A liberty interest in continued employment can arise when government action is so damaging to an employee's reputation that it impairs his or her chance of getting another job. In this case, **the college did not publicize either the letter informing the instructor he would not be rehired or the investigator's sexual harassment report.** The court affirmed the judgment for the college. *Phillips v. State*, 725 N.W.2d 778 (Minn. Ct. App. 2007).

◆ *A private college had to disclose certain records to the EEOC in the following case.*

A professor, who had been employed at a Pennsylvania private college for three years, was denied tenure after he was reviewed by the school's Professional Standards Committee. The committee, composed of the dean and five faculty members, recommended that tenure not be granted to the professor. The committee's recommendation was also reaffirmed by the college's grievance committee. The professor then filed a complaint with the EEOC alleging discrimination based on his French national origin. The EEOC issued a subpoena for the committee's records. Although the EEOC offered to accept the records with names deleted, the school refused to disclose them.

The EEOC then filed suit in federal district court to compel the college to comply with the subpoena. The district court ordered disclosure of the records and the college appealed. The court of appeals affirmed, holding that **although the disclosure might burden the tenure process or invade the privacy of other professors, the records had to be disclosed because they were "relevant" to the EEOC's case.** The college appealed to the U.S. Supreme Court, but its petition for review was denied. *Franklin & Marshall College v. EEOC*, 476 U.S. 1163, 106 S.Ct. 2288, 90 L.Ed.2d 729 (1986).

◆ *The U.S. Supreme Court required a university to comply with an EEOC subpoena seeking peer review information.*

After the University of Pennsylvania, a private institution, denied tenure to an associate professor, she filed a charge with the EEOC alleging discrimination based on race, sex and national origin in violation of Title VII. During its investigation, the EEOC issued a subpoena seeking disclosure of the professor's tenure-review file and the tenure files of five male faculty members identified as having received more favorable treatment. The university refused to produce a number of the tenure-file documents and asked the EEOC to modify the subpoena to exclude "confidential peer review information." The EEOC refused and successfully sought enforcement of its subpoena through a federal district court. The U.S. Court of Appeals, Third Circuit, affirmed and rejected the university's claim that policy considerations and First Amendment principles of academic freedom required recognition of a qualified privilege or the adoption of a balancing approach that would require the EEOC to demonstrate a showing of need to obtain peer review materials.

The U.S. Supreme Court then held that **a university does not enjoy a special privilege requiring a judicial finding of necessity prior to access of**

peer review materials. The Court was reluctant to add such a privilege to protect "academic autonomy" when Congress had failed to do so in Title VII. The Court also stated that "academic freedom" could not be used as the basis for such a privilege. The Court affirmed the lower court decisions. *Univ. of Pennsylvania v. EEOC*, 493 U.S. 182, 110 S.Ct. 577, 107 L.Ed.2d 571 (1990).

B. Hearings and Procedures

◆ *When a property right to employment exists, due process requires that the employee receive notice and an opportunity to be heard before being dismissed.*

In two consolidated cases, the U.S. Supreme Court considered what pretermination process must be afforded a public employee who can be discharged only for cause. In the first case, a security guard hired by a school board stated on his job application that he had never been convicted of a felony. Upon discovering that he had in fact been convicted of grand larceny, the school board summarily dismissed him for dishonesty in filling out the job application. He was not afforded an opportunity to respond to the dishonesty charge or to challenge the dismissal until nine months later. In the second case, a school bus mechanic was fired because he had failed an eye examination.

The mechanic appealed his dismissal after the fact because he had not been afforded a pretermination hearing. The Supreme Court held that **because the employees possessed a property right in their employment, they were entitled to a pretermination opportunity to at least respond to the charges against them**. The pretermination hearing need not fully resolve the propriety of the discharge, but should be a check against mistaken decisions. The Court held that in this case, the employees were entitled to a pretermination opportunity to respond, coupled with a full-blown administrative hearing at a later time. *Cleveland Board of Educ. v. Loudermill*, 470 U.S. 532, 105 S.Ct. 1487, 84 L.Ed.2d 494 (1985).

◆ *When the disciplinary action is something less than termination, the protections afforded by due process are not the same as required in* **Loudermill**.

A police officer employed by a Pennsylvania state university was arrested in a drug raid and charged with several felony counts related to marijuana possession and distribution. State police notified the university of the arrest and charges, and the university's human resources director immediately suspended the officer without pay pursuant to a state executive order requiring such action where a state employee is formally charged with a felony. Although the criminal charges were dismissed, university officials demoted the officer because of the felony charges. The university did not inform the officer that it had obtained his confession from police records and he was thus unable to fully respond to damaging statements in the police reports. He filed a federal district court action against university officials for failing to provide him with notice and an opportunity to be heard before his suspension without pay. The court granted pretrial judgment to the officials, but the U.S. Court of Appeals, Third Circuit, reversed and remanded the case.

The U.S. Supreme Court agreed to review the case, and stated that the court of appeals had improperly held that a suspended public employee must always receive a paid suspension under *Cleveland Board of Educ. v. Loudermill*, above. The Court held that **the university did not violate due process by refusing to pay a suspended employee charged with a felony pending a hearing**. It accepted the officials' argument that the Pennsylvania executive order made any pre-suspension hearing useless, since the filing of charges established an independent basis for believing that the officer had committed a felony. The Court noted that **the officer here faced only a temporary suspension without pay, and not employment termination as in *Loudermill***. The Court reversed and remanded the case for consideration of the officer's arguments concerning a post-suspension hearing. *Gilbert v. Homar*, 520 U.S. 924, 117 S.Ct. 1807, 138 L.Ed.2d 120 (1997).

◆   *An Ohio university football coach was allowed to discover and present information to a trial court before it resolved his breach of contract claim.*

The coach became aware that some of his players were conducting voluntary throwing sessions. He knew players could get hurt unless there was some organization to these workouts. An NFL scout arrived at the university looking for game films and information about a senior quarterback. During the visit, the coach allegedly directed the quarterback while the scout watched. The coach's supervisor reprimanded the coach in writing, stating that such contact with players outside NCAA-approved dates was unacceptable. The university investigated allegations that the coach violated the NCAA rules during a pre-season camp. After the investigation, the university suspended him.

The university held a hearing before a five-person faculty committee, then voted to dismiss the coach. He appealed through a grievance process, but the grievance committee rejected the appeal as untimely. The coach sued the university in a state court for breach of contract. The court awarded pretrial judgment to the university, and the coach appealed to the Court of Appeals of Ohio. There, he alleged the trial court had erred by granting judgment without providing him an opportunity to conduct the pretrial fact-finding process called "discovery." The court agreed, finding **the evidence was not developed in a way necessary to properly determine a motion for summary judgment**. It vacated the judgment and returned the case to the trial court to allow discovery. *Kaczkowski v. Ohio Northern Univ.*, No. 6-05-08, 2006 WL 1312401 (Ohio Ct. App. 5/15/06).

◆   *A federal district court held an Illinois university did not violate an employee's constitutional due process rights.*

The employee worked as the university's director of printing. He earned average or above-average job evaluations for 13 years. The university then conducted a financial analysis which showed the office of printing services had a deficit of over $1.1 million. The director's supervisor told him the deficit must be eliminated in one year, even though university policy usually allowed three years to do so. The director alleged most of the deficit was caused by a lease agreement for several hundred copiers. The supervisor and a financial affairs director then began to manage the university's photocopy business themselves.

A year later, the university fired the director. He sued the university in a federal district court, alleging it violated his due process rights. The director argued that the university had disregarded an investigatory recommendation. The court explained that the director had confused state-created procedural requirements with constitutionally protected interests. **A state statute or regulation must guarantee more than a right to certain procedures to rise to the level of a constitutionally protected right.** A right to notice, a hearing, an appeal or an investigation does not create a Fourteenth Amendment Due Process Clause right. The court dismissed the case. *Bant v. Board of Trustees of Univ. of Illinois*, No. 05-2132, 2006 WL 91327 (C.D. Ill. 1/12/06).

◆   *The Supreme Court of Nevada was liable to a tenured professor for breach of contract because it discharged him based on outdated evaluations.*

The university gave the professor consecutive unsatisfactory evaluations, which was cause for termination. It filed a complaint against the professor with its administrative code officer and scheduled a hearing. The parties reached a settlement under which the professor agreed to resign at the end of the academic year. The university agreed to cancel the hearing and offer him a non-tenured teaching contract. The professor refused to sign an employment contract without guaranteed language and sued the university for breach of contract in a Nevada trial court. The court prohibited the university from using the unsatisfactory evaluations as a basis for firing the professor. It ordered the university to continue the professor's employment unless it revoked his tenure.

The university filed another administrative complaint against the professor based on the unsatisfactory evaluations, which were now six years old. It decided its own six-month deadline for hearings did not apply to the time of the settlement and its present administrative complaint. After a hearing, the university fired the professor. He sued the university a second time, alleging the prior court order prohibited the university from using the old evaluations as a basis for termination. **The court held for the professor, and the university appealed. The Supreme Court of Nevada held the university breached the settlement by holding the hearing based on an outdated complaint that included the prior evaluations.** The court found the hearing violated the terms of the settlement agreement and held the university breached the agreement when it unilaterally determined it could proceed with a new hearing. *State of Nevada, Univ. and Community System v. Sutton*, 103 P.3d 8 (Nev. 2004).

◆   *The Court of Appeals of North Carolina held state law precluded administrative review of layoff actions involving state university employees.*

Permanent state funding reductions forced the University of North Carolina at Chapel Hill to eliminate staff positions in various departments. Three employees who were included in the reduction of force pursued grievances that were upheld under university procedures. All three employees filed petitions with the state office of administrative hearings (OAH), alleging they were improperly laid off. A state trial court denied the university's dismissal motions and held the OAH had jurisdiction to determine if just cause supported the layoffs. **The state court of appeals held the OAH only had jurisdiction to hear state employee cases involving demotion, retaliation for opposition to discrimination and disputes relating to veterans preferences.** The state legislature enacted a law that intentionally excluded reductions in force based on procedural violations from OAH jurisdiction. The court directed the trial court to grant the university's dismissal motions. *Univ. of North Carolina v. Feinstein*, 590 S.E.2d 401 (N.C. Ct. App. 2003).

◆ *A university was not liable for firing a professor for harassment prior to a hearing.*

A professor at a New York university was rumored to have sexually harassed a female student. Although no grievance or complaint was filed under the university's grievance procedures, the university took the student's information, gathered other information, and decided to fire the professor. When the student failed to appear at the arbitration hearings mandated by the collective bargaining agreement, the termination was rescinded and the charges against the professor were dismissed. He nevertheless sued the university for failing to follow its own rules when disciplining him. A jury awarded him $25,000 in damages, but the Second Circuit Court of Appeals reversed. Here, **the professor failed to show that the university was required to follow the grievance procedures exclusively when making a finding that an employee had engaged in illegal discrimination.** Because the university's grievance procedures gave it the flexibility to discipline the professor without formal hearings, there was no breach of duty by the university. *Garcia v. State Univ. of New York at Albany*, 320 F.3d 148 (2d Cir. 2003).

◆ *College officials were not entitled to immunity in a lawsuit brought by a teacher accused of misconduct and barred from campus.*

A music instructor at a Nebraska public college taught for 29 years before retiring. He directed a performance group called "Chorale" in addition to teaching, and continued to work in a part-time capacity after he retired until the college eliminated his position. At that time, the college informed him it was banning him from campus, pending an investigation into alleged embezzlement. The college's letter also accused him of permitting Chorale to have inappropriate sexual overtones in their performances. He sued the college and its officials under 42 U.S.C. § 1983, alleging violations of his substantive and procedural due process rights as well as his free speech and freedom of association rights under the First Amendment. **The college and officials asserted qualified immunity** and sought a dismissal. A federal court dismissed the substantive due process claims, but refused to dismiss the others.

The Eighth Circuit Court of Appeals affirmed. **The instructor was entitled to a name-clearing hearing because the accusations of dishonesty and immorality were stigmatizing and were known by faculty members at several campuses. He had a liberty interest in his name and reputation, and the college officials were not entitled to qualified immunity** after refusing to provide the hearing. Finally, since the college was a public forum, its officials should have determined whether banning the instructor from campus was the least restrictive way to serve a compelling interest. They were not entitled to qualified immunity on the First Amendment claims either. *Putnam v. Keller*, 332 F.3d 541 (8th Cir. 2003).

◆ *By seeking arbitration, a fired employee limited his judicial review rights.*

A physician at the University of Minnesota was accused of sexual harassment and was fired. He grieved the decision through three stages and, at Phase III, the termination was upheld. At that point, he requested Phase IV binding arbitration, which also resulted in an adverse decision. When the physician then challenged that decision before the Minnesota Court of Appeals, the court ruled that he could not do so. He either had to seek judicial review after Phase III or pursue his remedies under the federal Uniform Arbitration Act before a district court, both of which he failed to do. *Univ. of Minnesota v. Woolley*, 659 N.W.2d 300 (Minn. Ct. App. 2003).

◆ *A police officer whose contract was not renewed could not sue for due process violations.*

A Kentucky university hired a police officer under an annual contract. It later suspended him with pay for his involvement in the dubious arrest of several students. He did not challenge the suspension. When the university refused to renew his contract the following year, he sued it under 42 U.S.C. § 1983, asserting due process and equal protection violations. A federal court ruled in favor of the university, and the Sixth Circuit affirmed. It noted that he could not succeed because **he could not show that he had a legitimate expectation of continued employment with the university**. The university's personnel manual did not create a property interest in employment, nor did it require the university to reappoint him. *Baker v. Kentucky State Univ.*, 45 Fed. Appx. 328 (6th Cir. 2002).

◆ *An at-large professor might have been qualified for another position so as to avoid a reduction in force.*

A university hired a dean for its college of business and management, but because of a faculty restructuring, gave him an "at-large" executive appointment. Later, the college merged with the college of professional studies and he was retained as a tenured professor. Finally, a financial crisis caused a reduction in force (RIF), in which he lost his job. He sued the university, claiming that he should have been exempt from the RIF because of his status as an at large professor. The court ruled for the university, and the D.C. Court of Appeals affirmed in part. Here, **the university had the authority to conduct a RIF and release faculty members**. However, the university never made an initial finding as to whether the professor might have qualified for placement in another department because of his at large status. Thus, that issue had to be remanded to the university. *Hahn v. Univ. of Dist. of Columbia*, 789 A.2d 1252 (D.C. 2002).

◆ *Even if a university violated an employee's procedural due process rights, he did not suffer any harm so as to be entitled to judicial relief.*

A paraprofessional library assistant at a South Carolina university was accused of sexual harassment. Although no formal charges were filed, he was issued several reprimands, which were withdrawn from his file after he challenged them. Several years later, his new assistant accused him of gender discrimination and of making sexual advances toward males in a specific library. The director of the Equal Opportunity Programs (EOPs) office notified him of the allegations but failed to provide him with witness names or details. After yet another complaint, the university temporarily reassigned the employee, then issued him a reprimand and permanently reassigned him, still without providing him with witness names or details of its investigation.

The employee sued the university for violating his due process rights, and a federal court ruled against him. The Fourth Circuit affirmed, noting that even though the EOP office may have violated the employee's procedural due process rights, he could not show that he was deprived of a property interest in employment. **He only had a right to continued employment with the university, not to continued employment in a particular position. Also, he did not suffer a reduction in pay** upon his reassignment. *Parkman v. Univ. of South Carolina*, 44 Fed.Appx. 606 (4th Cir. 2002).

◆ *A North Dakota professor was properly fired where he was able to confront witnesses and challenge evidence in two hearings before his termination.*

A university professor served as chairman of the physics department until his relationships with other faculty members deteriorated and he was removed as chairman. He criticized the department in a number of letters that he sent to university officials and local newspapers. Subsequently, the university received numerous complaints from students about his poor teaching performance. More than 90% of his introductory students transferred out of his class in one semester. The university then sent him a letter of termination that listed six grounds for his firing, including his libelous conduct, his disciplinary record, and his lack of cooperation with faculty members. He obtained a hearing before a special review committee, which ruled in his favor, but the president of the university rejected the committee's findings.

The committee on faculty rights then upheld the dismissal. The professor sued the university in a federal district court under 42 U.S.C. § 1983 for violating his First and Fourteenth Amendment rights. The court ruled for the university, and the professor appealed to the Eighth Circuit. It noted that while two of the professor's letters addressed matters of public concern, most of them did not. The professor could not claim First Amendment protection for all the letters, and the allegedly libelous material in the unprotected letters could be used as a reason for termination. Also, **the professor received due process in that he was given notice of the charges against him and an opportunity to respond**. Thus, his Fourteenth Amendment claim could not succeed. *de Llano v. Berglund*, 282 F.3d 1031 (8th Cir. 2002).

◆ *A Wisconsin professor had six months to seek review of his tenure denial.*

The health, physical education, recreation and coaching department at a Wisconsin university evaluated an assistant professor it was considering recommending for tenure. Her teaching and service were above average, but her research was below average because none of the four articles she had submitted for publication had been published. The department decided not to recommend tenure. A grievance panel determined that the department should have considered her manuscripts. However, when the executive committee met, she had to submit revised drafts because she failed to keep copies of the originals. The committee refused to consider the revised drafts and voted to deny tenure. When she later sought judicial review, the university sought to dismiss her petition because it was not filed within the statutory 30-day deadline for contested tenure cases. A trial court dismissed the petition, but the Wisconsin Court of Appeals reversed. **Cases involving denial of tenure were not contested cases, but rather uncontested.** As such, she had six months to petition for review, and her petition was timely filed. The court remanded the case for further proceedings. *Hedrich v. Board of Regents of Univ. of Wisconsin System*, 635 N.W.2d 650 (Wis. Ct. App. 2001).

◆ *A ruling granting a grievance hearing to six non-tenured employees of the Tennessee state university and community college system was upheld.*

The plaintiffs were non-tenured support staff from different schools in the university system, holding such positions as roofer, security officer, custodian and library assistant. They were terminated for poor performance, but were denied grievance hearings. Each sued the university system, and the trial courts ruled that the university system acted arbitrarily by denying them grievance hearings in violation of Tenn. Code Ann. Section 47-8-117.

On appeal, the cases were consolidated. The university system argued that the plaintiffs were "at-will-employees" and could therefore be terminated at any time with or without good cause. The Tennessee statute addressing at-will employees requires educational institutions to establish a grievance procedure for their support staff for complaints relating to adverse employment actions such as "termination for cause." Termination for cause involves any termination in which the employee was fired for a job-related reason: for example, failure to follow a supervisor's directions, poor job performance or failure to execute assigned duties. However, an employee who has been terminated as part of a reduction in the work force has not been terminated for cause because the termination was not related to job performance. Here, **the plaintiffs were all fired for reasons related to their job performance, which entitled them to grievance hearings** under the statute. The decisions of the trial courts were upheld. *Lawrence v. Rawlins*, No. M1997-0223-COA-R3-CV, 2001 WL 76266 (Tenn. Ct. App. 2001).

◆ *Where no proof of actual injury was shown, a professor was only entitled to $1.00 in nominal damages.*

A tenured professor at a West Virginia university was issued a letter of reprimand by a dean, who cited a number of deficiencies, including that the professor's second job was interfering with his duties. The professor replied that the letter lacked specifics and was without a basis in fact. Subsequently, the university discharged him by letter. He appealed through the university's appeal system. After a hearing, it was determined that the discharge had been for just cause, but that the failure to hold a pre-termination hearing required the university to pay the professor back pay. The university appealed. The Supreme Court of Appeals of West Virginia held that **the university had improperly terminated the professor without providing him an opportunity to respond. This was a violation of his due process rights.**

However, the court then found that the termination was proper and that no proof of actual injury had been shown from the denial of procedural due process. As a result, the award of back pay was reversed, and the university only had to pay nominal damages of $1.00. *Barazi v. West Virginia State College*, 498 S.E.2d 720 (W.Va. 1997).

VI. WRONGFUL DISCHARGE

"Employment at-will" exists in the absence of an oral or written contract of employment. When an employee works "at-will," the law presumes the employment relationship may be terminated by either party at any time for any reason. However, an employer may not discharge an employee for an unlawful reason, such as reporting illegal or fraudulent conduct or agreeing to give testimony in an action that may be adverse to the employer's interests.

◆ *The Court of Appeals of Michigan interpreted the term "public body" broadly to allow an employee to pursue a whistleblower action.*

The U.S. Department of Education (DOE) investigated student financial assistance programs at a Michigan college. An administrator who cooperated with the DOE was later discharged. She sued the college in state court, relying on a state whistleblower statute to support her claim that she was fired for participating in the DOE investigation. The court held the college, finding the DOE was not a "public body" under the whistleblower law.

The administrator appealed to the Court of Appeals of Michigan, which noted the power to arrest was not the only factor to consider when determining whether an agency was a "law enforcement agency" under the whistleblower law. Instead, it was appropriate to consider the extent of the DOE's overall power to detect and punish legal violations. The DOE has broad investigatory powers, including the power to gain access to people and documents and to issue subpoenas. DOE officials are authorized to execute warrants and make arrests. **In light of the broad powers granted to the DOE, the appeals court concluded the DOE was a "law enforcement agency" within the meaning of the state whistleblower law.** It reversed and remanded the case for further proceedings. *Ernsting v. Ave Maria College*, 274 Mich. App. 506 (Mich. Ct. App. 2007).

◆ *A federal district court held a Connecticut College did not cause a director of development emotional distress during termination proceedings.*

After the director of development had worked for the college about two years, a newly hired vice president stated at a meeting that he perceived her position to be a "senior major gift officer" and not director of development. A month later, the acting vice president of development and alumni relations gave the director a negative performance evaluation. The college soon demoted her to a position designated "senior development officer of major gifts." The director's next performance evaluation was critical of her performance and a month later, the college discharged her. The director sued the college in a federal district court for negligently inflicting emotional distress, among other claims. The college moved for dismissal of the emotional distress claim.

The court stated the time period identified by the director as the basis for her emotional distress claim involved routine employment matters such as job performance evaluations, work assignments, job transfers and title transfers. While these actions may have played a part in the employment action, they did not occur during a "termination process." A claim for negligent infliction of emotional distress must be based on conduct during the termination itself, not during the time leading up to it. Since the employee offered insufficient evidence of negligent conduct by the university at a relevant time, the court dismissed the case. *Stitt v. Connecticut College*, No. Civ. A. 3:04 CV577 (CFD), 2005 WL 646218 (D. Conn. 2005).

◆ *The Supreme Court of Iowa held that opposition to a co-worker's discharge was not "protected activity."*

Drake University investigated a security officer for an arrest he made during the annual Drake Relays. The officer was placed on desk duty for three months, then discharged. A university shift sergeant defended the officer's actions and offered to testify on his behalf. The university asked the sergeant to stop discussing the incident with the press, but he continued to talk openly about it. The university then demoted him one rank, resulting in a pay cut. The sergeant resigned and sued the university in an Iowa court, asserting he was constructively discharged for engaging in protected activity. The court awarded the university summary judgment. The state appeals court affirmed.

The state supreme court held that **to succeed in a wrongful discharge claim, the sergeant had to establish his advocacy established a clearly defined public policy that would be undermined by his termination**. He would also have to show his termination resulted from his participation in a protected activity and for no other reason. **The court found that opposing a co-worker's wrongful termination was not a "protected activity" under state law.** While public policy protected employees offering truthful testimony at legal proceedings, there was no indication the discharged officer had intended to sue the university. The court affirmed the judgment for the university. *Shoop v. Drake Univ.*, 672 N.W.2d 335 (Iowa 2003).

◆ *A Florida District Court of Appeal held a whistleblower complaint was properly dismissed by the state human relations commission.*

After being discharged, a community college provost filed a complaint with the Florida Commission on Human Relations, accusing college trustees of violating the state whistleblower act. The commission dismissed her complaint because the college was not a "state agency" under state law. The provost appealed to a state district court of appeal. The court found the list of statutory terms for the definition of "state agency" included any official, officer, commission, board or department of the executive branch of state government. For the provost to establish the commission's jurisdiction to investigate her claim, she would have to show the board of trustees was part of the executive branch. However, state law described community colleges as state political subdivisions and emphasized the difference between political subdivisions and state agencies. As the board of trustees was not a board of the executive branch of state government, the commission lacked jurisdiction to investigate the complaint. *Caldwell v. Board of Trustees Broward Community College*, 858 So.2d 1199 (Fla. Dist. Ct. App. 2003).

◆ *An Illinois court denied a professor's claims against a university for defamation, breach of contract and invasion of privacy.*

A divinity school was considering an associate professor for tenure when the administration received complaints about the way he ran his classes. A tenure committee conducted an investigation and learned that students considered him rude and abrasive. They reported he deviated from class topics and was unprofessional. School administrators spoke with the professor several times about these concerns and warned him that failure to change his conduct would result in termination. The professor denied the charges and the school suspended him. He claimed the charges harmed his professional reputation and that communications to students and faculty about termination constituted defamation. He sued the school for defamation and breach of contract. The court dismissed the defamation claim and characterized the termination of his contract as a "buy-out," since it paid the professor in full.

The professor appealed. The Appellate Court of Illinois rejected contract claims relating to the university handbook, which allowed the interviewing of students about classroom decorum. **The university did not breach his contract by failing to renew it after extending the tenure review process.** Under the faculty constitution, notice of termination was to be given by March 1 of the year, except in cases of moral turpitude. Since the professor did not receive notice by this deadline, he argued colleagues and students would infer he was fired on grounds of moral turpitude. The court rejected his claim and affirmed the judgment. The invasion of privacy claim failed because the professor did not show the university put him in a false light. *Green v. Trinity Int'l Univ.*, 801 N.E.2d 1208 (Ill. App. Ct. 2003).

◆ *Project documents did not prevent a university from eliminating an employee's position.*

A university assigned an employee to work on a project updating the university's financial software system for Y2K compatibility. Several months later, the employee's position was eliminated as part of a reorganization and, after he unsuccessfully applied for a number of other jobs, he was fired. He sued the university for breach of contract, asserting that the project work plans amounted to a contract. The university asserted that the work plans did not constitute an employment contract and that, even if they did, it had not breached the contract. A court found in favor of the university, and the California Court of Appeal affirmed. **The work plans did not prohibit the university from conducting the reorganization or from firing the employee when it had no work for him.** *Jenkins v. California Institute of Technology*, No. B153627, 2002 WL 31529092 (Cal. Ct. App. 2002).

◆   *A fired university employee had to pursue administrative relief before she could sue for wrongful discharge.*

After a Texas university employee was fired, she sued the university for wrongful termination under the telephone hotline anti-retaliation provision of the Texas Workers' Compensation Act. Alternatively, she asserted violations of the state whistleblower act. The Texas Court of Appeals ruled against her, noting that **university employees were not entitled to judicial relief for employer retaliation under the workers' compensation act**. Also, her failure to comply with the administrative requirements of the whistleblower act meant that she could not sue under that statute either. *Univ. of Texas Medical Branch at Galveston v. Savoy*, 86 S.W.3d 782 (Tex. Ct. App. 2002).

◆   *A professor could sue an agency that supervised his grant work under the state's whistleblower act when it removed him from the project before he could release his results.*

A professor at the University of Louisville received a $500,000 grant to evaluate the effect of welfare reform on Kentucky families. The university then entered into a contract with the Cabinet for Families and Children (CFC) regarding the monitoring of the professor's research. As part of the contract, the CFC paid one-third of the professor's salary and benefits while he worked on the project. The university also reduced the professor's workload by one-third during the two years he was involved in the project. The results of the study indicated that welfare reform had a negative effect on black and Appalachian families, and the professor informed the CFC that he would release his report during a public hearing. Before that could happen, the CFC got the university to remove the professor from the project and return him to full-time teaching.

The professor sued the CFC under the state whistleblower act, and the Kentucky Court of Appeals found that he could do so. It rejected the CFC's argument that it was not the professor's employer, noting that **the CFC supervised the professor's work and paid part of his salary. Thus, it was an employer subject to the whistleblower act.** *Cummings v. Cabinet for Families and Children*, No. 2000-CA-001468-MR, 2002 WL 1943758 (Ky. Ct. App. 2002).

◆   *A university employee could not show that he was fired because of complaints he made about co-workers stealing.*

A receiving clerk in the maintenance department at a Florida university complained to university security officers that his supervisor and co-workers were stealing university property. He was then allegedly subjected to certain retaliatory actions, including a glued office lock, a smoke-filled office, and interference with his radio transmissions. He later asked to take a leave, but his request was rejected when the university determined that he had already exhausted his leave time. He took the time off anyway and was fired. **He sued the university for retaliation under the state whistleblower act**, and a state court ruled against him. The Florida District Court of Appeal affirmed. Here, even if the employee's complaint about stealing was protected speech, he failed to show a causal connection between his complaint and his firing. For being absent without leave, he would have been fired regardless of the complaint.

Also, as for the retaliatory actions, he was unable to prove that management was either implicated in the attacks or that it condoned them. *Amador v. Florida Board of Regents*, 830 So.2d 120 (Fla. Dist. Ct. App. 2002).

◆ *Although a coach should not have been fired for retaliating against a player, the university could still fire her for lying.*

A black basketball player at the University of Southern Florida filed a complaint with the university's Equal Opportunity Affairs (EOA) office, accusing her coach of race discrimination. She played basketball the following year, then was dismissed from the team after composing and singing a song implying that the coach was going to be removed from her job. She then filed a second EOA complaint, claiming she had been dismissed from the team in retaliation for the first complaint. During an investigation, the coach maintained that she did not know the student was involved in the first complaint against her. The university fired her for retaliating against the player and for dishonesty in her sworn statement that she did not know of the student's involvement. The Florida District Court of Appeal ruled that the university should not have fired the coach for retaliating against the player. **Since a year had passed between the first complaint and the player's dismissal from the team, there was no retaliation.** However, on remand, the university would be allowed to fire the coach for dishonesty if it so chose. *Winters v. Florida Board of Regents*, 834 So.2d 243 (Fla. Dist. Ct. App. 2002).

◆ *The Mississippi Court of Appeals held that neither coercion nor misrepresentation existed in the execution of a settlement agreement between a college and its provost.*

The provost of William Carey College was employed pursuant to an annual employment contract. After he disagreed with the board of trustees over the college's application for a federal education grant, the board determined that his actions undermined his relations with the college and decided not to renew his contract. Eventually, the provost and the college entered into a settlement agreement, under which the provost agreed not to file a civil action against the college or any of its officials. About two years later, the college entered into a settlement agreement with the U.S. Department of Justice following an investigation into alleged violations of the False Claims Act.

Upon learning of this agreement, the provost sued the college and its officials in a Mississippi court. The court granted pretrial judgment for the college, upon finding that the provost was unable to show that coercion or misrepresentation existed that would set aside his settlement agreement. The court of appeals upheld the ruling for the college. **A contractual employment relationship existed between the provost and the college, which was not the sort of relationship under which the school owed the provost fiduciary duties.** Even if the provost could have established a fiduciary relationship, he was unable to show that he was coerced into signing the agreement. In fact, the record revealed that in his capacity as a licensed attorney, the provost had "aggressively negotiated" the terms of the settlement agreement before signing it. *Braidfoot v. William Carey College*, 793 So.2d 642 (Miss. App. 2000).

◆ *An employee alleging retaliatory discharge was entitled to a trial.*

While conducting a study on the interaction between passive smoking and contact with radioactive materials for the University of Chicago, **an employee noticed that human test subjects had been exposed to dangerously high levels of radiation. After insisting that the matter be reported to the federal government, the employee was fired.** The employee filed suit, claiming that his termination was retaliatory, but a trial court dismissed the case because the employee did not allege that a criminal statute, state law or actual violation was involved. The Illinois Appellate Court reversed and remanded the case. It held that the employee merely had to allege that he had a good-faith belief that a violation of public policy occurred in order for the case to go to trial. *Stebbings v. Univ. of Chicago*, 726 N.E.2d 1136 (Ill. App. Ct. 2000).

◆ *A mold-sensitive employee could not prove that she was disabled under Michigan law.*

A Michigan university employee developed a pulmonary condition as a result of high concentrations of mold in her office. She was granted a medical leave, but her position was eliminated while she was on leave and she was terminated. She sued the university for damages. The case reached the Michigan Court of Appeals, which ruled that the university was not liable for an intentional tort because she failed to show that it knew she was unusually sensitive to mold and that she was certain to become ill because of that sensitivity. Also, she could not show that she was disabled under state law because **her breathing was usually impaired only when she was exposed to high concentrations of mold**. This was not a substantial limitation of a major life activity. However, she was entitled, as an at-will employee, to nominal damages for breach of contract. *Leonard v. Board of Governors of Wayne State Univ.*, No. 236210, 2003 WL 1919530 (Mich. Ct. App. 2003).

◆ *An adjunct music instructor was denied renewal of his employment contract based on his unprofessional conduct, not his organizational activities.*

Three adjunct music instructors at a Minnesota college distributed a survey to other adjuncts concerning salary and benefit issues. They presented the survey results to the department chairmen and informed them that they intended to hold elections for a formal committee. The adjuncts were elected to the Adjunct Faculty Committee (TAFC) and obtained recognition for it from the Faculty Affairs Committee. In light of the actions taken by the three organizers, one of the department chairmen recommended disciplinary action. The dean of the college declined, but decided to discuss professional expectations with each of the three instructors before offering them new one-year contracts. One instructor was not rehired, based on his conduct during his meeting with the dean. He filed a complaint with the National Labor Relations Board (NLRB), alleging the non-renewal was due to his organizing activities, in violation of federal law. An administrative law judge (ALJ) held the failure to extend a contract to him constituted an unfair labor practice. The NLRB adopted the ALJ's findings and ordered the college to reinstate the instructor.

The Eighth Circuit Court of Appeals rejected the NLRB's characterization of the instructors' meetings with the dean as a means of forcing them into abandoning their TAFC activities. Evidence from the dean's meeting with one of the retained instructors indicated they simply disagreed about the instructor's involvement with TAFC. In contrast, **the non-retained instructor used vulgarities and called the music department a "laughingstock" during his meeting with the dean**. The court found that the instructor's behavior during the meeting demonstrated unprofessional conduct and disrespect for the music department. Moreover, the court did not believe that the instructor's conduct was provoked. Because it was the instructor's conduct during the meeting that led to his termination, and not his organizing activities, the university met its burden of establishing that the termination decision would have been made regardless of the instructor's protected activities. The Eighth Circuit refused to enforce the NLRB's reinstatement order. *Carleton College v. NLRB*, 230 F.3d 1075 (8th Cir. 2000).

◆ *A wrongful discharge claim failed where the employee was paid through the end of his contract.*

A licensed veterinarian contracted with a Missouri private university to work for its animal facilities department from July 1989 through June 1990. The interim director ultimately notified him that his services would not be needed in 1990 but that he would remain on the payroll until the expiration of his current contract. The veterinarian filed a wrongful discharge lawsuit in a Missouri trial court, alleging that he had been discharged in retaliation for reporting infractions of the federal Animal Welfare Act. The trial court granted pretrial judgment to the university, and the court of appeals transferred the case to the Supreme Court of Missouri.

The supreme court held that only discharged at-will employees may state a wrongful discharge cause of action. Here, **because the veterinarian had not been discharged (his contract had expired), his claim had been properly dismissed**. Given the significant differences between employees at will and contractual employees, the court rejected the veterinarian's contention that the failure to renew an employment contract should be treated the same as the discharge of an employee at will. The court declined to consider whether a separate (as yet unrecognized) tort or theory of damages should have been alleged in place of the wrongful discharge claim. Whether liability exists for wrongful failures to renew contracts and what type of damages may be recovered for a breach of contract in "whistleblower" situations were still open questions. *Luethans v. Washington Univ.*, 894 S.W.2d 169 (Mo. 1995).

◆ *An employee's wrongful discharge claim failed where she could not show that her firing had been related to her reports of theft in the office.*

A Massachusetts private college employee reported the apparent theft of funds from the office in which she worked. She was employed at will, and after her reports of theft, she was discharged. She brought suit against the college and her former supervisor in the superior court, claiming wrongful discharge and intentional interference with her employment contract. The court granted pretrial judgment in favor of the college and her former supervisor. She appealed unsuccessfully to the Appeals Court and then appealed to the Supreme Judicial Court of Massachusetts.

The lower court had held that as an at-will employee, she could not obtain redress from her former employer when it discharged her for reporting the theft of funds. In certain circumstances, however, an at-will employee may maintain an action against her former employer for wrongful discharge. Public policy is violated when an employer discharges an employee for reporting criminal activity even if the reports were made only within the employing units. Here, there was no dispute that the woman was an at-will employee. She therefore had an obligation to support her claim that she was discharged for reporting criminal conduct to her superiors. However, **she had no facts to support her claim, and the record contained nothing showing that the college discharged her for a reason contrary to a well-established public policy.** Further, she failed to show that her supervisor intentionally interfered with her employment contract because she was unable to prove that he knowingly induced the college to break the contract, that his interference, in addition to being intentional, was improper in motive or means, and that she was harmed by his actions. Rather, the record stated several examples of problems she was having on the job. Therefore, the court affirmed the grant of pretrial judgment for the college and the supervisor. *Shea v. Emmanuel College*, 682 N.E.2d 1348 (Mass. 1997).

◆ *An employee was allowed to proceed in his lawsuit against a college for retaliation.*

A security officer employed by a Vermont private college sought workers' compensation benefits after he was injured on the job. The college denied his claim, but the state Department of Labor and Industry reversed and granted him benefits. The officer alleged the college then discriminated against him by badgering him to come back to work, changing his employment duties and responsibilities, requiring him to work night shifts in breach of a previous agreement, changing his work hours, giving him unfairly low job evaluations, and challenging his right to receive workers' compensation. He was also demoted and placed on probation for six months based on a student's complaint. The security officer did not return to work following his demotion, alleging stress-induced depression prevented him from working.

The college fired the officer after his short-term disability benefits ran out, and he sued it for retaliatory discrimination and intentional infliction of emotional distress. A state court granted pretrial judgment to the college, and the officer appealed. The Supreme Court of Vermont held that **employees have a private right of action under the workers' compensation act when an employer allegedly discharges them or discriminates against them for filing a workers' compensation claim**. Although the college articulated a legitimate, nondiscriminatory reason for the officer's discipline, the court found factual issues remained concerning whether he was discriminated against for filing a workers' compensation claim and whether the severity of the disciplinary action resulting from the student's complaint was the result of discriminatory treatment. Finally, the court dismissed the officer's intentional infliction of emotional distress claim. *Murray v. St. Michael's College*, 667 A.2d 294 (Vt. 1995).

CHAPTER SIX

Employment Practices and Labor Relations

I. PRIVACY RIGHTS

Courts reviewing public employee privacy cases typically balance the employee's reasonable expectations of privacy against the government employer's interest in supervision, control and workplace efficiency. In O'Connor v. Ortega, 480 U.S. 709 (1987), the U.S. Supreme Court held public employees have a reasonable expectation of privacy in their personal workspaces, desks and file cabinets. Acceptable use policies and other workplace rules place further limits on reasonable privacy expectations.

Security cameras create new issues of privacy for staff who may be recorded during surveillance activity. The Fourth Amendment standard of reasonableness applies to searches of public employees as well as their workspaces, offices and computers.

A. Electronic Data and Communications

◆ *Officials properly seized an Oklahoma university department head's personal laptop computer as part of a child pornography investigation.*

The case involved a department head at Oklahoma State University (OSU). Another OSU employee reported finding child pornography in a box belonging to the department head. A university dean and associate dean seized the box and turned it over to university police. After legal counsel was consulted, a decision was made to seize the desktop computer in the department head's office. Two members of the university's computer information services security office went to the office and saw a laptop computer on a table near his desk. Although the department head was not present, the laptop was running. The screen showed a university-supported e-mail program. The laptop also showed spreadsheets that appeared to include university records. The security specialists took the hard drive from the desktop computer and also seized the laptop. The contents were retained by the university's police department.

The department head sued university officials, including one of the security specialists, in a federal district court. He claimed the seizure violated the Fourth Amendment. The court relied heavily on the U.S. Supreme Court's ruling in *O'Connor v. Ortega*, above. **It found the search was reasonable, as the purpose was to investigate suspected misconduct involving the possibility that child pornography was being stored on computers located in an on-campus office.** The personal laptop computer was open and running when the security specialists entered the department head's office. **The laptop was showing an e-mail program that was supported by the university as well as spreadsheets that looked like they contained university records.** Under these circumstances, the search was justified at its inception, and its scope was reasonable. Therefore, the search did not violate the Fourth Amendment. The remaining state-law claim was dismissed. *Soderstrand v. State of Oklahoma*, 463 F.Supp.2d 1308 (W.D. Okla. 2006).

◆ *The Second Circuit upheld discipline against a New York state employee for downloading personal tax programs on the state-owned computer he used.*

The state had a policy prohibiting use of state equipment for personal business. The employee came under suspicion of neglecting his duties, and the state authorized an investigation of his computer usage. A list of file names revealed non-standard software was loaded on the computer, and additional searches determined the employee loaded a personal tax preparation program on it. The employee challenged the search of his computer in a federal district court. The court awarded pretrial judgment to the state.

On appeal, the U.S. Court of Appeals, Second Circuit, found no Fourth Amendment violation. The court held that **although the employee had a reasonable expectation of privacy in his office computer, the investigatory searches by the state were upheld as reasonable. The searches of his computer were reasonably related to the objectives of the search and not excessively intrusive** in light of the nature of his suspected misconduct. *Leventhal v. Knapek*, 266 F.3d 64 (2d Cir. 2001).

◆ *A North Carolina court held Congress clearly intended to abrogate sovereign immunity for federal wiretapping violations in actions against people or entities other than the U.S. government.*

A North Carolina university employee worked as a personal assistant for a department director. She learned the director had audio tape recorders and was taping the personal phone conversations of a co-worker. When the employee advised the director she knew about the recordings, he stated her conversations were not being taped. The director created a standard operating procedure for downloading recordings of phone calls that permitted access to a support technician and telecommunications supervisor. He later installed computer software that allowed him to eavesdrop on all department employee telephone conversations. The employee sued the director, other university officials and the university in a state court for violating federal wiretapping laws.

The court denied motions for pretrial judgment by the university and officials, and they appealed to the Court of Appeals of North Carolina. **The court held a state university and its officials are entitled to sovereign immunity in state court actions for federal law violations if Congress does not clearly express the intent to disallow immunity**. Congress had clearly stated the intent to abrogate sovereign immunity for federal wiretapping law violations in 18 U.S.C. § 2520(a). **The Electronic Communications Privacy Act of 1986 and the USA Patriot Act of 2001 broadened the wiretapping law to allow recovery against a person or entity other than the U.S. government.** The trial court had properly denied the director and university's claims to immunity, and the appeals court affirmed the judgment. *Huber v. North Carolina State Univ.*, 594 S.E.2d 402 (N.C. Ct. App. 2004).

◆ *While an Indiana university had no privacy rights, its administrators did.*

A professor at the University of Evansville was fired. He then created a Web site and e-mail addresses incorporating the letters "UE," a common abbreviation for the school's name, as well as portions of the names of the university president, vice president for academic affairs and dean of the college of arts and sciences. He sent e-mail messages that appeared to originate from those individuals, nominating them for positions at other schools, and placed articles on his Web site alleging wrongdoing by the president and other university employees. The university and the three administrators sued him for invasion of privacy, and a trial court granted a permanent injunction preventing the former professor from continuing that activity.

The Supreme Court of Indiana held that the university, as a corporate entity, had no right of privacy under state law. However, the administrators did have such rights, and the court largely upheld the injunction with respect to them. He could continue to send in nominations under his own name; he just could not do so where he was creating the appearance that they originated elsewhere. *Felsher v. Univ. of Evansville*, 755 N.E.2d 589 (Ind. 2001).

◆ *A teacher and a professor were held not to have violated the Electronic Communications Privacy Act in the following case.*

A private Delaware college employed a computer programmer who alleged the college president often mistakenly printed out e-mail messages in the office where the programmer worked, and that he would either return them to the president's assistant or place them in a folder beside the printer. After the programmer was discharged, he told a paralegal teacher that the college was foolish to fire him, as he had "seen things" on the computer screens. He mentioned he had seen an e-mail relating to an English professor's breach of contract lawsuit against the college. The teacher then called the English professor and recounted the conversation she had with the programmer. Neither the paralegal teacher nor the professor saw any e-mail until a lawsuit was filed against them and the programmer by the college. The college sued the teacher and professor for violations of the federal Electronic Communications Privacy Act (ECPA) and state law. They moved for dismissal.

The court held the ECPA prohibits people from attempting, intentionally intercepting, or procuring another to intercept any electronic communication. **A reasonable jury could not conclude that the teacher or professor took affirmative steps to intercept or access the president's e-mail, because there was no evidence that they possessed the capability to take those steps or join forces with someone who did.** Title I also prohibits any person from using or disclosing to any other person the contents of any electronic communication while knowing or having reason to know that the information was obtained through the illegal interception of an electronic communication. The court held that there was insufficient evidence to conclude that the teacher and professor should have known that the programmer intercepted the e-mail in violation of the ECPA. Also, the college had not shown that the programmer had acquired the e-mails while they were being transmitted. He could have merely seen them on the screen. This would not violate the ECPA. Fact issues precluded pretrial judgment with respect to the programmer. However, the court granted the teacher's and professor's motions for pretrial judgment. *Wesley College v. Pitts*, 974 F.Supp. 375 (D. Del. 1997).

◆   *A Florida high school teacher accused of exchanging sexually explicit e-mails with students did not have to turn over all his home computers for inspection by his school board for use in an employment termination hearing.*

The board suspended the teacher for misconduct for exchanging e-mails and instant messages with students that were sexually explicit and made derogatory comments about staff members and school operations. An administrative law judge issued an order allowing a board expert to inspect the hard drives of the teacher's home computers to discover if they had relevant data for use against him in a formal termination hearing.

The teacher appealed, arguing production of the home computer records would violate his Fifth Amendment right against self-incrimination and his privacy rights. He argued the production of "every byte, every word, every sentence, every data fragment, and every document," including those that were privileged, substantially invaded his privacy and that of his family. **The court noted that computers store bytes of information in an "electronic filing cabinet." It agreed with the teacher that the request for wholesale access to his personal computers would expose confidential communications and extraneous personal information such as banking records.** There might also be privileged communications with his wife and his attorney. The only Florida decision discussing the production of electronic records in pretrial discovery held **a request to examine a computer hard drive was permitted "in only limited or strictly controlled circumstances," such as where a party was suspected of trying to purge data.** There was no evidence that the teacher was attempting to thwart the production of evidence in this case. **The court held the broad discovery request violated the teacher's Fifth Amendment rights and his personal privacy, as well as the privacy of his family.** It reversed the administrative order allowing the board to have unlimited access to the teacher's home computers. *Menke v. Broward County School Board,* 916 So.2d 8 (Fla. Dist. Ct. App. 2005).

◆   *The Tennessee Court of Appeals applied Florida decisions in finding public school Internet records and e-mails were not open to public inspection.*

A Tennessee citizen made a written request to a county education board to view and inspect digital records of Internet activity, including e-mails sent and received, Web sites visited, and the identity of Internet service providers used during school hours or stored on school-owned computers. A trial court judge reviewed the requested records privately and found they were not accessible under the state Public Records Act (PRA).

The citizen appealed to the Court of Appeals of Tennessee, asserting the digital records or documents were open to public inspection because they had been made during business hours or were stored on the school's computers. **The court found the PRA's clear purpose favored the disclosure of public records. The PRA defined "public record" to include documents, papers, electronic data processing files and other material "made or received pursuant to law or ordinance or in connection with the transaction of official business by any governmental agency."** The PRA did not limit access to records based on the time a record was created or the place the record was produced or stored. The trial court judge had properly inspected documents in private to decide if they were "made or received pursuant to law or ordinance or in connection with the transaction of official business." **The Supreme Court of Florida has rejected arguments that placement of a document in a public employee's file made the document a "public record."** The Tennessee PRA definition of "public records" nearly matches the definition used in the Florida Law. The Tennessee court stated that while it was not bound by Florida decisions on public records, it found them well-reasoned and applicable. The trial court did not commit error in privately reviewing the records, and the judgment was affirmed. *Brennan v. Giles County Board of Educ.,* No. M2004-00998-COA-R3-CV, 2005 WL 1996625 (Tenn. Ct. App. 2005).

◆   *A Florida District Court of Appeal held personal e-mail fell outside the current definition of public records.*

The case involved a newspaper's request for e-mails sent from or received by municipal employees on government-owned computers. **The court of appeal held personal e-mail was not "made or received pursuant to law or ordinance." Although digital in nature, "there was little to distinguish a personal e-mail from personal letters delivered to public employees through a government post office box and stored in a government-owned**

desk." The court noted the state supreme court has held "only materials prepared 'with the intent of perpetuating and formalizing knowledge' fit the definition of a public record." The court denied a publisher's request to compel a municipality to release all e-mail sent from or received by two employees on their government-owned computers. *Times Publishing Co. v. City of Clearwater*, 830 So.2d 844 (Fla. Dist. Ct. App. 2002).

B. Employee Search and Seizure

Searches and seizures conducted by government employers implicate the Fourth Amendment. Because these searches are not carried out to enforce criminal laws, the courts consider them "administrative searches," which may be justified by the need to protect campus safety and ensure order.

◆ *The special needs of public employers justify allowing them to avoid the warrant and probable cause requirements of the Fourth Amendment.*

The U.S. Supreme Court held that the search of a public employee's office was reasonable when the measures adopted were reasonably related to the objectives of the search and not excessively intrusive in light of its purpose. The Court held that workplace searches by government employers "should be judged by the standard of reasonableness under all the circumstances."

The Court announced a case-by-case standard for evaluating employee privacy expectations, stating that a public employee's expectation of privacy in the workplace may be reduced by actual office practices, work procedures or rules. Acceptable use policies governing employee usage of computers and e-mail are examples of such workplace procedures or rules. *O'Connor v. Ortega*, 480 U.S. 709 (1987).

◆ *Three Ohio university police officers who arrested a school janitor for criminal menacing could not be sued for false arrest.*

The janitor reportedly lost his temper after the co-worker ignored a sign he had posted on a restroom door asking people to use a different bathroom. When the janitor told him to leave, the co-worker refused. Furious, the janitor went to their manager. The co-worker followed the janitor to the manager. The janitor threatened the co-worker, who called university police. The co-worker told the officers he was worried because he believed the janitor was capable of violence.

The officers arrested the janitor and charged him with criminal menacing. The janitor sued the university and nine employees in a federal district court. The court held the officers did not have qualified immunity, and they appealed. The U.S. Court of Appeals, Sixth Circuit, held public officials are protected by immunity unless they violate clearly established federal law. **It is clearly established that arrests based upon probable cause do not violate the Fourth Amendment. Sixth Circuit precedent allows police to base probable cause on credible eyewitness reports.** The co-worker stated the janitor had threatened him, and the manager verified his account. As the officers had probable cause for the arrest, the court reversed the judgment. *Franklin v. Miami Univ.*, 214 Fed.Appx. 509 (6th Cir. 2007).

C. Video Surveillance

◆   *A Massachusetts state college did not violate an employee's privacy rights by videotaping her without her knowledge.*

The employee worked in the college's small business development center. Many employees and volunteers had keys to the office and were allowed to enter and leave after business hours. Visitors did not have to check in at the front desk before entering. The college learned a former client who was being investigated for criminal activity had entered the building without permission after hours. Without informing the employee the college installed a hidden security camera on the rear wall of the office. For three weeks, she went to a rear work area, unbuttoned her blouse and applied ointment to a severe sunburn. The area was under video surveillance, but tape recordings did not show any images of her. The employee learned about the videotaping and sued the college in a state court for violating her Fourth Amendment privacy rights.

The court held the college was protected from liability by qualified immunity, and the employee appealed. **The Supreme Judicial Court of Massachusetts stated a person's constitutional right to privacy is violated only if an alleged invasion of privacy occurs where a person has a reasonable expectation of privacy.** Generally, a person's reasonable expectation of privacy on business premises is less than the expectation of privacy in a home. While the law recognizes some privacy interests in business premises, people cannot have a reasonable expectation of privacy in open places. The office was open to the public all day and visitors did not have to check in. Volunteers and employees could get into the office at any time with keys supplied by the college. There was no absolute guarantee of privacy, even when the employee locked the front door before she applied ointment. Despite her efforts to discreetly conduct personal and private acts in the office, she had no objectively reasonable expectation of privacy there. Accordingly, the court affirmed the judgment for the college. *Nelson v. Salem State College*, 446 Mass. 525, 845 N.E.2d 338 (Mass. 2006).

D. Personnel Records

State data privacy acts protect the confidentiality of public employee personnel files. Common law rules of defamation may also provide a basis for legal action against a school district or its officers for wrongful disclosure of private facts or erroneous factual statements.

1. Media Access

◆   *A Pennsylvania newspaper and reporter had a right to see current and past salary information for certain employees of a state university.*

The reporter asked the State Employees' Retirement System (SERS) for salary information on state university employees. The state Right to Know Act provides that "public records" kept by a government agency are accessible for inspection. A "public record" is "any account, voucher or contract dealing with the receipt or disbursement of funds by an agency." However, any record or document which would prejudice or impair a person's reputation or personal security is not considered a public record. Before SERS responded to the request, it notified the university. The university and employees claimed the salary information was private and protected from release by the Constitution.

The State Employees' Retirement Board granted the request, finding the information was a public record. The university and employees appealed to the Commonwealth Court of Pennsylvania. **The court held salary information was a "public record" because it was part of a contract dealing with the appropriation of public funds. Documents in the possession of SERS were public records.** The university and employees did not convince the court that the information was precluded from disclosure by the personal security exception of the act. Releasing the information did not threaten employee physical or economic security. Salary is not personal enough data to threaten personal security. The information did not violate the employees' privacy rights, as the reporter did not ask for social security numbers, phone numbers or addresses. The court affirmed the decision. *Pennsylvania State Univ. v. State Employees' Retirement Board*, 880 A.2d 757 (Pa. Commw. Ct. 2005).

◆ *The private consideration of applicants for a university president violated the Minnesota Open Meetings Law and Government Data Practices Act.*

The University of Minnesota Board of Regents searched for a new president for the university. Some applicants requested anonymity, and the board voted to screen them privately. The board denied information requests by media organizations about unsuccessful candidates. The organizations sued the board in the state court system for an order forcing disclosure of the information and enjoining the university from holding closed meetings. The court entered summary judgment for the media, and the board appealed.

The state court of appeals noted that **the government data privacy act made public all personnel data on current and former applicants for employment by a statewide agency.** The names of applicants were considered "private data," except for finalists. Since the university was a statewide agency, and because the candidates were deemed "finalists," the court held the data practices act applied to procedures for selecting a university president. The only exception to the open meetings law applied to disciplinary proceedings, and did not apply in this case. Accordingly, the court affirmed the decision to grant the media organizations' motion. *Star Tribune Co. v. Univ. of Minnesota*, 667 N.W.2d 447 (Minn. Ct. App. 2003).

2. Disclosure to Third Parties

◆ *Absent "truly exceptional circumstances," the University of Michigan had to release employee addresses and phone numbers to a professional union.*

The Michigan Federation of Teachers and School Related Personnel asked the University of Michigan for the names, home addresses, home phone numbers and job-related data of its employees. The university provided the names and job-related information, but limited its disclosure of home addresses and phone numbers to employees who were listed in its faculty/staff directory. The union sued the university in a Michigan court, seeking disclosure of the remaining information under the state Freedom of Information Act (FOIA). The court agreed with the university that disclosure of the information would result in a "clearly unwarranted invasion" of privacy, and the union appealed.

The Court of Appeals of Michigan explained that a FOIA exemption prevents disclosure of information of a personal nature, if disclosure would cause a "clearly unwarranted invasion" of personal privacy. Under the exemption, information is not "of a personal nature" unless it reveals "intimate and embarrassing details of an individual's private life." **The court held home addresses and phone numbers are not "information of a personal nature,"** as they usually do not reveal "intimate or embarrassing" information. The court also held disclosure would not be required if "truly exceptional circumstances" existed. For example, **the university would not be required to release the information if it could show disclosure would create a threat of physical danger.** Because it was improper to block the release of all the records without a more individualized inquiry, the court reversed the judgment. *Michigan Federation of Teachers & School Related Personnel, AFT, AFL-CIO v. Univ. of Michigan*, No. 258666, 2007 WL 861185 (Mich. Ct. App. 3/22/07).

◆ *A Missouri college did not violate an untenured professor's right to privacy by confirming to another institution that he was employed there.*

The professor signed a contract to be a full-time, tenure-track professor of business administration during his second year at the college. A representative from DeVry University called the college's human resources (HR) department. She gave the department the professor's Social Security number and asked if he was working full time at the college. The HR department confirmed that he was. The representative then asked the HR department if it knew the professor was on disability leave from DeVry. The HR department said it did not. The DeVry representative said the professor committed insurance fraud by claiming he was disabled when he was not. DeVry discharged the professor. The college soon reduced its staff and told the professor his contract would not be renewed.

The college's long-term disability carrier denied the professor's application for benefits. The professor was told to file another claim seeking benefits for a period during which he was not working and receiving a full salary. The professor continued to teach at the college, but sued the college and several officials in a state court for privacy rights violations. **The court found the only evidence the professor presented was the phone call between DeVry and the HR department. He did not indicate any confidential information was shared when the HR department confirmed he worked at the college.** The court granted the university's motion to dismiss the case. *Fish v. William Jewel College*, No. 05-00025-CV-W-DW, 2006 WL 2228975 (W.D. Mo. 8/3/06).

◆ *Statutory colleges operated by a private university had to comply with freedom of information requests.*

A New York citizen filed Freedom of Information Law (FOIL) requests on two statutory colleges that were technically part of the State University of New York system, but that were operated by Cornell University, a private institution. The colleges refused to disclose the information sought (on a possible agricultural technology park, and research on genetically modified organisms), and an Article 78 proceeding ensued, where the colleges were ordered to comply with the FOIL request. The New York Supreme Court, Appellate Division, affirmed. Even though the statutory colleges were operated by a private university, the legislature had authorized the dissemination of such information by Cornell, and **the requested information concerned a public interest**. Accordingly, the colleges had to release the requested information. *Alderson v. New York State College of Agriculture*, 749 N.Y.S.2d 581 (N.Y. App. Div. 2002).

II. LABOR RELATIONS

The National Labor Relations Act (NLRA), as amended by the Labor Management Relations Act (LMRA), 29 U.S.C. § 141, et seq., governs unionization and collective bargaining matters in the private sector, including private education. States are also subject to the dictates of the act. The NLRA was passed to protect the rights of employees to organize, or to choose not to organize, and to ensure that commerce is not interrupted by labor disputes. Managerial employees are unprotected by the NLRA.

A. Appropriate Bargaining Units

◆ *In certain circumstances, faculty members at private educational institutions can be considered managerial employees.*

Yeshiva University's faculty association had petitioned the National Labor Relations Board (NLRB) for certification as bargaining agent for all faculty members. The NLRB granted certification but the university refused to bargain. After the U.S. Court of Appeals declined to enforce the NLRB's order that the university bargain with the union, the NLRB appealed to the U.S. Supreme Court, which upheld the appeals court. The Supreme Court's ruling was based on its conclusion that Yeshiva's faculty were managerial employees. It stated:

> The controlling consideration in this case is that the faculty of Yeshiva University exercise authority which in any other context unquestionably would be managerial. **Their authority in academic matters is absolute.** They decide what courses will be offered, when they will be scheduled, and to whom they will be taught. They debate and determine teaching methods, grading policies, and matriculation standards. They effectively decide which students will be admitted, retained, and graduated. On occasion their views have determined the size of the student body, the tuition to be charged, and the location of a school. When one considers the function of a university, it is difficult to imagine decisions more managerial than these. To the extent the industrial analogy applies, the faculty determines within each school the product to be produced, the terms upon which it will be offered, and the customers who will be served.

The Court noted that its decision applied only to schools that were "like Yeshiva" and not to schools where the faculty exercised less control. **Schools** where faculty do not exercise binding managerial discretion do not fall within the scope of the managerial employee exclusion. *NLRB v.Yeshiva Univ.*, 444 U.S. 672, 100 S.Ct. 856, 63 L.Ed.2d 115 (1980).

◆ *An exclusive bargaining representative that is duly elected by school employees should have the sole voice in discussing employment-related matters with the employer.*

In a U.S. Supreme Court case, Minnesota community college faculty members brought suit against the State Board for Community Colleges. **The faculty alleged that a state statute requiring public employers to engage in official exchanges of views only with their professional employees' exclusive representatives on certain policy questions violated their First Amendment rights.** Under the statute, public employers were required to bargain only with the employees' exclusive bargaining representative. The statute gave professional employees, such as college faculty members, the right to "meet and confer" with the employer on matters outside the scope of the collective bargaining agreement.

The faculty members objected to the "meet and confer" provision, saying that rights of professional employees within the bargaining unit who were not members of the exclusive representative were violated. The Supreme Court held that the "meet and confer" provision did not violate the faculty members' constitutional rights. **There was no constitutional right to force public employers to listen to the members' views.** The fact that an academic setting was involved did not give them any special constitutional right to a voice in the employer's policymaking decisions. Further, the state had a legitimate interest in ensuring that its public employer heard one voice presenting the majority view of its professional employees on employment-related policy questions. *Minnesota Community College Ass'n v. Knight*, 465 U.S. 271, 104 S.Ct. 1058, 79 L.Ed.2d 299 (1984).

◆ *The Supreme Court held a public university could require faculty to emphasize undergraduate instruction without bargaining over the new rule.*

The Ohio legislature passed a statute requiring state universities to adopt faculty workload policies and made them an inappropriate subject for collective bargaining. The law was enacted to address the decline in the amount of time faculty spent teaching, as opposed to time spent on research. Any university policy prevailed over the contrary provisions of collective bargaining agreements. One university adopted a workload policy pursuant to the law and notified the collective bargaining agent that it would not bargain over the policy. As a result, **the professors' union filed a state court action, seeking an order that the statute violated public employee equal protection rights.** The Supreme Court of Ohio struck down the statute, finding the collective bargaining exemption was not rationally related to the state's interest of encouraging public university professors to spend less time researching at the expense of undergraduate teaching.

The U.S. Supreme Court accepted the university's appeal, and held that the state supreme court had not applied the correct standard of review under the Equal Protection Clause. In equal protection clause cases that do not involve fundamental rights or suspect classifications, there need only be a rational relationship between disparity of treatment and some legitimate government purpose. In this case, the disputed statute met the rational relationship standard. Ohio could reasonably conclude that the policy would be undercut if it were subjected to collective bargaining. **The state legislature could properly determine that collective bargaining would interfere with the legitimate goal of achieving uniformity in faculty workloads.** The Ohio Supreme Court decision was reversed and remanded. *Cent. State Univ. v. American Ass'n of Univ. Professors, Cent. State Univ. Chapter,* 526 U.S. 124, 119 S.Ct. 1162, 143 L.Ed.2d 227 (1999).

◆ *A District of Columbia court remanded an NLRB decision recognizing a bargaining unit for college faculty members.*

Approximately 60 full-time faculty members at LeMoyne-Owen College attempted to form a collective bargaining unit. The college denied the request because it considered them managerial employees who were exempt from NLRA coverage. The faculty petitioned the NLRB for recognition as a bargaining unit. The college opposed the petition, citing the Supreme Court's decision in *NLRB v. Yeshiva Univ.,* above, as controlling precedent. The NLRB regional director found the college's faculty were not managerial employees and certified the bargaining unit. The college sought review, arguing the regional director deviated from *Yeshiva* and other precedents.

The NLRB found the college guilty of an unfair labor practice when it refused to bargain with the new bargaining unit. The college petitioned for review of the NLRB's order. The District of Columbia Circuit Court remanded the case. While deference is generally afforded to the NLRB's authority to certify bargaining units, the decision in this case departed from precedent without explanation. The NLRB had an obligation to explain itself. The college made a reasoned argument based on the *Yeshiva* case. The regional director did not explain why the college's argument should be rejected. The court remanded the case to the NLRB for further proceedings. *LeMoyne-Owen College v. NLRB,* 357 F.3d 55 (D.C. Cir. 2004).

◆ *A Michigan court upheld a determination by the State Employment Relations Commission to deny a petition to merge two bargaining units.*

Kendall College of Art and Design is a sub-unit within Ferris State University. Kendall retains its own academic governance and operates autonomously. Although the university has the authority to make changes to Kendall, it has not exercised that power. The Ferris Faculty Association, which represented full-time faculty members at the university, petitioned to add the Kendall bargaining unit to its bargaining unit. The Kendall unit was composed of both full-time and part-time faculty members.

The Michigan Employment Relations Commission denied the petition, and the association appealed. The Court of Appeals of Michigan explained a commission's determination of appropriate bargaining units was factual, and could not be disturbed unless there was a lack of competent, material, and substantial evidence. In reaching its decision, the commission focused on Kendall's academic autonomy from the university and the differences between the two educational institutions. The court rejected the association's argument that the commission erred in considering the bargaining history of the Kendall union. **Bargaining history is a relevant factor in considering whether a bargaining unit is appropriate.** The commission acknowledged the need "to avoid fractionalization or multiplicity of bargaining units." As the Kendall bargaining unit served its members well, it was an appropriate bargaining unit. The commission's decision was affirmed. *Ferris Faculty Ass'n v. Ferris State Univ.*, No. 243885, 2004 WL 144671 (Mich. Ct. App. 2004).

◆ *A state labor relations board used incorrect tests to determine whether two employees were "confidential employees" who were ineligible for the union.*

A union sought to represent all classified and specialist employees at an Illinois college. In the representation election, the union won by a single vote. The college challenged the result, asserting that two of the employees should not have been allowed to vote because they were "confidential employees" under the state labor relations act. One was a secretary; the other was a research associate – both reported to an assistant vice president for administrative affairs. An administrative law judge determined that the employees were confidential employees, and the state labor relations board upheld that decision.

The Appellate Court of Illinois reversed and remanded the case, finding that the board used the wrong tests to determine whether the employees were "confidential." Here, **although the college asserted that the employees were going to be performing duties related to the collective bargaining process, they had not yet done so.** Thus, the board should have determined whether there was a reasonable expectation that future job duties would satisfy the definition of a confidential position. *One Equal Voice v. Illinois Educ. Labor Relations Board*, 777 N.E.2d 648 (Ill. App. Ct. 2002).

◆ *The Second Circuit refused to enforce a National Labor Relations Board (NLRB) order requiring a New York college to bargain with a union because supervisors belonged to the union.*

The Security Department Membership (SDM) is the organization certified by the NLRB to represent Quinnipiac College's security personnel in collective bargaining. Quinnipiac refused to bargain with SDM, maintaining the organization was improperly certified because it included supervisors, who are excluded from collective bargaining under the NLRA. SDM was certified to include six dispatchers, four traffic-control officers, two shift supervisors and 18 assistant supervisors, four of whom act as shift supervisors at certain times. Quinnipiac objected to the inclusion of the two shift supervisors and the assistant supervisors who acted as shift supervisors. The NLRB conducted a hearing in response to the college's objection, but concluded the shift supervisors were not "supervisors" under the act. The board ordered Quinnipiac to bargain with SDM, but the college refused. The NLRB petitioned the U.S. Court of Appeals, Second Circuit to enforce the order.

The NLRA defines "supervisor" as an employee who has the authority to hire, transfer, suspend, lay off, recall, promote, discharge, assign, reward, discipline or responsibly direct other employees, or address grievances. According to the Second Circuit, Quinnipiac's shift supervisors made assignment decisions based on their own expertise and experience, despite the existence of college procedures. Shift supervisors also disciplined employees. Although security directors had to review any disciplinary procedures taken by the shift supervisors, they still amounted to a supervisor's duty. Lastly, the shift supervisors responsibly directed other security employees. In declining to enforce the NLRB's order, the Second Circuit remanded the matter, with the suggestion that the board review the membership of SDM and consider eliminating the shift supervisors from the bargaining unit. *NLRB v. Quinnipiac College*, 256 F.3d 68 (2d Cir. 2001).

B. Agency Fees

Many states have authorized public employee unions and government employers to enter into "agency-shop agreements." These agreements entitle unions to assess "agency fees" upon employees who are not union members, but who enjoy the representation of unions. The U.S. Supreme Court has held public sector agency-shop arrangements raise First Amendment concerns by forcing individuals to contribute to unions as a condition of public employment.

In Abood v. Detroit Board of Educ., *below,* **the Court held unions cannot use agency fees collected from objecting nonmembers for ideological purposes that are unrelated to collective bargaining.**

◆ *The U.S. Supreme Court upheld a Washington law requiring public employee unions to obtain affirmative authorization from nonmember employees before using agency fees for election-related purposes.*

Washington law permits public employee unions to charge nonmembers who are in the collective bargaining unit an "agency fee" that is equivalent to full union membership dues. In 1992, state voters approved an initiative that prohibited unions from spending the agency fees collected from union nonmembers unless the expenditure was "affirmatively authorized by the individual" nonmember. The initiative became Section 760 of the Fair Campaign Practices Act. The Washington Education Association (WEA) faced separate state court actions claiming it used nonmember agency fees for election-related purposes without the affirmative authorization of union nonmembers. The cases were consolidated. The Supreme Court of Washington held the affirmative authorization requirement violated the First Amendment.

The State of Washington and other parties appealed to the U.S. Supreme Court. It held *Abood* **and later decisions did not require public sector unions to obtain affirmative consent before spending nonmember agency fees for purposes unrelated to collective bargaining**. The Court said Section 760 was a "modest limitation" on the extraordinary power of a private union over public employees to prohibit the use of agency fees for election-related purposes. This did not violate the First Amendment. In fact, the Court stated "it would be constitutional for Washington to eliminate agency fees entirely." The Court vacated the state court decision, finding Section 760 was a constitutional condition that presented no realistic threat of official suppression of ideas. *Davenport v. Washington Educ. Ass'n*, 127 S.Ct. 2372 (U.S. 2007).

◆   *Compelled agency fees cannot be used to support political viewpoints.*

In 1977, the U.S. Supreme Court held that the First Amendment prohibited states from compelling teachers to pay union dues or agency fees where their labor unions used the fees for purposes that were unrelated to collective bargaining. Compelled support of collective bargaining representatives implicated free speech, freedom of association, and freedom of religion concerns. However, some constitutional infringement on those rights was justified in the interest of peaceful labor relations. Thus, as long as the union acted to promote the cause of its membership, individual members were not free to withdraw their financial support. However, **compelled agency fees could not be used to support political views and ideological causes that were unrelated to collective bargaining issues**. *Abood v. Detroit Board of Educ.*, 431 U.S. 209, 97 S.Ct. 1782, 52 L.Ed.2d 261 (1977).

◆   *In order to justify agency fees, the activities for which the fees are collected must be germane to collective bargaining activity, be justified by the government's interest in labor peace (and the avoidance of free riders), and present only an insignificant burden on employee speech.*

The exclusive bargaining representative of the faculty at a state college in Michigan entered into an agency-shop arrangement with the college requiring nonunion bargaining unit employees to pay a service or agency fee equivalent to a union member's dues. Employees who objected to particular uses by the unions of their service fee brought suit under 42 U.S.C. § 1983, claiming that using the fees for purposes other than negotiating and administering the collective bargaining agreement violated their First and Fourteenth Amendment rights. A federal district court held that certain collective bargaining expenses were chargeable to the dissenting employees. The U.S. Court of Appeals affirmed, and the U.S. Supreme Court granted certiorari. The Court first noted that chargeable activities must be "germane" to collective bargaining activity and be justified by the policy interest of avoiding "free riders" who benefit from union efforts without paying for union services. It then stated that **the local union could charge the objecting employees for their** *pro rata* **share of costs associated with chargeable activities of its state and national affiliates, even if those activities did not directly benefit the local bargaining unit.** The local could even charge the dissenters for expenses incident to preparation for a strike, which would be illegal under Michigan law. However, lobbying activities and public relations efforts were not chargeable to the objecting employees. The Court affirmed in part and reversed in part the lower courts' decisions and remanded the case. *Lehnert v. Ferris Faculty Ass'n*, 500 U.S. 507, 111 S.Ct. 1950, 114 L.Ed.2d 572 (1991).

◆   *A union's objection procedures for challenging nonmembers' dues were constitutional.*

Two University of Alaska professors challenged their union's procedures for calculating nonmember dues. Under the collective bargaining agreement, if they declined union membership, they had a choice of either objecting to the use of their dues for unrelated union activities (and paying a reduced agency fee) or requesting arbitration to determine if the nonmember fee was accurate.

Under the second option, the arbitrator had the option of raising the amount. A federal court ruled that the union's procedure was constitutional, and the Ninth Circuit Court of Appeals affirmed. Here, the procedures complied with the requirements set forth by the U.S. Supreme Court in *Chicago Teachers Union v. Hudson*, 475 U.S. 292 (1986). **The professors received an adequate explanation of the basis for calculating the agency fee, and they were provided with a reasonably prompt opportunity to challenge the amount of the fee before an impartial decisionmaker.** *Carlson v. United Academics-AAUP/AFT/APEA AFL-CIO*, 265 F.3d 778 (9th Cir. 2001).

◆ *An Illinois local failed to provide adequate procedural protections to non-bargaining unit members who objected to its nonrepresentational activities.*

In federal court, a group of non-bargaining unit members, employed by a university as clerical employees, filed a class action suit against the union. The nonmembers asserted that the union's fair share fee collection procedure failed to provide sufficient safeguards, thereby violating the First and Fourteenth Amendments. The union moved to dismiss the complaint. The court interpreted the union's response as a pretrial judgment motion and ruled in favor of the union. The employees appealed.

The Seventh Circuit reversed. Pursuant to the Illinois Educational Labor Relations Act (IELRA), the amount of fair share fees "can neither exceed union dues nor include any costs related to supporting candidates for political office." In *Chicago Teachers Union v. Hudson*, 475 U.S. 292 (1986), the U.S. Supreme Court required a union to satisfy the following three prongs in collecting these fees: (1) provide "an adequate explanation of the basis for the fee"; (2) provide the nonmember with a reasonable opportunity to protest the fee amount; and (3) establish "an escrow account for the amounts in dispute." Here, the union had the university collect 100% of union dues from both members and nonmembers, even though the fair share fee calculated for two of the disputed years amounted to about 85% of full dues. When an objection was filed, the nonmember fees were then held in an escrow account, which could not be accessed by the union. **The collection of fees, based on an advance reduction approach, was not as problematic as the dispute resolution procedure.** Under the IELRA, objectors were deprived of 15% of their funds for a year, a portion of which was not even being disputed. In addition, the fee objections had to be renewed annually. These burdens violated the *Hudson* test. *Tavernor v. Illinois Federation of Teachers*, 226 F.3d 842 (7th Cir. 2000).

◆ *In response to challenges by nonunion public school and state university teachers against the union for assessing them certain agency fees, a court of appeals held that union officials' salaries were chargeable, but expenses related to a two-day strike by university faculty were not.*

Public school teachers and state university instructors sued the Massachusetts Teachers Association (MTA) for charging them agency fees for activities the teachers claimed were not part of doing business as a bargaining representative. The Massachusetts Labor Relations Commission examined the

MTA's expenditures for 1990–1991 to determine which expenses were chargeable to nonunion members and which were not. The commission concluded that the MTA had demanded $26.77 in excess service fees from each of the nonunion members.

The Massachusetts Court of Appeals largely upheld the commission's ruling, finding that unions are not required to submit evidence showing that each expense incurred for a conference or meeting is exclusively incurred in furtherance of a chargeable activity. The MTA's accounting expenses were chargeable, according to the court, except for the 14 hours the accounting staff devoted to non-chargeable activities. **The union president and vice president's salaries were overhead and therefore chargeable in proportion to the union's overall chargeable activities.** Discussions the union had about a statewide strike to publicize the condition of public education funding were not chargeable. Expenses related to two days in 1991 when faculty at the University of Massachusetts at Amherst withheld services to protest the lack of funding for their collective bargaining agreement were also not chargeable, even though the university administration approved of and participated in the protest. Because the faculty had withheld services, the two-day action was a strike, and the expenses incidental to it were not chargeable. Nor were the costs of flyers distributed during 1991 commencement exercises at the University of Massachusetts at Boston chargeable to nonunion members. Distribution of the flyers was a public relations activity not germane to the union's collective bargaining functions. However, expenses related to an article that appeared in a union magazine providing pointers on how to communicate during a strike or some other unusual event were chargeable. *Belhumeur v. Labor Relations Comm'n*, 432 Mass. 458, 735 N.E.2d 860 (Mass. App. Ct. 2000).

C. Collective Bargaining Agreements

◆ *A union's waiver of employee rights to negotiate an intellectual property policy survived the expiration of a collective bargaining agreement. For that reason, refusal to negotiate the policy was not an improper labor practice.*

The City University of New York (CUNY) adopted a policy in 1972 addressing intellectual property developed by its employees. The policy was not the subject of collective bargaining between CUNY and the Professional Staff Congress (PSC), which represented CUNY employees. The parties' 1996-2000 collective bargaining agreement expired, and PSC demanded that the intellectual property policy be negotiated. CUNY asserted Article 2 of the expired agreement constituted a waiver by the union to negotiate particular items, including the policy. Article 2 authorized CUNY's board of trustees to alter existing bylaws or policies "respecting a term or condition of employment" after giving PSC notice and an opportunity to consult. PSC filed an improper practice charge with the state public employment relations board (PERB). The parties reached a new agreement covering 2000-2002, and the PSC withdrew its proposal on the intellectual property policy. The new agreement carried forward Article 2, unchanged from the prior agreement. Just before expiration of the 2000-2002 agreement, PSC again sought to negotiate the intellectual property policy. An administrative law judge held CUNY committed an improper practice by refusing to negotiate the policy.

The PERB held PSC waived its right to negotiate the intellectual property policy in Article 2. The case reached the Court of Appeals of New York, which held the resolution of improper practice charges was generally within PERB's discretion. Article 2 granted CUNY the right to unilaterally alter bylaws and policies respecting terms or conditions of employment that did not conflict with the agreement. Article 2 explicitly referred to "terms and conditions of employment," and it was not confined to "management prerogatives." **The court held the intellectual property policy was squarely within the coverage of Article 2, since it was never a part of a collective bargaining agreement and did not conflict with any terms of the current agreement.** Civil Service Law Section 209-a(1)(e) required employers to continue all terms of an expired agreement while a new one was being negotiated. This enhanced the negotiating process by preserving the status quo pending a new agreement. As the PERB had correctly determined the status quo and found the Article 2 waiver remained in effect, the court reinstated its decision. *Professional Staff Congress-City Univ. of New York v. New York State Public Employment Relations Board*, 7 N.Y.3d 458, 857 N.E.2d 1108 (N.Y. 2006).

◆ *A California court rejected a nurse's claim that her dismissal from a student clinic violated her due process and collective bargaining rights.*

A nurse practitioner who worked at a university clinic examined a student and determined she was 24 weeks pregnant. The student wanted to abort the pregnancy, but the nurse recommended against it, saying the pregnancy was too advanced. The nurse later urged the student to put the baby up for adoption and told her that a colleague at the clinic was interested in adopting it. A supervisor learned of the plan and admonished the nurse for unethical conduct. The student later had the baby, and the colleague took it home from the hospital.

The university discharged the nurse, and her grievance was denied. She requested a hearing that was later cancelled by a union representative based on insufficient notice of witnesses and the university's refusal to allow her to issue subpoenas. A hearing was held in the nurse's absence, and the hearing officer upheld the dismissal. The nurse appealed to a state trial court, which dismissed the case. The Court of Appeal of California found the nurse had no right to invoke arbitration. It also rejected her claims that the hearing officer was biased and the proceedings were inherently unfair. The university's failure to provide her with a witness list seven days before the hearing did not prejudice her case. By then, the nurse had already gone through the grievance procedure and knew the identity of the witnesses. Her inability to subpoena witnesses did not render the process unfair. **Since the nurse voluntarily failed to appear for her hearing, she could not now complain it was unfair to hold it in her absence.** The judgment was affirmed. *Nelson v. Regents of the Univ. of California*, No. D040623, 2004 WL 339340 (Cal. Ct. App. 2004).

◆ *A union could use a university's e-mail system to contact members where the collective bargaining agreement did not prohibit it.*

The union representing Oregon University System employees negotiated a collective bargaining agreement that allowed union officers and stewards to "have access to electronic bulletin boards under specified conditions." The union then began using e-mail to transmit information to its members' work computers. The university objected to this practice, claiming that the bargaining agreement did not allow the union to use e-mail in that way. After two arbitrators determined that the university could prohibit union officials from using the e-mail system, the Oregon Court of Appeals determined that the union's use of e-mail neither violated the terms of the bargaining agreement nor breached its duty of good faith and fair dealing. **The bargaining agreement was silent with respect to the union's use of e-mail.** Thus, there was no breach of contract and no bad faith. *Oregon Univ. System v. Oregon Public Employees Union, Local 503*, 60 P.3d 567 (Or. Ct. App. 2002).

◆   *Adjunct faculty members were allowed to join a union in New Hampshire.*
A labor association seeking to represent 147 adjunct faculty members at a New Hampshire state college petitioned for certification by the Public Employees Labor Relations Board (PELRB). The university system opposed the petition, arguing that adjunct faculty are temporary employees who are excluded from bargaining because of their temporary status. A hearing officer granted the petition, allowing instructors who were currently teaching, and those who had taught two of the last three semesters, to join the union. The PELRB upheld that decision, and the adjunct faculty voted for the union.

The case reached the Supreme Court of New Hampshire, which found that there is some expectation that adjunct faculty members will return annually – they are compensated for longevity. The court affirmed the PELRB's decision that **adjunct faculty members are not temporary employees**. Even though the contracts they signed did not include an expectation of continued employment, that fact did not necessarily diminish the adjunct faculty members' **reasonable expectation of continued employment**. The fact that adjunct instructors taught one-third of the college's courses indicated that they were not just "last-minute" hires. The court remanded the case to consider who was eligible for union membership. The PELRB did not provide an explanation for why only adjuncts who were currently teaching or who had taught two of the last three semesters were eligible. *In re Univ. System of New Hampshire*, 795 A.2d 840 (N.H. 2002).

◆   *Hawaii could not enact a law eliminating state university employee rights to collectively bargain.*
A Hawaii law prohibited the state university system from negotiating over "cost items" during the 1999-2001 biennium. Because wages, hours, pensions, and other terms and conditions of employment were "cost items," public employee unions sued, seeking a declaration that the law was unconstitutional. The Hawaii Supreme Court struck down the law. Even though the state constitution gave the legislature the ultimate authority over collective bargaining "as provided by law," that authority was granted within the framework of existing **federal law that granted employees the right to bargain collectively**. Since the law would deny public employees the right to bargain collectively, it could not stand. *United Public Workers, AFSCME, Local 646, AFL-CIO v. Yogi*, 62 P.3d 189 (Haw. 2002).

◆ *The D.C. Circuit adopted a test for determining whether a religious institution can exempt itself from NLRB jurisdiction for collective bargaining.*

The University of Great Falls, which is operated by the Sisters of Providence (a Roman Catholic religious order) refused to recognize or bargain with the Montana Federation of Teachers. The university maintained that the NLRB lacked jurisdiction because the school was a religiously run institution, and also asserted that the Religious Freedom Restoration Act barred the NLRB from ordering it to engage in collective bargaining. The union petitioned the NLRB for relief, and the regional director examined the university's mission, courses and operation before ruling that the NLRB had jurisdiction. The NLRB upheld that determination, and the university appealed to the U.S. Court of Appeals, D.C. Circuit. The appellate court vacated the NLRB's decision and order. It stated that the NLRB had improperly engaged in an examination of the university's religious character.

The court adopted **a three-part test for determining whether an institution can avail itself of the exemption in** *NLRB v. Catholic Bishop of Chicago*, 440 U.S. 490 (1979) (see Chapter Four, Section I.B), where the Supreme Court held that the NLRB did not have jurisdiction over religious institutions. Under this test, an institution must: 1) provide a religious educational environment and hold itself out as such, 2) be organized by a nonprofit, and 3) be "affiliated with, or owned, operated or controlled directly or indirectly, by either a recognized religious organization or with an entity, membership of which is determined, at least in part, with reference to religion." Here, the university easily passed that test. As a result, the NLRB did not have jurisdiction, and the university did not have to bargain with the union. *Univ. of Great Falls v. NLRB*, 278 F.3d 1335 (D.C. Cir. 2002).

◆ *A law allowing Hawaii to postpone employees' pay by a few days was unconstitutional.*

To remedy a budget crisis, Hawaii passed a law authorizing the state to postpone by a few days, at six different times, the dates on which state employees were to be paid. It also declared that the postponements were "not subject to negotiation" by the state employees' unions. University of Hawaii faculty members and their union sued in federal district court to stop the state from implementing the law, and the district court granted the injunction. The case then reached the Ninth Circuit Court of Appeals, which affirmed. It held that **the law violated the U.S. Constitution's Contract Clause by substantially impairing the state's obligation to honor its collective bargaining agreements with the unions.** The law not only changed the employees' pay dates, but also removed "the whole subject from the bargaining table." It could not be justified as reasonable and necessary because there were less drastic ways to reduce the state's financial obligations. *Univ. of Hawaii Professional Assembly v. Cayetano*, 183 F.3d 1096 (9th Cir. 1999).

◆ *Where a no-smoking policy was not included in a collective bargaining agreement, a university did not have to bargain over the policy.*

The University of Alaska's Board of Regents adopted a policy that excluded smoking from university facilities that were open to the public. It later amended the policy to prohibit smoking in motor vehicles. Prior to the adoption of the policy, the union representing certain university employees formally requested bargaining. One union member learned of the revised smoking policy but continued to smoke in the vehicle assigned to him. He was censured for smoking in the vehicle and circulated a petition signed by 30 union members asking the union to negotiate the non-smoking policy.

The union presented the proposal to the university, which refused to bargain, asserting that the policy was a permissive subject for which it had no obligation to bargain. **The parties reached a collective bargaining agreement that was ratified by the union membership containing no express reference to the non-smoking policy.** The agreement contained a reservation of rights clause stating that bargaining unit members agreed to follow all university policies not specified in the agreement and reserving the right to change university policies. The union filed an unfair labor practice against the university, asserting that the non-smoking policy was a mandatory subject of bargaining. The state labor relations agency determined that the policy was a mandatory subject of bargaining, but that the union had contractually waived it by executing the collective bargaining agreement. On appeal, the Supreme Court of Alaska observed that **because the collective bargaining agreement contained no specific reference to the non-smoking policy, the union had contractually waived its right to bargain on that issue** by agreeing to the contract. The union could also be deemed to have waived its right to bargain under the reservation of rights section of the agreement. The court affirmed the agency ruling that the union had waived bargaining on the policy by entering into the agreement. *Univ. of Alaska v. Univ. of Alaska Classified Employees Ass'n,* 952 P.2d 1182 (Alaska 1998).

◆ *A law requiring Massachusetts employees to take days off or to work for deferred pay violated the Contract Clause of the Constitution by substantially impairing the state's obligations under the collective bargaining agreements. Such impairment was neither reasonable nor necessary.*

In the face of a perceived fiscal crisis, **Massachusetts implemented a mandatory furlough program for almost all state employees.** Under the program, employees could take unpaid days off, work without pay and receive bonus paid vacation days after the beginning of the next fiscal year, or work without pay and receive a lump sum payment upon terminating employment with the state. The amount of mandated days off increased with the amount of compensation an employee earned. After faculty and various professional staff at several of the state's community colleges, and unions representing employees in the state college system challenged the program, the case reached the Supreme Judicial Court of Massachusetts.

The court found that **the program violated the Contract Clause of the U.S. Constitution by substantially impairing the state's obligation to pay compensation to affected employees under their collective bargaining agreements.** Further, the state was unable to show that the impairment was both reasonable and necessary to serve an important state purpose. Because the increasing fiscal deficit problems were reasonably foreseeable at the time the state entered into the collective bargaining agreements with the employees, the substantial impairment of the employees' rights under those contracts (after the contracts were signed) could not be reasonable. The court struck down the mandatory furlough program. *Massachusetts Community College Council v. Comm'n*, 649 N.E.2d 708 (Mass. 1995).

◆ *Florida could not renege on a contract that promised pay raises to public employees.*

During the collective bargaining process, unions representing public employees in Florida reached an impasse with the state. The legislature resolved the impasse by authorizing a 3% pay raise, which the unions ratified. Subsequently, state officials projected a shortfall in public revenues, causing the legislature to convene a special session and postpone the pay raises. Several months later, the legislature responded to continuing revenue shortfalls by eliminating the pay raises altogether. When the unions sued, a state trial court ruled in their favor, and the state appealed. The Supreme Court of Florida affirmed the ruling against the state. **Here, the state had a fully enforceable agreement with the unions that it could not break unless there existed no other reasonable alternative means of preserving the contract, in whole or in part.** The state could not nullify the pay raises simply because that was the most expedient solution. By appropriating public money to fund the pay raises, the state and all its branches became bound by the agreement. The court ordered the state to take the necessary steps to implement the pay raises. *Chiles v. United Faculty of Florida*, 615 So.2d 671 (Fla. 1993).

D. Arbitration

◆ *An arbitrator wrongfully placed the burden on a Pennsylvania university to show it had good reason to deny tenure to a probationary faculty member.*

The university denied the professor tenure because she failed to demonstrate the requisite scholarly growth. Her professional union filed a grievance on her behalf under the relevant collective bargaining agreement (CBA). After the grievance was denied at all levels, the matter proceeded to arbitration, where an arbitrator held in the professor's favor. He ordered her reinstated as a probationary faculty member who was eligible for reconsideration for tenure. The university appealed to the state court system.

The case reached the Commonwealth Court of Pennsylvania, which noted courts generally defer to the decisions of arbitrators when parties have agreed via a CBA to use arbitration to resolve disputes. **However, an arbitrator's decision is not entitled to deference unless it "draws its essence" from the CBA.** In this case, the CBA did not expressly state which party bore the burden of proof in a grievance proceeding regarding tenure. **The agreement between the university and union specified that tenure candidates had the burden of showing requirements for tenure had been met.** The arbitrator should have consulted this agreement and placed the burden of proof on the professor. The arbitrator's award was vacated, and the case was remanded for additional proceedings. *Slippery Rock Univ. of Pennsylvania v. Ass'n of Pennsylvania State College and Univ. Faculties*, 916 A.2d 736 (Pa. Commw. Ct. 2007).

◆   *The Vermont State Colleges Federation did not unlawfully retaliate against a faculty member by declining to accommodate her scheduling request.*

The faculty member worked part time at a state college. The applicable collective bargaining agreement required the college to give priority to full-time faculty and administrators in scheduling matters. The faculty member filed a grievance when she was not assigned a schedule that accommodated her child care and commuting needs. She later complained about a new schedule. The department decided not to change the new schedule and she filed another grievance, this time for retaliation for her earlier grievance.

A grievance board found the college could have made some adjustments and was unlawfully motivated by the prior grievance. On appeal, the Supreme Court of Vermont found the faculty member did not present any direct evidence of a discriminatory motive. The court disagreed with the board's findings that the timing of the new schedule was suspicious, and that the college treated the faculty member less favorably than others. **The court noted an adverse employment decision following a successful grievance is not necessarily suspicious. The court said the faculty member presented no other evidence to infer the college retaliated because of her earlier grievance.** There was no basis to infer the timing was suspicious or that the college was unlawfully motivated. The court reversed the board's decision. *Grievance of Rosenberg v. Vermont State Colleges*, 852 A.2d 599 (Vt. 2004).

◆   *A Massachusetts employee association's decision not to invoke arbitration did not breach its duty of fair representation.*

The Massachusetts Maritime Academy employed an instructor under two one-year temporary appointment letters. He filed a grievance to protest the academy's decision denying him tenure. The Massachusetts State College Association represented academy employees and presented the case before a grievance committee. After the committee denied the grievance, the association decided not to invoke arbitration. The instructor filed a charge against the association with the state labor relations commission for unfair representation in refusing to proceed with his grievance to arbitration. The commission dismissed the charge, finding the association did not act arbitrarily.

The state appeals court affirmed the commission's decision. In reviewing the record, the court found the commission carefully reviewed the association's actions. **The association complied with its representational obligation under the terms of the collective bargaining agreement by filing the grievance, explaining the procedure to the instructor, and representing him before the grievance committee.** The decision not to invoke arbitration was a reasonable determination based on the evidence. The temporary appointment letters undermined the instructor's claim that he was promised tenure. The commission's decision was affirmed. *Gable v. Labor Relations Comm'n*, 59 Mass. App. 1101, 793 N.E.2d 1286 (Mass. App. Ct. 2003).

◆   *An Alaska university could raise nonunion salaries to redress past inequities in pay.*

The University of Alaska suspended a 3% salary increase for all employees due to a perceived financial crisis. A teachers' union filed a grievance, and union employees received the salary increase. Nonunion employees did not get the raise. Two years later, the university commissioned a study to identify underpaid employees, and decided to award certain nonunion employees a 2.6% salary increase. The union and six female faculty members filed another grievance, asserting that they were entitled to the 2.6% raise. Before that grievance was resolved, a third grievance was filed and settled, in which 26 faculty members received pay increases. The second grievance then went to arbitration, and the arbitrator found that the pay raise to nonunion employees was not motivated by illegal discrimination. However, he ordered the university to perform a new compensation study and apply a 2.6% pay increase to correct any identified inequalities.

The case reached the Supreme Court of Alaska, which refused to uphold the arbitrator's award. **The arbitrator committed "gross error" in finding that the university violated the collective bargaining agreement where there was no illegal discrimination.** The raise was an attempt to redress past salary inequities in a fair and equitable manner, not an attempt to discriminate against women or union members. *Univ. of Alaska v. Alaska Community Colleges' Federation of Teachers*, 64 P.3d 823 (Alaska 2003).

◆   *An arbitrator's decision was entitled to deference in a dispute over discovery of information.*

When a professor complained to her union that she was denied a merit compensation award based on her involvement with the union, the union filed a grievance on her behalf and requested from the university documentation regarding all merit applications and merit recommendations. The university denied the request. The grievance proceeded to arbitration, and the union filed an unfair labor practice charge against the university. During the arbitration, the union was supplied with the requested information. Ultimately, the arbitrator denied the professor's claim. The Delaware Public Employee Relations Board held the university committed an unfair labor practice by denying the request for discovery information. The Delaware Supreme Court held **the board should have deferred to the arbitrator's decision**. The collective bargaining agreement provided specific timelines under which the university had to comply with the arbitrator's requests for information, and the discovery and merit award issues were fully resolved by the arbitrator's ruling. *Delaware State Univ. Chapter of American Ass'n of Univ. Professors v. Delaware State Univ.*, 813 A.2d 1133 (Del. 2003).

◆   *The arbitration provision of a union-negotiated collective bargaining agreement was not enforceable in the following case.*

A clerical employee for New York University filed a discrimination suit against the school after she was fired for not returning to work when her leave under the Family Medical Leave Act expired. She claimed that the collective bargaining agreement, which governed the terms of her employment, explicitly prohibited discrimination by her employer. The university filed a motion to stay the action because the collective bargaining agreement stipulated that all disputes under the agreement would be arbitrated. The trial court denied the university's motion to stay pending arbitration and the university appealed.

The Second Circuit affirmed. Under *Alexander v. Gardner-Denver Co.*, 415 U.S. 36 (1974), an employee who is subject to a collective bargaining arbitration clause is not precluded from bringing suit in federal court. In addition, the Supreme Court's decision in *Wright v. Universal Maritime Service Corp.*, 525 U.S. 70 (1998), stated that **employees waive their rights under a federal statute only if a collective bargaining agreement explicitly states that is the case.** Here, the applicable agreement did not specifically state that employees waived their statutory right to bring discrimination claims in federal court. The Second Circuit ruled the arbitration clause was not "clear and unmistakable," as required by *Wright*. The fact that the agreement stated that discrimination laws were relevant – but did not explicitly state that discrimination claims must be arbitrated – demonstrated that the arbitration clause did not, under *Wright*, force the employee to waive her right to sue. *Rogers v. New York Univ.*, 220 F.3d 73 (2d Cir. 2000).

III. OVERTIME AND WAGE DISPUTES

The payment of wages is covered by contract but is also subject to the requirements of the Fair Labor Standards Act and state wage laws.

◆ *A Georgia university did not breach a professor's employment contract when it recalculated his salary following a demotion.*

When the professor acquired tenure, the university paid him an annual salary of $49,537. It then appointed him to an associate vice president position at a salary of $70,000. Over the next three years, the professor entered into a series of one-year contracts, each providing for a pay increase. The university then decided to eliminate the associate vice president position. It notified the professor in writing of its decision and gave him the option of returning to the classroom at an annual salary of $54,341. The professor argued his salary computation was wrong, but his appeal failed. He sued the university in a state court for breach of contract. The court awarded summary judgment to the university, and the professor appealed to the Court of Appeals of Georgia.

The court found the university had compared the professor's salary to the salaries of other faculty members in his department. The head of the department earned $59,472 for the same academic year and the salaries of three associate professors who worked for the university for similar or longer time periods than the professor were less than his. **The court found the terms of the professor's contract were unambiguous. Since the contract was clear, the trial court had the discretion to determine its terms.** The court affirmed the judgment. *Homer v. Board of Regents of the Univ. System of Georgia*, 613 S.E.2d 205 (Ga. Ct. App. 2005).

◆ *A California trade school qualified as an institution of higher learning, and its instructors were professionals who did not qualify for overtime pay.*

The school received state accreditation and became a degree-granting institution in 2002. Its instructors held certificates of authorization for service under the Education Code. The state division of labor standards enforcement notified the school its instructors were not exempt from overtime pay under an administrative wage order. The school sought a declaration that its instructors were exempt from overtime pay as professional employees. A state trial court agreed, and held the instructors were exempt from the overtime wage order. The state court of appeal held the school qualified as a "college." It complied with statutory requirements to obtain accreditation. **The "teaching exception" was not limited to institutions granting bachelor's or higher degrees.** The division relied on outdated records and evidence in arguing trade schools were not exempt as not meeting the definition of "higher learning." Instead, the boundaries of California's education system had expanded to include a much broader category of institutions. **Since the professional exemption was not limited to instructors at institutions granting baccalaureate degrees or higher, the school's instructors were entitled to the professional exception,** and the court affirmed the judgment. *California School of Culinary Arts v. Lujan,* 112 Cal.App.4th 16, 4 Cal.Rptr.3d 785 (Cal. Ct. App. 2003).

◆ *A New York court held that a fee required by medical schools from physicians as a condition of employment violated state Education Law.*

Ophthalmologists who worked as full-time assistant professors at Columbia University wanted to continue practicing ophthalmology and remain on the faculty. In exchange for allowing them to change their appointments to part time, Columbia requested that they pay a 10% "Dean's Tax" on all their practice income. When they refused, their appointments were terminated.

The doctors sued Columbia in a state trial court, which held in their favor. A state appellate division court held that the **payment of the "Dean's Tax" as a condition of employment constituted illegal fee-splitting**. Because the doctors were no longer employees, and because Columbia was no longer providing them with benefits, facilities or malpractice insurance, the request was a violation of law. The court directed Columbia to review the applications for part-time appointments and affirmed the judgment. *Odrich v. Trustees of Columbia Univ.,* 764 N.Y.S.2d 448 (N.Y. App. Div. 2003).

◆ *A teacher who also worked for the university as a nurse was entitled to an accounting over discrepancies in her pay.*

As part of her contract, a teacher at a Mississippi nursing school was required to work at a school-operated clinic. Although she would earn more income by doing so, she also had to contribute half of any earnings over $10,000 to the clinic. In practice, the clinic held her earnings until the end of the year, then paid her her share. The agreement between the parties specified that all disputes were to be arbitrated. When the teacher noticed that she received only $767 one year, while the clinic kept $6,000, she requested an explanation and an accounting. The dean refused the request and then fired the teacher when she refused to continue working at the clinic. She filed a petition for an accounting with the Mississippi Chancery Court, and the university sought to compel arbitration. The court held that **the teacher was entitled to an accounting** and that the university waived its right to demand arbitration. On appeal, the Mississippi Supreme Court ruled that the university did not waive its right to demand arbitration by delaying its demand. However, the teacher was entitled to an accounting, which was not subject to arbitration. *Univ. Nursing Associates PLLC v. Phillips*, 842 So.2d 1270 (Miss. 2003).

◆ *Two part-time Washington community college instructors were not entitled to overtime wages.*

Part-time instructors from five community colleges in Washington brought a lawsuit alleging that the colleges violated the state's Minimum Wage Act by failing to compensate them for overtime work. Their wages were determined by multiplying their classroom hours by a negotiated hourly rate that included payment for time spent on course preparation, grading and office hours. However, they asserted that they were not exempt professional employees paid on a salary basis because the colleges docked their pay for time missed after all their accrued sick and annual leave was exhausted. The case reached the Washington Supreme Court, which ruled against them. It noted that as long as **their predetermined wages were not subject to reduction because of variations in the quality or quantity of work performed**, they still could be considered salary-basis employees. Under U.S. Department of Labor regulations adopted by the court, deductions for missed time after accrued sick and annual leave expire do not alter an employee's professional status. *Clawson v. Grays Harbor College Dist. No. 2*, 61 P.3d 1130 (Wash. 2003).

◆ *A coach obtained over $135,000 for fraud and Fair Labor Standards Act (FLSA) violations after the athletic director who hired him refused to pay him.*

The athletic director at an Illinois community college hired a basketball coach in March 1999 and promised him a teaching position in physical education for the following fall. The coach began his duties right away, but was not paid. In August, he filled out paperwork for the teaching position. He also made informal complaints to the athletic director, then filed a formal complaint regarding the payment of wages. After the athletic director told him he would not be paid for the work he had done the previous seven months, he sued under the FLSA. A jury awarded him $10,562 on that claim, as well as $52,526 in compensatory damages for the athletic director's fraud and $75,000 in punitive damages. The district court judge reversed the fraud claim, but the Seventh Circuit Court of Appeals reversed the district court judge. It found sufficient evidence to support the jury's determination that **the coach had justifiably relied on the athletic director's misrepresentations to his detriment**. The award in favor of the coach was reinstated. *Hefferman v. Board of Trustees of Illinois Community College Dist. 508*, 310 F.3d 522 (7th Cir. 2002).

◆ *Probationary campus police officers were not entitled to overtime for attending EMT classes.*

A Massachusetts university hired four campus police officers as probationary employees. As a condition of employment, the officers were required to obtain and retain certification as emergency medical technicians within one year of their hire date. The four officers took the EMT course at the university and completed the course. Although they were not paid for attending EMT classes after work, they were compensated when EMT classes occurred during their regular working hours. They sued the university under the FLSA, seeking overtime pay for time spent working toward their EMT certification. A federal court ruled in their favor, but the First Circuit reversed. It noted that the Portal-to-Portal Act of 1947 precluded liability. **The Portal-to-Portal Act permits an employer to avoid paying an employee for activities that are "preliminary or postliminary" to the principal activities the employee is engaged to perform.** Here, that condition was satisfied because the officers were attending the EMT classes during their probationary period, and they did not perform any EMT-related work until after obtaining certification. Thus, they could be characterized as students during their probationary period for purposes of avoiding overtime compensation. *Bienkowski v. Northeastern Univ.*, 285 F.3d 138 (1st Cir. 2002).

IV. LEAVES OF ABSENCE

The Family and Medical Leave Act of 1993 (FMLA), 29 U.S.C. §§ 2601–2654, makes available to eligible employees up to 12 weeks of unpaid leave per year: 1) because of the birth of a son or daughter of the employee and in order to care for such son or daughter; 2) because of the placement of a son or daughter with the employee for adoption or foster care; 3) in order to care for the spouse, or a son, daughter, or parent, of the employee, if such spouse, son, daughter or parent has a serious health condition; or 4) because of a serious health condition that makes the employee unable to perform the functions of the position of such employee. 29 U.S.C. § 2612.

The FMLA exempts small businesses and limits coverage of private employers to those engaged in commerce or in activities affecting commerce and who employ 50 or more employees for each working day during each of 20 or more calendar workweeks in the current or preceding calendar year. To be eligible for leave, an employee must have been employed by the covered employer for at least 12 months, and must have worked at least 1,250 hours during the 12 month period preceding the start of the leave. 29 U.S.C. § 2611.

If the employer provides paid leave for which the employee is eligible, the employee may elect, or the employer may require the employee, to substitute the paid leave for any part of the 12 weeks of leave to which the employee is entitled under the act. When the need for leave is foreseeable, the employee must provide reasonable prior notice (generally, at least 30 days for birth or placement of a child, and at least 30 days for planned medical treatment, unless the employee does not have 30 days in which to provide notice). The employee also must make efforts to schedule the leave so as not to unduly disrupt the employer's operations. Further, where spouses are employed by the same employer, they can be limited to a total of 12 weeks of leave for the birth or adoption of a child or for the care of a sick parent. 29 U.S.C. § 2612.

An employer may require medical certification to support a claim for leave for an employee's own serious health condition or to care for a seriously ill child, spouse or parent. If the certification is for the employee's health condition, it must contain a statement that the employee is unable to perform the functions of his or her position. 29 U.S.C. § 2613. If the certification is for a child, spouse or parent, it must include an estimate of the amount of time the employee is needed to care for the family member.

Further, an employer may require, at its own expense, a second opinion. 29 U.S.C. § 2613. An employer also may require an employee on leave to report periodically to the employer on his or her leave status and intention to return to work. 29 U.S.C. § 2614. The regulations implementing the FMLA (29 CFR Part 825) define "serious health condition" to include treatment two or more times by a health care provider, and a period of absence to receive multiple treatments "for a condition that would likely result in a period of incapacity of more than three consecutive calendar days in the absence of medical intervention or treatment." 29 C.F.R § 825.114.

An employee needing leave for a serious health condition may, if medically necessary, take leave intermittently or on a reduced leave schedule that reduces the employee's usual number of hours per workweek or per workday. However, if an employee requests leave on such a basis, the employer may require the employee to transfer temporarily to an alternative position that better accommodates the intermittent or reduced leave, provided that the position has equivalent pay and benefits. 29 U.S.C. § 2613.

During leave, any preexisting health benefits provided to the employee by the employer must be maintained. However, **the employer is under no obligation to allow the employee to accrue seniority or other employment benefits during the leave period**. 29 U.S.C. § 2614. Upon return from leave, the employee must be restored to the same or an equivalent position. However, the statute contains an exemption for certain highly compensated employees, allowing an employer to deny restoration if: 1) such denial is necessary to prevent substantial and grievous economic injury to the operations of the employer, 2) the employer notifies the employee of its intent to deny restoration on such basis at the time the employer determines that such injury would occur; and 3) in any case in which the leave has commenced, the employee elects not to return to employment after receiving such notice. 29 U.S.C. § 2614.

It is unlawful for an employer to interfere with, restrain, or deny the exercise of or the attempt to exercise, any right provided under the FMLA. 29 U.S.C. § 2615. It is also unlawful for an employer to discharge or in any other matter discriminate against any individual for opposing a practice made unlawful under the act, or for participating in any inquiry or proceeding relating to rights established under the act. 29 U.S.C. § 2615.

Rights established under the FMLA are enforceable through civil actions. An employer who violates Section 2615 will be liable for money damages resulting from the violation, and an additional amount equal to the actual damages as liquidated damages. The employer also may be required to provide equitable relief, including employment, reinstatement or promotion. 29 U.S.C.

§ 2617. Where an employer can prove to the satisfaction of the court that it acted in good faith and had reasonable grounds to believe that its acts or omissions were not a violation, the court may, in its discretion, limit the employer's damages liability to the actual damages and refuse to award liquidated damages. 29 U.S.C. § 2617. The prevailing plaintiff in an action under the FMLA also is entitled to reasonable attorneys' fees, expert witness fees, and other costs of the action.

Actions brought under the FMLA must be brought not later than two years after the date of the last event constituting the alleged violation for which the action is brought, or within the last three years of the last event if the violation is willful. 29 U.S.C. § 2617. An employee's right to bring a civil action terminates if the Secretary of Labor files an action seeking relief with respect to that employee. 29 U.S.C. § 2617.

The FMLA further provides that it does not modify or affect any federal or state law prohibiting discrimination on the basis of race, religion, color, national origin, sex, age or disability. 29 U.S.C. § 2651. It also states that nothing in the act shall be construed to supersede any provision of any state or local law that provides greater family or medical leave rights than the rights established under the FMLA or any amendment to it. 29 U.S.C. § 2651. Further, **nothing in the FMLA is to be construed to diminish the obligation of an employer to comply with any collective bargaining agreement or any employment benefit plan or program that provides greater family or medical leave rights to employees than the rights established under the FMLA.** 29 U.S.C. § 2652. Nor shall rights established for employees under the FMLA be diminished by any collective bargaining agreement or by any employment benefit plan or program. 29 U.S.C. § 2652.

◆ *A federal appeals court held FMLA posting requirements are met when the employer posts notices on its intranet site.*

A Massachusetts employee was involved in an accident and took a leave of absence from his supervisory job. The employer sent him a letter that provided information about the FMLA and told him the leave was being counted as FMLA leave. The employer also asked the employee to provide a medical certification regarding his condition. He provided a disability claim form signed by a physician and was given 15 weeks of leave. The employer later discharged the employee after he failed to return to work. He filed a federal district court action claiming the employer failed to post FMLA notices.

The court held for the employer, and the employee appealed. The U.S. Court of Appeals, First Circuit, noted the employer posted an adequate FMLA notice on its intranet Web site. This defeated the claim that employees did not receive notice of their FMLA rights. The site was accessible to all employees while they were at work, and the employee admitted he had used it at work. The court rejected the claim that the employer violated the FMLA because the site could not be accessed from home. FMLA regulations only required that notice be posted at the workplace. The district court's decision was affirmed. *Dube v. J.P. Morgan Investor Services*, 201 Fed.Appx. 786 (1st Cir. 2006).

◆ *A New York college did not violate the FMLA or the Rehabilitation Act by refusing to provide accommodations for certain work-related injuries.*

The employee was a custodial assistant. He had a groin injury, which made it difficult for him to walk, stretch and do heavy lifting. The employee submitted notes from his doctor, which indicated he was under the doctor's care for an injury resulting from work-related trauma. The employee applied for leave under the FMLA. The college approved his request retroactively, and he returned to work. The employee continued to have back pains and asked to be transferred because he was being mistreated. The college denied his request.

The employee sued the college in a federal district court, alleging FMLA and Rehabilitation Act violations. **The court dismissed the FMLA claim on the basis of Eleventh Amendment immunity.** The court rejected the employee's Rehabilitation Act argument because he did not show he was "otherwise qualified" for the job by being able to perform essential job duties, with or without accommodations. **To prove retaliation in Rehabilitation Act cases, employees must show adverse employment action. Negative evaluations alone did not meet this standard.** *Jackson v. The City Univ. of New York*, No. 05 Civ. 8712(JSR), 2006 WL 1751247 (S.D.N.Y. 6/23/06).

◆ *An Iowa university did not violate the Equal Protection Clause by allowing mothers, but not fathers, the benefit of paid leave after childbirth.*

The university's parental leave policy allowed biological mothers to take sick leave for any pregnancy-related temporary disability. A male employee filed administrative complaints against the university, then sued the university in a federal district court. He alleged the policy violated the Equal Protection Clause of the Constitution. The case became a class action lawsuit when the employee was certified to represent similarly situated biological fathers who worked for the university. A federal district court held for the university, and the employee appealed to the U.S. Court of Appeals, Eighth Circuit.

The court found the policy did not allow mothers to use accrued sick leave after their disability ended. The time off was disability leave even though mothers often cared for a newborn during that time. The employee contended the university did not require proof of a disability for a leave, of six weeks or less. He submitted an affidavit from his wife that she fully recovered from childbirth in four weeks. **The court held the university reasonably established a period of presumptive disability. It did not need to review medical records for each employee. The court held the distinction between biological mothers and fathers was rationally related to legitimate concerns.** As the policy did not violate the Equal Protection Clause, the judgment was affirmed. *Johnson v. Univ. of Iowa*, 431 F.3d 325 (8th Cir. 2005).

◆ *An Illinois college did not retaliate against an employee by terminating her because she asked to take time off.*

The college instituted a dress code that prohibited employees from wearing shorts. The employee arrived at work wearing maternity shorts. The college denied her request for an exemption from the dress code and suspended her. The employee returned to work dressed in compliance with the dress code, but the college president told her that her conduct was "the grossest form of insubordination that he had seen in his 34 years at the College." The college board voted to approve the president's recommendation to fire the employee.

The employee sued the college in a federal district court, alleging it violated the FMLA by firing her before she became entitled to exercise her FMLA rights. To prevail on her FMLA claim, the court held she had to show the college fired her to prevent her from taking leave she was entitled to take. **Under the FMLA, an employee must provide sufficient notice to qualify for the leave. For leave that is foreseeable, such as for the birth of a child, the employee must give at least 30 days advance notice.** The employee said she told the college months in advance that she was pregnant and intended to take leave. **Employees are not required under the FMLA to mention the FMLA by name. They only need to give a college enough information to put it on notice that FMLA leave would be necessary. The court concluded the employee gave sufficient notice.** However, it did not find proof that she would not have been terminated had she not requested leave. As there was evidence of other reasons for the firing, the court held the college did not retaliate against the employee and dismissed the case. *Sample v. Rend Lake College*, No. 04-CV-4161-JPG, 2005 WL 2465905 (S.D. Ill. 10/5/05).

◆ *A federal district court decided to further consider the case of a Tennessee university employee whose son had attention deficit disorder (ADD).*

The university allowed the employee to start work an hour late so she could get her son on his school bus. Even with this accommodation, she had problems getting to work on time, and she eventually violated the university's absenteeism and tardiness policy. The employee was referred for written performance improvement counseling, but she continued to perform poorly. After the university warned her she would be fired if she did not improve, it followed through by terminating her employment. The employee sued the university in a federal district court for violated her rights under the FMLA.

The FMLA allows employees to take leave to care for a child's physical or psychological needs. The university said while ADD is a "serious health condition" as defined by the FMLA, it considered the request for leave to be only a request for a change in schedule. The court found information from the child's doctor could be read as a request for a schedule change, which was not provided by the FMLA. **The court found it unclear whether the employee had to be home to care for her son's physical or psychological needs – which were covered under the FMLA – or merely to get him on the bus, which was not.** A trial would have to be held to resolve these issues. *Wiseman v. Vanderbilt Univ.*, No. 3:04-0946, 2005 WL 3055661 (M.D. Tenn. 11/14/05).

◆ *A New York employee could proceed with his claim that a university violated his rights under the FMLA.*

The university hired the employee as a security guard and later promoted him to Director of Security Services. He began suffering from depression and anxiety due to personal and professional problems relating to a co-worker who had accused him of participating in administrative charges. The employee asked the university for a one-month vacation followed by a medical leave for mental health problems. After the employee left for his vacation, his supervisor sent him a letter discharging him immediately for poor performance and neglect of duties. The employee sued the university in a federal district court for FMLA violations by denying medical leave and firing him.

The court referred the case to a federal magistrate judge, who stated **the FMLA defines "serious health condition" as an illness, injury, impairment, or physical or mental condition that involves inpatient care in a hospital or continued treatment by a health care provider. Stress and depression can constitute a serious health condition for FMLA purposes.** The magistrate judge explained that because the evidence about the seriousness of the employee's health condition differed, summary judgment was improper. He recommended denial of the request for summary judgment. *Tambash v. St. Bonaventure Univ.*, No. 99CV967, 2004 WL 2191566 (W.D.N.Y. 2004).

◆ *A federal court held a New York university did not violate an employee's FMLA rights by terminating her position while she was on FMLA leave.*

A research nurse was placed on medical leave for being intoxicated at work. The university did not inform her it considered her leave to be under the FMLA. It sent the nurse a letter, stating the conditions of her leave and its concern with her performance. The university agreed to take no adverse action if she confirmed her admittance into a treatment program. The letter stated the university would consider the time she spent receiving treatment to be medical leave, and it continued to pay her for 12 weeks. The nurse applied for a professional assistance program, but the treatment center later reported she had relapsed. Doctors did not recommend she return to work, and the university discharged the nurse for failing to submit the reports required by the letter.

The nurse sued the university in a federal district court, alleging it interfered with her FMLA rights by firing her while she was on medical leave. She said the university violated the FMLA by not informing her she was being placed on FMLA leave, requiring the progress reports, and discharging her. The court held the nurse did not prove she was denied any FMLA benefits. The university granted her 12 weeks of paid leave, and **was not obligated to offer her a position after she took leave. The nurse was incapable of performing the job's essential functions. The university could discharge her while she was on leave, as long as it did not do so because she took FMLA leave.** The court dismissed the case. *Geromano v. Columbia Univ.*, 322 F.Supp.2d 420 (S.D.N.Y. 2004).

◆ *A New York university did not violate an employee's FMLA rights by denying his leave request.*

The employee had attendance problems, but no disciplinary action was taken against him. He stopped reporting to work and applied for workers' compensation benefits. When the employee's benefits were cut off, he applied for leave under the FMLA. He submitted an incomplete FMLA form request. The university rejected medical information supplied by his chiropractor and scheduled another physical examination. After the examination, the employee did not return to work. The university terminated his employment, and he sued the university in a federal district court for FMLA violations. The court granted the university's motion for summary judgment and the employee appealed.

The U.S. Court of Appeals, Second Circuit, noted the FMLA does not specifically define "willfully," but the U.S. Supreme Court has addressed the issue. Under the Supreme Court's rationale, if the university acted reasonably, but not recklessly, in determining its legal obligation to the employee, then its actions were not willful. The statute of limitations for bringing an FMLA claim differs depending on whether the employer's conduct is considered "willful." The employee filed his complaint against the university more than two years after the alleged incident occurred. If the university's behavior was considered willful, the employee had three years to file his claim. **Because the court found the university did not act willfully, the statute of limitations was only two years, and the judgment was affirmed.** *Porter v. New York Univ. School of Law*, 392 F.3d 530 (2d Cir. 2004).

◆ *A college employee could be fired for failing to return to work after her FMLA leave expired.*

A Morehouse College administrative assistant sustained injuries in a car accident and took leave under the FMLA and the college's similar family and medical leave policy. After returning to work, she notified the college that she was pregnant. A few months later, the college placed her on administrative leave while it investigated the office where she worked. It continued to pay her salary as well as full benefits. When the investigation ended, the office's director was fired for failing to follow directions and for running another business out of the office. However, because the assistant was due to give birth in a few weeks, the college kept her on administrative leave. After the birth of her child, the assistant failed to comply with the college's FMLA notification requirements. When she still had not returned to work five months after the birth of her child, she was fired for job abandonment. She sued the college under the FMLA for failing to give her timely notice of when her FMLA leave started and for refusing to allow her to select the starting date of her FMLA leave. She wanted the leave to start two months after the child was born so that the leave still would be under way at the time she was fired. A Georgia federal court ruled in favor of the college, finding that the FMLA leave started on the birth of her child even though she was not officially notified that the administrative leave had ended until after that time. Also, **the college could run her paid leave concurrently with her FMLA leave and require her to return to work after 12 weeks.** *Johnson v. Morehouse College*, 199 F.Supp.2d 1345 (N.D. Ga. 2002).

◆ *A professor on paid approved leave did not have to return monies paid for doing a seminar on the university's behalf.*

An Ohio university professor took an approved and paid faculty improvement leave, during which he participated in three seminars on the university's behalf. He was paid $4,230 for doing the seminars, but the university asked him to return the money on the grounds that state law prohibited him from receiving additional money while on paid faculty improvement leave. When the professor refused to pay the money to the university, a lawsuit ensued. A trial court ruled in favor the professor, and the Ohio Court of Appeals affirmed. Here, **the statute at issue did not require the professor to repay the seminar money because that money was not part of his salary**. The statute only provided that he could not be paid more than he would have been paid for performing his regular duties during the leave. Further, the professor had received payment for his involvement in the seminars throughout his 20-year tenure at the university and that money was not designated as salary. *Univ. of Akron v. Sellers*, No. 20627, 2002 WL 219568 (Ohio Ct. App. 2002).

◆ *An employee failed to show that she was discriminated against for requesting maternity leave.*

A university employee held a position classified as half-faculty/half-staff. When she requested maternity leave, she claimed that the university began to retaliate against her by requiring her to teach summer school and by reducing her accrued maternity leave. When she sued for discrimination under state law, the case reached the Minnesota Court of Appeals. The court held that even though the employee had presented a *prima facie* case, **the university had set forth a legitimate, nondiscriminatory reason for its adverse actions**. First, the employee had wrongly accrued maternity leave at the full-staff rate. Second, she was given the summer school assignment based on her past summer teaching experience. Because she could not show that the university's reasons for its actions were actually a pretext for discrimination, she could not succeed on her claim against it. *Cierzan v. Hamline Univ.*, No. C4-02-706, 2002 WL 31553931 (Minn. Ct. App. 2001).

V. EMPLOYEE BENEFITS

Like their counterparts in the public sector, many private schools offer a broad range of employment benefits to employees. These benefit programs are subject to federal civil rights laws such as Title VII and the Equal Pay Act as well as income tax laws. Employer-employee disputes concerning benefits will generally be resolved according to contract law rules (see Section I).

A. Retirement Benefits

◆ *A professor could not enroll in an early retirement program because he waited too long to submit his application.*

An Ohio state university instituted an early retirement incentive program, which Ohio law authorized as long as enrollment did not exceed 5% of eligible employees. A professor/associate dean applied for the program but then withdrew his application. He later attempted to resubmit his application, but the university denied his request. After resigning, the professor sued, seeking an order that he be enrolled in the early retirement program. A state court ruled in his favor, but the Court of Appeals of Ohio reversed. Here, the university had improperly expanded the program to allow more than 5% of eligible employees to participate. As a result, **even though the professor's initial application** would have placed him in the eligible 5%, his resubmitted application came after the 5% threshold had already been met. He was ineligible for the program. *Bee v. Univ. of Akron*, No. 21081, 2002 WL 31387127 (Ohio Ct. App. 2002).

◆   *A discharged professor could proceed with his lawsuit for unpaid pension benefits.*

After 10 years teaching, a tenured assistant professor was notified that he would be reassigned to an administrative position. While trying to agree on a position, the professor performed no services for the university, which then stopped paying his salary and began dismissal proceedings against him. The university did not complete the proceedings because it determined that he had abandoned his job. When he sued for reinstatement and back pay, a New York court dismissed the case on the grounds that he should have filed an Article 78 proceeding against the university. An appellate court reversed, but the lawsuit was dismissed when he failed to appear. He later sued for unpaid salary and pension contributions, asserting that the university had never formally fired him. A federal court dismissed the case, but the Second Circuit reversed in part, finding that **if his employment status claim was valid, he might be able to succeed on his pension claim**. However, his claim for unpaid salary had been properly dismissed. *Yoon v. Fordham Univ. Faculty and Administrative Retirement Plan*, 263 F.3d 196 (2d Cir. 2001).

◆   *Where a university reasonably modified a retirement plan, it was not liable for violating the Employee Retirement Income Security Act (ERISA).*

A professor employed by a New York private university retired in 1977 and began receiving benefits under the school's contributory retirement plan. The board of trustees amended the plan periodically to provide cost of living adjustments (COLAs) to plan members or their beneficiaries. Subsequently, the retirement committee amended the COLA, and the board of trustees amended the plan again to provide that "the retirement committee shall have exclusive authority and discretion to construe any disputed term." After the retirement committee denied the professor's claim for additional benefits, he filed suit against the retirement plan and the university under ERISA in a state trial court. The case was ultimately transferred to a U.S. magistrate judge. The magistrate judge granted the university's motion for pretrial judgment, and the professor appealed to the U.S. Court of Appeals, Second Circuit.

The retirement committee contended that it had properly modified the earlier increases by calculating what each retiree's monthly benefit would have been under the amended COLA, subtracting the value of increases actually given, and adding the difference to each retiree's monthly benefits. The professor contended that the base figure to which the above formula would be applied should include all prior COLAs. The court ruled that **the retirement committee had discretion to construe any uncertain or disputed term**. Consequently, the court applied the arbitrary and capricious standard of review. Because the retirement committee's interpretation of the statute was reasonable, the court affirmed the magistrate judge's ruling in favor of the university. *Jordan v. Retirement Committee of Rensselaer Polytechnic Institute*, 46 F.3d 1264 (2d Cir. 1995).

B. Welfare Benefits

◆ *A police instructor was not entitled to disability benefits because his injuries predated his membership in the state retirement system.*

The instructor was involved in two automobile accidents during his employment by a state university. He had been involved in an accident prior to his employment by the university that caused severe injuries to his spine, for which he underwent spinal fusion surgery and received psychiatric treatment for post-traumatic stress disorder. After going to work for the university, the instructor was involved in another motor vehicle crash and was diagnosed as having a sprain. His third accident occurred when he was going to work. After this accident, the instructor underwent a second cervical fusion operation. He applied for disability benefits based on his cervical injury and mental illness. A medical board denied his request, and a hearing officer upheld the denial. The hearing officer found the instructor's disability predated his university employment and his membership in the state retirement system.

The state retirement system adopted the hearing officer's findings, and the instructor appealed to the Court of Appeals of Kentucky. The court found medical testimony supported the hearing officer's finding that the instructor's physical and mental disabilities resulted from the first automobile accident and predated his university employment. The court rejected his argument that his injuries from the third accident occurred during the course of his employment because he changed his route to obtain water for use in his police training class. The record showed the instructor traveled just a mile out of his way and was not on campus when the accident occurred. **The university did not file an accident report or a workers' compensation claim, which would have indicated the accident was in the course of his employment.** The court affirmed the denial of benefits. *Morris v. Kentucky Retirement Systems*, No. 2002-CA-001570-MR, 2003 WL 21834980 (Ky. Ct. App. 2003).

◆ *The Court of Appeals of North Carolina upheld a decision to deny permanent and total disability benefits to a library assistant.*

A 55-year-old library assistant worked at North Carolina State University for 22 years before injuring herself when she slipped on a wet floor. The university workers' compensation disability benefits coordinator authorized health care, and a specialist diagnosed the assistant with a small wrist fracture. Another doctor diagnosed her with fibromyalgia and degenerative disc disease. Physicians explained that while these injuries were probably aggravated by the fall, the fall did not cause them. The university denied that the assistant's back injuries were related to her fall and the state industrial commission denied her claim for permanent total disability compensation.

The state appeals court noted only one physician had initially testified the assistant was permanently and totally disabled. However, after being asked if she met the statutory definition of "permanently and totally disabled," he retracted his statement. **Most of the medical testimony placed the assistant's disability at 5% to 10% permanent partial disability, indicating she could perform light-duty work with some restrictions.** The commission did not abuse its discretion by denying the assistant an opportunity to show a change in her condition. Since the commission's findings were supported by competent evidence, its decision was affirmed. *Hunt v. North Carolina State Univ.*, 582 S.E.2d 380 (N.C. Ct. App. 2003).

◆ *Community college teachers who did not work during the summer were not entitled to state-paid health care benefits.*

Two teachers at community colleges in Washington worked under contract for each quarter they taught at more than 50% of a full-time schedule. They did not teach during the summer. When the teachers sued to get state-paid health benefits for the summer months, a state trial court held they were not employees during the summer.

The Washington Court of Appeals found that while **the teachers worked a nine-month period, they did so under quarterly contracts and did not qualify as career seasonal/instructional employees**. Also, despite the fact that they did not qualify for unemployment in the summer (because they received reasonable assurances of employment for the following quarter), they were not technically employed during that time. *Mader v. Health Care Authority*, 37 P.3d 1244 (Wash. Ct. App. 2002).

◆ *A New Hampshire college could provide less insurance benefits for mental illnesses than for physical illnesses.*

A college professor was treated for depression through medication and outpatient medical care. The college funded its own health care plan, which contained an annual limit of $3,000 for outpatient mental health benefits and a lifetime cap of $10,000. After the professor reached the lifetime cap, he filed a grievance, arguing that the cap violated a state statute and the collective bargaining agreement by providing less benefits for mental illnesses than physical illnesses. An arbitrator ruled that neither the state statute nor the bargaining agreement had been violated, and the Supreme Court of New Hampshire upheld that decision. **Because the college was not an insurer, it was not subject to the statute requiring equal health insurance coverage for mental and physical illnesses.** *Marshall v. Keene State College*, 785 A.2d 418 (N.H. 2001).

◆ *A New Jersey college was forced to reinstate health insurance for an employee who failed to pay her premium after becoming mentally incompetent.*

The college offered a health plan that was governed by the Employee Retirement Income Security Act (ERISA) and the Consolidated Omnibus Budget Reconciliation Act (COBRA). An employee suffered from cerebral atrophy and became hospitalized and mentally incompetent. She failed to pay a premium, and her insurance was canceled. A representative notified her employer of her incompetency. Following the representative's judicial empowerment as legal guardian, he paid the premiums that would have come due. However, her employer contended that it could not be forced to reinstate coverage. The guardian sought reinstatement in a federal court.

Although ERISA and COBRA speak to the nonpayment of premiums, neither directly speak to nonpayment of premiums due to incompetency. The court considered the policies underscoring the statutes, which included "the continued well being and security of employees." Common law provides that the actions of an incompetent are disregarded. It followed that an incompetent's inaction should also be disregarded. Further, an earlier case ruled that an insured is not bound to give notice of a disability when made unable to do so by the disability insured against. **The employee was rendered unable to appreciate the fact that her premium was due. The court held the college could be required to accept the premium and reinstate coverage.** The motion for dismissal was denied and the case could proceed to trial. *Sirkin v. Phillips Colleges,* 779 F.Supp. 751 (D.N.J. 1991).

C. Discrimination

◆ *A California institute could not discontinue disability benefits to an employee who turned 65 because he was not receiving pension benefits.*

A research scientist at a California research and education institute was diagnosed with Parkinson's disease and took a medical leave of absence. He eventually became eligible to receive long-term disability benefits through the institute's insurance plan, but he retained his employee status and his right to return to work if his health improved. While still receiving his disability benefits, he turned 65 years old and became eligible for retirement. Had the scientist chosen to retire, his pension benefits would have been slightly more than his disability benefits. **Although he did not retire (and thus did not receive pension benefits), the institute offset his disability benefits with the amount of pension benefits he would have received by retiring, thereby reducing his income to zero.** The scientist filed suit against the institute in state court, alleging violations of the Age Discrimination in Employment Act (ADEA) and a state statute. The institute cross-claimed for the amount of disability benefits it had inadvertently paid him after he turned 65, removed the case to federal court and filed a motion to dismiss. The motion was granted and the employee appealed to the U.S. Court of Appeals, Ninth Circuit.

The court noted that this was not a case of double dipping, which the ADEA was designed to prevent. In order to preclude employees from receiving both long-term disability benefits and pension benefits for which the employee is eligible, the ADEA allows employers to offset the amount of disability benefits with the amount of pension benefits. The institute argued that since the employee was eligible to retire, he was eligible to receive the pension benefits, and therefore it could offset them. The court disagreed. **Because the employee had not retired, he was not receiving any pension benefits.** The court also noted that the ADEA expressly prohibits any employee benefit plan from requiring or permitting involuntary retirement. The primary effect of the institute's policy was to leave an employee without an income unless he or she retired, and the court held that a reasonable person in the employee's position would feel that he had no choice but to retire. Finding that **the offsetting of long-term disability benefits is only allowed when pension benefits are being paid concurrently,** the court found that the institute's disability plan violated the ADEA. The district court's decision was reversed. *Kalvinskas v. California Institute of Technology,* 96 F.3d 1305 (9th Cir. 1996).

D. Income Tax Laws

◆ *An employee welfare benefit plan established by an association of Christian schools was not entitled to tax-exempt status.*

The American Association of Christian Schools (AACS), a tax-exempt association of Christian schools located in all 50 states, established a "welfare plan" providing health, disability, and life insurance as well as other benefits to employees of member schools. The welfare plan, which was a separate legal entity, sued the IRS for a refund, contending that it was exempt from paying federal income taxes under Sections 501(c)(3), (4) and (9) of the Internal Revenue Code. The court observed that under Sections 501(c)(3), groups organized and operated exclusively for religious purposes were exempt from paying federal income taxes. The welfare plan did not meet the operational test of the provision because **it could not show that it was operated exclusively for a tax-exempt religious purpose.** Here, **the welfare plan essentially sold insurance coverage.** Because the welfare plan had a significant nonexempt purpose, it was not exempt under Sections 501(c)(3). The presence of a significant nonexempt purpose also prevented the welfare plan from being eligible for Sections 501(c)(4)'s "social welfare" exemption.

The welfare plan also argued that it was exempt from federal taxation because it was a voluntary employees' beneficiary association (VEBA) under Section 501(c)(9). The court observed that one of the requirements for being a VEBA is that the organization be controlled by either its membership, an independent trustee or a board of trustees, at least some of whom are designated by, or on behalf of, the employees themselves. Here, because the AACS welfare plan board was self-perpetuating, it failed to meet any one of these criteria. Even though school employees had some say in selecting the pastors of the churches, the court noted that when an employee selected a pastor who served on the board of trustees of the welfare plan, he or she was acting as a church member and not as an employee of the school. The welfare plan was not tax exempt, and its request for a refund was denied. On appeal, the decision was affirmed. *American Ass'n of Christian Schools Voluntary Employees Beneficiary Ass'n Welfare Plan Trust v. U.S.*, 850 F.2d 1510 (11th Cir. 1988).

◆ *A Wisconsin college was not entitled to a federal income tax refund paid on behalf of employees who received fringe benefits in lieu of higher salaries.*

Marquette University, a tax-exempt educational institution, provided certain fringe benefits to its employees from 1973 to 1978 with commensurate salary reductions, but did not withhold federal income tax on the amounts by which the salaries of participating employees were reduced. The university paid taxes on those amounts after they were assessed by the IRS and then sued the government seeking a refund. The Internal Revenue Code defines gross income as "all income from whatever source ... including ... compensation for services...." The court observed that this included income obtained in any form, whether services or property, and that the university would be obligated to locate a specific statutory section that allowed it to exclude the questionable amounts from "gross income." **The three benefits at issue were parking spaces, recreation center memberships and tuition payments by the**

university for certain employees' children at area high schools. The university claimed that the tuition payments remitted to the area high schools were scholarships and therefore were exempt from taxation.

The district court ruled, however, that the tuition payments were not scholarships since the payments had been deducted from the salaries of the employees and remitted to the high schools by the university and were therefore to be considered part of the employees' taxable gross income. The university also contended that waived parking fees and recreation center memberships were not taxable income. The district court observed that "entertainment, medical services, or so called 'courtesy' discounts furnished by an employer to his employee generally are not considered as wages subject to withholding if such facilities or privileges are of relatively small value and are offered by the employer merely as a means of promoting the health, goodwill, contentment, or efficiency of its employees." However, the court concluded that the benefits here did not meet the criteria since they were considered significant enough to be deducted from the employee's wages and were available only to employees who agreed to the salary reduction in return for the benefits. **The university's attempt to recover the taxes paid was rejected by the court.** *Marquette Univ. v. U.S.*, 645 F.Supp. 1007 (E.D. Wis. 1986).

VI. UNEMPLOYMENT AND WORKERS' COMPENSATION

A. Unemployment Benefits

The Federal Unemployment Tax Act (FUTA), 26 U.S.C. § 3301, et seq., establishes a federal program to compensate people temporarily unemployed. Although the federal Department of Labor oversees the program, states meeting specific criteria administer it. A major exemption from coverage, in Section 3309(b)(1) of the act, states: "This section shall not apply to service performed ... in the employ of (A) a church or convention or association of churches, or (B) an organization which is operated primarily for religious purposes and which is operated, supervised, controlled, or principally supported by a church or convention or association of churches."

◆ *A New York university adjunct professor could keep his benefits despite improperly stating he had no reasonable assurance of continued employment.*

The professor filed for and received unemployment insurance benefits after the end of the spring semester of 2004. On his application for benefits, he denied that he was filing the claim between academic terms or years. The university rehired the professor for two courses in the fall 2004 semester. An administrative hearing law judge (ALJ) then found the professor received a reasonable assurance of continued employment and willfully misrepresented this on his application for benefits. The ALJ held he was ineligible to receive benefits, charged him with a recoverable overpayment and assessed a penalty. The Unemployment Insurance Appeal Board found that because the professor's course load was cut by one-third for the fall 2004 semester, he could not earn at least 90% of what he had earned during the spring semester. He had not received reasonable assurance of continued employment within the meaning of Labor Law Section 590(10), so he could keep the employment insurance benefits he received. The board agreed with the ALJ that the professor had made willful misrepresentations on his application.

The university appealed to the New York Supreme Court, Appellate Division. **The court held New York Labor Law Section 590(10) precludes an employee from receiving unemployment insurance benefits during the time period between two successive academic years, or terms, where he or she had received a reasonable assurance that he would perform services in the same capacity for those academic years or terms.** Because the professor taught three courses during the spring 2004 term and only two courses during the fall 2004 semester, the appellate court agreed with the board. The professor could not meet the economic standard of earning in the fall 2004 semester of at least 90% of what he earned during the spring 2004 semester. He therefore could keep the benefits he had already received. *In re Kendall*, 30 A.D.3d 863, 817 N.Y.S.2d 715 (N.Y. App. Div.).

◆ *The Court of Appeals of Minnesota held a university was justified in firing an employee for repeatedly seeking loans from students.*

The employee worked at the university as a receptionist and administrative assistant. Her supervisor learned she was borrowing money from students. She told the employee this was inappropriate and instructed her not to do it again. The employee agreed and promised not to do it anymore. After the employee borrowed money from a student for a third time, the university fired her. The state department of employment and economic development denied her request for unemployment compensation benefits. The employee asked the Court of Appeals of Minnesota to review the commissioner's decision.

Under Minnesota Statutes Section 268.095, an employee discharged for misconduct does not qualify for unemployment compensation benefits. The statute says employment misconduct includes acts that evince a serious violation of the standards of behavior the employer has a right to reasonably expect of an employee. The court explained the university's policy about behavior did not have to be express. When the supervisor pointed out to the employee that her conduct was inappropriate, she made the employee aware of the behavior the school reasonably expected. The employee had agreed that borrowing money from students was inappropriate. When she continued to ask students for loans, she committed employment misconduct. The court affirmed the denial of unemployment compensation benefits. *Brown v. National American Univ.*, 686 N.W.2d 329 (Minn. Ct. App. 2004).

◆ *A professor not on tenure track and whose contract was not renewed was entitled to unemployment benefits.*

An Ohio university hired a visiting assistant professor under a one-year contract, which stated that it was not a tenure-track position and that it would not lead to a tenure-track position. At the end of the year, the university did not renew her contract, and she applied for unemployment compensation benefits. An administrative official determined that **she was entitled to benefits because the university's decision not to renew her contract resulted from**

lack of work. A review commission and a state court upheld that decision, and the Ohio Court of Appeals affirmed.

Despite the university's assertion that the professor should be ineligible for benefits because she voluntarily entered into a one-year contract, the court credited testimony by the university's director of employment relations that the university did not have any work available for the professor at the end of her contract. The professor was entitled to benefits. *Case Western Reserve Univ. v. Ohio Unemployment Compensation Review Comm'n*, No. 81773, 2003 WL 1924645 (Ohio Ct. App. 2003).

◆ *The Supreme Court of Hawaii held that a student, who was also a university employee, was not entitled to receive unemployment benefits.*

The student attended the University of Hawaii for five consecutive academic years. He was hired as a university peer counselor full-time during a summer when he did not attend school. The student resumed his studies at the university that fall. The next year, he filed an unemployment insurance claim. The state Department of Labor and Industrial Relations determined the wages from his summer job could be considered for the purpose of unemployment benefits, since he was not enrolled or regularly attending classes during the summer session. An appeals officer found the student's services could be considered for benefits. A state trial court noted Hawaii law made students ineligible for unemployment benefits if they were enrolled or regularly attended classes while working for a university. The court applied a "primary relationship test," which focused on the student's primary relationship to the university. It held the student's services were excluded from the unemployment statute's definition of "services." The Supreme Court of Hawaii held that **because the student attended classes full time for five consecutive academic years, his primary relationship was that of a student**. He would have been ineligible for summer work with the school without his status as a student. Since the summer job was excluded from the code's term "employment," the court affirmed the judgment. *Univ. of Hawaii v. Befitel*, 100 P.3d 55 (Haw. 2004).

◆ *Maryland's labor and employment statute does not require a finding of intent in cases of termination for misconduct to deny unemployment benefits.*

A senior lab technician employed by Johns Hopkins University (JHU) came to work one day armed with a hockey stick and began smashing desks, filing cabinets and other objects. Campus security and the Baltimore police were called. The technician was apprehended and taken to the emergency room. He was involuntarily admitted to JHU's affective disorder unit for observation and released nine days later. He was diagnosed with bipolar disorder. Based on this violent incident and other performance deficiencies, he was fired. He filed a claim for unemployment benefits, and a claims examiner denied them.

On appeal, a hearing examiner reversed that decision, finding competent evidence indicating that his bipolar disorder caused his actions and that they could not be characterized as intentional misconduct. A state court upheld this decision and JHU appealed. The Maryland Court of Special Appeals reversed. It reviewed the three grounds for disqualification – misconduct, gross misconduct and aggravated misconduct – and determined that the statutory language does not require intentional misconduct in order to be disqualified from receiving benefits. Moreover, the court distinguished civil cases from criminal cases, noting that criminal conduct involves an analysis of intent. However, **in civil cases, an individual is held accountable for his or her conduct regardless of whether that "conduct is a product of a mental deficiency."** Thus, the lower court erred in finding that the technician was entitled to unemployment benefits because his misconduct was not intentional. The appeals court concluded that the technician should have been temporarily disqualified from receiving unemployment benefits for a period of between five and 10 weeks. The judgment was reversed and the matter remanded for further proceedings. *Johns Hopkins Univ. v. Board of Labor, Licensing and Regulations*, 134 Md. App. 653, 761 A.2d 350 (Md. Ct. Spec. App. 2000).

B. Workers' Compensation

◆ *Missouri's labor and industrial relations commission erred in finding a sexual harassment incident could not trigger workers' compensation eligibility.*

The employee worked as a licensed practical nurse for about 21 years. Most of that time, she worked in the outpatient dialysis department. The employee was sexually harassed while administering dialysis treatment to a male patient. She notified the nurse in charge about the incident. After the employee left work that day, she broke down emotionally. She then took vacation time and began psychiatric treatment. The employee was diagnosed with depression and post-traumatic stress disorder. She took medication and received counseling. She resigned from her job because of the incident.

A vocational expert determined the employee was permanently and totally disabled due to emotional problems. The employee filed a claim for workers' compensation benefits. An administrative law judge (ALJ) found she failed to prove the stress was extraordinary and unusual. According to the ALJ, the employee had no physical injury and should be denied compensation. **The case reached the Missouri Court of Appeals, which explained that the employee's mental injury claim was based on a physical assault. Accordingly, it resulted from a traumatic incident, not work-related stress.** The employee was not required to prove the stress was extraordinary or unusual. The Missouri Workers' Compensation Act requires compensation of employees for personal injury arising out of and in the course of employment. The court reversed the decision and returned the case to administrative levels to determine if the employee deserved compensation. *Jones v. Washington Univ.*, 199 S.W.3d 793 (Mo. Ct. App. 2006).

◆ *The Court of Appeals of South Carolina held an administrative assistant who was hurt on the job could collect lifetime workers' compensation benefits.*

In 2000, the administrative assistant hurt herself when she fell at work. She had a previous history of injury, including a 1973 spinal injury from a car accident. As a result of the 2000 work accident, the assistant began using a walker and lost her ability to control her bowels. Because of these problems, the assistant became able to carry out only menial tasks and was unable to pursue additional vocational training. She sought lifetime medical care and weekly compensation benefits for life. The workers' compensation commission determined the assistant was entitled to lifetime benefits. The decision was largely based on the testimony of a treating physician. The university asked a state court to review the order, but the court affirmed it. The university appealed to the Court of Appeals of South Carolina.

The court of appeals held S.C. Code Section 42-9-10 provides that any person who is found totally and permanently disabled and is paraplegic from an injury is to receive workers' compensation benefits for life. The university argued the circuit court was wrong in determining the assistant was paraplegic because the statute did not differentiate between complete and incomplete paraplegia. The court of appeals found the circuit court had reasonably relied on the physician's testimony. The university offered no evidence to refute the court's interpretation that the term "paraplegic" included incomplete paraplegia. *Reed-Richards v. Clemson Univ.*, 631 S.C. 304, 638 S.E.2d 77 (S.C. Ct. App. 2006).

◆   *The Kentucky Workers' Compensation Board reasonably determined the disability benefits of a library assistant who was injured on the job.*

The library assistant felt pain and numbness in her right hand, arm, shoulder and neck while she was working on an exhibit. She reported the injury to her supervisor and missed a day of work before returning with restrictions. The employee continued to work until the university disallowed her from doing so because of her doctor's restrictions. She applied for workers' compensation benefits. A hearing was conducted by an administrative law judge (ALJ), who issued an opinion favoring the university. The employee appealed to the state Workers' Compensation Board, arguing the ALJ had erred by assigning only an 8% functional impairment rating instead of a "3 multiplier" to her benefits. She claimed the ALJ improperly determined the date of her maximum medical improvement (MMI). The board affirmed the MMI date and the 8% impairment findings. It reversed the finding on the multiplier and returned the case to the ALJ to reconsider the number applied.

The employee petitioned the Court of Appeals of Kentucky for review. She asserted that because the ALJ incorrectly assigned the MMI, she lost temporary total disability payments, which stop on the date of an employee's MMI. The court found the ALJ had based the MMI date on notes by the employee's orthopedic surgeon. The surgeon had stated the employee was able to return to work on a specific date, with restrictions. **The court affirmed the ALJ's decision on the MMI date, finding the ALJ had every right to believe the evidence of one doctor over another.** The court refused to review the issue of whether the correct multiplier was applied. The board had returned that issue to the ALJ, and the court was not authorized to direct the ALJ to make specific findings. *Crawford v. Univ. of Louisville*, No. 2005-CA-000137-WC, 2005 WL 2045940 (Ky. Ct. App. 8/26/05).

◆   *A deputy workers' compensation commissioner improperly allowed a claimant to introduce a cumulative injury theory at an administrative hearing.*

A University of Iowa custodian sought workers' compensation benefits for back injuries he suffered while dumping heavy trash at work. Based on his statements, the university prepared a defense to a specific injury theory. During a hearing, the custodian claimed he had previous back trouble and disputed the actual date of the injury. A deputy commissioner determined the custodian suffered a cumulative traumatic injury on the last day he worked. An Iowa trial court reversed the decision, finding the university was prejudiced by the new and unexpected theory. The Court of Appeals of Iowa affirmed. It stated **due process requires that a party receive notice of the issues to prevent surprise and to provide an opportunity to prepare**. The cumulative injury theory was raised for the first time at the workers' compensation hearing. As a result, the university was denied the opportunity to investigate and was unable to present expert witnesses to defend against the new theory. The trial court properly reversed the commissioner's decision. *Univ. of Iowa Hospitals and Clinics v. Waters*, 670 N.W.2d 432 (Iowa Ct. App. 2003).

◆ *A Delaware court reversed an award of benefits to a security guard that was made without considering her preexisting conditions.*

The University of Delaware hired a security service officer who soon suffered a ruptured disc in her lower lumbar spine. Following surgery, she returned to her position without restriction. Two years later, the officer needed additional surgery and several years after that, she injured her back at home. Following another surgery, the officer returned to work without restriction. She was then injured while trying to break up a fight on campus. She continued to work, but a few weeks later, her back stiffened and she underwent three additional surgeries to correct the problem. The officer became unable to perform her job duties and applied for workers' compensation benefits.

The state industrial accident board heard testimony from a university expert, who stated only half of the officer's prior injuries and surgeries were work related. The board rejected this allocation and decided to award the officer the entire amount of permanent impairment she claimed. **A state superior court held the officer's back problems were not the result of a natural degenerative condition. Therefore, an appointment provision applied, and she should have been awarded only half of the permanent partial impairment she claimed for work-related injuries.** The board's decision was reversed, and the case was remanded for further proceedings. *State of Delaware v. Neff*, No. Civ.A. 02A-12-006SCD, 2003 WL 22064099 (Del. Super. Ct. 2003).

CHAPTER SEVEN

Employment Discrimination

I.   RACE AND NATIONAL ORIGIN DISCRIMINATION

Title VII of the Civil Rights Act of 1964, later amended in 1991, 42 U.S.C. § 2000e, et seq., prohibits discrimination in employment based upon race, color, sex, religion or national origin. It applies to any institution, affecting commerce, which has 15 or more employees. Title VII exempts employment decisions based on religion, sex or national origin where these characteristics are "bona fide occupational qualifications reasonably necessary to the operations of that particular business or enterprise." The First Amendment also may preclude consideration of such claims against religious schools. However, no such exemptions exist for race-based discrimination. Other federal statutes cover discrimination based upon age and disability.

The prohibition against race and national origin discrimination in employment extends to all "terms or conditions of employment," including hiring and firing decisions, promotions, salary, seniority, benefits, and work assignments. Title VII applies to both public and private institutions.

A. Race Discrimination

◆ *Auburn University did not discriminate against an African-American employee by declining to reclassify her job.*

According to the employee, Auburn classified her position lower than for the same jobs performed by white employees. She also claimed the university failed to promote her and retaliated against her for complaining about disparities between African-American and white employee salaries and classifications. The employee sued Auburn in an Alabama federal district court, alleging it violated Title VII. In an attempt to support her claims, she compared herself to several other employees. **The court found comparison with one of the other employees inappropriate because that employee held a different position and worked in a different department. The employee did not identify other employees appropriate for comparison as they had different job duties.** The court also found no evidence to show any different treatment was based on race. The employee did not show a causal connection between her complaints about disparities and the failure to reclassify her position. As the university offered legitimate non-discriminatory reasons for its failure to reclassify the employee, the court awarded pretrial judgment to Auburn.

The employee appealed to the U.S. Court of Appeals, Eleventh Circuit, contending the district court erred by concluding the employees she compared to herself were not similarly situated. She said the other employees' job duties were essentially the same and that the university's reasons were a cover-up for race discrimination. The court determined the decision by the district court was proper and affirmed the judgment for Auburn. *Johnson v. Auburn Univ.*, 193 Fed.Appx. 955 (11th Cir. 2006).

◆ *A Pennsylvania university did not decline to rehire a former employee after an eight-year absence from work on the basis of his African-American heritage.*

The employee began work at the university faculty club in 1992. He suffered a work-related injury in 1995 and filed an employment discrimination claim against the university. That charge was settled after the employee sued the university. He also filed a separate workers' compensation claim and collected workers' compensation until March 2003. Meanwhile, he did not work for the university. The settlement agreement did not mention whether the university would reinstate the employee. The university paid him the amount specified in the settlement agreement and asked him to sign a resignation form. The employee refused. In September 2003, his doctor cleared him for full-time employment with some restrictions. The employee asked the university for his job back but was told the faculty club had closed in 1999. The university declined to reinstate him in another position, noting he had been invited to reapply for any position for which he was qualified but did not do so.

The employee filed another discrimination complaint, claiming the university denied him reinstatement to his former position. He then sued the university in a federal district court for Title VII violations. **The court found the employee did not prove a causal connection between any protected activity and his employment termination.** More than eight years had passed between the two events. Even if the employee had proven such a connection, the university articulated a legitimate, non-discriminatory reason for discharging him. The court dismissed the case. *Smith v. Univ. of Pennsylvania*, No. 05-525, 2006 WL 2645143 (E.D. Pa. 9/15/06).

◆ *The University of Minnesota did not deny promotions to an African-American employee based on his race or create a hostile work environment.*

The employee worked as a university delivery person. He was later rejected for promotion three times. The employee contended these rejections were based on his race. After his supervisor called him "tan" and he overheard a parking attendant saying the word "niggers," he filed discrimination charges with state and federal agencies. The complaints were dismissed, but the employee sued the university in a federal district court for race discrimination in violation of Title VII. The court awarded judgment to the university, and the employee appealed to the U.S. Court of Appeals, Eighth Circuit.

Courts rely on the test established in *McDonnell Douglas Corp. v. Green*, **411 U.S. 792 (1973), to analyze Title VII race discrimination claims. If the employer articulates a legitimate, nondiscriminatory reason for adverse employment action against an employee who is in a "protected class," the employee must show the reason is a pretext for discrimination.** The university stated it did not promote the employee because other applicants were more qualified. The court agreed, as the selected applicants were more qualified for the positions than the employee on specific test results and interviews. **Infrequent racial comments were not enough to create a hostile work environment.** As the employee did not prove the university was trying to cover up race discrimination, the court affirmed the judgment. *Sallis v. Univ. of Minnesota*, 408 F.3d 470 (8th Cir. 2005).

◆ *A Georgia university did not discriminate against a white female employee because of race when it discharged her.*

Emory University terminated a white female employee. She later sued the school in a federal district court for race discrimination in violation of Title VII.

The court held for the university, and the employee appealed. **The U.S. Court of Appeals, Eleventh Circuit, stated that to prevail on a Title VII claim for race discrimination, the employee had to show other employees were similarly situated in all relevant respects.** The employee claimed the university accused her of conduct similar to that of an African-American employee who kept her job. The university countered that it fired the employee because she performed poorly and because her conduct was not similar to that of the other employee. The African-American employee had several years of positive reviews. By contrast, the employee had just started working when the complaints were made. **The court found the conduct by the two employees was not sufficiently similar to compare them in a Title VII case.** The judgment for the university was affirmed. *Riley v. Emory Univ.*, 136 Fed. Appx. 264 (11th Cir. 2005).

◆   *A South Carolina college did not discriminate against a white employee who worked for a historically African-American college.*

The employee worked as an administrative assistant in the college athletic department under consecutive one-year contracts that permitted her discharge for any reason upon a 30-day notice. The college notified her she would not be rehired after a confidential source accused her of NCAA rules violations. The employee claimed she was replaced by an African-American female, and she sued the college in a federal district court for race discrimination under Title VII. The college argued the employee was not actually discharged. Rather, her position was eliminated because the athletic department reorganized. **The court concluded that a significant portion of the employee's duties were shifted within the department.** As she did not show the reasons stated for not rehiring her were a pretext for race discrimination, the court awarded summary judgment to the college. *Walters v. Benedict College*, No. 3:04-0952-JFA, 2006 WL 644442 (D.S.C. 3/10/06).

◆   *The Court of Appeals of Michigan ruled a university did not discriminate or retaliate against an African-American employee by firing him.*

The employee claimed the university violated the Elliott-Larsen Civil Rights Act, alleging it treated African-American employees differently from white employees. He claimed that over the course of five years, he asked the school to investigate his department because of alleged racial harassment and discrimination. He also told the school one of his supervisors allowed a relative to work overtime while denying his overtime request. The employee claimed the school retaliated against him after he complained about discrimination and filed a grievance alleging white employees discriminated against African-American workers. The university asserted it fired the employee for violating the absentee policy. It also pointed to his dishonesty.

A state court found the employee violated the school's absentee policy. It granted summary judgment for the school and the employee appealed. **The court of appeals explained an employee may establish employment discrimination by proving disparate treatment.** Here, the employee claimed he was treated differently. However, he failed to prove it by showing the school was predisposed to discriminate against him or that it actually acted on that predisposition. The employee presented no direct evidence of discrimination. He provided no information to show any white employees who were similarly situated were treated differently when they failed to provide proper notification of their absences and filed requests for leave. *Newlin v. Eastern Michigan Univ.*, No. 247751, 2004 WL 1533835 (Mich. Ct. App. 2004).

◆ *An Ohio university discharged an African-American computer systems analyst for poor performance, not because of his race.*

The employee consistently performed at the low end of the university's evaluation scale. After the university did not hire him for a promotion he sought, he was reprimanded for insubordination, lack of professionalism, lack of quality, and failing to timely complete assignments. The analyst complained of race discrimination to the Ohio Civil Rights Commission. The university later notified him he was not meeting his professional improvement goals and terminated his employment. The analyst sued the university in a federal district court for Title VII violations. The court dismissed the case, finding he did not submit evidence that the university would not have fired him if not for his civil rights complaint. **Considering the poor performance evaluations the analyst received, the court found a nine-month lag between the complaint and his termination too long to infer a causal connection.** *Tyson v. Univ. of Cincinnati*, No. 1:02-CV-907, 2005 WL 1075018 (S.D. Ohio 5/05/05).

◆ *An African-American assistant chancellor identified sufficient evidence of discrimination to avoid pretrial dismissal of her lawsuit.*

The assistant chancellor received merit increases and a contract extension during her first years with a Wisconsin university. She later criticized a university newsletter as offensive for its depiction of minorities, and advocated for a female basketball coach who was attempting to negotiate scheduling accommodations due to difficulties with her pregnancy. When the university's athletic director resisted making the accommodations, the assistant chancellor reminded him he had accommodated a male coach. She also informed the chancellor that the female coach might file a Title IX complaint. The assistant chancellor's contract was not renewed, allegedly because of staff complaints accusing her of micro-managing her office. She sued the university and officials in a federal district court for race and gender discrimination and for retaliating against her because she exercised her First Amendment rights.

The court found there were no substantial negative performance issues leading up to the decision not to renew the assistant chancellor's contract. There was sufficient evidence she was meeting expectations and the reasons for not renewing her contract were suspect to avoid pretrial dismissal of her race and sex discrimination claims. The remarks about the campus newsletter and coach's pregnancy accommodations constituted protected speech. **The court held that speech about compliance with the law is a matter of public concern. As there was evidence the university had retaliated against the assistant chancellor and stated false reasons for not renewing her contract, the court denied summary judgment** to the university and officials. *Walker v. Board of Regents of Univ. of Wisconsin*, 300 F.Supp.2d 836 (W.D. Wis. 2004).

◆ *The Eleventh Circuit held a student's poor performance during a residency program, and not his race, led to his dismissal from the program.*

The student was a native of the Netherland Antilles, and he was in a five-year surgical residency program at the University of South Florida. The department chair notified him he would have to repeat his fourth year due to his poor score on the national ABSITE examination. Eventually, the university allowed him to contract as a fourth-year resident while performing fifth-year work. It would review his performance after six months and promote him if his work was acceptable. However, the university dismissed the student for not attending conferences, low ABSITE scores and performance problems.

The student sued the university in a federal district court for breach of contract and race discrimination in violation of Title VII. The court held for the university. He appealed to the Eleventh Circuit. The court held the university was entitled to Eleventh Amendment immunity for the contract claim, as it did not clearly consent to being sued in federal court. **The student failed to show employment discrimination under Title VII, as he did not show similarly situated surgical residents were treated more favorably. He had significant performance problems including poor patient care and low ABSITE scores.** The court affirmed the judgment. *Maynard v. Board of Regents of Div. of Univ., Florida Dep't of Educ.*, 342 F.3d 1281 (11th Cir. 2003).

◆ *No discrimination occurred where a black security guard received a 75% tuition break while a white employee received a 100% deduction.*

A black security guard at a private university enrolled in classes at the campus and received a 75% tuition discount even though tuition remission was not normally offered to employees at that campus, and despite the fact that the university determined it would not benefit from his degree. He also was allowed to attend class while on duty and was compensated for his time in class. Later, the guard learned that a white administrative assistant at the campus was granted 100% tuition remission for classes taken outside her work hours because the university determined that her receipt of a bachelor's degree would benefit the university. After the guard complained, his duties and hours were briefly changed, and he was subjected to derogatory comments by several co-workers. He sued the university under Title VII for race discrimination and retaliation, but a federal court ruled against him. The Eighth Circuit affirmed, noting that **the guard failed to show he was treated less favorably than similarly situated white employees.** Also, the brief change to his hours and duties did not amount to an adverse employment action, and the stray comments were made by non-decision-makers. *Saulsberry v. St. Mary's Univ. of Minnesota*, 318 F.3d 862 (8th Cir. 2003).

◆ *Transfers of two employees to lateral positions could not be deemed race discrimination.*

Triton College employed a black woman as an associate vice president of affirmative action and human resources until she complained of stress. The college then reorganized the department she worked for and created a new position for her. She perceived the new position to be a demotion and, after a two-month leave for medical reasons, resigned without responding to the college's offer of the job. The college also employed a black computer systems specialist in its information systems department until a reorganization forced the employee's transfer to an audio-visual equipment assistant position with no reduction in pay or benefits. He also took a medical leave for six months and then resigned without responding to the college's offer.

The employees filed race discrimination charges with the EEOC, then sued the college under Title VII in an Illinois federal court. The court held for the college, and the Seventh Circuit affirmed. **Neither employee suffered an adverse employment action.** The first employee was transferred to a lateral position based on her complaints about stress, and the second employee did not suffer an adverse employment action because he did not lose any compensation or benefits. Also, neither employee could show that other similarly situated employees were treated more favorably. *Adams v. Triton College*, 35 Fed. Appx. 256 (7th Cir. 2002).

B. National Origin Discrimination

◆ *A Chinese-born professor failed to show he was denied tenure because of his race or national origin when a university did not select him for an award.*

The year before the assistant professor's tenure review, he won a teacher-of-the-year award. The next year, when the assistant professor was facing his tenure review, a tenured full professor said in a faculty meeting that he would no longer accept Chinese graduate students. The assistant professor claimed the department head retaliated against him by influencing faculty members to vote against him. The department head told the assistant professor he would not be granted tenure. The assistant professor sued the members of the board of trustees, alleging the university discriminated against him on the basis of race or national origin and violated his First Amendment speech rights.

A federal district court held for the university, and the assistant professor appealed. The U.S. Court of Appeals, Seventh Circuit, held he could not prove the department head or the professor who made the anti-Chinese remark had a final say in the tenure decision. The assistant professor had insufficient evidence to warrant a trial based on indirect discrimination. The university showed that a Caucasian assistant professor had superior credentials in terms of funding and invited presentations. By contrast, **the assistant professor had several identifiable weaknesses related to funding, scholarship, and supervising grad students**. Judgment had been properly granted on the First Amendment claim that his selection of an award recipient was protected speech and that the head retaliated against him. *Sun v. Board of Trustees of the Univ. of Illinois*, 473 F.3d 799 (7th Cir. 2007).

◆ *The removal of an instructor from a math course by a Kansas university was based on his inability to teach the course, not on his national origin.*

As part of his training, the instructor was assigned to teach a five-week math course under the mentorship of another instructor. When he began teaching, students began to complain about him almost immediately. The instructor improperly disclosed a student's personal academic information. As a result, he was removed from the course and told to retake an earlier portion of the training. The instructor sued the university in federal district court, alleging discrimination based on his Pakistani background. **The court rejected his claim because he could not show he was able to teach the course in a satisfactory manner. The university did not take an adverse action against the instructor when it instructed him that he needed to be retrained.** The retraining requirement did not significantly affect his employment status. Throughout the retraining, the instructor continued to receive pay. The court granted the university's motion for summary judgment. *Shinwari v. Univ. of Phoenix*, No. 05-1167-JTM, 2006 WL 3021116 (D. Kan. 10/23/06).

◆ *The U.S. Court of Appeals, Fifth Circuit, held a Texas university did not discriminate against two former employees based on their national origin.*

Two former employees asserted the university discriminated against them by assigning them poor performance reviews and initiating a disciplinary investigation. The Fifth Circuit affirmed a judgment for the university, finding the employees failed to show they suffered adverse employment action. **"Adverse employment action" means an ultimate employment decision like hiring or firing. The term does not apply to poor employment performance reviews or disciplinary investigations.** *Cardenas-Garcia v. Texas Tech Univ.*, 118 Fed.Appx. 793 (5th Cir. 2004).

◆ *A Jamaican-born employee was entitled to keep a $15,000 verdict in a federal discrimination lawsuit against an Illinois community college because she showed she was treated differently than an American-born employee.*

The employee worked for as coordinator of six child development centers run by the community college. One of her duties was to secure funding for the centers, including $500,000 from the Illinois Department of Human Services (IDHS). The college suspended the employee for 30 days without pay for taking a two-week vacation without completing the application for IDHS funding for the current school year. It then discharged her. The employee sued the college in a federal district court for national origin discrimination. The court denied the university's motion for pretrial judgment on the suspension claim. However, the college was entitled to judgment on her wrongful termination charge because there was evidence of insubordination. The suspension claim went before a jury. The employee presented evidence that an African-American supervisor said she thought the employee displayed a "plantation mentality." She also provided evidence that the university did not discipline a non-Jamaican employee who sent in a late application for an IDHS contract. The jury awarded the employee $15,000 on the suspension claim.

The university appealed to the Seventh Circuit, which found the evidence tended to show a difference of opinion as to whether the non-Jamaican employee was treated differently from the employee. It held the district court did not err in denying the college's motion for summary judgment on the suspension claim. **The district court ruling on the termination claim was upheld, as the employee did not counter evidence that she was unresponsive and insubordinate to instructions.** *Waite v. Board of Trustees of Illinois Community College Dist. No. 508*, 408 F.3d 339 (7th Cir. 2005).

◆   *An Illinois university did not discriminate against a professor of African descent for failing to abide by university regulations.*

The regulations permitted the discharge of employees who constituted a threat of harm to persons or property, or who represented an impediment to university operations. After being discharged for violating the regulations, the professor sued the university in a federal district court for national origin discrimination. **The court found the professor did not show the university treated any similarly situated employee more favorably than it treated him.** Even if he had shown this, he failed to show the university lied about his breach of regulations. As the professor did not show any national origin discrimination, the court dismissed the case. *Thompson v. Chicago State Univ.,* No. 04 C 6568, 2005 WL 3088440 (N.D. Ill. 11/16/05).

◆   *A federal district court held a Connecticut university did not discriminate against a professor by removing him from a position.*

The professor was a brown-skinned Asian-American from Nepal. He became a tenured associate professor and associate head of the department of civil engineering. The professor drafted and submitted a grant proposal for the university's space grant consortium. After it was accepted, the university named him the principal investigator for the Experimental Program to Stimulate Competitive Research Preparation Grant Program. The professor was also campus director and principal investigator for nine years. The university removed him as director for the consortium because of problems in his communication and interpersonal relations with other employees. The action did not change his status or salary as associate professor or associate department head. The university hired a white male as consortium director. The professor sued the university in a U.S. District Court under Title VII.

The university explained it removed the professor as campus director because he lacked interpersonal skills in communicating and working with others. Other professors complained he had been rude and condescending and said he consistently attacked the space grant management team. The university produced numerous e-mails from the professor to the space grant principal investigator, which demonstrated his difficulty in effectively communicating. **The court found the university had nondiscriminatory reasons for removing the professor. Nothing suggested the change occurred because of race, color or national origin.** The court dismissed the case. *Malla v. Univ. of Connecticut,* 312 F.Supp.2d 305 (D. Conn. 2004).

◆   *Where the reason for denying tenure may have been a pretext for discrimination, a university was not entitled to pretrial dismissal.*

An Ohio university employed an Iranian-born Muslim as a tenure track assistant professor. He was promoted to an associate professor and given his third year pre-tenure peer review. Although his review was largely positive, it also contained suggestions for improvement. Typically, faculty members on a pre-tenure track received a sixth-year review in addition to the third-year review. However, the professor did not receive his sixth-year review because the chairman of the department failed to notify the department that the review was due. A university grievance panel found that the professor should receive a proper review, but the university continued to deny him tenure on three different occasions. When the professor sued the university for **national origin and religious discrimination**, the university moved for pretrial judgment.

The court noted that although the professor was a member of a protected class and suffered an adverse employment action, genuine issues of material fact existed as to whether he was qualified to receive tenure. The evidence showed that the professor's research, publications, collaborative work, and service were adequate for tenure in the opinion of outside reviewers. Additionally, **some evidence existed that unprotected employees were treated differently**. Moreover, a material issue existed as to whether the university's proffered reasons for the denial of tenure were pretextual. The professor alleged that he met all university expectations prior to the chairman's membership in the faculty, and he provided evidence that the chairman gave preference to American-born or Jewish employees. Thus, the court denied pretrial judgment to the university. *Amini v. Case Western Reserve Univ.*, 5 F.Supp.2d 563 (N.D. Ohio 1998).

C. Individual Liability

◆ *University officials could be sued for race discrimination under 42 U.S.C. §§ 1981 and 1983.*

An East Indian math professor was denied several promotions and appointments. He sued the university and various officials under Title VII and 42 U.S.C. §§ 1981 and 1983, asserting race and national origin discrimination. A New York federal court dismissed his claims against the university, but held that he could proceed with his Section 1981 and Section 1983 claims against the officials. The court stated that **the Eleventh Amendment does not protect university officials who may have acted in violation of federal law because their actions would not be considered actions by the state**. *Kulkarni v. City Univ. of New York*, No. 01 CIV. 3019(DLC), 2001 WL 1415200 (S.D.N.Y. 2001).

◆ *In the following case, a federal court explained the reasoning behind why, in most jurisdictions, individuals cannot be held liable under Title VII.*

A white, Jewish, New Jersey woman worked as an assistant professor in the theater department of a private university. She alleged that the chairman of the department, a black, male professor, conspired with the dean and the president to deny her tenure. She further alleged that the chairman discriminated against her in numerous other ways. She filed an administrative complaint and later sued the university, the chairman and the two officials for racial, gender and religious discrimination in violation of Title VII. The defendants filed a motion to dismiss, arguing the chairman of the department and the two officials could not be held individually liable under Title VII.

Title VII defines an employer as "a person engaged in an industry affecting commerce that has 15 or more employees and any agent of such a person." The court noted that courts disagree over whether this provision allows individual liability, but it followed those courts that have held that the language imputes liability only on the employer and not on the employer's agents. It held **the statute does not cover businesses with fewer than 15 employees** to protect small entities from the costly burdens of discrimination claims. Therefore, it would be logical to assume that the statute also would protect individuals from these burdens. Further, in the Civil Rights Act of 1991, **damage awards are calibrated with regard to how many employees an employer has**. Because similar damages are not calibrated with regard to individuals, the court held that Congress had no intention of imposing individual liability. The court dismissed the claims against the chairman and the two university officials. *Schanzer v. Rutgers Univ.*, 934 F.Supp. 669 (D.N.J. 1996).

◆ *A temporary employee who was denied a permanent position failed in her claim of discrimination in the following case.*

A private college in New Hampshire hired a black woman as a temporary employee in its dining service program. When she applied for a permanent position, her application was rejected, ostensibly because she had accrued too many absences during her temporary employment. During that temporary employment, one of her supervisors made several comments that were derogatory and of a racial nature. The employee filed a charge of race discrimination, then brought suit against the college and certain supervisors with the Equal Employment Opportunity Commission (EEOC) and alleging both sex and race discrimination in violation of Title VII and Title IX.

The college and the supervisors argued the Title VII claim should be dismissed because the employee did not specifically claim discrimination on the basis of sex before the EEOC. The court granted this motion because **the employee failed to exhaust her administrative remedies** by claiming only race discrimination in the charge to the EEOC. Accordingly, only the Title VII race discrimination claim could proceed. The court also granted the supervisors' motion to dismiss because **there was no individual liability under Title VII in New Hampshire**. The court then dismissed the Title IX claim because the dining service program was not an education program or activity within the meaning of Title IX even though the dining service employed some students who were enrolled in federal work-study programs. **The employee did not allege that she was a student; thus, her Title IX claim failed.** The court dismissed in part the claims against the college and the supervisors. *Preyer v. Dartmouth College*, 968 F.Supp. 20 (D.N.H. 1997).

D.   42 U.S.C. § 1981

Section 1981 of the Civil Rights Act (42 U.S.C. § 1981) makes it unlawful for any person or entity to discriminate on the basis of race in the making and enforcement of contracts, therefore providing an alternative basis to Title VII for race discrimination claims. Section 1981 applies not only at the initiation of contracts, but also at any time during the life of the contract.

◆ *A Muslim job applicant failed to show an Ohio college based its decision not to hire him upon his race.*

The applicant was denied a full-time tenure-track position as an assistant professor of mathematics despite over 10 years of teaching experience and an extensive record of publishing. A hiring committee eliminated him from consideration because he had recently been denied tenure by another university and submitted outdated reference letters. One of the letters indicated concern about the applicant's performance. The college selected a white person for the position who had formerly studied under the department chair as a student. The applicant sued the college in a federal district court, alleging it violated Title VII of the Civil Rights Act and Section 1981. The court dismissed the case.

The applicant appealed to the Sixth Circuit, which held that **to prevail in a Section 1981 race discrimination case, there must be proof of intentional discrimination**. The applicant argued the district court did not properly consider preferential treatment for the white applicant as proof of intent to discriminate. The court disagreed, finding the department chair's preference for the white applicant, whom he knew personally, did not establish discrimination. The court accepted the college's position – that the applicant was not one of the most qualified candidates and that the former student was the most likely to succeed – as legitimate, non-discriminatory reasons for its actions. The judgment was affirmed. *Amini v. Oberlin College*, 440 F.3d 350 (6th Cir. 2006).

◆ *A North Carolina college did not discriminate against a white professor when it dismissed him for violating the college policy on grades.*

The professor asked the college registrar to change one of his student's grades, without giving a reason. Both times the dean rejected his requests. The professor stated a reason on the third request. His immediate supervisor approved the third request and passed it along to the dean. Because the reason given was unacceptable, the dean again rejected it. The dean met with the professor to discuss the grade change. The college then offered the professor a one-year terminal contract for disregarding the college policy.

The professor sued the college in a state court, alleging breach of contract and race discrimination under 42 U.S.C. § 1981. A jury found the college discriminated against the professor and the court awarded him $68,495. The college appealed to the Court of Appeals of North Carolina, which noted the professor had based his race discrimination claim solely on alleged different treatment from a similarly situated African-American employee. The court explained that the African-American employee was a department chair and the professor was not. They also did not have the same supervisor. **Because the employees were not similarly situated, the professor could not prove discrimination. The college offered a legitimate nondiscriminatory reason for offering the professor a terminal contract and there was no evidence of pretext.** The court vacated and remanded the judgment. *Miller v. Barber-Scotia College*, 605 S.E.2d 474 (N.C. Ct. App. 2004).

◆ *A university president may have violated Title VII by adjusting salaries for female and minority faculty on the basis of flawed statistical evidence.*

After conducting an investigation, an Arizona university determined that hiring and salary disparities existed with respect to female and minority faculty. The university's president increased salaries for female and minority faculty members whose salaries fell below the predicted salaries of similarly situated white males. Subsequently, an outside study concluded that the methodology employed in the investigation was flawed and that the statistical disparity was not significant enough to show gender or minority bias. A number of white male professors then sued the president under Title VII and 42 U.S.C. §§ 1981 and 1983 for violating their equal protection rights.

A federal court ruled for the president, but the Ninth Circuit reversed in part. It upheld the grant of qualified immunity on the Sections 1981 and 1983 claims, finding that even though **the president violated equal protection rights by adjusting salaries on the basis of race and gender without a compelling reason for doing so,** he did not understand that he was violating those rights at the time. However, with respect to the Title VII claims, the court found an issue of fact as to whether the salary increases had been necessary to eliminate a "manifest imbalance." This issue had to be litigated. *Rudebusch v. Hughes,* 313 F.3d 506 (9th Cir. 2002).

◆   *An Ohio professor's federal lawsuit against a university failed because he was not a member of a protected class under Section 1981 and similar laws.*

A professor at the University of Toledo was disciplined after the National Science Foundation accused him of plagiarism. The professor sued the university and various officials under 42 U.S.C. §§ 1981, 1983 and 1985(3). He also sued under state law. An Ohio federal court granted pretrial judgment to the university, and the Sixth Circuit affirmed. **The professor could not succeed on his Section 1981 and Section 1985(3) claims because he was not a member of a protected class.** Nor could he define himself as a class of one – this is allowed only under egregious circumstances, which were not present here. The court also held that his Section 1983 claim against the school could not succeed because universities are not "persons" under that statute, and the Eleventh Amendment bars suits against state entities in federal court. The Section 1983 claim against the various officials also failed because the professor did not specify that he was suing them in their individual capacities. The court refused to extend jurisdiction over the state-law claims and dismissed the lawsuit. *Underfer v. Univ. of Toledo,* 36 Fed.Appx. 831 (6th Cir. 2002).

◆   *The U.S. Supreme Court held that persons of Arab descent are protected from racial discrimination under 42 U.S.C. § 1981.*

The case involved an Arab-American Muslim professor who sued St. Francis College in a U.S. district court after St. Francis denied his tenure request. The Pennsylvania district court ruled that Section 1981, which forbids racial discrimination in the making and enforcement of any contract, does not reach claims of discrimination based on Arab ancestry. It held that Arabs were Caucasians, and that since Section 1981 was not enacted to protect whites, the Arab professor could not rely upon that statute. The professor appealed. The U.S. Court of Appeals, Third Circuit, reversed in favor of the professor, and St. Francis appealed to the U.S. Supreme Court.

Section 1981 states that "[a]ll persons shall have the same right to make and enforce contracts ... as is enjoyed by white citizens...." In affirming the court of appeals' decision, the Supreme Court noted that although Section 1981 does not use the word "race," the Court has construed the statute to forbid all racial discrimination in the making of private as well as public contracts. It observed that all who might be thought of as Caucasian today were not thought to be of the same race at the time Section 1981 became law. The Court cited several sources to support its decision that **for the purposes of Section 1981, Arabs, Englishmen, Germans and certain other ethnic groups are not to be considered a single race**. If the professor could prove that he was subjected to intentional discrimination because he was an Arab, rather than solely because of his place of origin or his religion, he would be entitled to relief under Section 1981. The court of appeals' decision in favor of the professor was affirmed, and the case was remanded for trial. *St. Francis College v. Al-Khazraji*, 481 U.S. 604, 107 S.Ct. 2022, 97 L.Ed.2d 749 (1987).

II. SEX DISCRIMINATION

Sex discrimination is prohibited by Title VII, the Equal Pay Act, and state statutes. These laws apply to public and private institutions of higher education. Colleges and universities may not engage in sexually discriminatory employment practices unless the employee's gender is a bona fide occupational qualification. The First Amendment may preclude sex discrimination claims against religious schools where the position involved is a religious one.

A. Different Treatment

◆ *A Pennsylvania labor foreman was provided further opportunities to show she was wrongfully denied a promotion because of her gender.*

Slippery Rock University posted a vacancy for a locksmith position. The posting stated that two years of experience was required. The foreman applied for the position along with three males. The university did not choose her for the vacancy, instead selecting a younger male carpenter. When the carpenter was later promoted, the university again posted the locksmith position. This time, it said three years of locksmithing experience was needed. However, it did not conduct interviews or fill the position on a permanent basis. The foreman sued the university, claiming it denied her the job based on her gender and age.

A federal district court rejected the claims, saying the foreman lacked the requisite experience for the job and was unqualified. She appealed, claiming the carpenter also lacked required experience. The U.S. Court of Appeals, Third Circuit, reversed the district court's decision. **The fact that a male without the "required experience" was hired for the job showed that something less than this was sufficient to meet the actual requirements.** As the district court mistakenly relied on the foreman's lack of experience to conclude she was not qualified for the job, the judgment was reversed and the case was remanded for further proceedings. *Scheidemantle v. Slippery Rock Univ. State System of Higher Educ.*, 470 F.3d 535 (3d Cir. 2006).

◆ *An Indiana university did not unlawfully discriminate against a female employee by treating her differently from her male co-workers.*

The university hired the employee to be the student coordinator of a scholars program. Program staff were university employees subject to university policies and procedures. The university disciplined the employee several times. One time she missed an appointment. On another occasion, the employee failed to arrange for the transportation of students from an event. The employee complained that her supervisor treated men differently from women. The university placed her on probation for three months based on her ongoing struggles with a supervisor. A memo specified the action was based on lack of attention to proper protocol, poor implementation of directives from the central office, and an inefficient use of time and resources. The memo also stated the employee did not try to get along with her supervisor. The university gave her a below-average raise because she had been reprimanded and was on probation.

Soon after that, the university discharged the supervisor. The employee applied for the job but the university hired another female applicant. The employee was told she was not selected because of her past job performance and the other applicant's superior performance during interviews and qualifications. The employee took family medical leave because of stress, depression and anxiety. When her doctors told her it would not be healthy for her to return to work, she resigned. The employee sued the university in a federal district court, alleging gender discrimination in violation of Title VII. She claimed the university was unjustified in reprimanding her because it did not reprimand her male co-workers for the same conduct. To survive a Title VII gender discrimination claim, the court held the employee had to show her male co-workers were "similarly situated." However, **there was no evidence to support her contention that her probation was unwarranted. The court held the employee did not show male co-workers had the same job responsibilities. It dismissed the case.** *Bragg v. Trustees of Purdue Univ.*, No. 1:05-CV-88-TLS, 2006 WL 1994456 (N.D. Ind. 7/13/06).

1. Defenses to Different Treatment

◆ *A Michigan English professor could not prove a community college rejected him for employment based on his sex.*

The professor applied for an English teaching position and was one of eight applicants invited to interview. The three highest-scoring candidates were invited to interview with the dean. The professor scored second and had an interview with the dean. The community college hired the candidate who scored highest. When the professor learned a woman had been hired instead of him, he wrote to the college board, complaining he was an "unfortunate victim of the mandates of Affirmative Action." He demanded to know if her qualifications were better than his. The community college soon posted another English department opening. The professor applied for it but was not asked to interview. Using the same hiring procedure, the committee again chose a woman. Like the other successful candidate, she held a master's degree, but she had only a year and a half of teaching experience. The professor sued the community college in a federal district court, alleging sex discrimination. The court held he could not show unlawful bias. The college presented evidence that its selection committee decided against hiring him because he was not a good fit. The college focused on teaching, while the professor apparently focused on research and publishing. Also, several committee members had reservations about his attitude. **The court stated, "an inference of discrimination does not arise merely because an employer has chosen between two qualified candidates."** *Catanzaro v. Oakland County Community College,* No. 06-10338, 2007 WL 142158 (E.D. Mich. 1/16/07).

◆ *A Maryland university did not fire an assistant professor based on gender.*

The head of the department considered the assistant professor to be a top-notch researcher. The university sometimes paid overload compensation, which must be recommended and approved by the dean's office and approved by the provost. It is paid when teaching or research exceeds the normal workload. The assistant professor asked the chair for overload compensation for overtime hours she claimed to have logged and for additional child care expenses. The chair strongly endorsed her request and noted her extraordinary efforts in attracting research grants and contracts. The university rejected the request for overload compensation. After that, the assistant professor's relationships with university staff and faculty members began to deteriorate. She accused the department head and other faculty members of sex discrimination. She filed a formal complaint with the Equal Employment Opportunity Commission.

The university received allegations that the assistant professor had engaged in scientific misconduct in connection with the grant for which she sought overload compensation. After an investigation, the university discharged her for professional misconduct and willful neglect of duty. The assistant professor sued the university and others in a federal district court for sex discrimination. **The court found no evidence of discrimination to support her claim. The university had a legitimate, non-discriminatory reason for every action it took.** The U.S. Court of Appeals, Fourth Circuit, affirmed the judgment in a brief opinion. *Britton v. Univ. of Maryland at Baltimore,* 206 Fed.Appx. 282 (4th Cir. 2006).

◆ *The discharge of a North Carolina campus police officer for various insubordinate acts did not violate Title VII.*

The officer refused to comply with an instruction to wear a tie, which was part of her uniform. The shift commander reported the incident to the department's captain, who issued the officer a written warning for unacceptable personal conduct. The officer filed a grievance to challenge the issuance of the written warning. After she filed the grievance, she was told that she was not eligible to do so because she was not a permanent employee. The officer later struck a guard rail while driving her patrol car on campus. A report indicated the officer did not contact her superior until she realized he had learned about the accident. A week after the accident, the officer met with a fellow officer at the university's cafeteria for breakfast during her shift. She did so even though officers were prohibited from eating with other officers while on duty.

A university police captain ordered the officer not to charge a student for a misconduct incident as this would have violated a university policy. Because the officer refused to do so, she was placed on administrative leave. After the investigation, the officer was discharged for unacceptable personal conduct and insubordination. After an unsuccessful internal appeal, the officer sued the university in federal district court. Her lawsuit accused the defendants of discharging her on the basis of her sex. **The court held the officer did not show she was performing her job in a satisfactory manner at the time of her discharge. She failed to follow instructions, violated a rule against eating with other officers while on duty, and issued two criminal citations to a university student even though she knew it was against a university policy to do so.** *Hooper v. North Carolina Cent. Univ.*, No. 1:04CV0014, 2006 WL 2850596 (M.D.N.C. 10/3/06).

◆ *A Florida graduate student was considered an "employee" under Title VII but could not prove employment discrimination by a university.*

The student conducted cancer research in a university professor's lab. The university gave her the highest possible performance rating in her first three reviews, but a professor voiced concerns about her attendance, lab notebooks and poor communication. He said the student failed to obey instructions, was argumentative, disrespected colleagues and lacked focus. She left a message for a school staff member that she needed time off because of a severe hand injury. The student never notified her professor, and the university replaced her with a male. The student sued the university for sex discrimination in violation of Title VII. The university argued Title VII did not apply because she was a student, not an employee. The court found she was an employee, but held the male was not a similarly situated or comparable employee and held for the university.

The student appealed to the U.S. Court of Appeals, Eleventh Circuit. The court applied the economic realities test to determine if the student was an employee for purposes of Title VII. The student worked in the lab to satisfy the lab work, publication and dissertation requirements of her graduate program. These factors led the court to view her as an employee. The decision not to renew the student's appointment was based on employment reasons, such as attendance, rather than academic reasons. She was paid for her work and received benefits, sick pay and annual leave. **The court held the university offered a nondiscriminatory reason for discharging her. The professor expressed his concerns about her performance months before she took a leave of absence.** Because she could not establish the university's nondiscriminatory reason for its action was a pretext, the court affirmed the judgment for the university. *Cuddeback v. Florida Board of Educ.*, 381 F.3d 1230 (11th Cir. 2004).

◆ *A Pennsylvania university did not discriminate against a male professor when it denied him a tenure-track position.*

The university dean stated he was not recommending the professor for a tenure-track position. He asked the department chair to contact the professor and see if he would be willing to accept a one-year appointment. The professor initially accepted, then told the chair he was not interested. The university contacted another candidate, who was female. When the search committee refused to recommend her, the university reclassified the position as a one-year position that was not tenure track. The professor sued the university in a state court for gender discrimination under Title VII.

The court held for the university, and the professor appealed to the Commonwealth Court of Pennsylvania. The professor said the university's stated reason for not offering him a tenure-track position was pretextual. The real reason, the professor said, was that he was male. The university said its decision had nothing to do with gender. It did not offer the professor a tenure-track position because she lacked scholarly growth. **The court held the university showed it had a legitimate nondiscriminatory reason for its action, and affirmed the judgment in its favor.** *Cummings v. Comwlth. of Pennsylvania, State System of Higher Educ., Bloomsburg Univ.*, 860 A.2d 650 (Pa. Commw. Ct. 2004).

◆ *A lesbian professor was denied tenure because of her poor teaching performance, not because of discriminatory motives.*

The professor was denied tenure by a New York college, allegedly because of numerous negative comments made by students on their evaluation forms. She sued the college in a federal district court, asserting sex discrimination and retaliation in violation of Title VII. The college moved for summary judgment, asserting that its reasons were not a pretext for unlawful discrimination. It said the denial of tenure was based on the professor's mediocre job performance. To support its decision, the college noted student evaluations describing her as "overly critical," "condescending," "insulting," "intimidating," and "rude."

The court found the student evaluations were gender-neutral, not biased against women and lesbians. She was regarded as a "modest scholar with an adequate service record" and many colleagues rated her as a below-average professor. These were legitimate, nondiscriminatory reasons for denying her tenure. The professor's advocacy for "greater sexual and racial diversity in the workplace" was not protected activity. **An employer's failure to follow an affirmative action policy is not an unlawful practice.** As the professor did not oppose any unlawful employment practice, there was no retaliation by the university. The university was entitled to summary judgment. *Byerly v. Ithaca College*, 290 F.Supp.2d 301 (N.D.N.Y. 2003).

2. Religious Entanglement

◆ *A Pennsylvania chaplain's sex discrimination claims against a Catholic university were dismissed under the Title VII "ministerial exception."*

The chaplain worked as director of the university's Center for Social Concerns. She then became the university chaplain. Allegations surfaced that the university's president had an affair with a subordinate, and he took a leave of absence. Another female employee accused him of sexual harassment. The chaplain claimed the university attempted to cover up the president's misconduct. The university demoted the chaplain by restructuring her position as head of the division and reduced much of her responsibilities and her decision-making authority. The chaplain sued the university in a federal district court, alleging it retaliated against her based on her conduct and her sex.

The court stated the ministerial exception precludes courts from questioning the reason for a religious university's employment decision. The chaplain was a ministerial employee in light of how important her role was in supporting the school's spiritual and pastoral mission. The court held she performed a "ministerial" function at the university, and declared it could not hear her Title VII claims. The U.S. Court of Appeals, Third Circuit, agreed to review the case. It joined seven other federal circuit courts that have recognized the ministerial exception. **Title VII exempts religious educational institutions from its anti-discrimination requirements to the extent that their decisions are based on religious preferences**. The chaplain's Title VII discrimination and retaliation claims were barred. As resolution of her fraudulent misrepresentation and breach of contract claims did not limit the university's free exercise rights, these claims were not precluded. However, the chaplain failed to plead fraud with sufficient particularity, and the claim was properly dismissed. The breach of contract claim required further consideration by the district court. *Petruska v. Gannon Univ.*, 462 F.3d 294 (3d Cir. 2006).

◆ *A Wisconsin civil rights act provided no protection to a female teacher whose contract with a seminary was not renewed. Because the position involved was a religious one, the statute did not apply.*

A part-time female teacher employed by a Wisconsin Roman Catholic theological seminary was selected to organize, develop, and lead the newly implemented department of field education. The purpose of the department was to increase seminary students' pastoral development outside the classroom. The Catholic Church promulgated an administrative policy requiring that directors of field education be experienced priests. Based on these policy guidelines, the seminary declined to renew the director's contract. The director challenged the seminary's action with the Labor Industry Review Commission, alleging sex discrimination in violation of the Wisconsin Fair Employment Act (WFEA). At a hearing, an administrative law judge determined that the seminary was wholly sectarian in purpose and ruled that the Equal Rights Division lacked jurisdiction over religious institutions such as the seminary. A Wisconsin trial court affirmed, and the director appealed.

The Court of Appeals of Wisconsin held the Equal Rights Division could investigate employment discrimination complaints but **could not enforce employment discrimination laws against religious associations when the employment position served a "ministerial" or "ecclesiastical" function**. As a general rule, if the employee's primary duties consist of teaching, spreading the faith, church governance, supervision of a religious order, or supervision or participation in religious ritual and worship, he or she should be considered ministerial or ecclesiastical. Because the director performed several of these duties, the Equal Rights Division was constitutionally precluded from enforcing the WFEA against the seminary. *Jocz v. Labor and Industry Review Comm'n*, 538 N.W.2d 588 (Wis. Ct. App. 1995).

◆ *An Equal Employment Opportunity Commission (EEOC) investigation and lawsuit was impermissibly entangled with religion, as they interfered with the selection and training of clergy.*

A Catholic university hired a nun as an associate professor. Her tenure application was denied, and she appealed to a school committee, alleging differential treatment. The university responded that her scholarship, measured primarily by her publications, was not up to its standards. She filed a complaint with the EEOC, which filed suit on her behalf against the university, alleging sex discrimination and retaliatory conduct. The trial judge dismissed the case, finding that the application of Title VII to the case would violate the Free Exercise and Establishment Clauses. The professor appealed.

The professor argued that the district court improperly used **the ministerial exception, which exempts the selection of clergy from Title VII,** and similar statutes. The court of appeals found that the exception did apply since the professor's duties included spreading the faith and participation in religious worship. The court held that the EEOC's investigation and lawsuit violated the First Amendment since they resulted in an impermissible entanglement with religious decision-making and interfered with a procedure of critical importance to the Catholic Church: its ability to select and train its clergy. The university's interest in employing faculty of its choice outweighed the government's interest in eliminating discrimination and, therefore, the professor's claims were barred by the Free Exercise and Establishment Clauses. The district court's decision was affirmed. *EEOC v. Catholic Univ. of America*, 83 F.3d 455 (D.C. Cir. 1996).

◆ *A female professor's liberal views on abortion could legitimately be considered in a hiring decision by a religious university.*

A female professor at Marquette University was repeatedly denied a position as associate professor of theology. The professor sued Marquette under Title VII of the Civil Rights Act of 1964, alleging that it had refused to hire her because she was a woman. She also claimed that Marquette had discriminated against her on the basis of her religious views, i.e., her liberal views on abortion. The district court ruled against the professor, holding that the First Amendment prohibited any court from considering her claim since Marquette's interest in the integrity of its theology department was an overriding factor. The court of appeals concluded that the professor's Title VII claim failed as a matter of law because **the record clearly indicated that she would not have been granted the associate position even if she were a man**. It agreed with the district court's observation that Marquette was exempt from Title VII under the provision that permits a university to hire and employ employees of a particular religion if it is owned by that religion. The professor's liberal abortion views could legitimately be considered in whether the professor ought to be hired as an associate professor. The district court's decision was upheld. *Maguire v. Marquette Univ.*, 814 F.2d 1213 (7th Cir. 1987).

3. Procedural Issues

◆ *The U.S. Supreme Court held that a Title VII "charge" did not have to be verified by oath or affirmation at the time it was filed with the Equal Employment Opportunity Commission (EEOC). As long as the charge was filed within the 300-day deadline, the oath or affirmation could come later.*

Five months after a Virginia college denied tenure to a professor, he faxed a letter to an EEOC field office claiming he had been subjected to gender, national origin and religious discrimination. He then filed charges with the state and, 313 days after the denial of tenure, he filed a verified "Form 5 Charge of Discrimination." When he sued the college under Title VII, the college sought to dismiss the case on the grounds that he had failed to comply with the 300-day statute of limitations. A federal court found that the faxed letter was not a "charge" of discrimination within the meaning of Title VII, and that the verification could not relate back to the letter. The Fourth Circuit agreed, but the U.S. Supreme Court reversed, noting that **the faxed letter to the EEOC could qualify as a "charge" under Title VII**, and that the verification could relate back to the letter. Nothing in Title VII required the charge to be verified at the time it was made. The Court remanded the case for further proceedings. *Edelman v. Lynchburg College*, 535 U.S. 106 (2002).

◆   *The Supreme Court held the statute of limitations for a Title VII case began to run on the date a teacher was denied tenure, not his final employment date.*

A black Liberian teacher taught at a state-supported Delaware college. A faculty committee on tenure recommended that he not be given tenure, and the college faculty senate and board of trustees agreed. The teacher then filed a grievance with the board's grievance committee, which took the case under advisement. The college offered him a one-year "terminal contract" in accordance with state policy. After the teacher had signed the terminal contract without objection, the grievance committee denied his grievance. The teacher then attempted to file a complaint with the EEOC. However, he was notified that he would first have to exhaust state administrative remedies if he wanted to file a claim under Title VII. After the appropriate state agency waived its jurisdiction, the EEOC issued a right-to-sue letter. The teacher then sued the college for discriminating against him on the basis of his national origin in violation of Title VII and 42 U.S.C. § 1981. The district court dismissed the teacher's claims as untimely because the Title VII complaint had not been filed with the EEOC within 180 days and the Section 1981 claim had not been filed in federal court within three years. The U.S. Court of Appeals, Third Circuit, reversed, holding that the limitations on Title VII and Section 1981 did not begin to run until the teacher's terminal contract expired.

The U.S. Supreme Court reversed the judgment, finding that **both the Title VII and Section 1981 claims were untimely**. The teacher's complaint did not state that the college discriminated against him on the basis of national origin; it simply concentrated on the college's denial of tenure. The teacher had failed to make out a *prima facie* case of employment discrimination under Title VII, because he had stated no continuing violation of his civil rights. In fact, the teacher had received essentially the same treatment accorded to other teachers who were denied tenure. The statute of limitations began to run when the teacher was denied tenure, specifically, on the date when the college had offered him a terminal contract. *Delaware State College v. Ricks*, 449 U.S. 250, 101 S.Ct. 498, 66 L.Ed.2d 431 (1980).

◆   *The Supreme Court compelled a private college to disclose employment records in an administrative proceeding before the EEOC.*

In *EEOC v. Franklin and Marshall College*, 775 F.2d 110 (3d Cir. 1985), a professor, who had been employed at a private school in Pennsylvania for three years, was denied tenure. The school's professional standards committee, composed of the dean and five faculty members, recommended that tenure not be granted to the professor. The committee's recommendation was reaffirmed by the college's grievance committee. The professor then filed a complaint with the EEOC, alleging discrimination based on his French national origin. The EEOC issued a subpoena for the committee's records. Although the EEOC offered to accept the records with names deleted, the school refused to disclose them. The EEOC then sued to compel the college to comply with the subpoena. The court ordered disclosure of the records. Before the court of appeals, the college argued that "the quality of a college and ... academic freedom, which has a constitutional dimension, is inextricably intertwined with a confidential peer review process." The court of appeals held that **although the disclosure might burden the tenure process or invade the privacy of other professors, the records had to be disclosed because they were "relevant" to the EEOC's case**. The records were ordered disclosed to the EEOC. The college appealed to the U.S. Supreme Court, but its petition for review was denied. *Franklin & Marshall College v. EEOC*, 476 U.S. 1163, 106 S.Ct. 2288, 90 L.Ed.2d 729 (1986).

◆   *The Supreme Court ruled that a state administrative proceeding on a Title VII discrimination claim filed in state court could be appealed to the federal court system when the state proceeding remained unreviewed by state courts.*

The University of Tennessee Agricultural Extension Service discharged a black employee, allegedly for inadequate work and misconduct on the job. The employee requested a hearing under the state Uniform Administrative Procedures Act to contest his termination. Before his administrative hearing took place the employee also filed a claim in a federal district court under federal civil rights laws, alleging that his dismissal had been racially motivated. The district court entered a temporary restraining order halting the state administrative hearing, but it later allowed the hearing to go forward. The hearing officer determined that the dismissal had not been racially motivated. The university moved to dismiss the employee's federal court lawsuit because it already had been resolved in the administrative hearing.

The district court agreed and dismissed the case. The Sixth Circuit reversed, allowing the case to remain in federal court. The university appealed the decision to the U.S. Supreme Court, which held that the case should be heard by the district court. It ruled that **a state administrative proceeding on a Title VII claim not reviewed by a higher state board could be heard in federal court**. Since the decision made at the employee's administrative hearing was not reviewed by the state courts, it had no preclusive effect. The employee had the right to introduce his claim anew. *Univ. of Tennessee v. Elliot*, 478 U.S. 788, 106 S.Ct. 3220, 92 L.Ed.2d 635 (1986).

◆   *In an employment discrimination lawsuit filed under Title VII, the aggrieved party bears the burden of proving employer pretext.*

In an employment discrimination case against a state college, a federal district court ruled that the college had discriminated against a professor on the basis of sex. The U.S. Court of Appeals, First Circuit, affirmed the decision, ruling that Title VII of the 1964 Civil Rights Act, 42 U.S.C. § 2000e, *et seq.*, required the college to prove absence of discriminatory motive. The U.S. Supreme Court held that this burden was too great. It ruled that **in an employment discrimination case, the employer need only "articulate some legitimate, nondiscriminatory reason for the employee's rejection."** In other words, the employee has the burden of proving that the reason for the employee's rejection was a mere pretext. The Court vacated the court of appeals' decision and remanded the case for reconsideration under the lesser standard. *Trustees of Keene State College v. Sweeney*, 439 U.S. 24, 99 S.Ct. 295, 58 L.Ed.2d 216 (1978).

B. Harassment

Sexual harassment is prohibited by Title VII of the Civil Rights Act of 1964 and by Title IX of the Education Amendments of 1972. The harassment must be severe or pervasive, and based on gender. In 1998, the Supreme Court held that in Title VII sexual harassment suits employers may have a defense where no tangible adverse action is taken against the employee. In such cases, the employer can avoid liability by showing that it exercised reasonable care to prevent and promptly correct any harassing behavior, and that the employee unreasonably failed to use those procedures or otherwise avoid harm.

1. Title VII

◆   *A court rejected a police officer's claim that a Pennsylvania university discriminated against her based on her need to produce breast milk at work.*

The university granted the officer's request for permission to express milk during breaks after she returned from maternity leave. However, supervisors refused to provide her a courtesy transport from her foot patrol to headquarters, where she expressed the milk. The officer claimed she was treated differently from colleagues in other ways and was assigned to menial tasks. She quit and sued the university in federal district court for race and pregnancy discrimination. The court held for the university, and the officer appealed.

The U.S. Court of Appeals, Third Circuit, explained that **to prove she was subjected to a hostile work environment, the officer had to show harassment that was so "severe or pervasive" that it changed the terms and conditions of her employment and created an abusive environment.** In addition, she needed to show she was subjected to conduct that was offensive both subjectively and objectively. It was clear that the conduct in this case was subjectively offensive. **However, the officer did not show she was subjected to conduct that a reasonable person in her position would have found to be hostile or abusive.** Other officers who were placed on light duty were also assigned menial tasks, and running errands for officers with greater seniority was a common practice. The university provided breaks to express breast milk and switched the officer to a patrol route that was closer to headquarters. As no reasonable jury could conclude the university created a hostile work environment in violation of Title VII, the court upheld the judgment. *Page v. Trustees of the Univ. of Pennsylvania*, 222 Fed.Appx. 144 (3d Cir. 2007).

◆ *A federal district court declined to dismiss a Wisconsin university employee's sexual harassment claim.*

The employee claimed her manager harassed her repeatedly during the three years that she worked for a university bookstore. She sued the university in a federal district court, alleging his conduct violated Title VII. The university admitted there had been a touching incident but denied anything further. It argued the manager's conduct was not sexual harassment under Title VII. The court held each case must be analyzed on its own facts to determine whether the conduct is actionable. **Factors to consider include the frequency and severity of the discriminatory conduct, whether the conduct was physically threatening or humiliating or merely offensive, and whether the harassment interfered with the employee's job performance.** The court held the employee presented enough evidence to proceed to trial. While each incident may not have seemed physically or verbally abusive, the conduct continued for a considerable time. The court denied the dismissal motion and set the case for trial. *Gray v. Board of Regents of the Univ. of Wisconsin System*, No. 04-C-562, 2006 WL 314416 (E.D. Wis. 2/9/06).

◆ *A Mississippi federal district court held an employee failed to establish a university did not promote her because of her sex.*

The university did not select the employee for the position of office manager. **She insisted that she was not chosen because she refused sexual advances by her supervisor.** The employee sued the university in a federal district court for discrimination based on her sex, claiming a violation of Title VII. The university argued the employee failed to establish sex discrimination because it selected another female applicant for the position. The supervisor testified that 20 applicants applied for the position and that he interviewed 16 females. The court rejected the employee's arguments. It said her alleged failure to accept the supervisor's advances were insufficient to support her claim that he sexually harassed her. *Turner v. Jackson State Univ.*, No. 3:04CV623LS, 2006 WL 1139931 (S.D. Miss. 4/25/06).

◆ *An Illinois university did not subject an employee to a sexually hostile environment or treat her differently from her male counterparts.*

The employee worked for the university as a building services worker. She claimed male supervisors called her degrading and obscene names, although not to her face. The employee also asserted that a male employee asked her to join him on his boat for "a weekend of drinking and other things." School officials suspended her for insubordination and failure to follow departmental guidelines and practices. The employee sued the university in a federal district court, alleging it violated Title VII for allowing a sexually hostile environment. **The court found the employee was not similarly situated to males who had been disciplined. She did not present any evidence that the university treated her less favorably than the males. While there had been offensive conduct, there was no showing this was frequent, severe, threatening or humiliating.** The court held for the university.

The employee appealed to the U.S. Court of Appeals, Seventh Circuit. **To establish a claim for Title VII sex discrimination, she had to show the**

university subjected her to adverse employment action. The court noted that adverse employment action is typically an economic injury, like suspension without pay. Because the employee voluntarily left her job, she was not subjected to economic injury. An employment action is "adverse" only if it alters the terms and conditions of employment. As the university did not change the terms or conditions of the employee's job, she could not prevail in a Title VII employment action. The court affirmed the judgment for the university. *Whittaker v. Northern Illinois Univ.*, 424 F.3d 640 (7th Cir. 2005).

♦   *The Supreme Court of Iowa reversed a trial court judgment ordering a university to pay $3 million to a student employee who was sexually harassed.*

The student attended a doctoral program and worked as a research assistant to a male professor. She accompanied him to Russia to help him run a month-long cultural and educational exchange program for high school students. When they arrived at their hotel, the student learned the professor had arranged for them to share a two-room suite with both beds in one room. The student told the professor she was uncomfortable with the sleeping arrangements and insisted one of the beds be moved to the other room. The professor was very angry, but relented. He later told the student she could "kiss her Ph.D. good-bye." At other times on the trip, the professor touched her and told her details of his sex life. When the student returned home, she filed a sexual harassment complaint against the professor. After he admitted his misconduct, the college reassigned the student to another professor. Although the college directed the professor to have no contact with the student, he continued to pester her, and she filed a formal complaint. The university found the professor violated its sexual harassment policy and suspended him. It tried to fire him, but it dropped the proceeding after he was diagnosed with terminal colon cancer.

The student sued the university in a state court for sexual harassment and retaliation in employment and education for failing to protect her from sexual harassment. A jury awarded her more than $3 million, and the university appealed. **The Supreme Court of Iowa held Title VII administrative procedures must be followed. Employees may sue a university for violating Title VII only after they exhaust available administrative procedures.** The court held that because the student did not allege retaliation in her complaints to the federal and state agencies, she failed to exhaust her administrative remedies. It reversed the jury verdict for the student and ordered a new trial on her sex discrimination claim. *McElroy v. State,* 703 N.W.2d 385 (Iowa 2005).

♦   *An Alabama university did not violate Title VII when it declined to renew a contract of a former dean of students.*

The dean claimed her supervisor made sexual advances and comments towards her. The supervisor never directly asked the dean for sex, but he implied it by asking about her house and bedroom. He told the dean he wanted to come visit her at home sometime, and that women sleep with their bosses to keep their jobs and get promotions. The supervisor denied he made sexual advances or comments towards the dean. After a poor performance evaluation, the supervisor told the dean the university was not renewing her contract, and she was placed on administrative leave until her contract expired.

The dean sued the college in a federal district court for violating Title VII. The university moved for summary judgment. **The court held sexual harassment is a form of sex discrimination which violates Title VII. Unwelcome sexual advances, requests for sexual favors, and comments of a sexual nature may constitute sexual harassment if they affect an individual's employment, or create an intimidating, hostile or offensive work environment.** The court found the dean did not present evidence that the supervisor threatened to fire her if she refused to comply. She never let the supervisor know she was uncomfortable about his sexual remarks. No evidence supported the dean's contention that the decision not to renew her contract was connected to sexual advances. Even after the dean turned down her supervisor's advances, he appointed her dean of students. The court granted the university's motion for summary judgment. *Hammons v. George C. Wallace State Univ.*, No. Civ. A. 04-0270-CG-M, 2005 WL 1907534 (S.D. Ala. 8/9/05).

◆   *A Louisiana women's basketball coach won a Title VII sexual harassment claim against a university based on the athletic director's misconduct.*

The athletic director was the coach's supervisor. She claimed he asked her out about once a month despite her repeated refusals, and made sexually oriented remarks about her appearance and clothing. The coach said the athletic director told her if she "was nice," she would not have to worry about losing her job and he would buy her nice things. According to the coach, after she continued to refuse the athletic director's advances, he began to interfere with her coaching. She sued the university in a state court for violating Title VII. A jury found the athletic director sexually harassed the coach, and the court held the university liable for his conduct. The university appealed.

The Court of Appeal of Louisiana explained that sexual harassment did not always come in the form of sexual advances. **Any harassment or unequal treatment that occurred only because of sex violated Title VII if it was sufficiently pervasive. Sexual harassment included unwelcome sexual advances, requests for sexual favors – and other conduct of a sexual nature – where the conduct unreasonably interfered with work performance or created an intimidating, hostile or offensive work environment.** The court agreed with the jury that the athletic director had subjected the coach to unwelcome sexual harassment, and affirmed the judgment. *Brooks v. Southern Univ.*, 877 So.2d 1194 (La. Ct. App. 2004).

◆   *An Oregon receptionist raised a valid retaliation complaint against a college after she complained of sexual harassment by her supervisor.*

The receptionist told her supervisor she needed to get a second job and was considering working as a cocktail waitress. Her supervisor told her she should be a stripper because she had a nice body and men would pay to see her dance. The supervisor later rubbed the receptionist's thigh and her boyfriend called the college president to report the incident. The president assured the boyfriend there would be an investigation. The supervisor discussed the allegations with his receptionist, and his concerns about the effects on his job and family. When the president learned the supervisor breached an agreement not to talk about the allegations, he fired him. A new supervisor compiled a list of the receptionist's performance problems and issued her a written warning. The receptionist told the college the new supervisor was retaliating against her. When the college did not respond, the receptionist sued it for sexual harassment and retaliation under Title VII and state laws. A federal district court stated Oregon anti-discrimination laws were interpreted like federal laws.

Conduct amounted to sexual harassment only if it unreasonably interfered with a person's work performance or created an intimidating, hostile or offensive work environment. The court held the circumstances of this case were not severe or pervasive enough to be considered a hostile work environment. The working environment must be perceived both subjectively and objectively as abusive. The court dismissed the federal and state sexual harassment charges against the college. However, it found sufficient evidence to raise the issue of whether the college's stated reasons for the adverse employment actions were a pretext for retaliation. The receptionist received her first warning of a performance problem only after the supervisor was fired. The college did not investigate or respond to her complaints. The court denied the college's request to dismiss the retaliation claims. *Payne v. Apollo College-Portland*, 327 F.Supp.2d 1237 (D. Or. 2004).

♦ *A professor did not suffer any adverse action under Title VII because she retained her position and benefits.*

A Georgia university assistant professor received excellent performance evaluations and was chosen for a candidate selection committee to fill a vacant position. She was upset by the majority's recommendation to hire a male for the position and allegedly shook her fist at other committee members. The faculty voted not to renew the professor's contract on the grounds that she was insulting and hostile to colleagues. School deans rejected the faculty's recommendation based on her previous positive performance evaluations. The faculty voted not to renew her contract the next year and the deans did not interfere with the decision. Although the faculty senate eventually voted to retain the professor, she sued the university and officials in a federal district court for First Amendment and Title VII violations.

The court granted summary judgment to the university, and the professor appealed. The Eleventh Circuit Court of Appeals found she suffered no serious or tangible effects from the university's actions. Moreover, any emotional distress was too insubstantial to be considered adverse employment action. **Since the professor did not suffer any adverse action under Title VII, there was no basis for a First Amendment retaliation claim. The court explained that "an important condition of employment" must be involved in a First Amendment retaliation claim.** She did not suffer a reprimand, demotion, or discharge, so the court affirmed the judgment. *Stavropoulos v. Firestone*, 361 F.3d 610 (11th Cir. 2004).

♦ *"A tangible employment action" occurs when a supervisor threatens an employee with discharge unless the employee acquiesces to sexual demands.*

A secretary for a California university began a sexual relationship with her supervisor. She later stated her belief that he would discharge her if she did not comply with his advances. After their relationship ended, she requested a transfer. The university denied the request and established a committee to investigate her sexual harassment allegations. The committee found insufficient evidence of sexual harassment, but it offered the secretary a position working for a female professor in a different department. She rejected the offer and sued the university and supervisor for sexual harassment. A federal district court awarded summary judgment to the university, finding the secretary did not suffer a "tangible employment action."

The secretary appealed to the Ninth Circuit, which held an employee can establish a "tangible employment action" by showing she complied with a supervisor's sexual demands to avoid termination. If there is a tangible employment action under Title VII, the employer can be held vicariously liable for the supervisor's unlawful conduct. The court found the secretary did not show her continued employment was conditioned upon consenting to sexual relations with the supervisor. Although he created an uncomfortable environment, there was no evidence establishing a connection between continuing employment and his request for sex. The court noted the university investigated the allegations as soon as it learned of them. Even though it did not think there was sufficient evidence of sexual harassment, it offered to transfer the secretary and asked the supervisor to resign. As the university took reasonable corrective measures, the court affirmed the judgment. *Holly D. v. California Institute of Technology*, 339 F.3d 1158 (9th Cir. 2003).

◆   *A North Carolina university police officer alleged sufficient facts to support Title VII claims that she was sexually harassed by a supervisor.*

The officer claimed the supervisor made lewd remarks, touched her inappropriately and accosted her in a parking lot. She complained to other supervisors, who offered her no assistance. The officer claimed the harassment caused her mental distress and depression. She received psychiatric treatment and eventually lost her job at the university. The officer sued the university in a federal district court under Title VII for hostile work environment, adding a Title IX claim for sexual harassment and a claim for constitutional rights violations by the university and its officials. The university moved for dismissal of the Title VII and constitutional claims.

The court relied on *Shaw v. First Union Nat'l Bank*, 202 F.3d 234 (4th Cir. 2000) to test the Title VII hostile work environment claim. It held the officer demonstrated harassment that was sufficiently pervasive or severe to create an abusive work environment. The supervisors who did not assist her had actual knowledge of harassing behavior which created an unreasonable risk of harm. While the supervisors were potentially liable for failing to act, punitive damages were unavailable against university officials. The university's motion to dismiss the case was denied. *Alston v. North Carolina A&T State Univ.*, 304 F.Supp.2d 774 (M.D.N.C. 2004).

◆   *An Alabama state university employee could sue for same-sex harassment under Title VII.*

A campus police officer at the University of Alabama claimed that his immediate supervisor, a male, subjected him to such severe sexual harassment that a hostile work environment was created. He sued the university under Title VII. The university sought to dismiss the case, arguing that it was immune from liability under the Eleventh Amendment. The court denied the motion for immunity, and the Eleventh Circuit Court of Appeals affirmed. Since **Title VII did not create new constitutional rights apart from those granted by the Equal Protection Clause**, Congress did not exceed its power when it enacted Title VII. As a result, the university was not entitled to immunity. Also, the court stated that the university could be liable for same-sex harassment under Title VII even though the discriminatory conduct did not have a sexual overtone. Where a supervisor displays hostility to members of the same sex in the workplace, a hostile work environment claim can be brought under Title VII according to the Supreme Court's decision in *Oncale v. Sundowner Offshore Services, Inc.*, 523 U.S. 75 (1998). The court remanded the case for further proceedings. *Downing v. Board of Trustees of Univ. of Alabama*, 321 F.3d 1017 (11th Cir. 2003).

◆ *Alabama college officials were entitled to qualified immunity in a suit alleging same-sex sexual harassment.*

Four security officers employed by an Alabama community college claimed their supervisor subjected them to sexual harassment over a 15-year period. They accused him of touching them and other male employees inappropriately and of constantly making sexual remarks and gestures. The officers sued the college and its officials in a federal district court, alleging the harassment violated their equal protection rights, and college officials violated their constitutional rights by failing to stop the misconduct. The court held the officials were entitled to qualified immunity.

The officers appealed to the Eleventh Circuit Court of Appeals, which held the officials were entitled to immunity unless they violated the officers' clearly established statutory or constitutional rights. **For a constitutional right to be clearly established, a governmental official must be aware an action is obviously wrong in the light of preexisting law.** Although a 1998 U.S. Supreme Court decision found a same-sex harassment claim actionable under Title VII against a private employer, the decision did not place governmental officials on notice that this conduct violated the officers' constitutional rights. **Since same-sex discrimination was not clearly a violation of the Equal Protection Clause at the time of the harassment, the officials were entitled to qualified immunity.** *Snider v. Jefferson State Community College*, 344 F.3d 1325 (11th Cir. 2003).

◆ *A university was liable for its agent's harassing behavior, but its good faith efforts to end the harassment prevented an award of punitive damages.*

A Louisiana woman worked as an office manager for a doctor at Tulane University and later began a consensual sexual relationship with him. After the relationship ended, she claimed that he began to harass her – breaking into her desk, searching her belongings and stripping some of her job duties. Her mental health suffered, and she eventually left Tulane. When she sued the doctor and the university under Title VII, a federal court dismissed the claims against the doctor, but allowed the claims against the university to go to a jury.

The jury awarded her $300,000 in compensatory damages as well as back pay and front pay of more than $128,000. The court dismissed her claim for punitive damages. On appeal, the Fifth Circuit affirmed, noting that there was sufficient evidence that the doctor harassed the manager because of her gender and not just because of the failed relationship. Since he was acting as an agent of the university by doing so, the jury verdict against the university was proper. Also, punitive damages had appropriately been denied because despite the doctor's behavior, **the university acted in good faith to end the harassment by putting her on paid administrative leave and seeking another position for her within the university system.** *Green v. Administrators of Tulane Educ. Fund,* 284 F.3d 642 (5th Cir. 2002).

2. Title IX

◆   *The former women's basketball coach for Delaware State University (DSU) lost her Title VII gender discrimination suit against the university because she should have filed a Title IX claim.*

Although DSU claimed the coach was fired for poor job performance, the coach maintained her termination was in response to her frequent complaints that the women's athletic program did not receive the same benefits as the men's program. The coach's lawsuit alleged gender discrimination and retaliation under Title VII of the Civil Rights Act of 1964. The U.S. District Court for the District of Delaware ruled that she failed to establish a *prima facie* case. The coach "confused discrimination based on her sex with discrimination based on her association with women's athletics." **She did not demonstrate that she was discriminated against for being a woman**, as opposed to being fired for her complaints about the women's athletic program. Additionally, the fact that she was replaced by a woman did not help her case. Her retaliation claim also failed because it addressed an activity protected under Title IX of the Educational Amendments of 1972, rather than Title VII. Despite the coach's claim that she suffered retaliation for complaining about a potential Title IX violation, **she did not show she suffered retaliation for complaining about discrimination based on her sex**, as required by Title VII. The court granted pretrial judgment to DSU. *Lamb-Bowman v. Delaware State Univ.,* 152 F.Supp.2d 553 (D. Del. 2001).

◆   *A professor's claim that Title IX was violated when a college fired him for sexual harassment failed.*

A Minnesota man working as a professor at a private college was accused of violating the college's sexual harassment policy because of his sexual contact with a student. He was later fired, and the student sued the professor and college. She later settled these claims, but the professor counterclaimed against the college and its president, alleging a violation of Title IX, breach of contract, defamation and tortious interference with contract. Both sides filed for pretrial judgment. The court noted that although courts have recognized a cause of action under Title IX on behalf of students who are discriminated against by educational programs, few courts have found that employees of educational institutions have a cause of action for damages under Title IX. **Because Title VII provides a comprehensive system for redressing employment**

discrimination, courts have refused to infer one in Title IX. The court dismissed that claim. However, it noted that the college did not follow the sexual harassment procedures contained in the faculty manual and therefore issues of fact existed on the breach of contract claim. The professor's motion was denied. The college's motion was granted in part and denied in part. *Cooper v. Gustavus Adolphus College*, 957 F.Supp. 191 (D. Minn. 1997).

◆ *A lawsuit against a university for harassment by a supervisor could not be dismissed where fact issues were in doubt as to what the university knew.*

A male supervisor at a Maryland private university allegedly sexually harassed two female employees. When they reported the incidents, they alleged that no action was taken and that one of them was assigned to a less desirable position. They also maintained that the university failed to distribute to them its policy manual prohibiting sexual harassment. They filed Title IX hostile work environment claims against the university in a Maryland federal court, which examined the university's motion for pretrial judgment and determined that claims brought under Title IX for abusive work environments should be analyzed under Title VII standards. It then found that the alleged conduct was severe and pervasive enough to warrant a trial on the facts. Here, **the university arguably had actual or constructive notice of the harassment**, and a jury would have to decide whether liability should be imputed to the university. *Ward v. Johns Hopkins Univ.*, 861 F.Supp. 367 (D. Md. 1994).

C. Equal Pay Issues

The Equal Pay Act (EPA) requires that employers pay males and females the same wages for equal work. Employees are protected by the EPA as long as the employer is engaged in an enterprise affecting interstate commerce. The EPA has been interpreted by the courts to require only that the jobs under comparison be "substantially" equal. Strict equality of the jobs under comparison is not required. The EPA requires equal pay for jobs involving "equal skill, effort, and responsibility, and which are performed under similar working conditions, except where such payment is made pursuant to (i) a seniority system; (ii) a merit system; (iii) a system which measures earnings by quantity or quality of production; or (iv) a differential based on any other factor other than sex." Many cases alleging disparate pay rates based on sex include claims under Title VII and analogous state laws. If employers can prove that the difference in pay is for a reason other than the difference in sex, they do not have to provide the same pay and benefits. It is for the employer to show that such a factor exists and that it is the real reason for the difference.

◆ *An Indiana university did not discriminate against a female professor who was denied a salary award given to some of her male peers.*

A university task force evaluated gender inequities at the university, with a particular focus on salary differences. After conducting a review, the task force reported that male professors tended to have higher mean salaries than female professors at all rank levels. It recommended a professional excellence program to reward tenured full professors who demonstrated excellence in scholarship, teaching and service. The professor was the only woman eligible in the college of liberal arts and sciences the first two years the awards were offered. The university made the awards only to male professors for both years. The professor filed a grievance with the faculty appeals committee, then sued the university for sex discrimination. A federal district court held for the university.

The professor appealed to the Seventh Circuit, which agreed with her argument that the denial of an award was an adverse employment action by the university. **Adverse employment actions include denial of a raise, failure to promote, and termination.** The court found the award was not a raise, but more closely resembled a bonus. The university contended it had a legitimate nondiscriminatory reason for not paying the award to the professor. For both years, it determined other professors exceeded her overall performance in the areas of teaching, scholarship and service. The professor alleged these reasons were a cover-up for sex discrimination. She said the existence of an "old boys' club" proved discrimination. **The court found the existence of an old boys' club did not in itself establish a cover-up. It accepted the university's reasons as legitimate and nondiscriminatory, and affirmed the judgment.** *Farrell v. Butler Univ.*, 421 F.3d 609 (7th Cir. 2005).

◆ *The U.S. Court of Appeals, Ninth Circuit, held a female professor failed to show a California university violated the Equal Pay Act.*

The professor claimed the university paid her male colleagues substantially more money than it paid her for the same kind of work. She sued the university in a federal district court for violating the EPA. The professor specifically pointed to a discrepancy between herself and the male employees in annual raises. The court dismissed the case, finding she did not show her total compensation was less than the average total compensation earned by her male colleagues for substantially equal work. **The district court said the comparison of annual raises alone does not violate the EPA, which compares "wages." The act defines wages to include all payments made to an employee and all forms of compensation.** The professor appealed to the Ninth Circuit, which agreed with the reasoning of the district court and affirmed the judgment. *Ghirardo v. Univ. of Southern California*, 156 Fed. Appx. 914 (9th Cir. 2005).

◆ *A Wisconsin university lecturer earned a trial to determine if a university violated the Equal Pay Act by paying males more than she received.*

The lecturer was an untenured senior lecturer in the university's business school who was not on a tenure track. She taught business statistics, a required course for all business school students. Three of her male colleagues earned more money per course than she did. Two taught management courses and one taught a marketing course. The lecturer asked the department chair to perform a gender equity review of her salary. The dean concluded her pay was appropriate. The lecturer sued the university in a federal district court, alleging it violated the EPA by paying more money to the male lecturers.

The court explained that to determine whether the university violated the EPA, it must compare job requirements, not individuals. Under the EPA, the university could lawfully pay the male lecturers more than the female lecturer based on seniority, a merit system, a system which measured earnings by production, or another reason besides sex. The university argued that the difference between the lecturer's salary and the salaries of the other three lecturers was valid because she did not teach in the core area of the business school. According to the lecturer, the university failed to prove her skill, effort and responsibility were different from those of the male lecturers. The court found a genuine issue of fact concerning whether the lecturer and the male lecturers had the same skill and responsibility and put forth the same effort. For that reason, it denied the university's motion for dismissal, and ordered that the case proceed to trial. *Mullins v. Board of Regents of the Univ. of Wisconsin System*, No. 05-C-581-S, 2006 WL 641079 (W.D. Wis. 3/10/06).

◆ *An Ohio university did not discriminate or retaliate against a female professor who was paid less than a male counterpart.*

The university hired the professor at $2,000 less per year than a newly hired male professor in the same department. When she learned of the salary difference two years later, the university honored her request to begin to adjust her salary so it would eventually equal his pay. Three years later, the professor was promoted to full professor. She took sabbatical leave, and over the next three and a half years, she taught at the university only one semester. The professor then sued the university in a federal district court, stating her salary was lower than eight other full-time professors in her department and $13,314 less than the male professor who was hired at the time of her hire.

The court held for the university, and the professor appealed to the U.S. Court of Appeals, Sixth Circuit. It held that **to prevail under a Title VII sex discrimination claim, the professor had to prove she was treated differently from similarly situated members of a non-protected class. The court found the university offered legitimate, nondiscriminatory reasons for paying her less than the male professor. The disparity was based on merit differences awarded during her absences and budgetary constraints.** Because the professor had no evidence to counter the university's nondiscriminatory reasons, the court affirmed the judgment. *Harrison-Pepper v. Miami Univ.*, 103 Fed.Appx. 596 (6th Cir. 2004).

◆ *A Minnesota assistant women's hockey coach lost his EPA and Title VII action because he did not prove he suffered any adverse employment action.*

The assistant coach learned the university paid him $13,000 per year less than a female assistant coach. He complained to the director of women's athletics, and then asserted the head coach retaliated against him and gave him a poor performance evaluation. The male assistant coach resigned and sued the university in a federal district court for EPA and Title VII violations. **The court noted the female assistant coach performed many job duties that the male assistant coach did not perform, such as recruiting and public relations. Their positions were not "substantially equal" under the EPA.**

The male assistant coach appealed to the Eighth Circuit, which upheld the EPA ruling. **It also rejected his Title VII retaliation claim because the performance evaluation was not an "adverse employment action."** The assistant's discomfort with the situation was not enough to create an adverse employment action under Title VII. As his working conditions were not so intolerable as to force his resignation, the court affirmed the judgment for the university. *Horn v. Univ. of Minnesota*, 362 F.3d 1042 (8th Cir. 2004).

◆   *A female volleyball coach will receive a jury trial in her Title VII sex discrimination and EPA actions against a Kansas university.*

The coach claimed the university paid her less than the school's male basketball coaches who had similar responsibilities and terms different from hers. **The EPA is limited to situations of equal work and equal skill. The court found coaching volleyball is substantially equal to coaching basketball.** It allowed the female coach's EPA and Title VII claims to go before a jury. *Mehus v. Emporia State Univ.*, 222 F.R.D. 455 (D. Kan. 2004).

◆   *A Louisiana professor failed to show an EPA violation because she did not show her job was "substantially equal" to a male professor's.*

The professor worked as an adjunct for nine years before becoming a tenured associate. The university turned her down twice for a full professorship before doing so after 11 years. She claimed the university violated the EPA by paying her less than a male professor doing the same work she did and that she was more experienced than anyone else in her department. The professor sued the university in a state court for EPA violations. The case went before a jury, which rejected the university's evidence that the pay disparity reflected the different starting dates and annual performance reports of the two professors. The university appealed to the Court of Appeal of Louisiana, which held the **professor did not show her job was substantially equal to that of the male professor or involved the same skills.** Because of this, she failed to show an EPA violation, and the court reversed the judgment. *Ramelow v. Board of Trustees of Univ. of Louisiana*, 870 So.2d 415 (La. Ct. App. 2004).

◆   *The Second Circuit affirmed a jury verdict of $117,929.98 to a female professor who sued Marist College under the EPA and Title VII.*

After the jury rendered its verdict for the professor, both sides appealed different aspects of the decision. The college argued that the verdict should be overturned because the professor did not make specific comparisons with her male counterparts, but rather the group as a whole. Thus, the university argued that the professor failed to state a *prima facie* case.

The professor claimed that a special jury verdict form erroneously instructed the jury to ignore her claim under Title VII if it found that any violation of the EPA by the college was not willful. The appeals panel rejected the college's argument, finding that the five variables the professor's expert used to isolate comparable positions were effective. The variables were rank, years of service, division, tenure status and degrees earned. Turning to the professor's argument on appeal, the circuit court pointed out that while the EPA and Title VII must be construed in harmony, particularly where claims made under the two statutes arise out of the same discriminatory pay policies, another consideration comes into play. One of the major differences between the EPA and Title VII is the requirement regarding intent. **Under Title VII, a plaintiff alleging disparate treatment must demonstrate discriminatory intent,**

while an EPA plaintiff does not have to make this showing. Accordingly, the jury verdict form was appropriate. The district court decision was upheld. *Lavin-McEleney v. Marist College*, 239 F.3d 476 (2d Cir. 2001).

D. Pregnancy Discrimination

Pregnancy discrimination is prohibited by Title VII, the Pregnancy Discrimination Act (42 U.S.C. § 2000e(k)), and analogous state laws.

◆ *Columbia University did not subject an employee to "adverse employment action" by changing her supervisor.*

The employee worked as an associate director for the university until the associate dean decided to restructure her department. The employee continued to report directly to the associate dean. Upon learning she was pregnant, she informed the executive director. The associate dean soon decided the employee was to report to the executive director as part of the restructuring. The employee suspected the decision was based on her pregnancy. She told the associate director she was having a high risk pregnancy, and she took disability leave. Meanwhile, the associate dean criticized her performance. The employee sued the university in a federal district court for pregnancy discrimination under Title VII, the Pregnancy Discrimination Act, and state law.

The court found the employee did not prove the university subjected her to adverse employment action. It said **the assignment to report to a different supervisor was not a demotion or an "adverse employment action."** The executive director was senior to the employee in title and grade, and the change did not affect her title, grade, salary or benefits. The court explained that criticizing an employee was not an adverse employment action. **"Adverse employment actions" include demotion, termination, or a change that results in significantly diminished material responsibilities.** As the employee did not establish any of these, the court awarded summary judgment in favor of Columbia. *Palomo v. Trustees of Columbia Univ. in City of New York*, No. 03 Civ. 7853 (DLC), 2005 WL 1683586 (S.D.N.Y. 7/20/05).

◆ *A federal district court let a pregnancy discrimination claim by an Oklahoma childcare employee proceed to trial.*

The employee worked as a childcare attendant at a university childcare center. She said her manager rolled her eyes and "congratulated' her in a hateful manner when she told her she was pregnant. The employee claimed after she became pregnant, the manager refused to consult with her and allowed other employees to harass her about her pregnancy. The employee gave her supervisors statements from a physician advising her to stop working because of pregnancy complications. She took FMLA leave and returned to work after the childbirth. The employee then gave her supervisors doctors' notes stating she could not lift over 20 pounds, which meant she could pick up infants but not toddlers. The center told her she could not work with restrictions.

The employee sued the university for pregnancy discrimination. The university moved for summary judgment, arguing she could not perform the job because lifting was required. The court disagreed, holding **the university**

did not conduct an independent evaluation to determine if the weight restrictions actually prevented the employee from performing her job duties. It denied the university's motion for summary judgment and scheduled the case for trial. *Borchert v. The State of Oklahoma*, No. 04CV0839 CVE/SAJ, 2006 WL 228913 (N.D. Okla. 1/30/06).

III. RELIGIOUS DISCRIMINATION

Title VII generally prohibits religious discrimination. However, religious hiring preferences are permitted if the institution is substantially "owned, supported, controlled, or managed" by a religious organization or if the curriculum "is directed toward the propagation of a particular religion."

◆ *A Missouri university did not discriminate against a doctor by refusing to rehire him because of license suspensions and criminal conduct.*

The doctor sued the university in a federal district court, alleging it violated Title VII when it did not hire him because the Catholic church did not approve of his divorce. **The university stated it did not rehire him because of medical license suspensions in Missouri and Illinois, criminal conduct, failure to provide a complete residency application, and past unprofessional conduct. The court found the school had legitimate non-discriminatory reasons for not rehiring the doctor.** He presented no evidence to show the decision was motivated by discrimination instead of the reasons it offered. The court granted the university's motion for summary judgment and dismissed the case. *Kaminsky v. Saint Louis Univ. School of Medicine*, No. 4:05CV1112 CDP, 2006 WL 2376232 (E.D. Mo. 8/16/06).

◆ *A physical altercation, not improper discrimination, motivated the discharge of a New York university employee.*

A supervisor accused the employee of punching the time card of a co-worker who was not at work. Their argument culminated in physical contact. The employee's union filed a grievance on her behalf but later declined to arbitrate it. The university determined the employee started the fight, but she denied this and sued the university in federal district court for discrimination based on her race, age, religion and color. The court held the employee did not state a claim of age discrimination. Because the university concluded she had struck the supervisor and that the supervisor had not struck her back, the two were not subject to the same disciplinary standards. There was no evidence to support the employee's claim that the person who investigated the incident was biased against her for any reason. The employee admitted that she struck the supervisor, and that act justified her termination.

The employee asserted she was discriminated against based on her Christian faith, and she supported this allegation by contending that a supervisor once said she disliked people who "pretend they're Christian." The employee further claimed that religious materials she left on a break room table were moved to the floor. **The court found these incidents did not prove**

religious bias by the university. It rejected the employee's remaining
claims and dismissed the case. *Mincey v. Univ. of Rochester*, No. 01-CV-
6159T, 2006 WL 3169108 (W.D.N.Y. 11/2/06).

◆ *A Georgia state university did not violate a Christian cheerleading
coordinator's constitutional right to the free exercise of her religion.*

Two Jewish cheerleaders complained to the athletic department that the
coordinator discriminated against them because of their religion. They said the
coordinator treated them unfavorably and used her position to encourage
students to pray, study the Bible and engage in other religious practices. The
university placed the coordinator on probation, and it informed her she would
be discharged if she continued to violate the university's policy on religious
discrimination. She read a statement to the cheerleading squad, stating a Jewish
cheerleader had accused her of religious discrimination and that the claim was
without merit. The university fired the coordinator, who filed a federal lawsuit.

**A federal district court held the university was entitled to Eleventh
Amendment immunity. The terms of the coordinator's probation letter
simply mandated that she keep her religious activities separate from the
cheerleading program. As the university did not compromise her religious
beliefs or prevent her from doing anything essential to exercising her
religion, the court dismissed the case.** *Braswell v. Board of Regents of the
Univ. System of Georgia*, 369 F. Supp. 2d 1371 (N.D. Ga. 2005).

◆ *A Minnesota business college discharged an instructor for his poor
performance, not his Muslim religion.*

The college hired the instructor to teach computer programming. There
were soon complaints about his teaching. A student complained that the
instructor did not respect students and refused to answer their questions.
Several students claimed his presentation and lecture styles were ineffective.
The college held an annual review and rated the instructor as "meeting
expectations" in all categories. His next annual review was unfavorable. The
university placed the instructor on probation and told him if he did not improve
his performance, he would be discharged. After he failed to follow the
conditions of his performance improvement plan, the college discharged him.
The instructor sued the college in a federal district court, alleging it
discriminated against him based on religion. The college argued the instructor
failed to adequately perform his job. **The court agreed, finding evidence that
he did not meet the legitimate employment expectations of the college. The
college was entitled to summary judgment.** *Eldeeb v. Career Educ. Corp.*,
No. Civ. 04-2932PAMRLE, 2005 WL 2105500 (D. Minn. 8/30/05).

◆ *A federal district court dismissed Title VII religious discrimination charges
by a former employee of the University of Rochester.*

The employee was Iranian and a Muslim. His supervisor was Jewish and
had lived in Israel. The supervisor noticed the employee's performance
problems during the first few months of his employment, and documented them
in a warning letter stating he might face termination if his work did not
improve. The employee stated the supervisor began treating him differently

after he found out he was Muslim and born in Iran. He sued the university in a federal district court for discrimination based on religion and national origin.

The court found examples of the employee's poor performance adequately demonstrated a nondiscriminatory reason for firing him. The employee offered no evidence to refute the university's explanation or to show its actions were actually a pretext for hostility towards Iran or Muslims. The firing of a Muslim employee two months after the September 11 terrorist attacks did not establish a connection between the decision to fire him and his religion or national origin. The court noted the employee's performance problems arose before September 11. This was not a case where a sudden change in a performance evaluation followed a precipitating event. The court granted the university's motion for summary judgment. *Sasannejad v. Univ. of Rochester*, 329 F.Supp.2d 385 (W.D.N.Y. 2004).

◆   *A Texas professor was unable to establish that a university improperly fired him based on his religious beliefs.*

The professor asserted that as the only Jewish professor in a predominantly Arab or Muslim department, he was subjected to a hostile work environment. He contended the university required him to teach a course on his Sabbath, while accommodating Muslim colleagues during Ramadan. A colleague observed the professor's class and found that he was not teaching or applying the required subjects. His supervisor rated his performance "unsatisfactory" and "unacceptable," and the university discharged him. The professor sued the university in a state court for age and religious discrimination. The court awarded the university summary judgment, and the professor appealed.

The Court of Appeals of Texas held that to prevail in his religious discrimination claim, the professor had to show the university knew of his good-faith religious beliefs, that they conflicted with a job requirement, and that he suffered an adverse employment action for failing to comply with the requirement. In view of the substantial evidence indicating the professor's performance was poor, the court concluded the university had legitimate, nondiscriminatory reasons for discharging him. Accordingly, summary judgment for the university was affirmed. *Brauer v. Texas A&M Univ.*, No. 13-01-868-CV, 2003 WL 22415369 (Tex. Ct. App. 2003).

◆   *An employee who quit under adverse conditions could proceed with her lawsuit for religious discrimination under Title VII.*

A recruiter for the University of Chicago Hospitals was an Evangelical Christian Baptist who recruited people at churches and church job fairs. She got a new boss who directed her to remove all religious items from her desk. She also was told that she could no longer recruit at churches and church job fairs. Although she had previously received good reviews, under the new boss, she was warned that she would be fired if her performance did not improve. Shortly before her vacation, another recruiter was hired to perform essentially the same duties. During a phone call while she was on vacation, she was asked about some missing applicant test scores, and was told that was the "last straw" and to "be prepared" when her leave was over. When she returned from vacation, she found her desk packed up and her office being used for storage. She resigned and filed a complaint with the Equal Employment Opportunity Commission (EEOC), which sued on her behalf for constructive discharge on the basis of religion. An Illinois federal court ruled for the hospitals, holding that she was not subjected to conditions that would make a reasonable person quit. The Seventh Circuit reversed, holding that **Title VII protects employees who have been told that termination is coming and who decide to quit rather than wait to be fired.** *EEOC v. Univ. of Chicago Hospitals*, 276 F.3d 326 (7th Cir. 2002).

◆ *A Massachusetts professor failed to show religious discrimination and also failed to timely file his claim.*

A tenured professor at a Massachusetts university was interrupted at home while observing the Jewish holy day of Yom Kippur. He complained to a dean and from then on was not disturbed while observing religious days at home. However, he claimed that the incident caused a hostile work environment to develop and resulted in retaliation against him. He filed a religious discrimination complaint against the university. The Superior Court of Massachusetts dismissed his claim because he had waited more than six months to file his claim. **There was no evidence that the professor experienced continuing harassment** that would allow him to pursue his case under the continuing violation doctrine. Moreover, he suffered no disciplinary action and was still employed by the university. *Berger v. Brandeis Univ.*, No. 01-04220, 2002 WL 31433433 (Mass. Super. 2002).

◆ *An Orthodox Jewish professor's claims of religious discrimination, hostile work environment and retaliation were allowed to go to trial.*

At the start of an Orthodox Jewish professor's first year as an associate professor in the School of Education at William Paterson College of New Jersey, her department chair allowed her to arrange her schedule around religious holidays and did not count as sick days the days she missed for religious holidays. During her third year of employment, she was charged sick days for religious holidays. She also was charged a sick day for a Jewish holiday that fell on a day she was not scheduled to teach. The professor was continually asked why she could not attend meetings on Friday nights and Saturdays, even though she had explained her wish to observe the Sabbath. After her termination, she sued under Title VII and the New Jersey Law Against Discrimination for religious discrimination, hostile work environment and retaliation. The district court granted pretrial judgment to the university, finding no intentional discrimination on the basis of religion.

The Third Circuit Court of Appeals reversed, noting that the district court applied the wrong standard when evaluating the professor's hostile environment claim. Rather than require a showing of discriminatory animus, the court should have asked **whether a reasonable fact finder could view the evidence as showing that the professor's treatment was attributable to her religion.** Although the college provided legitimate nondiscriminatory reasons for its decision not to retain the professor, she was able to cast doubt on the legitimacy of those reasons such that the lawsuit could proceed. *Abramson v. William Paterson College of New Jersey*, 260 F.3d 265 (3d Cir. 2001).

IV. AGE DISCRIMINATION

The Age Discrimination in Employment Act (ADEA), 29 U.S.C. § 621, et seq., prohibits age discrimination against individuals at least 40 years of age. As part of the Fair Labor Standards Act, it applies to institutions with 20 or more employees and which affect interstate commerce.

A. ADEA

◆   *The U.S. Supreme Court held employees may bring "disparate impact" actions under the ADEA. Disparate impact actions do not require proof of intentional age discrimination. Instead, they require an employee to show an employment policy has the effect of discriminating on the basis of age.*

The city of Jackson, Mississippi increased the salaries of all employees in 1999. Those with under five years of experience received comparatively higher raises than more experienced employees. The city justified the action as a way to remain competitive and "ensure equitable compensation to all employees." A group of veteran police officers, most over 40 years old, claimed the city's action constituted discrimination on the basis of age. The officers sued the city in a federal district court for ADEA violations, alleging both disparate treatment and disparate impact. The court held for the city, and the U.S. Court of Appeals, Fifth Circuit, affirmed the judgment.

The Supreme Court agreed to review the disparate impact claim. It compared the ADEA with Title VII of the Civil Rights Act of 1964. **Except for substitution of the word "age" for "race, color, religion, sex, or national origin," the language of the ADEA and Title VII was identical.** Title VII disparate impact claims have long been recognized by the Court. **The Court stated the ADEA authorizes potential recovery for disparate impact cases, in a manner comparable to Title VII disparate impact claims for race, religion or sex discrimination. Employees alleging an employer practice has a disparate impact on a class of employees need not show the practice is intentional.** While the Court held the officers were entitled to bring a disparate impact claim under the ADEA, they could not show the city violated the ADEA in this case. The Court noted the ADEA's coverage for disparate impact is narrower than that of Title VII. Under the ADEA, an employer can treat workers differently if the employer is motivated by reasonable factors other than age. The Court found Congress had narrowed the ADEA's scope because there is often a connection between age and ability to perform a job. The city's decision to make itself competitive in the job market was based on a reasonable factor other than age. As the employees could not prove the increase had a disparate impact on them, the Court affirmed the judgment for the city. *Smith v. City of Jackson*, 544 U.S. 228 (2005).

◆   *The U.S. Court of Appeals, Eighth Circuit, held that replacement by a substantially younger person is necessary to prove age discrimination.*

A Minnesota university promoted an employee to serve as a dean at the age of 62. He had a heart attack three years later, and learned of rumors indicating he wanted to retire and that a plan had been developed to replace him. The dean denied the rumors in a formal letter to the university president. He stated he was profoundly disturbed by the rumors and accused the president of trying to force his resignation. The next year, the university reorganized, and a newly hired provost/vice president soon recommended replacing the dean. The reasons stated were the dean's creation of a divisive environment, ineffective handling of conflicts, and favoritism and bias in personnel evaluations. The dean's permanent replacement was 64 years old at the time of his appointment. The dean sued the university in a federal district court for ADEA violations. The court held for the university, and the dean appealed.

The Eighth Circuit explained that the ADEA bars employers from taking age-based adverse employment actions against employees who are 40 or older. **The U.S. Supreme Court held in a 1996 case that the replacement of a 68-year-old by a 65-year-old was "very thin evidence" of discrimination.** The Eighth Circuit held the dean did not prove age discrimination based on his replacement by an employee who was only two-and-a-half years younger than he was. **The university had legitimate non-discriminatory reasons for demoting him, and the court did not "sit as a super-personnel department and second guess" its decisions.** The dean's other discrimination and retaliation claims failed for the same reasons. The court affirmed the judgment for the university. *Lewis v. St. Cloud State Univ.*, 467 F.3d 1133 (8th Cir. 2006).

◆ *A federal district court held a 56-year-old professor was fired because he was not qualified and did not follow university procedures.*

The professor had taught night classes as an adjunct professor in the university's college of business (COB) since 1985. His academic background was in the field of education. In 2002, the university hired a new dean for its COB and prepared for an accreditation visit. The university took steps to ensure that adjunct faculty were teaching courses in which they had academic and professional credentials. As a result, the university stopped using the professor to teach courses at its COB. He was given the chance to teach marketing courses at the university, but he failed to comply with a policy that required students to purchase their books from the student bookstore.

The university then discharged the professor, and he filed a federal court action for violation of the ADEA. **The court held age was not a factor in the university's decision. Instead, the discharge was based on the professor's lack of qualifications to teach the classes he formerly taught.** He also failed to order course books through the university's book store, as required by university policy. There was no violation of the ADEA. *Anhalt v. Cardinal Stritch Univ.*, No. 04-C-1052, 2006 WL 3692631 (E.D. Wis. 12/12/06).

◆ *The Supreme Court held state employees could not sue their employers under the ADEA.*

Two associate professors at the University of Montevallo sued the university in an Alabama federal court under the ADEA. They alleged that the university had discriminated against them on the basis of their age, that it had retaliated against them for filing charges with the Equal Employment Opportunity Commission, and that its College of Business, where they were employed, used an evaluation system that had a disparate impact on older faculty members. The university sought to dismiss the action on the grounds of Eleventh Amendment immunity, and the district court agreed, finding that the ADEA did not eliminate the state's immunity.

A group of current and former faculty and librarians of Florida State University and Florida International University filed suit against the Florida Board of Regents under the ADEA, alleging that the board refused to require the two state universities to allocate funds to provide previously agreed-upon market adjustments to the salaries of eligible university employees. They maintained that this failure had a disparate impact on the base pay of older employees with a longer record of service. The court refused to dismiss the action. On appeal, the Eleventh Circuit consolidated the cases and held the ADEA did not abrogate (do away with) state Eleventh Amendment immunity. The U.S. Supreme Court noted that **although the ADEA contains a clear statement of Congress' intent to eliminate the states' immunity under the Eleventh Amendment, such action exceeded Congress' authority under Section 5 of the Fourteenth Amendment** (which grants Congress the power to enact laws under the Equal Protection Clause). Although state employees cannot sue their employers for discrimination under the ADEA, they are not without remedies. Every state has age discrimination statutes, and almost all of them allow the recovery of money damages from state employers. *Kimel v. Florida Board of Regents*, 528 U.S. 62, 120 S.Ct. 631, 145 L.Ed.2d 522 (2000).

◆ *The U.S. Court of Appeals for the Second Circuit held a New York university did not assign fewer courses to a professor because of his age.*

The university assigned the tenured professor a courseload of four courses for an academic year. He believed his tenure entitled him to teach at least five courses, and he sued the university in a federal district court under the ADEA. The court ruled for the university, and the professor appealed. The Second Circuit held the professor did not establish adverse employment action. **The assignment of four courses was not a "materially adverse change" in the terms and conditions of his employment. Material changes include termination, a demotion evidenced by a decrease in wages, or a less distinguished title.** The average courseload for a tenured professor was fewer than four, and the professor claimed no wage loss. The court held that even if the professor had managed to show an adverse employment action, he submitted no evidence to support an inference that the assignment of classes was based on his age. The judgment for the university was affirmed. *Boise v. Boufford*, 121 Fed.Appx. 890 (2d Cir. 2005).

1. Applicability to Religious Schools

◆ *The ADEA did not to apply in the following case involving a seminary.*

A Missouri seminary allegedly dismissed an employee because of his age. He sued the seminary in a federal district court under the ADEA. The seminary brought a motion for pretrial judgment, stating that the ADEA was inapplicable because the institution was pervasively religious. The court agreed. It considered the U.S. Supreme Court's decision in *NLRB v. Catholic Bishop of Chicago*, 440 U.S. 490, 99 S.Ct. 1313, 59 L.Ed.2d 533 (1979), in which the

Court held the National Labor Relations Act (NLRA) inapplicable to church-operated schools. The court ruled that although the ADEA was a remedial statute rather than a regulatory statute such as the NLRA, the ruling in *Catholic Bishop* applied here. Because application of the ADEA could implicate enforcement by the EEOC, government regulatory powers were involved. Thus, **since the potential existed for impinging the seminary's religious freedoms, the court ruled that the ADEA was inapplicable.** It granted the seminary's motion for pretrial judgment. *Cochran v. St. Louis Preparatory Seminary*, 717 F.Supp. 1413 (E.D. Mo. 1989).

◆ *An Ohio federal court held that the ADEA could be applied to a religious institution.*

An employee at Xavier University, an institution operated by the Order of Jesuits, sued the university under the ADEA in an Ohio federal court. The university asserted that the court had no authority to rule on the case because the university, as a religious institution, was exempt from the ADEA's provisions. The court observed that because the ADEA gave no indication that religious institutions were exempt from its provisions, the issue became whether application of the ADEA to the university would violate the Free Exercise and Establishment Clauses of the First Amendment.

The court held for the employee, noting that the Fourth Circuit held in *Ritter v. Mount St. Mary's College*, 814 F.2d 986 (4th Cir. 1987), that **application of the ADEA to a religious institution did not present a significant risk of infringement on the institution's First Amendment rights.** Here, the facts gave no indication that enforcement of the ADEA would violate the religion clauses of the First Amendment. Accordingly, the university was not entitled to have the case dismissed. *Soriano v. Xavier Univ.*, 687 F.Supp. 1188 (S.D. Ohio 1988).

2. Releases and Settlements

◆ *A fired security officer could not use the Older Workers Benefit Protection Act (OWBPA) to avoid signing a settlement agreement.*

When the director of protective services at a New York university was fired at the age of 67 (after 16 years on the job), he sued under the ADEA for age discrimination. The university maintained that the real reasons for the firing were his poor communication skills and his inability to work with other employees and supervisors. During a settlement conference, no agreement was reached. But a second conference was held several months later, at which the employee agreed to accept $199,000 in exchange for a release of his claims prior to the settlement date. However, he later refused to sign the agreement on the grounds that he did not have enough time to consider it under the OWBPA. The court ordered him to sign the agreement because **the waiver was knowing and voluntary under the OWBPA.** He had had several months to consider the agreement between conferences, and had been represented by an attorney throughout the settlement process. *Manning v. New York Univ.*, No. 98 CIV. 3300 (NRB), 2001 WL 963982 (S.D.N.Y. 2001).

◆ *A private university could require a former employee to withdraw her Equal Employment Opportunity Commission (EEOC) claim in order to obtain a settlement award.*

A Tennessee woman who worked for a private university received a letter of reprimand and filed two grievances against her supervisors as a result. Subsequently, the head of the department and another supervisor asked her to sign a voluntary resignation letter and when she refused, she was discharged. Eight days later, she filed an age discrimination charge with the EEOC. The university conducted a grievance hearing before the associate dean of students who found no evidence of age discrimination or harassment. However, she recommended that the employee be placed on paid administrative leave for six months with a reasonable letter of recommendation to help her find another position within the university system. The university informed the employee that it would accept the recommendation of the hearing officer subject to the employee's agreement to withdraw her EEOC charge. When the employee refused to do so, the university declined to implement the recommended resolution. The employee then sued the university for retaliation in violation of the ADEA. The court held the university did not take adverse employment action against the employee. **Requiring an employee to withdraw an EEOC claim in order to have a recommended settlement award implemented is not an adverse employment action.** The court ruled for the university. *Hansen v. Vanderbilt Univ.*, 961 F.Supp. 1149 (M.D. Tenn. 1997).

3. Defenses

◆ *The U.S. Court of Appeals, Eleventh Circuit, held a Florida university did not reject an applicant because of his age.*

A 70-year-old white male applied for three positions at a university in Florida. The university rejected the applications. The applicant sued the university in a federal district court, alleging it refused to hire him because of his age, in violation of the ADEA. The court dismissed the case and the applicant appealed. The Eleventh Circuit found the university had legitimate, nondiscriminatory reasons for not hiring him. The university wanted to reduce turnover by filling the positions with faculty who had ties to the area. The applicant had no ties to central Florida, and one interviewer thought he was boring and unenthusiastic. **No evidence was presented to show the university lied about its reasons for not hiring him.** As the applicant failed to prove the reasons given by the university for not hiring him were untrue, the court affirmed the judgment. *Hillemann v. Univ. of Cent. Florida*, 167 Fed.Appx. 747 (11th Cir. 2006).

◆ *New York University did not discriminate against a 70-year-old teacher by firing him for making inappropriate comments.*

NYU refused to reappoint the teacher after learning he made inappropriate comments during a class and was rude to the staff. The university presented evidence that he had commented during class that his phone number was "just for girls." This violated NYU's internal sexual harassment policy. The teacher claimed the reasons alleged for the employment decision were false. He insisted the remarks were merely jokes and did not offend the other female students. NYU replaced him with a teacher who was substantially younger. The teacher sued the university in a federal district court for age discrimination.

The court said whether female students found the comments offensive was irrelevant, since the teacher's remarks violated the harassment policy. The teacher said the allegation he had been rude to members of the staff was a cover-up for unlawful age discrimination. He said he had always been polite and cooperative with staff. The court found the evidence supported the university's contention that the teacher was rude. It accepted NYU's legitimate, nondiscriminatory reasons for not reappointing him. As the teacher failed to prove the university's reasons were a cover-up for age discrimination, the court granted NYU's motion for summary judgment. *Chapkines v. New York Univ.*, No. 02CIV6355(RJH)(KNF), 2005 WL 167603 (S.D.N.Y. 1/25/05).

◆ *A Maryland employee did not prove a violation of the ADEA when she was laid off by a state university after 33 years of employment.*

The university laid off the employee, allegedly due to budget constraints. She later learned the university had not laid off younger employees and that the school had replaced her with a younger employee. The employee sued the university in a federal district court, alleging it discriminated against her because of her age. The employee alleged 10 of the 11 employees the university laid off for budget reasons were over 40. The university argued it was an arm of the state and was therefore protected from liability by the Eleventh Amendment. The court agreed, finding **Maryland courts have consistently held the state's public universities are arms of the state that are entitled to immunity**. The university's choice of autonomy from the University of Maryland did not deprive it of immunity. The court granted the university's request to dismiss the case. *Laney v. Morgan State Univ.*, No. Civ. CCB-04-1719, 2005 WL 1563437 (D. Md. 6/30/05).

◆ *The Supreme Court held that two employees could not pursue their age discrimination claims in state court because they waited too long to sue.*

Two University of Minnesota employees claimed that the university tried to force them to accept early retirement at the age of 52 and, when they refused to retire, reclassified their jobs to lower their salaries. They sued the university in federal court under the ADEA and also alleged age discrimination under the Minnesota Human Rights Act as a supplemental claim. A federal district court dismissed their lawsuit based on Eleventh Amendment immunity. The employees then sued the university in state court, alleging the statute of limitations was tolled during the time they were pursuing their federal court action. The case was removed to the federal court system, and it eventually reached the U.S. Supreme Court. The Court held that the federal law at issue here (which tolls the statute of limitations on certain state law actions while a plaintiff pursues a related claim in federal court) did not apply to claims that are dismissed under the Eleventh Amendment. **As the state had immunity in the federal action, there was no tolling of the state action.** *Raygor v. Regents of Univ. of Minnesota*, 534 U.S. 533, 122 S.Ct. 999, 152 L.Ed.2d 27 (2002).

4. Evidence of Discrimination

◆ *A Tennessee university did not violate the ADEA by changing a 69-year-old professor's position and decreasing his lab space.*

The professor had worked for the university for nearly 30 years when a newly hired pathology department chairman asked whether he would consider early retirement. The professor told him he had no intention of retiring any time soon, and claimed the chairman then began a series of retaliatory actions, including orders to vacate his lab and office space. The chairman offered him several employment options, but they all meant a lower salary and several included early retirement. The professor sued the university in a federal district court for age discrimination. The court dismissed the case, and he appealed to the Sixth Circuit. **The court found no adverse employment action under the ADEA. The reduction in lab space did not affect salary or job status. Any proposal to reduce the professor's salary was never carried out, and threats alone are not an adverse action.** The professor presented no evidence the job changes significantly decreased his responsibilities. As he could not prevail on his claim of age discrimination without evidence of an adverse employment action, the court affirmed the judgment for the university. *Mitchell v. Vanderbilt Univ.*, 389 F.3d 177 (6th Cir. 2004).

◆ *A District of Columbia university did not discriminate against a 47-year old African-American employee.*

The employee worked as director of reunions and events in the alumni relations office. She claimed that her relationship with a university vice president deteriorated after she expressed her opinion that the office was discriminatory. The university declined the employee's applications for several promotions. She sued the university in a federal district court for Title VII and ADEA violations. The court dismissed the case, and the employee appealed.

The U.S. Court of Appeals, District of Columbia Circuit, reviewed evidence that a university committee had interviewed six candidates for a promotion sought by the employee. Two were white men under the age of 50 and two were white women. The university selected a man for the position. The committee said it voted against the employee for the job because she lacked qualifications and interviewed poorly. **The court held she failed to present evidence to refute the university's legitimate nondiscriminatory reason for not promoting her.** As the employee presented no evidence to show any cover-up for retaliation, the court affirmed the judgment. *Carter v. George Washington Univ.*, 387 F.3d 872 (D.C. Cir. 2004).

◆ *A 61-year-old Illinois university administrator's ADEA claim failed because she did not show she was treated less favorably than younger persons.*

The administrator was promoted into a new position at the age of 61. Shortly after starting, she learned she had to work a significant amount of overtime to timely complete required financial reports. The administrator was unwillingly to put in these hours. A supervisor claimed she made mistakes because of her poor computer skills. Although he rated her performance "acceptable," he identified areas in which she could improve and noted she would have to work additional hours to meet her goals. After another similar evaluation, the administrator stormed out of a meeting with the supervisor, and he placed her on a 60-day performance improvement plan.

The administrator showed no signs of improvement after 60 days, and the university discharged her. She sued the university in a federal district court for age discrimination under the ADEA. The university argued she could not prove younger employees were treated more favorably than she was treated. The **court held that while discrimination may be implied by the hiring of a younger person for a position, the administrator made no such showing**. The university was entitled to summary judgment as the evidence did not support the complaint. *Vera v. Univ. of Chicago*, No. 02 C 9124, 2004 WL 1123817 (N.D. Ill. 2004).

B. Retirement

◆ *A federal district court held Cornell University did not discriminate against a professor because of her age.*

The professor received three consecutive five-year appointments. When she was 50 years old, the university told her she would not be offered a fourth five-year reappointment when her contract expired. Instead, it offered her a one-year assignment that would require travel between Ithaca and New York City. The university said the change was being made due to budget problems. Midway through the contract, the professor accepted the university's offer of early retirement. She continued to perform work for the university for several months. She then sent the university a $25,000 bill for her services. The university refused to pay the amount claimed by the professor, and she sued the university in a federal district court for ADEA violations. She claimed the university replaced her with a younger employee and that it fired six other females over 40 for budgetary reasons.

The court said the professor failed to show the university subjected her to an adverse employment action. **Action must be "more disruptive than a mere inconvenience or an alteration of job responsibilities" to be "adverse."** While termination is clearly an adverse employment action, the professor did not suffer adverse employment action because the university did not discharge her. Rather, it chose not to renew her appointment. The university extended the professor's employment for an additional year after the term of her reappointment expired, and kept her salary and benefits the same. She terminated her employment when she volunteered to resign and accept early retirement. The court granted the university's dismissal motion and the employee appealed to the U.S. Court of Appeals, Second Circuit. The court held the district court held her to too high a standard of proof in assessing the university's dismissal motion. **The complaint in an employment discrimination case is to be read liberally. In this case, the employee alleged an unofficial policy to guarantee her lifetime employment that was now being precluded on the basis of her gender and age**. She also asserted a valid Equal Pay Act claim, based on the assertion that male employees were paid more than she was for similar work. These allegations were sufficient to survive a pre-trial dismissal motion. While the employee had taken an early retirement package, she did so to preserve benefits she would have enjoyed if her job was secure. Two state law claims had been properly dismissed, but the discrimination claims were returned to the district court for further proceedings. *Leibowitz v. Cornell Univ.*, 445 F.3d 586 (2d Cir. 2006).

C. State Statutes

◆   *The Court of Appeals of Missouri upheld an award of more than $1.2 million to a baseball coach for age discrimination.*

The coach was over the age of 40 at the time of his hiring. His team had a winning record every year, and 80% of his players graduated. After he pursued an administrative charge of age bias in 1998, the university reduced his job to a half-time position, cut his pay in half and eliminated his benefits. It also moved his office to a basement near a swimming pool. During the same time his position was cut to part time, the university classified a younger compliance officer who worked 5.5 hours per day as a full-time employee. An assistant basketball coach who was under 40 and had far less experience than the baseball coach received a higher salary. The baseball coach sued the university in the state court system for violating the Missouri Human Rights Act. A jury awarded him $225,000 in actual damages and $1,050,000 in punitive damages.

On appeal, the court upheld the punitive damage award, finding that state law specifically authorized it. The court found the evidence was sufficient to support the punitive damages award. **Evidence showed younger employees were treated better with respect to pay, hours and benefits.** The baseball field did not comply with National Collegiate Athletic Association requirements, and coaches who were hired after the baseball coach were given nicer offices in an athletic complex. The amount of scholarship money allotted for baseball was low compared with the amount allotted for other sports. **The university discontinued the coach's medical insurance with knowledge that he was a cancer survivor.** The court rejected the university's argument that the amount awarded exceeded reasonable compensation for any injury he suffered. The verdict against the university was upheld. *Brady v. Curators of the Univ. of Missouri*, 213 S.W.3d 101 (Mo. Ct. App. 2006).

◆   *A Pennsylvania law school did not violate a state anti-discrimination act when it discharged an employee who was over 40 years old.*

The law school asked the employee to resign shortly before it merged with a Pennsylvania university. The law school and employee entered into a separation agreement and general release placing him on administrative leave at full salary with full benefits. In return for signing the agreement and giving up his right to unemployment benefits, the employee agreed not to make any claims under the Pennsylvania Human Relations Act (PHRA). However, he filed age discrimination charges against the university with state and federal civil rights agencies. Later, the employee sued the university and law school in a state court, alleging they violated the PHRA. He argued the agreement was invalid because it did not meet the requirements of the Older Workers Benefit Protection Act. The court held for the university and law school. The employee appealed to the Superior Court of Pennsylvania. **The court held the**

agreement was binding unless the employee proved fraud, duress or other circumstances to invalidate it. Contracts are interpreted according to their plain language, and the court found this contract was clear. It affirmed the judgment for the university and law school. *Griest v. Pennsylvania State Univ. & Dickinson School of Law*, 897 A.2d 1186 (Pa. Super. 2006).

◆ *A graduate student could not sue for discrimination under Kentucky's employment laws because she was not an employee of the university.*

A 44-year-old graduate student studying psychology received a Regent's Fellowship that provided her with full tuition and a yearly stipend. She lost her fellowship after her third year of study due to her failure to have her thesis proposal approved by a department committee. She remained in the graduate program for another year, but was subsequently dismissed. The student filed an unsuccessful grievance, then sued for sex and age discrimination in violation of Kentucky law and the university handbook.

A state court granted the university's motion for pretrial judgment, finding the student had no cause of action under the state discrimination statutes because she was not an employee of the university. The Kentucky Court of Appeals affirmed. **It rejected the student's assertion that her duties as a psychologist during her studies resembled employee duties, not academic work.** Although the student may have developed a therapist-patient relationship with one clinic patient, it was clear that nearly all of her duties and activities were in connection with her academic work rather than providing a service to the university, and therefore, an employer-employee relationship did not exist. *Stewart v. Univ. of Louisville*, 65 S.W.3d 536 (Ky. Ct. App. 2001).

◆ *State human rights laws mirror Title VII. They generally prohibit religious discrimination except by religious organizations.*

A Jewish vice president at a New York Catholic university was discharged, allegedly because of poor job performance. He filed suit in a New York trial court, alleging that he was subjected to increased scrutiny and then discharged because of his Jewish faith in violation of the Human Rights Law. The trial court granted pretrial judgment to the university, and the vice president appealed to the New York Supreme Court, Appellate Division. The appellate division affirmed, ruling that the university was exempt from the prohibition against religiously motivated discharges. The vice president appealed to the Court of Appeals of New York.

The court of appeals noted that the New York Human Rights Law permits religious organizations to "giv[e] preference to persons of the same religion" or "to promote the religious principles for which it is established or maintained." **However, the court held that the university could not "discriminate against the vice president for reasons having nothing to do with the free exercise of religion and then invoke the religious exemption as a shield against its unlawful conduct."** Here, disputed issues of fact as to whether the university engaged in unlawful discrimination precluded pretrial judgment in its favor. The holding of the appellate division was reversed. *Scheiber v. St. John's Univ.*, 84 N.Y.2d 120, 615 N.Y.S.2d 332 (N.Y. 1994).

V. DISABILITY DISCRIMINATION

Section 504 of the Rehabilitation Act of 1973, 29 U.S.C. § 794, prohibits discrimination against qualified individuals with disabilities in programs or activities receiving federal financial assistance. The Americans with Disabilities Act of 1990 (ADA), 42 U.S.C. § 12101, et seq., extends protection to both private and public employees. It also prohibits discrimination against employees who are associated with disabled individuals (for example, an employee with a disabled son or daughter).

A. Liability

◆ *The U.S. Court of Appeals, Fifth Circuit, held an employee with macular degeneration might be considered disabled under the ADA.*

Several doctors diagnosed the employee with Stargardt's disease, which is a form of macular degeneration. The impairment cannot be corrected with eyeglasses, contact lenses, or surgery. The employee's vision deteriorated enough that she had trouble reading information that was handwritten or typed in small fonts. She told her supervisors at the library about her condition and requested an accommodation. The library allowed her more time to complete her job tasks. The employee was offered a position as a research assistant with a university foundation to research prospective donors and maintain its donor files. When she started work for the foundation, she realized she was having a problem reading many of the materials. She told her supervisors and scheduled meetings with a vocational rehabilitation counselor and the university's ADA coordinator. However, the coordinator told the employee the university was discharging her. The employee sued the university in a federal district court.

The employee testified she did not believe it was safe for her to drive and that she had significant difficulty reading. A specialist in retinal degeneration testified the employee's visual impairment would continue to deteriorate. According to the specialist, while individuals with macular degeneration can often compensate with their other eye, the employee could not. The court held for the university, and the employee appealed to the U.S. Court of Appeals, Fifth Circuit. The court noted **the U.S. Supreme Court has held individuals who claim protection under the ADA must offer evidence that their limitation is substantial in terms of their own experience**. The Court has also held "mitigating measures must be taken into account in judging whether an individual has a disability." The Fifth Circuit found the testimony of the specialist and employee raised an issue regarding whether the employee was substantially limited in her ability to see. Because her impairment might qualify as a disability under the ADA, the court reversed the judgment and remanded the case to the district court for further proceedings. *Cutrera v. Board of Supervisors of Louisiana State Univ.*, 429 F.3d 108 (5th Cir. 2005).

◆ *The University of Pennsylvania did not violate the ADA when it denied a former employee's application for reemployment.*

The employee applied for any open administrative or clerical position. He submitted his résumé and described his prior work experience, but he did not mention he had been diagnosed with bipolar disorder. When the employee did not receive an interview, he sued the university in a federal district court for disability discrimination. The court ordered him to be examined by a psychiatrist. The employee then withdrew his claim that was based on an "actual disability" and preserved his ADA claim based on a "perceived disability." The court then ordered the applicant to undergo a psychiatric evaluation. After the applicant refused to undergo the evaluation, the court dismissed the case.

The employee appealed to the U.S. Court of Appeals, Third Circuit, asserting there was no need for a psychiatric evaluation. He said since the claim he was pursing focused on his "being regarded as disabled" – not on his actual abilities – the court had to focus on the reactions and perceptions of persons interacting with him. The court rejected this argument. It explained that **because the employee allegedly had a major psychiatric illness, the district court needed to evaluate whether he was "regarded as disabled."** Because he had been previously diagnosed as having bipolar disorder, his mental state was in controversy, and the judgment was affirmed. *Parker v. Univ. of Pennsylvania*, 128 Fed.Appx. 944 (3d Civ. 2005).

◆ *A Michigan university did not reject a job applicant based on her visual impairments.*

The university interviewed the applicant along with 18 others for an admissions counseling job. It contacted references the applicant had provided as part of its hiring process. One of the references was a doctor the applicant had worked for. The university hired one of the other applicants for the job. The applicant sued the university in a state court for disability discrimination. The university contended the applicant's blindness did not affect its decision. It said the person chosen was hired because he was the most qualified. The court awarded summary judgment to the university, and the applicant appealed.

In an attempt to prove her claim for disability discrimination, the applicant focused on the testimony of the doctor. The doctor had testified that the university's head of admissions seemed uncomfortable because the applicant was blind. The doctor said he spoke to the head of admissions about the applicant's use of adaptive technologies. He suspected some bias when the head of admissions did not ask details about how the applicant would carry out certain tasks. **The Court of Appeals of Michigan held the applicant did not submit sufficient evidence to refute the university's legitimate nondiscriminatory reasons for not hiring her, or show the reason was a cover-up for discrimination.** The judgment was affirmed. *Jackson v. Michigan State Univ.*, No. 261716, 2005 WL 1652195 (Mich. Ct. App. 7/14/05).

◆ *A District of Columbia university did not violate the ADA when it refused to assign an employee a permanent handicap parking space.*

After working for the university for 10 years, an employee was informed the department had decided to move her assigned parking space. The parking lot she had parked in was two blocks from her office building, and the new parking lot was eight blocks away. When the employee asked for a space in a closer parking space, the university told her no space was available. She learned other employees were assigned spaces in a closer lot. Despite the employee's repeated requests for a space in a closer lot, the university didn't grant her request until almost two years later. Based on her claims of health problems, the university assigned the employee a temporary handicap parking space in the lot adjacent to her office.

The employee sued the university in a federal district court, alleging it violated the ADA. To support her claim, she submitted a letter from a doctor. He stated the employee suffered from an illness that caused her to have a hard time breathing when she walked up the hill to her office. The doctor advised the employee to avoid activities that caused her shortness of breath to reduce the risk of a heart attack. **The court noted the university issued the employee a temporary space close to her office and made a reasonable request that she obtain a handicap parking permit. She failed to present evidence sufficient to establish the university discriminated against her because of a disability. The court dismissed the case.** *Drumgold v. Howard Univ.*, No. 1:99 CV 02255 (PLF), 2005 WL 975761 (D.D.C. 4/25/05).

◆   *A Harvard University staff assistant with bipolar disorder was permissibly discharged due to his egregious misconduct.*

The employee was diagnosed with bipolar disorder, and sometimes had periods of mania on the job. His disorder started to adversely affect his work after 15 years at Harvard. He established a Web site where he criticized the pay scale. The employee updated his web site at work on his personal laptop. Shortly after the employee created the Web site, he became severely manic. He was loud and animated as he told co-workers about Harvard's wage policies and invited them to view the Web site. In the university's main Museum lobby, he sang, clapped and danced to protest songs that were posted on his Web site. He was later hospitalized for an episode of paranoia. Soon after that, staff members and police officers approached the employee and asked him to leave. When he refused, the officers arrested him, and the university discharged him.

The employee sued Harvard in a state court for violating the ADA. He alleged he was fired because of his disability. Harvard contended the employee could not establish he was a "qualified handicapped person" under the ADA. Harvard relied on *Garrity v. United Airlines*, 421 Mass. 55 (1995). In *Garrity*, the Massachusetts Supreme Judicial Court said **if an employee engages in "egregious misconduct" that is adverse to the interests of the employer and violates employer rules, the employee may not claim ADA protection.** The court found the employee's misconduct was egregious and that Harvard fired him promptly after the misconduct. It granted Harvard's motion for summary judgment. *Mammone v. President and Fellows of Harvard College*, Civil Action No. 03-1402, 2004 WL 1982350 (Mass. Super. 2004).

◆   *A Massachusetts university librarian with rheumatoid arthritis was entitled to further opportunities to prove her claim of disability discrimination.*

The librarian's arthritis caused pain and exhaustion, and made it difficult for her to carry, lift and shelve materials. She asked the university to create an accommodation for her by assigning others her role of carrying materials, climbing stairs, and shelving articles and books. The university declined, even after a doctor sent a letter confirming the librarian had rheumatoid arthritis and should not lift over 10 pounds. The university insisted the librarian shelve books on a daily basis and never offered her an accommodation. Instead, it recommended she take a short-term disability leave.

The librarian sued the university in a state court for discrimination under the Massachusetts Civil Rights Act (CRA) and Massachusetts Equal Rights Act (MERA). The court dismissed the case and she appealed. **The Court of Appeals of Massachusetts considered whether shelving, paging and retrieval tasks were essential functions for the job, and whether the librarian could have performed these functions with a reasonable accommodation.** As the evidence about the job's essential functions was conflicting, and the trial court did not address the issue of reasonable accommodation, the order for summary judgment was inappropriate. The court vacated the judgment on the CRA claim, but affirmed the dismissal of the MERA claim, as this law created no independent right to sue. *Cargill v. Harvard Univ.*, 804 N.E.2d 377 (Mass. App. Ct. 2004).

◆   *After-acquired evidence of misconduct could not justify a discharge based on disability.*

A wheelchair-bound teacher at a North Carolina community college taught classes at a county jail preparing inmates to take their high school equivalency exams. After she broke her back and then her leg, she was told she would not be offered another contract at the jail because of the college's concerns about her safety and the school's liability if she were to suffer another accident at the jail. Less than 10 days later, the college received anonymous phone calls alleging misconduct by the teacher (including drug use, sex with inmates, providing prisoners with drugs and bullets, and carrying a loaded weapon).

The college notified the teacher that she was fired 10 days after she was notified her contract would not be renewed. She sued the college for disability discrimination under state and federal law, and the case eventually reached the North Carolina Court of Appeals. It noted that because the trial court had found that the teacher's disability was the reason for the termination, **it should not have used the after-acquired evidence of misconduct to dismiss the teacher's lawsuit.** However, the after-acquired evidence could be used to limit the relief available (like limiting back pay and barring reinstatement). *Johnson v. Board of Trustees of Durham Technical Community College*, 577 S.E.2d 670 (N.C. Ct. App. 2003).

◆   *A New York university employee raised material issues of fact concerning the university's ability to accommodate her disability.*

The employee had Systemic Lupus Erythematosus. Due to pain and fatigue, she was allowed to work only seven hours per day. During the next eight years, the employee took several leaves of absence for her disability and child care needs. The university warned her about excessive absences and tardiness, but promoted her to a departmental administrative position. The employee received a positive employment evaluation in her first year in the position, but her absences then increased dramatically. A university official said her absences were disruptive and ordered her to return to work by a specific date. The employee instead presented the university with a physician's note and requested an indefinite leave of absence. Her initial application for long-term disability benefits was denied, and the university discharged her.

Although the employee was later awarded long-term disability benefits and was reinstated on long-term disability leave, she sued the university in a federal district court for ADA violations. **The court focused on her ability to perform the essential functions of her position.** While the university contended the employee had to work for eight hours each day, she presented evidence she rarely needed to work overtime and that she had performed her essential job functions during a seven-hour shift for several years. The court accepted the employee's explanation that she was forced to apply for long-term disability benefits because the university did not offer her reasonable accommodations. Based on her employment history and inconsistencies in the parties' versions of events, the court denied the university's summary judgment motion. *James v. Trustees of Columbia Univ.*, No. 01 Civ. 8873(LBS), 2003 WL 23018797 (S.D.N.Y. 2003).

◆   *The U.S. Supreme Court concluded that Congress exceeded its authority by allowing monetary damage awards against states in ADA cases.*

Two Alabama state employees alleged that they were discriminated against by their employers in violation of the ADA. One was a state university nursing director who was demoted upon her return from a medical leave to undergo treatment for breast cancer. The other was a youth services department security officer with chronic asthma and sleep apnea who alleged that the department refused to provide him with reasonable accommodations to mitigate the effects of his disabilities. They sued the state in federal court for monetary damages under the ADA. The court consolidated the cases and granted judgment to the state. The U.S. Court of Appeals, Eleventh Circuit, reversed the judgment.

The U.S. Supreme Court reversed, holding that the ADA did not validly abrogate Eleventh Amendment immunity in lawsuits seeking monetary relief. The Eleventh Amendment ensures that no state may be sued in a federal court without first consenting to be sued. However, Congress may abrogate this immunity where it does so unequivocally and under a valid grant of constitutional authority. The Supreme Court noted that legislation enacted under Section 5 of the Fourteenth Amendment must demonstrate "congruence and proportionality between the injury to be prevented or remedied and the means adopted to that end." Here, there was no such congruence and proportionality. Congress identified negative attitudes and biases against individuals with disabilities as reasons for enacting the ADA, but did not identify a pattern of irrational discrimination by the states. **This limited evidence fell far short of showing a pattern of unconstitutional discrimination.** Congress thus exceeded its authority by authorizing suits for money damages under the ADA against the states. *Board of Trustees of Univ. of Alabama v. Garrett*, 531 U.S. 356, 121 S.Ct. 955, 148 L.Ed.2d 866 (2001).

◆   *The Fifth Circuit decided that a teacher at a community college in Texas raised sufficient factual issues to bring his ADA case to a jury.*

The instructor had slurred speech as the result of an accident, but never requested any accommodations. The president of the college transferred him from the college banking program, stating the program was not running well and that the instructor's handicap could have contributed to the problem. The next year, the instructor was informed that his contract was not going to be renewed, based on an allegation that he had been intoxicated while teaching, and that the banking program had improved since he had been removed.

An investigation revealed **the claim of intoxication had been based on the instructor's slurred speech and unsteady gait, both of which were due to his accident**. The instructor sued the college, alleging it discriminated against him on the basis of a perceived disability. A federal magistrate judge disagreed and entered judgment for the college. The Fifth Circuit, however, determined there were enough facts in dispute to entitle the instructor to bring his case to a jury. **There was evidence that the college perceived him to be disabled and transferred him to a full-time teaching position because of his limited speaking ability.** The case had to be presented to a jury. *McInnis v. Alamo Community College Dist.*, 207 F.3d 276 (5th Cir. 2000).

B. Defenses

◆ *A Florida professor's claim that he was discharged because his employer thought he was an alcoholic will not be dismissed prior to a trial.*

The professor began teaching as an adjunct professor and soon became a full-time associate professor. A few years later, he began missing meetings and showing signs of alcohol abuse. His divorce became final near this time. An associate dean arrived unannounced at the professor's residence and concluded he was under the influence of alcohol. The professor was placed on medical leave. The university told him he would be deemed to have resigned if he did not submit a leave of absence form and physician's certification by a specified date. It then discharged him after he did not submit the forms on time.

The professor sued the university under the Rehabilitation Act, claiming it discharged him because it "regarded" him as an alcoholic. Alcoholism can be a disability under the Rehabilitation Act when the individual claiming protection is not currently abusing alcohol. The court rejected the university's claim that pretrial judgment should be granted based on the professor's failure to actively participate on a dissertation review committee. A factual dispute existed as to whether active participation on the committee was an essential job function and as to whether he adequately performed it. **The court also rejected the university's argument that it accommodated the professor by placing him on leave and making its employee assistance program available to him. These steps did not conclusively establish it met its duty to reasonably accommodate him.** *Gardiner v. Nova Southeastern Univ.*, No. 06-60590 CIV, 2006 WL 3804704 (S.D. Fla. 12/22/06).

◆ *The U.S. Court of Appeals, Eleventh Circuit, held a Florida university could not claim Eleventh Amendment immunity under Title II of the ADA.*

Students at a Florida university requested sign language interpreters, auxiliary aids, and note-takers. When the requests were denied, a disability rights association sued the university in a federal district court, alleging it violated Title II of the ADA. The court found the university was immune from liability under the Eleventh Amendment. The association appealed to the Eleventh Circuit. The court stayed the appeal until the U.S. Supreme Court decided *Tennessee v. Lane*, 541 U.S. 509 (2004), which concerned the ability of disabled citizens to sue for access to the courts under Title II.

In *Lane*, the Supreme Court decided Title II constituted a valid exercise of Congressional power under the Fourteenth Amendment in cases implicating the fundamental right of access to the courts. The Eleventh Circuit then took up the appeal by the Florida students. **The court held Title II of the ADA constituted a valid exercise of Congress's enforcement power under the Fourteenth Amendment in cases involving access to public education.** Since Congress had acted within its power, Eleventh Amendment immunity was abrogated. The court reversed the judgment and remanded the case to the district court for further proceedings. *Ass'n for Disabled Americans v. Florida Int'l Univ.*, 405 F.3d 954 (11th Cir. 2005).

◆ *An alcoholic employee could be fired for failing to comply with a return to work agreement.*

An administrative employee took several unauthorized leaves of absence and eventually told his supervisors that he was an alcoholic and that he needed to enter a treatment program. He continued to have problems, missing meetings and failing to return messages. He was finally offered a "return to work" agreement detailing conditions he had to satisfy in order to retain his job. Under the agreement, he had to supply documentation that he had successfully completed a treatment program and also provide weekly progress reports after his in-patient treatment ended. He provided the documentation regarding the treatment program, but failed to supply the weekly progress reports, and the university fired him. When he sued under the ADA and the Rehabilitation Act, a federal court dismissed the lawsuit. Here, **the university had provided a legitimate nondiscriminatory reason for the termination** – his failure to comply with the return to work agreement. *Mayo v. Columbia Univ.*, No. 01 Civ. 2002 (LMM), 2003 WL 1824628 (S.D.N.Y. 2003).

◆ *A New York university could fire a dyslexic security officer for unsatisfactory performance.*

A state university hired a security officer as a probationary public safety officer. Under civil service laws, he could be fired at any time after two months of employment and before completion of his 52-week probationary period. His two-month review was satisfactory, but his next review was not. During a discussion of the second review, the officer admitted for the first time that he was dyslexic. University officials offered him training opportunities and increased his responsibilities. Although his third evaluation showed some improvement in his recordkeeping, university officials became concerned about his judgment and ethics after two incidents involving campus parking violations. The university fired the officer, who sued under the ADA and the Rehabilitation Act. A federal court dismissed the lawsuit, noting **the officer was neither disabled nor regarded as disabled**. Here, the termination was because of unsatisfactory performance. *Smith v. State Univ. of New York*, No. 1:00-CV1454, 2003 WL 1937208 (N.D.N.Y. 2003).

◆ *An employee suing for disability discrimination under state law should have filed a charge with the state agency rather than the Equal Employment Opportunity Commission (EEOC).*

A groundskeeper at a Texas university medical center was responsible for maintaining an area of ground near a large bird sanctuary. After contracting histoplasmosis – a disease caused by inhaling spores from an organism that thrives in areas enriched by bird droppings – she complained about the environmental risks caused by the birds. She claimed that she was then offered the choice of resigning or being fired. She quit, then filed a charge with the EEOC. Later, she sued in federal court under state law and had her lawsuit dismissed. When she sued again in state court for disability discrimination, **her lawsuit was again dismissed because she failed to exhaust her administrative remedies**. Reporting her disability discrimination claim to the EEOC was not the same as reporting it to the Texas Commission on Human Rights. *Smith v. Univ. of Texas Southwestern Medical Center*, 101 S.W.3d 185 (Tex. Ct. App. 2003).

◆ *A professor fired for unprofessional conduct failed in his ADA lawsuit against the university.*

An Arizona university hired an adjunct professor and later promoted him to chair of the College of Arts and Sciences. The professor insisted on employing a veteran with a service-related knee injury, gout, hepatitis C and other ailments to a computer assistant position. He then began accumulating reprimands for unprofessional conduct and was demoted before eventually being fired. He sued the university under the ADA, asserting that he had been retaliated against for advocating on behalf of a disabled student. An Arizona federal court ruled in favor of the university. It noted that although none of the student's conditions necessarily supported a finding of disability under the ADA, his conditions were sufficient for the professor to have a reasonable belief that he was advocating on behalf of a disabled person. However, **the university set forth a legitimate, nondiscriminatory reason for its actions – the professor's unprofessional conduct**. Here, in contravention of university policy, he had allowed a dog to ride in a university van, allowed students to take their own vehicles on a field trip, and allegedly drank with students at a bar. *Garber v. Embry-Riddle Aeronautical Univ.*, 259 F.Supp.2d 979 (D. Ariz. 2003).

◆ *A narcoleptic hospital resident could be fired where he couldn't perform his duties due to his impairment.*

An anesthesiology resident at a New York university hospital failed to respond to his emergency beeper on three occasions and was fired. He was later diagnosed with narcolepsy. He then sued the hospital and various physicians for disability discrimination, and the defendants sought to have the case dismissed. After a trial court dismissed the doctors from the suit, the New York Supreme Court, Appellate Division, dismissed the hospital. Although the resident suffered from a disability, which caused the behavior that got him fired, **the hospital had asserted a legitimate reason for firing him** – his narcolepsy prevented him from performing the essential functions of the job. *Timashpolsky v. SUNY Health Science Center at Brooklyn*, 761 N.Y.S.2d 94 (N.Y. App. Div. 2003).

◆ *Generally, a seniority system takes precedence over ADA accommodation.*
In a case involving an airline employee with a bad back, who was seeking a mailroom position, **the U.S. Supreme Court held that as a general rule, an accommodation under the ADA is not reasonable if it conflicts with an employer's seniority rules**. However, employees may present evidence of special circumstances that make a "seniority rule exception" reasonable in a particular case. *US Airways, Inc. v. Barnett*, 535 U.S. 391, 122 S.Ct. 1516, 152 L.Ed.2d 589 (2002).

C. Contagious Diseases

In 1998, the U.S. Supreme Court held that a person with HIV was protected by the Americans with Disabilities Act (ADA), despite the fact that she was not yet exhibiting symptoms of the disease. Since HIV substantially impaired her ability to reproduce, she could not be excluded unless her condition presented a direct threat to the health and safety of others. Bragdon v. Abbott, *524 U.S. 624, 118 S.Ct. 2196, 141 L.Ed.2d 540.*

◆ *The Supreme Court held that a person with a contagious disease was entitled to the protections of the Rehabilitation Act.*
A Florida elementary school teacher was discharged because of her continued recurrence of tuberculosis. She sued the school board under Section 504 of the Rehabilitation Act. A federal district court dismissed her suit, but the Eleventh Circuit held persons with contagious diseases fall within Section 504's coverage. The case then reached the U.S. Supreme Court, which held that **tuberculosis was a disability under Section 504**. The disease attacked the teacher's respiratory system and affected her ability to work. It would be unfair to allow an employer to distinguish between a disease's potential effect on others and its effect on the afflicted employee in order to justify discriminatory treatment. Accordingly, she was entitled to reinstatement or front pay if she could show that despite her disability, she was otherwise qualified for her job with or without a reasonable accommodation. *School Board of Nassau County v. Arline*, 480 U.S. 273, 107 S.Ct. 1123, 94 L.Ed.2d 307 (1987).

◆ *The transfer of an HIV-positive employee was not discriminatory where the employee had committed infractions that resulted in risks to others.*
A New York medical college employed a phlebotomist who was HIV positive. The college had a policy in place requiring employees to wear gloves on both hands when drawing blood. After the employee violated that policy on at least three occasions, the college reassigned her to the billing department. The employee brought suit against the college in a state trial court, alleging that it had discriminated against her based on her HIV-positive disability. The case was transferred to the New York Supreme Court, Appellate Division, which

held that **the college did not discriminate against the employee by reassigning her**. The court noted that the employer was unaware of any similar infractions by any other employees. Thus, it had provided a legitimate, nondiscriminatory reason for the transfer that was supported by substantial evidence. *Friedel v. New York State Division of Human Rights*, 632 N.Y.S.2d 520 (N.Y. App. Div. 1995).

VI. RETALIATION

A. Generally

Title VII prohibits an employer from retaliating against an employee for opposing an unlawful employment practice, or for making a charge, testifying, assisting, or participating in any manner in a discrimination investigation, proceeding or hearing.

In Robinson v. Shell Oil Co., *519 U.S. 337 (1997),* **the Supreme Court held a former employee of a corporation could bring a retaliatory discrimination lawsuit against his former employer after he was given a negative employment reference following his filing of an Equal Employment Opportunity Commission complaint.**

◆   *The U.S. Supreme Court held the reassignment of a female to more arduous and dirtier work was evidence of retaliation by her employer.*

The employee worked in the maintenance way department of a railway company. Her primary responsibility was to operate a forklift. The employee was the only woman in her department. She complained that her immediate supervisor told her women should not be working there. The company disciplined the supervisor but also transferred the employee from forklift duty to standard track laborer tasks. The employee who transferred her said the reassignment reflected co-workers' complaints that a "more senior man" should have the "less arduous and cleaner job of forklift operator." The employee filed two complaints with the Equal Employment Opportunity Commission (EEOC), claiming that the company discriminated against her in violation of Title VII. She was suspended without pay for insubordination but was later reinstated with back wages. The employee sued the company in a federal district court for unlawful retaliation under Title VII. Following a jury trial, the jury held in favor of the employee. The U.S. Court of Appeals, Sixth Circuit, affirmed the judgment and the U.S. Supreme Court agreed to review the case.

The Court held the anti-retaliation provision of Title VII provides that an employer may not discriminate against an employee or job applicant because he or she has opposed a practice prohibited by Title VII. The Sixth Circuit had held that to prevail on a Title VII retaliation claim, employees must show they suffered an "adverse employment action." **An "adverse employment action" is defined as a "materially adverse change in the terms and conditions" of employment. The Court held the scope of the anti-retaliation provision extended beyond workplace or employment-related retaliatory acts and harm.** The anti-retaliation provision must prohibit employers from action that is serious enough to deter victims of discrimination from complaining to the EEOC. Petty slights, minor annoyances, and simple lack of good manners will not create such a deterrence. The Court found sufficient evidence to support the jury's verdict on the retaliation claim. The jury had correctly found the employer's actions were "materially adverse." The reassignment was more arduous and dirtier, and the forklift position required more qualifications. An indefinite suspension without pay could act as a deterrent to complain, even though the employee was later reinstated. *Burlington Northern & Santa Fe Railway Co. v. White*, 126 S.Ct. 2405 (U.S. 2006).

◆ *A Utah instructor failed to prove a university failed to renew her three-year teaching contract based on her gender, national origin or retaliation.*

The instructor claimed the university declined to renew her contract because she assigned some students poor grades. She said the failure to renew her contract was based on her gender and/or national origin, and she added a claim for hostile work environment.

The instructor sued the university in a federal district court. It stated that to prove discrimination, she needed to show that she was doing satisfactory work. The instructor failed to satisfy this requirement. The facts showed she could not establish and maintain authority in her classroom. The instructor failed to respond to messages from the chair of her department. There were no facts showing the employment environment at the university was objectively hostile. **To prove retaliation, the instructor had to show she had engaged in a protected activity. The instructor claimed she was retaliated against for academically penalizing students. The court held this was not protected behavior that can support a retaliation claim.** *Mejia v. Univ. of Utah*, No. 1:05-CV-53 TS, 2007 WL 391586 (D. Utah 2/1/07).

◆ *The U.S. Supreme Court held the broad prohibition of discrimination on the basis of sex in Title IX extends to retaliation claims.*

An Alabama teacher worked in Birmingham public schools for over 10 years, where he taught physical education and coached basketball. He was transferred to a high school after six years, where he discovered the girls' team did not receive the same funding or access to equipment and facilities as boys' teams enjoyed. The teacher claimed his job was made difficult by lack of adequate funding, equipment and facilities, and began complaining to supervisors. He stated the district did not respond to his complaints, and that he began to receive negative evaluations and was ultimately removed as girls' coach. The teacher sued the school board in a federal district court, claiming the loss of his supplemental coaching contracts constituted retaliation in violation of Title IX of the Education Amendments of 1972. The court dismissed the case, and its decision was affirmed by the Eleventh Circuit.

The Supreme Court held **Title IX covers retaliation against a person for complaining about sex discrimination. Retaliation is an intentional act that is a form of discrimination, since the person who complains is treated differently than others.** A program that retaliates against a person based on a sex discrimination complaint intentionally discriminates in violation of Title IX. The Court held a private right of action for retaliation was within the statute's prohibition of intentional sex discrimination. **Title IX did not require the victim of retaliation to also be the victim of discrimination.** Retaliation against individuals who complained of sex discrimination was intentional conduct violating the clear terms of Title IX. The Court found a reasonable school board would realize it could not cover up violations of Title IX by retaliating against teachers. It reversed and remanded the case to allow the teacher a chance to prove the board retaliated against him. *Jackson v. Birmingham Board of Educ.*, 544 U.S. 167 (2005).

◆ *An Oregon university may have retaliated against an employee after she reported her supervisor was discriminating against her.*

An Oregon university hired the employee as an apprentice electrician. She was the only female in the electrical shop. Over the next four years, the employee continued to have problems with her supervisor. Finally, the supervisor forced the employee to quit her position on a workplace safety committee because he felt she "shouldn't be telling his journeymen what to do safety-wise." Several months later, the university laid her off. When a journeyman electrician position opened at the university two years later, the employee applied. The university declined to interview her.

The employee sued the university in a state court, alleging it laid her off in retaliation for her opposition to the school's allegedly discriminatory practices. The court granted the university's motion to dismiss the case and the employee appealed to the Court of Appeals of Oregon. The university argued that the employee could not have lost her job based on her complaints, as her job was temporary and would have ended when she received her journeyman's license. The court noted the employee continued work for three months after her apprenticeship ended. **A jury could reasonably find the university retaliated against her**, and the court reversed and remanded the case for a jury trial. *Boynton-Burns v. Univ. of Oregon*, 105 P.3d 893 (Or. Ct. App. 2005).

◆ *A Massachusetts university did not fire a professor in retaliation for supporting his wife's sexual harassment claim against a department head.*

The professor and his wife worked in the university's biochemistry and molecular biology department. A department head criticized the professor for certain fees charged by the research lab founded by the professor and his wife. He said imposing such fees indicated the professor lacked a cooperative spirit and collegiality. The professor and wife filed a grievance, asking the university to remove the information from their personnel files. The grievance was resolved when the department head agreed his letter was a private communication that did not belong in university files. The university later reduced the professor's teaching assignments after he received negative comments on student evaluations. His evaluations remained poor for several years, and the university eventually held hearings and decided to fire him.

The professor sued the university and two department heads in a Massachusetts trial court for retaliation in violation of Title VII and a Massachusetts anti-discrimination law. The court awarded judgment to the university and department heads, and the professor appealed to the Supreme Judicial Court of Massachusetts. He argued a court could infer the causal connection between support of his wife's complaint and the actions taken against him from the timing and sequence of events. **The court held the professor did not prove a causal link merely by showing that one event followed another. His performance and department funding problems began before his wife filed her complaint.** As the time span between endorsing the sexual harassment complaint and adverse employment action was too long, the court affirmed the judgment. *Mole v. Univ. of Massachusetts*, 442 Mass. 582, 814 N.E.2d 329 (Mass. 2004).

◆ *A business professor claimed Kentucky State University (KSU) retaliated against her for filing a federal wage and sex discrimination lawsuit.*

The professor taught business courses at KSU for 15 years. For most of that time, she was the only female professor in her division. Her salary was 31% less than her male counterparts and 13% less than males in lower-ranking positions. KSU justified the professor's lower salary as the result of her very low incoming salary. The professor claimed KSU retaliated against her after she sued the university in a federal district court for unequal pay. She contended the dean of the business school threatened to discharge her after she filed the complaint. The professor filed a second action against the university in a federal district court for gender-based discrimination and retaliation.

The court granted the university's request for summary judgment, and the professor appealed to the U.S. Court of Appeals, Sixth Circuit. **The court found significant evidence from which a court could decide that intentional gender discrimination was a substantial factor in the pay disparity at KSU. The professor presented enough conflicting evidence to support inferences that the dean's actions were retaliatory.** The conflicting evidence called for a trial, not summary judgment. The court reversed the summary judgment and remanded the case for a trial. *Smith v. Kentucky State Univ.*, 97 Fed.Appx. 22 (6th Cir. 2004).

◆ *The U.S. Court of Appeals, Tenth Circuit, held the University of Kansas had legitimate, nondiscriminatory reasons for denying tenure to an adjunct professor and did not retaliate against her on the basis of disability.*

A University of Kansas assistant professor was denied tenure, then discharged. She sued the university in a federal district court for discrimination under Title VII. She was then appointed to an adjunct lecturer position, but was denied principal investigator (PI) status, which would have allowed her to act as a director of grant applications. Meanwhile, a jury ruled for the university in her discrimination lawsuit. The next month, the professor applied for an administrative position with the university, but was not interviewed for it. Claiming the university denied her the administrative position and PI status in retaliation for filing her Title VII lawsuit, she brought a second action against the university in a federal district court for retaliation. The court granted summary judgment to the university, and the professor appealed.

The U.S. Court of Appeals, Tenth Circuit, held that to establish adverse employment action under Title VII, the professor had to show the university acted in a way that meant a significant change in her employment status. The court found the decisions to confer the adjunct lecturer title on the professor and deny her PI status were not significant changes in employment. The university's decision not to hire the professor as an administrator was not retaliation. **The university presented legitimate, nondiscriminatory reasons for declining to hire her for that position. Because the professor offered no evidence to show the school's nondiscriminatory reasons were a pretext for discrimination or retaliation, the court affirmed the judgment.** *Annett v. Univ. of Kansas*, 371 F.3d 1233 (10th Cir. 2004).

B. Defenses

◆ *A District of Columbia university did not discriminate against an employee when it moved his office and gave him a poor performance evaluation.*

The employee attended a meeting where he discussed the treatment of African-Americans with university officials. Ten weeks later, his office was moved to a basement cubicle. The employee resigned 22 months later, after the university placed him on probation for poor performance. The employee sued the university in a federal district court, alleging it violated Section 1981 by moving his office and giving him a poor performance evaluation in retaliation for speaking out against the university's treatment of African-Americans.

The university maintained it had moved the employee's office as part of an office reorganization. The employee stated the associate vice president called him "arrogant nigger" and "asshole" and gave him a jazz recording, saying "you probably like this kind of music." **The university offered a legitimate nondiscriminatory reason for its decision to move his office. The court rejected the assertion that he was assigned a poor performance evaluation in retaliation for what he said at the meeting. It said 22 months between the two events was too long to infer a connection between them.** The reorganization affected many university employees, not just African-Americans. The court granted the university's motion for summary judgment. *Sullivan v. Catholic Univ. of America*, 387 F.Supp.2d 11 (D.D.C. 2005).

◆ *An Alabama university did not retaliate against an employee for reporting sexual harassment by her supervisor.*

The employee claimed her supervisor subjected her to unwelcome sexual attention. She said he implied he would allow her to obtain further training opportunities only if she gave in to his sexual demands and that he threatened to fire her. The employee sought a higher-paying position, but she did not mention any problems with her supervisor. Later, the supervisor refused to sign the employee's time sheet. She complained about him to the university's human resource department. For the first time, the employee told the university her supervisor had made sexual advances toward her. The university placed her on paid leave and instructed her to file a written statement about the harassment.

The university investigated the complaint and interviewed the supervisor. He stated he had engaged in consensual sex with the employee. The university reassigned the employee to a different supervisor. She sued the university in a federal district court for retaliation. **The court held an employer can only be held liable for a Title VII sexual harassment claim if there is a tangible**

employment action, such as discharge or demotion, or the harassment was sufficiently severe to change the employee's working conditions. The court agreed with the university that there was no adverse employment action in this case. Although the supervisor apparently threatened to fire the employee, no evidence was presented to show he actually tried to do this. The court granted the university's motion for summary judgment. *Arnold v. Tuskegee Univ.*, No. 3:03CV-515-F, 2006 WL 47507 (M.D. Ala. 1/9/06).

◆ *A three-year lapse between reported sexual harassment and the discharge of a Wisconsin professor doomed her retaliation claim.*

A research scientist with the U.S. Department of Veteran Affairs (VA) worked part time as an associate professor of neurology at a Wisconsin medical college. When she charged another professor with sexual harassment, her supervisor at the college warned her filing a sexual harassment charge could be a "career limiting move." However, the supervisor investigated her complaint. Three years later, the professor lost her VA research position. The college then discharged her because her VA research responsibilities were the basis of her faculty appointment. The professor sued the college in a federal district court for retaliation in violation of Title VII. The court granted the college's motion for summary judgment and the professor appealed.

The U.S. Court of Appeals, Seventh Circuit stated that **a Title VII claim based on retaliation required evidence of statutorily protected activity that results in adverse employment action. The professor's retaliation claim failed because of the time lapse between her sexual harassment complaint and her discharge three years later.** The delay was too great to imply a causal connection between protected activity and adverse employment action. The supervisor's comment that a complaint could be a "career limiting move" was not direct evidence of retaliation. As the professor did not show she was treated less favorably than similarly situated employees, the court affirmed the decision. *Myklebust v. Medical College of Wisconsin*, 97 Fed.Appx. 652 (7th Cir. 2004).

◆ *A math teacher assigned to remedial and introductory courses failed to show that the assignments were retaliatory.*

A mathematics instructor of Burmese origin worked for a community college in Washington and did some things that angered his fellow instructors, like changing the grade of a student who was not in his class. He received a written reprimand for that action. However, he later obtained tenure despite a "no" vote from the tenure review committee when he appealed to the board of trustees. Afterward, he received teaching assignments for remedial courses as well as a few introductory college-level and post-calculus courses. He sued the college for discrimination and retaliation (for challenging the tenure denial).

A state court let the discrimination claim proceed, but granted pretrial judgment to the college on the retaliation claim. The Court of Appeals of Washington found the instructor did not engage in protected activity when he challenged the tenure decision. And even if he did, his class assignments were not adverse employment action. **The college had a legitimate reason for making the assignments.** His teaching style differed from the "Harvard reform calculus method" recently adopted by the math department. *Tan v. State of Washington*, No. 27937-1-II, 2003 WL 1849185 (Wash. Ct. App. 2003).

◆ *A Texas state court agreed with a private religious university that it could not consider an employment case that was previously brought in federal court.*

A former university department chair sued the university in federal court for Title VII violations based on his removal from office and retaliation for an earlier lawsuit he filed against the university. Before the federal court ruled on the case, the employee filed a breach of contract and fraud action against the university in the state court system.

The federal court awarded the university summary judgment, declaring that religious education institutions are exempt from Title VII. The Court of Appeals of Texas then held the state court action was barred by the equitable doctrine of *res judicata*, which precludes actions that have already been litigated between the same parties and involve the same factual basis. *Bishop v. Baylor Univ.*, No. 10-01-080-CV, 2003 WL 22996902 (Tex. Ct. App. 2003).

◆ *A retaliation claim failed because the university had proffered a legitimate nondiscriminatory reason for its non-renewal of the professor's contract.*

A female assistant professor was denied tenure by a New York private university, allegedly because she lacked a Ph.D. and a sufficient record of scholarly research. The professor rejected several offers for part-time adjunct positions and filed a complaint against the university with the New York Human Rights Commission, alleging that she had been denied tenure on the basis of her sex. She was permitted to teach in adjunct status without a contract for an additional two years, despite the university's policy of not allowing persons to teach without signed contracts. During settlement negotiations, the university offered her a five-year adjunct contract with a 60% pay increase in exchange for her withdrawal of the sex discrimination complaint. The professor declined the offer, and the university unconditionally refused to consider her for additional available adjunct positions.

The professor filed a second complaint with the commission, alleging that the university had retaliated against her for not withdrawing her sex discrimination complaint. The commission held that the university had retaliated against the professor but dismissed the discrimination claim. The case reached the Court of Appeals of New York. It held **the record was devoid of evidence that the university had a subjective retaliatory motive for the non-renewal**. The professor's failure to agree to any of the university's adjunct offers over the course of two years belied her assertion that the non-renewal was in retaliation for her failure to withdraw the discrimination claim. Rather, her adjunct status was not renewed because of her protracted tactical decisions not to execute a series of adjunct contracts, in favor of her relying completely on her achieving full tenure in the pending discrimination proceeding. Moreover, the university's enforcement of its policy prohibiting adjuncts from teaching without a signed contract was a legitimate nondiscriminatory reason for the non-renewal. *Pace Univ. v. N.Y. City Comm'n on Human Rights*, 85 N.Y.2d 125, 647 N.E.2d 1273 (N.Y. 1995).

C. Causal Connection

◆ *The U.S. Court of Appeals, Sixth Circuit, upheld a jury verdict finding a Tennessee community college discharged an African-American professor in retaliation for accusing the college of unlawful discrimination.*

The professor complained of racial discrimination during his 25-year career and filed several complaints with the college affirmative action office. He also filed racial discrimination charges with the U.S. Equal Employment Opportunity Commission. The college received criticism from the professor's students and colleagues about how he managed a psychology course. The department removed the professor from that class and eventually relieved him of his teaching duties for unsatisfactory performance. He attempted to meet the requirements of a performance plan but was not given the entire fall term, as promised, to complete it. The college discharged the professor and he appealed to the Chancellor of the Tennessee Board of Regents. The Chancellor upheld the termination. The professor sued the college, and others, in a federal district court, alleging it violated Title VII by opposing an unlawful employment practice enumerated under Title VII. The district court dismissed the action but the U.S. Court of Appeals, Sixth Circuit, returned the case to the district court for further consideration. A jury awarded the professor $320,000 in compensatory damages, and the college appealed again to the Sixth Circuit.

The court concluded the professor presented sufficient evidence for a reasonable jury to have found the college unlawfully retaliated against him in violation of Title VII. The court explained that to succeed on a Title VII retaliation claim, an employee must demonstrate he or she was fired in retaliation for opposing a discriminatory practice. **The professor presented ample evidence to support a causal connection between his termination and retaliation for his discrimination complaints against the college.** The court found that awarding front pay was appropriate to compensate the professor for future loss. *Cox v. Shelby State Community College*, 194 Fed.Appx. 267 (6th Cir. 2006).

◆ *A Mississippi university may have discriminated against an employee by eliminating her job and choosing a male for a newly created position.*

The university hired the employee as a vice president of student services and enrollment. Before she started the job, the title was changed to vice president of student affairs (VPSA). After enrollment at the university declined by 30%, the university began to search for a new dean of enrollment. At the same time, the university hired a new president, who decided to combine student services with enrollment management and create a position titled "vice president of student services." The employee alleged this position was not newly created, but was in reality the job she had been hired for. A search committee was formed, and it recommended a male for the job.

The employee filed a discrimination complaint with the U.S. Equal Employment Opportunity Commission (EEOC). Days later, the university discharged her. The employee sued the university in a federal district court, alleging Title VII violations. The court held the case should proceed to trial. **The university did not prove the male chosen for the position was more**

qualified than the employee or that the university did not retaliate against her for complaining to the EEOC. *Stephens v. Mississippi Univ. for Women,* No. Civ.A. 1:04 CV 226, 2005 WL 3591812 (N.D. Miss. 12/30/05).

◆ *A New Jersey university could be liable for firing a Hispanic employee in retaliation for her previous complaints of race and gender discrimination.*

The employee worked as an emergency medical technician. She filed complaints of sexual harassment and race and gender discrimination against the university at various times in her career. The university fired the employee for driving an ambulance off the road. She sued the university in a federal district court, alleging retaliation for her previous complaints in violation of Title VII and state law. The university moved for summary judgment, arguing the employee did not show retaliation. The employee countered with testimony by a hospital director who stated the university had allowed other employees who committed similar acts to return to work. **The court found a jury could conclude the university's stated reason for firing the employee was a cover-up for retaliation.** It sent the case to a jury to determine whether university was motivated by retaliation for her previous complaints. *Cortes v. Univ. of Medicine and Dentistry of New Jersey,* 391 F.Supp.2d 298 (D.N.J. 2005).

◆ *Discrimination and retaliation charges against a college were dismissed.*

The college assigned the employee to advise students in a center operated by the Chicago Public Schools (CPS). He claimed the center mistreated him because he wore dreadlocks and a kofi to observe his religion. The employee filed an administrative complaint alleging race discrimination against CPS. He later claimed the college discharged him in retaliation for filing the claim. The employee then sued CPS in a federal district court for Title VII violations. The case was dismissed because CPS had never been his employer.

The employee filed a new action against the college for race and religious discrimination and retaliation. The complaint alleged the college retaliated against him after it learned of his discrimination claim against CPS. The court noted the discrimination charges referred to only retaliation and said nothing about the college engaging in discriminatory practices. It therefore dismissed the race discrimination claim. **The court said that in a Title VII retaliation claim, the retaliatory actions must be those of the employer or an agent of the employer. Since the college and CPS were separate and independent from one another, charges against one could not be imputed to the other.** For that reason, the court dismissed the retaliation claim. *Flowers v. Columbia College Chicago,* No. 03 C 9247, 2004 WL 1459346 (N.D. Ill. 2004).

◆ *A former assistant director of development alleged sufficient facts to survive a motion to dismiss her retaliatory discharge action.*

The assistant director worked for the Gene Siskel Film Center at the Art Institute of Chicago. She agreed to post names of the Siskel family on a donor wall as a condition for accepting a donation by the family. A vice president of the center admonished her for listing more than one name in violation of the Institute's "one gift, one name" policy, even though the president and four other officials had approved the action. Two days before a public dedication, the director of the center instructed the assistant director to "steer ... Gene Siskel's widow ... away from the donor wall during the press preview." She refused to comply with the directive and was discharged for insubordination.

The assistant director sued the institute in a federal district court for retaliatory discharge. **The court held the critical factor in this case was whether the assistant director reasonably believed her supervisors were involved in an illegal or unlawful act.** The institute had accepted the donation on the condition that the entire Siskel family would be listed on the donor wall. Supervisors instructed her to remove their names just two days before the dedication and without discussing the change with the family. The sudden change in plans was sufficient for the assistant director to reasonably believe the institute was engaging in fraudulent activity. She presented sufficient evidence to survive the institute's motion to dismiss the case. *Tanzer v. Art Institute of Chicago*, No. 02 C 8115, 2003 WL 21788850 (N.D. Ill. 2003).

◆ *A three-year span between a sexual harassment complaint and an adverse employment decision was too great to permit an inference of retaliation.*

A teacher at a Kansas university accused the vice president of academic affairs of improper sexual advances. The university resolved the complaint through a settlement in which she dropped the charges in exchange for a three-year lecturer position. In that position, she received positive reviews, and the university decided to make the position a tenure position. However, she was not selected for it because she lacked the requisite background in educational technology. She sued the university for retaliation, but a federal court ruled against her. The Tenth Circuit affirmed, noting that she relied too much on inference to try to prove retaliation. Even though the five-member search panel had been chaired by a good friend of the vice president, **her mere speculation about the vice president's influence was not sufficient to prove retaliation.** Also, three years had passed since she had made the complaint. Finally, the candidate selected was qualified for the position. *Adams v. Washburn Univ. of Topeka*, 66 Fed.Appx. 819 (10th Cir. 2003).

CHAPTER EIGHT

Intellectual Property

I. COPYRIGHT LAW

State and federal copyright laws protect original works of authorship by creating exclusive rights for the owner to make copies of the work, prepare derivative works, distribute copies of the work, and perform or display the work publicly. See 17 U.S.C. § 106. Copyright protection for an original work exists even if no copyright is registered. See 17 U.S.C. § 408(a). Registration is required in order to initiate a copyright infringement action. Employers are presumed to own the copyright to works prepared by their employees within the scope of their employment, unless a specific written agreement says otherwise.

A. Fair Use

Educators and others are entitled to make "fair use" of copyrighted works for the purposes described in 17 U.S.C. § 107. The statute lists four factors to assure such use is not for commercial purposes. In Stewart v. Abend, *495 U.S. 207 (1990), the U.S. Supreme Court held the primary factor in fair use cases is the effect that use will have on the work's potential market or value.*

17 U.S.C. § 107 states:

The fair use of a copyrighted work, including such use by reproduction in copies … for purposes such as criticism, comment, news reporting, teaching (including multiple copies for classroom use), scholarship, or research, is not an infringement of copyright. In determining whether the use made of a work in any particular case is a fair use the factors to be considered shall include—

(1) the purpose and character of the use, including whether such use is of a commercial nature or is for nonprofit educational purposes;
(2) the nature of the copyrighted work;
(3) the amount and substantiality of the portion used in relation to the copyrighted work as a whole; and
(4) the effect of the use upon the potential market for or value of the copyrighted work.

◆   *A New York university defeated a media foundation's claims for copyright infringement and breach of contract.*

The parties contracted to produce public service announcements. The foundation alleged the university breached the contract by refusing to pay additional compensation as a condition of producing the announcements. It also contended the university violated federal copyright law by displaying copyrighted material at a fundraiser for a commercial purpose. The foundation sued the university in a federal district court for breach of contract and violation of the "fair use" provision of copyright law. The court allowed the case to go before a jury, and after a trial, it found for the university. The foundation appealed to the U.S. Court of Appeals, Second Circuit, which held it breached the contract with the university by demanding extra compensation.

To determine if the university satisfied the fair use requirements of 17 U.S.C. § 107, the court considered: 1) the purpose and character of the use, including whether such use is of a commercial nature or is for nonprofit educational purposes; the 2) nature of the copyrighted work; 3) the amount and substantiality of the portion used in relation to the copyrighted work as a whole; and 4) the effect of the use upon the potential market for or value of the copyrighted work. The court determined the fair use issue was properly presented to the jury. **Copyright law permits the reproduction or distribution of a copyrighted work as long as it is not done for commercial reasons.** The judgment was affirmed. *New York Univ. v. Planet Earth Foundation*, 163 Fed.Appx. 13 (2d Cir. 2005).

◆   *The U.S. Supreme Court has held that publishing companies must obtain permission from freelance writers before reusing their works in electronic databases.*

In 2001, the U.S. Supreme Court determined that permission was required for inclusion of freelancers' works in electronic databases. Copyright law allows publishers to reuse free-lancers' contributions when a collective work, such as a magazine issue or an encyclopedia, is revised, but the Court said that **massive databases such as NEXIS do not fit within that provision of the law because they are not revisions of previously published collective works**.

The decision was the result of a lawsuit that was filed against New York Times Co., Newsday Inc., Time Incorporated Magazine Co., LEXIS/NEXIS and University Microfilms International, alleging violation of freelance writers' copyrights in articles they wrote that were included in complete issues of the publishers' products. *New York Times Co., Inc. v. Tasini*, 533 U.S. 483, 121 S.Ct. 2381, 150 L.Ed.2d 500 (2001).

◆ *By refusing to pay permission fees to copyright holders, a copy shop violated the Copyright Act.*

A commercial copy shop reproduced substantial segments of copyrighted works and bound them into "coursepacks," which were sold to students so that they could fulfill reading assignments given by professors at the University of Michigan. The copy shop acted without the permission of the copyright holders, claiming that the fair use doctrine eliminated the need for it to obtain permission. The fair use doctrine states that the fair use of a copyrighted work for teaching, scholarship or research, among other uses, is not an infringement of copyright. In this case, a number of copyright holders sued the copy shop claiming that its reproduction of material was not fair use. A federal court agreed and awarded damages against the copy shop. It also found that the infringement was willful.

On appeal, the U.S. Court of Appeals, Sixth Circuit, noted that by reproducing copies for students without paying the copyright holders the permission fees that other copy shops paid, **the copy shop was reducing the potential market for or the value of the copyrighted works**. Since one of the potential uses of a copyright is to grant a license to reproduce part of the work for use in a classroom, and since the copyright holders were willing to grant those licenses, by refusing to pay the permission fees, the copy shop violated the Copyright Act. The court also noted that the purpose and character of the use was of a commercial nature, that the material being reproduced was creative in nature, and that the amount and substantiality of the reproduced segments in relation to the works as a whole were quite large (between 5 and 30%). The court affirmed the finding that the copy shop had infringed the copyright holders' rights. However, **it refused to find that the infringement had been willful**. It remanded the case for reconsideration of the damages. *Princeton Univ. Press v. Michigan Document Services*, 99 F.3d 1381 (6th Cir. 1996).

◆ *A copy shop violated the Copyright Act by copying excerpts from books and putting them in course packets. This was not "fair use" under the act.*

Several New York publishers sued Kinko's for copyright infringement as a result of the store's **policy of copying excerpts from books, compiling them into course "packets," and selling them to college students**. Kinko's admitted that it copied the works, but asserted that doing so was a fair use under the Copyright Act, and that since it had been doing this type of copying for 20 years, the publishers could not now claim copyright infringement.

A federal district court held that Kinko's had infringed the copyrights. First, the usage was commercial in nature, rather than for nonprofit educational use. Second, the amount and substantiality of the copied works weighed against Kinko's because the portions copied were critical parts of the copyrighted works. Third, and most importantly, **the effect of the use on the value of and market for the works weighed against Kinko's**. Thus, the copying did not amount to fair use under the Copyright Act. Further, the court accepted the publishers' assertion that although they had known Kinko's was copying their works for 20 years, they did not know that Kinko's had been infringing on their copyrights all that time. It ordered Kinko's to obtain permission in the future, to pay any licensing fees required, and to pay $510,000 in statutory damages for past infringement. *Basic Books, Inc. v. Kinko's Graphics Corp.*, 758 F.Supp. 1522 (S.D.N.Y. 1991).

◆ *The U.S. Court of Appeals for the First Circuit rejected a Tufts University visiting lecturer's claims based on the terms of a publishing contract involving a publisher and a professor at another college.*

The lecturer had co-authored the second and third editions of an undergraduate textbook with a professor and director of the graduate nutrition program at another college. The third edition agreement assigned all present and future copyrights of the third and future editions to the book's publisher. The lecturer and professor contracted with the same publisher for a fourth edition that increased the lecturer's share of royalties from 25 to 40%. The professor failed to meet deadlines set by the agreement, and the publisher suggested she assign more work to the lecturer. The professor refused, and the lecturer notified the publisher she was withdrawing from the project. She also stated her revisions could not be used without her permission. The publisher sent the lecturer an acknowledgement that she would receive 12.5% of the fourth edition royalties – half her compensation under the third edition agreement. She signed the acknowledgement, but later discovered her revisions were included in the fourth edition and that the professor was listed as its sole author.

The lecturer copyrighted her revisions and brought a multi-count federal district court complaint against the publisher and professor for copyright infringement and breach of contract. The court held the lecturer had assigned her copyright interest to the publisher under the fourth edition revisions. The publisher was not obligated to terminate its contract with the professor when she failed to meet her deadlines. The First Circuit affirmed the decision, holding the lecturer could not claim a copyright interest in her fourth edition revisions. Based on the terms of the third and fourth edition agreements, she had "assigned ... all present and future copyrights" of the third and future editions to the publisher. **The publisher was the sole copyright owner of the third edition, and consequently the fourth "revised edition." There was no breach of contract by the publisher, because it had the option to extend the deadlines and did so for legitimate financial reasons.** *Zyla v. Wadsworth*, 360 F.3d 243 (1st Cir. 2004).

B. Work-For-Hire

Employers are presumed to own the copyright to works prepared by their employees within the scope of their employment, unless they have agreed otherwise in writing. See 17 U.S.C. § 201(a), also referred to as Section 201(b) of the Copyright Act of 1976. The work of independent contractors is considered "work for hire" under a written agreement for specially ordered or commissioned work used as a contribution to a collective work, part of a motion picture or other audiovisual work, a translation, supplementary work, compilation, instructional text, test or test answer, or an atlas.

Agency principles help determine whether a professor's work is covered by the work-for-hire doctrine. Section 228 of the Restatement (Second) of Agency deems a work to be "for hire" only if the work is of the type the faculty member was hired to create, was created substantially within the space and time limits of the job, and was motivated at least partly by a purpose to serve the university. Higher education employees are expected to produce intellectual property in the scope of their employment. In consideration for this expectation, professors who conduct research, write and publish scholarly articles and create other forms of intellectual property receive better performance evaluations, more promotional opportunities and higher pay.

◆ *The Supreme Court of Kansas held the work-for-hire doctrine did not prevent a state university and the employee association representing its faculty from entering into a memorandum of agreement on intellectual property rights.*

The university and Kansas Board of Regents proposed a policy to retain ownership and control over any intellectual property created by the faculty. The faculty association rejected the policy. The board responded it was not required to negotiate over the policy because intellectual property rights were not a "condition of employment." According to the board, the question of intellectual property rights was a management prerogative and was preempted by state and federal law. The board then adopted a policy giving some intellectual property rights to faculty, but without meeting and conferring with the association.

The state public employee relations board (PERB) held the university had no duty to meet and confer with the faculty association, because the subject was preempted by state and federal law. The case reached the Supreme Court of Kansas, which found neither state nor federal law preempted the subject of intellectual property from being included in a memorandum of agreement. **The work-for-hire doctrine was only a presumption regarding the ownership of copyrights, and it allowed parties to contract for particular ownership rights. The doctrine operated as a default provision, unless the parties agreed otherwise.** The court found Congress contemplated that parties could negotiate the ownership of a copyright. The federal Patent Act also allowed parties to assign patent ownership rights. **Federal law did not preempt any kind of intellectual property rights from being covered by a memorandum of understanding or other written agreement.** The court reversed the decision with directions to return the case to the PERB for further proceedings. *Pittsburg State Univ./Kansas National Educ. Ass'n v. Kansas Board of Regents/Pittsburg State Univ.*, 280 Kan. 408, 122 P.3d 336 (Kan. 2005).

◆ *In a case filed by a New York high school teacher claiming ownership of materials he prepared for students, the U.S. Court of Appeals, Second Circuit, explained that federal copyright law considers an employer to be the "author" of a work, if an employee prepares it in the course of employment.*

The teacher was suspended for inappropriate conduct with students. When he refused to clean out his classroom to make it available to his successor, the school district removed some personal property in his absence. The teacher claimed the district confiscated tests, quizzes and homework problems he had stored in the classroom. He sued the school district in a federal district court for unlawful search and seizure and copyright violations. The court dismissed the case, and the teacher appealed to the U.S. Court of Appeals, Second Circuit.

The court affirmed the dismissal of the teacher's Fourth Amendment claims for unlawful search and seizure. He did not show he had a reasonable expectation of privacy in his classroom, as many persons had access to the classroom. The teacher acknowledged his property was commingled with school materials throughout the room. Whatever privacy expectation the teacher may have had ended with his suspension. **The court held the tests, quizzes and homework problems he stored in his classroom and files were the property of the district. Federal copyright law considers an employer the "author" of a work, if it is prepared by an employee in the course of employment.** The court stated the academic tradition of granting university professors ownership of published scholarly works did not apply to teaching materials that were not explicitly prepared for publication. *Shaul v. Cherry Valley-Springfield Cent. School Dist.*, 363 F.3d 177 (2d Cir. 2004).

◆ *Brown University retained its copyrights to photographs taken by a member of its staff under the "works for hire" doctrine.*

Brown University hired a full-time professional photographer to capture images of academic life and natural campus settings for its publications. He was also allowed to shoot pictures on his own initiative. The university purchased photographic equipment for him, arranged for student assistants, and provided him with access to the university's darkroom. Brown's copyright policy contained a provision regarding the ownership of copyrightable materials. After 24 years, Brown severed its relationship with the photographer as part of a reduction in force. He sued Brown in a federal district court, claiming ownership of 97 photographs in his possession.

The court focused on several sections of the Copyright Act of 1976. **Under Section 201(b), titled "Works Made for Hire," the court explained that ownership rights of works by an employee typically vest with the employer.** It determined the photographs were "works for hire" owned by Brown. **The court distinguished between the photographs and the "faculty exception" from the works for hire rule.** Equitable considerations often mandate that a scholar retain the copyright to works, notwithstanding the works for hire doctrine. **The faculty exception did not apply in this case because Brown officials often directed what images should be photographed.** There was no document indicating a conveyance of ownership rights by Brown to the photographer. The language of the policy was too imprecise to use as evidence to support the photographer's claim of such a transfer. By his own admission, he did not think about copyright ownership in the photos until after his relationship with Brown was severed. The court granted summary judgment to Brown. *Foraste v. Brown Univ.*, 290 F.Supp.2d 234 (D.R.I. 2003).

C. Standardized Tests

◆ *New York's Standardized Testing Act requires testing agencies to file reports on standardized tests with the Commissioner of Education and also requires the filing of copyrightable test questions.*

The American Association of Medical Colleges (AAMC), a nonprofit educational association, sponsors a medical school testing program, the central feature of which is the MCAT exam. The AAMC holds copyrights in the MCAT test forms, test questions, answer sheets, and reports. When the state of New York enacted the Standardized Testing Act, requiring disclosure of this copyrighted information, the AAMC sued to enjoin the application of the act. It claimed that the Act was preempted by the federal Copyright Act and moved for pretrial judgment, which the court granted. The court found that the purpose and character of the use was noncommercial and educational, and that disclosure of the test questions would prevent their reuse.

The Second Circuit Court of Appeals reversed, finding that there were issues of fact that precluded a grant of pretrial judgment. If the disclosure of material were considered "fair use," then there would be no Copyright Act violation. However, if the state act facilitated infringement, then the Copyright Act would preempt it. **Here, the state's goal of encouraging valid and objective tests was laudable, and there was a question of fact as to whether the test questions could be used again after being disclosed.** As a result, the fourth and most important fair use factor – the effect of the use upon the potential market for or value of the copyrighted work – did not necessarily weigh in favor of the AAMC. The court remanded the case for further proceedings. *Ass'n of American Medical Colleges v. Cuomo*, 928 F.2d 519 (2d Cir. 1991).

◆ *A federal district court agreed with four educational testing agencies, including the College Entrance Examination Board, that the required disclosure of test questions under a New York law violated federal copyright law.*

New York education law requires college testing services to file copies of their test questions and statistical reports with the state education commissioner. A number of testing agencies claimed that the statute violated federal copyright law, and filed a lawsuit against the governor and other state officials. In view of the result in a similar case filed by the Association of American Medical Colleges, the parties entered into a stipulation under which the testing agencies disclosed questions for only some of the tests administered in the state and were allowed to administer a fixed number of undisclosed tests. The court then considered a motion by the agencies for temporary relief. The agencies argued that the compelled disclosure of the test questions violated federal copyright law and did not meet the fair use exception to federal copyright law. The state argued that **the public had an interest in ensuring the fairness and objectivity of standardized admission tests** and had a strong need to evaluate the scoring process. It also claimed that disclosure did not violate copyright laws because of the lack of any commercial purpose.

The court agreed with the testing agencies that the disclosure of test questions violated federal copyright law and issued a preliminary injunction. The court also found that the agencies were entitled to the presumption of irreparable injury that normally accompanies the showing of copyright infringement. However, because of the many factual issues existing in the case, the court issued an order preserving the status quo, under which only some tests administered in the state would be subject to the disclosure law pending further proceedings. *College Entrance Examination Board v. Pataki*, 889 F.Supp. 554 (N.D.N.Y. 1995).

Three of the testing agencies sought an order completely barring enforcement of the state law or alternative relief. A fourth agency submitted a statement indicating that it would comply with the order by disclosing three testing forms administered in New York during the test year and an additional form traditionally administered in the state in low-volume administrations.

The testing agencies asserted that the wording of the preliminary order would prevent the Graduate Record Examination (GRE) program from offering at least one administration in the state, and that the status quo provision of the order did not account for changing circumstances in testing from year to year. They further asserted that the preliminary order contravened **the principle in copyright infringement cases that the status quo sought to be preserved is the state of non-infringement**.

The court held that the preliminary order struck the correct balance between competing interests, including that of the students who would take the examinations. There was no need to strictly comply with the rule that the status quo to be preserved is a state of non-infringement, since the parties had agreed by stipulation to provide for limited disclosure of test forms. The court modified the preliminary order to accommodate the GRE program's phase-out of paper and pencil administrations. *College Entrance Examination Board v. Pataki*, 893 F.Supp. 152 (N.D.N.Y. 1995).

D. Immunity

◆   *A public university in Texas was entitled to immunity in a lawsuit filed by an author who asserted copyright violations.*

The author asserted that the University of Houston violated federal copyright law by publishing her book without consent and violated the Lanham Act by naming her as the selector of plays in another book without her permission. She sued the university in a federal court, which refused to dismiss the case on the basis of immunity. The Fifth Circuit held that the university had impliedly waived Eleventh Amendment immunity by contracting with the author, because Congress had imposed statutory waivers of immunity in both the Copyright and Lanham Acts.

The U.S. Supreme Court remanded the case for reconsideration under *Seminole Tribe of Florida v. Florida*, 517 U.S. 44 (1996), which held that abrogation of a state's Eleventh Amendment immunity requires an expression of Congressional intent and a constitutionally valid exercise of power. On remand to the Fifth Circuit, the court held that under *Seminole Tribe*, a state's waiver of immunity cannot be implied simply because the state conducts business in an area subject to federal regulation. **The express provisions of the Copyright and Lanham Acts purporting to require this consent were outside the power of Congress under Article I.** The author's statutorily created right to protect her name from misappropriation under the Lanham Act was not a protected property interest. **Congress had no power to subject states to federal court lawsuits for Lanham Act violations.** The copyright claim was one for breach of contract, which could not be treated as a procedural due process violation in federal court. The claims against the university had to be dismissed. *Chavez v. Arte Publico Press*, 157 F.3d 282 (5th Cir. 1999).

Subsequently, the Supreme Court decided *Florida Prepaid Postsecondary Educ. Expense Board v. College Savings Bank*, 527 U.S. 627, 119 S.Ct. 2199, 144 L.Ed.2d 575 (1999) and *College Savings Bank v. Florida Prepaid Postsecondary Educ. Expense Board*, 527 U.S. 666, 119 S.Ct. 2219, 144 L.Ed.2d 605 (1999). The Fifth Circuit again considered the case and held that the Copyright Remedy Clarification Act was not a valid exercise of legislative authority as applied to the states. As a result, the university was entitled to be dismissed from the suit under the Eleventh Amendment. *Chavez v. Arte Publico Press*, 204 F.3d 601 (5th Cir. 2000).

E. Due Process Issues

◆   *A tenured University of Michigan professor had an insufficient property interest in an idea to gain any protection of it as his intellectual property.*

In 1995, the professor wrote drafts for a design center in the university's Department of Aerospace Engineering. The drafts were revised by another professor and turned into an abstract. The first draft proposal listed two co-authors, and the second listed three others. The proposal identified a design center with resident visitors of different specialties, with a focus on Russian designers. The university obtained funding for the center and built it in 1999. The professor sued the university in the state court system asserting violation of his due process and intellectual property rights. The court held for the university, and he appealed. On appeal, the Court of Appeals of Michigan held the university had no fiduciary duty to the professor. A fiduciary relationship exists only "when there is confidence reposed on one side and a resulting superiority and influence on the other." The court disagreed with the professor's claim to a property interest in the design center. He prepared drafts for the center in 1995 with various others. The proposal indicated there were already programs for visiting designers. The university had previously hired retired designers to teach courses. **The court held the protection of an idea under a property theory "requires that the idea possess property-like traits."**

Moreover, **"ideas themselves are not subject to individual ownership or control. They do not rise to the level of property and are not in themselves protected by law."** The professor could not "own the idea" of a design center or a visiting designer program that already existed in other forms. The professor asserted the university's rules and policies made him "automatically the principal investigator" of the proposal. The court disagreed, finding no such rule or policy "promising or even hinting at how those benefits accrued to him." **In order to have a constitutionally protected interest, a person must have more than an abstract need or desire for it. There must be a legitimate claim of entitlement.** A party's unilateral expectation is insufficient to create a property interest protected by procedural due process. The court held that as the professor did not show any legitimate property interest in his idea, he could not allege a due process claim. *Kauffman v. Univ. of Michigan Regents*, No. 257711, 2006 WL 1084330 (Mich. Ct. App. 4/25/06). The Supreme Court of Michigan denied further review. *Kauffman v. Univ. of Michigan Regents*, 477 Mich. 911, 722 N.W.2d 823 (Mich. 2006).

II. PATENTS

A patent is a legally protected property interest that gives the owner the right to exclude others from making, using, selling, offering for sale, or importing the invention covered by the patent. Patents generally run for a period of 20 years from the effective filing date of the patent application. To be patentable, an invention must be useful, new or novel, and non-obvious.

Unlike copyright law, there is no federal patent law provision on work-for-hire. Patent ownership is instead resolved by common law. The federal Patent Act also allows parties to assign patent ownership rights. In determining who owns the patent rights to an invention, courts look at the nature of the relationship between the inventor and the employer. Where the inventor is hired to invent something, the employer retains all patent rights; and where the inventor is hired under a general contract of employment, the inventor will retain ownership rights. However, most cases fall somewhere in between these two: for example, where a university hires a professor or a graduate student to teach and do research. The ambiguity this creates has led colleges and universities to enter into pre-employment assignments of intellectual property rights that specifically lay out the rights of both parties. Sometimes this is done by written agreement – other times, by use of a faculty handbook.

With respect to patent rights, professors usually are required to assign creations and patent rights to the colleges and universities that employ them in exchange for a percentage of the royalties. The issue becomes trickier when dealing with graduate students. Some universities require graduate students to assign patent rights, while others do not.

A number of states have enacted statutes to limit the extent to which employers can claim an interest in employee inventions. However, those statutes generally provide that if the employer provides resources, or if the invention relates to the employer's business, the employer can require assignment of intellectual property rights. It is only where the employer has no involvement at all that the employee can claim full rights to an invention.

A. Ownership and Inventorship

◆ *A patent licensee could pursue claims against a competitor under the California unfair competition law and the Lanham Act, but not the Florida Deceptive and Unfair Trade Practices Act.*

Optivus Technology claimed to be the exclusive licensee of two proton beam therapy system patents. The University of Florida signed a non-binding letter of intent with Optivus regarding the proton beam therapy systems. After the letter expired, Florida considered other vendors and awarded a contract to Ion Beam Applications (IBA), which competed with Optivus in the same market. Optivus sued IBA in a federal district court for infringement of the patents. Loma Linda University Medical Center, as assignee of Optivus, became a party. Optivus added claims against IBA for unfair competition under

California and Florida law, as well as violation of the Lanham Act. IBA counterclaimed against Optivus, seeking an order declaring the proton beam patents invalid in view of a neutron therapy facility in use at the University of Washington. The California unfair competition claim was based on the theory that IBA marketed a medical device that was not approved by the U.S. Food and Drug Administration (FDA). The district court refused to consider the California unfair competition law claim. The court held for IBA on the Florida Unfair Trade Act and Lanham Act claims, as well as a claim for intentional interference. The court found both patents invalid and ruled there was no patent infringement. Optivus appealed to the U.S. Court of Appeals, Federal Circuit.

The court agreed with Optivus that the district court should have ruled on the significance of an FDA letter. The district court had thus improperly dismissed the California state law unfair competition claim. The court considered the claim under the Florida Unfair Trade Act and noted the University of Florida had selected IBA as its vendor after the expiration of the letter of intent with Optivus. **At the time IBA was selected, only a "consumer" could bring a claim under the Florida Deceptive and Unfair Trade Practices Act.** For this reason, the district court properly awarded summary judgment to IBA on Optivus' Florida law claim. **The district court had found Optivus did not show a business relationship existed after the letter of intent expired. The court of appeals found no error in this conclusion.** Any business relationship between Optivus and Florida ended with the expiration of the letter. **The court stated that to prevail on its Lanham Act claim, Optivus would have to show IBA made a false and material statement of fact that caused the University of Florida to award the contract to IBA.** The court disagreed with the district court's findings in favor of IBA regarding false statements about financing. It reversed the judgment on the Lanham Act claim for further consideration of IBA's alleged statements. Loma Linda asserted the lower court improperly found the patents invalid. It claimed modification of the University of Washington's neutron therapy facility would result in a "death ray." The court disagreed, finding the combination of prior art references by the district court had been proper. **The patent was invalid as obvious, in view of Washington's neutron therapy facility.** The patent for a safety system for a multi-room proton beam therapy facility was written with expansive, highly inclusive language. **As Loma Linda did not rebut this evidence, the judgment of patent invalidity was correct.** *Optivus Technology, Inc. v. Ion Beam Applications, S.A.*, 469 F.3d 978 (Fed. Cir. 2006).

◆   *A federal district court denied a request for a protective order to prevent a university from taking depositions in a lamb cloning patent dispute.*

A University of Massachusetts employee submitted a patent application to clone non-human animals using "nuclear transfer" with "a cycling non-quiescent donor cell." This application resulted in U.S. Patent No. 5,945,577. Advance Cell Technologies became the assignee of the 577 Patent and cloned two heifers. Three years later, an employee of Roslin Institute submitted a patent application, U.S. Patent Application No. 09/650, 194 to clone non-human animals using "nuclear transfer" with "a quiescent donor cell." From this patent, Geon Corporation and Exeter Life Sciences, as assignees of the patent, cloned a lamb. Advanced initiated interference proceedings with Geon and Exeter to determine who owned the animal cloning technology and the nuclear transfer technology. The purpose of these proceedings was to decide which patent holder was actually entitled to hold the patent and which one was interfering with the legitimate patent holder's patent. After the proceedings, the Board of Patents Appeals and Interferences found for the Institute, Geon and Exeter as to its patented method for cloning animals and for its nuclear transfer technology. The university appealed the decision to a federal district court.

The university asked to depose a named inventor and a witness who had submitted a declaration in the interference actions. The Institute, Geon and Exeter moved for a protective order to prevent the depositions from going forward. Under Fed. R. Civ. P. 26(c), protective orders are issued for good cause and to prevent annoyance, embarrassment, oppression, undue burden, or expense. **"Good cause" is established only when the one asking for the protective order can show the failure to grant a protective order would cause a clearly defined and serious injury.** Under Fed. R.Civ.P. 26(b)(1), the scope of permissible evidence includes any matter relevant to the claim or defenses of any party. The court found the Institute, Geon and Exeter did not show the depositions were not reasonably calculated to lead to the discovery of admissible evidence, or would cause clearly defined and serious injury to them. Because they failed to prove "good cause" for a protective order, the court denied their motion. *Univ. of Massachusetts v. Roslin Institute*, 437 F.Supp.2d 57 (D.D.C. 2006).

◆ *A medical school student at a private New York university did not prove he contributed to a professor's patented treatment for glaucoma.*

The university owned a patent involving the use of prostaglandins in treating glaucoma. A long-time professor at the university was the named inventor of the patent. In 1980, the professor agreed to a proposal by the student to perform a one-semester ophthalmology research elective. He directed the student to begin his project by reviewing a faculty member's papers on prostaglandins and intraocular pressure (IOP). At the time, the professor had published several papers on the effects of prostaglandins on the IOP in animals such as rabbits and owl monkeys. The student conducted experiments in the lab that showed topical application of single doses of prostaglandin reduced IOP in rhesus monkeys and cats. After the student left the university, the professor conceived the patent while studying the effects of repeated prostaglandin application on the IOP in rhesus monkeys. He applied for the patent in 1982, and it was issued in 1986. When the student found out about the patent, he sued the university and professor in a federal district court, asking to be added as a co-inventor. The trial court granted summary judgment for the university and the professor. It found the student failed to present evidence of inventorship.

On appeal, **the U.S. Court of Appeals, Federal Circuit, held the student had to show he contributed to the conception of the invention in order to be considered one of the inventors of the patent.** The court found the student did not have an understanding of the claimed invention. He also did not discover that prostaglandins have an effect on IOP, or conceive of the idea of the use of prostaglandins to reduce IOP in primates. Furthermore, the student did not collaborate with the professor in developing a glaucoma treatment. **He simply carried out an experiment done previously by the professor on different animals.** The court held the student's contribution was insufficient to support his claim of co-inventorship and affirmed the judgment. *Stern v. Trustees of Columbia Univ. in the City of New York*, 434 F.3d 1375 (Fed. Cir. 2006).

◆ *A federal district court held a Yale University chemistry professor defrauded Yale of a patent for an invention.*

The professor claimed he invented a chemical mass spectometry device and that its patent was issued to him in July 1992. However, Yale's internal patent policy gave it the right of first refusal to patent any faculty inventions. The professor sued Yale in a federal district court, alleging it violated the Connecticut Unfair Trade Practices Act. Yale counterclaimed for an accounting and assignment of the patent. It also said the professor breached his contract and committed fraud and theft. After a trial, the court held the professor did not prove his claims. There were significant issues concerning Yale's remaining allegations, and the parties were ordered to further brief the court.

Yale alleged the professor's actions amounted to embezzlement or appropriation by false pretenses, which would make him liable for larceny and theft under state law. The professor argued he acted under a good-faith claim of right to the patent and never intended to permanently deprive Yale of the patent. **The court noted it had already found the professor breached Yale's internal patent policy, to which he was contractually bound. Yale was entitled to patent the invention and receive all related royalties.** The court found the professor misrepresented the importance and commercial viability of the invention. He discouraged Yale from preparing and filing a patent application while secretly preparing an application in his own name. The professor refused to assign the patent to Yale, in breach of the internal patent policy. The court found he purposefully engaged in fraud and committed larceny and civil theft, and ordered him to assign his rights as patent holder to Yale. *Fenn v. Yale Univ.*, Nos. Civ.A. 396 CV (CFD), Civ.A. 396 CV 990 (CFD), Civ.A. 396 CV 1647 (CFD), 2005 WL 327138 (D. Conn. 2/8/05).

◆ *A pharmaceutical company had to pay $54 million in damages for fraudulently obtaining a patent based on work by university researchers.*

Two University of Colorado researchers worked under an agreement with a pharmaceutical company. They discovered certain multivitamins were not supplying proper amounts of iron to pregnant women and published an article suggesting a reformulation to increase iron absorption. The researchers sent an advance copy to the doctor they had been working with at the company. The company then obtained a patent on the reformulation of the multivitamin without notifying the university. It copied and plagiarized portions of the article in the patent application. The university foundation sued the company in a federal district court for wrongfully obtaining the patent. The court found the company liable for fraudulent nondisclosure. It noted the company would have had to pay the university for the rights to the reformulation, and calculated the royalty rates at approximately $22 million. The court held the university could recover equitable damages for unjust enrichment of $23 million. It also ordered exemplary damages in the amount of $500,000 for each inventor, based on the company's "clandestine and deceptive conduct," and "fraud, malice, and willful and wanton misconduct." *Univ. of Colorado Foundation v. American Cyanamid Co.*, 216 F.Supp.2d 1188 (D. Colo. 2002).

The U.S. Court of Appeals, Federal Circuit, rejected the company's argument that the damage award for unjust enrichment created a state-based patent law that was inconsistent with the federal statutory scheme. The court held this was not the issue in this case. The unjust enrichment claim was based on the wrongful use of research and did not interfere with the federal patent scheme. The researchers satisfied state law requirements for unjust enrichment, as it would be unjust to allow the company to retain profits acquired through misconduct. **The district court had properly awarded damages based on incremental profits that were directly attributable to the misconduct. The court upheld the district court's findings establishing inventorship.** Clear and convincing evidence indicated the researchers were the sole inventors of the patent. Substantial evidence supported the damage award, including the award of exemplary damages, and the court affirmed the judgment for the researchers and university. *Univ. of Colorado Foundation v. American Cyanamid Co.*, 342 F.3d 1298 (Fed. Cir. 2003).

◆   *A university's patent policy validly required two researchers to assign all rights to their inventions to the university.*

The University of New Mexico's patent policy stated that all inventions developed during the course of research funded by the university or employment at the university belonged to the university. The policy also required the inventors to cooperate with the university in the patent process. Two researchers of chemical compounds completed work that led the university to submit 11 different patent applications regarding two compounds. The researchers assigned their rights in the patents to the university.

Two years later, the university submitted five continuation-in-part patent applications, and the researchers did not assign their rights under these applications to the university. When the university entered into a licensing agreement with a company regarding the two compounds, a dispute arose over the ownership of the patents. A New Mexico federal court assigned a special master, who concluded that the researchers had to assign their rights to one of the compounds to the university. With respect to the second compound, the court conducted a trial and determined that the university owned those patents as well. On appeal, the Federal Circuit largely affirmed. The researchers were to be listed as inventors, but **the university's patent policy, which was incorporated into the researchers' employment contracts, clearly made the university the owner of the patents.** *Regents of the Univ. of New Mexico v. Scallen*, 321 F.3d 1111 (Fed. Cir. 2003).

◆   *The corporate sponsor of genetic research at a state university was the rightful owner of a patentable invention.*

A molecular biologist assigned all intellectual property rights arising out of his research at Washington State University (WSU) to WSU by agreeing to the terms of WSU's faculty manual. WSU had in turn assigned its intellectual property rights to a corporate sponsor under a research collaboration agreement. The biologist began research on a plant fat metabolism project, for which he also used a laboratory at Ohio State University (OSU). He discovered the FAD2 gene, one of several genes that encoded the fatty acid desaturase enzyme. The sponsor and biologist entered into an agreement recognizing him and another scientist as the inventors of the FAD2 gene and assigning his entire right, title and interest in the gene to the sponsor. The biologist further agreed to cooperate with the sponsor's patent application. He later refused to cooperate until he received a reasonable royalty. The sponsor sued the biologist in a federal district court for a declaratory judgment that it exclusively owned the FAD2 gene, and to enforce his contract duties. The biologist counterclaimed for a declaration that he was the sole owner and inventor of the FAD2 gene and requesting rescission of his assignment. The court held for the sponsor.

On appeal, the Sixth Circuit held that while the Federal Circuit has exclusive jurisdiction over federal patent law, this was a contract dispute. It held **inventorship is an issue of patent law, but ownership of a patent is not a federal patent law question. The WSU faculty manual established a legally binding contract between the biologist and WSU.** Faculty members assigned their ownership of intellectual property to WSU, which in turn assigned ownership to the sponsor under the research collaboration agreement. The consequence of these two agreements was that all rights to the FAD2 patent were transferred to WSU, and then to the sponsor. OSU had waived any rights to the FAD2 patent. Even if it did not, **the faculty manual obligated the transfer of the biologist's intellectual property rights to WSU.** Summary judgment for the sponsor was affirmed. *E.I. Du Pont de Nemours & Co. v. Okuley*, 344 F.3d 578 (6th Cir. 2003).

◆   *A West Virginia university could not compel a student to assign second-generation patents to it under the university's patent policy.*

The student created a "half-wave bifilar contrawound toroidal helical antenna." He asked the university to submit patent applications for the antenna, and it did so. The student changed his mind and received a patent for the same invention. He then filed another application to provoke an interference with the university's application for second-generation patents. The university sued the student in a federal district court for breaching his duty to assign the patent as required by a university policy, and the student counterclaimed for breach of an implied contract. The district court issued an order for the university.

On appeal, the Federal Circuit held the student in breach of his obligation to assign the applications. He refused to sign the university's assignment forms and drafted new ones that only conveyed the rights to patent applications listed in the district court order. The court granted the university's motion to enforce the order and denied the student's motion for relief. The case reached the Federal Circuit again. The university argued the student's assignments failed to include three second-generation patents. **The court held the original assignment covered only the exact invention, its "immediate lineal descendants" and similar categories. The second-generation patents were excluded from these categories,** and the professor was not obligated to assign them to the university. **The university could not use its patent policy to compel assignment of the**

second-generation patents. As the ownership of these patents had not been decided yet, the case was reversed and remanded. *Univ. of West Virginia v. VanVoorhies,* 342 F.3d 1290 (Fed. Cir. 2003).

♦ *A university could not employ the "experimental use" defense in a patent infringement action filed against it by a former professor.*

Duke University hired a research professor from Stanford who had obtained two patents for devices/technology used in his lab: a "microwave electron gun" and a "free-electron laser oscillator." The professor worked as the director of Duke's laser research lab and, along with the university, contracted with another school to build a "microwave gun test stand" under a government contract awarded to the other school. After a disagreement over management of the lab and use of lab equipment, the professor was removed as director and eventually resigned from the university. He then sued Duke for patent infringement resulting from the continued use of equipment that incorporated his patented technology. A federal district court dismissed the case, finding Duke was entitled to the "experimental use" defense. The Federal Circuit reversed in part, noting that the lower court had improperly drawn a distinction between a research grant and a government contract for services. The court noted that **the experimental use defense should be applied in limited circumstances where use was "for amusement, to satisfy idle curiosity, or for strictly philosophical inquiry."** It did not matter that Duke was a nonprofit entity. The court remanded the case for an evaluation of the grant and a determination of which uses of the electron gun fell within the scope of the grant. *Madey v. Duke Univ.,* 307 F.3d 1351 (Fed. Cir. 2002).

♦ *A university showed that a company infringed its patent by surreptitiously disassembling a prototype device and stealing the design.*

Kent State University, through two subsidiaries, developed a "polymer-free liquid crystal display device" commonly used in digital watches and notebook computer screens. The university later learned that a company was using a similar polymer-free liquid crystal display device and sued to enforce its patent. The company responded by seeking a declaratory judgment that the university's patent was invalid. After a company engineer testified that he and others surreptitiously disassembled a prototype, photographed its component parts and then reassembled the device, a jury found that the company had infringed on the university's valid patent and awarded the university $1.5 million in damages.

A federal court upheld jury findings that **the company had infringed the university's patent**, noting that the patent was not "invalid for indefiniteness." The terms used in the patent application were not indefinite when construed in the context of the entire patent document. Also, even though the jury found that the company had committed both **literal infringement** (misappropriation of all essential elements in the patent) and **infringement under the doctrine of equivalents** (infringement that involves a device performing the same function as the patented device in substantially the same way to achieve the same result), the court found no inconsistency and simply reformed the verdict to show a finding of literal infringement. The court did, however, lower the damage award to $175,000 based on a reasonable royalty determination at the time the infringement occurred. *Advanced Display Systems, Inc. v. Kent State Univ.*, No. 3-96-CV-1480-BD, 2002 WL 1489555 (N.D. Tex. 2002).

B. Validity of Patents

When competing applicants for a patent on the same invention cannot settle their differences privately, either party may seek to have the matter resolved by the U.S. Patent and Trademark Office via a procedure known as a patent interference proceeding. The purpose of these proceedings is to determine priority of invention between competing applicants. Sometimes, an applicant can ask that an interference proceeding be conducted even after the patent it seeks has been granted to another applicant.

◆ *A patent claimed by a New York university was invalid because it did not comply with the written description requirement of federal patent law.*

Researchers at the University of Rochester developed a method for identifying a prostaglandin synthesis inhibitor. The university received two U.S. patents, one of which was based on a method that inhibited PGHS-2 prostaglandins. After four pharmaceutical manufacturers began using the method, the university filed a federal district court action against them for patent infringement. The court held the patent did not meet statutory written description requirements and merely described a theory, not an invention. The patent did not satisfy statutory enablement grounds, as it did not allow those skilled in the art to make and use the invention without undue experimentation.

The university appealed to the Federal Circuit. It held **the patent failed the written description requirement, as its description was "vague." It did not disclose the structure or physical properties of any compounds.** While it was not necessary for the university to describe the exact chemical compound of an inhibitor, its description of a non-steroidal compound that inhibits the activity of the PGHS-2 gene product was insufficient for statutory purposes. **It would not provide a researcher, skilled in this area, with sufficient information to understand what it claimed to accomplish and how to perform the method.** The court affirmed the judgment for the manufacturers. *Univ. of Rochester v. G.D. Searle & Co.*, 358 F.3d 916 (Fed. Cir. 2004).

◆ *Inventions by a pharmaceutical concern and a university were separately patentable as their molecules had different chemical structures.*

Eli Lilly and Co. filed a reissue application surrendering a patent covering deoxyribonucleic acid (cDNA), a sequence code for human protein C. At the same time, Lilly filed a patent interference claim against the University of Washington concerning a university-held patent that also related to the sequence of human protein C. The university denied any interference, asserting the cDNA molecules had different chemical sequences. The Board of Patent Appeals and Interferences agreed, finding Lilly's invention was not the same as the university's. Lilly was dissatisfied with the board's ruling and moved to define the interfering subject matter by proposing two alternative constructions of the cDNA: a narrow construction and a broad construction. The board applied a two-part test and rejected Lilly's contentions. Regardless of whether the claim was construed as a genus or a species, Lilly's reissue application and the university's claim did not define the "same patentable invention." There was no interference-in-fact, and the matter was dismissed. Lilly appealed to the Federal Circuit, which explained that under 37 C.F.R. § 1.601(n), the "'same patentable invention' means that the one invention of one party anticipates or renders obvious the other party's invention." Since the claimed interference involved genus/species inventions, it was unclear whether the genus claim or the species claim was invented first.

The court found it possible that both a genus claim and a species claim could be separate, patentable inventions. The director resolved the issue by presuming that both Lilly's invention and the university's invention were "prior art." This meant that the university's invention was assumed to be prior art of Lilly's invention and vice versa. Although the court acknowledged Lilly's assertion that a one-way test should be applied, it was within the director's discretion not to accept it. The court upheld the use of the two-way test and affirmed the board's decision. *Eli Lilly & Co. v. Board of Regents of Univ. of Washington*, 334 F.3d 1264 (Fed. Cir. 2003).

◆   *A university and its licensee could not patent a discovery about the best time to harvest and eat certain vegetables.*

Johns Hopkins University owned three patents based in part on the discovery of the beneficial effects of harvesting and eating broccoli and cauliflower at the two-leaf stage, when they contain the highest levels of glucosinates and Phase 2 enzymes, which reduce the risk of developing cancer. The patents also contained a method for preparing the sprouts in order to increase their protective properties. The university licensed the patents to a company, then joined the company in a lawsuit against competitors for violating the patents. The defendants asserted that the portions of the patents that referred to the eating and growing of sprouts should be invalidated by prior art. A Maryland federal court ruled in favor of the defendants. On appeal, the Federal Circuit Court of Appeals noted that under 35 U.S.C. § 101, a patent can be obtained for inventing or discovering any new composition of matter or any new improvement thereof.

The university and its licensee did not create a new kind of sprout or develop a new growing method. They merely discovered that the vegetables contained glucosinates and Phase 2 enzymes (anti-cancer agents). Those elements were inherent in the sprouts. Since prior art unquestionably included growing, harvesting and eating the sprouts, the patents were invalidated to the extent they tried to protect that activity. The judgment was affirmed. *Brassica Protection Products, LLC v. Sunrise Farms*, 301 F.3d 1343 (Fed. Cir. 2002).

◆   *Two researchers lost their right to continuing royalties when the patent on minoxidil expired.*

Two Colorado university researchers discovered that minoxidil stimulates hair growth. At approximately the same time, a drug company discovered the same thing. Because of competing patent claims, the Patent & Trademark Office held an interference proceeding, which resulted in the parties entering into an "interference settlement agreement." The agreement granted the researchers a minimum of $100,000 a year for the first six years after minoxidil was available commercially. After six years, with the researchers having received more than $26 million in royalties, the drug company's patent expired, and the royalty payments ceased. The researchers sued, asserting that they were entitled to three more years of royalty payments, but a federal court ruled against them. The Tenth Circuit Court of Appeals affirmed. **Even if the settlement agreement was ambiguous, the royalty payments terminated with the expiration of the patent.** The federal Hatch-Waxman Act did not extend the term of the patent for three more years. It merely permitted the Food and Drug Administration "to grant a drug manufacturer an extended 'exclusivity' period." Since the act was enacted four months after the parties signed their agreement, the parties could not have intended for its provisions to apply. *Grant v. Pharmacia & Upjohn Co.*, 314 F.3d 488 (10th Cir. 2002).

C. Defenses

The Eleventh Amendment to the U.S. Constitution generally bars claims against state defendants, including state colleges and universities. States can waive immunity from suit. In this case, a federal appeals court held that a state university could not claim Eleventh Amendment immunity in a patent dispute, because it chose to invoke the jurisdiction of the federal courts.

◆   *The Eleventh Amendment bars federal court lawsuits by private parties against states under the Patent Remedy Act and the Lanham Act.*

In 1999, the Supreme Court decided two cases involving the same parties and the same dispute. In *Florida Prepaid Postsecondary Educ. Expense Bd. v. College Savings Bank*, 527 U.S. 627, 119 S.Ct. 2199, 144 L.Ed.2d 575, **the Court held that Congress' abrogation, under the Patent Remedy Act, of states' sovereign immunity from patent infringement suits was not constitutional**. Building on its earlier decision in *Seminole Tribe of Florida v. Florida*, 517 U.S. 44, 116 S.Ct. 1114, 134 L.Ed.2d 252 (1996), where it held that Congress does not have the power to abrogate a state's sovereign immunity under Article I of the Constitution, the Court found that Congress had overstepped its bounds. Although patents can be considered property within the meaning of the Due Process Clause, there was no indication here that the Patent Remedy Act had been enacted under the authority of the Fourteenth Amendment. Rather, the legislation was authorized by Article I and thus improperly removed states' sovereign immunity.

The case arose after College Savings Bank, which owned and marketed a patented investment methodology designed to finance the costs of college education, discovered that the state of Florida was selling a similar product. The bank brought separate actions against the state for patent infringement and false advertising under the Lanham Act. In the patent infringement action, the Court determined that Florida could not be sued without its consent where it had merely engaged in interstate commerce. In the false advertising action, the Court held that **the Trademark Remedy Clarification Act also did not validly abrogate states' Eleventh Amendment immunity from a suit**

brought under the Lanham Act. Although Congress may remove a state's sovereign immunity under Section 5 of the Fourteenth Amendment, there must be a property interest involved for it to do so. However, there was no property interest at stake in a false advertising suit under the Lanham Act. Further, the state of Florida had not constructively waived its immunity by engaging in interstate commerce. *College Savings Bank v. Florida Prepaid Postsecondary Educ. Expense Board,* 527 U.S. 666, 119 S.Ct. 2219, 144 L.Ed.2d 605 (1999).

◆ *A state university that voluntarily submits itself to the jurisdiction of the federal court system waives its Eleventh Amendment immunity with respect to the claims involved.*

The University of Missouri filed an application for a patent of an unspecified invention. While the application was pending, a company filed an application to patent the same invention. The company's application proceeded more quickly, and it was granted while the university's remained pending. The university responded by instituting an interference proceeding. After a six-year interference proceeding, the U.S. Patent and Trademark Office held the company was not entitled to the patent. The university was awarded priority and the office held it was entitled to the patent. The company appealed to a federal district court. The university moved for dismissal, arguing it was immune from suit in the federal courts under the Eleventh Amendment.

The district court agreed with the university, and the company appealed. The U.S. Court of Appeals, Federal Circuit, explained that a state does not waive its Eleventh Amendment immunity merely by participating in the federal patent system. In this case, however, the university asked the U.S. Patent and Trademark Office to conduct litigation-type activity, and it participated in that activity without claiming immunity. **When a state voluntarily submits itself to the jurisdiction of the federal court system, it waives its state immunity with respect to the claims raised.** In this case, an appeal to federal court was built into the U.S. Patent and Trademark Office proceeding by statute. Therefore, by instituting and participating in the proceeding, the university subjected itself to federal court jurisdiction. The appeals court reversed the decision and remanded the case for further proceedings. *Vas-Cath, Inc. v. Curators of the Univ. of Missouri,* 473 F.3d 1376 (Fed. Cir. 2007).

III. TRADEMARKS

A trademark, defined at 15 U.S.C. § 1127, is any word, name, symbol or device, or any combination thereof used to identify and distinguish goods, including a unique product, from those manufactured or sold by others, and to indicate the source of the goods, even if the source is unknown. Service marks are identical to trademarks in all respects except that they are intended to indicate the origin of services, rather than goods. Trade dress is defined as the total image of a product, and includes features such as size, shape, color, color combinations, texture, graphics or sales techniques. Although trademark issues arise in higher education, they occur much less frequently than copyright and patent issues.

◆   *Section 43(a) of the Lanham Act, 15 U.S.C. § 1125(a), creates a federal cause of action for unfair competition in interstate commercial activities. It forbids unfair trade practices involving infringement of trade dress, service marks or trademarks, even in the absence of federal trademark registration. See, for instance, Two Pesos, Inc. v. Taco Cabana, Inc., 505 U.S. 763 (1992). Under Section 43(a), civil liability exists in cases where a person "on or in connection with any goods or services, ... uses in commerce any word, term, name, symbol, or device, or any combination thereof, or any false designation of origin, false or misleading description of fact, or false or misleading representation of fact, which—*

> *(A) is likely to cause confusion, or to cause mistake, or to deceive as to the affiliation, connection, or association of such person with another person, or as to the origin, sponsorship, or approval of his or her goods, services, or commercial activities by another person, or (B) in commercial advertising or promotion, misrepresents the nature, characteristics, qualities, or geographic origin of his or her or another person's goods, services, or commercial activities..."*

According to one court, the "touchstone test" for a violation of Section 43(a) is the likelihood of confusion resulting from the defendant's adoption of a trade dress similar to the plaintiff's. See Original Appalachian Artworks, Inc. v. Toy Loft, Inc., 684 F.2d 821 (11th Cir. 1982).

◆   *Texas Tech University won a $3.1 million judgment against a retailer who continued to sell unlicensed university merchandise after the termination of a longstanding contract between the parties.*

The retailer was one of 450 university licensees that sold a total of $8 million in licensed products annually. He failed to account for the university's share of royalties, and the license was terminated in 2003. However, the retailer continued selling unlicensed merchandise through 2005, when Texas Tech sued him in a federal district court for trademark infringement, unfair competition, breach of contract, trademark dilution and injury to business reputation.

The court first sought to determine if the trademarks qualified for protection. **The relevant factors for the court to consider were functionality, distinctiveness and secondary meanings of a mark. If the use of a mark was likely to create confusion in the marketplace, the owner qualified for protection.** The court held Texas Tech's marks were protectable under trademark law because they were distinctive and not functional. The color scheme of Texas Tech apparel and merchandise identified and distinguished it. The scheme was associated with the university since the 1920s. The products were easily recognized, and they signalled to the public that they were licensed by Texas Tech. The commercial impression created by the unlicensed products was identical to the impression created by the university's products. The strength of the marks was undeniable, and they deserved broad protection. In addition, the retailer sold licensed products right alongside unlicensed ones. Consumers were likely to be confused by the sales of similar goods at the same stores. Each of the factors regarding the potential confusion for consumers presented by the retailer's use of the trademarks weighed in favor of the university. Texas Tech was also entitled to judgment on the unfair competition claims, for the same reasons that supported the trademark infringement claims. **Unfair competition occurs when an individual passes off the products of another by virtue of their substantial similarity.** The retailer had sold unlicensed products with identical marks since the license was revoked in 2003. The retailer clearly breached his contract with Texas Tech by continuing to sell licensed products after the contract was terminated. He further breached the contract by trying to register the phrases "Wreck 'em Tech" and "Raiderland" with the U.S. Patent and Trademark Office. **The Lanham Act permits the owner of a violated trademark to recover all the infringer's profits plus any damages and costs.** Texas Tech showed the retailer's profits during 2004–05 totalled more than $2.8 million. The university was entitled to the full amount of these profits as well as the royalties due under the contract. The university was awarded summary judgment on its trademark dilution and breach of contract claims. The court awarded Texas Tech damages of more than $3.1 million. *Texas Tech Univ. v. Spiegelberg*, 461 F.Supp.2d 510 (N.D. Tex. 2006).

◆   *The Nebraska Supreme Court denied an apparel store owner's claim for damages and injunctive relief against the University of Nebraska for wrongful use of a registered trade name.*

In late 1995, the Nebraska Athletic Department created an Authentic Shop, which would sell to the public apparel and equipment identical to that used by its teams and staff. The university began this process by test-marketing the idea to gather purchasing statistics for a new store. That same year, the university's board of regents filed an application with the Nebraska secretary of state to register the trade name "Husker Authentics" for the purpose of selling licensed goods. However, because the university did not file the requisite proof of publication of the name with the secretary and the county clerk as required by law, the registration was canceled without notice to the university. Taking all this in was Brent White, who owned and operated two businesses, Nebraska Spirit and Team Spirit Industries. White was well aware of the university's plans to open a store in 1997, which would, he believed, be a direct competitor with his stores. The day White learned that the university's registration of the trade name had been canceled because of improper publication, he filed his own application for registration of the trade name Husker Authentics. The Collegiate Licensing Company (CLC), the university's exclusive licensing agent, then got involved in the dispute. White had the CLC's approval to produce and manufacture the university's indicia from 1995 to 1998. The CLC sent White a letter claiming he was in violation of his license agreement and that failure to transfer his registration to the university within 15 days would result in immediate termination of his licensing agreement. White then canceled his agreement with CLC. Ignoring White's preemptive strike, the university opened a store called Husker Authentic on Aug. 27, 1997. Seven days later, White filed a petition requesting that the school be enjoined from using the disputed trade name. Later that month, White added a damages claim.

The university argued, among other things, that there had been a violation of common-law and statutory trade name and trademark rights. A state district court considered the arguments and found for the university, concluding that White's registration had been improperly granted because he had not actually used the trade name prior to registration. White appealed. The Nebraska Supreme Court found the district court's decision to be correct, but on different grounds, citing the work the university had done in test-marketing the concept. It further concluded that this afforded the school the common-law right to the trademark and any subsequent registration was therefore invalid. **Because the university owned the common-law right to "Husker Authentics," White could not properly register the disputed trademark.** The lower court's cancellation of White's registration was upheld. *White v. Board of Regents of the Univ. of Nebraska*, 260 Neb. 26, 614 N.W.2d 330 (Neb. 2000).

◆   *The practice of registering a domain name that is a common misspelling of someone else's domain name was found to violate the Anticybersquatting Consumer Protection Act in the following case.*

The Third Circuit concluded "Typosquatting" – the registration of Internet domain names that are misspellings of trademarks or service marks belonging to others – violates the Anticybersquatting Consumer Protection Act (ACPA). Joseph C. Shields operates the Web site www.joecartoon.com, which receives more than 700,000 hits per month. Additionally, products bearing Shields' work have been sold nationally in gift shops and online. On an issue of first impression, the Third Circuit ruled that John Zuccarini violated the ACPA by registering several variations on Shields' domain name, including joescartoon.com, joecarton.com, joescartons.com, joescartoons.com and cartoonjoe.com. "A reasonable interpretation of conduct covered by the phrase 'confusingly similar' is the intentional registration of domain names that are misspellings of distinctive or famous names, causing an Internet user who makes a slight spelling or typing error to reach an unintended site," the appeals court wrote. The circuit court characterized Zuccarini's conduct as an example of conduct the ACPA was developed to address. *Shields v. Zuccarini*, 254 F.3d 476 (3d Cir. 2001).

◆   *Villanova University was granted a preliminary injunction against its athletic booster club barring the organization from using various trademarks associated with its sports teams, "The Wildcats."*

In 1995, the Blue White Club (previously the Wildcat Club) and Villanova executed an agreement that formally affiliated the two entities, detailed their specific roles and outlined the organization's use of Villanova's sports trademarks. The agreement expired in 1996. After failing to reach a new agreement, the club's members voted to become an independent entity, and the university officially terminated the affiliation agreement. It told the organization that it was no longer authorized to solicit funds for the university, its athletic programs or athletic scholarships. On May 23, 2000, **the university notified the club's legal counsel that the club must cease and desist all use of the University's names and marks.** Since the termination of the parties' affiliation, the club changed its mission to raising funds for non-athletic scholarships. It continued to solicit funds and to use the designations "Wildcat

Club," "Villanova Alumni Educational Foundation," "Villanova Alumni," "Villanova," and "Villanova Wildcats," as well as the image of a wildcat.

Villanova then sued the Blue White Club, alleging that since the university had disassociated itself from the club, the club engaged in "service mark infringement, service mark dilution, tortious interference with prospective contractual relations and breach of contract." The school also filed a motion for a preliminary injunction, requesting that the booster club cease use of the trademark words or any other name or mark "confusingly similar thereto." The Blue White Club maintained that it was free to use the designations. The club contended that the suit was merely an attempt to divert its significant credit card royalty income to the university. Villanova claimed that it sued only because the club ignored its repeated requests to stop using its trademarks.

The club filed a countersuit against Villanova, seeking a court order giving the club the right to use the Wildcat designations without university approval. In addition, it sought more than $1.2 million in endowment funds that it claimed to have raised for the university. The Blue White Club alleged that after its repeated refusals to submit itself to the university's jurisdiction, Villanova's president, the former university athletic director, and the former vice president for development conspired to tortiously interfere with the club's fund-raising activities to cause it to go out of business. **The court granted a preliminary injunction to Villanova, barring the club from using the "Villanova" and "Wildcat" designations.** The university and club were competing with each other in their fund-raising efforts, and the club's use of university designations could easily confuse outside parties. *Villanova Univ. v. Villanova Alumni Educ. Foundation, Inc.*, 123 F.Supp.2d 293 (E.D. Pa. 2000).

CHAPTER NINE

School Liability

I. NEGLIGENCE

Negligence refers to acts or omissions demonstrating a failure to use reasonable or ordinary care. There must be a legal duty in order to impose liability on a person or an institution. The existence of a legal duty is determined by the foreseeability of the risk of harm that leads to an injury.

If an injury is a foreseeable result of negligent or intentional conduct, courts impose a legal duty upon the actor, and liability may follow. A pattern of negligence by schools and colleges that shows a conscious disregard for safety may be deemed "willful misconduct," a form of intentional conduct discussed in Section II of this chapter.

A. Duty of Care

Most personal injury lawsuits brought against colleges and universities assert negligence, which has four general components: 1) a duty on the part of the school or school officials to protect others from unreasonable risk of harm, 2) failure to exercise the duty of care appropriate to the risk involved, 3) an injury or loss caused by such failure, and 4) damages.

◆   *The Court of Appeals of Ohio rejected a student's claim that a university was liable for failing to protect her from being attacked and raped on campus.*

The student was attacked and raped by a stranger at 9:00 a.m., when she was studying in a university lecture hall. She sued the university in a state court for negligence. The court held for the university, and the student appealed to the Court of Appeals of Ohio. The court of appeals held that to find the university negligent, she had to prove it was reasonably foreseeable she would be raped in a classroom on a weekday morning when final exams were going to be given. It looked to the totality of circumstances to determine if the university should be held liable. The evidence suggested that one rape took place on campus in a restroom more than a year earlier. The earlier rape, the court concluded, was not enough to give the university reason to know the student would likely be raped in a classroom while she studied at 9:00 a.m. **Because the university could not have reasonably foreseen what happened, it could not be liable for breaching a duty of care to the student.** The court affirmed the judgment. *Kleisch v. Cleveland State Univ.*, No. 05AP-289, 2006 WL 701047 (Ohio Ct. App. 3/21/06).

◆   *An Ohio university was not liable for the rape of a student that took place in a university dormitory because the rape was not foreseeable.*

The student lived in a co-ed dorm with separate communal bathrooms for male and female students. She was raped while she was taking a shower in a dorm bathroom. Her attacker was never caught. The student sued the university in a state court for negligence, asserting it breached a duty of care by failing to install locks on the bathroom or shower doors. The court held for the university, but the Court of Appeals of Ohio reversed the judgment. It found the trial court had improperly admitted testimony by an expert witness. When the case was retried, the trial court held the university liable for negligence and awarded the student $100,000 for her injuries, pain and suffering. The university brought another appeal to the Court of Appeals of Ohio. According to the university, it did not owe the student a duty to protect her from rape by an unknown intruder. It claimed it was not liable because the attack was unforeseeable.

The court noted that while the university had a duty to warn or protect its students from known criminal conduct of third persons, it was not an insurer of student safety. If the attack was not foreseeable, the university was not liable for negligence. To determine whether an incident was foreseeable, Ohio courts apply the "totality of circumstances test" described in *Kleisch v. Cleveland State Univ.*, above. **This test considers prior similar incidents, the propensity for criminal activity to occur on or near the location, and the character of the business.** In this case, the trial court had found evidence that the university knew criminal activities occurred on campus, in classrooms, and in dorms, presenting a risk of harm to female students in a co-ed dorm. The court of appeals rejected these findings, as **the evidence was not specific enough to show the university could have foreseen this attack. The university did not breach its duty of care to the student,** and the court reversed the judgment. *Shivers v. Univ. of Cincinnati*, No. 06AP-209, 2006 WL 3008478 (Ohio Ct. App. 10/24/06).

◆   *The Supreme Court of Louisiana held a student's suicide note could not be admitted as evidence to support a negligence claim against a university.*

The student committed suicide at her parents' home by hanging herself. According to the parents, the university failed to properly supervise fraternal organizations on campus, and fraternity members sexually assaulted and raped her. The parents sued a fraternity, the university, and others in a state court, alleging their negligence caused the student to kill herself. She had written a suicide note that said "[a]ll I wanted was to forget about what happened & all it brought me was debt." The university and the fraternity challenged the parents' right to have the suicide note admitted into evidence. The court allowed most of the letter into evidence. The rest of the note was inadmissable because it was not a "dying declaration," which is an exception to the evidence rule on hearsay. The case reached the Supreme Court of Louisiana.

The court explained that hearsay statements are unreliable when admitted through someone other than the person who actually said them. Dying declarations are exempt from the hearsay rule because the likelihood that people will lie at the time of death is highly improbable. To be admitted into evidence, a dying declaration must address impending death, when a person realizes he or she is going to die immediately. The control of the student over her fate distinguished the suicide note from a true dying declaration. A suicide note is planned and in anticipation of death. **The court held the parents failed to show a connection between the rape and the suicide. The student killed herself months after the rape.** The supreme court held the lower court erred in allowing the note to be admitted as a dying declaration into evidence. It reversed the judgment and sent the case back to the district court to determine if the fraternity or the university should be held negligent. *Garza v. Delta Tau Delta Fraternity National*, 948 So.2d 84 (La. 2006).

◆   *The Court of Appeals of Ohio held in favor of a university that faced a student's claim of negligence.*

A student was injured when he tripped over a wire traffic cable in a school parking lot. He sued the university in a state court for negligence. According to the student, he did not see the cable until after he fell. He claimed the university was negligent in failing to discover, correct and/or repair the hazardous condition and in failing to warn the public of it. The university moved for pretrial judgment, asserting the cable was "open and obvious" had the student merely looked in front of him. The trial court granted the motion.

The student appealed to the Court of Appeals of Ohio, where he argued that a jury should determine whether an unmarked steel cable across a vehicular and pedestrian thoroughfare was open and obvious when encountered at night and with minimal lighting. **Ohio courts have held that open and obvious dangers serve as their own warning. Such dangers are not hidden or concealed from view.** The court emphasized that the dangerous condition did not actually have to be observed by the student for it to be "open and obvious." What matters is that it is observable. The court held that **darkness is always a warning of danger**, and it affirmed the judgment. *Springer v. Univ. of Dayton*, No. 21358, 2006 WL 1717906 (Ohio Ct. App. 6/23/06).

◆   *The Supreme Court of Utah held a university was not liable for injuries to a student who fell on an icy sidewalk during a class field trip.*

As part of an earth sciences curriculum, the student attended a field trip to examine fault lines in Salt Lake County. An instructor told students to walk on icy and snowy sidewalks through a condominium complex. The student fell and was injured when a classmate slipped and grabbed him for support. The student sued the university in a state court for negligence. The case reached the Supreme Court of Utah, which reviewed whether the university had a special relationship with the student that created a legal duty of care.

The court held a special relationship can be created between an instructor and a student in higher education settings, because a college student will at times defer to an instructor's superior knowledge, skill, and experience. In this case, the instructor's directive that students cross the condominium sidewalk was not a command the student should have felt he had to obey. The court found it was unreasonable to believe the student would think his academic success could be affected if he refused to take a dangerous route so he could view fault lines. **The instructor did not exert the type of control in an academic setting required to create a special relationship.** As no special relationship existed, the court held the university had no legal duty to protect the student, and could not be held liable for his injuries. *Webb v. Univ. of Utah*, 125 P.3d 906 (Utah 2005).

◆   *A Minnesota university was not liable for injuries to a cheerleader who injured her spine while participating in a pyramid stunt during a practice.*

The cheerleader fell and suffered a cervical spine fracture when the squad tried to perform a pyramid stunt. She later admitted she knew the stunt was risky, but felt pressured to attempt it. The cheerleader sued the university for negligence in a state court. The court found the university had no duty to protect her and held for the university. The cheerleader appealed to the Court of Appeals of Minnesota. **The court held that to prevail on her negligence claim, the cheerleader had to establish first that the university owed her a duty of care. A university is not required to guarantee student safety.**

The court found that courts in Utah, Indiana and Louisiana have found no special relationship exists between a university and a student-athlete. While the university handled some administrative tasks for cheerleading programs, it exerted minimal control over cheerleaders. The university did not provide a coach to direct practices or otherwise impose rules on participants. The court noted the university did not profit from cheerleading programs. The university was not in a position to protect the student and could not have been expected to do so. Nothing suggested the cheerleader was vulnerable. Because there was no special relationship in this case, the university did not owe her a duty of care, and the court affirmed the judgment. *Vistad v. Board of Regents of Univ. of Minnesota*, No. A04-2161, 2005 WL 1514633 (Minn. Ct. App. 6/28/05).

◆   *The Superior Court of Delaware held a university was not liable for injuries sustained by a student who was attacked off campus.*

The university rented rooms from a local inn to temporarily house students because it ran out of dorm rooms. Students were expected to move back on campus as soon as room became available. The student was attacked and shot by an ex-boyfriend of one of his friends. He never contacted the university's security office or other officials to let them know about the incident.

The student sued the university in a Delaware superior court, alleging the university negligently failed to protect students who lived at the inn. **The court held the university had a duty to safeguard only against attacks that were foreseeable.** The university could only have foreseen the attack if it knew or had reason to know the attack was likely to occur. The inn had not reported any criminal incidents over the past three years. The court noted the attack by the ex-boyfriend was not generally the type deterred by security patrols, and could have taken place anywhere and at any time. **The court found the university could not be held liable for the attack because it was unforeseeable.** It awarded summary judgment to the university. *Rogers v. Delaware State Univ.*, No. Civ. A. 03C-03-218-PLA, 2005 WL 2462271 (Del. Super. Ct. 10/05/05).

◆ *A Delaware university was not negligent when its security officers responded to a student's 911 call within two minutes.*

The student heard someone outside the door of her dormitory room about 5:00 a.m. She called campus security, but by the time the security office picked up the call, she had hung up. The student was afraid the person would get in, so she jumped out her window, injuring herself. She crawled back into the building and hid in a men's room on the first floor. A university security officer arrived at the dorm room less than two minutes after the call was received.

When security arrived at the room, no one answered and there were no signs of an attempted break-in. Officers searched the grounds nearby. About an hour later, the student emerged from the men's room and the university quickly transported her to a hospital. The student sued the university in a Delaware trial court, alleging the school security personnel were negligent by failing to promptly respond to her 911 call. **The court held that to prevail on her claim of negligence, the student had to show the university owed her a duty of care and that it breached the duty.** While the university owed a duty to the student to protect her in her dorm, she failed to present any evidence of a breach of that duty. Evidence indicated university personnel acted professionally and effectively in responding to the incident. The court granted the university pre-trial judgment. *Pochvatilla v. Univ. of Delaware*, No. Civ.A. 03C-11-015 SCD, 2005 WL 434495 (Del. Super. Ct. 2/03/05).

◆ *A Massachusetts university was not liable for the death of a student at a campus health center.*

The health center was staffed by a registered nurse on Saturdays under a university protocol. Nurses were directed to make an initial assessment and consult an off-site, on-call doctor if needed. The student came to the health center on a Saturday with a dry cough, nausea, dizziness, upper abdominal discomfort, lower back pain, and general malaise. The nurse did not consult a doctor, concluding the student had influenza. She released the student to her dorm room and told her to follow up with the health center if her symptoms persisted. The student instead went home to New Jersey, where she died a week later of acute anemia triggered by acute myelogenous leukemia.

The student's estate sued the university for negligence in a Massachusetts trial court. The parents alleged the university negligently staffed the health center on weekends with inexperienced and untrained personnel who were allowed to practice beyond the scope of their professional licenses. A jury found the university was negligent and was liable for the student's death. The university appealed to the Appeals Court of Massachusetts. **The court said expert testimony was required to find the university negligent. Determinations about whether the center was adequately staffed on weekends required medical judgment beyond what a lay person knew.** The trial court allowed expert evidence that the nurse had deviated from the applicable standard of care. While the evidence was sufficient to find the nurse negligent, it was irrelevant concerning the university's negligence. Since the parents offered no evidence to prove the university was negligent, the court found the verdict was unsupported and reversed the judgment. *Goldberg v. Northeastern Univ.*, 805 N.E.2d 517 (Mass. App. Ct. 2004).

◆   *The Supreme Court of Montana held a state university was liable for injuries to a child who fell on library stairs.*

The child slipped between the stairway balusters of a second story open stairwell and fell approximately twenty feet to the concrete floor. He suffered three skull fractures from the fall. The mother sued the state in a Montana trial court, alleging negligence. The court found the state had a duty of care to the child and breached that duty, so it was liable for the fall. The state appealed to the Supreme Court of Montana. **To decide if a legal duty existed, the court considered whether the state could have foreseen the risk involved. The court held the state had a duty to maintain the balcony and staircase at the university library so they were safe for ordinary public use.** The court found the risk of falling was foreseeable because the state knew the distance between the staircase balusters was 11 to 12 inches. As the state failed to cure, remove or warn the public about the stairway defect, the court affirmed the judgment. *Henricksen v. State of Montana*, 84 P.3d 38 (Mont. 2004).

◆   *The Court of Appeals of Tennessee held a state university was not liable to a non-student actress who fell during a rehearsal.*

The play took place in a theater in the round with several concentric descending steps encircling the theater. Glow tape was placed on set pieces to help actors and stagehands place sets and props on the stage during blackouts. During a rehearsal, a cast member complained she could not see well enough to make out the entrances and that more glow tape was needed near her entrance. A non-student actress then broke her ankle after attempting to stand on the darkened stage. The actress sued the state, claiming the university negligently failed to place glow tape on the edge of the stage.

The Tennessee Claims Commission found the actress 100% at fault for her injuries. She appealed to the Court of Appeals of Tennessee, which agreed with her argument that theaters owed a duty to actors and actresses to exercise reasonable care. However, that did not make them liable for risks that could not be reasonably foreseen. **The court found the actress did not prove the university knew or should have known she would fall because no glow tape was on the edge of the stage.** The other cast member's complaint that glow tape should be placed on set pieces did not put the university on notice there was a dangerous condition in another part of the stage. When the theater was blacked out, the actors were not supposed to be on stage. The court held the actress failed to establish the state was negligent. *Fox v. State of Tennessee*, No. E2003-02024-COA-R3-CV, 2004 WL 2399822 (Tenn. Ct. App. 2004).

◆ *A New York university was not liable for a student's gunshot injuries because even if it was negligent, it did not cause the harm.*

A student at the University of Rochester attended several fraternity and sorority parties on campus in an area named fraternity quad. Due to a rash of robberies in the prior week, the university had placed 19 security guards on patrol. Eight security guards patrolled the quad area. The student was shot by a non-student while the security guard assigned to that part of the campus was in an office doing paperwork. The student sued the university for negligence. The New York Supreme Court, Appellate Division, ruled that the university was not liable for the gunshot injuries. The student **failed to show that any negligence on the part of the university was a proximate cause of his injuries**. Even if the university owed him a duty to protect him from criminal activity, and even if the university breached its duty to provide adequate security, this breach was not the proximate cause of his injuries. *Colarossi v. Univ. of Rochester*, 770 N.Y.S.2d 237 (N.Y. App. Div. 2003).

◆ *A California college was not liable for a student's injuries sustained during an off-campus assignment.*

A student at a California community college was thrown from a pickup truck while on a homework assignment for a course designed to train guides for horse-packing trips. The assignment required her to camp and map out a route for a three-day "pack trip." She became a paraplegic and sued the college and instructor, alleging negligence in planning and supervising the assignment. A trial court found that the defendants had no duty to ensure the student had a safe means of transportation. Also, the defendants were immune. The California Court of Appeal affirmed, determining that the college had no duty to protect the student during the off-campus assignment. **As a general rule, colleges and their employees are not liable for off-campus student injuries. Here, neither the instructor nor any other school employee supervised the assignment.** *Stockinger v. Feather River Community College*, 4 Cal. Rptr. 3d 385 (Cal. Ct. App. 2003).

◆ *A university did not have a greater duty to protect a 15-year-old student than it had to its other students.*

A 15-year-old matriculated at the University of Alabama and performed well her first semester. However, she then began drinking, doing drugs, and was rumored to be engaged in sexual activity with football and basketball players. On two occasions, university officials confronted her about the rumored sexual activity, which she denied. Later, she stopped attending classes and failed out of school. She then sued the university under Title IX, alleging that the university had a duty to prevent her from engaging in sexual activity that interfered with her classroom performance, which it breached. She asserted that the college stood *in loco parentis* (in the place of her parents) because of her age. An Alabama federal court disagreed. **Even though high schools stand *in loco parentis*, and even though she was of high school age, the university did not have increased obligations toward her.** Further, she had denied engaging in any sexual activity when confronted by university officials. Thus, the court dismissed the case. *Benefield v. Board of Trustees of Univ. of Alabama at Birmingham*, 214 F.Supp.2d 1212 (N.D. Ala. 2002).

◆   *An Alabama veterinary student will receive an opportunity for a jury trial to consider whether a university knew she could be hurt in class.*

A veterinary instructor sedated a cow for a surgical procedure, and the student tried to secure it. When the student realized the cow was resisting the procedure, she called to the instructor for help. The instructor gave the cow more sedatives. Another student, who was having a hard time injecting the cow, also asked the instructor for help. The cow continued resisting the procedure. The instructor realized the cow had previously suffered a spinal fracture. She told the students not to perform the surgical procedure at the cow's spinal level, and demonstrated a modified procedure. The instructor then left. The cow kicked the student when she attempted to perform the assigned procedure.

The student sued the university in a federal district court for negligence and negligent supervision. **The court found evidence that the university knew the cow could harm someone.** The instructor had to attend to the cow three times on the day of the incident because students were having a hard time controlling it. **A jury could find the university failed to exercise due care, since the instructor could have taken additional safety precautions to prevent the cow from kicking.** Because the district court believed a jury could find the university was negligent, or was negligent in its supervision of the instructor, it denied the university's request for summary judgment and ordered that the case proceed to a jury trial. *Molinari v. Tuskegee Univ.*, 339 F.Supp.2d 1293 (M.D. Ala. 2004).

◆   *A Montana State University researcher could not prevail in a negligence case based on erroneous advice from the university legal services office.*

In 1996, a citizen of China was granted American resident status and hired by the university as an HIV researcher. In 1997, he and his wife were involved in a domestic dispute, and he was arrested and charged with assault. The couple went to the university's legal services office for advice. An employee there advised the researcher to plead guilty to "Family Member Assault." She had been told by an attorney that the Immigration and Naturalization Service (INS) would not deport the researcher until he was convicted of two misdemeanors; however, in 1996, Congress amended immigration law to allow the deportation of immigrants who were convicted of domestic violence. The researcher pled guilty to family member assault, and the INS notified him that he was subject to deportation. The researcher hired a new attorney, withdrew his guilty plea, and then pled guilty to violating the state's assault statute. Based on the new conviction, a federal judge ordered him deported. The researcher then sued the employee and the university's legal services office for professional negligence.

The case reached the Supreme Court of Montana. The researcher argued his second guilty plea was not a violation of the state's domestic violence statute and therefore could not warrant deportation. The court disagreed, noting that the federal judge who ordered deportation concluded the second offense was just as violent a crime as the initial offense. **Although the employee had misinformed the researcher, her advice did not lead to his current predicament**, which was based on his second plea, made on the advice of his new attorney. Thus, the researcher could not prove that he would have avoided deportation if it had not been for the employee's advice, and his professional negligence claim was not viable. *Fang v. Bock*, 28 P.3d 456 (Mont. 2001).

◆   *An Iowa university had no special duty of care to a student who committed suicide, even though officials were aware of his earlier suicide attempt and did not notify his parents.*

University of Iowa resident assistants (RAs) were called to an off-campus dormitory to defuse a situation between an 18-year-old freshman and his girlfriend regarding the student's alleged attempt to commit suicide. The RAs suggested the student go to a counselor, which he agreed to do. The next day, another university official suggested to the student that he arrange for counseling from the university's counseling service. He again agreed. The student refused to allow his parents to be contacted. About three weeks later, the student committed suicide in his dorm room. His parents filed a wrongful death lawsuit against the university, claiming that it negligently failed to notify them of the student's previous suicide attempt. A trial court ruled for the university, and the Iowa Supreme Court affirmed. The university did not have a "special duty of care" toward the student as a result of its knowledge of his previous suicide attempt. Here, the university tried to help the student by referring him to counseling, offering encouragement and seeking permission to inform his parents of the situation. **The university neither increased the risk that the student would commit suicide nor led him to abandon other avenues of relief.** *Jain v. State of Iowa*, 617 N.W.2d 293 (Iowa 2000).

◆   *A Florida university owed a student a duty to use reasonable care in assigning her to a practicum location.*

A graduate student in psychology at a private Florida university was assigned to an internship (practicum) at a family services agency that was about 15 minutes away from the university's campus. One evening, while leaving the agency, the student was abducted at gunpoint, robbed and sexually assaulted. She sued the university, alleging that it had been aware of a number of criminal incidents that had occurred at or near the agency's parking lot and that it had breached its duty of care to her by assigning her to an unreasonably dangerous internship site. The university sought to dismiss the case, arguing that it did not owe the student a duty of care because it did not own, operate or control the parking lot where the abduction had taken place. A trial court agreed.

The case reached the Florida Supreme Court. It noted that **because the university required the student to take the internship, and because it**

assigned her to a specific location, it also assumed the duty of acting reasonably in making that assignment. Since the university had knowledge that the internship location was unreasonably dangerous, a jury would now have to decide whether the university acted reasonably in placing the student there. The jury also would have to consider the student's knowledge that the internship site was unreasonably dangerous, and assess fault accordingly. *Nova Southeastern Univ. v. Gross*, 758 So.2d 86 (Fla. 2000).

◆ *A university psychology professor could be liable for negligence where he failed to refer a student to someone qualified in suicide prevention.*

A university student with a history of psychological problems sought the guidance of a professor of psychology, who also was a psychologist. The professor discovered that the student suffered from depression and had experienced suicidal fantasies almost since elementary school. He only saw the student three times, pursuant to the university's policy of providing only short-term care, and then gave him a list of four people that he could contact for further treatment. None of them were psychiatrists or specialists in suicide prevention. The student selected a specialist in eating disorders, whom he met with for over two years. However, he then terminated his treatment and committed suicide. His mother sued the professor for negligent referral and the university on the basis of *respondeat superior* as the professor's employer.

The court refused to let the case go to the jury, and the mother appealed to the Supreme Court of Rhode Island. The supreme court remanded the case for further proceedings on whether the professor negligently referred the student. **A jury could have reasonably concluded that the professor was negligent in failing to refer the student to someone qualified in suicide prevention** or to someone who could prescribe medication that would reduce his suicidal inclinations. *Klein v. Solomon*, 713 A.2d 764 (R.I. 1998).

B. Premises Liability

◆ *A Tennessee university could be liable for injuries contractors sustained while performing repairs on the school's premises.*

A maintenance supervisor discovered a malfunctioning switchgear in an electrical equipment cabinet and called in outside help when he discovered unusually high voltage was present. He told the contractor's service manager that high voltage was present but did not relay this information to the two contractors who arrived to fix the problem. The two men began to work on the equipment and were injured when a high-voltage arc of electricity generated a flash of light and ball of fire. Both men sued the university in the state court system for negligence, claiming it misstated the voltage. They also faulted the university for failing to provide warning signs and failing to maintain its electrical equipment. The case reached the Supreme Court of Tennessee.

The court explained that a premises owner who hires an independent contractor and offers information regarding the repair has a duty to make sure the information is accurate. If the university employees told the contractors that the equipment carried only 480 volts, the university had a duty to make sure that information was correct. The university was also potentially liable to the contractors on a theory of negligent misrepresentation. Under that theory, a person or entity that supplies false information to others with respect to business transactions can be liable for losses suffered as a result of reliance on the information. In this case, a disputed issue remained as to whether university employees supplied false information to the contractors about the voltage in the equipment. It would be improper to award pretrial judgment to the university. The case was remanded for additional proceedings. *Bennett v. Trevecca Nazarene Univ.*, 216 S.W.3d 293 (Tenn. 2007).

◆ *The U.S. Court of Appeals, Second Circuit, held a college was not liable for a student's attack in her dorm.*

A student attended a college in New York. She was assaulted at knifepoint in her dorm room by an attacker who was wearing a mask. The student had left the door to her room slightly ajar. At the time of the attack, the college had a security policy that required all outer doors to its residential halls be locked 24 hours a day. The policy also required visitors to register in the lobby. Despite the policies, students held and propped open doors so people could enter without registering. The student sued the college in a federal district court for negligence. The court dismissed the complaint, and the student appealed.

The U.S. Court of Appeals, Second Circuit, disagreed with the district court's conclusion that the attack was unforeseeable because of the low history of on-campus crime. **In each of the previous five years, there had been significant events and a security reporting firm reported there were other assaults on campus that were not documented.** The district court's analysis of foreseeability was flawed because it assumed that only actual prior crimes could put the college on notice of the risk of future crimes. **A jury could reasonably find suggestions by a security company hired by the college were enough to alert the school to the possibility that intruders might commit a crime.** While the court found the attack was foreseeable, the student failed to establish a causal connection between negligence by the college and her attack. Because the attacker was never caught or identified, the student did not show the university caused her attacker to gain access to the building. While New York law did not require her to identify her assailant, she had to provide some evidence that her attacker was an intruder, and she failed to do so. The judgment was affirmed. *Williams v. Utica College of Syracuse Univ.*, 453 F.3d 112 (2d Cir. 2006).

◆ *The Court of Appeals of Mississippi held a university was not liable for a visitor's shooting of a student on campus.*

A Mississippi state university had welcome centers located at the main and rear entrances to the campus. During the hours the centers were open, a member of the campus police department was stationed at each center and was to log in each non-student visitor who entered the campus. The police officers were allowed to suspend the log-in process during public events. One evening, three non-students entered the campus in a car. They were not asked to log in. The non-students rode around the campus and came across four female students in another car. The non-students threw beer bottles at students and became involved in a number of fights. One of the non-students drew a gun and shot into a crowd that had gathered to watch the fighting. A bullet hit a student and he underwent surgery to remove it. The student sued the university in a Mississippi trial court for negligence. The court denied a motion to dismiss the case on grounds of whether the campus police department acted in reckless disregard of the student's safety when it allowed the non-students to enter the campus without signing in. The court held the university had a duty to protect its students and breached that duty. However, even if campus police had recorded information in the log book, they would not have searched the car for weapons. The campus police manual does not call for pat downs or searches.

The student could not prove a connection between the reckless disregard by the police officers and the student getting shot. He appealed to the Court of Appeals of Mississippi, contending that had the police conducted log-in procedures, they would have become suspicious and would not have admitted the non-students. The court disagreed. It emphasized that because the log-in procedure did not require a search for weapons, the outcome would have been the same. **The court agreed with the trial court that the student failed to prove a causal connection between the police officers' conduct and his injuries.** It affirmed the judgment. *Johnson v. Alcorn State Univ.*, 929 So.2d 398 (Miss. Ct. App. 2006).

♦   *A Maryland university was not negligent when it assigned a student to live with a roommate who had a prior record of fighting.*

The student was in the process of moving out of the room when the roommate accused him of breaking a fish tank. The roommate hit the student in the jaw, requiring him to undergo surgery and have his mouth wired shut. The student sued the university for negligence in a state trial court. The case went before a jury. The student presented evidence of the roommate's disciplinary history at the university. He had been involved in fights with other students. The university had suspended the roommate and allowed him to return only after he completed a conflict resolution counseling program.

The Court of Special Appeals of Maryland held the university and student had a landlord-tenant relationship. As a landlord, the university had to take reasonable security measures to eliminate foreseeable harm. **The university could not have foreseen the incident based on the roommate's prior fights with other students. No previous fights had taken place in a dormitory, nor were there weapons incidents or criminal charges.** The university did not breach its duty to protect the student from injury. On further appeal, the Court of Appeals of Maryland held the university could not have reasonably foreseen what happened. The roommate had no history of violence under similar circumstances. Even the student did not believe the roommate was dangerous. He knew about the roommate's prior incidents and did not ask for a new room or roommate. The judgment for the university was affirmed. *Rhaney v. Univ. of Maryland Eastern Shore*, 388 Md. 585, 880 A.2d 357 (Md. 2005).

♦   *The Court of Appeals of Georgia held a college could not be held liable for the abduction of a student from a campus parking lot.*

The student had parked her car in a campus parking lot. When she returned to her car the next afternoon, an assailant reached into the window and punched her several times in the face. He then forced his way in, drove to another area and raped the student. She escaped when the car stopped at a red light. The student later sued the college in a state court for negligence. The court denied her motion for pretrial judgment, and she appealed to the court of appeals.

A college is generally not liable for the criminal acts of a third party unless it could have reasonably foreseen such an act. The assault would be considered foreseeable if it was substantially similar to previous criminal activities that occurred on or near the premises, and a reasonable person would have taken ordinary precautions to protect persons from the risk. **Courts review the location, nature and extent of prior criminal activities and their likeness, proximity or other relationship to the crime in question. The previous activity must have attracted the college's attention to a dangerous condition.** The court found no evidence of similar occurrences in the campus parking lot. The college could not have foreseen the attack. The lot was a common area used by many students, and a confrontation with an attacker could be very brief. The court affirmed the judgment for the college. *Agnes Scott College v. Clark*, 273 Ga.App. 619, 616 S.E.2d 468 (Ga. Ct. App. 2005).

◆ *A Kentucky college was not held negligent for failing to warn visitors about a dangerous condition on the property.*

A woman slipped and fell from a cliff overhang on college property. Members of her party sued the college in a federal district court for negligence. They claimed the college should have posted signs to prohibit trespassing and warn climbers of the danger of falling. The college argued the risk of falling off the cliff was open and obvious. The court found the woman was familiar with the area. The danger of slipping and falling from the edge of a cliff is open and obvious. **The court found the college was not negligent because it had no duty to warn the woman about the cliff or to make the property totally safe. An owner of property does not have a duty to warn visitors if a dangerous condition is so open and obvious that a person could have discovered it.** The college was entitled to summary judgment. *Blust v. Berea College*, 431 F.Supp. 2d 703 (E.D. Ky. 2006).

◆ *A professor could proceed with a negligence claim against an Illinois university for failing to light an area where he was injured.*

The professor ran into a concrete post in an unlit area of campus. He sued the university for negligence in a federal district. **The court held that to prevail on his negligence claim, the professor had to show the university owed him a duty of reasonable care concerning its premises.** The university argued it had no duty to protect or warn the professor of the dangers associated with the posts because they were open and obvious. The court explained that a property owner could be held liable for harm resulting from an obviously dangerous condition if an injury could be reasonably anticipated. **The court found a reasonable jury could conclude the lack of lighting in the area caused the post to become a concealed danger.** The concrete post was not so open and obvious in the dark that it relieved the university of a duty to warn or protect the professor from danger. The court denied the university's request for dismissal and directed the case to proceed to trial. *Pollard v. Univ. of Chicago*, No. 04C7946, 2006 WL 681046 (N.D. Ill. 3/14/06).

◆   *The Court of Appeals of Texas held a university was not liable for the death of a child who drowned while playing in a creek on its property.*

The child's mother sued the university in a Texas trial court under the attractive nuisance doctrine. The court granted the university's request for summary judgment and the mother appealed to the Court of Appeals of Texas. **The court explained an attractive nuisance may exist if a property owner maintains a device or machinery on property that is unusually attractive to children. Children are not considered trespassers in such cases.** A property owner then has a duty to exercise ordinary care to keep its property in a reasonably safe condition. The doctrine applies only to artificially created and maintained things, not to natural conditions.

The university argued the creek was a naturally occurring condition, so the attractive nuisance doctrine did not apply. The child's mother argued the creek had been artificially altered when the school constructed parking lots, drainage ditches, houses, and buildings around the property where the drowning occurred. **The court found the university had no control over the residential and commercial development around its property. It had not modified the creek or the surrounding area, so there was no attractive nuisance.** Because there was no attractive nuisance, the court held the university could not be held liable for the drowning. *Woolridge v. East Texas Baptist Univ.*, 154 S.W.2d 257 (Tex. Ct. App. 2005).

◆   *The Court of Appeals of Nebraska held a state university was not liable to a visitor who fell on some stairs at a stadium.*

The visitor slipped and fell on a wet, slimy substance on the stairs at a stadium where she attended a concert. She sued the university for negligence in a Nebraska district court. The court dismissed the case, and the visitor appealed to the Court of Appeals of Nebraska, arguing the spill was foreseeable and the university did not assign adequate personnel to monitor the stadium.

The court stated a property owner has a duty to exercise reasonable care to its visitors. It looked to whether the university could have foreseen the possibility that the visitor would have been harmed under the circumstances. An events director testified the university had staffed the event with 50-60 employees, six or eight police officers, three maintenance employees, three custodial employees, and eight to 10 Red Cross volunteers. There was testimony that event supervisors reported spills to custodial employees, and that stairs were cleaned regularly. A yellow stripe was painted along the edge of the steps. The court found the visitor failed to prove the university knew of the dangerous condition or created the risk. It affirmed the judgment. *Knittel v. State of Nebraska*, No. A-03-098, 2004 WL 2216488 (Neb. App. 2004).

◆   *A university was liable for a pedestrian's injuries where it did not maintain a walkway properly, even though a safer route was available.*

A pedestrian was walking through a New York university's campus courtyard when she slipped and fell on ice. She sued the university for negligence in maintaining its courtyards and pathways. A jury found that the university could not be held liable because it had a direct and safer alternative path on campus and the pedestrian chose to take the more dangerous one. The

Supreme Court, Appellate Division disagreed. It held that the university had to act reasonably in maintaining the campus property and ensuring it is kept in a safe condition. Just because there was a safer alternative route on campus did not mean the university did not have to maintain the pathway where the pedestrian fell. The university was liable for the pedestrian's injuries. *Witherspoon v. Columbia Univ.*, 777 N.Y.S.2d 507 (N.Y. App. Div. 2004).

◆ *A university and its contractor weren't vicariously liable for the negligent acts of a subcontractor.*

A deliveryman sued a university and its contractor for injuries he received when a door fell on him while he was making a delivery on school grounds. The door had not yet been installed and was leaning against a wall. The university had hired a contractor to install the door, and the contractor had subcontracted the installation. The trial court granted summary judgment for the school and its contractor, and the New York Supreme Court, Appellate Division, affirmed. **When a property owner hires an independent contractor for a job, it is not liable if that contractor is negligent unless there is a duty or the owner knows about an inherent danger**. The university and contractor offered evidence to show that none of their employees supervised or were involved in the door's installation. Since the deliveryman failed to submit evidence to the contrary, there was no liability. *Laecca v. New York Univ.*, 777 N.Y.S.2d 433 (N.Y. App. Div. 2004).

◆ *A college that leased premises to a professor did not breach its duty to inspect or repair the property.*

A professor moved into faculty housing, which she leased from her employer, Marymount College. When she called the management service to complain about a leaking toilet and a non-working dishwasher, the service fixed the toilet but not the dishwasher. After the second visit to repair the dishwasher, she found her kitchen flooded. As she crossed the kitchen floor to turn the water valve off, she slipped on the wet linoleum floor and injured herself. She sued Marymount and the service for negligence and premises liability, claiming they failed to properly inspect the premises and remove dangerous plumbing materials. A trial court ruled for the defendants, and the Court of Appeal of California affirmed. Marymount's obligation to inspect was limited to only those defects or dangerous conditions that could be discovered by a reasonable inspection. Even if the service had not inspected her unit, **she failed to show the leak could have been detected via a reasonable inspection**. *Henowick v. Marymount College*, No. B158103, 2004 WL 604138 (Cal. Ct. App. 2004).

◆ *A negligence claim filed by an injured food service worker was rejected because the university did not control the area where the fall took place.*

An employee of a company that provided food services at Fordham University fell down an interior staircase that connected the kitchen of the cafeteria to the basement of the student center. She claimed the steps were slippery because that is where they took down the garbage. She also said the metal strip at the edge of the step was worn away. She suffered injuries and sued the university and the Jesuits of Fordham. The New York Supreme Court, Appellate Division, noted that control of the stairway was the critical issue in assessing liability. The evidence was unrefuted that **the Jesuits did not own, manage, or control the student center where the employee fell**. Only company employees handled the kitchen trash, and no member of the Fordham maintenance staff handled kitchen trash or used the stairway. Moreover, there was no evidence that the university had either actual or constructive notice of the stairway's alleged defective condition. *Garcia v. Jesuits of Fordham, Inc.*, 774 N.Y.S.2d 503 (N.Y. App. Div. 2004).

◆ *A Texas university was not liable for a diver's injuries under the Recreational Use Statute.*

A member of the public, who paid a nominal fee to use the East Texas Baptist University outdoor pool, injured her back while attempting to dive. She claimed the diving board "double bounced." She sued the university for premises liability, negligence, and gross negligence, arguing the diving board's lever support was improperly positioned. The trial court granted the university's motion for summary judgment. The Court of Appeals of Texas affirmed, finding that it did not breach its duty of care to the diver under the Recreational Use Statute. The university was only "liable for injuries incurred through its willful, wanton, or grossly negligent conduct." Although the university acknowledged that the lever would shift after extensive use, the shifting did not cause problems suggesting that divers were at risk. A university lifeguard testified that in her 10 years of lifeguarding she never received any complaint that the diving board was functioning improperly, and never observed any defects or problems with the diving board, either before or after the injury. *Howard v. East Texas Baptist Univ.*, 122 S.W.3d 407 (Tex. Ct. App. 2003).

◆ *A student failed to show that snow and ice on a sidewalk constituted a nuisance per se.*

A student at Eastern Michigan University slipped on a snow-covered sidewalk and hit his head. He sued the university, alleging that snow, ice and debris that accumulated on the sidewalk constituted a nuisance per se. The university moved for summary judgment. The trial court determined the sidewalk did not constitute a nuisance per se. The Court of Appeals of Michigan affirmed. By definition, a nuisance per se is "an activity or condition, which constitutes a nuisance at all times and under all circumstances, without regard to care." Based on this definition, the snowy, icy sidewalk did not constitute a nuisance per se. *Hajek v. Eastern Michigan Univ. Board of Trustees*, No. 245574, 2004 WL 136746 (Mich. Ct. App. 2004).

◆ *A university might be liable for injuries sustained by a student who mistakenly walked into a glass panel.*

A student at the University of Southern California mistakenly walked into a large glass panel that flanked the exit doors. The glass shattered, and falling glass shards injured her. She sued the university for negligence, claiming that the glass panels that were too thin to resist the impact of walking into them. A trial court found that the student was unable to establish causation because the breach did not result in her injuries. The California Court of Appeal reversed in part. It found that the trial court erred in its analysis of the causation issue. **Causation required a showing that the university's act or omission was a "substantial factor" in causing the injury**. Here, the width of the glass panels did not meet Building Code standards in 1968, which indicated that the glass panels should have been 5/16 inch thick rather than 1/4 inch thick. The university's negligence contributed to the injury enough to be a "substantial factor." Although the student admitted that she was not watching where she was going, this admission did not negate the causation element. Instead, it merely raised an issue of comparative negligence. A trial was required. *Chin v. Univ. of Southern California*, No. B161246 2003 WL 21696282 (Cal. Ct. App. 2003).

C. Defenses

1. Immunity

◆   *A Kentucky university was immune to a claim of negligence in the case of a student who was assaulted, raped and set on fire in her dormitory room.*

Three days after being brutally attacked in her dorm room at Western Kentucky University, the student died from her injuries. Two men who were not residents of the dorm were later charged in the case. The administrators of the student's estate filed negligence claims in a suit against the university in state court. The court dismissed the case, and the state appeals court affirmed the judgment. The case reached the Supreme Court of Kentucky.

The court explained that **governmental immunity extends to state agencies that perform governmental functions. At the same time, immunity does not extend to state agencies that are not created to perform a governmental function.** Officials of state agencies can also be entitled to immunity if the agency itself is immune to suit. When sued in their official capacities, these officials enjoy the same immunity as the state agency. The university operated the dorm as part of its statutory duty to provide college instruction, and therefore it was not performing a proprietary function. **As the dormitory operation was a discretionary function, the university was entitled to immunity.** Because the claims against the university were barred by immunity, the claims against the officials in their official capacities were also barred. *Autry v. Western Kentucky Univ.*, 219 S.W.3d 713 (Ky. 2007).

◆   *Texas State University was immune to a student's claim for negligence after she was sexually attacked on campus.*

A student was attacked and raped at knifepoint after leaving the campus library at 11:00 p.m. She sued Texas State in a state district court, claiming employees negligently implemented campus safety policies. The student also contended Texas State did not use ordinary care to keep the campus safe, properly lit, and free from criminal trespassers. The court held Texas State was protected from liability by governmental immunity, and the student appealed.

The Court of Appeals of Texas stated that the Texas Tort Claims Act makes state entities liable for personal injury if, as a private person, it would be liable according to Texas law. **The student did not show a connection between the alleged defect and her injuries**, which is a necessary element of a personal injury claim. **The court found the actions of the student's attacker, not the alleged safety problems, were what caused her to be harmed.** The court rejected her argument that governmental immunity was waived because the university negligently implemented a security-related safety policy. It said that **negligent implementation of a security policy does not itself waive governmental immunity.** The court affirmed the judgment. *Dimas v. Texas State Univ. System*, 201 S.W.3d 260 (Tex. Ct. App. 2006).

◆ *A Texas university was not liable for injuries a student suffered when she fell on her way back to her seat after receiving her diploma.*

The student was hurt when her foot became caught between a platform and the floor when she was returning to her seat with her diploma. She sued the university in a state court, claiming it failed to provide a warning about the floor's condition and failed to properly maintain and inspect the floor. The student also argued the university failed to use due care when it designed and placed a mat on the floor. The university sought to have the complaint dismissed based on state law immunity. The court denied the motion, and the university appealed. On appeal, the Court of Appeals of Texas explained that state law generally immunizes governmental entities from claims for injuries.

The law also provides exceptions to immunity for injuries caused by the condition or use of real property and for claims arising due to defective premises. However, the exceptions do not apply when the governmental unit makes a discretionary decision. **A decision is discretionary if it involves the exercise of judgment. Decisions relating to the design of municipal premises and buildings are discretionary.** In addition, there is no immunity if injury results from a governmental entity's negligent implementation of a policy or its negligent maintenance of its premises. In this case, the student conceded that the decision to use a raised floor was discretionary. But she said there should be no immunity because the implementation of the decision created a dangerous condition. Although an expert said the university should not have used a raised platform, there was no showing that the raised floor or mat were defective. **Because the decisions relating to the design of the floor were discretionary, the university had immunity** and the case was properly dismissed. *Univ. of Houston v. DeLuna*, No. 01-06-00448-CV, 2007 WL 1119916 (Tex. Ct. App. 4/12/07).

◆ *A Kansas state university was immune from liability in a case filed by a student who slipped and fell on an icy crosswalk.*

The student stated it was snowing lightly at the time of her fall. She testified that snow that had fallen earlier had been pushed off the crosswalk. She thought the snow had probably refrozen to form ice. The university had 13 landscaping employees responsible for snow removal. Most of them started work at 6:30 a.m. and were instructed to begin their shifts by walking the campus in search of any hazardous conditions needing immediate attention. Employees were to sprinkle ice melting compound on hazardous spots, remove the ice, or report the problem to a manager.

The student stated the employees negligently failed to inspect and treat the crosswalk on the morning she fell, and sued the university in a state court. The court granted summary judgment to the university, finding it was immune from liability under the Kansas Torts Claims Act. The student appealed to the Court of Appeals of Kansas. **The court agreed with the university that the only exception to state immunity is injury caused by an employee's affirmative act. By contrast, an employee's failure to act has no bearing on liability.** As the student did not allege any affirmative act by a university employee, the court held the university was immune from liability under the act and affirmed the judgment. *Owoyemi v. Univ. of Kansas*, 91 P.3d 552 (Kan. Ct. App. 2004).

◆ *A Texas university was not entitled to sovereign immunity for injuries caused by a sprinkler because its placement was not discretionary.*

A Texas woman and her husband were cycling along a trail adjacent to the shot put field on the campus of Stephen F. Austin University. Unexpectedly, she was struck by a stream of water shooting out of a sprinkler head located on the shot put field. The water hit the right side of her head with such force that she was knocked off her bicycle. As a result of the fall, she sustained injuries. She sued the university under the state's tort claims act. The university moved to dismiss, asserting that sovereign immunity barred the action. A trial court denied the motion, finding the placement and operation of the sprinkler system constitutes policy implementation under the tort claims act. Such activity was not protected by sovereign immunity. The Court of Appeals of Texas affirmed. Although the decision to water the campus was discretionary, making the university immune on that issue, **the decision as to how and when to water the campus was not discretionary**. Instead, it was a maintenance activity conducted at the operational level. *Stephen F. Austin State Univ. v. Flynn*, No. 12-03-00240-CV, 2004 WL 100395 (Tex. Ct. App. 2004).

◆ *A dormitory at a public university did not satisfy the "public-building" exception to governmental immunity.*

A student at the University of Michigan lived in a dormitory that was locked 24 hours a day. In order to gain entrance, students used a courtesy telephone at the top of a short stairway outside the residence. After using the telephone, the student lost her balance and fell down the stairs, injuring herself. She sued the university, claiming that the telephone was placed too close to a narrow step and that its location created a defective and dangerous condition. Because the university was protected by sovereign immunity, she asserted that the dormitory was a public building under the public building exception to sovereign immunity. The Supreme Court of Michigan held that **the public building exception did not apply to a residence hall at a public university**. Mere public ownership was insufficient to meet the public building exception. The critical issue was whether the university intended to limit the public's access to the dormitory. Here, public access was limited by the courtesy telephone and that entry was granted only by a resident. The university was entitled to sovereign immunity. *Maskery v. Board of Regents of Univ. of Michigan*, 664 N.W.2d 165 (Mich. 2003).

◆ *The design immunity provision of California's government code barred recovery to a concert-goer injured in a fall.*

The concert-goer fell down a few stairs at UCLA and sued for premises liability, claiming that the steps were a dangerous and hazardous condition and were in violation of the safety codes. UCLA moved for summary judgment, arguing that the design immunity provision of the government code barred the plaintiff's recovery. The trial court granted UCLA's motion. The California Court of Appeal affirmed. The stairs met building code and safety requirements, and the lack of guardrails and barriers was part of the design. The campus fire marshal approved the plans for the stairway and testified that a guardrail or barrier was not necessary for a riser less than 30 inches tall. The stairway plans were based on a reasonable design. **The design immunity provision does not require that the building be perfectly designed.** *Ying v. Regents of the Univ. of California*, No. 2d Civil No. B162112, 2003 WL 21983727 (Cal. Ct. App. 2003).

◆ *A state university could not be held liable for a resident advisor's murder at the hands of a student.*

A graduate student at Purdue University worked as a resident advisor (RA) and reported to campus police that a student had marijuana in his dorm room. He later discovered that the student's roommate had cocaine on him and reported that to the police as well, despite a death threat from the roommate. Later, the roommate shot the RA, then killed himself. The RA's estate sued the university, the campus police and various officials for wrongful death, asserting violations of 42 U.S.C. § 1983. A trial court dismissed the action, but the Indiana Court of Appeals reversed in part. Although **the university and the campus police were "arms of the state" under Section 1983 and thus immune from liability under the Eleventh Amendment**, the university officials and individual police officers were "persons" under Section 1983 and could be sued. The court also noted that the state never assumed a duty to protect the RA, and it did not have a "special relationship" with him such that a duty to protect could be inferred. The court remanded the case for further proceedings against the individual defendants. *Severson v. Board of Trustees of Purdue Univ.*, 777 N.E.2d 1181 (Ind. Ct. App. 2002).

◆ *A state university was entitled to charitable immunity in a lawsuit brought by a student.*

A student at Montclair State University fell down an amphitheater staircase on campus, fracturing his ribs and elbow. He spent several days in the hospital and sued the university for damages. The university asserted that it was immune under the New Jersey Charitable Immunity Act, and a trial court agreed. Because the student was a "beneficiary" under the act, the university was entitled to charitable immunity. The appellate division court reversed that decision, but the New Jersey Supreme Court reinstated the trial court's ruling. Here, the university was formed for a nonprofit purpose; it was organized for educational purposes; and it was promoting those goals at the time the student (beneficiary) was injured. **Nothing in the act required that an entity be a private nonprofit institution in order to qualify for charitable immunity.**

As a result, the public university was entitled to have the lawsuit against it dismissed. *O'Connell v. State of New Jersey*, 795 A.2d 857 (N.J. 2002).

◆ *The associate housing director at Murray State University was not entitled to immunity in a lawsuit brought by the mother of a student who died in a dormitory fire.*

A fire started in the dorm where the student lived. His mother contacted the associate director of the university's housing office, who allegedly described the incident as "minor" and assured her that the fire was "nothing to worry about." Five days later, another fire was set in the same location. This time, the student was unable to escape and died of smoke inhalation. His mother later learned that the suspected cause of both fires was arson. As a result, she sued the associate director for negligent misrepresentation, claiming that if he had told her the school suspected arson was the cause of the fires, she would have removed her son from the dorm after the first fire. The suit also claimed that the director of public safety at the university breached his duty to ensure the safety of the students by not having an adequate security system in place. The defendants moved to dismiss the suit, claiming immunity because they did not knowingly commit a wrongful act. The defendants argued that since the mother's complaint alleged "negligent misrepresentation," they were immune. The district court agreed and dismissed the suit.

On appeal, the U.S. Court of Appeals, Sixth Circuit, upheld the district court's dismissal of the claims against the director of public safety, but found the associate director of the housing office was not entitled to immunity. Despite the fact that the mother was suing for negligent misrepresentation, the court interpreted her allegation as claiming that the associate director intentionally misrepresented the cause of the first fire. **Since the facts alleged by the mother were sufficient to support a claim for intentional misrepresentation, the associate director was not entitled to immunity.** *Minger v. Green*, 239 F.3d 793 (6th Cir. 2001).

◆ *A university was entitled to qualified immunity where the students suing it could not show that they had been deprived of a property interest in their education.*

Two student-athletes at an Illinois state university were accused of raping another student. They maintained that the sex had been consensual, and that the accusation of rape had followed from the refusal by one of them to continue a relationship with the student. One of the student athletes was acquitted of all criminal charges, and the other was never charged. Both were, however, required to appear before a hearing board, where one was expelled and the other was suspended indefinitely. The student-athletes sued the university and various officials, alleging that they were deprived of a property interest in their education without due process of law. An Illinois federal court dismissed the case, finding that the university was entitled to qualified immunity because the student athletes failed to show that the university violated a clearly established constitutional right, and also that the Eleventh Amendment barred their suit. They appealed to the Seventh Circuit Court of Appeals, which affirmed. **Even if children have a property interest in attending elementary and secondary**

public schools, the student-athletes had not shown that Illinois state law provided them with a property interest in higher education. The court also noted that the university, as an arm of the state, was immune from suit under the Eleventh Amendment. *Lee v. Board of Trustees of Western Illinois Univ.*, 202 F.3d 274 (7th Cir. 2000).

◆ *Two students who were injured while traveling to another college to play a soccer game could not sue their college because of state law immunity.*

Two members of a community college soccer team were injured when the van they were riding in was involved in a highway accident. While traveling to another college for a soccer match in a van owned by the community college and driven by an assistant coach, the van blew a tire. The coach lost control of the vehicle, causing it to travel across two lanes of oncoming traffic and to flip several times. The players sued the college and the coach to recover for their injuries. The college claimed it could not be sued, citing a California statute that granted immunity to colleges for field trips or excursions in connection with school-related social, educational, cultural, athletic or college band activities to and from places. The statute provided that **persons taking such field trips or excursions are deemed to have waived all claims against the college or the state for any injuries that might result**. The California Court of Appeal affirmed the trial court's grant of pretrial judgment in favor of the college. Since extracurricular sports programs are "school-related athletic activities," the trip to the other college was covered by the immunity statute, and the students' lawsuit could not succeed. *Barnhart v. Cabrillo Community College*, 90 Cal.Rptr.2d 709 (Cal. Ct. App. 1999).

2. Assumption of Risk

Assumption of risk is an affirmative defense to a claim of negligence. If the defense is proven, the claimant cannot recover on a negligence claim. To prove the defense, a university or college must show the claimant had knowledge of the risk, appreciated the risk, and voluntarily confronted it. Because the risk of injury is inherent and obvious in many sports, assumption of risk often bars recovery in negligence actions brought by student-athletes.

◆ *The parent of a Maryland student was unable to pursue a negligence case because she assumed the risk of injury by trying to cross an icy parking lot.*

The parent drove to the university to deliver gas money and other supplies to her daughter after about 22 inches of snow had fallen in the vicinity. As soon as she drove into the parking lot near her daughter's dormitory, she noticed it had not been cleared of ice and snow. Although the parent made it to her daughter's room safely, she fell and broke her leg in the icy lot while returning to her car. She sued the university in state court for negligent failure to clear the lot of snow and ice. She also claimed negligent hiring, training and supervision based on the failure of university employees to clear the lot in a timely manner. A Maryland trial court held the parent voluntarily assumed the risk of injury by walking on the snow and ice. The state court of special appeals reversed the decision, finding that a jury should decide whether to bar her negligence claim.

On appeal, the Court of Appeals of Maryland held the parent had voluntarily assumed the risk of injury when she chose to cross the icy lot. She could have found another way to get the money to her daughter. There was no evidence that the parent was forced to confront the danger of walking on ice and snow against her will. She understood she was taking a chance when she chose to cross the lot. **It was clear that a person of normal intelligence would have understood the risk presented. In assumption of risk cases, the claimant relieves the defendant of its duty of care by voluntarily choosing to encounter a known risk.** For that reason, the university's failure to clear the lot was irrelevant. The decision against the university was reversed. *Morgan State Univ. v. Walker*, 397 Md. 509, 919 A.2d 21 (Md. 2007).

◆   *A California college was not liable to a student injured during a peace officer training class where he practiced arrest and control techniques.*

The student attended a class called "Arrest Communications and Firearms," which satisfied requirements prescribed by the state Commission on Peace Officer Standards and Training. Students performed techniques and maneuvers for controlling suspects by role-playing in teams of two. One student played the role of an officer and the other played a suspect. Three police officers taught the class. One of the officers demonstrated four maneuvers the students were to carry out. An officer saw the student perform each maneuver at least once. The student was injured when his partner pulled him down. He hit his neck on the partner's knee, causing a herniated cervical disc. The student sued the college in a state court for negligence. The court held for the college and the student appealed to the Court of Appeal of California.

The court discussed the doctrine of primary assumption of risk, which applies to activities or sports where "conditions or conduct that otherwise might be viewed as dangerous often are an integral part of the sport itself." Skiing is an example of such a sport. Careless conduct by others could also be an inherent risk in a specific sport or activity. **The court explained that during dangerous activities, the integral conditions of the sport or the inherent risks of careless conduct by others render the possibility of injury obvious and negate the duty of care usually owed for those particular risks.** The takeover maneuvers in the student's class bore a similar risk of injury inherent in many sports. The court found careless conduct by others was an inherent risk. Imposing a duty to eliminate the risk of injury from the activity in this situation would chill vigorous participation in learning the maneuvers. Because of the nature of the classroom activity and the lack of evidence that the college acted recklessly, the court held the action was barred by the doctrine of primary assumption of the risk. The judgment for the college was affirmed. *Saville v. Sierra College*, 133 Cal.App.4th 857, 36 Cal.Rptr.3d 515 (Cal. Ct. App. 2005).

◆   *A Rhode Island university was not liable for injuries to a student who fell while walking at night on campus.*

The student lived in a university dormitory. He fell while on an unlighted pathway on an unpaved embankment on the side of a road on campus. The student sued the university in a state trial court for negligence. The case was heard by a jury. It ruled in favor of the university. The student filed a motion for a new trial. After the court denied the motion, he appealed to the Supreme Court of Rhode Island. The student argued the trial court overlooked evidence about defects in the asphalt where he fell. He also claimed the area was commonly used by students. The court held the trial court judge had properly reviewed the evidence and assessed the credibility of the witnesses. The judge had found the student was not credible. The court agreed with the trial court's finding that the student tripped on crumbled asphalt, not a defect in a campus walkway. **The trial court made a well-supported finding that the area of the fall was not an existing pathway and the student could have used an existing route instead of the one he chose.** The judgment for the university was affirmed. *Candido v. Univ. of Rhode Island*, 880 A.2d 853 (R.I. 2005).

◆ *A student's personal injury action was barred because she signed the university's release.*

A student registered for a seven-week basic rock-climbing course at Cornell University. As part of the registration process, she watched a safety video and signed a release, which precluded her from holding the university liable for any injuries caused by use of the climbing wall and for injuries that resulted from her own negligence. She also signed a contract promising not to climb above a yellow "bouldering" line without required safety equipment. On the day of her fall, she was climbing above the yellow "bouldering" line without safety equipment. She lost her footing and fell, then sued the university for her injuries. The university moved to dismiss the matter based on the release. The trial court granted the university's motion, and the New York Supreme Court, Appellate Division, affirmed. **The release language was unambiguous. It pointed out the dangers of rock climbing, and it clearly stated that the university could not be held responsible.** *Lemoine v. Cornell Univ.*, 769 N.Y.S.2d 313 (N.Y. App. Div. 2003).

◆ *Where a student signed waivers assuming the risk of injury, she could not sue a university after sustaining an injury.*

After signing two waivers of liability and an authorization of medical treatment, an Indiana university student participated in a motorcycle training course for beginners. She drove a motorcycle provided by the university into a tree, breaking her arm. She then sued the university for negligence, including failure to provide appropriate equipment and failure to provide appropriate instruction. A state court granted pretrial judgment to the university, and the student appealed. The Court of Appeals of Indiana held that the waivers were not void as against public policy. Here, **the student had agreed that she assumed the risk of injury by participating in the class.** Further, the university did not owe her a statutory duty that voided the waivers she signed. Because the waivers were valid, the university was not liable for the student's injury. *Terry v. Indiana State Univ.*, 666 N.E.2d 87 (Ind. Ct. App. 1996).

◆ *A university was not liable for injuries a student sustained while sledding into a parking lot.*

When a rare winter snowstorm hit northern Louisiana, a university student went sledding with some fellow students. While riding on a plastic garbage can lid, the student (on his eighth trip down the hill) collided with the concrete base of a light pole in the football stadium parking lot. He sustained head and back injuries resulting in permanent paralysis from the mid-chest down. He and his parents sued the university and the state for negligence, asserting that the university had encouraged dangerous sledding activities and had failed to put cushions on the light poles. A state court granted pretrial judgment to the defendants, finding that the danger of striking a fixed object while sledding was apparent and obvious. The court of appeal reversed.

The Supreme Court of Louisiana noted that a number of people had testified that the light poles were visible, and that they had tried to warn the student that he was approaching the pole. **Because the conditions of the property were not unreasonably dangerous, and because the dangers of the light poles were apparent and obvious, the university did not have a duty to protect the student.** Further, the university encouraged sledding only in proper areas and with the use of good judgment. Finally, there was no special relationship between the university and the school that created a duty to protect. The supreme court reversed the lower court decision and ruled in favor of the university. *Pitre v. Louisiana Tech Univ.*, 673 So.2d 585 (La. 1996).

D. Damages

The nature and extent of damage awards generally depends upon the nature of the injury and the conduct of the parties. Compensatory damages serve to compensate an injured party for his or her injuries such as medical expenses or pain and suffering.

Punitive damages, on the other hand, are not designed to compensate for loss. Instead, they serve to punish the offending party because of the party's willful and wanton conduct.

◆   *A Louisiana university was liable for failing to protect patrons from getting hit by foul balls when they entered a baseball park.*

A visitor went to a baseball game held on a university baseball field. She was struck in her right eye by a foul ball near the ticket booth along the third-base side of the field. The visitor suffered a fracture and permanent ocular blindness resulting in permanent 10/200 vision in her right eye. She sued the university in a state trial court for negligence. The court awarded the visitor $485,000, and the university appealed to the Court of Appeal of Louisiana.

The court explained that ballpark owners cannot be held responsible for every foul ball in common areas. There are certain areas of a ballpark where protection is required. One such area is the main entrance, where people have to enter to buy a ticket. **The court said the university could have reasonably anticipated there would be foul balls in the main entrance area. There was sufficient evidence to support the jury's finding that the baseball park presented an unreasonably dangerous condition to those who entered and that the university had notice of the defect.** The court affirmed the judgment. *Reider v. Louisiana Board of Trustees for State Colleges and Universities*, 897 So.2d 893 (La. Ct. App. 2005).

◆   *The Court of Appeals of Ohio held a university was liable for injuries to an operations manager of a mobile production unit.*

The manager got hurt when he was on the university's campus setting up for television coverage of a basketball game. He spoke to a university representative, who told him to run cables beside two large air conditioning units. The units were housed inside a dimly lit brick enclosure. Based on what the university representative told him, the manager thought the power was on the other side of the enclosure. He tossed the cable over a wall and over one of the air conditioner units, but it fell short. The manager entered into the darkness, took two steps and fell into a large pit. He injured his head, wrist and elbow. After two surgeries, the manager got a staph infection. He sued the university for negligence in a state trial court. The court found the university had breached its duty of care to the manager and caused his injuries.

The university appealed to the Court of Appeals of Ohio, arguing expert medical testimony was required to establish a connection between the manager's original injuries and the staph infection. The court of appeals disagreed. **Expert testimony is needed only where the internal complexities of the body are at issue.** The court found the staph infection was not internal or elusive, so the trial court needed to focus only on the location and nature of the infection to determine a connection. A court could sufficiently understand the infection and its connection to the surgery without expert medical testimony. **The court also rejected the university's contention that the operations manager played a part in getting hurt by stepping into the brick enclosure.** It was unclear whether a university representative lulled him into a false sense of safety by directing him to the area without warning him of the danger of the pit. The court affirmed the judgment. *Dixon v. Miami Univ.*, No. 04 AP-1132, 2005 WL 3316963 (Ohio Ct. App. 12/8/05).

◆   *A Vermont university was liable for over $2 million in damages for hazing.*

A five-year veteran of the Navy enrolled in the Military College of Vermont of Norwich University under a Navy Reserve Officer Training Corps scholarship. He lasted for only 16 days, during which he was subjected to, and observed, repeated instances of hazing by upperclassmen. After withdrawing from school, he sued the university for assault and battery, infliction of emotional distress and negligence, asserting that it was vicariously liable for the actions of the upperclassmen. A jury returned a verdict in the student's favor, awarding him almost $500,000 in compensatory damages and $1.75 million in punitive damages. The Supreme Court of Vermont affirmed the compensatory damage award against the university, but reversed the award of punitive damages, finding no evidence of malice on the university's part. Here, **the university had charged the upperclassmen with "indoctrinating and orienting" the student**. As a result, this was not a simple case of student-on-student hazing for which the university could not be held liable. Because the upperclassmen were acting as agents of the university, it breached its duty of care toward the student. The court also found that the nearly $500,000 in compensatory damages awarded by the jury was not clearly erroneous. *Brueckner v. Norwich Univ.*, 730 A.2d 1086 (Vt. 1999).

II. INTENTIONAL CONDUCT

Institutions may be found liable for the intentional acts or omissions of their personnel. Courts have found colleges and universities liable for intentional acts of third parties on or near campuses. In those cases, courts may hold the institution should have foreseen the potential for misconduct.

A. Instructor Misconduct

Common lawsuits against university instructors include those claiming intentional infliction of emotional distress, defamation, or sexual misconduct. Often, accusations of inappropriate sexual behavior may result in civil as well as criminal action against the instructor.

◆ *Yale University defeated a student's claim that her drama instructor's vulgar behavior intentionally inflicted emotional distress upon her.*

The student was on stage when her instructor announced he changed the title of a play to "Metamorphosis Revisited Or Rock Out with Your Cock Out." He instructed male actors to simulate masturbation as they stood next to the student. After they carried out the simulation, the instructor called out "that was great!" The student complained to the department chair and questioned the artistic value and justification for the activities. She claimed that the rest of the year, faculty and students subjected her to macho and "frat house" behavior.

The student sued the university in a federal district court for intentional infliction of emotional distress. **The court explained that liability for intentional infliction of emotional distress requires proof of conduct that exceeds "all bounds usually tolerated by decent society." Conduct that is merely insulting or displays bad manners or results in hurt feelings is insufficient to prove intentional infliction of emotional distress.** The court held a reasonable jury could not find the conduct here constituted extreme and outrageous behavior. Connecticut courts have generally held that mere insults or verbal taunts do not rise to the level of extreme and outrageous conduct. While the adaptation of the play may have been tasteless, it did not subject the student to conduct that exceeded all bounds tolerated by decent society. The court granted the university's motion for dismissal. *Greenhouse v. Yale Univ.*, No. 3:05 CV1429 (AHN), 2006 WL 473724 (D. Conn. 2/28/06).

◆ *If a professor's spanking of a student was sexual in nature, then the university could be liable to the student under Title IX.*

While enrolled in a biology class at a Virginia university, a female student took a make-up examination, which her professor immediately evaluated. After reviewing the exam, the professor told her that her performance was unsatisfactory and invited her to his office to review the test. The professor, after reviewing the test with the student, placed her over his knees and spanked her repeatedly with his hand. He then told her that she could retake the test the next day, but that she should bring a hairbrush with her because he was going to spank her again, even harder, if she did not achieve a certain score. The student left the professor's office and sought medical treatment for sore buttocks. She initiated criminal and administrative proceedings against the professor, which resulted in the professor's conviction for misdemeanor assault and placement on probation by the university.

The student sued the university under Title IX, asserting *quid pro quo* sexual harassment (that she was required to submit to the harassment as a condition of receiving an educational benefit). The university sought pretrial judgment. The U.S. District Court for the Eastern District of Virginia held that **there were questions of fact as to whether the professor's actions in spanking and threatening to spank the student were sexual in nature. However, there was no question that the university was liable for the professor's actions.** Thus, if the spanking and threatened spanking amounted to *quid pro quo* sexual harassment, the university would be liable. The court refused to grant pretrial judgment to the university. *Kadiki v. Virginia Comwlth. Univ.*, 892 F.Supp. 746 (E.D. Va. 1995).

◆ *When a student settled a slander claim against a college, he could not pursue the claim against the professor who committed the act.*

A sociology professor allegedly ordered a student to leave his classroom, then slandered him in a 30-minute tirade to the remaining students. Subsequently, the student entered into a settlement agreement with the college, which released the college, its officers, agents and employees from any liability for any alleged slander committed by the professor. The release did not prevent the student from suing the professor for actions outside the scope of his authority as an employee. When the student sued the professor for slander, a state trial court granted pretrial judgment to the professor.

The Supreme Court of Montana affirmed the judgment, finding that **the student was statutorily barred in his suit against the professor by reason of his settlement with the college. A Montana state law provided that recovery against a governmental entity barred recovery against the employee whose wrongful act caused the harm.** *Stansbury v. Lin*, 848 P.2d 509 (Mont. 1993).

◆ *An Idaho university could not be held liable for a professor's "battery" against a woman.*

While at a woman's house as a social guest, a university professor walked up behind the woman and touched her back with both of his hands, mimicking the movement of pressing and releasing the keys of a piano keyboard. He did this to demonstrate the sensation of the movement by a pianist, not to cause any harm. However, the woman sustained injuries as a result of the touching and sued the university under the Idaho Tort Claims Act. The university asserted that it was immune from liability because the touching amounted to a "battery" under the law. The university, as a governmental entity, was immune from liability for any injuries arising out of a battery committed by an employee.

The case reached the Supreme Court of Idaho, which held that for a civil battery to be committed, there need not be any intent to cause harm; there need only be an act that causes an intended contact with another person that is not permitted and that is harmful or offensive. **Here, the professor's touching of the woman was without her permission, intentional and, despite intent to**

the contrary, harmful. As a result, it was battery. The university could not be held liable for battery under the state tort claims act. *White v. Univ. of Idaho*, 797 P.2d 108 (Idaho 1990).

B. Employee Misconduct

◆ *A discharged university employee could not proceed with a claim of intentional infliction of emotional distress against university officials.*

The employee, who was female, discovered that a male university employee was earning nearly $10,000 more annually for performing essentially the same job. She filed administrative claims of discrimination against the university, then sued the university, supervisors and a human resources representative in federal district court. The employee claimed violations of the Equal Pay Act, the Fair Labor Standards Act, Title VII, and the state fair employment practices act. She added a state law claim for intentional infliction of emotional distress, saying supervisors had continuously harassed her for filing the administrative complaint. The employee claimed supervisors denied her access to files she needed to do her job and took away significant job responsibilities. She said they had a "shadow" follow her around at work and subjected her to discipline without cause. According to the employee, these actions caused her to suffer from sleeplessness and anxiety.

The court held that to prevail on an emotional distress claim, the employee had to show conduct that was extreme and outrageous, and that it caused her to suffer severe emotional distress. The court rejected the claim, because she did not show the conduct was extreme or outrageous. **The employee's allegations did not indicate conduct that "transcend[ed] the bounds of civilized society," and she did not allege she was subjected to any public ridicule or humiliation.** In short, she did not allege facts sufficient to support her claim of intentional infliction of emotional distress. The motion to dismiss the claim was granted. *Jamilik v. Yale Univ.*, No. 3:06 CV 0566 (PCD), 2007 WL 214607 (D. Conn. 1/25/07).

◆ *A university instructor's physical assault of a student did not result in school liability because the assault was not in furtherance of the school's business and therefore fell outside the scope of employment.*

A student at a New York university enrolled in a non-credit karate course offered during the summer session. The class was held in the school's physical education building. According to the student, he was told by the instructor to do a reverse push-up. After he refused, believing that it was unsafe, the instructor struck him several times. He was taken to the hospital and later sued the school in the Court of Claims for his injuries. The school asserted that it should not be held vicariously liable for the student's injuries because the instructor was not an employee but an independent contractor.

The court noted that although there was an issue as to whether students could reasonably believe that the instructors of the non-credit courses were employees of the school, it did not need to resolve this issue since the karate instructor's conduct was outside the scope of his employment. **The school did not authorize the use of violence and such actions were not within any**

discretionary authority given to the instructor. The assault was not in furtherance of the school's business and therefore fell outside the scope of employment. The school could not be held vicariously liable for such actions. *Forester v. State*, 645 N.Y.S.2d 971 (N.Y. Ct. Cl. 1996).

C. Third-Party Misconduct

Liability for third-party misconduct can arise when someone connected with a university is injured by a third party off campus, or when an individual not affiliated with the institution enters campus and injures someone connected with the institution. Typically, third-party misconduct involves some type of criminal behavior, such as physical or sexual assault.

◆ *A Texas student's claims against a university arising from sexual assault were dismissed on grounds of state immunity and untimeliness.*

The student was sexually assaulted by an acquaintance who was also a student at the university. The student obtained an emergency protective order, which she presented to an associate dean. She was unaware that the associate dean knew the attacker. According to the student, the associate dean tried to convince her not to pursue charges against the attacker and to forgive him. Eventually, the associate dean admitted that she knew the attacker. She added that if the student did not drop her claim against the attacker, she would find continuing at the medical school to be difficult. The attacker was disciplined under the Student Code of Conduct. Two years later, the victim sued the university, the associate dean and the attacker, alleging assault, intentional infliction of emotional distress, retaliation and constitutional rights violations.

A federal district court noted the Eleventh Amendment shields states from claims for money damages unless Congress has abrogated that immunity. This did not happen here. **Since the university was a state entity, it was entitled to Eleventh Amendment immunity.** The associate dean was also entitled to immunity because she was sued in her official capacity as an employee of the university. The court then turned to the issue of timeliness and determined the student had waited too long to file her lawsuit. All of the events described in the complaint occurred more than two years before the student sued. Even though administrative proceedings had taken place at the university within that two-year period, the statute of limitations was not tolled, because those proceedings did not prevent the student from exercising her legal right to sue. The court dismissed the claims against the university defendants. *Maltbia v. Coffie*, No. H-06-834, 2007 WL 43793 (S.D. Tex. 1/5/07).

◆ *A Massachusetts university was not liable for the murder of a student in his off-campus apartment because the risk of injury to him was not foreseeable.*

The student leased the apartment where he was murdered from a private landlord. On the day of the murder, another tenant let the perpetrators into the building. The student's estate sued the university for wrongful death and negligence. The court granted the university's motion for pretrial judgment on grounds that **the university had no duty to provide security for the student or to prevent his murder. Although there had been four burglaries at the**

building in the six months before the murder, there was no evidence that they involved violence or that any other violence occurred in the building. The building was privately owned and managed, and the university was not in the best position to take the steps needed to ensure the student's safety. *Doyle v. Gould*, 22 Mass.L.Rptr. 373 (Mass. Super. Ct. 2007).

◆ *A New York university was not liable for injuries to a student who was injured when another student struck him with a chain.*

The student was injured when another student hit him on the head with a tow-truck chain during a fight on campus. Another fight involving different students had occurred on campus earlier that day. The university campus security officers went to the location of the second fight immediately after it started and apprehended the student with the chain. They called police and emergency medical services to the scene, and they appeared within minutes of the call. The student sued the university in a state court for negligence. The court denied the university's motion for pretrial judgment, and it appealed.

A New York appellate division court explained that **as a property owner, the university had a duty to exercise reasonable care to protect the student from reasonably foreseeable criminal or dangerous acts committed by third persons on campus.** The university did not breach its duty because it could not have foreseen the attack on the student. The other fight involving different students could not have put the university on notice of the fight between the student and his attacker. Even if the university had known of the later fight, the student failed to show what could have been done to stop it. The trial court should have granted the university's motion, and the judgment was reversed. *Ayeni v. County of Nassau*, 794 N.Y.S.2d 412 (N.Y. App. Div. 2005).

◆ *The Supreme Court of Texas held a state university was not liable for the stabbing of a student actor during a school play.*

The university had no theater curriculum, but it offered a voluntary student drama club whose members received no grades or class credit for participating. The club director and his wife told actors to use a real knife in a play, in violation of a university policy prohibiting deadly weapons on campus. During the second performance of the play, an actor missed a stab pad worn by the student and drove the knife into the student's chest, puncturing his lung. The student sued the university in a Texas court, alleging the university was liable for his injuries. The court held for the student, and the university appealed.

The state court of appeals reversed the decision, finding the director, his wife, and the club's faculty advisors were not considered "employees" under the Texas Tort Claims Act. For that reason, the university was protected by governmental immunity. The Supreme Court of Texas reviewed the case, and found the advisors were university employees under the act. However, the director and his wife had no employment contract with the university. **The university had only a minimal degree of control over them that did not indicate employee status. The court held the university was protected from liability by governmental immunity.** It reversed the judgment and dismissed the case. *Texas A&M Univ. v. Bishop*, 156 S.W.3d 580 (Tex. 2005).

◆ *An Ohio appellate court held a university was entitled to question a student who started a fire in a dormitory.*

The fire killed another student who was asleep in his dorm room. Investigators determined the fire was caused by a student who lit paper towels in a stairwell of the dorm. The father of the student who died sued the university, alleging its negligence contributed to his son's death. The university sued the student who started the fire for contribution. A settlement was reached between the student who set the fire and the father. The student asserted that because he entered into an agreement with the father in good faith, the court should dismiss the university's action against him. The university contended the court should permit it to question the student to evaluate whether the agreement was entered into in good faith. The court denied the university's request to question him about the incident. It found the student entered into a settlement agreement with the father in good faith, and it dismissed the action against him. The university appealed to the Court of Appeals of Ohio.

According to the university, the trial court erred by declining its request to question the student to determine if the agreement was completed in good faith. **The court held the university should be allowed to assess whether the settlement agreement was in good faith.** If it was not, the university could seek contribution. The court reversed the judgment and remanded the case to the trial court for further proceedings. *Cohen v. Univ. of Dayton*, 164 Ohio App.3d 29, 840 N.E.2d 1144 (Ohio Ct. App. 2005).

◆ *An Alabama district court found a state university was not liable for the murder of a freshman residing in a dormitory.*

The student was a freshman at the university and lived in a dormitory room. A stranger entered the dormitory without authorization and murdered her in her room. Her parents sued the university in a federal district court for civil rights violations. They argued the student's relationship with the university was involuntary, such that it had a "special relationship" to her. This meant the university would have a duty to protect her from violence by a third party. The parents argued this relationship arose from a university requirement that all freshmen live on campus. The court disagreed. **The student voluntarily attended the university and was not in its custody.** She was able to retain her liberty and therefore had no special relationship to the university. The court also rejected the parents' due process claim based on deliberate indifference to a risk of serious injury to the student. **The university did not know about or disregard a risk to the student's health and safety.** The court found the university was entitled to qualified immunity and dismissed the case. *Griffin v. Troy State Univ.*, 333 F. Supp.2d 1275 (D. Ala. 2004).

◆ *Lawsuits filed against Texas A&M after a tragic bonfire accident were allowed to continue by a federal appeals court.*

In 1999, a bonfire stack collapsed on the campus of Texas A&M University, killing 12 students and injuring 27 others. A university special commission report exonerated university officials, finding that their actions did not rise to the level of deliberate indifference. However, numerous lawsuits arose, alleging violations of 42 U.S.C. § 1983 under a state-created danger theory. A federal district court dismissed the lawsuits, but the Fifth Circuit reversed and remanded the case. The court held the record supported a finding of deliberate indifference. The plaintiffs presented evidence that university officials allowed the bonfire stack to increase over the years to a pile of burning trash weighing more than 3 million pounds. A university official had described the stack as the "most serious risk management activity at the university." Nevertheless, university officials did not use their authority to control the stack's building or destruction. The plaintiffs even asserted that the university encouraged students to add to the stack as a "marketing tool to lure prospective students" and to gain alumni donations. Based on all this evidence, the Fifth Circuit found that the plaintiffs established their Section 1983 claim. The district court's decision was reversed, and the case was remanded. *Scanlon v. Texas A&M Univ.*, 343 F.3d 533 (5th Cir. 2003).

◆ *The University of Maine may have been negligent in failing to prevent a sexual assault that occurred in one of its dorms because, under state law, it has a duty as a business to protect its "invitees."*

A student participated in a pre-season summer soccer program at the University of Maine. The university allowed participating students to live on campus during the program. The student stayed in a dorm and attended a fraternity party, after which a young man offered to escort her back to her dorm. When she reached her room, the man followed her in and sexually assaulted her. The student and her parents sued the university for negligence and breach of an implied contract. The court granted pretrial judgment to the university. She appealed. The Supreme Judicial Court of Maine reversed the dismissal of the negligence claim. It found that the university owed a duty of care to the student. Under Maine law, **a business (such as the university) has a duty to protect its "invitees" from reasonably foreseeable danger. A sexual assault in a college dormitory is foreseeable** and is one of the reasons the university went through the trouble of establishing safety measures in the dorms. Here, the student had never seen or met with the resident assistant on her floor; there were no group meetings offering instruction on rules and regulations regarding safety within the dorms; and there were no signs posted in the dorms informing residents who should or should not be allowed in. The negligence claim was allowed to proceed, but the court affirmed dismissal of the contract claim. *Stanton v. Univ. of Maine System*, 773 A.2d 1045 (Me. 2001).

◆ *A New York college could declare an alumnus "persona non grata" and bar him from campus.*

Over the course of his nine years at a college, a student exhibited disruptive behavior on campus and began receiving psychiatric treatment. His mother allegedly warned a nurse that he might act violently at his graduation ceremony, and security guards questioned him shortly before the ceremony began. However, the ceremony took place without any trouble. A month later, the student was declared "persona non grata" by the college and was barred from the campus. He eventually sued the college and the nurse. A state court ruled for the defendants, and the New York Supreme Court, Appellate Division, affirmed. Here, **since he had graduated, he was no longer a student and was**

not entitled to due process as a result of the college barring him from campus. Further, his claims against the nurse could not succeed because he could not show that she breached a duty to keep information confidential. *Godinez v. Siena College*, 733 N.Y.S.2d 262 (N.Y. App. Div. 2001).

III. BREACH OF CONTRACT

Colleges and universities can be liable for breach of contract even where they have immunity from lawsuits for negligence or other torts. In order for a contract to exist, there must be some enforceable promise, not just general representations of the kind typically found in student handbooks.

◆ *Representations to incoming students in a university's medical department brochure were not sufficiently definite to form an enforceable contract.*

A Massachusetts Institute of Technology student overdosed on Tylenol with codeine during her freshman year. She was hospitalized and admitted to a psychiatric hospital for one week. While receiving treatment there, the student revealed she suffered from mental health problems and had cut herself when she was in high school. A psychiatrist at the university's mental health services department diagnosed the student with adjustment disorder. He recommended further therapy when she returned for her sophomore year. When the student returned after summer break, she told a dean she was thinking about suicide.

The dean sent her to the mental health department for an immediate assessment. The psychiatrist stated the student had passive suicidal ideation but he did not believe she was at risk of hurting herself. Her mental health problems resurfaced about five months later. The psychiatrist decided the student should be admitted for observation at the university infirmary. After she was examined, she was allowed to return to the dorm. Shortly thereafter, the student died from self-inflicted thermal burns. Her parents sued the university in a state court, asserting representations in the university's medical department brochure and in its medical department bylaws created an enforceable contract. **The court held the representations in the brochure and bylaws were only generalized representations of the purpose and medical services available to the school community. Such statements are not definite and are too vague to form an enforceable contract**. There was no evidence of specific promises made by the university. The court held there was no contract and awarded the university pretrial judgment. *Shin v. Massachusetts Institute of Technology*, 19 Mass. L. Rptr. 570 (Mass. Super. 2005).

◆ *The receipt of funds from a state is just one factor to consider in determining whether a state university is entitled to immunity.*

The Rosa Parks Legacy contracted with Troy University to use the name and image of Rosa Parks in connection with the operation of the Rosa Parks Library and Museum. A dispute developed between the parties, and the Parks Legacy sued the university in a state court for breach of contract. It sought to block the university from using Rosa Parks' name or image and particularly from making a movie that was to feature her image. The Parks Legacy named the university's president as a party, and it sought compensatory and punitive damages. The university and president filed motions to dismiss the action based on the immunity provisions of the Alabama Constitution. The court denied their motions, and they sought review by the Supreme Court of Alabama.

The court noted the state's constitution broadly immunizes state defendants from liability. The state "shall never be made a defendant in any court of law or equity." This provision barred claims not only against the state but against state agencies, employees and officials, including state institutions of higher learning. The Parks Legacy argued the university was not immune from suit because it was not wholly funded by the state. The court rejected this argument, noting **the receipt of funds from the state is just one factor to consider in determining whether an entity is a state entity.** The university president also enjoyed immunity. The nature of the claims against her showed she was being sued in her official capacity, and a suit against a state agent in his or her official capacity is essentially a suit against the state. *Ex parte Troy Univ.*, No. 1051318, 2006 WL 3759341 (Ala. 12/22/06).

◆ *A North Carolina university could be sued for breach of contract, but not for an intentional tort.*

The dealer for a piano manufacturer entered into a contract with a North Carolina university to loan the university a number of pianos in exchange for the right to service the university's other pianos. When the contract ended, the dealer and the manufacturer sued the university for breach of contract, conversion and property damage, claiming that the university returned the pianos in damaged condition and that the university improperly retained 14 pianos. The university sought to dismiss the lawsuit on grounds of sovereign immunity. The North Carolina Court of Appeals noted that the state's tort claims act allows state entities to be sued for negligence. However, conversion is an intentional tort (wrongfully depriving another of it property) and that action had to be dismissed. The breach of contract action, on the other hand, could continue because **when the university entered into the contract, it impliedly agreed to be sued for damages if it breached the contract.** Also, the property damage claim was a breach of contract claim that could proceed. The court remanded the case. *Kawai America Corp. v. Univ. of North Carolina at Chapel Hill*, 567 S.E.2d 215 (N.C. Ct. App. 2002).

◆ *A public college was shielded from liability by the state tort immunity act.*

An employee at an Illinois public college worked under a series of one-year contracts. He complained to college officials that his supervisor subjected him to physical and verbal abuse that caused him physical and psychological problems. When the supervisor gave him a negative evaluation, his contract was not renewed. He then sued the college for breach of contract, battery and intentional infliction of emotional distress. He also sued the supervisor. A jury returned a verdict in his favor, but the Appellate Court of Illinois reversed in part. The court found that **the Illinois Tort Immunity Act shielded the college from liability for the battery and emotional distress claims.** Also, the college was not liable for breach of contract. Here, the college had to provide three months' notice of non-renewal to avoid a breach. The court held that it did so by postmarking the notice on March 31 – the last day it could provide notice. Even though the employee did not receive the notice until early April, it was deemed timely because it was postmarked in March. Finally, however, the court held that the supervisor could be held liable for battery and emotional distress. *Valentino v. Hilquist*, 785 N.E.2d 891 (Ill. Ct. App. 2003).

♦ *A university was determined to have breached its agreement with a philanthropist; it could not claim that the money was a gift.*

A private California university asked a philanthropist to endow a professional chair at one of its research centers. After a number of conversations and the exchange of several letters, the philanthropist agreed to endow the chair. However, the university later selected an existing faculty member for the chair in violation of the endowment terms and also failed to fund the chair. The philanthropist sued for breach of contract, promissory fraud and misappropriation. A state trial court dismissed the action, finding that no contract existed and that the philanthropist made a gift to the university. The California Court of Appeal reversed, finding that **the contract (partially verbal and partially written) existed**. The letters confirmed the verbal agreement; they did not make up the agreement exclusively. The philanthropist could sue the university. *Glenn v. Univ. of Southern California*, No. BC 236256, 2002 WL 31022068 (Cal. Ct. App. 2002).

IV. INSURANCE

Insurance policies may provide coverage for both first- and third-party claims. Third-party claims generally involve liability policies and lawsuits against schools for negligence of school employees. Unless an exclusion in the policy specifically exempts a claim from coverage, an insurer may be required to defend and indemnify the school in any lawsuit arising from an injury to a third party. First-party claims generally involve property and casualty policies, and direct claims of loss by the school.

♦ *The U.S. Court of Appeals, Third Circuit, held a private college's breach of contract claim against its insurance carrier could proceed to trial.*

The college purchased a policy that covered repairs necessary to return property to pre-fire condition. It bought a separate "Ordinance and Law Endorsement" that covered loss to the undamaged portion of a building if it had to be fixed to comply with any ordinance or law. The insurance carrier denied coverage for fire damage caused to the upper floors of a dormitory. The college sued the carrier in a federal district court for breach of contract, contending the endorsement provided coverage for repair and renovation costs required by the Americans with Disabilities Act (ADA). It asserted that the endorsement covered numerous accessibility upgrades made to the building because they had to be done to comply with the ADA. The court held the protections of the ADA did not apply to dormitory space on the second, third and fourth floors of the building. It found they were akin to apartments. The court held for the carrier, and the college appealed to the U.S. Court of Appeals, Third Circuit.

The court held the repairs to the dormitory were alterations within the meaning of the ADA because they included remodeling, renovation or reconstruction. **The court agreed with the college's contention that because dorms are part of boarding colleges, they are places of education.** The ADA prohibited denying disabled students reasonable accommodations that would allow them to live in its dorms. The court held the ADA applied to all four floors of the dormitory. It reversed the judgment. *Regents of Mercersburg College v. Republic Franklin Insurance Co.*, 458 F.3d 159 (3d Cir. 2006).

◆ *A liability insurer did not have to defend a university accused of fraud.*

A Florida university failed to disclose in its catalog that its physical therapy program's accreditation status was probationary. When the applicable accrediting organization withdrew the program's certification, the students who had enrolled in the program became ineligible to take the physical therapy licensing examination. They sued the university for breach of contract, fraud in the inducement, and violation of the Florida Deceptive and Unfair Trade Practices Act. The university sought to have its liability insurer defend and indemnify it in the action, but the Florida District Court of Appeal ruled in favor of the insurer. Here, the insurance policy covered any bodily injury caused by an occurrence, and defined "occurrence" as an accident. However, **the students were alleging intentionally fraudulent conduct by the university. Fraud in the inducement could not be accidental.** Thus, the university would have to defend itself in the action. *Barry Univ. v. Fireman's Fund Insurance Co. of Wisconsin*, 845 So.2d 276 (Fla. Dist. Ct. App. 2003).

◆ *A Missouri medical school could not obtain reimbursement from its insurer for a settlement.*

The medical school agreed to buy land from an energy company that it intended to convert into a parking lot. Before the sale closed, the school's contractor began working on the site, struck and ruptured an underground storage tank, and caused the release of coal tar wastes. The company sued the school and contractor for negligence and trespass, and the school's insurer initially defended it. It withdrew from the defense after a federal court concluded it had no duty to defend. That decision was later reversed. After a court found that the contractor had not trespassed because it had implied permission to work on the site, a settlement was reached. The school then sued its insurer for indemnification. A federal court ruled in favor of the insurer, and the Eighth Circuit affirmed. Here, the policy excluded environmental contamination claims, and the contractor was found not to have trespassed (the only claims the insurer could have been liable for). Thus, **even though the insurer breached its duty to defend the school, it did not have to indemnify the school for the settlement**. *Royal Insurance Co. of America v. Kirksville College of Osteopathic Medicine*, 304 F.3d 804 (8th Cir. 2002).

◆ *A university was entitled to insurance coverage for damage that occurred during a flood.*

After a record rainfall, the Red River flooded, and the city of Grand Forks shut down two sanitary sewer lift stations that serviced the University of North

Dakota campus. As a result, water entered 22 campus buildings through the sewer system and damaged boiler and machinery equipment. The university's insurer denied coverage on the grounds that the sewer backup actually was caused by flooding, which was excluded by the policy. The university asserted that the damage was caused instead by the sewer backup, and that the policy therefore provided coverage. In the lawsuit that followed, a jury ruled in favor of the university, finding that the flood was not the efficient proximate cause of the damage. (Efficient proximate cause is the predominating cause of the loss, though not necessarily the last act in the chain of events, nor the triggering cause of the loss.) **The jury determined that the sewer backup, not the flood, was the efficient proximate cause of the damage.** The North Dakota Supreme Court affirmed, noting that the jury had properly considered the evidence before finding that the sewer backup caused the loss. Accordingly, the court upheld the jury's award of $3.35 million to the university. *Western National Insurance Co. v. Univ. of North Dakota*, 643 N.W.2d 4 (N.D. 2002).

◆   *An excess insurer had to contribute to the defense costs when a university was sued.*

A Colorado professor sued a university in state court for denial of tenure, wrongful termination, defamation and breach of contract, among other claims. Eighteen months later, she filed a second lawsuit against the university in federal court, but chose not to include the defamation claim. The lawsuits were consolidated in federal court, and a question of insurance coverage then arose – namely, which insurer (primary or excess) had to pay the costs of defending the university. The primary insurer was held to have the responsibility for defending the first lawsuit because of the defamation claim – the only claim it was potentially liable for paying. **The excess insurer had to contribute $50,000 to the second lawsuit** (where no defamation claim was presented and the primary insurer could not be liable) even though the two cases were consolidated. Here, even though the cases were consolidated and the primary insurer had the primary obligation to defend the lawsuit, the second lawsuit retained its separate identity for purposes of allocating defense costs. *Farmington Casualty Co. v. United Educators Insurance Risk Retention Group, Inc.*, 36 Fed.Appx. 408 (10th Cir. 2002).

◆   *By giving its insurer late notice of an occurrence that could lead to a lawsuit, a university lost coverage.*

Vanderbilt University conducted a study in the 1940s to track the absorption of iron in pregnant women. The women unknowingly ingested a solution containing radioactive iron isotopes. In the 1960s, a follow-up study revealed a higher incidence of cancer among the participants. In 1985, the Department of Energy requested information relating to the study for a congressional hearing. In 1994, the women and their children filed a class action lawsuit against Vanderbilt, which was settled for $10 million in 1998.

When Vanderbilt sought insurance to cover the loss, its excess insurer denied coverage because of the late notice. A federal court ruled in favor of the insurer, and the Sixth Circuit Court of Appeals affirmed. **Under the policy, Vanderbilt had to notify the insurer of an "occurrence" as soon as possible.**

Here, the occurrence was deemed to have happened in the 1960s when the follow-up study was conducted (or at the very latest, in 1985). By failing to give notice until the lawsuit was filed in 1994, Vanderbilt prejudiced the insurer's ability to defend and thus was not entitled to be reimbursed for the settlement. *U.S. Fire Insurance Co. v. Vanderbilt Univ.*, 267 F.3d 465 (6th Cir. 2001).

◆ *City University of New York (CUNY) did not have to compensate Carnegie Hall Corporation for damages the hall's insurance company paid after a student fell during a graduation ceremony.*

CUNY's licensing agreement with Carnegie Hall allowed CUNY to use the hall for the 1994 graduation ceremony of the university's technical college. The agreement required CUNY to obtain comprehensive general liability insurance to cover any claims arising out of the event, but CUNY never obtained the required coverage. During the ceremony, a graduating student fell on a staircase and sued Carnegie Hall for failing to keep the staircase in a reasonably safe condition. The hall's insurance company ultimately paid $41,987 in settlement fees and defense costs.

Carnegie Hall and the insurance company sued CUNY for reimbursement because the university failed to get insurance coverage, as mandated by the license agreement. A New York claims court determined that CUNY owed the hall's insurer compensation and granted pretrial judgment in the plaintiffs' favor, but the New York Supreme Court, Appellate Division, disagreed. The court held neither Carnegie Hall nor the insurer had any basis for recovery against CUNY. Carnegie Hall had no ground to seek damages from CUNY because it did not incur any financial loss – its insurer paid the expenses related to the student's lawsuit. In addition, **the insurer was not entitled to recover settlement and defense costs. It was not a party to the license agreement, and it did not claim to be a third party to the agreement.** Therefore, any basis for recovery was based on its status as the subrogee of Carnegie Hall. New York's high court previously has ruled that recovery for the breach of a contract requiring the purchase of insurance is limited to the cost of obtaining substitute coverage, and not defense costs. Accordingly, the case was dismissed. *Carnegie Hall Corp. v. City Univ. of New York*, 729 N.Y.S.2d 93 (N.Y. App. Div. 2001).

◆ *An insurer could seek reimbursement for a student's medical expenses by joining the student's individual action.*

A University of Tennessee student was permanently injured while participating in a track meet. The student and his parents filed a claim against the university with the Tennessee Claims Commission. The matter was settled between the parties, except for the student's subrogation claim seeking $1,026,666 in reimbursement to his insurer for medical expenses. The Claims Commission denied the subrogation claim because the student did not assert the claim in his pleadings and because his insurer was not joined as a party to the action. Initially, the Tennessee Court of Appeals affirmed the commission's determination and found that the insurer should file its own claim to obtain compensation. The student then notified the Claims Commission that he was joining the insurer to the action, but the commission denied the joinder request as too late. The appellate court reversed the commission's decision. It held that the commission was in error when it struck the student's pleadings regarding joinder of the insurer, even though the pleadings were untimely. The panel noted that **the University of Tennessee was previously advised of the subrogation claim and would not be prejudiced if the claim was included, since the commission had not yet decided whether the insurer was entitled to reimbursement**. The case was remanded for a trial on the merits of the insurer's claim. *Hartman v. Univ. of Tennessee*, 38 S.W.3d 570 (Tenn. Ct. App. 2000).

◆ *A public university in Oregon could not deny health insurance coverage to domestic partners of homosexual employees.*

The Oregon Court of Appeals determined that a public health sciences university violated the state constitution's privileges and immunities clause by maintaining **a practice of denying health insurance coverage to the domestic partners of its homosexual employees**. The case arose after three university nurses applied for insurance coverage for their domestic partners. The benefits manager refused to process the application because the university provided health insurance to spouses, not unmarried partners. After the state employee benefits board upheld the denial of benefits, the nurses sued. The court of appeals stated that Oregon's employment discrimination statute protected the nurses on the basis of their sexual orientation. However, the university did not violate that statute. Rather, the university violated the state constitution's privileges and immunities clause (which requires governmental entities to make benefits available on equal terms to all Oregon citizens). **Because homosexuals cannot marry under Oregon law, the university's health insurance benefits were made available on terms that, for gay and lesbian couples, were a legal impossibility.** *Tanner v. Oregon Health Sciences Univ.*, 971 P.2d 435 (Or. Ct. App. 1998).

V. PRIVATE INSTITUTIONS

Like their public counterparts, private colleges and universities are not liable for negligence unless they breach a legal duty. A claimant must show the breach of duty proximately caused injury and damages. Private institutions have no duty to shield students from injuries caused by sudden, unexpected, or unforeseeable acts. Institutions organized exclusively for religious, charitable, or educational purposes may be entitled to claim charitable immunity.

◆ *Private institutions must exercise reasonable care to protect students from foreseeable criminal or dangerous acts by third persons.*

A New York private college student was punched in the face by a classmate during a classroom altercation. He sued the college in the state court system for negligently failing to prevent the attack. The court held for the college, and the student appealed. The New York Supreme Court, Appellate Division, held that **to prove negligence, there must be a breach of a legal duty that** proximately caused damages. **The court noted that colleges generally have no duty to shield students from dangers presented by other students.** However, **they must exercise reasonable care to protect students from reasonably foreseeable criminal or dangerous acts committed by others,** including other students. In this case, the college did not breach any duty, because the injury was the result of a "sudden, unexpected, and unforeseeable act." Because the attack was not foreseeable, the college's failure to prevent it was not negligent. The judgment was affirmed. *Luina v. Katharine Gibbs School New York*, 830 N.Y.S.2d 263 (N.Y. App. Div. 2007).

◆ *A private Connecticut university was not liable for harassment of a student based on his religion.*

The student attended a doctoral program in management systems. He claimed one of his professors suggested he adopt some Chinese heritage and culture, and that another remarked that he had a "mind like a computer." The student told the professor his mental abilities came from God. The professor responded, "It doesn't come from God, it comes from David, from the Jewish religion." A third professor allegedly made a remark about the student being Catholic. The student claimed several other faculty members also harassed him, delayed his presentation of his doctoral thesis, and prevented him from taking classes. He sued the university, claiming it violated state and federal laws when it harassed him based on his religion. The student alleged the university violated his federal civil rights, as protected by 42 U.S.C. § 1983. **The university argued it was a private entity that could not be sued for federal civil rights violations.** The student contended that as the university received some federal funding, the court should further determine if its acts or decisions would be considered functions of the state. The court agreed with the university and granted its motion for summary judgment. *Martin v. Univ. of New Haven*, 359 F.Supp.2d 185 (D. Conn. 2005).

◆ *A student who was shot could proceed with his lawsuit against a college and a fraternity for negligence.*

A Missouri student enrolled in a private college for the summer semester and moved into a fraternity house. After a confrontational phone call, the student attempted to lock the front door, but the latch malfunctioned and popped open. Ten minutes later, two men entered the house and shot him. He sued the college and the fraternity for negligence, asserting that they breached a duty to maintain the premises in good repair. The college and fraternity maintained that they had no duty to prevent a third person from performing an intentional criminal act, and that even if they had a duty to maintain and repair the house, the student could not show that a breach of that duty caused his injuries under the law. A state court granted pretrial judgment to the defendants, but the Missouri Supreme Court reversed. It found issues of fact as to **whether the student was in a landlord-tenant relationship with either of the defendants so as to impose a duty of care.** There also was a jury question as to whether the breach of that duty was the proximate cause of the student's injuries. *Letsinger v. Drury College*, 68 S.W.3d 408 (Mo. 2002).

◆ *Where an insured board member at a private college made misrepresentations to the board of trustees to obtain a personal advantage for his company, and where the college lost $2 million as a result, the college's errors and omissions policy did not provide coverage for the loss.*

A Texas Christian College purchased a "school leaders errors and omissions" policy that insured it against wrongful acts committed by directors and officers of the school. Subsequently, a member of the board of trustees convinced the board to invest $2 million of its endowment funds in a company that accepted accounts receivable as security for short-term loans. However, he did not disclose that the company had a negative net worth, that he was a 49% owner of the company, or that he also was a salaried employee of the company. **When the investment failed, the college obtained the board member's resignation, then sued him and his company for misrepresentation of certain facts and for making false statements.**

The college obtained a judgment against the board member for $1.8 million and against the company for $2 million. Unable to collect on the judgments, it sought to collect under its errors and omissions policy. The insurer denied coverage under the "fraud or dishonesty" exclusion and the "personal profit or advantage" exclusion. A Texas federal court held that the two exclusions applied to bar coverage, and the college appealed to the U.S. Court of Appeals, Fifth Circuit. The appellate court affirmed. It noted that **the exclusion for "any claim arising out of the gaining in fact of any personal profit or advantage to which the Insured is not legally entitled" applied to bar coverage**. Here, the board member clearly gained a personal advantage by his company's receipt of the $2 million in endowment funds from the college. Despite the fact that the board member did not ultimately make a profit, he did gain a personal advantage by his wrongful acts. As a result, the insurer had no obligation to pay out under the policy. *Jarvis Christian College v. National Union Fire Insurance Co.*, 197 F.3d 742 (5th Cir. 1999).

◆ *A Virginia college and professor were not entitled to charitable immunity where the professor was not acting on behalf of a charitable institution at the time he injured a beneficiary.*

A professor at a Virginia college established a program with the Boys and Girls Club of Hampton Roads, under which students in the professor's recreation programming class were required to spend six hours observing the children and volunteering at the club. The students were required to return to the classroom, design programs for the children, then implement the programs at the club. The professor went to the club to observe his students and help them out when needed. While he was there observing one day, a student asked him to watch a door leading to the weight room. She was giving a talk on wellness and body conditioning to 13- to 18-year-olds and wanted to keep younger students not involved in the program out of the room. The professor closed the door, amputating the right thumb of a minor who had his hand on the doorframe. The minor sued the professor and the college, who sought to dismiss the action on the basis of charitable immunity.

The Supreme Court of Virginia noted that the club was a charity and that the minor was a beneficiary of the club. However, **it refused to award the** defendants charitable immunity because, at the time of the injury, the **professor was not engaged in the work of the charity. Rather, he was carrying out his duties as a professor**, observing a student and acting as a "doorkeeper." The court remanded the case for further proceedings. *Mooring v. Virginia Wesleyan College*, 514 S.E.2d 619 (Va. 1999).

◆ *The New Jersey charitable immunity statute provided protection to a religious university in a negligence lawsuit arising from the university's operation of a pub on campus.*

A Catholic university in New Jersey operated a pub on campus solely for students and their guests. The pub was not operated for profit, it was subsidized by the student government association, and its employees were students. A 21-year-old senior at the university went with several friends to the pub and slipped in a puddle that was apparently left when a serving cart was moved. He sued the university in a state trial court seeking to recover for his injuries. The court denied the university's motion for a directed verdict, and a jury returned a verdict in favor of the student. The university appealed to the Superior Court of New Jersey, Appellate Division.

On appeal, the court noted that the university had deemed the pub to be part of a student's socialization process and a factor in the development of a well-rounded person. The question was whether the state's charitable immunity statute applied to the university while it was running the pub for students and their guests. **Under the statute, nonprofit corporations, societies or associations organized exclusively for religious, charitable, or educational purposes could not be held liable for negligence where the person injured as a result of the negligence was a beneficiary, to whatever degree, of the works of the nonprofit corporation, society or association.** Because the student was a beneficiary of the university to some degree while patronizing the pub, the university was entitled to charitable immunity under the statute. The court noted that the fact that the pub had since been replaced by a campus coffee house was not critical to the immunity analysis. Since the university had reasonably concluded that a campus experience ought to include opportunities to mature in an environment enriched not only by study and classes, but by diverse forms of social interchange within the university setting, the student was a beneficiary at the time of his injury, and the university was entitled to immunity. *Bloom v. Seton Hall Univ.*, 704 A.2d 1334 (N.J. Super. Ct. App. Div. 1998).

◆ *Patients who never faced a medically verified substantial risk of contracting HIV did not suffer recognizable damages.*

Six patients received various treatments from several students at an Illinois private university's dental clinic during 1990 and 1991. In July of 1991, the university sent a letter to the patients informing them that a dental student who provided care to the patients was infected with HIV. While the university stated that it was unlikely that they were infected with HIV, it strongly recommended that the patients be tested for the virus. The patients sued the university and the dental student in a state court, which dismissed their claim. The patients appealed to the Appellate Court of Illinois, First District, which held that **in the**

absence of a particularly substantial risk of HIV infection, their reasonable fears were not severe enough to warrant compensation. Because the patients never faced a medically verified substantial risk of contracting HIV, they did not suffer recognizable damages. Therefore, the court affirmed the judgment dismissing the complaint. *Doe v. Northwestern Univ.*, 682 N.E.2d 145 (Ill. App. Ct. 1997).

◆   *A private college did not become liable for a priest's sexual assault of a boy because it was not reasonably foreseeable.*

A priest employed as a campus minister by a private college and as a chaplain at a hospital was accused of sexually assaulting a boy. The priest knew the boy and his family through the boy's school and parish. The alleged assaults took place in the evening at the priest's residence, where the boy was staying because of his family's friendship with the priest. The boy was neither a patient at the hospital nor a student at the college. After the assault, the boy's parents sued the college and the hospital, alleging *respondeat superior* liability and negligent supervision. The college and the hospital filed motions to dismiss, which the trial court granted.

The parents appealed to the Court of Appeals of Ohio, which noted that **for an employer to be liable under the theory of *respondeat superior*, the employee's act must be committed within the scope of employment**. This means that it must be calculated to facilitate or promote the business for which the person was employed. Here, the court held that sexual assault diverted from the straight and narrow performance of the priest's job, as it was not reasonably foreseeable to the college or hospital that the priest would commit such an act against someone who was neither a student at the college nor a patient at the hospital. His relationship with the boy was in no way related to his roles as campus minister or hospital chaplain. The court also found no liability as to the negligent supervision claim. The trial court's decision was affirmed. *Gebhart v. College of Mt. St. Joseph*, 665 N.E.2d 223 (Ohio Ct. App. 1995).

VI. VICARIOUS LIABILITY

The doctrine of "vicarious liability," also known as "respondeat superior," makes employers liable for the wrongful conduct of their employees that occurs within the scope of their employment or official responsibilities.

◆   *A Mississippi court ruled a university could be sued for negligence by a student who suffered a burn injury during an iron pour demonstration.*

The professor was invited to give a lecture and demonstrate an iron pour and he asked the student to participate. The pour was conducted in an outdoor area, and the ground was wet. The student was burned when the molten iron overflowed onto the ground and began popping up into the air. She suffered a third-degree burn on her ankle, which required multiple surgeries and left her with hypersensitivity and a limited range of motion. The student sued the university and professor in a state court for negligence. At trial, the professor admitted there would have been less of a chance for metal to pop off the ground if he had put down some dry sand in the area of the pour. The student's expert witness testified the popping and flying of the metal was directly caused by the failure to put sand down. There was also evidence that recognized safety standards call for a layer of dry sand to be placed under and around furnaces whenever molten metal is being handled. The court held the university owed the student no duty of care in light of her age and experience with iron pouring. The professor was immune from suit under state law because he was acting within the course and scope of his employment. The university also had immunity. The student appealed to the Court of Appeals of Mississippi.

The court held the university was responsible for the negligence of its employees acting in the course and scope of employment. The professor had a duty to take ordinary and reasonable precautions to protect students from an unreasonable risk of injury when he prepared for the iron pour. He breached this duty when he failed to place dry sand on the wet ground. The evidence also showed this failure caused the student's injury. Under applicable state law, governmental entities and their employees are generally entitled to immunity on claims arising from the performance or failure to perform a "discretionary function." Although his actions involved an element of choice or judgment, they were not based on considerations of public policy, and the university had no immunity. The judgment was reversed, and the case was remanded to determine the amount of damages to award the student. *Pritchard v. Von Houten*, No. 2005-CA-00710-COA, 2007 WL 333190 (Miss. Ct. App. 2/6/07).

◆ *The District Court of Appeal of Florida held a college was not liable for the conduct if a teacher who got into a traffic accident on a class trip.*

At the end of the school year, the student, her teacher, and the student's daughter went on a trip to celebrate the end of the course. The teacher lost control of the van and it rolled over. The student was injured and her daughter died. The student sued the college in a state court for negligence. The court held for the college, and the student appealed to the District Court of Appeal of Florida. According to the student, the teacher was acting in the course and scope of his employment when the accident occurred. The college contended it did not authorize the trip and that the teacher was not performing official duties. The college term had ended and the trip had no educational purpose.

The court held that to show the teacher was acting in the scope of his employment at the time of the accident, the student had to show his conduct was of the kind he was hired to perform. She further had to show this conduct occurred substantially within the time and space limits of his work and was in some way related to serving the college. **As the accident occurred the day after the term ended, the court found the teacher was not acting within the course and scope of his employment with the university** at the time of the accident. The judgment for the college was affirmed. *Fernandez v. Florida National College*, 925 So.2d 1096 (Fla. Dist. Ct. App. 2006).

◆ *The Court of Appeals of Michigan held a university was not liable for a student's injury in an on-campus accident with a university vehicle.*

The accident occurred when the driver of another vehicle failed to obey a stop sign and crashed into the student's motorcycle as he drove through an intersection. The student suffered a dislocated shoulder, injuries to both knees and traumatic chestwall syndrome. The driver was employed by the university and was driving a university-owned vehicle. The student claimed he suffered serious impairment of his body functions and sued the university in a state court, alleging it was vicariously liable for the driver's negligence. The court found he had not suffered a "serious impairment of body function," and did not establish the threshold requirement for non-economic damages under the state No-Fault Act. The student appealed to the Court of Appeals of Michigan.

The student his injuries prevented him from snowboarding, mountain-biking, and rollerblading, and impaired his ability to work in a bike shop. He said his restrictions left him grossly underemployed and unable to complete a course, delaying his ability to obtain a degree in graphic design. Surgery did not correct the injuries, and the student claimed this resulted in serious impairment of body function. **The court found no medical evidence that the nature of the injuries was such that the student would have to endure a lifetime of pain, instability and weakness.** To determine whether the impairment affected his course of normal life, the court compared his life before and after the accident and considered the extent to which the injuries affected his overall life. The court explained that merely showing impairments that interrupted part of the student's life was not enough to prove they affected the course of his life. A reduction in athletic activity did not change the course of his life and his failure to earn a graphic design degree had nothing to do with the injuries. The student did not explain why he could not finish the course or what efforts he made to complete it. As for any impact on his employment, the court found they were self-imposed. The court affirmed the judgment. *Chambers v. Lehmann*, No. 262502, 2005 WL 2291889 (Mich. Ct. App. 9/20/05).

◆   *A college was not liable for negligence when a resident assistant did not get medical assistance for a student's guest, who had passed out.*

An Iowa college student's guest drank at least 12 shots of vodka and passed out. The student informed the resident assistant (RA) of the guest's condition and was instructed to watch her. At some point, the student engaged the guest in sexual intercourse, which he claimed was consensual. The guest claimed it was sexual assault. The student also allegedly permitted two friends to fondle the guest's breasts. She brought a damages action against Simpson College for negligence under the theory of respondeat superior, based on the failure of the RA to obtain medical attention for her. A federal court granted the college summary judgment. The Eighth Circuit affirmed. It refused to find that the RA assumed a legal duty to come to the guest's aid. Since the RA did not specifically act to take control of the guest, he had no legal duty to obtain medical aid for her. *Freeman v. Busch*, 349 F.3d 582 (8th Cir. 2003).

◆   *A university employee was not entitled to immunity for sexual harassment where his conduct was outside the scope of his employment.*

An employee of the Ohio Department of Surgery Corporation worked with an employee of Ohio State University (OSU). She claimed that the OSU employee subjected her to sexual harassment and created a hostile work environment. She accused him of calling her a "worthless slut," an "ignorant slut," and a "pushy bitch." She sued him and OSU in the Court of Claims, seeking a determination regarding the employee's immunity. The court found that the OSU employee was entitled to immunity because, although his conduct was "boorish," he did not act with malice, in bad faith, or in a wanton or reckless manner. The Court of Appeals of Ohio reversed. **A state employee is not entitled to immunity if his conduct is manifestly outside the scope of his employment or official responsibilities, or if he acts with malicious purpose, in bad faith, or in a wanton or reckless manner**. From the record, the court concluded that the OSU employee's remarks did not further the interests of the state. Consequently, he was acting "manifestly outside the scope of his employment" and was not entitled to immunity. *Oye v. Ohio State Univ.*, No. 02AP-1362, 2003 WL 22511511 (Ohio Ct. App. 2003).

◆   *A university was not liable for the conduct of a research assistant, who hit a car while driving drunk.*

A research assistant at a California university drove to the home of her supervising professor, with whom she also was romantically involved. Although she intended to work at his house, she discovered that he had been in a car accident and instead went to the hospital. She later brought him back to his house and consumed a bottle of vodka while there. When she drove home in the evening, she crossed the median of a highway and collided with another vehicle. She was charged with driving under the influence. The driver of the other vehicle sued the university for his damages, asserting that it was liable under the doctrine of *respondeat superior*. A state court dismissed the lawsuit. The California Court of Appeal affirmed. **The research assistant had not been acting within the scope of her employment at the time of the crash.** Thus, the crash was not foreseeable as a part of her work, and the university could not be held vicariously liable for her actions. *Williams v. Regents of the Univ. of California*, No. GO29601, 2002 WL 31873790 (Cal. Ct. App. 2002).

◆   *Faculty members who volunteered to serve as advisors to Texas A&M's drama club were still considered university employees.*

A student actor was accidentally stabbed with a bowie knife by another student during the final scene of a performance. The injured student sued the university, the director of the play, the choreographer and the faculty advisors for negligence because Texas A&M prohibits deadly weapons on campus. The trial court held the university liable for the incident, but the court of appeals reversed, finding that Texas A&M could not be legally responsible because the director and choreographer were independent contractors, and the faculty advisors were considered volunteers in their roles as advisors to the drama club.

The Texas Supreme Court overturned the appellate decision. It ruled that **although the faculty members were not paid additional compensation for their work as advisors to the drama club, they were still considered employees of the university for the purposes of liability under the state's Tort Claims Act**. Even though the faculty members were not directly paid for their role as advisors and were not required to act as advisors, Texas A&M considered their drama club involvement when calculating their salaries. The court did not address whether the director and choreographer were considered university employees because they settled with the injured student out of court. The university was held liable for the faculty advisors' failure to ensure that the university's no-weapons policy was enforced. *Bishop v. Texas A&M Univ.*, 35 S.W.3d 605 (Tex. 2000).

◆ *A university may be liable if it is deliberately indifferent to student-on-student sexual harassment.*

Two female students at the University of Colorado who participated in the Reserve Officer Training Corps (ROTC) program alleged that a fellow student (a higher-ranking cadet in the ROTC program) committed acts that created a hostile work environment. When they reported the acts to a superior ROTC officer, he retaliated against them by denying them further opportunities in the ROTC program and subjected them to other acts of sexual harassment. They then reported the harassment to university officials and asserted that the university did not take adequate measures to respond to their allegations. They sued the university in federal court under Title IX, where the university maintained that it could not be held liable because ROTC members were not agents of the university and it did not exercise control over them. The court dismissed the case against the university, and the students appealed to the U.S. Court of Appeals, Tenth Circuit. The court of appeals reversed, finding that the lawsuit should not have been dismissed. Here, **the students had adequately pled that the ROTC program was a university-sanctioned program, that they had been harassed by members of that program, and that the university did not take remedial action when notified of the harassment.** The case was remanded for further proceedings. *Morse v. Regents of the Univ. of Colorado*, 154 F.3d 1124 (10th Cir. 1998).

◆ *Where an Army officer who instructed ROTC students was not an agent of a college, the college could not be liable for any negligence on his part.*

A Georgia college student enrolled in a military science Mountaineering Techniques class injured his ankle while practicing rappelling techniques. He sued the college, asserting that the instructor had negligently instructed him, causing the injury. The college maintained that the instructor had not been negligent and that, even if he had, he was not an agent of the college because he was a full-time Army officer who was assigned to the college to teach ROTC courses. The trial court held that the college had the right and authority to control the details of the sergeant's work, but chose not to do so. Accordingly, the sergeant was an agent of the college, which was potentially liable for the student's injury. The Georgia Court of Appeals reversed. It stated that **under the cross-enrollment agreement for the establishment of ROTC instruction, the college did not have the right to control the time, manner and method of the Army's performance**. Because the Army provided the rappelling tower, uniforms, textbooks, ropes and other equipment, and because the training procedures were the Army's, the instructor was an independent contractor rather than an agent of the college. The student's lawsuit was dismissed. *Armstrong State College v. McGlynn*, 505 S.E.2d 853 (Ga. Ct. App. 1998).

CHAPTER TEN

University Operations

I.   GOVERNMENT REGULATION

A.   Public Records and Freedom of Information

◆   *A Michigan university police incident report was not entirely exempt from public disclosure.*

Three men were arrested in connection with an assault on the campus of Michigan State University (MSU). A news organization asked MSU for a copy of its police incident report related to the incident. The request was filed under the state Freedom of Information Act (FOIA). The organization had already published a story with the names of three men who were arrested for the assault, but it wanted additional information from the report, such as personally identifiable information relating to victims, witnesses, and police officers. The report also included photographs and statements from the responding officers and others. MSU officials denied the request, saying disclosure would violate individual privacy rights and interfere with the law enforcement investigation.

The case reached the Michigan Court of Appeals, which held MSU did not show FOIA privacy and law enforcement exemptions applied. **It was not enough for MSU to show disclosure might cause retaliation or interfere with the investigation.** The court said MSU needed to show disclosure actually would cause retaliation or unduly disrupt law enforcement proceedings. **The privacy exemption does not apply unless disclosure would cause a "clearly unwarranted" invasion of privacy.** In this case, disclosure might shed light on issues of public concern, such as MSU's security policies and government response to crime. The trial court had wrongfully failed to review the report to decide if parts of the report could be separated and disclosed without violating individual privacy rights or interfering with the investigation. The case was remanded to the trial court for further proceedings. *State News v. Michigan State Univ.*, 274 Mich. App. 558 (Mich. Ct. App. 2007).

◆   *The Supreme Court of Iowa held a state university could not shield its financial records from public view by outsourcing certain university functions to a private foundation.*

University financial records were managed by a private nonprofit foundation that had been incorporated by the university in 1958. In 2002, the university and foundation renewed an elaborate service agreement. In the agreement, the university expressed its desire to engage the expertise of the foundation as an independent contractor to provide advice, coordination, and assistance in fundraising, development, and in the operation, accounting and fund investment management of those areas. A group of citizens sought a state court order to view university tax and financial records under the Iowa Freedom of Information Act, I.C.A. § 22.1, *et seq.* The act creates a public right to view governmental records. The court held the foundation was not a government body under the act, so its documents were not "public records."

The citizens appealed to the Supreme Court of Iowa. It stated "public records" included documents or other information belonging to the state, school corporation, or nonprofit corporation whose facilities are supported with property tax revenue, and relate to the investment of public funds. **The court held the foundation was performing a government function through the contract with the university, so its records were subject to public disclosure. It said a government body may not outsource its functions to a private corporation and then keep the information from the public.** In executing the service agreement, the university, a government body, contracted away its ability to raise money and manage its finances to what was assumed to be a nongovernment body. **The university had attempted to do indirectly what it could not do directly – avoid disclosure of what would otherwise be public records.** The court held the Freedom of Information Act prevented this result, and it reversed the judgment. *Gannon v. Board of Regents of State of Iowa*, 692 N.W.2d 31 (Iowa 2005).

◆   *Massachusetts' highest court held incident reports and other documents held by a private university police department were not "public records."*

A student newspaper asked two municipal police departments and Harvard University's police department for all records related to certain incidents listed on the university department's weekly log of complaints, including incident reports and correspondence. The municipal police departments supplied the documents to the newspaper, but the university asserted it did not have to comply with the public records law because it was not a public entity.

The newspaper asked a state court for an order requiring the university to release the documents. The court dismissed the case, ruling that private university officers were not governmental employees. Accordingly, documents they made or received were not "public records." The newspaper appealed to the Supreme Judicial Court of Massachusetts, arguing the appointment of some university officers as special state police officers or deputy sheriffs vested them with broad police powers. Under this theory, they were subject to public records law requirements. **The court held the university records were not covered by the state public records law, and did not have to be disclosed.** The judgment for Harvard was affirmed. *Harvard Crimson v. President and Fellows of Harvard College*, 445 Mass. 745, 840 N.E.2d 518 (Mass. 2006).

◆   *A federal district court held the U.S. Department of Agriculture (USDA) failed to properly document a refusal to disclose information to a university under the federal Freedom of Information Act (FOIA).*

An Illinois university requested documents under the FOIA from the USDA. When the USDA failed to respond more than a year later, the university sued it in a federal district court. The USDA admitted it did not respond to the request and provided the documents the university had asked for. The USDA then argued the case was moot because it had complied with the FOIA. The court noted the U.S. Court of Appeals, District of Columbia Circuit, held in *Vaughn v. Rosen*, 484 F.2d 820 (D.C. Cir. 1973), **that a federal agency must submit an index to explain the reasons why information was withheld or redacted.** This index is known as a "Vaughn index." Because the USDA failed to submit a Vaughn index, the court could not assess whether its reasons for redacting information or refusing to disclose materials were legitimate. The court denied the university's motion for summary judgment and ordered the USDA to submit a Vaughn index. *Northwestern Univ. v. U.S. Dep't of Agriculture*, 403 F.Supp.2d 83 (D.D.C. 2005).

◆   *New York's Freedom of Information Law required disclosure of animal testing information to a citizen group.*

A citizen group sued the Board of Trustees of the State University of New York under the state's Freedom of Information Law (FOIL) to obtain certain records relating to biomedical research on cats and dogs. A New York appellate court held that the facility was not an "agency" under the FOIL when it maintained the random source certifications because it was doing so to comply with federal law. However, the New York Court of Appeals held the group was entitled to the research information. **The facility was an "agency" for purposes of the FOIL because the certifications were being kept in connection with the research conducted by the facility, and that research was fulfilling the state university system's statutory mission – a state governmental function.** Since the board of trustees had not shown that the information being sought was subject to any exception, the FOIL required that the information be disclosed. *Citizens for Alternatives to Animal Labs v. Board of Trustees of SUNY*, 703 N.E.2d 1218 (N.Y. 1998).

◆   *A university had to disclose faculty booklists to a competitor of the campus bookstore under the New York Freedom of Information Law .*

A bookstore seeking to compete with the on-campus bookstore run by Barnes & Noble attempted to obtain faculty booklists. When informal attempts failed, it got an advisory opinion stating that the lists constituted records under New York's Freedom of Information Law (FOIL), then submitted formal requests to university faculty members and the university's records access officer. A few faculty members responded, but the records officer did not. The following semester, the same result was achieved. The bookstore then sued the university to compel it to comply with the FOIL, and a trial court dismissed the action. The supreme court, appellate division, reversed. **Course syllabi and written booklists constitute "records" under the FOIL because they are held by an agency.** It did not matter that the lists were kept by individual faculty members. Regardless of whether the university required the lists to be turned in to the records office, if they existed and someone requested them, they had to be made available. Here, the records existed, and the records officer was required to make them available. *Mohawk Book Co. Ltd. v. SUNY*, 732 N.Y.S.2d 272 (N.Y. App. Div. 2001).

B. Aliens and Immigration

◆   *A California court found no conflict between federal immigration statutes and a state law permitting undocumented aliens to qualify for resident tuition.*

The California Legislature enacted Assembly Bill 540, which became Section 68130.5 of the state Education Code. The law exempted some students without lawful immigration status from non-resident tuition rates at public institutions of higher learning. Section 68130.5 placed those seeking to legalize their immigration status on the same footing as students who had graduated from California high schools, students who had attended a California high school for at least three years, and current students registered at state institutions of higher education. A group of university students who could not claim resident status under Section 68130.5 sued the state university system in a California superior court. **The court explained that California and nine other states have similar laws allowing certain undocumented students to apply for in-state tuition rates at public universities and colleges. However, the federal government, including the Secretary of Homeland Security, had yet to offer any opinion on the validity of these state laws. The court held federal immigration laws did not preempt Section 68130.5.**

The court held the state law did not confer a benefit based on residency in California. The complaining parties did not show the law violated the Equal Protection Clause or the Privileges and Immunities Clause of the state and federal constitutions. Section 68130.5 did not classify people on the basis of alienage or residency. Nothing in Section 68130.5 supported the contention that the section discriminated against U.S. citizens. The state had a legitimate governmental purpose in helping high school students who were likely to remain in California. **There was no evidence that the legislature was trying to promote immigration or naturalization through Section 68130.5.** The complaining parties did not show the law was discriminatory under the state civil rights act. The court made other pretrial rulings and denied a request by other parties to intervene in the case. *Martinez v. Regents of Univ. of California*, No. CV 05-2064, 2006 WL 2974303 (Cal. Super. Ct. 10/4/06).

◆ *The U.S. Department of Homeland Security was ordered to make a final decision regarding a Muslim scholar's visa within 90 days.*

The American Academy of Religion (AAR) and the American Association of University Professors (AAUP) sued the Department of Homeland Security (DHS) in a federal district court, challenging the exclusion of Tariq Ramadan from the U.S. Ramadan is a well-known Muslim scholar who shuns violence as a form of activism and has spoken out against terrorism and radical Islamists. However, the U.S. revoked his visa in July 2004. AAR and AAUP sought an injunction requiring DHS to immediately adjudicate Ramadan's pending visa application, or permit him to enter the U.S. on a visa waiver program for up to 90 days. As a Swiss citizen, Ramadan was eligible for the waiver program.

The DHS claimed Ramadan's visa application was never denied because the revocation was only a "prudential" revocation, which is not a denial but a means of cancelling a visa while the government investigates. It said the visa application was still pending. **The court explained that if the government had a legitimate reason for excluding Ramadan, then it could do so. However, it was unable to determine whether the reason was legitimate or bona fide because the DHS did not explain why it excluded Ramadan.** Federal regulations require a statement of the reasons for a visa revocation. The court directed the DHS to issue a formal decision on Ramadan's pending visa application within 90 days. *American Academy of Religion v. Chertoff*, 463 F.Supp.2d 400 (S.D.N.Y. 2006).

◆ *Yale University could no longer employ an alien student because students who are not enrolled are ineligible for on-campus employment.*

Yale had hired the student, who is a Turkish citizen, to work as a full-time research assistant. According to the student, Yale breached the terms of contracts when it refused to pay him money it allegedly owed him. The student had dropped the only course he had been enrolled in, which meant he lost his status as a student. The Appellate Court of Connecticut upheld the trial court's decision in favor of Yale. **It could no longer employ or pay the student because immigration law provides that once a student is no longer enrolled, he is ineligible for an on-campus employment benefit.** *Keles v. Yale Univ.*, 98 Conn. App. 901, 908 A.2d 28 (Conn. App. Ct. 2006).

◆ *The right to rebut a presumption of nonresidence extends even to aliens with visas living in state.*

The University of Maryland granted "in-state" tuition status only to students domiciled in Maryland, or, if a student was financially dependent on the student's parents, to students whose parents were domiciled in Maryland. The university also could deny in-state status to individuals who did not pay the full spectrum of Maryland state taxes. The university refused to grant in-state status to a number of students, each of whom was dependent on a parent who held a "G-4 visa" (a non-immigrant visa granted to officers and employees of international treaty organizations and members of their immediate family). The university stated that the holder of a G-4 visa could not acquire Maryland domicile because the holder was incapable of showing an essential element of domicile – the intent to live permanently or indefinitely in Maryland. After unsuccessful appeals at the administrative level, the students brought a class action lawsuit in federal court seeking declaratory and injunctive relief. The students alleged that university policy violated the Equal Protection Clause.

A federal district court granted relief, stating that the G-4 visa could not create an irrebuttable presumption of nondomicile. On appeal, the U.S. Supreme Court stated that the case was controlled by the principles announced in *Vlandis v. Kline*, this chapter, that **when a state purports to be concerned with domicile, it must provide an individual with the opportunity to present evidence bearing on that issue.** Federal law allows aliens holding a G-4 visa to acquire domicile in the United States. However, the question of whether such domicile could be acquired in Maryland was a question of state law. Since no controlling precedent had been decided by the state's highest court, the Supreme Court declined to rule and certified the question to the Maryland Court of Appeals for resolution. *Elkins v. Moreno*, 435 U.S. 647, 98 S.Ct. 1338, 55 L.Ed.2d 614 (1978).

◆   *The Supreme Court struck down a university policy that restricted an alien's right to acquire domicile in a state and thus qualify for in-state tuition.*

The University of Maryland's student fee schedule policy denied students whose parents held non-immigrant alien visas in-state status, even if they were domiciled in the state, thus denying them preferential fee and tuition schedules. The U.S. Supreme Court found the policy to be in violation of the Supremacy Clause of the U.S. Constitution. The Court stated that the university's policy conflicted directly with the will of Congress as expressed in the Immigration and Nationality Act of 1952. In passing the Immigration and Nationality Act, Congress explicitly decided not to bar non-immigrant aliens such as these the right to acquire domicile in the United States. **The university's policy denying these aliens "in-state" status, solely on the basis of their immigration status, amounted to a burden not contemplated by Congress** in admitting them to the United States. Thus, the University of Maryland's student fee schedule, as applied to these aliens, was held to be unconstitutional. *Toll v. Moreno*, 458 U.S. 1, 102 S.Ct. 2977, 73 L.Ed.2d 563 (1982).

C. Residency

◆   *The University of Illinois violated its own regulation by refusing to classify a student as a state resident.*

The student's family resided in Iowa, but his mother was a faculty member at a community college in Illinois. A university regulation governing residency defined "resident" to include any dependent of a faculty member who worked at an Illinois state-supported institution of higher education on at least a quarter-time basis. The university refused to classify the student as an Illinois resident on grounds that community colleges were not state-supported public institutions of higher learning. The student's father presented information from the state community college board which indicated the college received 35.4% of its annual budget from state funds. He also sent the officials a definition of "public institutions of higher education" from the Illinois Code that included both four-year and community colleges. University officials maintained that only dependents of employees at four-year universities qualified for in-state tuition reduction. The parents appealed the university's decision to an Illinois circuit court. The court upheld the decision, and the parents appealed.

The Appellate Court of Illinois found the university's regulation defined "resident" to include the dependent of someone employed at least one-quarter time as a faculty member of a "state-supported institution of higher education in Illinois." State support for four-year public universities had fallen so much in recent years that it was questionable whether they received more funding from the state than community colleges. The university received about 31% of its total revenue from the state, while the community college received 34% of its revenue from the state. The college's receipt of local funding did not negate its status as a "state-supported institution." Community colleges were both state supported and locally supported, and they were not excluded from being considered state-supported public institutions under the regulation. **The court held the university's board was bound to comply with its own regulation.** It rejected the university's additional reasons for denying the student resident status and reversed the judgment. *Dusthimer v. Board of Trustees of Univ. of Illinois*, 368 Ill.App.3d 159, 857 N.E.2d 343 (Ill. App. Ct. 2006).

◆   A *Maryland state university's presumption against in-state residency for all students who depended upon out-of-state sources did not violate equal protection principles. However, university administrators may not have applied the presumption in a constitutional manner.*

Four students who were enrolled in professional and post-graduate degree programs at a state university sued the university board of regents in a state court, claiming the board violated their constitutional rights by refusing to classify them as in-state residents. This decision denied them a substantial tuition reduction offered to Maryland residents, which the students claimed was a violation of equal protection principles. The university system presumed that students who were not financially independent were residing in the state primarily for the purpose of attending a college or university, if they remained financially dependent upon a nonresident. A state court held for the board and the students appealed to the Court of Special Appeals of Maryland.

The court stated no single definition could mechanically determine a person's domicile. The most important factors for determining domicile were where a person actually lived and where he or she voted, although a number of other factors also had weight. **The court held the university system's presumption was valid. The source of a student's financial support was related to the issue of residence.** However, there was evidence that some administrators did not allow students to challenge the presumption by treating the financial dependency presumption as irrebuttable. **The absence of uniformity in standards or criteria under the tuition policy violated equal protection principles.** The students were in the state during the time they attended the university, and each satisfied many other traditional domicile factors. The court vacated the lower court order for the board and remanded the case for further activity. *Bergmann v. Board of Regents of the Univ. System of Maryland*, 167 Md. App. 237, 892 A.2d 604 (Md. Ct. Spec. App. 2006).

◆   *State residency requirements for favorable tuition rates are subject to the*
due process right of students to present evidence about their residency.

Connecticut required nonresidents enrolled in the state's university system
to pay tuition and other fees at a higher rate than state residents. It also created
an irreversible and irrebuttable statutory presumption that if the legal address of
a student, if married, was outside the state at the time of application for
admission or, if single, was outside the state at some point during the preceding
year, the student remained a nonresident as long as the student remained
enrolled in Connecticut schools. Two students, one married, one single, who
were both residents of Connecticut, challenged the presumption, claiming that
it violated the Fourteenth Amendment's guarantee of due process and equal
protection. A three-judge district court panel upheld the students' claim.

The U.S. Supreme Court held that **the Due Process Clause does not**
permit states to deny a student the opportunity to present evidence that the
student is a bona fide resident of the state, and thus entitled to in-state
tuition rates, on the basis of an irrebuttable presumption of nonresidence. Such
a presumption is not necessarily true, and the state had reasonable alternatives
in making residency determinations. *Vlandis v. Kline*, 412 U.S. 441, 93 S.Ct.
2230, 37 L.Ed.2d 63 (1973).

◆   *A New Jersey state university's decision to deny a student in-state tuition*
eligibility was held arbitrary and unreasonable.

The student was born in the U.S., but lived with her parents in Korea before
returning to New Jersey for high school. She graduated from a New Jersey high
school. The student's parents paid for her educational expenses related to her
attendance at a state university as an undergraduate. This made her a dependent
student under state law. The student applied for in-state tuition status. To
support her application, she submitted detailed certification describing her
activities in and contacts with New Jersey. She attached a copy of her driver's
license, automobile registration, local voter registration identification card, and
federal and state personal income tax returns for two years. Although all the
documents reflected New Jersey residency, the university rejected the student's
request for in-state tuition. It stated that the residence of the parents of an
undergraduate student, not the residence of the student, dictates tuition status.

A state court upheld the university's decision, and the student appealed to
the Superior Court of New Jersey, Appellate Division. Under N.J.S.A. § 18A:
62-4, a person is presumed to be domiciled in New Jersey for the purposes of
in-state tuition treatment if he or she has been a resident of state for 12 months.
A person is not considered to be domiciled in New Jersey if residence was
established only to attend a particular educational institution. **Dependent**
students might overcome the presumption that they share their parents'
place of residence by presenting evidence of residency. Such evidence could
include a student's state income tax return, ownership of or long-term
lease on a permanent residence in the state, a state driver's license or
motor vehicle registration, or a state voter registration card. The court
found the university did not evaluate the student's documentation to determine
if she demonstrated her decision to relocate from Korea to New Jersey was not
solely to attend the university. Instead, it exclusively based the decision on an

incorrect assumption that the only way she could establish she was eligible for in-state tuition was to prove she was financially independent from her parents. The court reversed the judgment and returned the case to the university to reevaluate its decision. *Shim v. Rutgers-The State Univ. of New Jersey*, 385 N.J. Super. 200, 896 A.2d 1118 (N.J. Super. Ct. App. Div. 2006).

◆   *The Court of Appeals of Kansas held that a student who moved to Kansas to attend law school could not claim resident tuition status.*

The student, who was born in England, came to Kansas in May 1999 and moved to Colorado in July 1999. He lived there until March 2002. He signed a contract to build a house in Kansas, contingent on his acceptance to the law school there. He was accepted and he and his wife finalized the purchase of a house in Kansas in June 2002. The university denied the student's application to be reclassified as a Kansas resident for the 2003 fall semester. The residence committee found he did not satisfy the residency requirements and denied his appeal. A state district court agreed, and the student appealed.

The court of appeals noted several state law factors determined if a student was a Kansas resident. **These included a continuous presence in Kansas, employment in the state, payment of resident income taxes, reliance on in-state sources of financial support, commitment to an education program indicating an intent to remain permanently, and owning a home in Kansas.** The committee found the purchase of the house was contingent on the student's acceptance to the law school. This did not demonstrate an intent to remain in Kansas permanently. All of the other factors could be considered routinely performed by temporary residents of Kansas. The court found the committee's decision was supported by substantial competent evidence and it affirmed the district court judgment. *Lockett v. The Univ. of Kansas, Residence Appeals Committee*, 33 Kan. App.2d 931, 111 P.3d 170 (Kan. Ct. App. 2005).

◆   *The Board of Regents of the University of Wisconsin System had immunity against a student's equal protection challenge.*

The student attended a Wisconsin state university for five semesters after graduating from a high school in Colorado. The university charged him the nonresident tuition rate of $9,000 per semester. At the same time, the tuition for residents was about $2,500 per semester. Tuition for students who were residents of Minnesota was only slightly higher because of a reciprocity agreement between Wisconsin and Minnesota. The student sued the board of regents in a federal district court, claiming the tuition policy violated the Equal Protection Clause of the Constitution.

The court held the board of regents was immune from liability under the Eleventh Amendment and dismissed case. The student appealed to the U.S. Court of Appeals, Seventh Circuit. The court held that the board was an arm of that state that qualified for immunity under the Eleventh Amendment. As Congress did not surrender state immunity in Section 1983 actions, the student's action against the board was barred, and the judgment was affirmed. *Joseph v. Board of Regents of the Univ. of Wisconsin System*, 432 F.3d 746 (7th Cir. 2005).

◆ *A Virginia court held a student did not qualify for in-state tuition just because she lived in the state at the time she attended school.*

A student moved from New York to attend Virginia Commonwealth University. She met Virginia requirements for residency including continuous residence in the state for one year, filing and paying state income tax and possessing a state driver's license. She also registered as a Virginia voter, had a job in the state and owned property there. However, **to be eligible for in-state tuition, a student arriving from another state must show the intention of living in Virginia for the long-term and not merely to attend school.**

A university residency appeals committee found the student's primary reason for moving to Virginia was to attend the university and denied her request for in-state tuition. The student appealed to a state circuit court, which noted the Virginia Code limited its powers of review to whether the committee's decision was arbitrary, capricious or otherwise contrary to law. The court reviewed evidence that the student had applied to school in South Carolina as well as Virginia. She did not move to Virginia until after she was accepted to the university. As the committee's decision was not arbitrary, capricious or contrary to law, the court denied the appeal. *Gauthier v. Virginia Comwlth. Univ.*, No. CH03-1896-1, 2004 WL 1386321 (Va. Cir. 2004).

◆ *A student's lawsuit for breach of contract should not have been dismissed where questions of fact existed.*

A Georgia high school student applied for a scholarship at a Mississippi university pursuant to a 1997 catalogue and application. Under those terms, the university waived the out-of-state tuition rate, and the student was to receive $1,000 per year. When the student attended the orientation, he was given a 1998 catalogue, which listed the scholarship amount at $500 per year, and was informed that he no longer qualified for the nonresident tuition waiver. He sued for breach of contract. A federal court dismissed his lawsuit, but the Mississippi Court of Appeals reversed. On further appeal, the Supreme Court of Mississippi reversed and remanded the case. **Neither party received a fair evaluation as to whether a contract for a scholarship existed between the student and the university based on the terms of the school catalogue.** The trial court improperly dismissed the case, and the court of appeals improperly refused to allow the university to present a defense. *Aronson v. Univ. of Mississippi*, 828 So.2d 752 (Miss. 2002).

D. Zoning and Land Use

◆ *The Court of Appeals of North Carolina upheld a decision to grant a university's request for an order to close a road running along its property.*

The university asked the Town of Chapel Hill to close part of Laurel Hill Road to promote safety, unify the grounds of the North Carolina Botanical Garden, and provide better teaching and visitor experiences. The town council adopted an order to permanently close a section of the road. A nearby property owner filed a state court petition to vacate the order. The court dismissed the petition and affirmed the order of the town council. The owner appealed to the Court of Appeals of North Carolina. He contended the trial court erred in failing to conduct an evidentiary hearing and in refusing to allow him to present evidence at the hearing on his petition. The court noted the owner did not contest the procedures at the town hearing and did not contend the trial court violated other applicable local requirements. **The town held three public hearings on the proposed road closing in two months. Those hearings were the proper place for the owner to present evidence, not the trial court.** The court affirmed the judgment upholding the town's decision. *Houston v. Town of Chapel Hill*, 177 N.C.App. 739, 630 S.E.2d 249 (N.C. App. 2006).

◆ *A New York court held a city commission had no rational basis to deny an application by Cornell University to build a parking lot in a historic district.*

Cornell intended to replace some existing residence halls with new housing and create a parking lot nearby. The city planning board approved the building proposal, but it denied the request for a parking lot. Two years later, the commission designated a new historic district that included the parking lot site. The historic district consisted of about 10 acres of land and three buildings in an area zoned exclusively for educational use. Near the buildings were a shared lawn and other landscaping. Cornell proposed to place the parking lot in a wooded area. The Ithaca city landmarks preservation commission denied the application, but a state trial court annulled the commission's decision.

The commission appealed to the New York Supreme Court, Appellate Division. Under the Ithaca city code, proposed improvements within a historic district may be approved if they will not have a substantial adverse effect on the aesthetic, historical or architectural significance and value of the landmark. The court found the parking lot, which was to be located within the wooded area, would have a minimal effect on the original landscape. It would not be visible to the public, and 85% of the existing lawn would be retained. **The court rejected the commission's argument that the parking lot was not a valid educational use. Colleges and universities are generally allowed to locate facilities for accessory uses on their properties that are reasonably related to their educational purposes.** The parking lot was a qualified accessory use to the student residences and instructional facilities. The commission did not consider what conditions could reasonably be imposed to mitigate any adverse effect on the landscape. Instead, it simply assumed the public would be offended by a change to the landscape. The court held the commission's decision was arbitrary and capricious, and it affirmed the judgment for Cornell. *Cornell Univ. v. Beer*, 16 A.D.3d 890 (N.Y. App. Div. 2005).

◆ *A federal district court upheld a District of Columbia zoning board order concerning a campus plan.*

The District zoning board approved the university's campus plan for 2000-2010, but its order imposed several conditions, including a cap on student enrollment. The university had already admitted a substantial number of its students for the next semester. The order also directed that if the university failed to meet a requirement to house 70% of buildings on campus, it would be barred from erecting nonresidential buildings on campus while it was noncompliant. A federal district court granted the university's request to prevent enforcement of the order. The board then issued a corrected final order that also imposed a cap on housing with certain housing requirements for undergraduates. The university amended its federal district court complaint to include a due process claim. The court found the board's order was not rationally related to its legitimate purpose and violated due process. The U.S. Court of Appeals, D.C. Circuit, reversed in part, noting that **the zoning board did not violate the university's substantive due process rights by imposing the housing restrictions.** Since students are not a suspect class deserving of heightened protections, the board's zoning regulations would be constitutional if they were rationally related to a legitimate governmental interest. Preservation of the residential character of an adjoining neighborhood was a legitimate governmental interest, and the zoning restrictions were upheld. *George Washington Univ. v. Dist. of Columbia,* 318 F.3d 203 (D.C. Cir. 2003). The case was remanded to the district court, where the university argued the board's final order was an unconstitutional taking of its property.

To determine if government action amounts to a taking of property, a court considers the economic impact, any interference with reasonable investment-backed expectations, and the character of government action. The court found the final order did not deprive the university of all economic benefits from the property. The university did not show the order diminished the property value. The court held the order did not interfere with the university's reasonable investment-backed expectations because it knew the property was subject to governmental regulation. To assess the character of the government's action, courts consider whether the action advances a "common good" or "public purpose." Because of the potential impact on the surrounding neighborhood, the court held the board's order advanced a common good or public purpose. **The conditions imposed by the order did not constitute a taking of property,** and the court dismissed the university's complaint. *George Washington Univ. v. Dist. of Columbia,* 391 F.Supp.2d 109 (D.D.C. 2005).

◆ *A Massachusetts zoning board's density regulation was invalid as applied to a college campus under state law.*

Boston College (BC) applied to the Newton Board of Aldermen for special permits to construct three buildings. It also sought an exemption from the parking requirements of a local zoning ordinance. The purpose of the construction project was to provide additional space for academic functions, faculty offices and dining facilities. The board denied the application and BC sued the board in a state court, alleging violation of the Dover Amendment, a state law barring zoning ordinances that prohibit or restrict the use of land for educational purposes. The court held the board unreasonably applied its dimensional and density regulations to the building project, but was reasonably justified in denying a parking waiver. The parties appealed.

The Court of Appeals of Massachusetts noted that **a municipality could reasonably regulate parking, open spaces, and buildings used for educational purposes.** The floor area ratio density requirement of the local zoning ordinance was invalid as applied to the BC middle campus. The entire middle campus was "nonconforming" under the ordinance, with the practical result that enforcement would require BC to always secure a special permit to construct any building there. **Strict compliance with the density requirement**

would thwart an "educational use" and was invalid. The trial court correctly found the denial of a waiver for more parking spaces was unreasonable. The court affirmed the decision. *Trustees of Boston College v. Board of Aldermen of Newton*, 793 N.E.2d 387 (Mass. App. Ct. 2003).

◆ *A university could turn a campus building into a child development center under a zoning order.*

The D.C. Board of Zoning Adjustment approved a Georgetown University building as a "mixed-use main campus education/educational support" facility under a campus plan. This approval included "accessory uses" as permissible uses for the building. Subsequently, the university sought to turn the building into a child development center to be used exclusively by the university's faculty, staff and students. A group of residents challenged the issuance of the final permits, but the board held that the childcare center supported the university's mission and was a proper function of the university. Therefore, it was exempted from R-3 zoning restrictions. The D.C. Court of Appeals upheld the board's decision. **Conversion of the building into a childcare center was a use consistent with the uses permitted under the "mixed-use" campus plan previously approved.** Because the childcare center would be for the exclusive use of the university community, it satisfied the definition of "accessory use." *Georgetown Residents Alliance v. Dist. of Columbia Board of Zoning Adjustment*, 816 A.2d 41 (D.C. 2003).

◆ *A city could require certain landlords of college students to comply with a lodging house ordinance.*

Six owners of condominium units in the city of Worcester leased the units to students at the College of Holy Cross. Four unrelated students lived in each unit. When the condo owners refused to obtain permits as operators of lodging houses, the city filed complaints against them in housing court. The court found the lodging ordinance unconstitutionally vague, but the Appeals Court of Massachusetts vacated that opinion and found the ordinance valid. Here, **the ordinance clearly defined a lodging house as a "dwelling unit that is rented to four or more persons not constituting a family."** Moreover, the ordinance was rationally related to a legitimate governmental interest: creating quiet neighborhoods and limiting the number of unrelated people living together. The condo owners were subject to the ordinance. *City of Worcester v. Bonaventura*, 775 N.E.2d 795 (Mass. App. Ct. 2002).

◆ *If a city improperly targeted a private university for designation as a historic district, it could be liable for an equal protection violation.*

The city of Evanston, Illinois, asked Northwestern University to voluntarily contribute to the cost of city services. Northwestern refused to do so. A group of citizens then formed an association that sought to designate parts of the city and parts of the university as a National Historic District. The Department of the Interior approved the designation over Northwestern's objections. Northwestern then sued the city under 42 U.S.C. § 1983 for violating its constitutional rights, and the city moved for dismissal. The district court granted the motion in part. However, it found that Northwestern could proceed on two causes of action. First, under the "vindictive action equal protection" part of the lawsuit, **Northwestern alleged that the city had an improper motive (hostility to the university) and that it was treated unequally as a result.** This claim had to proceed to trial. Also, Northwestern claimed that the city imposed an unconstitutional condition on its right to be exempt from property taxation under the charter granted to it by the state in 1851. It asserted that an alderman suggested university property could be excluded from the historic district if the university agreed to surrender its tax-exempt status. This claim also deserved a trial. *Northwestern Univ. v. City of Evanston,* No. OOC7309, 2002 WL 31027981 (N.D. Ill. 2002).

◆ *An ordinance that prohibited educational uses of property in a historic district owned by a New York private college was struck down as unconstitutional.*

The private college owned property adjacent to its campus that developed into a distinctive, turn of the century residential neighborhood listed on the National Register of Historic Places. The city adopted a zoning ordinance encompassing the property, which limited property uses and restricted special permit uses to public utility facilities, substations and structures. All other special uses, including educational uses, were foreclosed. The college proposed that the ordinance be amended to allow special permit use for faculty offices, administrative offices and homes for visiting dignitaries and guests of the college. The city's Historic Districts Commission and the New York State Office of Parks, Recreation and Historic Preservation both projected that the proposed amendment would have a deleterious effect on the historic preservation of the property. The college then discontinued its pursuit of an amendment and filed a declaratory judgment action in state court against the city, its mayor and city council, seeking a declaration that the ordinance was unconstitutional. The court granted the college pretrial judgment, and the appellate division affirmed. Appeal was then taken to the Court of Appeals of New York, the state's highest court.

The court noted that **proposed educational uses must be weighed against the interest in historical preservation as well as other legitimate, competing interests to determine how best to serve the public welfare.** Here, depriving the college of the opportunity to have its presumptively beneficial educational use weighed against competing interests, and thereby wholly excluding educational uses from the property, bore no substantial relation to the public welfare. Therefore, it was beyond the city's zoning authority. Moreover, neither the variance nor the amendment process allowed the zoning board to balance a particular applicant's educational use against the public interest in historical preservation. The judgment of the appellate division was affirmed. *Trustees of Union College v. Schenectady City Council,* 667 N.Y.S.2d 978 (N.Y. 1997).

◆ *The U.S. Supreme Court found the Religious Freedom Restoration Act (RFRA) unconstitutional as applied to state actions.*

The case involved a building permit for the enlargement of a church. It was denied on the ground that the church building was part of a historical district.

The Supreme Court held that the church could not use the RFRA to obtain the permit because the RFRA proscribed state conduct that the Fourteenth Amendment did not even prohibit. However, the Supreme Court did not address the question of whether the RFRA was unconstitutional in all respects. It limited its analysis to state actions. Accordingly, the RFRA still may provide protections against federal actions. *City of Boerne, Texas v. Flores*, 521 U.S. 507, 117 S.Ct. 2157, 138 L.Ed.2d 624 (1997).

E. State and Local Regulation

◆   *The Supreme Court of Alabama held a lower court should have dismissed an action to determine the term of office for an Auburn University trustee.*

The dispute centered on whether the appointment of a replacement trustee was intended to complete the unexpired term of a previous trustee or was instead for a full seven-year term. After receiving an opinion from the state attorney general, the university determined the trustee was serving out the remainder of his predecessor's term, not a full seven-year term. The trustee agreed to give up his seat. When the governor sought to fill the vacancy, another trustee of the university filed a state court action, seeking a declaration that the trustee was entitled to serve a full seven-year term. The trial court restrained the governor's appointing committee from meeting or acting to appoint a new trustee. **The supreme court reversed the judgment, finding the individual who filed the action had no standing to bring it.** He could not show any actual injury to his rights as a public official, and he was not prevented from performing his duties. *Ex parte Richardson*, 957 So.2d 1119 (Ala. 2006).

◆   *The Court of Appeal of California held a community college was required to perform an environmental study before moving a campus shooting range.*

The college proposed a new site for a shooting range used for firearms courses offered in its criminal justice programs. It obtained approval by county and city governments, but a report indicated high levels of lead contamination at the new site. A public interest group alleged violation of state Environmental Quality Act requirements for an environmental study. A state superior court disagreed, finding the site change was not a "project" under the act.

The Court of Appeal of California stated that under the act, **a "project" is defined as "an activity which may cause either a direct physical change in the environment, or reasonably foreseeable indirect physical change in the environment" by a person or agency receiving public funds**. Even though dismantling and removing the range would be accomplished incrementally, these actions were all part of a single project. The college argued the lead abatement aspect of the move was exempt from the act, as the cleanup would cost less than $1 million. The court held that while lead abatement was exempt, this did not relieve the college of its responsibility to conduct an initial study of the project. **The decision was reversed and remanded with instructions for an environmental study.** *Ass'n for a Cleaner Environment v. Yosemite Community College Dist.*, 10 Cal.Rptr.3d 560 (Cal. Ct. App. 2004).

◆ *A state court must decide whether the University of Utah can prohibit students, faculty and staff from carrying concealed weapons on campus.*

Utah residents can apply for concealed weapon permits. The University of Utah prohibits most students, faculty and staff members from possessing or carrying firearms on campus. When the state attorney general issued an advisory opinion that stated in a footnote that the university's policy was invalid and should not be enforced, the university sued the attorney general in federal court for an order allowing it to uphold the policy. It asserted that the First and Fourteenth Amendments allowed it to enact the firearms policy as part of its commitment to ensuring academic freedom. It also asserted that the Utah Constitution permitted it to enact the policy in order **to protect campus order and discipline, and to promote an environment consistent with the educational process.** The attorney general sought to have the lawsuit dismissed. The U.S. District Court of the District of Utah refused to consider the federal claims, and remanded the case to state court for a decision on the legality of the policy under the Utah Constitution. *Univ. of Utah v. Shurtleff*, 252 F.Supp.2d 1264 (D. Utah 2003).

◆ *New York City was not allowed to ban a private educational institution's distribution of free magazines via news racks because the proposed ban arbitrarily singled out certain kinds of publications.*

A private institution that offered short, nonaccredited courses in New York City sought to distribute its magazine free of charge by way of news racks placed on city sidewalks. The city contended that the news racks were unsightly, unsanitary and unsafe. It also asserted that the magazine was "commercial speech," which is entitled to a lesser degree of First Amendment protection, and that the ban on all commercial speech through sidewalk news racks was constitutional. The New York Court of Appeals observed that the city's arguments missed the central point in the case: **"a government official or employee may not exercise complete and unregulated discretion, in the absence of duly enacted guidelines, ... to decide which publications may be distributed via [news racks]."** Here, the city's action against the institution was taken without the benefit of any regulatory guidelines. The city's action therefore violated the First Amendment, which requires that government action regulating "speech" be undertaken pursuant to clear guidelines that leave little room for arbitrary decisions. The decision to ban the sidewalk magazine news racks was illegal. *City of New York v. American School Publications*, 509 N.E.2d 311 (N.Y. 1987).

◆ *In 1982, the Supreme Court ruled that a Pennsylvania taxpayer group lacked standing to challenge a governmental conveyance of surplus property to a private religious college. The Court ruled that the group could show no injury to itself or any of its members as a result of the conveyance.*

Congress enacted the Federal Property and Administrative Services Act, 40 U.S.C. § 471, *et seq.*, to dispose of surplus property and authorize its transfer to public or private entities. This statute authorized the education secretary to dispose of surplus real property for schools. The secretary was permitted to take into account any benefit accruing to the U.S. from any new use of the transferred property. In 1973, the Secretary of Defense and General Services Administration declared a Pennsylvania army hospital site surplus property. In 1976, the secretary conveyed part of the property to a Christian college. Although the appraised value of the property was $577,500, the secretary computed a 100% public benefit allowance, permitting the college to acquire the property for no cost. **A taxpayer group advocating the separation of church from state learned of the conveyance and sued the college and U.S. government**, claiming that the conveyance violated the Establishment Clause. The court dismissed the complaint, ruling that the taxpayers lacked standing under prior decisions of the U.S. Supreme Court. The U.S. Court of Appeals, Third Circuit, reversed the decision, and the Supreme Court agreed to hear an appeal by the college and the U.S. government

The Court stated that Article II of the Constitution limited the judicial power of courts to cases and controversies. Litigants were entitled to bring a lawsuit only by showing some actual or threatened injury. Without such a showing, lawsuits were to be dismissed for lack of standing. In this case, the taxpayers had alleged injury from deprivation of fair and constitutional use of their tax dollars. This allegation was insufficient to confer standing in federal courts. Taxpayers were proper parties only to allege the unconstitutionality of congressional actions under the Taxing and Spending Clause and were required to show that the action went beyond the powers delegated to Congress. **Courts were not available to taxpayers to vent generalized grievances of government conduct or spending.** The complained-of statute arose under the Property Clause, and therefore the taxpayers had no standing to complain about the property transfer. The Court reversed the court of appeals' decision. *Valley Forge Christian College v. Americans United for Separation of Church and State*, 454 U.S. 464, 102 S.Ct. 752, 70 L.Ed.2d 700 (1982).

F. Licensing

◆   *The Michigan Department of Education could deny a license to operate to the owner of a trade school teaching casino gambling.*

A Michigan resident applied to the proprietary school unit of the department of education for a license to operate a private trade school teaching casino gambling. The board denied his application because gaming was considered criminal behavior in Michigan. The applicant appealed to a Michigan trial court. The trial court reversed, and the board of education appealed to the Court of Appeals of Michigan.

The court of appeals noted that public policy did not completely prohibit casino gambling as evidenced by the legislature's decision to legalize millionaire parties and to allow casino gambling on Indian reservations. On further appeal, the Supreme Court of Michigan reversed. It adopted the dissenting opinion from the lower court, which stated that **licensing the proposed school would violate public policy**. If the school were allowed to teach casino gambling, it would be teaching behavior that was currently defined as illegal under Michigan law. *Michigan Gaming Institute v. State Board of Educ.*, 547 N.W.2d 882 (Mich. 1996).

♦ *A corporation that provided review courses for nursing school graduates had to pay an annual renewal licensing fee for each location.*

The corporation offered courses that prepared nursing school graduates for state certification exams. It operated at five different locations in the state. The review courses were held in hotel meeting rooms, college auditoriums or hospital conference rooms. The California legislature modified the Private Postsecondary and Vocational Education Reform Act to increase the annual renewal fee for nondegree granting institutions from $225 to a range of $600 to $1,200, depending on size. The corporation made a single $1,200 payment but refused to make a separate payment for each of its course sites.

A lawsuit arose, and a California trial court found that a separate fee could be charged for each location. The California Court of Appeal, First District, noted that because the corporation's educational sites were 50 miles from corporate headquarters and were held in places such as hotel conference rooms, they were neither branches nor satellites subject to separate annual fees under the act. However, since the legislature provided that each site be inspected by the governing council, the court inferred a legislative intent to require separate annual fees for each site. **As long as the governing council used some "reasonable method" of estimating the administrative costs of the entire program, its annual fee interpretation was reasonable.** Thus, the court of appeal required the corporation to pay an annual fee for each site. *RN Review for Nurses, Inc. v. State*, 28 Cal.Rptr.2d 354 (Cal. Ct. App. 1994).

♦ *A New York appellate court upheld the denial of a license to a school that had operated illegally.*

A New York private school that had received a warning for improper conduct from the New York Secretary of Education sought to open another facility. The school began operations at an unlicensed facility and enticed students to enroll with promises of employment. Both of these practices are illegal, but they continued despite orders to desist. Finally, the secretary denied the school a license to operate.

The New York Supreme Court, Appellate Division, held that **the secretary may lawfully deny a private for-profit school a license to operate if the secretary has good cause**. The secretary's decision should not be overturned unless it is arbitrary and capricious. The first issue questioned whether the school had received due process. The school in this case had been given an opportunity to refute the authority's findings, and that opportunity was held to be adequate to satisfy the requirements of due process. The court then observed that the school's conduct was clearly unlawful. The license denial was reinstated. *Blake Business School, Inc. v. Sobol*, 575 N.Y.S.2d 955 (N.Y. App. Div. 1991).

♦ *A board for community colleges should have provided an occupational school with a hearing prior to terminating the school's license.*

A private Colorado occupational school was licensed to do business by the State Board for Community Colleges and Occupational Educations. A new statute revised licensing requirements, and the school was required to renew its license. The board's vice president rejected the school's application because it had not employed an independent accountant or utilized accepted accounting procedures as required by the new statute. The school filed a 42 U.S.C. § 1983 action in a Colorado district court against the vice president and the board. It alleged that both had failed to provide a hearing prior to terminating the school's license and had failed to provide an impartial tribunal.

The school sought damages and injunctive relief requiring the board to restore its license. A trial court determined that neither the board nor its vice president could be sued under 42 U.S.C. § 1983 and dismissed the case. The Colorado Court of Appeals found that the board was a state regulatory body that was entitled to immunity from suits for damages. Next, the court determined that **the vice president's failure to grant the school a pre-deprivation hearing was not a clear violation of its constitutional rights**. The vice president therefore had immunity on the claim for damages under Section 1983. However, the board's refusal to grant the school a pre-deprivation hearing potentially violated its statutory rights. On remand, the school could sue for injunctive relief. *National Camera, Inc. v. Sanchez*, 832 P.2d 960 (Colo. Ct. App. 1991).

◆   *Because a cease and desist order amounted to a license revocation, the board that issued the order should have provided procedural safeguards.*

A corporation operated an association of career schools in Florida. These schools were licensed by the Board of Independent Postsecondary Vocational Trade and Business Schools (board). The board became concerned with the school's advertisement practices and issued the school a cease and desist order that prohibited further advertisement, enrollment of students, or acceptance of further tuition payments. The school contended that the board had in effect revoked the school's license without following the required procedural safeguards. The school appealed directly to the District Court of Appeal of Florida, which noted that the board had the discretion to take the actions included in the cease and desist order. However, other Florida legislation deals directly with revoking or limiting a school's license, and mandates compliance with specific procedural safeguards in the event of an emergency suspension. The school argued that these procedures should be followed because the cease and desist order had the same effect as revoking the school's license. The court agreed. It then held that **the board had not set out specific facts showing the necessity of actions, published an evaluation of the fairness of the action, or provided a prompt hearing**. The court quashed the cease and desist order. *Allied Educ. Corp. v. State, Dep't of Educ.*, 573 So.2d 959 (Fla. Dist. Ct. App. 1991).

◆   *A state tuition refund rule was held to be constitutional such that a school could be denied a license renewal for failing to comply with the rule.*

A Florida correspondence school offered courses of instruction for home study with optional training at its Florida training school. Florida Department of Education rules required a tuition refund policy identical to or more liberal than the refund policy recognized by the U.S. Office of Education. Sanctions for failure to comply with the rule included non-renewal of licensing. The school operated in several states, maintaining 44 field offices.

The field offices utilized 22 separate contract forms to comply with various state regulations while minimizing the tuition refund to dropout students. In each case, the minimum refund corresponded to student domicile state law rather than Florida law. The Florida Department of Education notified the school that it intended to deny its license renewal application for failure to comply with the state tuition refund rule. The District Court of Appeal rejected the school's argument that the refund rule burdened interstate commerce, because **the rule put nonresident students in the same position as resident students concerning tuition refunds.** Since the rule did not burden out-of-state students but placed them on exactly the same footing as Florida students with respect to refunds of prepaid enrollment charges, it was clear that there was no discrimination. Students would no longer be subject to different tuition refunds depending upon their state's law. *Associated Schools v. Dep't of Educ.*, 522 So.2d 426 (Fla. Dist. Ct. App. 1988).

G. Desegregation

◆ *A longstanding court battle to end racial segregation in Alabama colleges and universities could not be used to force the state to change its funding of K-12 schools. The case was about segregation in higher education.*

The suit was filed in 1981, when a group of black citizens claimed the state perpetuated a segregated university system. They said admissions standards at historically white institutions disqualified disproportionate numbers of black applicants. The citizens claimed historically black institutions were plagued by unfair funding and facility policies. In 1991, a federal district court ordered the state to encourage greater racial integration at its colleges and universities. Four years later, it entered a decree that ordered numerous additional changes to the state's higher education policies. Among other things, it required more flexible admissions policies and increased integration of faculty and administration at all state colleges and universities. The court also required the state to increase its funding of historically black institutions. Over the following eight years, the state and the plaintiffs "worked tirelessly" to make the changes required by the court's orders. From 1990 to 2004, the state increased its annual funding of higher education by about $340 million. During the same time period, undergraduate and graduate degrees awarded to black students increased by more than 96%. The plaintiffs filed a motion for additional relief in 2003, seeking an order to require the state to provide better funding for K-12 schools.

The plaintiffs sought an order invalidating property tax limitations imposed by the state constitution. They said a funding crisis in the state's K-12 schools resulted in segregation at its colleges and universities. The district court denied the motion, and the plaintiffs appealed. On appeal, the U.S. Court of Appeals, Eleventh Circuit, explained that the case had always been about segregation in the state's higher education system. The plaintiffs' motion was about reforming the state's K-12 school funding system. Because the motion raised a claim relating to school finance rather than desegregation, it could not be pursued. The plaintiffs tried to link the inadequacy of K-12 funding with segregation at higher levels by proposing a chain of causation. Property tax limitations resulted in underfunded public schools, leading to the diversion of higher education funds to lower education. This diversion resulted in higher tuition rates and decreased black student enrollment at state colleges and universities. **Under *U.S. v. Fordice*, below, race-neutral state policies governing higher education can be challenged under the Constitution if they are traceable to a system of segregation.** The court found the asserted relationship between the underfunding of the state's K-12 schools and segregation in Alabama colleges and universities was too attenuated and based on too many unpredictable premises. The judgment for the state was affirmed. *Knight v. Alabama*, 476 F.3d 1219 (11th Cir. 2007).

◆   *Where a state perpetuates policies and practices that can be traced to a segregative system and that have segregative effects, the policies will be considered unconstitutional unless there is sound educational justification for them and it is not practical to eliminate them.*

Mississippi maintained a dual system of public education at the university level – one set of universities for whites, and another set for blacks. In 1981, the State Board of Trustees issued "Mission Statements" to remedy this, classifying the three flagship historically white institutions (HWI) as "comprehensive" universities, redesignating one of the historically black institutions (HBI) as an "urban" university and characterizing the rest as "regional" institutions. However, the universities remained racially identifiable. A federal court found that state policies need merely be racially neutral, developed in good faith, and not contribute to the racial identifiability of each institution. It held that Mississippi was currently fulfilling its duty to desegregate. The U.S. Court of Appeals, Fifth Circuit, affirmed. The U.S. Supreme Court granted review.

The Supreme Court held that the district court had applied the wrong legal standard in ruling that Mississippi had brought itself into compliance with the Equal Protection Clause. **If a state perpetuates policies and practices traceable to its prior dual system that continue to have segregative effects, and such policies are without sound educational justification and can be practicably eliminated, the policies violate the Equal Protection Clause.** This is true even if the state has abolished the legal requirement that the races be separated and has established neutral policies. The proper inquiry is whether existing racial identifiability is attributable to the state. Applying the proper standard, several surviving aspects of Mississippi's prior dual system were constitutionally suspect. First, the use of higher minimum ACT composite scores at the HWIs, along with the state's refusal to consider high school grade performance was suspect. Second, the unnecessary duplication of programs at HBIs and HWIs was suspect. Third, the mission statements' reflection of previous policies to perpetuate racial separation was suspect. Finally, the state's policy of operating eight universities had to be examined to determine if it was educationally justifiable. *U.S. v. Fordice*, 505 U.S. 717, 112 S.Ct. 2727, 120 L.Ed.2d 575 (1992).

On remand, a Mississippi federal court **entered a remedial decree prohibiting the state from maintaining remnants of the prior segregated system** and mandating specific relief in areas of admissions and funding. However, the court refused to order the relief requested by the complaining parties, which would significantly increase the number of African-Americans accepted for regular admission at state universities. The complaining parties claimed that the district court order's reliance on a summer remedial program to boost African-American admissions was inappropriate, and the parties appealed to the U.S. Court of Appeals, Fifth Circuit. The court agreed with the complaining parties that the district court's order affirming the elimination of many remedial courses had to be reconsidered, along with its finding that use of college entrance scores as a criterion for scholarships was not traceable to the illegal system of segregation. The court remanded for clarification the status of a proposal to merge two universities to eliminate unnecessary program duplication, as well as questions of increasing the other-race presence at two HBIs and issues of accreditation and funding. The court affirmed many aspects of the district court decision as consistent with the *Fordice* decision, significantly affirming its decision to maintain admissions standards that ensured educational soundness. *Ayers v. Fordice*, 111 F.3d 1183 (5th Cir. 1997).

H. Delegation of Police Power

◆   *The Appeals Court of Massachusetts held in favor of a university that faced charges it had illegally arrested a university alumnus.*

A student at the university had an abuse prevention order against a university alumnus, which required him to stay at least 30 yards away from her. However, as she was leaving a university building one day, she spotted the alumnus parked in a car across the street. The student went back inside the building and called university police to report a violation of the protection order. She gave a description of the car. The alumnus had left the campus area by then. University police officers confirmed there was an order and saw where the student said the alumnus had been parked. The area was within 30 feet of where the student had been at the time. Based on information he had been given, a university police officer stopped and arrested the alumnus on a public street near the university. The university sent him a letter notifying him he was barred from entering campus. The alumnus sued the university in a trial court, alleging the university police lacked the authority to arrest him, among other claims. He asserted a brochure titled "Benefits for Alumni of Boston University" created a contract between himself and the university.

The court awarded summary judgment to the university. The alumnus appealed to the Appeals Court of Massachusetts. He contended university police were not authorized to arrest him on a public street near the university. **The court found the university officer who arrested the alumnus was appointed as a special state police officer, with the same power to make arrests as regular police officers for any criminal offense committed in or about university property.** The officer had probable cause to arrest the alumnus, and the letter barring him from campus did not breach any contract, as he alleged. The court found the officer's authority extended to the area surrounding the campus, and it affirmed the judgment for the university. *Young v. Boston Univ.*, 64 Mass. App. Ct. 586 (Mass. App. Ct. 2005).

II. ACCREDITATION

Regional and other accrediting institutions have been sued by private schools upon withdrawal of accreditation. The cases suggest: 1) actions of accrediting institutions do not constitute "state action" triggering due process requirements, 2) a school may maintain a breach of contract lawsuit against an accrediting institution if the institution fails to follow its own rules and procedures, and 3) if an accrediting institution's procedures are fair, its decision to revoke accreditation will likely be upheld.

A. Grants of Accreditation

◆ *A federal court refused to force the American Bar Association (ABA) to provisionally accredit a law school.*

After a religious university acquired a non-accredited law school, it applied for provisional accreditation from the ABA. The ABA rejected the application. The following year, the university applied again, and again was rejected. A group of graduates, students and instructors then sued the ABA seeking a preliminary injunction to force provisional accreditation. The university also filed a third application for provisional accreditation. A Florida federal district court refused to grant the injunction, finding no evidence that irreparable harm would befall the plaintiffs if the injunction was not granted. While the third application was pending, **graduates still could be admitted to practice in other states, and they could seek a waiver of the 12-month rule on sitting for the Florida Bar Exam** from the state supreme court. *Staver v. American Bar Ass'n*, 169 F.Supp.2d 1372 (M.D. Fla. 2001).

◆ *Where an accreditation foundation's denial of accreditation was supported by substantial evidence, it did not qualify as arbitrary or unreasonable.*

In 1995, Savannah College of Art & Design sought accreditation for its interior design program from the Foundation for Interior Design Education Research. Although a team of evaluators' report generally praised the program, it recommended the denial of accreditation. The foundation's board of trustees accepted the recommendation. Savannah College appealed, and a second on-site evaluation also recommended denial of accreditation for poor student achievement. Believing it had been treated unfairly, Savannah turned to the foundation's appeals panel, which determined that the denial of accreditation was supported by substantial evidence and consistent with other schools' accreditation reports. After the college threatened legal intervention, the foundation sued for a declaration that its decision to reject accreditation was lawful. In response, the college filed counterclaims against it. A federal court granted pretrial judgment to the foundation and dismissed all of the counterclaims. The school appealed to the Sixth Circuit.

The court held the foundation's denial of accreditation was neither arbitrary nor discriminatory. Savannah College argued that the foundation's method of evaluation deviated from the usual evaluative process and was therefore discriminatory. The court agreed that the process in this case differed, but to the college's favor. The foundation would not normally send a second evaluation team, but it did so in this case to ensure fairness. Savannah's final argument claimed the foundation acted arbitrarily because the college's interior design program closely resembled other accredited programs. The court disagreed and affirmed the judgment, finding the foundation's decision was based on substantial evidence. *Foundation for Interior Design Educ. Research v. Savannah College of Art & Design*, 244 F.3d 521 (6th Cir. 2001).

◆ *An Oregon law allowing certain schools to be exempted from requirements that out-of-state schools were not exempted from, was struck down.*

A private Washington university with a branch campus in Oregon was accredited by the Northwest Association of Schools and Colleges (NASC). Following NASC accreditation, the Oregon Office of Educational Policy and Planning (OEPP) continued to review non-Oregon schools every three years. The statute provided that "no school ... shall confer ... any degree ... without first having submitted the requirements for such degree to the [OEPP] and having obtained the approval of the director." However, an amendment exempted Oregon schools in good standing with the NASC from OEPP review. The university filed suit in an Oregon circuit court, seeking a declaration that the statute violated the Commerce Clause. The circuit court held for the university and severed a portion of the amendment. The court of appeals affirmed but invalidated the exemption in its entirety. The Oregon Supreme Court allowed the university's petition for review solely on the issue of remedy.

The university contended that the entire amendment had been improperly invalidated. The supreme court disagreed, ruling that the statute as severed was not capable of being executed in accordance with legislative intent. The legislature had intended both to continue the exemption from OEPP authority for Oregon schools that were members of the NASC and to remove the exemption from OEPP authority for out-of-state schools, even if those schools were NASC members. However, the dominant intent of the amendment was to ensure that Oregon branch campuses of the out-of-state schools had the same level of faculty and facilities as their main campuses. **Because a partial severance would subject these out-of-state schools to lesser scrutiny, the court ordered the amendment severed in its entirety.** The court of appeals' ruling was affirmed. *City Univ. v. Office of Educ. Policy*, 885 P.2d 701 (Or. 1994).

◆ *Denial of accreditation by an association of schools was not state action that would trigger application of the Constitution.*

The Medical Institute of Minnesota, a private technical school training students for careers as medical and dental assistants, received accreditation from the National Association of Trade and Technical Schools for a five-year period commencing in 1977. In 1983, the institute's application for reaccreditation was denied, and an association hearing panel upheld the denial. The institute then sued the association in federal court, claiming a violation of its constitutional rights. The case reached the U.S. Court of Appeals, Eighth Circuit, which held that the **denial of accreditation was not "state action" that triggered application of the U.S. Constitution. The court also refused to substitute its judgment for the association's with respect to a purely**

educational matter. It further noted that although the institute had been given an opportunity to justify its deficiencies, it had been unable to do so. The institute's action could not succeed. *Medical Institute of Minnesota v. NATTS*, 817 F.2d 1310 (8th Cir. 1987).

B. Claims of Fraud

◆ *A university's failure to gain accreditation for its Master of Social Work program did not violate students' due process rights.*

Governor's State University instituted a Master of Social Work Program in 1997. Three years later, university officials informed graduate students enrolled in the program that the National Council of Social Work Education had denied the university's application for accreditation. As a result, graduates were not permitted to sit for a licensing examination in Illinois. Graduating students discussed the accreditation problem with university officials at a board meeting. Additional students remained outside, protesting. A month later, graduate students were invited to an alumni fundraising dinner. The university limited the number of entrances and exits and permitted the students to picket only in the vestibule area. Instead of attending the dinner, the students peacefully protested the university's actions. Security guards removed the students from the premises and refused to allow them to re-enter the grounds.

A group of students sued the university, its president and trustees in a federal district court for due process and speech rights violations. The court held for the university, and the students appealed to the U.S. Court of Appeals, Seventh Circuit. **The court held the students did not show any arbitrary government action in violation of the Due Process Clause. While the university was responsible for ensuring its programs were accredited, the students had adequate remedies at law to resolve their complaints.** The trustees were not involved in the dinner event, and did not prevent the protesters from attending. The university president did not retaliate against the students for their protests. The actions of university security guards were merely a response to overcrowding. The court held summary judgment was properly entered for the university and its officials. *Galdikas v. Fagan*, 342 F.3d 684 (7th Cir. 2003).

◆ *A class of students was allowed to sue an accrediting agency for fraud after the agency extended the accreditation of a school without checking to see if the school met the agency's standards.*

A District of Columbia vocational school applied to an accrediting agency for accreditation in 1985. The agency granted the school an accreditation that was to expire in two years. Despite areas of concern, including curriculum, instructional materials, clarity of the school's mission statement and the school's financial status, the agency granted the school a series of automatic extensions until November of 1988. A number of students who had enrolled during this period began to notice that the school did not carry through on all of its promises. The students filed suit against the accrediting agency in the U.S. District Court for the District of Columbia, alleging that the agency was liable for fraud because it extended the accreditation of the school without any knowledge of whether the school met its standards for accreditation.

On cross-motions for pretrial judgment, the court determined that **the class of students had established a *prima facie* case of fraud** under District of Columbia law. The elements of a cause of action for fraud are 1) a false representation, 2) in reference to a material fact, 3) made with the knowledge of its falsity, 4) with the intent to deceive, and 5) on which action is taken in reliance upon the representation. Here, there were issues of fact that precluded the granting of pretrial judgment for either party. The motions for pretrial judgment were denied. *Armstrong v. Accrediting Council for Continuing Educ. & Training, Inc.*, 961 F.Supp. 305 (D.D.C. 1997).

◆ *A fraud claim brought by nursing students against a school that had allegedly misrepresented its accreditation status failed where the students could not show that they relied on the school's misrepresentation.*

A Missouri nursing school graduated its first class of students in 1984. The school was accredited by the Missouri State Board of Nursing. It also was a "candidate for accreditation" with the North Central Association for Colleges and Schools (NCA). The NCA recommended that the school's brochure state that it was a "candidate for accreditation by the NCA." However, the brochure actually stated that the school "has ... been granted [NCA] candidacy for review status" and that "accreditation for [the school] is expected in 1983." In 1981, a letter from the student services coordinator restated the above-quoted information to the class of 1984. However, the students were not apprised of the NCA accreditation status prior to their graduation, and the school was not formally accredited until 1987. This accreditation status did not apply retroactively to the class of 1984. Several members of the class of 1984 filed suit in a Missouri trial court, alleging that the school intentionally misrepresented its accreditation status, which limited their job prospects, advanced education and future earning power.

The trial court granted the school's motion for pretrial judgment, and the students appealed. The Missouri Court of Appeals held that **although misrepresentation of a material fact by silence may amount to actionable fraud, the students failed to show that they relied on the school's allegedly fraudulent statements in enrolling or remaining enrolled in the program**. Because the students failed to establish the reliance element of fraud, the court refused to address the issue of whether the school had a duty to disclose all material facts related to the anticipated accreditation. The holding of the trial court was affirmed. *Nigro v. Research College of Nursing*, 876 S.W.2d 681 (Mo. Ct. App. 1994).

C. Negligence

◆ *Students were allowed to sue accrediting agencies for negligence in the following case. The Higher Education Act (HEA) did not preempt their lawsuit.*

An Arizona private technical school made certain positive representations to several prospective students about the school's accreditation status as well as the education, jobs and benefits they would receive during school and after they graduated. Based on these representations, the students obtained loans and enrolled at the school. They could not have obtained the loans if the school had not been accredited. The school went out of business prior to the students' graduation, leaving them with thousands of dollars in student loans to repay. The students filed a negligence lawsuit against the accrediting agencies in a U.S. district court, **alleging that they had negligently accredited and failed to monitor the school**. The court ruled that the HEA preempted the students' negligence lawsuit and held for the agencies. The students appealed to the Ninth Circuit. The court of appeals noted that the HEA did not expressly preempt state common law tort claims against accreditors. It also declined to find an implied preemption. Consequently, the HEA did not preempt the students' claims. Rather, state courts had to decide whether to recognize a cause of action for negligent accreditation. *Keams v. Tempe Technical Institute Inc.*, 39 F.3d 222 (9th Cir. 1994).

◆ *However, the lawsuit for negligence failed when the U.S. Court of Appeals held that the accrediting agencies did not have a duty to the students.*

In a subsequent case, a group of students, who had taken out federally guaranteed student loans in order to attend the Arizona technical institute, filed suit against the institute and the accrediting agencies in federal district court. They alleged that the agencies negligently accredited and monitored the institute, causing them monetary damages. The district court dismissed their lawsuit for failure to state a claim upon which relief could be granted, and the students appealed to the U.S. Court of Appeals, Ninth Circuit. The court of appeals noted that to establish a cause of action for negligence under Arizona law, **a plaintiff must establish that the defendant has a duty, recognized by law, to conform to a certain standard of conduct**. This duty can be imposed when both the person to whom the duty is owed and the risk are foreseeable to a reasonable person. The students argued that it was foreseeable to the agencies that the negligent performance of their duties would cause the alleged damages. The court disagreed, finding that the students had not sufficiently shown that the agencies had given them false information. It also found no Arizona cases that recognized a duty of care in this type of situation or held that accrediting agencies owe a duty to students attending the institutions that they accredit. The court affirmed the district court's decision. *Keams v. Tempe Technical Institute, Inc.*, 110 F.3d 44 (9th Cir. 1997).

D. Withdrawal of Accreditation

◆ *A Texas court upheld provisions of the state education code requiring all private, post-secondary educational institutions to obtain accreditation.*

The Texas legislature amended the state Higher Education Coordinating Act in 1975 to stem the operation of private post-secondary educational institutions as "degree mills" and to preserve the integrity of post-secondary degrees. New provisions required all private post-secondary educational institutions to obtain a certificate of authority from the Texas Higher Education Coordinating Board before awarding credits or degrees. HEB Ministries operated three Christian post-secondary educational institutions in Texas. The

Board informed HEB it was required to obtain accreditation before issuing credits or degrees. HEB sued the board in a state court, seeking a declaration that the act violated the Establishment and Free Exercise Clauses. The court upheld the law and a $170,000 penalty against HEB, and HEB appealed.

The Court of Appeals of Texas upheld Section 61.304 of the state Education Code. Its language was facially neutral and it did not censor any religious subject or philosophy. **The provision had no hidden motivation targeting religious educational institutions and secular. Religious institutions of higher education were treated the same as others.** There was no government inquiry into the religious beliefs of HEB Ministries. There was no evidence to suggest that the legislature intended to thwart any religious sect in drafting the provision. The court upheld the $170,000 fine and imposed another $3,000 penalty on HEB. *HEB Ministries v. Texas Higher Educ. Coordinating Board*, 114 S.W.3d 617 (Tex. Ct. App. 2003).

◆ *A Florida business school was entitled to an injunction to stop an accrediting council from suspending its accreditation where it would suffer irreparable harm if the suspension were allowed and where it was likely to prevail on the merits of the case.*

The school was accredited by a council of independent schools and colleges. The council used a list of criteria in its accreditation decisions. In determining whether to continue accrediting the school, the council conducted an on-site evaluation and found that the school was not in compliance with a number of the listed criteria. Most importantly, less than 50% of the school's students had a high school diploma or its equivalent, and the number of students enrolled in nonbusiness programs exceeded the number enrolled in business programs. The school failed to adequately explain its noncompliance, the council suspended its accreditation, and a review board approved this decision. The school filed an emergency motion for injunctive relief in the U.S. District Court for the Southern District of Florida.

The court noted that its review was limited to whether the council's decision was arbitrary and unreasonable or supported by substantial evidence. Although the school had originally reported that most of its students did not have high school diplomas, it later discovered that the report was wrong because of a computer error. Actually, less than 50% of its students were without a diploma. The school also argued that it believed its cosmetology and nursing programs qualified as business programs based on language in the council's accreditation manual and the practices of other accrediting agencies. Because the school would not receive federal funding and would be closed if it did not receive accreditation, **the court found it would suffer irreparable harm. This harm outweighed the harm that the council would suffer.** The court also found that the school showed a substantial likelihood of success on the merits. It granted the preliminary injunction and remanded the case for further proceedings. *Florida College of Business v. Accrediting Council for Independent Colleges and Schools*, 954 F.Supp. 256 (S.D. Fla. 1996).

◆ *Where a decision to withdraw accreditation was not arbitrary, a federal court should not have ordered the agency to continue the accreditation.*

The Commission on Occupational Education Institutions (COEI) is part of the Southern Association of Colleges and Schools (SACS). It was set up to accredit postsecondary, nondegree granting institutions. In March 1988, COEI conducted an on-site inspection of a cosmetology school's campuses to determine whether to reaffirm accreditation. After finding various problems (violations of dual accreditation and of refund and disclosure policies, and failure to submit an annual report for 1986), COEI dropped the school's accreditation. Since this was a prerequisite for the students' receipt of federal financial assistance, the school sued COEI and SACS to stop the disaccreditation. A federal court issued an injunction preventing SACS from withdrawing the school's accreditation for at least one year, and it further ordered SACS to pay the school's attorneys' fees and costs.

During the SACS appeal to the U.S. Court of Appeals, Fifth Circuit, five of the school's six campuses closed. The school voluntarily relinquished SACS accreditation for the other campus. This rendered the validity of the injunction moot. However, the court of appeals found that it had to reach the merits of the case because of the question of attorneys' fees and costs. The court then noted that **there had been clear evidence that the school had been in violation of the dual accreditation policy set by COEI**. The district court had incorrectly found that COEI's policy language was vague. It should have accorded COEI's accreditation decisions greater deference. Thus, the court reversed the district court's award to the school and held that it was not entitled to attorneys' fees and costs. *Wilfred Academy v. Southern Ass'n of Colleges and Schools*, 957 F.2d 210 (5th Cir. 1992).

III. CONSTRUCTION AND OUTSIDE CONTRACTS

◆ *The U.S. Supreme Court held a choice of law clause in a construction contract superseded arbitration rights found in the Federal Arbitration Act.*

An electrical contractor contracted with a California university to install conduits. The contract contained a clause in which the parties agreed to arbitrate disputes relating to the contract. The contract also contained a choice-of-law clause that stated that it would be governed by the law of the place of the project's location. A dispute arose concerning overtime compensation, and the contractor made a formal request for arbitration. The university sued the contractor in a California trial court for fraud and breach of contract. **The contractor claimed that it was entitled to arbitration under the contract and the Federal Arbitration Act (FAA).** The court granted the university's motion to stay arbitration under a California statute that permits a stay when arbitration is the subject of pending court action. The contractor appealed to the California Court of Appeal, which affirmed the trial court's decision. The court of appeal acknowledged that although the contract affected interstate commerce, the California statute applied because of the contractual choice-of-law clause. The California Supreme Court denied the contractor's petition for discretionary review, but the U.S. Supreme Court agreed to hear its appeal.

On appeal, the contractor reiterated its argument that the court of appeal's ruling on the choice-of-law clause deprived it of its federally guaranteed right to arbitration under the FAA. The Supreme Court ruled that **the FAA did not confer a general right to compel arbitration. Rather, it guaranteed the right to arbitrate according to the manner provided for in the parties' contract.** The court of appeal had correctly found that the contract incorporated California law. The FAA was not undermined by the state law that permitted a stay of arbitration. The Court affirmed the court of appeal's decision for the university. *Volt Information Sciences v. Board of Trustees of Leland Stanford Junior Univ.*, 489 U.S. 468, 109 S.Ct. 1248, 103 L.Ed.2d 488 (1989).

◆ *A university that did a thorough environmental impact evaluation of a construction project did not have to file an environmental impact statement.*

A New York state university planned five separate campus housing projects, including a 116-unit building for which it filed a full environmental assessment form that was supported by an environmental site assessment report. A lawsuit nevertheless ensued, seeking to compel the university to file an environmental impact statement and seeking a temporary injunction to prevent construction until such statement was filed. The New York Supreme Court, Appellate Division, ruled that the university did not have to file an environmental impact statement because its thorough study of the environmental effects of construction concluded that there would not be an adverse impact on wetlands, cultural resources, groundwater, air quality, solid waste, removal of vegetation, wildlife or open space such that the project should be stopped. **In light of the university's thorough evaluation, the project could proceed.** *Forman v. Trustees of State Univ. of New York*, 757 N.Y.S.2d 180 (N.Y. App. Div. 2003).

◆ *A university was entitled to money from a contractor who underbid a project and then sought to recoup its losses as additional work.*

The University of Alaska solicited bids for fixing a drainage problem involving an access road and gravel pad surfaces at a research facility. **It accepted the lowest bid but then experienced problems with the contractor.** The contractor first obtained a one-week extension, then sought approval for extra materials, extra work and the payment of additional money. The university rejected the claims. When the contractor failed to finish the project on time, the ground froze, and it was unable to complete the project. Both the university and the contractor sought financial reimbursement, and a hearing officer determined that the contractor underbid the project, then sought to recover its losses as additional work. However, the university also owed some additional monies to the contractor.

The case reached the Supreme Court of Alaska, which largely upheld the hearing officer's determinations. It refused, however, to grant the university liquidated damages because the university had entered into an agreement with the contractor's bonding company regarding the hiring of another contractor to finish the project. *Lakloey, Inc. v. Univ. of Alaska*, No. 5-9690, 2002 WL 1732561 (Alaska 2002).

◆ *Fact issues prevented a court from granting pretrial judgment to a university on a breach of contract claim involving an electrical contractor.*

A New York university hired an electrical contractor to perform work on a biomolecular medicine and residential tower. Shortly after the contract was signed, the project fell behind schedule. The electrical contractor blamed the construction manager and inadequate security, which led to vandalism and theft, forcing the electrical contractor to redo some work. Eventually, a lawsuit was filed, with the electrical contractor asserting that the university breached the contract by failing to pay for work performed, and the university asserting that it had to correct and complete work the electrical contractor was supposed to finish. A New York court granted pretrial judgment to the university, but the Supreme Court, Appellate Division, reversed. **Evidence existed indicating that the electrical contractor performed its obligations under the contract.** The court remanded the case for further proceedings. *F. Garofalo Electric Co. v. New York Univ.*, 754 N.Y.S.2d 227 (N.Y. App. Div. 2002).

◆ *A coffee shop breached its lease agreement with a university by refusing to pay rent after a competitor opened a shop on campus.*

An Ohio university entered into a 10-year lease with a coffee shop for one of the sections of its food court. The university agreed that competition between like products among shops would be strongly discouraged. Later, another coffee seller opened a location in the student center, and the coffee shop stopped paying rent. The university sued it for breach of contract, and the coffee shop defended by asserting that the university breached the non-compete agreement of the lease by allowing the competitor onto the university campus. The Ohio Court of Claims ruled for the university, finding it only had a duty not to allow competitors into the food court. **Since the competitor was not located in the court with the coffee shop, the university did not breach the non-compete agreement.** The court ordered the coffee shop to pay the university over $37,000 in damages for past-due rent and common area charges. *Kent State Univ. v. Univ. Coffee House, Inc.*, 776 N.E.2d 583 (Ohio Ct. Cl. 2002).

◆ *A university could not recover from a contractor for an explosion and fire several years after the construction of a power plant.*

The University of Colorado contracted with a construction company to build a co-generation power facility on its Boulder campus. The contract contained a provision stating that **acceptance of the work would constitute a release of all claims against the company**, and also contained a 12-month warranty period. However, the university purchased an extended five-year warranty from the subcontractor that furnished the gas turbine engines for the facility. After the facility had been in operation for three and, a half years, a combination of events caused a backup in one engine, resulting in an explosion and fire. The university sued the contractor and subcontractor for breach of contract, breach of warranty, negligence and strict liability. A state court ruled for the defendants, and the Colorado Court of Appeals affirmed. Here, the contractor's warranty and the release clearly protected it from liability. Also, with respect to the subcontractor, the jury's ruling was not unsupported by the evidence. *Regents of the Univ. of Colorado v. Harbert Construction Co.*, 51 P.3d 1037 (Colo. Ct. App. 2001).

♦   *West Virginia's highest court set forth five factors to be used in determining whether a construction project is a public project.*

West Virginia University and the West Virginia University Foundation (a private, nonprofit corporation) began planning and developing a layout for the construction of a building to be known as the University Services Center. After a bidding process, a developer agreed to build the center at its own cost and risk. The foundation would then purchase the site and lease the building to the university. When an affiliation of construction trades sued for a declaration that the proposed construction was a public project governed by state wage and competitive bidding laws, the university and the nonprofit foundation moved for pretrial judgment. A state court granted the motion, finding that the foundation was not a state agency, and its connection to the university did not convert the construction into a public project. The West Virginia Supreme Court of Appeals affirmed. It listed five factors to be used in determining whether a construction project is a public project and held that **the lower court record was not sufficiently developed to determine whether public funds had been used on the project**. Further, the building was now completed, and there was no indication of wage violations. *Affiliated Construction Trades Foundation v. Univ. of West Virginia Board of Trustees*, 557 S.E.2d 863 (W. Va. 2001).

♦   *The University of Connecticut's suit against the state Department of Public Utility Control survived dismissal.*

In 1989, Charter Communications of Northeast Connecticut entered into a 10-year contract with the university to provide cable services to its campus, using the university's conduits to bring in cable wires both outside and inside campus buildings. Over the 10-year period, the conduits became either full or clogged in several buildings. After unsuccessful negotiations to renew the arrangement, the contractual relationship between the parties terminated when the contract expired. Subsequently, Charter filed a request with the state Department of Public Utility Control, (DPUC) seeking a declaratory ruling regarding its rights to provide cable services to the campus. The DPUC determined that Charter had a right to access the university's buildings and to provide cable services. When the university appealed, Charter moved to dismiss the action.

The court denied the motion. In appealing an administrative decision, the university had to establish that it was "aggrieved." Here, the school demonstrated a specific personal and legal interest that was adversely affected by the DPUC decision. The university argued that permitting Charter's wires to remain in place clogged its conduits. Moreover, the university asserted that a portion of the $750,000 used to create HUSKYvision, its own cable system, was spent because of the presence of Charter's wires in its conduits. **This evidence was sufficient for the court to conclude that the university showed it was aggrieved, and Charter's motion to dismiss was denied.** *Univ. of Connecticut v. Dep't of Public Utility Control*, No. CV 9904978265, 2000 WL 1409799 (Conn. Super. Ct. 2000).

CHAPTER ELEVEN

School Finance

Page

I. PUBLIC ASSISTANCE TO SCHOOLS

A. Federal Funding

1. Compliance

◆ *A federal court lacked jurisdiction to determine whether the U.S. Department of Education (DOE) improperly listed a college as closed.*

A Puerto Rico college participated in the Pell Grant program under a Program Participation Agreement (PPA). In February 1995, the Puerto Rico Treasury Department shut down the school due to a tax debt. The department placed locks on the college's doors, and students were forced to vacate the premises. The college reopened about two weeks later. As a result, the DOE placed the college on a list of "closed schools" and stopped treating it as a participating school in the Pell Grant program. The college claimed the DOE breached its PPA contract and sued the DOE. The U.S. Court of Federal Claims dismissed the complaint, but the U.S. Court of Appeals for the Federal Circuit vacated the decision and remanded the case to the lower court. On remand, the court again dismissed the case. The DOE did not breach any contract with the college by failing to provide it with a hearing. Under federal regulations governing PPAs, the agreement automatically expired when the college failed to hold classes for two weeks. **As the agreement automatically expired, no hearing was needed. The court also held it lacked jurisdiction to determine whether the DOE improperly placed the college on its list of closed schools.** *San Juan City College v. U.S.*, 74 Fed.Cl. 448 (Ct. Claims 2006).

◆ *The Supreme Court stated that federal assistance may be based on compliance with federal laws. Thus, a statute mandating compliance with the Selective Service System's requirements as a prerequisite to federal aid did not violate the Fifth Amendment's protection from self-incrimination since no student is compelled to apply for federal aid.*

Section 12(f) of the Military Selective Service Act denied federal financial assistance under Title IV of the Higher Education Act to male students between the ages of 18 and 26 who failed to register for the draft. Applicants for assistance were required to file a statement with their institutions attesting to their compliance with the Selective Service Act. A group of students who had not registered for the draft sued the selective service system to enjoin enforcement of Section 12(f). A federal district court held that the act was a bill of attainder (a law that imposes a penalty on a group of people without a trial) because it singled out an identifiable group that would be ineligible for Title IV aid based on their failure to register. The court also held that the compliance requirement violated the Fifth Amendment.

On appeal, the Supreme Court rejected the claims that the law was a bill of attainder and upheld the law. **The law clearly gave non-registrants 30 days after receiving notice of ineligibility for federal financial aid to register for the draft and thereby qualify for aid.** Furthermore, the bill of attainder prohibition in the Constitution applies only to statutes that inflict punishments on specified groups or individuals such as "all Communists." The Court also held that the denial of aid based on these requirements was not "punishment." The Court stated that **if students wish to further their education at the expense of their country, they cannot expect the benefits without accepting their fair share of governmental responsibility.** Finally, the law did not violate the Fifth Amendment because there was nothing forcing students to apply for federal aid. *Selective Service System v. Minnesota Public Interest Research Group*, 468 U.S. 841, 104 S.Ct. 3348, 82 L.Ed.2d 632 (1984).

◆ *Private schools whose students receive federal funds are deemed to be recipients of federal assistance. Therefore, even a college with an unbending policy of rejecting all forms of government assistance was required to comply with federal laws because its students received federal grants and loans.*

A private college, which had an "unbending policy" of refusing all forms of government assistance in order to remain independent of governmental restrictions, was asked by the Department of Education (DOE) to supply "assurance of compliance" with Title IX, which the college refused to do on the ground that it was receiving no federal funding. The DOE disagreed, saying that because the school enrolled large numbers of students receiving federal Basic Educational Opportunity Grants (BEOGs), it was receiving financial assistance for purposes of Title IX. The DOE then cut off student financial assistance based on the college's failure to execute the assurance of compliance. Four students and the college brought suit challenging the termination of financial assistance.

The Supreme Court held that the college was a recipient of federal financial assistance and was thus subject to the statute prohibiting sex discrimination. This was so despite the fact that only some of the college's

students received BEOGs and even though the college did not receive any direct federal financial assistance. Thus, the college was obliged to submit assurance of compliance, but only with regard to the administration of its financial aid program, in order for students to continue to receive federal aid. *Grove City College v. Bell*, 465 U.S. 555, 104 S.Ct. 1211, 79 L.Ed.2d 516 (1984).

◆ *The U.S. Supreme Court held that the government may show a violation of Title IV of the Higher Education Act without proving specific intent to injure or defraud by a defendant.*

A private, nonprofit technical school in Indiana participated in the Guaranteed Student Loan (GSL) program authorized by Title IV of the Higher Education Act. The program required the school to make refunds to the lender if a student withdrew from school during a term. If the school failed to refund loans to the lender, the student – and if the student defaulted, the government – would be liable for the full amount of the loan. The treasurer of the school conferred with the school's owners and initiated a practice of not making GSL refunds. As a result, the school owed $139,649 in refunds.

After the school lost its accreditation, a federal grand jury indicted the treasurer for "knowingly and willfully misapplying" federally insured student loan funds in violation of 20 U.S.C. § 1097(a). A federal district court dismissed the indictment because it lacked an allegation that the treasurer intended to injure or defraud the U.S. The Seventh Circuit reinstated the prosecution, and the U.S. Supreme Court affirmed the decision. The Court held Section 1097(a) did not require the specific intent to injure or defraud. **If the government can prove the defendant misapplied Title IV funds knowingly and willfully, that is sufficient to show a violation of Section 1097(a).** *Bates v. U.S.*, 522 U.S. 23, 118 S.Ct. 285, 139 L.Ed.2d 215 (1997).

◆ *A former university recruiter may proceed on his claim that an Indiana university violated the False Claims Act.*

One of the requirements for a university's eligibility for Higher Education Act (HEA) funding is to refrain from paying recruiters contingent fees for enrolling students. On a phase-one HEA application, a university assured the U.S. Department of Education (DOE) that it complied with the rule against contingent fees. A former recruiter claimed the university lied. He said he had received contingent fees as a university recruiter and later as its director of admissions. The recruiter sued the university in a federal district court under the federal False Claims Act (FCA).

An FCA violation requires proof that a university's allegedly false certification was the reason it received federal subsidies. The case reached the U.S. Court of Appeals, Seventh Circuit, which found the DOE would not have granted phase-two applications had the university told the truth. **All the disbursements depended on the phase-one finding that the university was an eligible institution.** The court reversed the judgment and remanded the case to the district court for further proceedings. *U.S. ex rel. Main v. Oakland City Univ.*, 426 F.3d 914 (7th Cir. 2005).

2. Government Authority

◆   *A government agency could seek a refund of grant money to equalize the amounts spent by it and by the university foundation awarded the grant.*

A nonprofit foundation for a California university submitted a project proposal designed to retrain defense engineers for positions in small businesses or manufacturing. The estimated cost of the program was $1,179,544, and the foundation sought $593,166 from a federal grant program administered by the National Science Foundation (NSF). The NSF awarded the foundation $550,000 under a three-year grant that required the foundation to essentially match the grant funds, and to maintain detailed accounting records of all costs as well as of the matching funds. When the NSF later suspected that the foundation was not meeting its financial obligations, an audit was conducted, and a recommendation was made that the NSF should seek a refund of approximately $140,000. The foundation sued to prevent the NSF from obtaining a refund, but a Virginia federal court ruled in favor of the NSF.

The U.S. Court of Appeals, Fourth Circuit, affirmed the judgment, finding that **the foundation had breached the terms of the grant regarding its obligation to fund or obtain funding for approximately half the costs of the program**. The foundation also had improperly stated certain amounts paid to the engineers as matching funds. As a result, the lower court had properly required the foundation to refund part of the grant money to the NSF. *California State Univ. Fullerton Foundation v. National Science Foundation*, 26 Fed.Appx. 263 (4th Cir. 2002).

◆   *A private university did not meet the eligibility requirements for student financial assistance programs under Title IV of the Higher Education Act.*

In 1991 and 1992, the DOE found the university system, Sistema Universitario Ana G. Mendez, was not eligible for Title IV programs dealing with Pell grant programs. As a result of the DOE's finding, **the university system was responsible for refunding to the federal government $1,712,540 in student grant funds** that were dispersed from 1989 to 1991. The secretary of education's determination was based on the fact that the university system failed to license its additional campuses. When filling out its Title IV application forms, the university system did not report these campuses under the "additional locations" section. It also failed to obtain prior approval from the Puerto Rico Commission on Higher Education for most of the satellite locations. The university system filed an administrative challenge, but a DOE administrative law judge affirmed its $1.7 million liability. The university system appealed to a federal district court, which reversed the administrative decision, finding the satellite campuses were licensed. However, it also found that the certifications did not necessarily constitute legal authorization under the Higher Education Act. On remand, the DOE determined that the certifications did not constitute legal authorization. The district court affirmed.

The university system then asked the U.S. Court of Appeals for the First Circuit to determine whether the Higher Education Act gives the secretary of education the final word on whether a university program is legally authorized by a state under the act and is therefore eligible for Title IV funding. The First

Circuit held that **the Higher Education Act does not explicitly give either the secretary of education or the states the exclusive right to determine "legal authorization."** However, the court reasoned that it is not impermissible or unreasonable to allow the secretary to make that determination. The DOE's finding of liability was affirmed. *Sistema Universitario Ana G. Mendez v. Riley*, 234 F.3d 772 (1st Cir. 2000).

◆   *A federal court upheld a U.S. Department of Education classification of prisoner-students, finding federal law allowed distinctions among students.*

An accredited for-profit vocational-technical school in Texas entered into an agreement with certain privately operated prison facilities to provide training programs for prisoners. The prisoners were not obligated to provide funding; however, the school received compensation by having the prisoners obtain federal Pell Grants based on the amounts it normally charged nonprisoner students, with an adjustment for the shorter prison programs. The school received a total of about $8.1 million. The U.S. Department of Education (Department) determined that because the prisoner students were under no obligation to pay tuition, there was no tuition "charge" that could be offset by a Pell Grant. Also, the school could not include "expenses" since the prisoners did not pay for books or other materials, and the state of Texas paid for their living arrangements. Thus, the school was required to reimburse the Department. The school sued the Department, and the case reached the U.S. Court of Appeals, Fifth Circuit.

The Higher Education Act (HEA) defines the tuition and fees component of a student's "cost of attendance" as those "normally charged" at the institution. The Department determined that for prisoner students, to whom the school was required to provide classes free of charge, the tuition "normally charged" was zero. Thus, the school was not entitled to receive reimbursement for tuition in the form of a Pell Grant. The court upheld the Department's subclassification of the prisoner students, finding that the HEA plainly allowed distinctions between groups of students who are normally charged different amounts. **The court held that the school had reasonably and detrimentally relied on the Department's previous interpretation, which indicated that tuition and fee waivers did not affect the "cost of attendance" for Pell Grant purposes, and did not require the school to reimburse the tuition portion of the awards.** However, the school remained liable for reimbursement of the expense allowance portion of the awards. Because the students incurred no expenses, the school was never entitled, nor could it ever have believed it was entitled, to make awards based on those amounts. *Microcomputer Technology Institute v. Riley*, 139 F.3d 1044 (5th Cir. 1998).

◆   *The U.S. Court of Appeals, Second Circuit, upheld federal regulations published under Title IV of the Higher Education Act as representing a reasonable interpretation of the statute.*

Title IV of the Higher Education Act, 20 U.S.C. § 1091b(a), requires college and post-secondary vocational training schools that receive federal funds for student financial aid programs to establish a fair and equitable policy for refunding unearned tuition and other costs when a student receiving such aid fails to enter or prematurely leaves the intended program. Subsection (b) declares that an institution's refund policy shall be considered fair and equitable if the refund is at least the largest of the amounts provided under state law, the institution's nationally recognized accrediting agency formula, or the statutorily described formula for pro rata refunds.

A regulation issued by the Secretary of Education (found at 34 C.F.R. § 668.22(b)(4)) provided that schools had to deduct "any unpaid charges owed by the student for the period of enrollment for which the student has been charged." Former regulations had put the risk of student nonpayment on the government. A coalition of vocational training schools in New York sought a federal district court injunction against the operation of the regulation. The court granted the injunction, but the U.S. Court of Appeals, Second Circuit, vacated the injunction and stated that **Section 668.22(b)(4) represented a reasonable interpretation of the statute**. The statute set a minimum refund amount but did not bar the secretary from asking for a larger amount. *Coalition of New York State Career Schools Inc. v. Riley*, 129 F.3d 276 (2d Cir. 1997).

B. State Funding

◆   *The New York Supreme Court, Appellate Division, held that the state could review a nonpublic educational institution's certification of a student's eligibility for a state grant.*

A New York private college accepted and certified a group of students who had previously attended a local community college as eligible for state Supplemental Tuition Assistance Program (STAP) grants. The STAP grants provided tuition assistance to New York students whose educational deficits were so great that they would not be considered admissible to a college-level program. The state denied the college's request for STAP award and a New York trial court affirmed the denial. On appeal by the college, the appellate division court held that **the state had both the authority and the obligation to review a nonpublic educational institution's certification of a student's eligibility for a STAP grant**. The regulatory scheme did not contemplate awards to students with successful college experience who had previously received funds pursuant to the Tuition Assistance Program. The appellate court affirmed the trial court's denial of STAP funds. *Touro College v. Nolan*, 620 N.Y.S.2d 558 (N.Y. App. Div. 1994).

◆   *A university could not maintain a race-based scholarship program where past discrimination did not justify it.*

The University of Maryland maintained a merit scholarship program open only to African-American students. It alleged that the program redressed prior constitutional violations against African-American students by the university, which had formerly been segregated by law. A student of Hispanic descent attempted to obtain a scholarship under the program, but was denied on the basis of his race. He filed a lawsuit against the university and a number of its officials in the U.S. District Court for the District of Maryland. The court granted summary judgment to the university, and the student won reversal from the U.S. Court of Appeals, Fourth Circuit. On remand, the parties again filed cross motions for summary judgment, and the district court again awarded summary judgment to the university.

The case was again appealed to the court of appeals. It determined that the district court had improperly found a basis in the evidence for its conclusion that a remedial plan of action was necessary. It also had erroneously determined that the scholarship program was narrowly tailored to meet the goal of remedying past discrimination. The court had misconstrued statistical evidence presented by the parties and had erroneously found a connection between past discrimination and present conditions at the university. **The reasons stated by the university for maintaining the race-based scholarship – underrepresentation of African-American students, low retention and graduation rates and a negative perception among African-American students – were legally insufficient.** The court reversed the summary judgment order for the university and awarded summary judgment to the student. *Podberesky v. Kirwan*, 38 F.3d 147 (4th Cir. 1994).

C. Student Default

Section 523(a)(8) of the U.S. Bankruptcy Code does not allow the discharge of student loans in bankruptcy. However, a bankruptcy court may permit the discharge of student loan debt if the student can show it would impose an undue hardship to repay the loans. In addition to the test for "undue hardship," a bankruptcy court may consider exceptional circumstances that strongly suggest a continuing inability to repay, such as a disability, and a student's failure to take advantage of forebearances or deferments.

◆ *The U.S. Department of Education could intercept a 67-year-old disabled Washington man's Social Security benefits to offset a delinquent student loan.*

The man failed to repay federally reinsured student loans he incurred between 1984 and 1989 under the Guaranteed Student Loan Program. The loans were reassigned to the Department of Education, which certified the debt to the U.S. Department of Treasury through the Treasury Offset Program. The U.S. began withholding a portion of the man's Social Security benefits to offset his debt, part of which was over 10 years delinquent. He sued the U.S. in a federal district court, alleging the offset was barred by the 10-year statute of limitations contained in the Debt Collection Act of 1982. The federal district court dismissed the case, and the U.S. Court of Appeals, Ninth Circuit, affirmed. The U.S. Supreme Court agreed to review the case.

The court noted the Debt Collection Act permits U.S. agency heads to collect an outstanding debt by "administrative offset." However, Section 407(a) of the Social Security Act limits the availability of benefits to offset a debt. The Court explained that the Higher Education Technical Amendments of 1991 "sweepingly eliminated time limitations as to certain loans." This included the student loans in this case. The Debt Collection Improvement Act of 1996 clarified that, notwithstanding any other law, including Section 407, all payments due under the Social Security Act were subject to offset. **The Court**

held the Debt Collection Improvement Act clearly made Social Security benefits subject to offset. Moreover, the Higher Education Technical Amendments removed the 10-year limit that would otherwise bar an offset of Social Security benefits. The Court rejected the man's argument that Congress could not have intended in 1991 to repeal a statute of limitations as they concerned Social Security benefits that were not made available for offset until 1996. Congress did not have to foresee all the consequences of a statutory enactment. It was also unnecessary for Congress to explicitly mention Section 407 in the Higher Education Technical Amendments. The Court concluded that the Debt Collection Improvement Act gave the U.S. the authority to use Social Security benefits to offset debts. The retention of the 10-year limit on debt collection in the Higher Education Technical Amendments did not apply in all contexts, including this administrative offset. It affirmed the judgment for the U.S. *Lockhart v. U.S.*, 546 U.S. 142 (2005).

◆ *An Ohio university failed to recoup a tuition subsidy it provided to a medical student who broke her promise to practice medicine in the state.*

Tuition subsidies are available to out-of-state residents who attend Ohio University and agree to practice medicine in Ohio for at least five years after they complete an in-state medical program. A California resident completed the program but returned to California without fulfilling the five-year obligation. The university sued her for breach of contract, seeking to recover about $94,000 – the subsidized cost of educating her. It obtained a default judgment on its claim. Before the university could collect on the judgment, the student filed for bankruptcy, seeking to discharge the debt to the university.

Under Chapter 7 bankruptcy law, a debtor generally remains obligated to repay an educational loan or an "educational benefit." The bankruptcy court held for the student, finding that her obligation was not a loan or the repayment of an educational benefit. The university then appealed to the Bankruptcy Appellate Panel (BAP) of the Ninth Circuit. The BAP held that **to qualify as a "loan," the agreement must indicate definite repayment terms. In addition, the repayment obligation must be a reflection of the benefit received.** As the contract did not require the student to repay the value of the educational services she received, the subsidy did not qualify as an "educational benefit" within the meaning of the bankruptcy law. The Ninth Circuit adopted the opinion of the BAP. *In re Hawkins*, 469 F.3d 1316 (9th Cir. 2006).

◆ *The Georgia state medical education board could recoup a scholarship awarded to a student who breached a contract.*

The student received more than $40,000 in return for an agreement with the board to practice medicine in a Georgia community with a population of 15,000 or less. She claimed she could relocate to a qualifying community only if the board paid her "funds necessary to rent a building, purchase equipment and hire competent staff." **The Court of Appeals of Georgia found no merit to the student's claim that the board was obligated to help her find work in a qualifying community.** There was no evidence that the board breached the contract by not paying her all the funds due under the contract or rescinded the contract. In an earlier order, the court of appeals held that state law authorized the award of treble damages under the contract. It reversed a lower court order limiting the board to the amount of her scholarship. *Calabro v. State Medical Educ. Board*, 283 Ga.App. 113, 640 S.E.2d 581 (Ga. Ct. App. 2006).

◆ *Noting that the debtor listed manicures for her dogs among her expenses, a bankruptcy court refused to excuse more than $62,000 in student loan debt.*

The court acknowledged that repayment of student loan debt can be excused when it would result in undue hardship for the debtor. Because the Bankruptcy Code does not define "undue hardship," the court applied the "totality of the circumstances" test. This test required it to consider the debtors' past, current and future resources, their reasonable and necessary living expenses, and any unique facts and circumstances. If the debtors could repay the debt and still maintain a minimal standard of living, repayment of the debt could not be excused. Applying this test, **the court determined that the expenses claimed were more than needed to maintain a minimal standard of living**. The cable television expense was unnecessary and unreasonable. The court reduced the allowable amounts claimed for pet care and costs of entertainment. After adjusting the allowable expenses, the court determined the couple was left with disposable income of $434 per month. In combination with the fact that the wife could increase that amount by working, at least on a part-time basis, the court refused to excuse the couple from repaying the student loan debt. *In re McLaughlin*, 359 B.R. 746 (W.D. Mo. 2007).

◆ *A Massachusetts bankruptcy court declined to discharge a student's school loans because she failed to show repayment would cause undue hardship.*

The student immigrated from Haiti in 1990. English was her second language. She earned a bachelor's degree in 1996 and received a master's degree in public administration in 1997. When the student graduated, she had a hard time finding a job. She held various data entry and health assistant jobs at rates ranging from 10 to 15 dollars per hour. As of 2004, her income was $2,400 a month. In addition to her income, the student received $25,000 from a settlement. She put the money in a savings account where it continued to earn interest. The student did not use any of the money to pay off her loans.

The student sued the university and Educational Credit Management Corporation (ECMC) in a bankruptcy court for discharge of her loans. The university agreed she could discharge its loans because of undue hardship. The student still owed seven loans held by ECMC totaling $53,000 which were not discharged. The ECMC asked the court to deny the request for discharge. The court noted **the bankruptcy code does not define "undue hardship" and that courts have struggled with its meaning. It concluded the student failed to prove that repaying her seven loans would impose an undue hardship or that her prospect for future income increases was so poor as to warrant a discharge.** *In re Paul*, 331 B.R. 730 (Bkrtcy. D. Mass. 2006).

◆ *A South Carolina graduate could not discharge an educational loan because she did not prove repayment imposed an undue hardship upon her.*

The graduate had $11,688 in government-guaranteed educational loans issued by the Educational Credit Management Corporation (ECMC). After graduating from a university in 1993, she worked in a variety of low-paying jobs. The graduate moved to South Carolina to take care of ailing family members. She then became self-employed and reported income of less than $11,000 for two years. The graduate filed for bankruptcy under Chapter 7 of the Bankruptcy Code and filed an adversary complaint against ECMC to discharge her student-loan debt as an undue hardship under 11 U.S.C. § 523(a)(8). The bankruptcy court found the graduate proved an "undue hardship" under 11 U.S.C. § 523(a)(8) and discharged the student-loan debt. The district court affirmed, and the ECMC appealed to the U.S. Court of Appeals, Fourth Circuit.

The court stated that government-backed student-loan debt is ordinarily not discharged under Chapter 7. **Congress expressly excluded this debt unless repayment would impose an undue hardship on a debtor.** To determine if a debtor may claim undue hardship, many courts have adopted a test established in *Brunner v. N.Y. State Higher Educ. Services Corp.*, 46 B.R. 752 (S.D. N.Y. 1985). The Fourth Circuit joined these courts and found nothing indicated the graduate or her son had any physical or mental disabilities. **Having a low-paying job does not in itself cause undue hardship, especially when the debtor has not tried to get a job that pays more.** The court found the graduate did not make good-faith efforts to repay her loans, and it reversed the judgment. *In re Frushour*, 433 F.3d 393 (4th Cir. 2005).

◆   *A Missouri law school graduate was allowed to discharge over $31,000 of his student loans, which totalled $110,000.*

The graduate was fired from his position as a state legislative researcher after he failed the Missouri bar exam. He made no payments on his student loans and did not seek a deferment or forbearance, even though he was eligible for one. His wife was also unemployed. The graduate asked a federal bankruptcy court to discharge his student loan debt under Title 11. At the time, he was 28 years old and had no disabilities or medical conditions that would limit his earning ability. **The court stated the Eighth Circuit applies the "totality of the circumstances" test to determine undue hardship.**

The courts consider whether the debtor's reasonable future financial resources will sufficiently cover payment of the student loan debt – without reducing what the debtor and his dependents need to maintain a minimal standard of living. The court referred to *Gill v. Nellnet Loan Services*, 326 B.R. 611 (E.D. Va. 2005), where the court articulated the requirements needed to meet a minimum standard of living. **"Minimum standard of living" means sufficient resources for food, shelter, clothing and medical treatment.** Even though the graduate was unemployed at the time of trial, the court found he had a significant earning capacity. The graduate was eligible to take the bar exam again and offered no good reason he had not done so. The court concluded his prospects of future earning – combined with any part-time income his wife could earn – suggested he could repay his student loans in the future. The court discharged loans totalling $31,761 because the bank that held those loans failed to answer the complaint. However, the totality of the circumstances indicated no undue hardship and the balance of the debt was nondischargeable. *In re Shadwick*, 341 B.R. 6 (W.D. Mo. 2006).

II. ESTABLISHMENT CLAUSE ISSUES

The Establishment Clause of the First Amendment prohibits Congress from making any law respecting an establishment of religion. It has been construed by the U.S. Supreme Court as prohibiting direct financial assistance by government agencies to religious schools and colleges. In 1997, the Court decided Agostini v. Felton, *521 U.S. 203, 117 S.Ct. 1997, 138 L.Ed.2d 391, an important private school finance case in which the Court abandoned the presumption that the presence of public employees on parochial school grounds creates a symbolic union between church and state that violates the Establishment Clause. Under* Agostini, *government assistance to private schools must not result in government indoctrination or endorsement of religion. The recipients of government assistance must not be defined by reference to their religion, and the assistance must not create excessive entanglement between church and state.*

◆ *The U.S. Supreme Court approved of the state of Washington's choice to exclude devotional theology candidates from a state scholarship program.*

Washington law created the Promise Scholarship Program, which made state funds available to qualified students for their educational costs. To be eligible, students had to meet certain performance standards and income limits, and enroll at least half-time in an eligible postsecondary institution in the state. The program excluded scholarships for theology majors, but students who attended religiously affiliated schools could still obtain scholarships so long as they did not major in theology and the institution was accredited. A student who received a Promise Scholarship enrolled as a double major in pastoral ministries and business at a private Christian college. A college financial aid administrator advised him he could not use the scholarship to pursue a devotional theology degree and could only receive program funds by certifying he would not pursue a theology degree. The student sued state officials in a federal district court for violating the Free Exercise, Establishment, Speech and Equal Protection Clauses. The court awarded summary judgment to the state, but the Ninth Circuit reversed the decision.

The U.S. Supreme Court held **the program was not a state expression of disfavor against religion**, as the student argued. The program did not impose civil or criminal sanctions on any type of religious service or rite. **There was no Free Exercise Clause violation, as the program did not require students to choose between their religious beliefs and a government benefit.** The state had only chosen not to fund a distinct category of instruction. The training of ministers was essentially a religious endeavor that could be treated differently than training for other callings. There was no evidence of state hostility toward religion. **The program permitted funding recipients to attend pervasively religious schools, and nothing in its text or the state constitution suggested anti-religious bias.** The state interest in denying funds to theology majors was substantial, and the program placed only a minor burden on recipients. The Court reversed the judgment. *Locke v. Davey*, 540 U.S. 712, 124 S.Ct. 1307, 158 L.Ed.2d 1 (2004).

◆   *The Court of Appeals of Missouri held that St. Louis University's use of*
public funds to build a sports arena did not violate the state constitution.

The university sought state tax increment financing (TIF) for a 13,000-seat
arena. The city of St. Louis enacted ordinances to establish the TIF assistance
under a state law that provided real property tax increment funding for urban
renewal projects. It agreed to pledge TIF revenues to special funds that "would
ultimately be funnelled to the developer to pay for the development costs
incurred." Groups opposed to the project sued the city in a federal district court
to prevent it from going forward. The university was not a party to the case.
Instead, it filed a new action in the state court system, seeking a declaratory
judgment that the TIF ordinances did not violate the Missouri Constitution. The
state court awarded summary judgment to the university and city, finding no
violation of state or federal law. The project opponents appealed.

The Court of Appeals of Missouri explained that the Missouri Constitution
is more restrictive than the Establishment Clause of the First Amendment.
Article IX, Section 8 forbids any Missouri city from appropriating or paying
public funds "in aid of any religious creed, church, sectarian purpose, or to help
to support or sustain any private or public school" that is "controlled by any
religious creed, church or sectarian denomination." The court sought to
determine whether the university was "controlled by a religious creed, church
or sectarian denomination" under the state constitution. The Supreme Court of
Missouri has identified the significance of independent governance as a factor
of "control" under Article IX, Section 8. Schools that had independent boards
would not be subject to the "control" provision. **While St. Louis University**
maintained a Jesuit heritage, it was controlled and operated by an
independent, lay board of trustees. University bylaws limited Jesuit
membership to a minority of board members. The constitutional language
"controlled by any religious creed" indicated an intent to include institutions
that "inculcate a doctrine and faith of a denomination, not those institutions that
merely identify with a religious heritage." St. Louis University intended to use
the TIF revenues to build a facility for secular purposes, such as sports events
and graduation ceremonies. **The grant of public benefits was for a valid**
public and secular purpose that did not violate the state constitution. *St.*
Louis Univ. v. Masonic Temple Ass'n of St. Louis, No. ED 86804, 2006 WL
2805606 (Mo. Ct. App. 10/3/06).

◆   *In 1986, the U.S. Supreme Court held that the First Amendment to the U.S.*
Constitution did not prevent the state of Washington from providing financial
assistance directly to an individual with a disability attending a Christian
college. However, the Supreme Court of Washington then held on remand that
the assistance violated the state constitution.

A visually impaired Washington student sought vocational rehabilitative
services from the Washington Commission for the Blind pursuant to state law.
The law provided that individuals with visual disabilities were eligible for
educational assistance to enable them to "overcome vocational handicaps and to
obtain the maximum degree of self-support and self-care." However, because the
plaintiff was a student at a Christian college intending to pursue a career of
service in the church, the Commission for the Blind denied him assistance. The

Washington Supreme Court upheld this decision on the ground that the First Amendment to the U.S. Constitution prohibited state funding of a student's education at a religious college. The U.S. Supreme Court took a less restrictive view of the First Amendment and reversed the Washington court. The operation of Washington's program was such that the Commission for the Blind paid money directly to students, who could then attend the schools of their choice. **The fact that the student in this case chose to attend a religious college did not constitute state support of religion because "the decision to support religious education is made by the individual, not the state."** The First Amendment was therefore not offended. *Witters v. Washington Dep't of Services for the Blind*, 474 U.S. 481, 106 S.Ct. 748, 88 L.Ed.2d 846 (1986).

On remand, the Washington Supreme Court reconsidered the matter under the **Washington State Constitution, which is far stricter in its prohibition on the expenditure of public funds for religious instruction than is the U.S. Constitution. Vocational assistance funds for the student's religious education violated the state constitution because public money would be used for religious instruction.** The court rejected the student's argument that the restriction on public expenditures would violate his right to free exercise of religion. The court determined that the commission's action was constitutional under the Free Exercise Clause because there was no infringement of the student's constitutional rights. Finally, denial of the funds to the student did not violate the Fourteenth Amendment's Equal Protection Clause because the commission had a policy of denying any student's religious vocational funding. The classification was directly related to the state's interest in ensuring the separation between church and state as required by both state and federal constitutions. The court reaffirmed its denial of the student's tuition. *Witters v. State Comm'n for the Blind*, 771 P.2d 1119 (Wash. 1989).

◆   *For more than a generation, courts have analyzed Establishment Clause cases under the framework established by the U.S. Supreme Court in* Lemon v. Kurtzman. *The test has been criticized by legal experts and by members of the Court itself, but it remains important for assessing the validity of government programs under the Establishment Clause.*

In *Lemon v. Kurtzman*, the Court invalidated Rhode Island and Pennsylvania statutes that provided state money to finance the operation of parochial schools. The Rhode Island statute provided a 15% salary supplement to parochial school teachers who taught nonreligious subjects using public school teaching materials. The Pennsylvania statute authorized payment of state funds to parochial schools to help defray the cost of teachers' salaries, textbooks and other instructional materials. Reimbursement was limited, however, to the costs of secular subjects, which also were taught in the public schools. The Supreme Court evaluated the Rhode Island and Pennsylvania programs using its **three-part test: First, the statute must have a secular legislative purpose; second, its principal or primary effect must be one that neither advances nor inhibits religion, finally; the statute must not foster "an excessive government entanglement with religion."**

Applying this test to the two state programs in question, the Court held that the legislative purpose of the programs was a legitimate, secular concern with maintaining high educational standards in both public and private schools. The Court did not reach the second inquiry because it held that the state programs failed under the third inquiry. The Rhode Island salary supplement program excessively entangled the state with religion because of the highly religious nature of the Catholic schools that were the primary beneficiaries of the program. The teachers who received the salary supplements provided instruction in classrooms and buildings containing religious symbols such as crucifixes. In such an atmosphere, even a person dedicated to remaining religiously neutral probably would allow some religious content to creep into the ostensibly secular instruction. Similar defects were found in the Pennsylvania program. The Court also observed that in order to ensure that the state-funded parochial school teachers did not inject religious dogma into their instruction, the state would be forced to extensively monitor the parochial school classrooms. This would result in excessive state entanglement with religion. Consequently, **the salary supplement programs were held to violate the Establishment Clause of the First Amendment**. *Lemon v. Kurtzman,* 403 U.S. 602, 91 S.Ct. 2105, 29 L.Ed.2d 745 (1971).

◆   *The Supreme Court held that the "secular side" of a college could be distinguished from sectarian programs, making it permissible for a state to provide funding to a religiously affiliated college, where the assistance goes only to a college's secular side.*

The state of Maryland enacted a program that authorized annual, noncategorical grants to religiously affiliated colleges. The program was challenged by taxpayers who alleged that state money was being put to religious uses by the schools, which had wide discretion in spending the funds. The Supreme Court noted *Hunt v. McNair* requires (1) that no state aid at all go to institutions that are so "pervasively sectarian" that secular activities cannot be separated from sectarian ones, and (2) that if secular activities can be separated out, they alone may be funded."

The colleges involved in this case were not found to be pervasively sectarian even though they were affiliated with the Catholic Church. The Court held that the "secular side" of the colleges could be separated from the sectarian and found that **state aid had only gone to the colleges' secular side**. It was admittedly somewhat difficult to ensure that the colleges and the Maryland Council for Higher Education would take care to avoid spending state funds on religious activities, but the Court expressed its belief that those entities would spend the money in good faith and avoid violating the First Amendment. *Roemer v. Board of Public Works,* 426 U.S. 736, 96 S.Ct. 2337, 49 L.Ed.2d 179 (1976).

◆   *The Supreme Court held that the receipt of Higher Education Facilities Act funds by four religious colleges did not violate the Establishment Clause.*

The Higher Education Facilities Act of 1963 contained an exclusion for any facility used for sectarian instruction or as a place of religious worship or any facility that is used primarily as part of a school divinity department. Federal education officials had powers to enforce the statute for a 20-year time period during which they could seek to recover funds from violators. A group of Connecticut taxpayers filed a federal district court action against government officials and four religious colleges that received Higher Education Facilities Act funds, seeking an order against the release of funds to sectarian institutions that used federal funds to construct libraries and other facilities. The court held the act did not have the effect of promoting religion.

The U.S. Supreme Court reviewed the case and held that the statute had been carefully drafted to ensure that no federal funds were disbursed to support the sectarian aspects of these institutions. **The four colleges named as defendants in this case had not violated any of the restrictions in the statute, as they had placed no religious symbols in facilities constructed with the use of federal funds, and had not used the facilities for any religious purposes.** There was no evidence that any of the colleges maintained a predominantly religious atmosphere, and although each of them was affiliated with the Catholic Church, none excluded non-Catholics from admissions or faculty appointments, and none of them required attendance at religious services. The receipt of funds by the colleges did not violate the Establishment Clause. The Court held, however, that the 20-year limit on federal oversight created the potential for religious use of the facilities after the 20 years expired. Because of the risk of use of the facilities for advancing religion, the court invalidated this portion of the legislation. *Tilton v. Richardson*, 403 U.S. 672, 91 S.Ct. 2091, 29 L.Ed.2d 790 (1971).

◆ *A city development board could issue tax-exempt bonds to a sectarian university for a building project.*

A Christian university began a renovation project and sought $15 million in low-interest loans from the Industrial Development Board for Nashville, Tennessee. The board approved the loan and issued tax-exempt bonds to the university. A group of taxpayers sued, asserting that the bond issuance impermissibly benefited a religious university in violation of the Establishment Clause. A federal court ruled that the university was so pervasively sectarian that no state aid could go to it. The Sixth Circuit Court of Appeals reversed, noting that **the tax-exempt bonds did not violate the Establishment Clause.** First, public funds were not used to issue the bonds; the university had to arrange for private financing; and bond purchasers only had recourse against the university. Second, the bonds were issued in a neutral manner to nonprofit organizations. Third, the bonds advanced the secular objective of promoting economic development. The university was entitled to receive the tax-exempt bonds. *Steele v. Industrial Development Board of Metropolitan Government of Nashville*, 301 F.3d 401 (6th Cir. 2002).

◆ *A Wisconsin program allowing unrestricted telecommunications access grants to sectarian schools and colleges violated the Establishment Clause.*

A 1997 Wisconsin law created the Technology for Education Achievement (TEACH) Board, which administered the Education Telecommunications Access program. The TEACH board approved access for data lines and video links under a heavily subsidized program in which both public and private schools participated. A taxpayer group objected to the program on constitutional grounds because $58,873 of the program's annual total of over

$1.9 million was awarded to nine religiously affiliated Wisconsin schools and private colleges. The taxpayers sued state education officials, including the TEACH board, challenging the program as unconstitutional. The court held that the program as a whole did not violate the Constitution, but found that unrestricted cash grants to private, sectarian schools violated the Establishment Clause's prohibition on state support of religion.

The parties appealed unfavorable aspects of the decision to the Seventh Circuit. The taxpayers dismissed their appeal concerning the constitutionality of the full program in view of the U.S. Supreme Court's intervening decision in *Mitchell v. Helms*, 530 U.S. 793 (2000). In *Mitchell*, the Supreme Court upheld the constitutionality of a state-aid program that helped parochial schools acquire computers, televisions, and laboratory equipment. The Seventh Circuit proceeded to the question of grants to religious schools, noting that **the Wisconsin law violated the third *Agostini* criteria, because in the absence of any restriction on the expenditure of public funds by the schools, the expenditures had a primary effect that advanced religion**. The subsidies could easily be used for maintenance, chapels, religious instruction, or connection time to view religious Web sites. The law did not bar schools from using the grants for these and other constitutionally impermissible purposes. Because direct aid from the government to a sectarian institution in any form is invalid, the court affirmed the district court's finding that the direct subsidies to religious schools were unconstitutional. *Freedom From Religion Foundation Inc. v. Bugher*, 249 F.3d 606 (7th Cir. 2001).

◆   *The Fourth Circuit determined a college operated by the Seventh-Day Adventist Church was eligible for state aid for secular programs.*

Maryland's Joseph A. Selinger program gives public aid to private colleges in the state. Qualifying colleges receive direct payments from the state to be used for secular purposes. In 1990, Columbia Union College applied for Selinger funds, but the Maryland Higher Education Commission denied the application because it believed the college was too sectarian. A few years later, the school sought reconsideration of its application in view of *Rosenberger v. Rector and Visitors of the University of Virginia*, 515 U.S. 819 (1995), which emphasized the importance of neutral criteria in determining eligibility for public aid. The commission continued to reject the school's application. In 1996, Columbia Union applied for Selinger aid to specifically fund its math, computer science, clinical laboratory science, respiratory care and nursing programs, but again the request was denied. The school sued, alleging constitutional and statutory violations. The district court applied the reasoning in *Roemer v. Board of Public Works*, 426 U.S. 736 (1976) to find Columbia Union was not "pervasively sectarian." Thus, it was eligible for Selinger funds.

The commission appealed, arguing that the district court wrongly concluded the school was not pervasively sectarian. Columbia Union countered that whether an institution is pervasively sectarian is no longer relevant when determining an institution's eligibility for public aid, in light of *Mitchell v. Helms*, 530 U.S. 793 (2000). In *Mitchell*, the Supreme Court upheld the constitutionality of a state-aid program that helped parochial schools acquire computers, televisions, and laboratory equipment. The Supreme Court used the test outlined in *Agostini v. Felton*, 521 U.S. 203 (1997), examining whether the program had a secular purpose and whether it had the primary effect of inhibiting or advancing religion. The court ruled that **giving Selinger funds to Columbia Union had a secular purpose and did not advance religion because the aid had to be used for secular purposes.** Although the college had a mandatory worship policy, it applied only to a minority of students. Also, the college's traditional liberal arts classes were not taught with the primary objective of religious indoctrination. Although the Seventh-Day Adventist Church had a strong influence over college affairs, and the college preferred to hire and admit members of that faith, these factors by themselves were not enough to make the college pervasively sectarian. *Columbia Union College v. Oliver*, 254 F.3d 496 (4th Cir. 2001).

◆ *A Virginia Christian school could constitutionally raise funds for new facilities through the issuance of revenue bonds under a state program.*

Regent University is a private Christian university that applied for assistance under the Educational Facilities Authority Act, seeking financing for various construction projects including new classrooms, administrative space, a communication and arts complex, and an events center. The Virginia College Building Authority (VCBA) approved the application and issued the requested revenue bonds. As a result, members of Americans United for Separation of Church and State, an advocacy group, challenged VCBA's action. A state trial court held that Regent was ineligible for participation in the VCBA program because it is a "pervasively sectarian institution and because its primary purpose is 'religious training'." The Virginia Supreme Court reversed. Even though Regent was "pervasively sectarian" both in policy and practice, the court focused on the secular purpose of the university and found that its receipt of bonds did not violate the Establishment Clause of the First Amendment.

The court distinguished seminaries, which educate students for religious vocations, from church-related colleges, which offer various degrees for secular vocations. Here, the school offered over 20 different graduate degrees in the areas of business, education and journalism. It also was approved by the Southern Association of Colleges and Schools to award masters' and doctoral degrees, and its law school was accredited by the American Bar Association. Because the bond proceeds did not involve governmental aid (the bonds were purchased by private investors who chose to invest in VCBA bonds), the university was eligible to participate in the bond program. **Since no taxpayer dollars flowed into the bonds, VCBA's approval of Regent's application did not involve "excessive government entanglement with religion."** Further, the VCBA program could not reasonably be viewed as an endorsement of religion. *Virginia College Building Authority v. Lynn*, 260 Va. 608, 538 S.E.2d 682 (Va. 2000).

◆ *The Supreme Court of Virginia held that a university with a pervasively religious mission could not receive the proceeds of a city bond issue without violating the Establishment Clauses of the U.S. and Virginia Constitutions.*

Liberty University is a private, sectarian institution that is closely related to a local Baptist church. It required all of its students and faculty to comply with clearly spelled out religious requirements. The Lynchburg, Virginia, city council and Industrial Development Authority (IDA) approved the issuance of up to $60 million of Educational Facilities Revenue Bonds in order to assist Liberty University in building and developing academic and administrative facilities in Lynchburg. The validity of the bond issue with respect to both the U.S. and Virginia Constitutions came under question. The IDA filed an action to answer those questions. A Virginia trial court validated the bond issue, and a group of opposing taxpayers appealed to the Supreme Court of Virginia.

The main issue was whether the bond issuance violated the Establishment Clauses of the U.S. or Virginia Constitutions. The First Amendment states, "Congress shall make no law respecting the establishment of religion." The court turned to a number of decisions in which the U.S. Supreme Court has allowed comparable arrangements for other church-related schools. Those decisions involved schools that imposed no religious requirements for admission or employment, or religious requirements for students or faculty while affiliated with the school. The court contrasted Liberty's policies and found the bond issuance unconstitutional. Liberty had published policies requiring specific church attendance six times per week. Academic freedom also was limited. **The court found Liberty to be "a religious mission" with a "pervasive aim [of] equipping young people for evangelistic ministry." Because of this pervasiveness, the bond issue could only have the effect of establishing religion.** The trial court judgment was reversed. *Habel v. Industrial Development Authority*, 400 S.E.2d 516 (Va. 1991).

III. PRIVATE SCHOOL TAXATION

The U.S. Supreme Court has infrequently considered federal income tax cases involving private schools. In Bob Jones Univ. v. U.S., *461 U.S. 574, 103 S.Ct. 2017, 76 L.Ed.2d 157 (1983), it held that private schools must comply with the strong federal interest against race discrimination and that federal tax exempt status can be denied to schools maintaining discriminatory policies. More recently, in* Camps Newfound/Owatonna, Inc. v. Town of Harrison, Maine, *520 U.S. 564, 117 S.Ct. 1590, 137 L.Ed.2d 852 (1997), the Court found no reason why nonprofit status should exempt a private entity from laws regulating commerce, including local property tax laws.*

A. Federal Income Taxation

◆   *The U.S. government's strong public policy against racial discrimination was held sufficient to deny tax-exempt status to an otherwise qualified private college.*

Section 501(c)(3) of the Internal Revenue Code (IRC) provides that "corporations ... organized and operated exclusively for religious, charitable ... or educational purposes" are entitled to tax-exempt status. The Internal Revenue Service routinely granted tax exemption under IRC Section 501(c)(3) to private schools regardless of whether they had racially discriminatory admissions policies. In 1970, however, the IRS concluded it could no longer grant tax-exempt status to racially discriminatory private schools because such schools were not "charitable" within the meaning of Section 501(c)(3). In *Bob Jones Univ. v. U.S.*, two private colleges whose racial admissions policies were allegedly rooted in their interpretations of the Bible sued to prevent the IRS from interpreting the federal tax laws in this manner. The Supreme Court rejected the colleges' challenge and upheld the IRS's interpretation.

The Court's ruling was based on a strong federal public policy against racial discrimination in education. **Because the colleges were operating in violation of that public policy, the colleges could not be considered "charitable" under Section 501(c)(3). Thus, they were ineligible for tax exemption. The Court held that in order to fall under the exemption of Section 501(c)(3) an institution must be in harmony with the public interest.** It also held that the denial of an exemption did not impermissibly burden Bob Jones' alleged religious interest in practicing racial discrimination. *Bob Jones Univ. v. U.S.*, 461 U.S. 574, 103 S.Ct. 2017, 76 L.Ed.2d 157 (1983).

B. State and Local Taxation

◆   *Office space leased by a bank from a university was exempt from property taxation because it was used for a "school purpose."*

The University of Delaware contracted with a bank to develop a student student identification card that could also be used as a debit card for services. The university provided office space to the bank for the project. The local land use department discontinued the university's property tax exemption for the space and assessed taxes on it. A county board of assessment review upheld the assessment, but its decision was reversed by a state superior court, which found the space was used for a school purpose under state law.

The Supreme Court of Delaware noted the term "school purpose" was undefined by 9 Del. C. Section 8105. Under that section, college or school property used for educational or school purposes was not subject to taxation. The court rejected the county's argument that Section 8105 must be read narrowly. Statutes exempting educational institutions from taxation are generally "construed more liberally than other tax exempting statutes." The trial court had correctly determined the bank served a "school purpose." **The court held "school purposes" included use of school-owned property that contributed to the legitimate welfare, convenience, and/or safety of the school community or its members.** The judgment was affirmed. *New Castle County Dep't of Land Use v. Univ. of Delaware*, 842 A.2d 1201 (Del. 2004).

◆   *A North Carolina court denied tax-exempt status to a restaurant that claimed to be an institution of higher learning.*

A taxpayer purchased a restaurant and named it the University for the Study of Human Goodness and Creative Group Work. He applied for tax-exempt status as an educational institution, describing the restaurant as a learning laboratory with a three-member faculty and a one-year program with four curriculum tracks. The university was not accredited by any organization, and a local tax review board denied the application. The North Carolina Property Tax Commission also denied the taxpayer's appeal.

The Court of Appeals of North Carolina credited the board's findings that **the restaurant lacked the characteristics typical of an educational institution. It had no formal curriculum and did not issue academic grades. It appeared the restaurant was operated predominantly as a business** with a substantial amount of patronage. The North Carolina Supreme Court had previously held that a spiritual center was not entitled to tax-exempt status because mediation did not qualify as a learning activity. In another case, a day care center was denied tax-exempt status because it was not a "traditional school and not 'wholly and exclusively' used for educational purpose." Based on the evidence and case law, the court upheld the commission's decision. *Matter of Univ. for Study of Human Goodness and Creative Group Work*, 582 S.E.2d 645 (N.C. Ct. App. 2003).

◆ *A university's bus service was not entitled to a credit for fuel taxes for its campus bus service.*

An Ohio public university owned a campus bus service that provided free transportation within the university campus. It also transported disabled students to and from the airport, and serviced the city of Kent and neighboring townships. However, it did not operate under a contract with the city or any other regional transit authority. When it applied for reimbursement of motor vehicle fuel taxes, claiming eligibility for the credits because its buses were transit buses, the tax commissioner and the Board of Tax Appeals ruled that its buses did not meet the statutory definition of "transit buses." The Supreme Court of Ohio upheld that determination. Here, even though the buses benefited non-students as well as students, **the bus service did not meet the requirement that it be operated by or for a municipal corporation**. The bus service was not entitled to the tax reimbursement. *Campus Bus Service v. Zaino*, 786 N.E.2d 889 (Ohio 2003).

◆ *A city was allowed to proceed in its lawsuit against a Catholic university for back taxes.*

The city of Scranton and its school district sued the University of Scranton, a Roman Catholic institution, for payment of back business privilege and/or mercantile taxes since 1995. The city asserted that the university gained income in those years from the sale of books and food, from parking lot revenue and from other sources. Since those income-generating activities took place in the city, the university ought to have to pay mercantile taxes. The university sought to dismiss the suit, **asserting that it was a charitable institution under the state's Purely Public Charity Act**, and the court of common pleas agreed. However, the Pennsylvania Commonwealth Court reversed, finding issues that required the lawsuit to proceed. As a result, the university had to answer the city's complaint. *School Dist. of City of Scranton v. Univ. of Scranton*, No. 2345 C.D. 2001, 2002 WL 876980 (Pa. Commw. Ct. 2002).

◆ *An office building owned by teaching doctors of Midwestern University did not qualify for real estate tax exemptions.*

The primary activities taking place at the property constituted billing, collection, data processing, accounting, administration, management, payroll and related functions for the physician group. When a state court held that the physician group did not qualify for the "charitable purposes" or "school" exemptions under Illinois law, appeal reached the Appellate Court of Illinois. **Under Illinois law, a property entitled to an exemption must be used exclusively for charitable purposes and owned by a charitable organization.** Here, the group failed to meet either requirement. The Appellate Court did not allow the group to use its relationship with the university to cast itself as a charitable organization. No patient care, medical research or instructional classes took place on the property. *Midwest Physician Group, Ltd. v. Dep't of Revenue of Illinois*, 711 N.E.2d 381 (Ill. App. Ct. 1999).

◆ *A university could not claim tax-exempt status for a parking garage or parts of a building leased to for-profit companies.*

A university owned a four-story building with an attached parking garage, and leased space to five tenants. Two tenants were nonprofit organizations, and the other three tenants were for-profit companies. The Board of Tax Appeals found that the building and the land under it were exempt from taxation, but the garage and land under it were not. The Cleveland Board of Education filed a notice of appeal, wanting the whole property to be taxed.

The Supreme Court of Ohio affirmed the Board of Tax Appeals decisions regarding the tax exemption for the space leased by the two nonprofit organizations, and the non-tax-exempt status of the garage and the land under it. It reversed exemptions given to the university for the space held by the for-profit tenants and vacant areas in the building. **The garage did not qualify for tax-exempt status because it was not an essential and integral part of the university's or nonprofit tenants' charitable and/or educational activities.** *Case Western Reserve Univ. v. Tracy*, 84 Ohio St.3d 316, 703 N.E.2d 1240 (Ohio 1999).

◆ *A religious college was required to pay a development fee in order to build an addition. The fee was not a tax for which the college could claim an exemption because it was not compulsory. It was only applied upon development of property.*

A Catholic private college in California acquired an adjacent tract of land in order to build a postgraduate business school and parking structure. The college intended to move its existing business school to the new building, resulting in no increase in students or faculty. Before construction could begin, the college needed a permit that would not be issued unless the college paid a school development fee. Under state statute, any school district can levy a fee against any commercial, industrial or residential development project for the purpose of funding the construction of school facilities. The only exceptions are facilities used exclusively for religious purposes or facilities owned and occupied by agencies of federal, state, or local government. The college paid the fee under protest and then filed a petition for writ of mandamus in state court. The trial court found for the college, and the school district appealed to the California Court of Appeal, Second District.

The college argued that the development fee qualified as a tax, which it should not be required to pay as a nonprofit, educational institution. The court agreed that the college was exempt from state taxes because of its status, but found that the development fee was not a tax. It was not compulsory, like a tax, but was imposed only when a property owner decided to develop. Furthermore, **the California Supreme Court has held that exemptions from taxes refer only to property taxes**. The court also found that the development was not going to be used exclusively for religious purposes. The college did not fall into any of the exceptions to the statute and therefore it had to pay the development fee. *Loyola Marymount Univ. v. Los Angeles Unified School Dist.*, 53 Cal.Rptr.2d 424 (Cal. Ct. App. 1996).

◆ *Land used by a seminary for recreational purposes and as a buffer zone was exempt from taxation.*

A North Carolina county reviewed several parcels of land owned by a seminary and determined that they were not eligible for tax exemptions because they were not used for educational or religious purposes. After the state property tax commission held that exemptions applied to three parcels, the county appealed. The North Carolina Court of Appeals affirmed the decision in favor of the seminary. **Although the land was used essentially for recreational purposes, and as a buffer between the campus and commercial development surrounding the campus, it served to provide and maintain a relaxed campus atmosphere.** Further, the seminary's attempt to rezone one of the parcels for commercial development so that it could sell the land for a profit was a planned future use, which did not change the present exempted use of the land. *In the Matter of Southeastern Baptist Theological Seminary*, 135 N.C.App. 247, 520 S.E.2d 302 (N.C. Ct. App. 1999).

◆ *The Commonwealth Court of Pennsylvania held a college was entitled to exemption from real estate taxes because it was maintained as a public charity.*

A Pennsylvania educational institution founded by the Presbyterian Church in the 18th century developed into a nonsectarian, private, coeducational four-year college. Students were admitted based on academic qualifications and irrespective of sex, race, color, creed or national origin. No criterion based on financial need was established as a condition of enrollment, but if a student was unable to pay the tuition he or she would not be allowed to complete his or her education. The college's board of trustees served without compensation, and the salaries of the college's employees were not excessive. Nearly 80% of the students received financial aid, and the college regularly had an operating loss, although the market value of its endowment fund was over $50 million. The state board of assessment denied the college's application for a real estate exemption. On appeal by the college, a Pennsylvania trial court affirmed the board's decision. The college appealed.

The Commonwealth Court of Pennsylvania held that the college qualified as a purely public charity. It advanced a charitable purpose, donated a substantial portion of its services, and benefited a substantial and indefinite class of persons who were legitimate subjects of charity. For example, the college offered a program to academically underprivileged youth, awarded substantial grants based on academic and financial need to students, enrollment was open, and students were admitted pursuant to a nondiscriminatory admissions policy based on merit. The court also held that the college relieved the government of some of its burdens and operated free from the private profit motive. **Because the college was founded and was maintained as a purely public charity, it was entitled to a real estate tax exemption.** The commonwealth court reversed the trial court judgment. *City of Washington v. Board of Assessment*, 666 A.2d 352 (Pa. Commw. Ct. 1995).

◆   *The Commonwealth Court of Pennsylvania held that property owned by the private college in the following two cases was tax exempt because the college was a public charity under state law and the property was regularly used for the purposes of the college.*

A Pennsylvania nonprofit private college owned a house occupied by its grounds crew leader. The college charged the grounds crew leader a discounted rent that averaged about 70% of the fair market value. In exchange for the discount, the grounds crew leader agreed to be available on a 24-hour basis to respond to emergencies and nighttime calls. He was allegedly called to campus after-hours six times in both 1991 and 1992 for snow and ice removal and to remove fallen tree limbs. The Delaware County Board of Assessment Appeals determined that the house was not exempt from property taxes. On appeal by the college, a Pennsylvania trial court reversed, finding the house exempt from taxation. A local public school district appealed the finding to the Commonwealth Court of Pennsylvania.

Article VIII of the **Pennsylvania Constitution provides that the general assembly can exempt real property of public charities "regularly used for the purposes of the institution."** Section 204 of the General County Assessment Law exempts all college property "necessary for the occupancy and enjoyment of the same." The commonwealth court stated that the college need not prove that the property was absolutely necessary to its needs for the exemption to apply. Rather, it was required to show only that it had a reasonable need for the property. Here, emergency personnel were essential to the college community. The grounds crew leader was able to respond much quicker to an emergency than personnel who were living off campus. The college properly chose to forego the additional rental revenues to provide these needed services. Further, the alleged infrequency of emergency situations did not render the house incidental to the college's purposes. **Because emergency services were directly related to the proper functions of the college, the trial court did not err in concluding that the house was tax exempt.** *In Re Swarthmore College*, 645 A.2d 470 (Pa. Commw. Ct. 1994).

The college also owned a large house designed for entertaining. The college's vice president for alumni development lived in the house rent-free and was not charged for utilities. The house was used for meetings, special events, receptions and to entertain potential donors from whom one-third of the college's yearly income was derived. The county Board of Assessment Appeals determined that the house was not exempt from property taxes. The Commonwealth Court of Pennsylvania stated that the **college was not required to prove that the property was absolutely necessary to its needs for the exemption to apply. Rather, it was required to show only that it had a reasonable necessity for the property.** Here, the vice president was required to live in the house, use it to cultivate personal relationships with donors, and utilize it for numerous college functions. These uses were directly related to the proper functions of the college. Consequently, the vice president's house was tax-exempt. *In re Swarthmore College*, 643 A.2d 1152 (Pa. Commw. Ct. 1994).

◆   *The Court of Appeal of Louisiana held that state law does not require private colleges to substantiate their tax-exempt status except as set forth by the state legislature.*

A Louisiana church operated a private university that offered a variety of secular undergraduate and graduate programs. The Louisiana Board of Regents notified the university that it had failed to complete and submit the required licensure application and was therefore in violation of state law. Consequently, it sought to close the school. **Although degree-granting institutions were generally required to be registered and licensed by the board, institutions granted a tax exemption under the Internal Revenue Code were exempted from these requirements.** Previously such private universities were required to supply only basic information to obtain a license. The state attorney general filed suit in a Louisiana trial court, seeking to enjoin the church's operation of the university based on its noncompliance with the board's procedural requirements. The trial court found that because the Internal Revenue Code does not require churches to obtain recognition of their exempt status, the board was prohibited from requiring the organization to do so. It denied the state's request for injunctive relief, and the state appealed.

The Court of Appeal of Louisiana affirmed the decision, noting that the state legislature chose to defer to federal law in this procedural area. Federal law, pursuant to the Internal Revenue Code, granted churches automatic exempt status without the necessity of paperwork. Absent a contrary directive from the state legislature, the court refused to read additional requirements into the law. *Ieyoub v. World Christian Church*, 649 So.2d 771 (La. Ct. App. 1994).

◆   *The Supreme Court of Iowa upheld tax-exempt status for property owned by a private university because it was used solely for the university's purpose of providing Catholic education for its students.*

A private Catholic university in Iowa was organized for charitable, scientific, religious, and educational purposes. The university acquired property adjacent to the campus and converted it into a child care center. The purpose of the child care center was to enable parents of preschool-age children to attend the university. Priority admission to the center was given to students, then to faculty, then to the general public. The university vice president, a Catholic priest, also was provided rent-free housing at a location apart from the central campus of the university. This property also served as an office and conference center for the school. The university sought an exemption from general property taxation for both parcels. The district court held that the child care facility was exempt but that the university vice president's residence was not exempt. The university appealed to the Supreme Court of Iowa.

The supreme court noted the statutory requirements for exemption. First, the **property must be used by literary, scientific, charitable, benevolent, agricultural or religious institutions and must not be operated for profit.** Because the child care facility was nonprofit and the university had a religious affiliation, these requirements were satisfied. Next, the property must be used "solely for its appropriate object." Here, the child care facility was properly used to enable students to attend the university and to enable university employees to further their goal of educating the students. The court also noted that the university vice president was a priest, and was therefore "necessary" to further the stated purposes of the university. Consequently, **both the child care facility and the rent-free housing were solely for the university's object of providing an education based on the Catholic religion.** Both properties were exempt from general property taxation. The holding of the district court was affirmed in part and reversed in part. *St. Ambrose Univ. v. Board of Review*, 503 N.W.2d 406 (Iowa 1993).

◆ *The Court of Appeals of Washington held that property owned by a religious order was of an educational nature as that term was defined in Washington law. The college was therefore entitled to exempt the property from state property taxation.*

An order of Benedictine monks established a small liberal arts college in Washington in the late 1800s. The religious order maintained the college in that same location since its inception. In 1985, the Washington Department of Revenue denied the college's application to exempt certain portions of its campus from real property taxation. After several unsuccessful administrative appeals, the college appealed to a Washington trial court.

The land in question was an undeveloped and unmaintained area of the campus that served essentially as a buffer zone. The students and faculty were free to utilize the property for recreational purposes, but the property was also occasionally used for classes. Additionally, religion students periodically entered the property to meditate. The trial court reversed the administrative decisions and determined that the property was entitled to be exempted from real property taxation. The department appealed the adverse decision to the Court of Appeals of Washington.

On appeal, the department conceded that the property was smaller in size than the maximum acreage permitted by statute (to still be eligible for an exemption), and that the property in question incidentally furthered an educational purpose. However, it contended that the exemption was unwarranted because the property was essentially unused, empty land that was not reasonably necessary for achievement of the educational, athletic or social programs of the college. The court found that the utilization of the property was of an educational nature as that term was defined in Washington law.

The purposes of a religious educational institution could be better carried out in a pleasant atmosphere that was conducive to the contemplation of nature than it could be in a crowded urban setting. The court found it significant that several state colleges and universities also were surrounded by green belts and buffer zones. **Since the property had been and continued to be an integral part of the college campus, the application for tax exemption should not have been denied. The court affirmed the trial court's decision in favor of the college.** *St. Martin's College v. State Dep't of Revenue*, 841 P.2d 803 (Wash. Ct. App. 1992).

IV. PRIVATE ASSISTANCE TO SCHOOLS

Colleges and universities often rely on financial boosters to support their athletic programs. But when questions arise as to how money is being raised and spent, relationships between booster organizations and schools can go sour. In the following case, an Iowa court rejected a college's claim that the head of a booster club mishandled funds and engaged in other unauthorized activities.

◆ *Members of nonprofit organizations are not liable for the debts of an organization unless they engage in intentional misconduct.*

Over the course of his long tenure as a benefactor, Charles Talbot personally donated more than $45,000 and helped raise more than $97,000 for Indian Hills Community College. Talbot approached the school to discuss the creation of a more formal tax-exempt booster club in 2001. The school told Talbot it would need to endorse such a move, but he went ahead and formed a nonprofit corporation without asking for approval. The relationship between Talbot and the school began to sour. The president told the group they needed to run the booster club funds through a school-audited account, but the group refused to do so. They also refused to provide the college access to the club's financial records. In April 2004, the college sued Talbot and the booster club in a state court. The suit accused Talbot and the club of conversion, and it claimed he had engaged in unauthorized acts. The trial court held for Talbot, relying on state law immunity for members of nonprofit organizations and corporations.

On appeal, the Court of Appeals of Iowa held the trial court had correctly applied state law immunity provisions to block the college's claims. **Members of nonprofit organizations were not liable for debts or obligations of the organization unless they engaged in intentional misconduct, knowingly violated the law, or derived an "improper personal benefit" from a transaction.** There was no showing that any actions taken by Talbot were illegal or inappropriate Therefore, he could not be held liable for any of the allegedly improper actions taken on behalf of the booster club. The trial court decision against the college was affirmed. *Indian Hills Community College v. Indian Hills Booster Club*, No. 06-0392, 2007 WL 911890 (Iowa Ct. App. 3/28/07).

◆ *Vanderbilt University could not change the name of its dormitories in violation of an agreement with a donor organization.*

In 1905, trustees of the Peabody Education Fund voted to direct $1 million to create a permanent endowment for a college of higher education for teachers in the southern states. Trustees of the college voted to buy several properties adjacent to Vanderbilt University. The United Daughters of the Confederacy (UDC) entered into a contract with college trustees to raise $50,000 to construct the women's dorm on the new campus. In return for the gift, the college had to allow female descendants of Confederate soldiers nominated by the UDC to live in the dorm rent-free. In 1927, the college and UDC entered into a second contract specifying that a Confederate Memorial Hall be constructed on the campus. From 1935 until the late 1970s, female descendants of Confederate soldiers nominated by the UDC lived in the dorms rent-free. The college started experiencing financial difficulties. To raise money, college trustees leased two dorms, including Confederate Memorial Hall, to Vanderbilt. When the college's financial situation became worse, it merged with Vanderbilt. A year after the renovation of Confederate Memorial Hall, some Vanderbilt students, faculty and staff expressed dissatisfaction with the building name. They emphasized demographic changes over the years. The chancellor of Vanderbilt decided to change the name to "Memorial Hall" without consulting the UDC. The UDC sued Vanderbilt in a state court for breach of contract. The court awarded summary judgment to Vanderbilt. It found it impractical and unduly burdensome for Vanderbilt to continue to perform the terms of the contract. The UDC appealed to Court of Appeals of Tennessee.

Vanderbilt argued it already had substantially fulfilled its obligations because it had allowed many women to live in the dorms rent-free over the years and had kept the building's original name for almost 70 years. Moreover, the university should no longer be obligated to keep the name because it would be inconsistent with laws prohibiting racial discrimination. **The court held the intent of the UDC was for the funds to be a conditional gift. Generally, if the university failed to comply with the conditions, the donor would recover the gift.** However, since the value of a dollar was different now from when the money was given, returning the gift would be unfair to the UDC. **The court held that as Vanderbilt had refused to abide by the conditions of the gift, the present value of the gift must be returned, or the university would have to agree to abide by the conditions.** The court reversed the judgment and returned the case to the trial court to calculate the gift's present value. *Tennessee Division of United Daughters of the Confederacy v. Vanderbilt Univ.*, 174 S.W.3d 98 (Tenn. Ct. App. 2005).

Generally, when private parties donate money to schools, they have to be careful to specify how that money will be used or the schools will be able to put the money into their general operating funds.

◆ *A university had to identify donors to its new arena who purchased luxury suites.*

Fresno State University built a new $103 million arena primarily with private donations and created a nonprofit association to operate it. The association leased the arena's luxury suites to interested donors. Prices for the suites ranged from $45,000 to $63,000 per year (with terms of 5, 7 or 10 years). The association promised some of the donors they would remain anonymous. However, when a newspaper sought documents containing the names of the donors who obtained leases, the university and association sought to withhold the information on the grounds that disclosure would cause a decrease in future donations. A state court determined that the documents were public records under the California Public Records Act and thus had to be disclosed. The California Court of Appeal affirmed, noting that **the purchase of luxury suites was more a business transaction than a traditional donation**. People making such a purchase have placed themselves in public view and have a diminished expectation of privacy. Further, because the arena was financed with $8 million in public funds, there was a legitimate public interest in the fairness of the transactions. *California State Univ. v. Superior Court*, 108 Cal.Rptr.2d 870 (Cal. Ct. App. 2001).

◆   *The Court of Appeals of Kentucky denied a claim to property by a college under a property owner's will.*

A Kentucky property owner bequeathed property to a relative. However, the will stated that if the relative died without children, the property was to pass to the relative's younger sister and her heirs. The will also provided Georgetown College would receive the proceeds from the sale of 71 acres of farmland, to be used to fund a permanent endowment at the college. Any additional money would be paid to the college for the endowment fund. Both the relative and her sister died without children. A state court distributed $1.3 million from the estate in three equal shares to the sister's heirs, finding the college was only covered under a specific item in the will. The state appeals court rejected the college's argument that the devises to the sisters were substitutional. **When the property owner died, the court explained, the interest in her property vested in the sister's heirs. The college's reasoning would lead to a finding that the property owner had died without heirs.** As this result was disfavored, the court affirmed the judgment for the heirs. *Georgetown College v. Alexander*, 140 S.W.3d 6 (Ky. Ct. App. 2003).

◆   *A university hospital named as an alternate beneficiary could not get money bequeathed to another institution even though a condition of the will was illegal.*

A doctor associated with the Keswick Home in Baltimore provided for four annuitants in his will and, after the death of the last of them, directed that the remainder of his estate (nearly $29 million) go to the Keswick Home for the acquisition or construction of a new building in his name for "white patients who need[ed] physical rehabilitation." If Keswick found the bequest unacceptable, the money was to pass to the University of Maryland Hospital to be used for physical rehabilitation. A lawsuit developed over the funds, with the university hospital arguing that the illegal racial restriction required the money to be awarded to it. A trial court agreed, but the Maryland Court of Appeals reversed. It excised the illegal condition attached to the will and awarded the money to Keswick. *Home for Incurables of Baltimore City v. Univ. of Maryland Medical System Corp.*, 797 A.2d 746 (Md. 2002).

APPENDIX A

UNITED STATES CONSTITUTION

Provisions of Interest to Higher Educators

ARTICLE I

Section 1. All legislative Powers herein granted shall be vested in a Congress of the United States, which shall consist of a Senate and House of Representatives.

* * *

Section 8. The Congress shall have Power To lay and collect Taxes, Duties, Imposts and Excises, to pay the Debts and provide for the common Defence and general Welfare of the United States; but all Duties, Imposts and Excises shall be uniform throughout the United States;

To borrow money on the credit of the United States;

To regulate Commerce with foreign Nations, and among the several States, and with the Indian Tribes;

To establish an uniform Rule of Naturalization, and uniform Laws on the subject of Bankruptcies throughout the United States;

* * *

To promote the Progress of Science and useful Arts, by securing for limited Times to Authors and Inventors the exclusive Right to their respective Writings and Discoveries;

* * *

To make all Laws which shall be necessary and proper for carrying into Execution for the foregoing Powers, and all other Powers vested by this Constitution in the Government of the United States, or in any Department or Officer thereof.

* * *

Section 9. * * * No Bill of Attainder or ex post facto Law shall be passed.

* * *

Section 10. No State shall * * * pass any Bill of Attainder, ex post facto Law, or Law impairing the Obligation of Contracts, or grant any Title of Nobility.

ARTICLE II

Section 1. The executive Power shall be vested in a President of the United States of America. * * *

ARTICLE III

Section 1. The judicial Power of the United States, shall be vested in one supreme Court, and in such inferior Courts as the Congress may from time to time ordain and establish. The Judges, both of the supreme and inferior courts, shall hold their Offices during good Behaviour, and shall, at stated Times, receive for their Services a Compensation, which shall not be diminished during their Continuance in Office.

Section 2. The judicial Power shall extend to all Cases, in Law and Equity, arising under this Constitution, the Laws of the United States, and Treaties made, or which shall be made, under their Authority; - to all Cases affecting Ambassadors, other public Ministers and Consuls; - to all Cases of admiralty and maritime Jurisdiction, - to Controversies to which the United States shall be a party; - to Controversies between two or more States; - between a State and Citizens of another State; - between Citizens of different States; - between Citizens of the same State claiming Lands under the Grants of different States, and between a State, or the Citizens thereof, and foreign States, Citizens or Subjects.

* * *

ARTICLE IV

Section 1. Full Faith and Credit shall be given in each State to the public Acts, Records and judicial Proceedings of every other State. * * *

Section 2. The Citizens of each State shall be entitled to all Privileges and Immunities of Citizens in the several States.

* * *

Section 4. The United States shall guarantee to every State in this Union a Republican Form of Government, and shall protect each of them against Invasion; and on Application of the Legislature, or of the Executive (when the Legislature cannot be convened) against domestic Violence.

ARTICLE V

The Congress, whenever two thirds of both Houses shall deem it necessary, shall propose Amendments to this Constitution, or, on the Application of the Legislatures of two thirds of the several States, shall call a Convention for proposing Amendments, which, in either Case, shall be valid to all Intents and Purposes, as part of this Constitution, when ratified by the Legislatures of three fourths of the several States, or by Conventions in three fourths thereof, as the one or the other Mode of Ratification may be proposed by the Congress; Provided that no Amendment which may be made prior to the Year One thousand eight hundred and eight shall in any Manner affect the first and fourth Clauses in the Ninth Section of the first Article; and that no State, without its Consent, shall be deprived of its equal Suffrage in the Senate.

ARTICLE VI

* * *

This Constitution, and the Laws of the United States which shall be made in Pursuance thereof; and all Treaties made, or which shall be made, under the Authority of the United States, shall be the supreme Law of the Land; and the Judges in every State shall be bound thereby, any Thing in the Constitution or Laws of any State to the Contrary notwithstanding.

The Senators and Representatives before mentioned, and the Members of the several State Legislatures, and all executive and judicial Officers, both of the United States and of the several States, shall be bound by Oath or Affirmation, to support this Constitution; but no religious Test shall ever be required as a Qualification to any Office or public Trust under the United States.

* * *

AMENDMENT I

Congress shall make no law respecting an establishment of religion, or prohibiting the free exercise thereof; or abridging the freedom of speech, or of the press; or the right of the people peaceably to assemble, and to petition the Government for a redress of grievances.

* * *

AMENDMENT IV

The right of the people to be secure in their persons, houses, papers, and effects, against unreasonable searches and seizures, shall not be violated, and no Warrants shall issue, but upon probable cause, supported by Oath or affirmation, and particularly describing the place to be searched, and the persons or things to be seized.

AMENDMENT V

No person shall be held to answer for a capital, or otherwise infamous crime, unless on a presentment or indictment of a Grand Jury, except in cases arising in the land or naval forces, or in the Militia, when in actual service in time of War or public danger; nor shall any person be subject for the same offence to be twice put in jeopardy of life or limb; nor shall be compelled in any criminal case to be a witness against himself, nor be deprived of life, liberty, or property, without due process of law; nor shall private property be taken for public use, without just compensation.

AMENDMENT VI

In all criminal prosecutions, the accused shall enjoy the right to a speedy and public trial, by an impartial jury of the State and district wherein the crime shall have been committed, which district shall have been previously ascertained by law, and to be informed of the nature and cause of the accusation; to be confronted with the witnesses against him; to have compulsory process for obtaining witnesses in his favor, and to have the Assistance of Counsel for his defense.

AMENDMENT VII

In Suits at common law, where the value in controversy shall exceed twenty dollars, the right of trial by jury shall be preserved, and no fact tried by jury, shall be otherwise re-examined in any Court of the United States, than according to the rules of the common law.

AMENDMENT VIII

Excessive bail shall not be required, nor excessive fines imposed, nor cruel and unusual punishments inflicted.

AMENDMENT IX

The enumeration in the Constitution, of certain rights, shall not be construed to deny or disparage others retained by the people.

AMENDMENT X

The powers not delegated to the United States by the Constitution, nor prohibited by it to the States, are reserved to the States respectively, or to the people.

AMENDMENT XI

The Judicial power of the United States shall not be construed to extend to any suit in law or equity, commenced or prosecuted against one of the United States by Citizens of another State, or by Citizens or Subjects of any Foreign State.

* * *

AMENDMENT XIII

Section 1. Neither slavery nor involuntary servitude, except as a punishment for crime whereof the party shall have been duly convicted, shall exist within the United States, or any place subject to their jurisdiction.

Section 2. Congress shall have power to enforce this article by appropriate legislation.

AMENDMENT XIV

Section 1. All persons born or naturalized in the United States, and subject to the jurisdiction thereof, are citizens of the United States and of the State wherein they reside. No State shall make or enforce any law which shall abridge the privileges or immunities of citizens of the United States; nor shall any State deprive any person of life, liberty, or property, without due process of law; nor deny to any person within its jurisdiction the equal protection of the laws.

* * *

Section 5. The Congress shall have power to enforce, by appropriate legislation, the provisions of this article.

APPENDIX B

Subject Matter Table of United States Supreme Court
Cases Affecting Higher Education

Note: Please see the Table of Cases (located at the front of this volume) for Supreme Court cases reported in this volume.

Academic Freedom

Univ. of Pennsylvania v. EEOC, 493 U.S. 182, 110 S.Ct. 577, 107 L.Ed.2d 571 (1990).

Epperson v. Arkansas, 393 U.S. 97, 89 S.Ct. 266, 21 L.Ed.2d 228 (1968).

Sweezy v. New Hampshire, 354 U.S. 234, 77 S.Ct. 1203, 1 L.Ed.2d 1311 (1957).

Meyer v. Nebraska, 262 U.S. 390, 43 S.Ct. 625, 67 L.Ed.2d 1042 (1923).

Arbitration

Volt Information Sciences v. Board of Trustees of Stanford Univ., 489 U.S. 468, 109 S.Ct. 1248, 103 L.Ed.2d. 488 (1989).

Athletics

NCAA v. Tarkanian, 488 U.S. 179, 109 S.Ct. 454, 102 L.Ed.2d 469 (1988).

NCAA v. Smith, 525 U.S. 459, 119 S.Ct. 924, 142 L.Ed.2d 929 (1999).

Attorneys' Fees

Webb v. Board of Educ., 471 U.S. 234, 105 S.Ct. 1923, 85 L.Ed.2d 233 (1985).

Smith v. Robinson, 468 U.S. 992, 104 S.Ct. 3457, 82 L.Ed.2d 746 (1984).

Civil Rights

Farrar v. Hobby, 506 U.S. 103, 113 S.Ct. 566, 121 L.Ed.2d 494 (1992).

St. Francis College v. Al-Khazraji, 481 U.S. 604, 107 S.Ct. 2022, 97 L.Ed.2d 749 (1987).

Grove City College v. Bell, 465 U.S. 555, 104 S.Ct. 1211, 79 L.Ed.2d 516 (1984).

Rendell-Baker v. Kohn, 457 U.S. 830, 102 S.Ct. 2764, 73 L.Ed.2d 418 (1982).

Collective Bargaining

Davenport v. Washington Educ. Ass'n, 127 S.Ct. 2372 (U.S. 2007).

Cent. State Univ. v. American Ass'n of Univ. Professors, Cent. State Univ. Chapter, 526 U.S. 124, 119 S.Ct. 1162, 143 L.Ed.2d 227 (1999).

Compulsory Attendance

Wisconsin v. Yoder, 406 U.S. 205, 92 S.Ct. 526, 32 L.Ed.2d 15 (1972).

Pierce v. Society of Sisters, 268 U.S. 510, 45 S.Ct. 571, 69 L.Ed. 1070 (1925).

Continuing Education

Austin ISD v. U.S., 443 U.S. 915, 99 S.Ct. 3106, 61 L.Ed.2d 879 (1979).
Harrah ISD v. Martin, 440 U.S. 194, 99 S.Ct. 1062, 59 L.Ed.2d 248 (1979).

Corporal Punishment

Ingraham v. Wright, 430 U.S. 651, 97 S.Ct. 1401, 51 L.Ed.2d 711 (1977).

Court Intervention in School Affairs

Epperson v. Arkansas, 393 U.S. 97, 89 S.Ct. 266, 21 L.Ed.2d 228 (1968).

Criminal Activity

Bates v. U.S., 522 U.S. 23, 118 S.Ct. 285, 139 L.Ed.2d 215 (1997).

Desegregation

U.S. v. Fordice, 505 U.S. 717, 112 S.Ct. 2727, 120 L.Ed.2d 575 (1992).
Freeman v. Pitts, 503 U.S. 467, 112 S.Ct. 1430, 118 L.Ed.2d 108 (1992).

Disabled Students

Florence County School Dist. Four v. Carter, 510 U.S. 7, 114 S.Ct. 361, 126 L.Ed.2d 284 (1993).
Zobrest v. Catalina Foothills School Dist., 509 U.S. 1, 113 S.Ct. 2462, 125 L.Ed.2d 1 (1993).
Dellmuth v. Muth, 491 U.S. 223, 109 S.Ct. 2397, 105 L.Ed.2d 181 (1989).
Honig v. Doe, 484 U.S. 305, 108 S.Ct. 592, 98 L.Ed.2d 686 (1988).
City of Cleburne, Texas v. Cleburne Living Center, 473 U.S. 432, 105 S.Ct. 3249, 87 L.Ed.2d 313 (1985).
Honig v. Students of California School for the Blind, 471 U.S. 148, 105 S.Ct. 1820, 85 L.Ed.2d 114 (1985).
Burlington School Committee v. Dep't of Educ., 471 U.S. 359, 105 S.Ct. 1996, 85 L.Ed.2d 385 (1985).
Smith v. Robinson, 468 U.S. 992, 104 S.Ct. 3457, 82 L.Ed.2d 746 (1984).
Irving Independent School District v. Tatro, 468 U.S. 883, 104 S.Ct. 3371, 82 L.Ed.2d 664 (1984).
Board of Educ. v. Rowley, 458 U.S. 176, 102 S.Ct. 3034, 73 L.Ed.2d 690 (1982).
Univ. of Texas v. Camenisch, 451 U.S. 390, 101 S.Ct. 1830, 68 L.Ed.2d 175 (1981).
Pennhurst State School and Hospital v. Halderman, 451 U.S. 1, 101 S.Ct. 1531, 67 L.Ed.2d 694 (1981).
Southeastern Community College v. Davis, 442 U.S. 397, 99 S.Ct. 2361, 60 L.Ed.2d 980 (1979).

Discrimination, Generally

Edelman v. Lynchburg College, 532 U.S. 106, 122 S.Ct. 1145, 152 L.Ed.2d 188 (2002).

Raygor v. Regents of Univ. of Minnesota, 534 U.S. 533, 122 S.Ct. 999, 152 L.Ed.2d 27 (2002).

Alexander v. Sandoval, 531 U.S. 1049, 121 S.Ct. 1511, 141 L.Ed.2d 517 (2001).

Board of Trustees of the Univ. of Alabama v. Garrett, 531 U.S. 356, 121 S.Ct. 955, 148 L.Ed.2d 866 (2001).

Kimel v. Florida Board of Regents, 528 U.S. 62, 120 S.Ct. 631, 145 L.Ed.2d 522 (2000).

Texas v. Lesage, 528 U.S. 18, 120 S.Ct. 467, 145 L.Ed.2d 347 (1999).

Lane v. Pena, 518 U.S. 187, 116 S.Ct. 2092, 135 L.Ed.2d 486 (1996).

Jett v. Dallas Independent School Dist., 491 U.S. 701, 109 S.Ct. 2702, 105 L.Ed.2d 598 (1989).

Carnegie-Mellon Univ. v. Cohill, 484 U.S. 343, 108 S.Ct. 614, 98 L.Ed.2d 720 (1988).

School Board of Nassau County v. Arline, 480 U.S. 273, 107 S.Ct. 1123, 94 L.Ed.2d 307 (1987).

Hazelwood School Dist. v. U.S., 433 U.S. 299, 97 S.Ct. 2736, 53 L.Ed.2d 768 (1977).

DeFunis v. Odegaard, 416 U.S. 312, 94 S.Ct. 1704, 40 L.Ed.2d 164 (1974).

Due Process

Gilbert v. Homar, 520 U.S. 924, 117 S.Ct. 1807, 138 L.Ed.2d 120 (1997).

Univ. of Tennessee v. Elliot, 478 U.S. 788, 106 S.Ct. 3220, 92 L.Ed.2d 635 (1986).

Memphis Community School Dist. v. Stachura, 477 U.S. 299, 106 S.Ct. 2537, 91 L.Ed.2d 249 (1986).

Cleveland Board of Educ. v. Loudermill, 470 U.S. 532, 105 S.Ct. 1487, 84 L.Ed.2d 494 (1985).

Perry v. Sindermann, 408 U.S. 593, 92 S.Ct. 2694, 33 L.Ed.2d 570 (1972).

Board of Regents v. Roth, 408 U.S. 564, 92 S.Ct. 2701, 33 L.Ed.2d 548 (1972).

Employment

Burlington Northern & Santa Fe Railway Co. v. White, 126 S.Ct. 2405 (U.S. 2006).

Smith v. City of Jackson, 125 S.Ct. 1536 (U.S. 2005).

Corporation of the Presiding Bishop of the Church of Jesus Christ of Latter-Day Saints v. Amos, 483 U.S. 327, 107 S.Ct. 2862, 97 L.Ed.2d 273 (1987).

O'Connor v. Ortega, 480 U.S. 709 (1987).

Franklin & Marshall College v. EEOC, 476 U.S. 1163, 106 S.Ct. 2288, 90 L.Ed.2d 729 (1986).

NLRB v. Catholic Bishop of Chicago, 440 U.S. 490, 99 S.Ct. 1313, 59 L.Ed.2d 533 (1979).

Federal Aid

Traynor v. Turnage, 485 U.S. 535, 108 S.Ct. 1372, 99 L.Ed.2d 618 (1988).

Selective Service System v. MPIRG, 468 U.S. 841, 104 S.Ct. 3348, 82 L.Ed.2d 632 (1984).

Bell v. New Jersey and Pennsylvania, 461 U.S. 773, 103 S.Ct. 2187, 76 L.Ed.2d 312 (1984).

Grove City College v. Bell, 465 U.S. 555, 104 S.Ct. 1211, 79 L.Ed.2d 516 (1984).

Valley Forge Christian College v. Americans United for Separation of Church and State, 454 U.S. 464, 102 S.Ct. 752, 70 L.Ed.2d 700 (1982).

Board of Educ. v. Harris, 444 U.S. 130, 100 S.Ct. 363, 62 L.Ed.2d 275 (1979).

Wheeler v. Barrera, 417 U.S. 402, 94 S.Ct. 2274, 41 L.Ed.2d 159 (1974).

Tilton v. Richardson, 403 U.S. 672, 91 S.Ct. 2091, 29 L.Ed.2d 790 (1971).

Freedom of Religion

City of Boerne, Texas v. Flores, 521 U.S. 507, 117 S.Ct. 2157, 138 L.Ed.2d 624 (1997).

Edwards v. Aguillard, 482 U.S. 578, 107 S.Ct. 2573, 96 L.Ed.2d 510 (1987).

Ansonia Board of Educ. v. Philbrook, 499 U.S. 60, 107 S.Ct. 367, 93 L.Ed.2d 305 (1986).

Freedom of Speech

Garcetti v. Ceballos, 126 S.Ct. 1951, 164 L.Ed. 2d 689 (U.S. 2006).

Board of Regents of Univ. of Wisconsin System v. Southworth, 529 U.S. 217, 120 S.Ct. 1346, 146 L.Ed.2d 193 (2000).

Board of Educ. of Westside Community School v. Mergens, 496 U.S. 226, 110 S.Ct. 2356, 110 L.Ed.2d 191 (1990).

Board of Trustees of the State Univ. of New York v. Fox, 492 U.S. 469, 109 S.Ct. 3028, 106 L.Ed.2d 388 (1989).

Hazelwood School Dist. v. Kuhlmeier, 484 U.S. 261, 108 S.Ct. 562, 98 L.Ed.2d 592 (1988).

Rankin v. McPherson, 483 U.S. 378, 107 S.Ct. 2891, 97 L.Ed.2d 315 (1987).

Bethel School Dist. v. Fraser, 478 U.S. 675, 106 S.Ct. 3159, 92 L.Ed.2d 549 (1986).

Wayte v. U.S., 470 U.S. 598, 105 S.Ct. 1524, 84 L.Ed.2d 547 (1985).

Connick v. Myers, 461 U.S. 138, 103 S.Ct. 1684, 75 L.Ed.2d 708 (1983).

Board of Educ. v. Pico, 457 U.S. 853, 102 S.Ct. 2799, 73 L.Ed.2d 435 (1982).

Givhan v. Western Line Consolidated School Dist., 439 U.S. 410, 99 S.Ct. 693, 58 L.Ed.2d 619 (1979).

Mt. Healthy City School v. Doyle, 429 U.S. 274, 97 S.Ct. 568, 50 L.Ed.2d 471 (1977).

Papish v. Board of Curators, 410 U.S. 667, 93 S.Ct. 1197, 35 L.Ed.2d 618 (1973).

Grayned v. City of Rockford, 408 U.S. 104, 92 S.Ct. 2294, 33 L.Ed.2d 222 (1972).

Police Dep't v. Mosley, 408 U.S. 92, 92 S.Ct. 2286, 33 L.Ed.2d 212 (1972).

Tinker v. Des Moines, 393 U.S. 503, 89 S.Ct. 733, 21 L.Ed.2d 733 (1969).

Pickering v. Board of Educ., 391 U.S. 563, 88 S.Ct. 1731, 20 L.Ed.2d 811 (1968).

Whitehill v. Elkins, 389 U.S. 54, 88 S.Ct. 184, 19 L.Ed.2d 228 (1967).

Keyishian v. Board of Regents, 385 U.S. 589, 87 S.Ct. 675, 17 L.Ed.2d 629 (1967).

Elfbrandt v. Russell, 384 U.S. 11, 86 S.Ct. 1238, 16 L.Ed.2d 321 (1965).

Baggett v. Bullitt, 377 U.S. 360, 84 S.Ct. 1316, 12 L.Ed.2d 377 (1963).

Cramp v. Board of Public Instruction of Orange County, 368 U.S. 278, 82 S.Ct. 275, 7 L.Ed.2d 285 (1961).

Shelton v. Tucker, 364 U.S. 479, 81 S.Ct. 247, 5 L.Ed.2d 231 (1960).

Slochower v. Board of Educ., 350 U.S. 551, 76 S.Ct. 637, 100 L.Ed. 692 (1955).

Adler v. Board of Educ., 342 U.S. 485, 72 S.Ct. 380, 96 L.Ed. 517 (1952).

Intellectual Property

New York Times Co. Inc. v. Tasini, 533 U.S. 483, 121 S.Ct. 2381, 150 L.Ed.2d 500 (2001).

Florida Prepaid Postsecondary Educ. Expense Board v. College Savings Bank, 527 U.S. 627, 119 S.Ct. 2199, 144 L.Ed.2d 575 (1999).

College Savings Bank v. Florida Prepaid Postsecondary Educ. Expense Board, 527 U.S. 666, 119 S.Ct. 2219, 144 L.Ed.2d 605 (1999).

Labor Relations

Lehnert v. Ferris Faculty Ass'n, 500 U.S. 507, 111 S.Ct. 1950, 114 L.Ed.2d 572 (1991).

Fort Stewart Schools v. Federal Labor Relations Authority, 495 U.S. 641, 110 S.Ct. 2043, 109 L.Ed.2d 659 (1990).

Minnesota State Board for Community Colleges v. Knight, 465 U.S. 271, 104 S.Ct. 1058, 79 L.Ed.2d 299 (1984).

NLRB v. Yeshiva Univ., 444 U.S. 672, 100 S.Ct. 856, 63 L.Ed.2d 115 (1980).

NLRB v. Catholic Bishop of Chicago, 440 U.S. 490, 99 S.Ct. 1313, 59 L.Ed.2d 533 (1979).

Abood v. Detroit Board of Educ., 431 U.S. 209, 97 S.Ct. 1782, 52 L.Ed.2d 261 (1977).

Maternity Leave

Richmond Unified School Dist. v. Berg, 434 U.S. 158, 98 S.Ct. 623, 54 L.Ed.2d 375 (1977).

Cleveland Board of Educ. v. La Fleur, 414 U.S. 632, 94 S.Ct. 791, 39 L.Ed.2d 52 (1974).

Cohen v. Chesterfield, 414 U.S. 632, 94 S.Ct. 791, 39 L.Ed.2d 52 (1974).

Private School Funding

Agostini v. Felton, 521 U.S. 203, 117 S.Ct. 1997, 138 L.Ed.2d 391 (1997).

Board of Educ. of Kiryas Joel Village School Dist. v. Grumet, 512 U.S. 687, 114 S.Ct. 2481, 129 L.Ed.2d 546 (1994).

Witters v. Washington Dep't of Services for the Blind, 474 U.S. 481, 106 S.Ct. 748, 88 L.Ed.2d 846 (1986).

Aguilar v. Felton, 473 U.S. 402, 105 S.Ct. 3232, 87 L.Ed.2d 290 (1985).

Grand Rapids School District v. Ball, 473 U.S. 373, 105 S.Ct. 3216, 87 L.Ed.2d 267 (1985).

Mueller v. Allen, 463 U.S. 388, 103 S.Ct. 3062, 77 L.Ed.2d 721 (1983).

Valley Forge Christian College v. Americans United for Separation of Church and State, 454 U.S. 464, 102 S.Ct. 752, 70 L.Ed.2d 700 (1982).

Committee for Public Educ. and Religious Liberty v. Regan, 444 U.S. 646, 100 S.Ct. 840, 63 L.Ed.2d 94 (1980).

New York v. Cathedral Academy, 434 U.S. 125, 98 S.Ct. 340, 54 L.Ed.2d 346 (1977).

Wolman v. Walter, 433 U.S. 229, 97 S.Ct. 2593, 53 L.Ed.2d 714 (1977).

Roemer v. Board of Public Works, 426 U.S. 736, 96 S.Ct. 2337, 49 L.Ed.2d 179 (1976).

Meek v. Pittenger, 421 U.S. 349, 95 S.Ct. 1753, 44 L.Ed.2d 217 (1975).

Wheeler v. Barrera, 417 U.S. 402, 94 S.Ct. 2274, 41 L.Ed.2d 159 (1974).

Sloan v. Lemon, 413 U.S. 825, 93 S.Ct. 2982, 37 L.Ed.2d 939 (1973).

Committee for Public Educ. and Religious Liberty v. Nyquist, 413 U.S. 756, 93 S.Ct. 2955, 37 L.Ed.2d 948 (1973).

Hunt v. McNair, 413 U.S. 734, 93 S.Ct. 2868, 37 L.Ed.2d 923 (1973).

Levitt v. Committee for Public Educ. and Religious Liberty, 413 U.S. 472, 93 S.Ct. 2814, 37 L.Ed.2d 736 (1973).

Early v. Di Censo, 403 U.S. 602, 91 S.Ct. 2105, 29 L.Ed.2d 745 (1971).

Lemon v. Kurtzman, 403 U.S. 602, 91 S.Ct. 2105, 29 L.Ed.2d 745 (1971).

Flast v. Cohen, 392 U.S. 83, 88 S.Ct. 1942, 20 L.Ed.2d 947 (1968).

Racial Discrimination

Grutter v. Bollinger, 123 S.Ct. 2325 (2003).

Gratz v. Bollinger, 123 S.Ct. 2411 (2003).

St. Francis College v. Al-Khazraji, 481 U.S. 604, 107 S.Ct. 2022, 97 L.Ed.2d 749 (1987).

City of Pleasant Grove v. United States, 479 U.S. 462, 107 S.Ct. 794, 93 L.Ed.2d 866 (1987).

Wygant v. Jackson Board of Educ., 476 U.S. 267, 106 S.Ct. 1842, 90 L.Ed.2d 260 (1986).

Regents of the Univ. of California v. Bakke, 438 U.S. 265, 98 S.Ct. 2733, 57 L.Ed.2d 750 (1978).

Runyon v. McCrary, 427 U.S. 160, 96 S.Ct. 2586, 49 L.Ed.2d 415 (1976).

Lau v. Nichols, 414 U.S. 563, 94 S.Ct. 786, 39 L.Ed.2d 1 (1974).

Norwood v. Harrison, 413 U.S. 455, 93 S.Ct. 2804, 37 L.Ed.2d 723 (1973).

Recognition of Student Organizations

Bender v. Williamsport Area School Dist., 475 U.S. 534, 106 S.Ct. 1326, 89 L.Ed.2d 501 (1986).

Healy v. James, 408 U.S. 169, 92 S.Ct. 2338, 33 L.Ed.2d 266 (1972).

Release Time

Zorach v. Clauson, 343 U.S. 306, 72 S.Ct. 679, 96 L.Ed. 954 (1952).

McCollum v. Board of Educ., 333 U.S. 203, 68 S.Ct. 461, 92 L.Ed. 649 (1948).

Religious Activities in Public Schools

Rosenberger v. Rector and Visitors of Univ. of Virginia, 515 U.S. 819, 115 S.Ct. 2510, 132 L.Ed.2d 700 (1995).

Lamb's Chapel v. Center Moriches Union Free School District, 508 U.S. 384, 113 S.Ct. 2141, 124 L.Ed.2d 352 (1993).

Lee v. Weisman, 505 U.S. 577, 112 S.Ct. 2649, 120 L.Ed.2d 467 (1992).

Karcher v. May, 484 U.S. 72, 108 S.Ct. 388, 98 L.Ed.2d 327 (1987).

Wallace v. Jaffree, 472 U.S. 38, 105 S.Ct. 2479, 96 L.Ed.2d 29 (1985).

Widmar v. Vincent, 454 U.S. 263, 102 S.Ct. 269, 70 L.Ed.2d 400 (1981).

Stone v. Graham, 449 U.S. 39, 101 S.Ct. 192, 66 L.Ed.2d 199 (1980).

Chamberlin v. Dade County Board of Public Instruction, 377 U.S. 402, 84 S.Ct. 1272, 12 L.Ed.2d 407 (1964).

Abington School Dist. v. Schempp, 374 U.S. 203, 83 S.Ct. 1560, 10 L.Ed.2d 844 (1963).

Residency

Martinez v. Bynum, 461 U.S. 321 103 S.Ct. 1838, 75 L.Ed.2d 879 (1983).

Toll v. Moreno, 458 U.S. 1, 102 S.Ct. 2977, 73 L.Ed.2d 563 (1982).

Elkins v. Moreno, 435 U.S. 647, 98 S.Ct. 1338, 55 L.Ed.2d 614 (1978).

Vlandis v. Kline, 412 U.S. 441, 93 S.Ct. 2230, 37 L.Ed.2d 63 (1973).

School Liability

Gebser v. Lago Vista Independent School Dist., 524 U.S. 274, 118 S.Ct. 1989, 141 L.Ed.2d 277 (1998).

Regents of Univ. of California v. Doe, 519 U.S. 425, 117 S.Ct. 900, 137 L.Ed.2d 55 (1997).

Sex Discrimination and Harassment

Jackson v. Birmingham Board of Educ., 125 S.Ct. 1497 (U.S. 2005).

United States (Brzonkala) v. Morrison, 529 U.S. 1062, 120 S.Ct. 1740, 144 L.Ed.2d 658 (2000).

Davis v. Monroe County Board of Educ., 526 U.S. 629, 119 S.Ct. 1661, 143 L.Ed.2d 839 (1999).

U.S. v. Virginia, 518 U.S. 515, 116 S.Ct. 2264, 135 L.Ed.2d 735 (1996).

Franklin v. Gwinnett County Public Schools, 503 U.S. 60, 112 S.Ct. 1028, 117 L.Ed.2d 208 (1992).

Ohio Civil Rights Comm'n v. Dayton Christian Schools, 477 U.S. 619, 106 S.Ct. 2718, 91 L.Ed.2d 512 (1986).

Mississippi Univ. for Women v. Hogan, 458 U.S. 718, 102 S.Ct. 3331, 73 L.Ed.2d 1090 (1982).

Cannon v. Univ. of Chicago, 441 U.S. 677, 99 S.Ct. 1946, 60 L.Ed.2d 560 (1979).

Trustees of Keene State College v. Sweeney, 439 U.S. 24, 99 S.Ct. 295, 58 L.Ed.2d 216 (1978).

Student Loans

Lockhart v. U.S., 126 S.Ct. 699 (U.S. 2005).

Student Privacy

Owasso Independent School Dist. No. I-011 v. Falvo, 534 U.S. 426, 122 S.Ct. 934, 151 L.Ed.2d 896 (2002).

Gonzaga Univ. v. Doe, 536 U.S. 273, 122 S.Ct. 2268, 153 L.Ed.2d 309 (2002).

Student Searches

Vernonia School Dist. 47J v. Acton, 515 U.S. 646, 115 S.Ct. 2386, 132 L.Ed.2d 564 (1995).

New Jersey v. T.L.O., 469 U.S. 325, 105 S.Ct. 733, 83 L.Ed.2d 720 (1985).

Student Suspensions

Regents v. Ewing, 474 U.S. 214, 106 S.Ct. 507, 88 L.Ed.2d 523 (1985).

Board of Educ. v. McCluskey, 458 U.S. 966, 103 S.Ct. 3469, 73 L.Ed.2d 1273 (1982).

Carey v. Piphus, 435 U.S. 247, 98 S.Ct. 1042, 55 L.Ed.2d 252 (1978).

Board of Curators v. Horowitz, 435 U.S. 78, 98 S.Ct. 948, 55 L.Ed.2d 124 (1978).

Wood v. Strickland, 420 U.S. 308, 95 S.Ct. 992, 43 L.Ed.2d 214 (1975).

Goss v. Lopez, 419 U.S. 565, 95 S.Ct. 729, 42 L.Ed.2d 725 (1975).

Taxation

Camps Newfound/Owatonna, Inc. v. Town of Harrison, Maine, 520 U.S. 564, 117 S.Ct. 1590, 137 L.Ed.2d 852 (1997).

Allen v. Wright, 468 U.S. 737, 104 S.Ct. 3315, 82 L.Ed.2d 556 (1984).

Bob Jones Univ. v. United States, 461 U.S. 574, 103 S.Ct. 2017, 76 L.Ed.2d 157 (1983).

Mueller v. Allen, 463 U.S. 388, 103 S.Ct. 3062, 77 L.Ed.2d 721 (1983).

Ramah Navajo School Board v. Bureau of Revenue, 458 U.S. 832, 102 S.Ct. 3394, 73 L.Ed.2d 1174 (1982).

California v. Grace Brethren Church, 457 U.S. 393, 102 S.Ct. 2498, 73 L.Ed.2d 93 (1982).

Gordon v. Lance, 403 U.S. 1, 91 S.Ct. 1889, 29 L.Ed.2d 273 (1971).

Askew v. Hargrave, 401 U.S. 476, 91 S.Ct. 856, 28 L.Ed.2d 196 (1971).
Doremus v. Board of Educ., 342 U.S. 429, 72 S.Ct. 394, 96 L.Ed. 475 (1952).

Teacher Termination

Patsy v. Board of Regents, 457 U.S. 496, 102 S.Ct. 2557, 73 L.Ed.2d 172 (1982).
Chardon v. Fernandez, 454 U.S. 6, 102 S.Ct. 28, 70 L.Ed.2d 6 (1981).
Delaware State College v. Ricks, 449 U.S. 250, 101 S.Ct. 498, 66 L.Ed.2d 431 (1980).
Beilan v. Board of Public Educ., 357 U.S. 399, 78 S.Ct. 1317, 2 L.Ed.2d 1414 (1958).

Textbooks

Norwood v. Harrison, 413 U.S. 455, 93 S.Ct. 2804, 37 L.Ed.2d 723 (1973).
Board of Educ. v. Allen, 392 U.S. 236, 88 S.Ct. 1923, 20 L.Ed.2d 1060 (1968).
Cochran v. Louisiana State Board of Educ., 281 U.S. 370, 50 S.Ct. 335, 74 L.Ed.2d 1929 (1930).

Transportation

Kadrmas v. Dickinson Public Schools, 487 U.S. 450, 108 S.Ct. 2481, 101 L.Ed.2d 399 (1988).
Wolman v. Walter, 433 U.S. 229, 97 S.Ct. 2593, 53 L.Ed.2d 714 (1977).
Everson v. Board of Educ., 330 U.S. 1, 67 S.Ct. 504, 91 L.Ed. 711 (1947).

Weapons

U.S. v. Lopez, 514 U.S. 549, 115 S.Ct. 1624, 131 L.Ed.2d 626 (1995).

The Judicial System

In order to allow you to determine the relative importance of a judicial decision, the cases included in *Higher Education Law in America* identify the particular court from which a decision has been issued. For example, a case decided by a state supreme court generally will be of greater significance than a state circuit court case. Hence a basic knowledge of the structure of our judicial system is important to an understanding of higher education law.

Almost all the reports in this volume are taken from appellate court decisions. Although most education law decisions occur at trial court and administrative levels, appellate court decisions have the effect of binding lower courts and administrators so that appellate court decisions have the effect of law within their court systems.

State and federal court systems generally function independently of each other. Each court system applies its own law according to statutes and the determinations of its highest court. However, judges at all levels often consider opinions from other court systems to settle issues that are new or arise under unique fact situations. Similarly, lawyers look at the opinions of many courts to locate authority that supports their clients' cases.

Once a lawsuit is filed in a particular court system, that system retains the matter until its conclusion. Unsuccessful parties at the administrative or trial court level generally have the right to appeal unfavorable determinations of law to appellate courts within the system. When federal law issues or Constitutional grounds are present, lawsuits may be appropriately filed in the federal court system. In those cases, the lawsuit is filed initially in the federal district court for that area.

On rare occasions, the U.S. Supreme Court considers appeals from the highest courts of the states if a distinct federal question exists and at least four justices agree on the question's importance. The federal courts occasionally send cases to state courts for application of state law. These situations are infrequent and, in general, the state and federal court systems should be considered separate from each other.

The most common system, used by nearly all states and also the federal judiciary, is as follows: a legal action is commenced in district court (sometimes called trial court, county court, common pleas court or superior court) where a decision is initially reached. The case may then be appealed to the court of appeals (or appellate court), and in turn this decision may be appealed to the supreme court.

Several states, however, do not have a court of appeals; lower court decisions are appealed directly to the state's supreme court. Additionally, some states have labeled their courts in a nonstandard fashion.

In Maryland, the highest state court is called the Court of Appeals. In the state of New York, the trial court is called the Supreme Court. Decisions of this court may be appealed to the Supreme Court, Appellate Division. The highest court in New York is the Court of Appeals. Pennsylvania has perhaps the most complex court system. The lowest state court is the Court of Common Pleas. Depending on the circumstances of the case, appeals may be taken to either the Commonwealth Court or the Superior Court. In certain instances the Commonwealth Court functions as a trial court as well as an appellate court. The Superior Court, however, is strictly an intermediate appellate court. The highest court in Pennsylvania is the Supreme Court.

While supreme court decisions are generally regarded as the last word in legal matters, it is important to remember that trial and appeals court decisions also create important legal precedents. For the hierarchy of typical state and federal court systems, please see the diagram below.

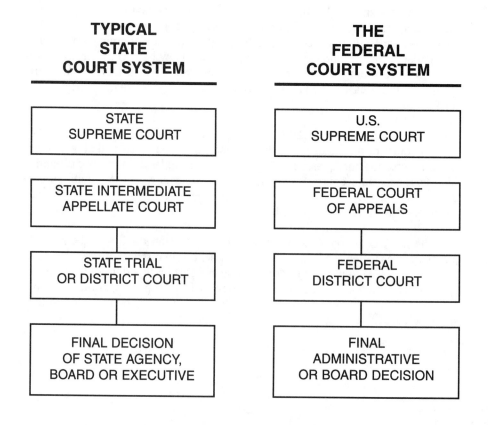

TYPICAL STATE COURT SYSTEM

STATE SUPREME COURT

STATE INTERMEDIATE APPELLATE COURT

STATE TRIAL OR DISTRICT COURT

FINAL DECISION OF STATE AGENCY, BOARD OR EXECUTIVE

THE FEDERAL COURT SYSTEM

U.S. SUPREME COURT

FEDERAL COURT OF APPEALS

FEDERAL DISTRICT COURT

FINAL ADMINISTRATIVE OR BOARD DECISION

Federal courts of appeals hear appeals from the district courts that are located in their circuits. Below is a list of states matched to the federal circuits in which they are located.

First Circuit — Puerto Rico, Maine, New Hampshire, Massachusetts, Rhode Island

Second Circuit — New York, Vermont, Connecticut

Third Circuit — Pennsylvania, New Jersey, Delaware, Virgin Islands

Fourth Circuit — West Virginia, Maryland, Virginia, North Carolina, South Carolina

Fifth Circuit — Texas, Louisiana, Mississippi

Sixth Circuit — Ohio, Kentucky, Tennessee, Michigan

Seventh Circuit — Wisconsin, Indiana, Illinois

Eighth Circuit — North Dakota, South Dakota, Nebraska, Arkansas, Missouri, Iowa, Minnesota

Ninth Circuit — Alaska, Washington, Oregon, California, Hawaii, Arizona, Nevada, Idaho, Montana, Northern Mariana Islands, Guam

Tenth Circuit — Wyoming, Utah, Colorado, Kansas, Oklahoma, New Mexico

Eleventh Circuit — Alabama, Georgia, Florida

District of Columbia — Hears cases from the U.S. District Court for the District of Columbia.

Federal Circuit — Sitting in Washington, D.C., the U.S. Court of Appeals, Federal Circuit hears patent and trade appeals and certain appeals on claims brought against the federal government and its agencies.

How to Read a Case Citation

Generally, court decisions can be located in case reporters at law school or governmental law libraries. Some cases also can be located on the Internet through legal Web sites or official court Web sites.

Each case summary contains the citation, or legal reference, to the full text of the case. The diagram below illustrates how to read a case citation.

case name (parties) case reporter name and series court location
Sanders v. City of Minneapolis, 474 F.3d 523 (8th Cir. 2007).
volume number first page year of decision

Some cases may have two or three reporter names such as U.S. Supreme Court cases and cases reported in regional case reporters as well as state case reporters. For example, a U.S. Supreme Court case usually contains three case reporter citations.

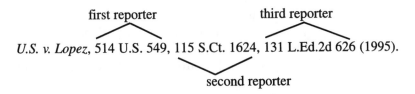

first reporter   third reporter
U.S. v. Lopez, 514 U.S. 549, 115 S.Ct. 1624, 131 L.Ed.2d 626 (1995).
second reporter

The citations are still read in the same manner as if only one citation has been listed.

Occasionally, a case may contain a citation that does not reference a case reporter. For example, a citation may contain a reference such as:

case name   year of decision   first page   date of decision
Maltbia v. Coffie, No. H-06-834, 2007 WL 43793 (S.D. Tex. 1/5/07).
court file number   WESTLAW[1]   court location

The court file number indicates the specific number assigned to a case by the particular court system deciding the case. In our example, the Texas Court of Appeals has assigned the case of *Maltbia v. Coffie* the case number of "H-06-834," which will

---

[1] WESTLAW® is a computerized database of court cases available for a fee.

serve as the reference number for the case and any matter relating to the case. Locating a case on the Internet generally requires either the case name and date of the decision, and/or the court file number.

Below, we have listed the full names of the regional reporters. As mentioned previously, many states have individual state reporters. The names of those reporters may be obtained from a reference law librarian.

P. **Pacific Reporter**
Alaska, Arizona, California, Colorado, Hawaii, Idaho, Kansas, Montana, Nevada, New Mexico, Oklahoma, Oregon, Utah, Washington, Wyoming

A. **Atlantic Reporter**
Connecticut, Delaware, District of Columbia, Maine, Maryland, New Hampshire, New Jersey, Pennsylvania, Rhode Island, Vermont

N.E. **Northeastern Reporter**
Illinois, Indiana, Massachusetts, New York, Ohio

N.W. **Northwestern Reporter**
Iowa, Michigan, Minnesota, Nebraska, North Dakota, South Dakota, Wisconsin

So. **Southern Reporter**
Alabama, Florida, Louisiana, Mississippi

S.E. **Southeastern Reporter**
Georgia, North Carolina, South Carolina, Virginia, West Virginia

S.W. **Southwestern Reporter**
Arkansas, Kentucky, Missouri, Tennessee, Texas

F. **Federal Reporter**
The thirteen federal judicial circuits courts of appeals decisions. *See The Judicial System, p. 499* for specific state circuits.

F.Supp. **Federal Supplement**
The thirteen federal judicial circuits district court decisions. *See The Judicial System, p. 499* for specific state circuits.

Fed. Appx. **Federal Appendix**
Contains unpublished decisions of the U.S. Circuit Courts of Appeal.

U.S. **United States Reports**
S.Ct. **Supreme Court Reporter** ⟩ U.S. Supreme Court Decisions
L.Ed. **Lawyers' Edition**

GLOSSARY

Ad Valorem Tax - In general usage, a tax on property measured by the property's value.

Age Discrimination in Employment Act (ADEA) - The ADEA, 29 U.S.C. § 621, *et seq.*, is part of the Fair Labor Standards Act. It prohibits discrimination against persons who are at least 40 years old, and applies to employers that have 20 or more employees and that affect interstate commerce.

Americans with Disabilities Act (ADA) - The ADA, 42 U.S.C. § 12101, *et seq.*, was signed into law on July 26, 1990. Among other things, it prohibits discrimination against a qualified individual with a disability because of that person's disability with respect to job application procedures, the hiring, advancement or discharge of employees, employee compensation, job training, and other terms, conditions and privileges of employment. The act also prohibits discrimination against otherwise qualified individuals with respect to the services, programs or activities of a public entity. Further, any entity that operates a place of public accommodation (including private schools) may not discriminate against individuals with disabilities.

Bill of Attainder - A bill of attainder is a law that inflicts punishment on a particular group of individuals without a trial. Such acts are prohibited by Article I, Section 9 of the Constitution.

Bona fide - Latin term meaning "good faith." Generally used to note a party's lack of bad intent or fraudulent purpose.

Claim Preclusion - (see Res Judicata).

Class Action Suit - Federal Rule of Civil Procedure 23 allows members of a class to sue as representatives on behalf of the whole class provided that the class is so large that joinder of all parties is impractical, there are questions of law or fact common to the class, the claims or defenses of the representatives are typical of the claims or defenses of the class, and the representative parties will adequately protect the interests of the class. In addition, there must be some danger of inconsistent verdicts or adjudications if the class action were prosecuted as separate actions. Most states also allow class actions under the same or similar circumstances.

Collateral Estoppel - Also known as issue preclusion. The idea that once an issue has been litigated, it may not be re-tried. Similar to the doctrine of *Res Judicata* (see below).

Due Process Clause - The clauses of the Fifth and Fourteenth Amendments to the Constitution which guarantee the citizens of the United States "due process of law" (see below). The Fifth Amendment's Due Process Clause applies to the federal government, and the Fourteenth Amendment's Due Process Clause applies to the states.

Due Process of Law - The idea of "fair play" in the government's application of law to its citizens, guaranteed by the Fifth and Fourteenth Amendments. Substantive due process is just plain *fairness*, and procedural due process is accorded when the government utilizes adequate procedural safeguards for the protection of an individual's liberty or property interests.

Employee Retirement Income Security Act (ERISA) - Federal legislation that sets uniform standards for employee pension benefit plans and employee welfare benefit plans. It is codified at 29 U.S.C. § 1001, *et seq.*

Enjoin - (see Injunction).

Equal Pay Act - Federal legislation that is part of the Fair Labor Standards Act. It applies to discrimination in wages that is based on gender. For race discrimination, employees paid unequally must utilize Title VII or 42 U.S.C. § 1981. Unlike many labor statutes, there is no minimum number of employees necessary to invoke the act's protection.

Equal Protection Clause - The clause of the Fourteenth Amendment that prohibits a state from denying any person within its jurisdiction equal protection of its laws. Also, the Due Process Clause of the Fifth Amendment that pertains to the federal government. This has been interpreted by the Supreme Court to grant equal protection even though there is no explicit grant in the Constitution.

Establishment Clause - The clause of the First Amendment that prohibits Congress from making "any law respecting an establishment of religion." This clause has been interpreted as creating a "wall of separation" between church and state. The test now used to determine whether government action violates the Establishment Clause, referred to as the *Lemon* test, asks whether the action has a secular purpose, whether its primary effect promotes or inhibits religion, and whether it requires excessive entanglement between church and state.

Ex Post Facto Law - A law that punishes as criminal any action that was not a crime at the time it was performed. Prohibited by Article I, Section 9, of the Constitution.

Exclusionary Rule - Constitutional limitation on the introduction of evidence that states that evidence derived from a constitutional violation must be excluded from trial.

Fair Labor Standards Act (FLSA) - Federal legislation that mandates the payment of minimum wages and overtime compensation to covered employees. The overtime provisions require employers to pay at least time-and-one-half to employees who work more than 40 hours per week.

Federal Tort Claims Act - Federal legislation that determines the circumstances under which the United States waives its sovereign immunity (see below) and agrees to be sued in court for money damages. The government retains its immunity in cases of intentional torts committed by its employees or agents, and where the tort is the result of a "discretionary function" of a federal employee or agency. Many states have similar acts.

42 U.S.C. §§ 1981, 1983 - Section 1983 of the federal Civil Rights Act prohibits any person acting under color of state law from depriving any other person of rights protected by the Constitution or by federal laws. A vast majority of lawsuits claiming constitutional violations are brought under § 1983. Section 1981 provides that all persons enjoy the same right to make and enforce contracts as "white citizens." Section 1981 applies to employment contracts. Further, unlike § 1983, § 1981 applies even to private actors. It is not limited to those acting under color of state law. These sections do not apply to the federal government, though the government may be sued directly under the Constitution for any violations.

Free Exercise Clause - The clause of the First Amendment that prohibits Congress from interfering with citizens' rights to the free exercise of their religion. Through the Fourteenth Amendment, it also has been made applicable to the states and their sub-entities. The Supreme Court has held that laws of general applicability that have an incidental effect on persons' free exercise rights are not violative of the Free Exercise Clause.

Incorporation Doctrine - By its own terms, the Bill of Rights applies only to the federal government. The Incorporation Doctrine states that the Fourteenth Amendment makes the Bill of Rights applicable to the states.

Individuals with Disabilities Education Act (IDEA) - 1990 amendment to the Education of the Handicapped Act (EHA) that renames the act and expands the group of children to whom special education services must be given.

Injunction - An equitable remedy (see Remedies) wherein a court orders a party to do or refrain from doing some particular action.

Issue Preclusion - (see Collateral Estoppel).

Jurisdiction - The power of a court to determine cases and controversies. The Supreme Court's jurisdiction extends to cases arising under the Constitution and under federal law. Federal courts have the power to hear cases where there is diversity of citizenship or where a federal question is involved.

Labor Management Relations Act (LMRA) - Federal labor law that preempts state law with respect to controversies involving collective bargaining agreements. The most important provision of the LMRA is § 301, which is codified at 29 U.S.C. § 185.

Mill - In property tax usage, one-tenth of a cent.

National Labor Relations Act (NLRA) - Federal legislation that guarantees to employees the right to form and participate in labor organizations. It prohibits employers from interfering with employees in the exercise of their rights under the NLRA.

Negligence per se - Negligence on its face. Usually, the violation of an ordinance or statute will be treated as negligence per se because no careful person would have been guilty of it.

Occupational Safety and Health Act (OSHA) - Federal legislation that requires employers to provide a safe workplace. Employers have both general and specific duties under OSHA. The general duty is to provide a workplace that is free from recognized hazards that are likely to result in serious physical harm. The specific duty is to conform to the health and safety standards promulgated by the Secretary of Labor.

Overbroad - A government action is overbroad if, in an attempt to alleviate a specific evil, it impermissibly prohibits or chills a protected action. For example, attempting to deal with street litter by prohibiting the distribution of leaflets or handbills.

Per Curiam - Latin phrase meaning "by the court." Used in court reports to note an opinion written by the court rather than by a single judge or justice.

Preemption Doctrine - Doctrine that states that when federal and state law attempt to regulate the same subject matter, federal law prevents the state law from operating. Based on the Supremacy Clause of Article VI, Clause 2, of the Constitution.

Prior Restraint - Restraining a publication before it is distributed. In general, constitutional law doctrine prohibits government from exercising prior restraint.

Pro Se - A party appearing in court, without the benefit of an attorney, is said to be appearing pro se.

Remand - The act of an appellate court in returning a case to the court from which it came for further action.

Remedies - There are two general categories of remedies, or relief: legal remedies, which consist of money damages, and equitable remedies, which consist of a court mandate that a specific action be prohibited or required. For example, a claim for compensatory and punitive damages seeks a legal remedy; a claim for an injunction seeks an equitable remedy. Equitable remedies are generally unavailable unless legal remedies are inadequate to address the harm.

Res Judicata - The judicial notion that a claim or action may not be tried twice or re-litigated, or that all causes of action arising out of the same set of operative facts should be tried at one time. Also known as claim preclusion.

Section 504 of the Rehabilitation Act of 1973 - Section 504 applies to public or private institutions receiving federal financial assistance. It requires that, in the employment context, an otherwise qualified individual cannot be denied employment based on his or her handicap. An otherwise qualified individual is one who can perform the "essential functions" of the job with "reasonable accommodation."

Section 1981 & Section 1983 - (see 42 U.S.C. §§ 1981, 1983).

Sovereign Immunity - The idea that the government cannot be sued without its consent. It stems from the English notion that the "King could do no wrong." This immunity from suit has been abrogated in most states and by the federal government through legislative acts known as "tort claims acts."

Standing - The judicial doctrine that states that in order to maintain a lawsuit a party must have some real interest at stake in the outcome of the trial.

Statute of Limitations - A statute of limitation provides the time period in which a specific cause of action may be brought.

Summary Judgment - Also referred to as pretrial judgment. Similar to a dismissal. Where there is no genuine issue as to any material fact and all that remains is a question of law, a judge can rule in favor of one party or the other. In general, summary judgment is used to dispose of claims that do not support a legally recognized claim.

Supremacy Clause - Clause in Article VI of the Constitution that states that federal legislation is the supreme law of the land. This clause is used to support the Preemption Doctrine (see above).

Title VI, Civil Rights Act of 1964 (Title VI) - Title VI prohibits racial discrimination in federally funded programs. This extends to admissions, financial aid, and virtually every aspect of the federally assisted programs in which private schools are involved. Codified at 42 U.S.C. § 2000d.

Title VII, Civil Rights Act of 1964 (Title VII) - Title VII prohibits discrimination in employment based upon race, color, sex, national origin, or religion. It applies to any employer having 15 or more employees. Under Title VII, where an employer intentionally discriminates, employees may obtain money damages unless the claim is for race discrimination. For those claims, monetary relief is available under 42 U.S.C. § 1981.

Title IX - Enacted as part of the Education Amendments of 1972, Title IX prohibits sexual discrimination in any private school program or activity receiving federal financial assistance. Codified at 20 U.S.C. § 1981, *et seq.*

U.S. Equal Employment Opportunity Commission (EEOC) - The EEOC is the government entity that is empowered to enforce Title VII (see above) through investigation and/or lawsuits. Private individuals alleging discrimination must pursue administrative remedies within the EEOC before they are allowed to file suit under Title VII.

Vacate - The act of annulling the judgment of a court either by an appellate court or by the court itself. The Supreme Court generally will vacate a lower court's judgment without deciding the case itself, and remand the case to the lower court for further consideration in light of some recent controlling decision.

Void-for-Vagueness Doctrine - A judicial doctrine based on the Fourteenth Amendment's Due Process Clause. In order for a law that regulates speech, or any criminal statute, to pass muster under the doctrine, the law must make clear what actions are prohibited or made criminal. Under the principles of the Due Process Clause, people of average intelligence should not have to guess at the meaning of a law.

Writ of Certiorari - The device used by the Supreme Court to transfer cases from the appellate court's docket to its own. Since the Supreme Court's appellate jurisdiction is largely discretionary, it need only issue such a writ when it desires to rule in the case.

INDEX

511